Research Methods in Criminal Justice and Criminology

Fourth Edition

Frank E. Hagan
Mercyhurst College

Allyn and Bacon
Boston • London • Toronto • Sydney • Tokyo • Singapore

Editor-in-Chief, Social Science: Karen Hanson
Series Editorial Assistant: Jennifer Jacobson
Marketing Manager: Karon Bowers
Composition and Prepress Buyer: Linda Cox
Manufacturing Buyer: Megan Cochran
Cover Administrator: Linda Knowles
Editorial-Production Service: Shepherd, Inc.

Hagan, Frank E.
    Research methods in criminal justice and criminology / Frank E.
Hagan. -- 4th ed.
      p.   cm.
    Includes bibliographical references (p. 460) and index.
    ISBN 0–205–19351–X
    1. Criminology—Research—Methodology.   2. Criminal justice,
Administration of—Research—Methodology.   3. Criminology-
-Statistical methods.   I. Title.
    HV6024.5.H33 1997
    364′.072—dc20   96–28508
                                    CIP

Printed in the United States of America

10 9 8 7 6 5 4 3 2 1 01 00 99 98 97 96

To MaryAnn and Shannon

Brief Contents

Detailed Contents

Chapter 13 Policy Analysis, Evaluation Research, and Proposal Writing 381

Preface

The first edition of *Research Methods in Criminal Justice and Criminology* was prepared in the early 1980s when no comprehensive research text existed that directly addressed the areas of criminal justice and criminology.

The text remains a comprehensive one, emphasizing sources and resources of classic and contemporary research in the field. There continues to be an acceleration of publications in the field employing increasingly more sophisticated and esoteric research designs and statistical analysis. The intent of the fourth edition remains the same as the first three: to reduce the gap that exists between the types of materials appearing in professional journals and publications in the field and the ability of students and professionals to understand them. The approach is to use criminological and criminal justice studies to illustrate research methods because it is as important to become familiar with examples of research in the field as it is to learn fundamental research skills.

This edition features major revisions throughout, while retaining a vital core of material from the first three editions. The organization of the work will carry the student through the sequence of the research process. Instructors may wish to shuffle the order of the chapters, however, to suit their syllabus or research style.

The first chapter introduces the reader to the area of criminological and criminal justice research while attacking commonsense approaches to research. Chapter 1 also outlines the steps in research elaborated on in Chapters 3 through 11. Following the issue of problem formulation in the first chapter, Chapter 2 examines the important issue of research ethics. Research designs and the experimental model, the latter being a benchmark with which to compare all other research in criminal justice, is detailed in Chapter 3. The third chapter includes an expanded treatment of time-series designs, a subject of major importance in recent research.

In Chapter 4, alternative data-gathering strategies are introduced, and the *Uniform Crime Reports* and its recent major revision are examined. Chapter 5 looks at sampling strategies as well as survey research, particularly mail questionnaires and self-report studies. Chapter 6 concentrates on interviews and telephone surveys, particularly recent developments in victim surveys. Participant observation and case studies are the subject of Chapter 7. Such field studies represent some of the most fascinating literature in the field.

Chapter 8 explores the interesting world of nonreactive or unobtrusive techniques, which include criminal justice and criminological applications involving secondary and content analysis, physical trace analysis, the use of official data, and observational strategies—all of which are useful cost-effective means of gathering data. Alternative means of data gathering such as surveys, field studies, and unobtrusive methods often contain strengths missing in experimental research. The important issues of validity and reliability are detailed in Chapter 9, the triangulated strategies are proposed as the single most logical path by which to resolve these questions. In all of these chapters, examples of both classic and contemporary research in criminal justice and criminology are used as illustrations. In addition to providing an overview of research methods, this text also presents a review and analysis of research literature.

Chapter 10 discusses scaling and index construction and features new and expanded coverage of crime severity scales, salient factor scores, and prediction scales.

Data analysis is the subject of Chapters 11 and 12, with Chapter 11 examining data management activities such as coding, keyboard entry, and table reading and Chapter 12 providing a user's guide to statistics. The latter is intended as a quick reference guide to many of the major statistical techniques presented in the literature. Although the primary goal of this chapter is to provide the reader with the ability to recognize and interpret the meaning of statistics, "pop quizzes" and additional appendixes have been added to assist in improved comprehension. Chapter 13 discusses evaluation research and proposal writing and features a section on policy analysis that reflects the growing interest of the social sciences in this subject in the past few years.

It is hoped that the style of presentation will convert many readers who may begin the course with apprehension into relatively fluent users of "researchese," a valuable and useful international language.

In addition to updating tables, figures, references, and examples, some principle changes have been made in this edition in response to reviewer and user suggestions. A number of exhibits have been added to illustrate or provide more detail on research issues. These include: Merton's "Matthew Effect" in Science, feminist research methods, PAVNET online, the Kansas City Gun Experiment, Child Abuse Victims and Violence, the Project on Human Development, Shock Incarceration, the National Incident-Based Recording System, Flaws in Public Opinion Polls, the Redesigned National Crime Victimization Survey, American Skinheads, Studies of Gangs, the National Archive of Criminal Justice Data, and The Drug Use Forecasting Program update. In addition, updates on the Revised Uniform Crime Reports, Computers and Software in Research, and CART (Continuous Audience Response Technology) in Focus Groups have been included. Also featured is an all-new SPSS-PC Appendix, which was revised by Laure Weber Brooks (University of Maryland).

I would like to thank the many people who assisted me in various ways in writing the editions of this text. Senior Editor Karen Hanson was very helpful and encouraging in getting this fourth edition underway. I would also like to thank editorial assistant, Jennifer Jacobsen for her help as well as Kelly Bechen and Lora Kalb at Shepherd, Inc. for their patient copyediting. To Tim Jacoby and Jack Mayleben who encouraged me to undertake the first edition, I remain indebted. To Chris Cardone, I particularly owe a debt for her encouragement and counsel throughout the second and third editions. I would also like to thank Howard Abadinsky, John Hudzik, and John Smykla for their helpful reviews of the first edition, as well as James A. Adamitis, the University of Dayton; Rosy A. Ekpenyong, Michigan State University; Randy Martin, Indiana University of Pennsylvania; Robert J. Mutchnick, Indiana University of Pennsylvania; Shirley R. Salem, Southern University at New Orleans; and Frank Schmalleger, Ph.D., Editor of *The Justice Professional* for their many fine suggestions for the second edition. For their reviews of, suggestions for, and comments concerning the third edition, I would like to thank Pamela Tontodonato, Kent State University; Laure Weber Brooks, University of Maryland; James A. Adamitis, The University of Dayton; William E. Thornton, Loyola University; and Malcolm D. Holmes, University of Texas at El Paso. Mike Blankenship, William McDonald, Gary Sykes, and William Wilbanks are acknowledged for their encouragement and/or for providing materials, as are Peter Benekos, Shirley Williams, and my colleagues in the Criminal Justice Department. I also once again express my gratitude to Marie Haug and Marvin Sussman for providing my early training in research. Although much of what is good about this book is due to the many fine suggestions of the reviewers, the author is solely responsible for any shortcomings.

Finally, I would like to thank my wife, MaryAnn, whose continuing support, editing, typing, and encouragement made completion of this new edition possible. It is to MaryAnn and our daughter Shannon that I dedicate this work.

I would like to encourage students as well as faculty to contact me with any questions, comments, or suggestions via e-mail: hagan@paradise.mercy.edu.

F.E.H.

CHAPTER

1 Introduction to Criminal Justice Research Methods: Theory and Method

Most students of criminal justice or criminology approach a course in research methods with the enthusiasm of a recalcitrant patient in a dentist's office. Even in the experience is not going to be painful, it most certainly is not anticipated to be exciting or interesting. Being primarily people oriented or pragmatically oriented, the criminal justice student at best expects to mildly tolerate an experience that seems quite remote from the real world and practical, everyday problems in criminal justice.

Scientific Research in Criminal Justice

Critics of may applications of scientific research to the criminal justice system view such efforts as either elucidation of the irrelevant, obscure

1

jargonizing, or academic intimidation—a detailed elaboration of what any person with common sense knows. To make matters worse, all of these efforts take place at substantial cost, usually to the taxpayer, at a time when needed action-oriented programs that really count are being cut back.

Some recent research findings are illustrative:

1. Females and the elderly fear crime because they are the most heavily victimized of all groups.
2. Victims of crime seldom know or recognize their offenders.
3. The typical criminal offender is either unemployed or on welfare.
4. The larger the city, the greater the likelihood its residents will be victims of crime.
5. In general, residents of large cities believe that their police are doing a poor job.
6. African Americans and Hispanics are less likely than the population as a whole to report personal crimes to the police.
7. Most residents of large cities think that their neighborhoods are not safe.
8. African Americans are overrepresented on death rows across the nation; however, this overrepresentation is more pronounced in the South than in other regions.
9. Crime is an inevitable product of complex, populous, and industrialized societies.
10. White-collar crime is nonviolent.
11. Regulatory agencies prevent white-collar crime.
12. The insanity defense allows many dangerous offenders to escape conviction.

What could be more obvious or a matter of common sense than these findings? If anything, all that we have learned is that Uncle Sam continues to waste tax money on useless studies. The real purpose of presenting these findings, although devious, was to make a point: *Sometimes common sense is nonsense.* Each of the preceding statements is incorrect and represents a myth about crime (U.S. Department of Justice, 1978; Bohm, 1987; Pepinsky and Jesilow, 1984; Walker, 1989; and Wright, 1985). The actual findings were as follows:

1. Rates of victimization are higher for males than females and for younger rather than older people.
2. In a large proportion of violent crimes, particularly domestic violence, victims know and recognize their offenders.
3. Knowledge of imprisoned criminals indicates that most persons who engage in crime have jobs and very few are welfare dependent.
4. The residents of smaller cities have higher rates than those of our largest cities for certain crimes such as assault, personal or household larceny, and residential burglary.

5. The opinions of residents of numerous cities across the nation indicate that the vast majority is satisfied with the performance of their police, with four out of five residents of the twenty-six cities surveyed giving ratings of good or average.

6. The offenses experienced by African Americans and Hispanics, by and large, are just about as apt to be reported as are crimes against victims in general.

7. Nine out of ten persons living in twenty-six large cities surveyed felt very or reasonably safe when out alone in their neighborhoods during daytime. A majority (54 percent) felt the same at night.

8. African American overrepresentation on death row is less pronounced in the South than in the other major regions of the country.

9. Crime is not a major concern in some developed countries, and in Japan it has actually decreased in the post–World War II period (Clinard, 1978; and Adler, 1983).

10. Unsafe work conditions and the marketing of unsafe products kill and maim more Americans yearly than street muggers and assailants (Hills, 1987).

11. Regulatory agencies have been understaffed, underfinanced, and inadequate in controlling white-collar crime (Clinard and Yeager, 1979).

12. Despite media attention, insanity defense cases are rare and successful ones even more rare (Morris, 1987).

Common Sense and Nonsense

Common sense   A number of works attempts to tackle the *common sense* issue head-on, such as *Sense and Nonsense about Crime* (Walker, 1989), *Myths That Cause Crime* (Pepinsky and Jesilow, 1984), *The Great American Crime Myth* (Wright, 1985), and *The Mythology of Crime and Justice* (Kappeler, Blumberg, and Potter, 1993).

What was assumed to be obvious in our example appeared so after the results were presented. If people agreed with the findings, they considered them obvious, whereas if they disagreed, they viewed the findings as unscientific because common sense told them so. Hirschi and Stark (1969) in "Hellfire and Delinquency" found a very weak relationship between church attendance and nondelinquency. In speaking to a "damned if you do and damned if you don't" phenomenon, they indicate that had they found a strong relationship as common sense would have suggested, they would have been accused of wasting time on the obvious. Because their study countered common sense, it was attacked as false, stupid, or an illustration of inadequate methods.

Brown and Curtis (1987, p. 3) indicate that:

Many practitioners within criminal justice have met with repeated failure over the years because they relied upon only their common sense. Thus, millions of dollars have been spent on police patrol efforts that do not reduce crime, judicial practices that are widely perceived as unfair, rehabilitation programs that do not rehabilitate offenders and countless other failures.

Evans in *The Natural History of Nonsense* (1958) outlines numerous examples of common sense–nonsense issues that have hindered human progress. The beliefs that the earth was flat and that it was the astrological center of the universe are but two examples. In testimony before Congress protesting threatened drastic cuts in funding for social science research and in response to attacks on the social sciences as employing obscure jargon and explicating the obvious or common sense. Herbert Simon counterattacked, asserting that the common sense of the social sciences is not a mirror of society but a result of research:

> The social sciences are often discounted because much of what they learn seems to be common sense. Well, it is common sense today to say that if you drop a feather and a rock together in a vacuum, they will fall at the same pace. It was not common sense before Galileo . . . [O]ne of the basic aims of the social sciences must be to take knowledge that comes out of the laboratory—knowledge that may be stated in language that is hard to understand—and make it part of the common sense of our society [Prewitt and Sills, 1981, p. 6].

Many of the terms used in everyday conversation originated in social science research; however, little credit is given for these theoretical accomplishments because the discoveries, once labeled, were quickly absorbed into the conventional wisdom.

In an essay celebrating twenty-five years of criminal justice research sponsored by the National Institute of Justice (the research arm of the U.S. Department of Justice), Blumstein and Petersilia (1994, p. 36) state:

> When compared to the public debate about these issues, which is still often focused on ideological issues and simplistic solutions to complex problems, it is clear that the thinking resulting from research, backed up by strong evidence, is very sophisticated, but it still has a long way to go to become an important part of the public debate. Researchers must also remember that the revolution in thinking brought about by Galileo and Copernicus took far longer than twenty-five years to become widely diffused to European thinking.

The most interesting phenomenon about those who propose a commonsensical approach to criminal justice is that the debunker often simply substitutes his or her own subjective biases and experience for the more scientific approach found lacking. Wilkins addresses himself to those who argue the antiscientific view wherein each individual is unique and defies measurement and prediction:

> The objection states that prediction is useless (or dangerous?) because the individual is unique. Prediction is said to be either (or both) impossible or undesirable, and this argument rests on the complexity of human relationship . . . If the case is unique, what experience can the clinician use to guide

him? . . . Statistical experience can be based on samples of the population which we know to be unbiased. A clinician has only his own sample to guide him with no guarantee of its lack of bias. . . . If these features are "intangible," how can we know that they exist? How in fact does the clinician take them into account? Can they not be described in words? If not, are they more than the prejudices of the observer? [Wilkins, 1978, pp. 233–236].

As we will see in Chapter 9, verbal descriptions of phenomena are a little different than numerical measures of some entity; the latter simply force the analyst to be more precise and rigorous, while thinking through the concept under study in a more disciplined manner. Thus, common sense and experience certainly serve an important function in sensitizing us to a subject; however, our separate experiences might better be viewed as limited case studies of a subject matter that may not be entirely generalizable to the universe of such subjects, or as observations that may be limited by time, place, and the subjective biases of the observer. Related to the commonsense approach to research, but of vital importance in criminal justice, are the questions "So what?" "Of what practical use are these findings?" This subject will be discussed in detail in Chapter 13 in the sections on evaluation research and policy analysis.

Why Study Research Methods in Criminal Justice?

Why study research methods?

Rather than viewing certain elementary research concepts and procedures in scientific methodology as a foreign element, the criminal justice professional may, once he or she has mastered them, discover a very valuable tool for assessing current and future directions in the field.

Once familiarity with these tools is gained, much of the anxious sanctimony bestowed upon technical reports, academic concepts, and research findings can be dispensed with. Many readers of this text have a healthy cynicism or critical and suspicious approach to research findings and probably know and employ more about research methodology than they are aware. In most cases they simply lack conceptual frameworks, scientifically acceptable tags, or sufficient knowledge of the language of research methods to defend their views in an appropriate manner. Research methods provide the tools necessary to approach issues in criminal justice from a more rigorous standpoint and enable a venture beyond opinions based solely on nonscientific observations and experiences (see Black, 1993).

Although many readers may never undertake their own research, all will be consumers or recipients of findings and policies based upon research findings. It is not unusual to find students as well as professionals in criminal justice who are unable to fully understand reports and journal articles in their own field. Other fields may have this same problem: however, one might certainly be wary of a surgeon who is performing an operation without an understanding of the latest article on the procedure in the *Journal of the American Medical Association.* Similarly, in striving for professional status, it is imperative that criminal justice professionals comprehend and critically evaluate new developments in their field (Hagan, 1975). Mastery of this material will assist in this endeavor. A very interesting outcome upon completion of the material is that many find themselves carefully reading and interpreting the tables presented in studies and skipping much of the prose. This procedure, which reverses the usual pattern at the beginning of the course, results in a great economy of time and effort.

Much of what appears in this text as research methods in criminology and criminal justice is, of course, not unique to criminal justice, but is, in fact, borrowed from the other social sciences and applied to criminal justice topics and examples. The techniques are applicable to a wide variety of areas and in that sense are excellent broad-based skills.

The Emergence of Science and Criminal Justice

Emergence of science

Humankind's long stride toward understanding and explaining the universe might be viewed as a marathon that has accelerated into a 100-yard dash in the past two centuries. In an attempt to provide a stage for our purposes and avoid philosophical discourses, which could occupy far too much time for our purposes, this development can be described succinctly. Human beings, through the creation of symbols or abstractions such as language, are able to develop knowledge. *Knowledge* is what people create symbolically to represent reality.

Knowledge

Knowledge might also be viewed as our presently accepted level of ignorance. There is no guarantee that what one historical generation considers wise policy or procedure will not be considered gross ignorance by the next generation. Less than 100 years ago "feebleminded" persons were locked up permanently for the protection of society because "feeblemindedness causes crime" (McCaghy, 1976, p. 10). Not long before that, the physically ill were bled to "cure" their illness.

The early French sociologist Auguste Comte described the "progression of knowledge as being one from predominantly theological or supernatural explanations of reality to metaphysical or philosophical ones and finally to scientific approaches" (Comte, 1877). Rather than looking to otherworldly explanations, philosophy sought explanations in worldly events through a new spirit of inquiry—rationality and logical explanation.

Science

Science combined this spirit of rational explanation with method—empiricism, experimentation, or what has come to be called the scientific method. The scientific orientation emphasized observation, measurement, replication (repetition of observation), and verification (checking on the validity of observations). Science subjects ideas or theories to tests through observation, quantification, and empirical analysis. Unlike the philosopher's often sole reliance on logic and argumentative reasoning, all scientists can be said to be from Missouri, the "Show Me" state. **Replication** is

Replication

Verification the repetition of experiments or studies utilizing the same methodology. **Verification** is confirmation of the accuracy of findings or attainment of greater certitude in conclusions through additional observations.

Systematic application of the scientific method to research problems provided major breakthroughs in the development of knowledge. While the scientific era has enabled mankind to take giant strides in explaining and harnessing physical reality, more recently the social sciences, of which criminal justice is a progeny, have attempted to apply these same procedures to their subject matters—society, human behavior, politics, or, of concern in our enterprise, crime and criminal justice.

Because we have gained mastery over simpler, more controllable physical reality, why, as intelligent humans, is not possible to gain the same explanation, prediction, and control over such recurring social phenomena as crime, violence, and their many ramifications?

Criminal justice as an interdisciplinary discipline draws upon many fields, both academic and applied, and, in terms of appropriate research methodology, has not only borrowed and adapted but has made many of its own contributions as will be presented throughout this book. Whether criminal justice is a science is argued even by practitioners within the field. Criminal justice researchers, unlike physical scientists, find their subject matter a topic of popular discussion in which the layperson's experience is viewed as just as good a guide to policy as that of the researcher. The same people who would not dream of arguing about molecules, atomic weights, or quasars feel quite qualified to address issues of crime and punishment. In this writer's view the appropriate employment of scientific methodology and procedure qualifies a discipline to claim scientific status. Although this topic is certainly worthy of debate elsewhere, the approach throughout this text is a very pragmatic one—we are employing scientific procedures and therefore contributing to the development of a young science.

Probabilistic Nature of Science

Probabilistic nature of science As social scientists, criminologists, and criminal justice researchers assume that the subject matter they study is probabilistic—i.e., they believe that effects will most often occur when certain causes are present, but not in every single case. In predicting general patterns, trends, and relationships among groups, social scientists do not expect these patterns to hold in each individual case or do not expect absolute determinism. If researchers show a relationship between rising unemployment rates and suicide rates, they are not assumed to be or considered to be wrong if most newly unemployed do not commit suicide. Researchers do attempt to estimate the probability of their predictions being accurate. For example, there is an 85 percent chance that a Savings and Loan thief such as Charles Keating will be white, upper-middle class, and a college graduate.

Proper Conduct of Critical Inquiry

Bayley (1978) offers three suggestions for improving criminal justice research:

1. Research requires interdisciplinary efforts as well as the tackling of field-oriented, practical problems.
2. Researchers should cease giving speeches to practitioners about the value of research and attack their practical concerns with a realistic appraisal of error proneness of any research endeavor.
3. It is time to be done with "methodological narcissism," methods for methods' sake.

The latter is aptly illustrated by the well-known Martinson Report, which was published in the early 1970s. Martinson (1974) raised quite a storm in the field of corrections when, based on his evaluation of rehabilitation programs throughout the United States, he concluded that none of these programs reduced recidivism or rehabilitated clients. Later, in retracting his own previously devastating "almost nothing works" critique of corrections research, Martinson (1978, p. 4) advised that it was time to avoid "methodological fanaticism" (what Bayley called **"methodological narcissism"**), in which substance is overlooked in the name of method. Preferred rigor in research design is seldom realized in criminal justice field studies. This does not justify throwing out "the baby with the bath water." Instead, such problems represent challenges to the criminal justice researcher, rather than a justification for self-defeating pessimism and methodological capitulation.

Hirschi and Selvin give sound advice to those either doing research or criticizing the research of others. The proper conduct of critical inquiry requires that "those concerned with good research should be objective and vigilant as well as sympathetic" (Hirschi and Selvin, 1973, pp. 273–274). *Objectivity* entails value neutrality or a dispassionate approach to the subject matter that holds constant personal bias (Weber, 1949). *Vigilance* involves a concern for accuracy and efforts to eliminate error. Error, however, is ever present in research. The only perfect research is no research, which suggests the last point, sympathy. In critiquing the research of others, *empathy* or a willingness to put oneself in the role of the researcher is important. *If a student of research is afraid of making errors in research, then he or she probably should do none, because error is omnipresent.* One could even argue that the only perfect research is no research. In criticizing other research, one often need not go far to find some error. For example, in an analysis of the quality of publications in criminology, Wolfgang, Figlio, and Thornberry (1978) concluded that the methodological sophistication was very low and that greater concern for adequate study design and execution should be a requirement for publication in the field. The question is not whether errors are present, but,

Methodological narcissism

Objectivity

Vigilance

Empathy

rather, whether reasonable attempts were made to acknowledge and/or eliminate the most glaring errors. Only when such errors so grossly compromise the accuracy of findings and conclusions thereof, should one scathingly attack other research.

Exhibit 1.1 presents Robert Merton's concept of the "Matthew effect" in science in which he alleges that judgments regarding the quality of scientific

---

EXHIBIT 1.1

Merton's "Matthew Effect" in Science

For unto every one that hath shall be given, and he shall have abundance: but from him that hath not shall be taken away even that which he hath.

—Matthew 13: 11–12

Robert Merton (1968) identified the "Matthew Effect" in science as the tendency for those who are published to get published. Rather than scientists being entirely objective and neutral in evaluating new works, the "Matthew effect" proposes the hypothesis that there is a tendency on the part of established camps of scholars or scientists to cite each other and to reject new ideas by those who are outside their clique or challenge the established paradigm. Science becomes a small circle of mutual admiration societies that reject unconnected newcomers and their new ideas. The most celebrated example of such censorship was the unwillingness of physics journals to publish the work of Immanuel Velikovsky and his *Worlds in Collision* (1950) theory of the origins of the universe.

Merton's hypothesis has inspired a number of observations. A.J. Lotka observed that half of all scientific publications are written by less than ten percent of scientists, while another cynically advises: "Don't pick an important problem; don't challenge existing beliefs; don't obtain surprising results; and don't write clearly" (Sobel, 1989, p. 27). While some of these remarks may reflect a sour grapes reaction to academic rejection, there is some empirical support for such an effect.

Psychologist Michael Mahoney gave seventy-five reviewers of a psychology journal five versions of a fictitious but technically sound article on child behavior. One version supported orthodox behaviorism, another contradicted it, a third offered no results, and the remaining two had mixed findings. Those who had received the positive article all accepted it with high praise, while the negative article was rejected and panned for its methodology. "When reviewers learned what Mahoney had done, three participants tried to have him fired or at least reprimanded by the American Psychological Association" (ibid.). Neither took place and his work was eventually published.

Douglas Peters and Stephen Ceci took twelve previously published articles and resubmitted them to the same journals where they had appeared two years earlier. The titles were changed and the names of the authors and their universities were altered, the latter done to reflect less prestigious institutions. Three of the resubmissions were recognized, but eight of the remaining nine were rejected. While the study itself was published, one of the authors nearly lost tenure because of it (ibid.).

Source: Merton, Robert K. "The Matthew Effect," *Science* 159 (January 1968): 56–63; Sobel, David. "The Matthew Effect." *Omni* (August, 1989): 27; Immanuel. Velikovsky, *Worlds in Collision.* New York: Doubleday, 1950.

contributions do not always take place as a result of purely objective standards and that established cliques may reject new ideas by those who are not part of this established network.

Approaches to Theory and Method in Criminal Justice

Theory   Theory in criminal justice represents an attempt to develop plausible explanations of reality, which in this case is crime and the criminal justice system. Theory attempts to classify and organize events, to explain the causes of events, to predict the direction of future events, and to understand why and how these events occur (Turner, 1974, p. 2). It represents a reasonable and informed guess as to why things are as they appear and to explain their underlying nature and meaning. Much criminological theory possesses a global or sensitizing quality that alerts us to critical issues, but often lacks the quality of formally testable, scientifically verifiable propositions (Hagan, 1990, p. 121). Without the generation of useful theoretical explanations, a field is intellectually bankrupt; it becomes merely a collection of war stories and carefully documented encyclopedic accounts. It fails to explain, summarize, or capture the essential nature of its subject matter. Theory asks: What is the point of all of this? What does it mean? Why are things this way? Willis (1983), in a review of twenty-five criminal justice textbooks, noted almost a "trained incapacity" or unwillingness to deal with theoretical issues and a tendency to concentrate on what fictional character Joe Friday, in the old television series *Dragnet,* called "just the facts."

In *The Structure of Scientific Revolutions,* Thomas Kuhn (1970) describes how the evolution of new knowledge, rather than being slow and incremental, is often dependent upon new paradigms that may stand previous assumptions on their heads. A paradigm is "some implicit body of intertwined theoretical and methodological belief that permits selection, evaluation, and criticism" (ibid., pp. 16–17). A new paradigm represents a new model or revolutionary schema with which to view reality. Paradigms organize reality by giving structure, a framework, and perspective from which to investigate reality. Kuhn viewed scientific knowledge as achieving breakthroughs by revolutions fueled by the inability to explain anomalies by means of the existing scientific tradition. The old paradigm (normal science) is made obsolete by the new paradigm through this process of revolution. In a related phenomenon, sometimes new knowledge takes place or is discovered by a process of serendipity, a wholly unanticipated and surprising discovery. In the process of doing research on one topic, a discovery is made that addresses some different topic.

Edwin Sutherland's concept of "white-collar crime" (1940) serves as an example of a paradigm revolution in criminology, a radical reorientation in theoretical views of the nature of criminality. After Sutherland, crime was no longer viewed solely as an activity of the underclass. Copernicus' astronomical theory of the universe made totally irrelevant the previous paradigm of astrology. Walker (1992, pp. 72–73) indicates:

> Finally, Kuhn's perspective cautions adherents of the prevailing paradigm to recognize that there is nothing permanent or timeless about their viewpoint. This paradigm, which organizes their thinking, research, and policy proposals, was the product of a scientific revolution that replaced an earlier paradigm. Science, however, like time, marches on. We cannot predict what kind of scientific revolution lies in the future and will overthrow the assumptions shared by virtually everyone reading this article.

Methodology   **Methodology,** on the other hand, involves the collection of accurate facts or data regarding the nature of crime and criminal justice policy. *In short, while theory addresses the issue "why," methodology concerns itself with "what is."* There usually exists in any field a certain division between those who are primarily interested in generating theory and who view their efforts as classical scholarship akin to philosophy and those (methodologists) who are viewed as technical and scientific in their approach. Good criminal justice requires both. These differences are common to a variety of fields as indicated by the following humorous observation:

> Not long ago in social psychology, the methodologist was viewed as an unpleasant fact of life—a necessary tool in the development of the discipline, but certainly not someone that anybody would want his sister to marry. Today, attitudes and practices have changed to the extent that the one common feature of almost all the current generation of social psychologists is their training in research methodology [Crano and Brewer, 1973, Preface].

Demise of Criminological Imagination   In an article entitled "The Demise of Criminological Imagination," Williams (1984) laments the lack of any new, imaginative, theoretical contributions to the field since the 1960s. He attributes this "hiatus in theory" to three factors:

1. *A recent lack of sociological imagination.* The creative generation of new theory has been stymied by an overemphasis on "empirical scientism," an overconcentration on methodological precision, at the expense of theoretical development.
2. *A critical intellectual environment* nurtured in the 1960s that emphasized the analysis of differences between theories at the expense of the integration of theoretical concepts.
3. *The rise of criminal justice* as a discipline in part as a result of federal funding, which attracted intellectual energy to the issue of crime control systems and to programmatic efforts to improve its efficiency.

If Williams' diagnosis is correct, these developments may spell intellectual rigor mortis for both criminology and criminal justice, which will become disciplines satisfied to serve in the role of technician for existing crime control policies and ideology. These disciplines come to emphasize technical proficiency and the development of narrow techniprofessionals, ultimately leading to "rigor professionis" (Reiff, 1971), a state in which technical skill tends to predominate at the expense of the theoretical and intellectual core of knowledge essential for the higher professions (Hagan, 1987). In many fields, publications in professional journals seem to favor mathematical olympians, no matter how narrow the theoretical topic, rather than nonquantitative theoretical works.

Bernard and Ritti (1990, pp. 18–19) note:

> The alternation between theory and research is an interactive process that results in the falsification of some theories and the accumulation of knowledge within the context of other theories—i.e., in progress within the discipline. . . . The failure of criminology to progress as a discipline, it seems to us, comes from the failure to take theory seriously in designing and implementing research. Too much emphasis is placed on the sophistication of methodological and analytical techniques, and too little attention is paid to the careful specification of the theoretical issue that is being addressed. No matter how sophisticated the research techniques, progress in criminology as a science cannot occur unless that research is based on explicit and intelligent theory.

Theory devoid of method—explanation without accurate supportive data—is just as much a ritualistic dead end as method devoid of theory. The former resembles armchair theorizing, while the latter resembles a fruitless bookkeeping operation. Both theory and method should be viewed as means to an end, the end being sound criminal justice knowledge.

Pure versus Applied Research

Pure research

Applied research

    Pure (basic) research is concerned with the acquisition of new knowledge for the sake of science or the development of the field, whereas **applied research** is practical research concerned with solving immediate policy problems. Although we addressed the issue of common sense briefly by means of "myths of crime," there still exists the broader issue: Criminal justice has experienced conflict between two camps, *the applied practitioner* and *the nonapplied academic.* Although this division is in part stereotypical, as mutual exclusivity is not in fact the case with these groups, for heuristic purposes we consider these as "ideal types."[1] Being on the front lines of the criminal justice system, practitioners are most interested in *applied research,* studies, and findings that speak directly to policy issues.

[1]Weber (1949) viewed "ideal types" as useful analytic devices that extract pure or overgeneralized elements of a reality, but seldom exist in pure form. Wilson's (1968) "Watchman," "Service," and "Legalistic" styles of policing are an illustration.

Academics, on the other hand, are more concerned with *pure research,* which may have no immediate applicability but contributes to the knowledge base and scientific development of the discipline. Although the practitioner may view the pure scientific researcher as off in a closeted ivory tower or a likely candidate for Senator Proxmire's Golden Fleece Award for irrelevant research,[2] the pure scientific researcher may view many of the policy recommendations of applied research as shamanism, or quackery, an attempt to give advice or guide policy without adequate theoretical or methodological support. In speaking to the issue of premature application Friedman (1980) puts it succinctly: "If you eat the cookies before they are ready you can get sick."

In reality, neither pure nor applied research fits these neat stereotypical views (Rabow, 1964). Some of the most apparently obscure and abstract research projects may produce the critical discoveries that in the long run produce more applied payoffs than hundreds of premature applied projects. On the other hand, many existing projects require informed decisions, which, although not perfect or entirely supported by research findings, represent the best we have to offer at the time. A study of state correctional agency practitioners (Light and Newman, 1992) found that while such practitioners strongly supported social science research, they reported using it very little in comparison with other types of information and knowledge.

Many of the major and important scientific discoveries of ancient and modern times were made not by the kings' wizards commissioned to immediately perform alchemy or other applied magic, but by abstract "tinkers"— Galileo, Copernicus, Einstein, and Pasteur. What is regarded as renegade, pure, and ivory-tower research of one epoch often finds itself the basis for important applied breakthroughs in the next. As mentioned previously, in the late 1970s, in an attempt to point out wasteful government funding of "irrelevant" research projects, Senator Proxmire periodically would publicize and give his infamous Golden Fleece Award. To the layperson, obscure sounding studies such as "The Sex Life and Mating Habits of Bees in the Upper Amazon Basin" appear to be projects deserving of derision and attack until at a later date scientists speculate that "killer bees" that are resistant to existing chemical insecticides may invade North America and result in human deaths.

The National Institute of Justice (NIJ), a research branch of the U.S. Department of Justice, was established in 1979 with the mission to encourage policy-relevant research that might be useful in preventing or reducing

---

[2]In the late 1970s, Senator William Proximire attracted considerable publicity by presenting awards to government-sponsored research projects with esoteric titles that he viewed as irrelevant. Proximire was the subject of an $8 million libel and slander suit by experimental psychologist Dr. Ronald R. Hutchinson as a result of his being identified as a recipient. See "Golden Fleece Suit Reaches Supreme Court," *Footnotes,* American Sociological Association, 7 (May 1979), 5.

crime. In enunciating the practitioner's perspective, then Director of NIJ James Stewart (1983, pp. iv–v) points out:

> The fact remains that those charged with administering the criminal justice system are forced by the flow of events to make decisions, to implement new policies and alter operations often without the benefit of the best available knowledge. Their world is not the world of the laboratory experiment. It is one instead of crisis, action and reaction. Thus, while they concede the serendipitous nature of some research and the need for time, their quid pro quo is the support for more immediate, analytical research and the development of mechanisms that can inform and guide their decisions. This is a task well within the capability of the research community. . . .
>
> . . . Criminal justice research and practice is at an important stage in its development. While still in embryonic form, criminal justice could evolve like the fields of health and engineering where those who conduct research and those who practice essentially share similar paradigms and look naturally to each other for information and guidance.

An Ad Hoc Committee on the Future of Justice Research (1982, p. 1) recognized the views of and role of practitioners in the setting of a federal research agenda:

> Practitioners appreciate the need for a mixed strategy in funding research. They feel both basic and applied research should be sponsored by the federal government, though emphasis should be on applied research that is policy relevant. They see a need for employing a greater range of methodological approaches in research. The controlled experiment should not be the only method used.
>
> Practitioners desire an equal role with academicians and other researchers in establishing research agendas, practitioners also feel they have a role to play in peer review of proposals, in serving as test beds or sites for research projects and experiments, and in disseminating the results of research.

Evaluation research *Evaluation research,* which will be discussed in detail in Chapter 13, is a branch of applied research that examines public programs and policies. Do programs work? How well do they work? How can they be made to work better? These are some of the questions asked in evaluation research.

Qualitative and Quantitative Research

Quantitative research In **quantitative research** concepts are assigned numerical value, whereas in **qualitative research** concepts are viewed as sensitizing ideas or terms **Qualitative research** that enhance our understanding. Research methods in the social sciences, of which criminal justice is heir, have followed two basic philosophical traditions. *The first legacy* reflects a historical, intuitive, or observational

Verstehen

Positivism

Historicism

Scientism

approach and suggests that the physical and social sciences are distinct entities.[3] It emphasizes a *qualitative approach* to understanding the reality under investigation. Classic sociologist Weber described it as a **verstehen** (in German, *understanding* or *empathy*), in which researchers hope to immerse themselves in the subject matter and develop "sensitizing concepts" that enhance their understanding and explanation of reality (Weber, 1949). Many field studies and participant observation studies, in which the researcher lives with and experiences a group's way of life from the group's perspective, serve as examples. Qualitative research offers the investigator the opportunity to alter and even add data collection processes during the study (Haar, 1992, p. 6). This grounded theory approach enables a shifting of gears to focus upon issues that were not previously assumed to be of importance at the time of the beginning of the project.

Positivism, a natural science approach, is often used to describe the *second legacy.* This empirical orientation suggests that the same approach applicable to studying and explaining physical reality can be used in the social sciences. This second tradition is a *quantitative approach* and is concerned with measuring social or, in our case, criminal justice reality. Although both legacies as pure ideal types may represent dead ends in criminal justice research, moderate expressions of either of these strategies have, as we will discover in Chapter 3, a role in enhancing our understanding of criminal justice. An extreme qualitative approach would provide **historicism**—*seeing all* social events as a distinct chronicle of unique happenings. This would involve a denial that any scientific generalities could be drawn from the world of human events. Such as stance is antiscientific. On the other polar extreme is **scientism** or extreme positivism, in which the researcher takes the stance that "if you cannot measure it, it is not worth studying or commenting on." Although historicism may jade those from the traditional humanities in their view of criminal justice as a discipline, scientism is most often the orientation of physical scientists, who may view fields such as criminal justice as a pretender to the scientific throne or one of a score of "Johnny-come-lately" pseudosciences. Such physical scientists may feel that unless criminal justice or social science researchers can attain the same rigorous control over the conditions of study as in the physical sciences, they are somehow involved in an inferior enterprise, an amateur imitation of real science. Obviously, social phenomena cannot be put in a test tube or maze.

Criminal justice as an emergent, interdisciplinary, applied scientific field requires for its mature development a full array of qualitative and quantitative approaches, pure and applied research efforts, and theoretically incisive as well as methodologically sound studies and evaluations to gain the academic respectability it both aspires to and deserves.

---

[3]The qualitative approach is illustrated by such writers as Weber (1949), Garfinkel (1967), and Blumer (1969) and by groups that advocate "symbolic interactionism" or "ethnomethodology."

Researchese: The Language of Research

Sprechen Sie Researchese? To the uninitiated, the language of research is almost like being exposed to a foreign language. How often have we heard a frustrated reader of a report say, in despair and disgust. "Why don't these people write in English?" This common reaction might even be described, to coin a phrase, as **research shock**—a sense of disorientation experienced by a person when suddenly confronted with an unfamiliar style of presentation and research language. What one is reacting to is not complexity or the unlearnable, but merely the unfamiliar. Those of you who are in-service, criminal justice professionals or you who have taken only a few courses in criminology or criminal justice, or any major for that matter, soon discover that you have accumulated much of the specialized language of the field. When you use this argot around others not in the field you may be surprised that others are unaware of these terms. This, incidentally, explains why many occupational groups cling together socially because others cannot fully appreciate their jargon or ideology. It also explains why many spouses at parties request in despair, "Please stop talking shop!" So, even though at first much of the terminology seems clumsy, stick with it, and by the completion of this text you too will be able to read, write, and think **researchese** (the language of research), a valuable international language and a useful tool for negotiating and understanding the latest literature in your field.

Research shock

Researchese

The notion of causality, a complex subject in philosophy, is the very essence of scientific inquiry. Science assumes that elements of reality can be isolated, defined, explained, and predicted—that science holds the key to unlocking the mysteries of the ages. Scientific investigation assumes that causal principles and laws underlie reality and that by discovering these elements, science can predict and control reality (Wilkins, 1976). This process begins by naming things.

Concepts

Concepts

Concepts are abstract tags put on reality and are the beginning point in all scientific endeavors. Not to be confused with reality itself, concepts are symbolic human creations or constructs that attempt to capture the essence of reality. In coming up with a name for some phenomenon, we are attempting to describe, understand, classify, or become more sensitized to some element of reality. Examples of concepts that are used in criminological and criminal justice studies include crime, recidivism, cynicism, intelligence, risk on parole, defendant's appearance, and police patrol. Age, sex, race, religion, and social class are other concepts with which we are quite familiar. Concepts may be viewed as qualitative, sensitizing/global notions or they can be converted into *variables* through *operationalization*.

Operationalization

Operationali-
zation

Operationalization defines concepts by describing how they will be measured. *Working definition* or *operational definition* are other terms used to refer to this process. The notion of operationalization can be defined in response to the statement. "I measured it by _____." Completion of this sentence constitutes the operationalization of the concept. This process of operationalization has now quantified (assigned numerical values to) a concept and converted it from an abstract, verbal entity to a measurable quantity or variable.

Variables

Variables

Variables are concepts that have been operationalized or "concepts that can vary" or take on different values of a quantitative nature. They are the mortar and brick of scientific investigation. Theoretically, variables can be of a qualitative nature. For example, qualitative distinctions could be made regarding a person's age as old or young, but the measurement of actual chronological age would be regarded as more exact. Crime may be operationalized in a study as having been measured by official police statistics, surveys of victims, or self-admission reports. Different measures may yield slightly different pictures and therefore should be defined. Similarly, recidivism may be defined by means of rearrest rates, reincarceration (imprisonment or jail) rates, or other measures that could produce quite different assessments of the success or failure of programs. Table 1.1 provides some illustrations of the conversion of various concepts into variables by means of operationalization.

Dependent and Independent Variables

Dependent
variables

The **dependent** (*outcome*) **variable** is the variable one is attempting to predict and by convention is denoted by the letter Y. Common outcome variables in criminal justice are concepts such as crime or recidivism. Table 1.1 illustrates that ordinarily the dependent variable is some behavior or attitude that is usually the subject of one's study. The **independent** (or *predictor*) **variable** is the variable that causes, determines, or precedes in time the dependent variable and is usually denoted by the letter X (or any letter other than Y). An independent variable in one study may become a dependent variable in another. For example, a study of the impact of poverty (X) upon crime (Y) finds poverty as a predictor (independent) variable, whereas a study that looks at race (X) as a predictor of poverty (Y) finds poverty as an outcome (dependent) variable. The treatment variable is always an independent variable as are demographic variables such as age, sex, and race.

Independent
variables

TABLE 1.1 Researchese: Basic Terms

Concept	Operationalization	Variable
Cynicism	A Cynicism Scale consisting of 20 questions (ranging for each from 1—low cynicism to 3—high cynicism)	Cynicism Score 20 (low) to 60 (high)
Intelligence	Administration of an intelligence test that compares mental age (scores on a test) with chronological age	IQ (Intelligence Quotient), for example, range of below 55 to 145+
Risk on parole	A Parole Risk Prediction Scale called "Salient Factor Score"	Parole Risk Score ranging from 0 (poor risk) to 10 (very good risk)
Defendant's appearance	Raters used a scale and rated defendants from 0 (poor) to 10 (excellent)	Appearance Rating Score 0 (poor) to 10 (excellent)
Police patrol	Precincts were assigned to either proactive (increased patrol), reactive (decreased patrol), or control (same as usual patrol)	Police Patrol Strategy: proactive reactive control

Independent (Predictor)* Variable (*X*)	Dependent (Outcome) Variable (*Y*)
(usually demographic variable or a treatment)	(usually behavior/attitudes)
e.g., Appearance, Police Patrol, Age, Sex, Race, Social Class	e.g., Crime, Recidivism, Cynicism, Intelligence, Risk on Patrol

*Identification of independent and dependent variables has been oversimplified for heuristic purposes.

Theories/Hypotheses

Theories

Theories were described previously as *attempts to develop plausible explanations of reality.* They are usually general or broad statements regard-

Hypotheses

ing the relationship between variables. **Hypotheses** *are specific statements regarding the relationship between* (usually two) *variables* and are derived from more general theories. A *research hypothesis states an expected relationship between variables in positive terms.* For example: poverty causes crime. The *null hypothesis* is a *hypothesis* of *no difference* and is the one actually tested statistically. For example: poverty is not related to crime. One approach to research involves formulation of hypotheses—specific predicted relationships between independent and dependent variables—the operationalization or measurement of these variables, and the testing or bringing of evidence to bear upon these. Hypothesis testing will be explored in Chapter 12. Figure 1.1 outlines a model of the research process.

Examples of the Research Process

A brief description of this process can be illustrated by Durkheim's (1951) classic study of suicide, which was originally conducted in 1897 and was one of the first empirical studies in deviant behavior. At the time Durkheim

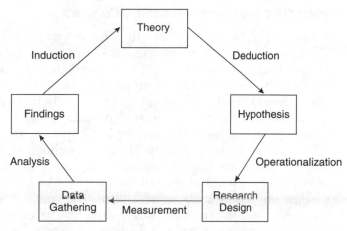

Figure 1.1   A Model of the Research Process.

performed his study— in the late nineteenth century—little in the way of empirical analysis had been undertaken in the social sciences. Contrary to popular views of the time, Durkheim proposed the general theory that group membership affects suicide. From this he deduced the specific hypothesis that religious denomination, marital status, and the like would affect suicide rates. He operationalized his key variables or indicators of group member- ship by assuming that married people have greater group ties than singles, or that Judaism and Catholicism required greater group religious orientation than Protestantism which was more individualistic. Proceeding to analyze the available official suicide records in European countries at the time, he simply compared rates for each variable subcategory. Drawing the general conclusion that singles and Protestants had higher suicide rates than mar- ried people and Jews and Catholics, he inferred from these findings a now modified theory: Group membership does affect suicide.

In examining Figure 1.1 as well as our example, note that reasoning may proceed by means of an a priori assumption (before-the-fact reasoning), wherein a theoretical idea precedes any attempt to collect facts or use an a posteriori assumption (after-the-fact reasoning). The former is an example of a deductive process of reasoning, with reasoning based on hypothesis or the- ory, and the latter illustrates the inductive process, with reasoning based on inference of facts or particulars to general principles or theory. Thus, theory to fact is *deduction* and fact to theory is *induction*. **Deduction** involves mov- ing from a level of theory to a specific hypothesis, whereas **induction** entails inferring about a whole group on the basis of knowing about a case or a few cases. Sherlock Holmes' famous compliment to Dr. Watson, "Brilliant deduction, my dear Watson," should probably have read "induction" because Watson, in helping Holmes solve a case, was proceeding a posteri- ori from specific facts or evidence to a conclusion or theory.

Deduction

Induction

Recidivism among Juvenile Offenders

In order to further illustrate the research process, let us examine a hypothetical example. In an experimental correction program called Salvation House, half of those scheduled for incarceration are sent instead to this new community-based treatment program on the basis of a very general *theory* that offenders better adjust, or are more likely to become rehabilitated, in a community rather than in prison. A specific *hypothesis* derived from this theory (using, as we will describe in Chapter 3, an interrupted time-series design) is that the Salvation House experimental group will experience lower recidivism than the control group of incarcerateds. The *dependent variable* (*Y*) is recidivism, and the predictor or *independent variable* (*X*) is assignment to jail or Salvation House. The concept "recidivism" is defined as a reduction in both the quantity and quality (seriousness) of crime commission over a one-year period after release compared with a similar period prior to assignment to either correctional program.

Suffice it to say that each group was examined before and after treatment. *Data gathering* involved the simple examination of official statistics kept by police and probation/parole agents on violations, as well as weighting of the seriousness of these offenses. Let us suppose the *analysis* demonstrated a "suppression effect"—a decline in both the quantity and seriousness of offenses of the Salvation House assignees. We might now draw the empirical generalization that less recidivism is demonstrated as a result of community-based corrections, at least in our limited case study. We thus lend support to our original theory that correction in the community appears to be more successful than isolated incarceration, at least in bringing about some decline in the quality and quantity of offenses. The theory is not set up for reanalysis and investigation.

An actual evaluation of juvenile intensive aftercare probation for serious offenders in Philadelphia (Sontheimer and Goodstein, 1993) found it had a major impact on reducing the frequency of subsequent offenses, but not the incidence of recidivism. Had only the latter been used to operationalize recidivism, then a successful project would have been evaluated as showing no difference.

Simon and Burstein offer sage advice:

> There is never a single, standard, correct method of carrying out a piece of research. Do not wait to start your research until you find out the proper approach, because there are always many ways to tackle a problem—some good, some bad, but probably several good ways. There is no single perfect design. A research method for a given problem is not like the solution to a problem in algebra. It is more like a recipe for beef stroganoff; there is no one best recipe. [Simon and Burstein, 1985, p. 4]

Although some methodological narcissists would disagree with this view, the method employed should follow from the theory and research problem

Margin notes: Hypothesis; Data gathering

rather than research topics avoided because they do not lend themselves to a favored method. Subject determines method rather than method dictating subject.

General Steps in Empirical Research in Criminal Justice

Although research varies considerably in scope, style, and procedure, most studies—particularly those of a more quantitative nature—follow these general **steps in research:**

Steps in research

1. *Problem formulation.* Review, selection, and specification of the area to be investigated.
2. *Research design.* Type of experimental or nonexperimental approach, studies of a group (or groups) at one time or over a period of time, and use of control groups.
3. *Data collection methods.* Choice of a variety of methods such as observation, reanalysis of existing data, questionnaires, and interviews.
4. *Analysis and presentation of findings.* Summarizing, reporting, statistically analyzing where appropriate and presenting findings.
5. *Conclusions, interpretations, and limitations.* What the researcher believes the study has to say.

Despite the neat, logical appearance of the research reported in journal articles, it is the rare project that follows these steps in a straightforward fashion. Some research, for instance, is exploratory and hypothesis generating rather than hypothesis testing in nature. The steps remain, however, a useful heuristic device for explaining the process at this stage in a simple manner. Although we will discuss problem formulation next, the organization of the text is designed to follow these steps. The next chapter examines ethics in research, Chapters 3–8 look at different data-gathering methods, and subsequent chapters discuss the presentation of findings and their interpretation. By combining these steps with the model of the research process described in Figure 1.1, we find that the investigator is often faced first with the issue of finding a research problem.

Problem Formulation: Selection of Research Problem

Problem formulation

Problem formulation may be guided by many concerns including personal experiences. Take your gut feelings seriously and pursue them. Chances are that each of us has unique experiences or sensitivities that give us an edge in terms of interest or feel for a subject. This is an advantage that should be capitalized upon. Practical concerns may govern one's decision—data are available on the job, our agency needs to have a similar study done, or the subject is manageable and likely to be completed in the time allotted. The latter is certainly an important consideration in academic theses and dissertations.

In selecting a research problem one should look for gaps in theory or the current state of the art, feasibility of doing the research, ambiguous and conflicting findings in the current literature, as well as the potential timeliness of policy implications. Additionally, the availability of funding and sponsorship is an important consideration, particularly in large-scale projects. The NIJ has an active research agenda and specified the following areas for funding for fiscal year 1995–1996 (NIJ, 1994):

Reducing violent crimes
    Studies of offenders and offenses
    Violent situations
    Firearms violence
    Response to violent offenders
    Violence against women
Reducing drug- and alcohol-related crime
    Substance abuse and criminal behavior
    Substance abusing offenders and the criminal justice system
    Treatment and aftercare evaluations
    Drug use forecasting (DUF) research
    Drug enforcement
Reducing the consequences of crime
    Assessing victim needs
    Program evaluations
    Criminal justice system response to victims
    Victimization patterns
    Impact of crime on victims
    Impact of crime on service delivery
Improving the effectiveness of crime prevention programs
    Crime prevention for high-risk youths
    Developing community-based crime prevention partnerships
    Location-specific crime prevention programs
    Crimes and offender behavior
    Crime by and related to illegal aliens
Improving law enforcement and the criminal justice system
    Law enforcement
    Prosecution, defense, and adjudication issues at pretrial stage
      New approaches
      Drug courts

> Juvenile justice
> Community and institutional corrections
>> Boot camps
>> Sanctions and punishments
>> Meeting offender needs
>> Preserving safety
>> Managing change
> Systemwide issues
>> Consequences of decisions on system responses
>> Sentencing
>> Illegal aliens
>> White-collar and organized crime
> Developing new technology for law enforcement and the criminal justice
>> system
> Forensic sciences
> Less-than-lethal technology
> Science and technology
> Drug testing

Other sources that may influence one's choice of research problem include administrative decision-making needs, scientific or intellectual interests, or attempts to ameliorate crime or injustice. Minority and feminist scholars have charged that much research and scholarship in criminology and criminal justice has ignored minorities and females and has spoken primarily from a white, androcentric (male-centered) bias (Chesney-Lind, 1989; Mann, 1993; and Russell, 1992). Exhibit 1.2 examines some of these issues.

Problem Formulation: Specification of Research Problem

The mere selection of a subject for investigation is only the beginning. One must now formulate hypotheses, define key concepts, indicate appropriate operationalization or decide upon a qualitative sensitizing approach, decide upon research strategies, and finally relate one's research problem to broader issues in criminal justice.

One key way to search for research problems is, of course, through a literature review (O'Block, 1992). Such a search will more likely than not hone what may have begun as a simple, vague hunch. Many novice researchers, anxious to get on with the task, view the problem formulation and literature review stages of a research project as a waste of precious time or a painful

EXHIBIT 1.2

Feminist Perspectives and Research Methods

Feminist theory has emerged as a major force in criminology and criminal justice. While it has many expressions, it draws on Marxist, interactionist, and critical theory and advocates a methodology that differs from the dominant empirical positivism. Some feminist writers view the latter as failing to include gender as a central force and as being blind to its own ideological bias, an androcentrism that ignores females as a central part of crime and justice issues. "Observers are gendered beings, and the research act is a gendered production. Feminism lays positivism to rest in the human disciplines" (Denzin, 1989, pp. 66–67; and Denzin, 1984). In calling for nonsexist research methods, Eichler (1988) speaks of "gender insensitivity" in social science research. This involves an ignoring of gender as an important social variable.

Others attack "malestream" approaches to empirical criminal justice and argue that feminist writings and voices should be incorporated into the mainstream of criminal justice education (McDermott, 1992; and Renzetti, 1993). Such inclusion of feminist methods in social research (Reinharz, 1992) can be illustrated by a study by Elizabeth Stanko (1990), *Everyday Violence: How Women and Men Experience Sexual and Physical Dangers,* in which she used in-depth interviews to tap women's experiences that do not turn up in standard surveys. Feeling that much nonfeminist research is sexist due to cultural beliefs and a preponderance of male researchers, feminists question perspectives that assume traditional gender roles. This bias particularly has expressed itself in the past in writings on topics such as rape and domestic violence.

In a content analysis of twenty-two introductory criminal justice texts in print in 1989, Dorworth and Henry (1992) found that women and blacks were underrepresented in photographs as authorities. While women were overrepresented as victims, blacks were overrepresented as offenders. Criminology has omitted black females by equating "woman" with white woman and "black" with black male (Rice, 1990). McDermott (1992, pp. 247–248) enjoins:

> The newer feminist perspectives suggest that reality isn't clean and tidy, and that experiences don't come in little boxes that are ready to be labeled and counted. . . . It is frightening but necessary to begin to understand knowledge as situated and as socially constructed, and to view our methods of obtaining knowledge as potentially biased. We should encourage our students to consider the potential contributions of newer perspectives and to acknowledge that the issues surrounding methodology and epistemology [how we come to know] exist and are real. There is no other way to move forward.

process preceding the actual research. In reality this is the most important period of a study, because it refines that which is to be examined and relates it to current and past inquiries, thus preventing the reinvention of the wheel or rediscovery of a dead end. Table 1.2 lists selected journals and abstracts that are useful in a literature review in criminal justice and criminology. Sources of existing data are treated in more detail in the section on uses of available data in Chapter 8. Appendix A contains instructions on "How to Write a Research Report."

Exhibit 1.3 provides an illustration of the growing online services available on computer networks and the electronic highway.

TABLE 1.2   Literature Review Sources

Selected Journals Relevant to Criminal Justice and Criminology[a]

American Criminal Law Review
American Journal of Criminal Justice
American Journal of Police
American Journal of Sociology
American Sociological Review
British Journal of Criminology
British Journal of Sociology
Canadian Journal of Criminology
Corrections Digest
CJ International
Crime and Delinquency
Crime and Social Justice
Criminal Justice and Behavior
Criminal Justice Ethics
Criminal Justice Newsletter
Criminal Justice Policy Review
Criminal Justice Review
Criminology
Federal Probation
International Journal of Criminology and Penology
Journal of Contemporary Criminal Justice
Journal of Crime and Justice
Journal of Criminal Justice
Journal of Criminal Law and Criminology

Journal of Family Violence
Journal of Justice Issues
Journal of Law and Society
Journal of Legal Studies
Journal of Police Science and Administration
Journal of Quantitative Criminology
Journal of Research in Crime and Delinquency
Journal of Society Administration
Judicature
Justice Quarterly
Law and Society Review
NIJ (National Institute of Justice) Reports
Police Chief
Police Studies
The Public Interest
Public Opinion Quarterly
Social Forces
Social Problems
Social Science Quarterly
Sociological Inquiry
Sociology and Social Research
Victimology
Violence and Victims

Abstracts/Indexes[b]

Abstracts on Police Science
Crime and Delinquency Abstracts
Criminal Justice Abstracts
Criminal Justice Periodical Index
Criminology and Penology Abstracts
Document Retrieval Index
Encyclopedia of Crime and Justice
New York Times Index

Police Science Abstracts
Psychological Abstracts
Reader's Guide to Periodical Literature (for popular
   sources only)
Social Science Index
Social Sciences Citation Index
Sociological Abstracts

[a]This list is only a selection of journals and not an exhaustive list.
[b]These are among the many abstracts that are available in the reference section of the library. For more detail on sources of information in criminal justice and criminology, see Chapter 8.

EXHIBIT 1.3

PAVNET Online

Partnerships **A**gainst **V**iolence **NET**work (PAVNET) **Online** is a new approach to give users information about techniques for combating violence in American society. It represents the cooperation of multiple Federal agencies to quickly bring information on anti-violence programs to State and local officials. It is designed to relay the latest information in the most rapid way possible—via electronic media.

PAVNET was created in response to a report by the Interdepartmental Working Group on Violence to the President and the Domestic Policy Council in January 1994. That report recommended that the Federal Government "develop online computerized information about Federal resources, and produce new resource guides and how-to manuals about promising activities to reduce violence."

PAVNET Online on the Internet

The most common pathway to the information superhighway is currently provided by the *Internet*. The Internet is a worldwide system of thousands of computers organized into networks. One estimate indicates 2 million computers are connected to the Internet in 45,000 networks serving between 10 and 25 million Internet users.

Today's Internet is a global resource that began as a Department of Defense (DOD) experiment over 20 years ago. Later, the National Science Foundation (NSF) decided to link its six supercomputer centers, using a new protocol established by the DOD. The network of six supercomputers, known as NSFNET, became the foundation of Internet, and by 1989 Internet included 14 networks. Today numerous additional networks are part of the Internet including those at many universities, government agencies, and commercial organizations.

Internet users can perform four basic functions:

1. Send and receive electronic mail.
2. Transfer files from one computer to another.
3. Participate in discussion groups.
4. Search for information.

The discussion in this Guide is limited to the fourth function of searching for information.

PAVNET Online is located on Federal Government computers linked into the Internet. A prosecuting attorney in Ohio might obtain information on a violent offender prosecution program in California by connecting with PAVNET Online in Washington, D.C., through an Internet connection in Ohio.

There are several reasons why the Internet has become so popular as a research tool:

- It provides access to many sources of information, not just those close to home or work.
- It uses electronic speed to search for information. For example, it is analogous to searching dozens of library reference card catalogs in seconds.
- It allows users to narrow their searches to selected topics. For example, a search for promising programs could be narrowed to "juvenile intensive supervision programs for violent offenders."
- It offers direct access to information about reducing violence in America. By having information available on the Internet, PAVNET Online provides a faster search routine for materials related to violence.

Information in PAVNET Online

The following three major categories of information are currently in PAVNET Online:

- Promising Programs.
- Information Sources and Technical Assistance.
- Funding Sources.

Full discussion of PAVNET Online, access to Internet via navigational tools, gopher systems, telnet, and file transfer protocol are too lengthy for discussion here; but full explanation can be obtained free by consulting the sources cited at the end of this exhibit. Once on the PAVNET system through Internet the user selects from various menu boards and can "download" (print out entire documents) on their personal computer.

The main menu under PAVNET Online looks like this; (note the back slash [/] after an item means that another menu will appear if you select this item):

```
PAVNET ONLINE: Partnerships
Against Violence
Page 1 of 1

1 About PAVNET Online/
2 Latest Additions to PAVNET
  Online/
3 PAVNET Online's Search Routine
4 Promising Programs/
5 Funding Sources for Violence
  Prevention/
6 Information Sources and
  Technical Assistance/
7 Other Violence Prevention
  Program Resources/
8 Other Internet Resources/
```

```
Enter Item Number, SAVE, ?, or
BACK: 1
```

You may want to start by finding some background information on PAVNET Online. When you select item 1, you will find all the chapters of this manual plus whatever may have been added since the manual's publication.

```
About PAVNET Online
Page 1 of 1

1 What is PAVNET Online?
2 How to Access PAVNET Online
3 How to Use PAVNET Online
4 PAVNET Online Clearinghouses
  and Resource Centers
5 Selected Bibliography
6 Glossary

Enter Item Number, SAVE, ?, or
BACK: 3
```

Sources: "PAVNET Online User's Guide." National Institute of Justice Research in Action, March 1995, NCJ 152057.

The information in PAVNET Online is also available in a two-column Partnerships in Violence Resource Guide and on diskette in Word Perfect 5.1 or ASCII. Call NCJRS at 1-800-851-3420 for more information.

Summary

In this introductory chapter we discussed why those who attack criminological or criminal justice research as being common sense often deceive themselves with nonsense, substituting their own personal bias or ignorance for objective, scientific information. The study of research methods was described as an invaluable tool for understanding the latest developments in criminal justice as well as in society. *Knowledge* is what people create symbolically to represent reality and was described by Comte as "progressing through three stages": theological (supernatural), metaphysical (philosophical, rational), and scientific (rational plus scientific method or proof). Criminal justice strives for scientific status. Scientists rely upon probabilistic knowledge, that is, predicting general trends, not each case.

In conducting or critiquing studies, researchers are advised to avoid *methodological narcissism* (fanaticism for one method or method for method's sake). Those concerned with good research should be objective, vigilant (for error), and sympathetic (because all research is infested with error). *Theory* represents an attempt to develop plausible explanations of reality, whereas *methodology* is an attempt to collect accurate facts or data. Both are indispensable in providing sound criminal justice knowledge. New knowledge often takes place due to paradigm shifts. A paradigm is a model or scheme with which reality is viewed. *Pure research* is directed at the acquisition of new knowledge for its own sake, whereas *applied research* is interested in knowledge for the practical resolution of existing problem. *Quantitative research* (positivism) is concerned with measuring social reality using the scientific method.

Researchese, the language of research, includes *concepts* (abstract tags put on reality), *operationalization* (defining concepts by describing how they will be measured), *variables* (operationalized concepts or concepts that vary), *theories* (general statements regarding relationships between variables), and *hypotheses* (specific statements regarding the relationship between variables). Variables may be *dependent* (*outcome*) (the variable one is attempting to predict, denoted by the letter Y) and *independent* (the predictor variable, denoted by the letter X or any letter other than Y).

The *research process* was illustrated as a circular process from theory to hypothesis to research design to data gathering to findings and then back to theory.

The *general steps in empirical research in criminal justice* are: problem formulation, research design, data-collection methods, analysis/presentation of findings, and conclusions/interpretations/limitations. The first step—problem formulation—was discussed; the remaining steps will be the subject of subsequent chapters.

The feminist perspective on research methods offers an alternative to androcentric bias in criminology. Finally, PAVNET Online was presented as an example of the proliferating search services available through Internet.

Key Concepts

Replication	Verstehen	Dependent Variable
Verification	Historicism	Independent Variable
Methodological	Scientism	Hypotheses
Narcissism	Research Shock	Deduction
Theory	Researchese	Induction
Methodology	Concepts	Steps in Research
Pure Research	Operationalization	Problem Formulation
Applied Research	Paradigm	Serendipity
Quantitative Research	PAVNET	Feminist Perspectives
Qualitative Research	Variables	

Review Questions

1. Name a myth or inaccurate common sense view of crime or criminal justice other than one presented in this chapter. Indicate how research has clarified this misconception.
2. Are criminology and criminal justice sciences? Discuss some developments that support their claim to scientific status.
3. What is the role of theory in criminological/criminal justice research, and why has there been such a shortage of new theory since the 1960s?
4. Choose a recent journal article and identify: (a) the research problem, (b) research design, (c) data-gathering strategy, (d) dependent variable/s, (e) independent variable/s, and (f) operationalization of the key dependent and independent variables.
5. What is the feminist perspective on research methods? Why is there a need for such a perspective? How does it differ from the "malestream?"
6. What is the purpose of PAVNET Online? How does it operate and of what benefit is it to criminal justice researchers?

2 | Ethics in Criminal Justice Research

Ethical Horror Stories

Biomedical Examples

Unethical
biomedical
experiments

Nazi doctors tortured, maimed, and murdered innocent captive subjects. Some scientists have purposely allowed subjects to suffer and even die of a disease while withholding a known cure. As part of other experiments, researchers have deceived people into believing that they were electrocuting people; they have created an artificial prison in which participants become hostile and aggressive; or they have spied on secret sexual activity and later showed up at the subjects' homes and invaded their privacy as part of a scientific survey. Intelligence agencies have employed social scientists to gather data on dissidents in Third World countries and, along with the military, have employed researchers and scientists (including former Nazis) to conduct often bizarre and dangerous experiments on unknowing subjects. If all of these things sound like plots for a Stephen King gothic novel, they are not. Each is an actual example of a project that has raised ethical controversies.

Major ethical concerns about the use of human subjects in research originally arose as a result of the outrageous examples of inhuman Nazi experiments during World War II. Dr. Josef Mengele, the "Angel of Death," performed horrifying human experiments in which captive subjects were tortured and killed in the name of scientific research. These experiments were cold blooded and inhumane. In the name of medical research, people were infected with diseases, used as guinea pigs to test new drugs, administered poisons, and exposed to extreme temperatures and decompression to test reactions to high altitudes (Katz, 1972). After the war the Nuremberg trials defined such behavior as war crimes and crimes against humanity. The

Nuremberg Code

Nuremberg Code set forth principles governing the use of human subjects in research, including the requirement that such subjects "voluntarily consent" to participate in a study (Wexler, 1990, p. 81).

Tuskegee Syphilis Study

In the infamous *Tuskegee Syphilis Study* (Brandt, 1978) the U.S. Public Health Service withheld penicillin, a known cure for syphilis, from 425 uneducated Black male sharecroppers who suffered from and eventually died of untreated syphilis. This study, which began in 1932 before a cure for syphilis was available, was completed in the 1970s, well after such medicine was developed. Such inhumane biomedical research on unsuspecting subjects did not end with the Tuskegee Study (Jones, 1982). In the 1960s live cancer cells were injected into elderly patients at a Brooklyn hospital without their knowledge. The U.S. military services, during and after World War II, exposed their own soldiers to mustard gas and nuclear radiation, resulting in cases of chronic ailments and premature death. During the

Cold war experiments

post-World War II cold war era, American intelligence agencies, with the cooperation of the scientific community, performed bizarre and dangerous experiments on unknowing subjects. In the early years of the cold war, American intelligence agencies had become convinced that the Communists had developed secret mind control and brainwashing techniques and that it was necessary in this battle for human minds and world domination to pull out all the stops (Scheflin and Opton, 1978; Hagan, 1990).

This explains, but does not condone, the following abuses:

- Government researchers slipped LSD into the drink of an unsuspecting government employee, who then committed suicide. Later, the government refused to tell his grief- and guilt-stricken family what really happened.

- In the 1950s, using code names like Bluebird, Artichoke, and MKUltra, the CIA, FBI, and U.S. military experimented with behavior-control devices and interrogation techniques, including ESP, drugs, polygraphs, hypnosis, shock therapy, surgery, and radiation. These experiments involved secret testing on unsuspecting citizens and, if death or injury occurred, a cover-up (Cousins, 1979; Simon and Eitzen, 1996).
- In 1988 the CIA agreed to pay damages to eight Canadian citizens who had been victims of experiments at a Montreal mental hospital (Witt, 1988, p. 2A). As an example, a Canadian teenager seeking medical treatment for an arthritic leg was first given LSD, and then was subjected to electroshock therapy and forced to listen to taped messages saying, "You killed your mother." Such studies were conducted on more than 100 Canadians and were financed by the CIA and conducted by an American doctor who had been the former president of the American Psychiatric Association.
- In 1986 the House Energy and Commerce Subcommittee uncovered the fact that during a thirty-year period beginning in the mid-1940s, federal agencies had conducted exposure experiments on American citizens, including injecting them with plutonium, radium, and uranium. These studies included feeding radium or thorium to elderly patients during an experiment at the Massachusetts Institute of Technology, irradiating inmates' testes with x rays, and exposing people to open-air fallout tests and feeding them real fallout from a Nevada test site (Lawrence, 1988). It was later revealed that the U.S. military even employed former Nazi doctors and scientists, using them to conduct chemical experiments on U.S. military personnel at Fort Dietrick (Aberdeen, Maryland).

Social Science Examples

Most of the foregoing examples have been *biomedical* in nature; but because social and behavioral research likewise puts subjects at risk, its activities have led to similar ethical concerns. Many social scientific studies related to crime and deviance have come under scrutiny. The three social scientific studies that seem to be cited in the literature most often are: Stanley Milgram's *Obedience to Authority* (1974), Philip Zimbardo's simulated prison experiment (1972, 1973, 1974), and Laud Humphreys' *Tearoom Trade* (1970).

Social science examples

In his classic *Obedience to Authority* study, Stanley Milgram had one very important objective: He wanted to discover the causes of the Holocaust. During the Nazi era in Germany, some people performed their gruesome duties as if it was "just another day at the office." How and why do average, "normal" people commit the most monstrous acts? In Milgram's study, which was designed to answer this question, volunteer subjects were recruited and paid to act as "teachers" while "confederates" (fake subjects who were really in on the study) acted as "pupils." The subjects (teachers) were then deceived into believing that each time they

Milgram's study

threw a lever on a shock apparatus, they were administering gradually more painful electric shocks to pupils, whom they could hear but not see. When the pupils failed to answer a question correctly, the teachers were to administer shocks. Despite protests from the pupils, teachers were willing to administer levels of voltage which they believed to be dangerous, particularly when assured by lab assistants, who appeared as scientific authorities, that such behavior was necessary. Subjects experienced personal turmoil both during and immediately after the experiment, although debriefing (explaining the purpose of the study after-the-fact) seemed to have resulted in no long-term harm. In the name of science do experimenters have the ethical right to deceive and put subjects in a position of emotional stress?

Zimbardo's simulated prison

In Philip Zimbardo's *simulated prison study*, male, undergraduate, paid volunteers assumed the roles of either guard or prisoner. A mock prison was constructed in the basement of a Stanford University building; and prisoners and guards assumed their respective roles, complete with uniforms, nightsticks, and mirrored sunglasses for the guards, and numbers and prison garb for the prisoners. Whereas the experiment was to have lasted at least two weeks, individuals became so carried away with the roles—passivity and hostility by prisoners and aggressive and dehumanizing behavior by guards—that Zimbardo cancelled the study after six days rather than risk harm to the participants.

The possibility of such potential harm is even worse if the subjects do not consent to participate in a study; in such experiments observation usually takes place in private settings and the behavior involves activity which society may regard as immoral or illegal. All of these factors were present in

Humphrey's Tearoom Trade

Laud Humphreys' controversial study, *Tearoom Trade* (1970), one involving secret male homosexual behavior in public restrooms. Pretending to be a "watchqueen" (voyeur), Humphreys served as both a lookout and as a hidden observer of such behavior. He copied license numbers and traced them to the owners' homes. Changing his appearance, Humphreys showed up at their homes under the guise of a mental health researcher.

Although Humphreys' research was important to the criminal justice system, which gained important insights into the nature of such participants who engage in impersonal homosexual liaisons in public places, was the obtaining of such knowledge justified given the risk for potential harm to subjects if their secret sexual behavior were to become known to legal authorities, family, or employers? Even though Humphreys claimed to have taken great precautions to protect the anonymity of the subjects, did he have the right to put them in harm's way without their permission? Is there any way of studying such behavior without using deceit and deception? Should criminological researchers study only volunteers?

What if the researchers are themselves the subject of deception? Through various fronts during the 1960s and 1970s, the CIA, apparently without the knowledge of the recipients, funded social psychological research by such names as Sherifs, Orne, Rogers, Osgood, and Goffman (Marks, 1979, p. 121), and it financed the publication of more than one thousand books, pretending that they were the products of independent scholarship (Cook, 1984, p. 287).

Project Camelot

In *Project Camelot* (Horowitz, 1965), for example, U.S. researchers studied student and peasant insurgency movements in Chile. Because this was an area of the world where government opponents routinely "disappeared," many subjects were justifiably suspicious of this effort, and they feared the data it would generate. Believing that the "Yanqui" researchers were gathering this information for intelligence purposes, they thought the study would have a chilling effect on dissent. Although the researchers denied such CIA involvement at the time, some of the researchers later discovered that their data were in fact being gathered for intelligence purposes. The government of Chile, which had been unaware of the project, expelled the researchers and brought to an end the infamous *Project Camelot*. Among the many questions raised by this study are: Should researchers do the bidding of intelligence agencies, thus acting as spies? Whose side is social research on? Should researchers refuse certain sponsorship or specify the conditions under which sponsorship will be accepted?

There has been no shortage of such ethical horror stories, including those involving correctional research on prisoner "volunteers" (Cassell and Wax, 1980, p. 260). Mitford in *Kind and Unusual Punishment* (1973) documents abuse of inmates by medical researchers. Such human experimentation has been condemned by the American Correctional Association (1976).

Researcher Fraud and Plagiarism

A fundamental expectation of any piece of scientific research is that it be accurate, honest, and properly referenced. This, incidentally, is the reason that professors harp upon these themes when correcting student papers; and those who ignore these lessons may become haunted by them later in life.

Research fraud

Research fraud occurs when researchers purposely fabricate or misrepresent their findings. Despite the pressure on researchers to "publish or perish"—tenure and grants are often dependent on their success in getting published in research publications—the actual number of cases of research fraud are relatively rare. In 1989, however, the Department of Health and Human Services started an Office of Scientific Integrity to address this issue (Neuman, 1991, p. 438 l; "Fraud in Research," 1994).

Perhaps the most celebrated case of researcher dishonesty was that of Sir Cyril Burt, a famous British psychologist, whose studies on twins had demonstrated the inherited nature of intelligence. But after his death other researchers discovered that he had faked his data and that he had even created nonexistent coauthors (Wade, 1976). It should be noted, however, that more recent investigations of the Burt affair have drawn differing conclusions (Hearnshaw, 1979), with some reviewers indicating that Burt was innocent of outright fraud and that some of his detractors may have been guilty of character assassination (Joynson, 1989; and Fletcher, 1991). In 1995 Dr. Gerald L. Gerson, after examining Louis Pasteur's 102 laboratory notebooks, charged

---

EXHIBIT 2.1

Legendary Research Scams

Most famous cases of research fraud have taken place in medicine and the physical sciences, but two cases in the social sciences have raised considerable controversy: the "Piltdown Hoax" and the "Tasaday Hoax." The Piltdown Hoax was perpetrated in England in 1911 with the claim that the fossil remains of the evolutionary "missing link" between apes and humans had been discovered. The unearthed bones had some features of humans and some features of apes. In the 1950s researchers using carbon dating were able to document that the remains were of recent origin, that the human skull had simply been combined with portions of the jaw of an orangutan, and then the entire remains were treated to appear to be very old in origin (Broad and Wade, 1983; Weiner, 1955; and Spencer, 1990).

A similar outright fraud took place in the 1970s in the Philippines. Television documentaries and large-scale media exposure was given to the discovery of a lost tribe, the Tasaday, a peaceful, "Stone Age" community that had no previous contact with the modern world. Later investigations revealed that no humans had probably ever lived on the supposed Tasaday Island and that the entire hoax had involved government officials encouraging local peasants to pretend to be primitives in order to attract tourists or other publicity (Marshall, 1989).

Pasteur had misled, lied, secretly stole a rival's techniques, and otherwise deceived the scientific world in order to receive grants, patents, and awards (Altman, 1995). Exhibit 2.1 depicts two legendary research scams.

Plagiarism   **Plagiarism,** as most college students know, is a type of fraud in which a writer presents the ideas or work of someone else as his or her own. Prominent figures such as Senator Joseph Biden, Alex Haley, John Hersey, and Martin Luther King, Jr., have been accused of plagiarism. Researchers should be very careful to properly acknowledge—and therefore not take credit for or steal—the ideas of others (Broad and Wade, 1993; and LaFollette, 1992).

The Researcher's Role

Ethical concerns in criminal justice research raise potential problems for the researcher with respect to the various roles she or he must often play. The role of researcher as scientist may intersect with, and sometimes conflict with, the role of criminal justice practitioner, the role of citizen, and the role of humanitarian. Rabow (1980), for instance, sees the conflict of scientific and treatment roles in corrections as hindering the effort to improve and apply treatment successfully.

Researcher's role   The **role of researcher** requires that one be objective and "value free" in approaching and reporting on the subject matter. As was indicated, particularly in our previous treatment of participant observational studies of criminals, such a stance often impinges on one's concept of the proper role of a criminal justice practitioner. The practitioner is involved in programmatic efforts to prevent, rehabilitate, and otherwise process criminals and/or crime. Such a role obviously conflicts with the role of neutral observer and scientist. Similar conflicts may take place with one's role as citizen or humanitarian, wherein one is concerned with cooperating with public officials or expressing concern and supporting efforts for eliminating inequitable social conditions or human maladies. In a classic statement, Polsky directs himself to the moral issues of field studies of criminals:

> If one is effectively to study adult criminals in their natural settings, he must make the moral decision that in some ways he will break the law himself. He need not be a "participant" observer and commit the criminal acts under study, yet he has to witness such acts or be taken into confidence about them and not blow the whistle. . . . According to Yablonsky, nonmoralizing on the part of the researcher, when coupled with intense interest in the criminal's life, really constitutes a romantic encouragement of the criminal. . . . [Polsky feels] the burden of proof rests upon those who claim that abstention from moralizing by the field investigator has any significantly encouraging effect on criminal's lifestyles, and they have not supplied one bit of such proof. Finally, our society at present seems plentifully supplied with moral uplifters in any case, so one needn't worry if a few sociological students of crime fail to join the chorus. . . . The majority of criminologists are social scientists only up to a point . . . and beyond that point they are really social workers in disguise or else correction officers manqués. . . . This is not to deny his right as an ordinary citizen to be "engaged" and make value judgments about crime, politics, sex, religion, or any other area of moral dispute. . . . But, what of one's duty as a citizen? Shouldn't that take precedence? Well, different types of citizens have different primary duties. And our very understanding of "citizenship" itself is considerably furthered in the long run if one type of citizen, the criminologist conceives his primary duty to be the advancement of scientific knowledge about crime even when such advancement can be made only by "obstructing justice" with respect to particular criminals in the short run (Polsky, 1967, pp. 139–143).

The National Advisory Committee on Criminal Justice Standards and Goals addresses the intersection of researcher as scientist, researcher as criminal justice practitioner, and researcher as citizen:

> Criminal justice researchers who are funded by, work closely with, or are employees of agencies whose functions include law enforcement can encounter ethical problems when they appear to assist in law enforcement activities. Although most researchers would support the objective of enhancing the effectiveness of the criminal justice system and recognize their duties as citizens to do so, the progress of research may nonetheless be undermined by failure to distinguish between their roles as researcher and the roles of other criminal justice personnel. The burden of maintaining this distinction falls on both researchers and agencies, but researchers who study any type of organization should guard against having to assume any nonresearch roles or even appearing to do so (National Advisory Committee, 1976, p. 131).

In self-mediating the potential conflicting roles of the criminal justice researcher, it is incumbent on the investigator to enter the setting with eyes wide open. A decision must be made beforehand on the level of commitment to the research endeavor and the analyst's ability to negotiate the likely role conflicts. Although there are no hard and fast rules and each research enterprise is in many ways a unique reality, the *researcher's primary role is that of scientist.* This is not to say that this role should in all cases take total precedence over other agenda; however, the researcher should determine limits and priorities and subject accountability as soon as practicable in embarking on a study (Punch, 1986; Reynolds, 1982).

Research Targets in Criminal Justice

Research targets in criminal justice

Criminal justice research focuses on a variety of **targets** or subject matter: the criminal, the victim, the criminal justice system and practitioners, as well as the general public. Each of these topics raises unique ethical problems or concerns for the investigator. One group that has been a traditional source of research subjects and of increasing controversy has been the incarcerated.

A national prison research commission report questioned the legitimacy and ethicality of prison research in the United States. They doubted whether prisoners' voluntary decisions to participate in studies reflect volunteerism or fear that not to "volunteer" would bring reprisals. Instead of banning all such investigations the committee called for a review by outside boards that would be made up of various constituencies including prisoners, prisoner advocates, and representatives of racial and cultural minorities (Branson, 1977).

Ethical Relativism

Denzin succinctly isolates the relative nature of ethicality in research:

There seems to be general agreement that ethics (and values as well) refer to an "ought" world. When researchers make a decision to study prisoners and not prison officials, they are making a value decision. But [when] they say that the relationship between X and Y is negative, they are making a scientific statement. Science is "an *is world,* a set of facts growing out of a consensus among a small group" (Dalton, 1964, p. 60). When I say that all sociologists *should* honor their relationship with subjects, I am making an ethical statement. When some sociologists honor these relationships, they are branded as unethical. It must be remembered that ethics and values, like scientific findings, are not statements that come from an invariant source. They do not reside in a world of abstract ideals. Rather, ethics (like all plans of action) consists of symbolic meanings subject to the most complex political arguments. Hence, when I speak of values and ethics in the scientific process, I refer to meanings that are subject to negotiation and redefinition. What is ethical in one period, one university, one profession, or one group may be unethical in another (Denzin, 1989, p. 325).

Amoral

In reality science itself is *amoral*—ethically neutral—but scientists are not *amoral* (Babbie, 1983, p. 461). Criminologists and criminal justice researchers as social scientists strive for acceptance as *professionals*. The regulation of ethically acceptable research conduct may take one of three forms:

Codes of ethics and institutional review boards, which are adopted by professional associations or institutions doing research such as universities.

Procedures imposed by the federal government (primarily to regulate biomedical research, but with bearing on social research).

Legal regulation in the courts (Reynolds, 1982, p. 100).

Ethics and Professionalism

Following what has been identified as the "classic professionalism model," occupations and occupational incumbents attempt to convince the public, lawmakers, and other professionals that they are deserving of high respect, prestige, autonomy, privilege, and remuneration on the basis of two key elements (Hagan, 1975). The first is that the occupation begins to generate its own esoteric and useful knowledge. Many of the methodological issues addressed in this text are illustrative of major steps that have been taken in this direction. Unless, however, criminologists and criminal justice researchers view themselves as simply efficient, bureaucratic technocrats or social accountants, it is essential in order to convince others that the discipline is deserving of power, prestige, and independence, that its incumbents ascribe to a code of ethics, a dedication to service or science in which trust, integrity, and ethicality is assumed. *Thus, on the basis of the knowledge and service (ethics) dimensions, occupations may claim or be granted autonomy or high professional regard.* Public askance of claims by car sales personnel, insurance agents, morticians, florists, and the like basically questions the relevance or applicability of this model to all who aspire. Criminologists and criminal justice investigators, unless they wish to be regarded as in the same league as used car salespeople with a gimmick, must encourage the highest of ethical ideals not only in dealing with clients, but also in conducting research. Furthermore, such regulation of conduct must be mandated from within the profession, rather than solely being imposed by outside government funding agencies (Hagan, 1975).

Professional ethics

Some take strong issue with this view and see **professional ethics** as "a deceit and a snare," a means by which the establishment within an occupation can control and hide its activity from the public and thereby create a monopoly. Even if the occupation takes its self-policing seriously, it is used as a club to control deviance of the more creative nonestablishment members whose new ideas are vital, particularly for young professions (Douglas, 1979, p. 13). Douglas feels that ethical rules are created for outside public consumption, so that an occupation can gain a monopoly, and have little impact within the group. On the other hand, this view may be overly cynical because, if a group refuses to set its own standards, whether rigid or flexible, it is solely at the mercy of, and invites, outside regulatory groups such as government agencies to set standards for it. Douglas seems to view codes of ethics as a pincer attack on field studies by quantitative researchers within and government bureaucrats without. Revisions of the Department of Health and Human Services (HHS) guidelines to be discussed shortly may, in part, have calmed these fears.

Ethics in Criminal Justice Research

Ethical principles for criminal justice research

There is no universally accepted "code of ethics" or biblical-type description to which all criminal justice researchers must adhere. This presentation is given very much in the same spirit used by the National Advisory Committee on Criminal Justice Standards and Goals in describing its **Ethical Principles for Criminal Justice Research.**

> The intent . . . is not to propose a rigid set of guidelines for each researcher to follow. Rather, the principles and recommendations call attention to contemporary issues that neither policymakers nor researchers may have considered in a systematic manner. The application of these principles and recommendations must be tailored to the needs of each individual research project according to the unique conditions that surround it (National Advisory Committee, 1976, p. 38).

The last statement cannot be emphasized enough. Much of the academic guerrilla warfare taking place regarding ethical codes is a reaction to a view of the Orwellian "big brother" dictating and controlling the research enterprise. Rigid commandments will only invite subterfuge and hypocrisy. Reynolds (1982, p. 103) indicates that "the development of federal procedures for prior review of research with human participants is dramatic evidence of the failure of associations to convince the public that their members are to be trusted as individuals or that the associations are to be trusted to control them."

HEW guidelines for protection of human subjects

Historically, the most important source of guidance for ethical research in the United States was the **Department of Health, Education, and Welfare's (HEW) Institutional Guide to DHEW Policy on Protection of Human Subjects** (1971), which requires that any grant recipients abide by its stipulations. Since 1980 the most important source has been that of the Department of Health and Human Services. Both the codes of ethics of professional associations (internal controls) and federal requirements (external controls) are constantly changing.

History of Federal Regulation of Research

Until revision of the HHS guidelines in 1981, bitter debate took place between the social science research community and federal officials with respect to the applicability of informed consent requirements (at that time, HEW guidelines) to much of social science research. Initiated in the 1960s and eventually extended to all federally funded research, the guidelines required the informed consent of research participants as well as prior review by Institutional Review Boards (IRB) weighing the costs to participants versus the benefits to science and society. Although each agency, including the Department of Justice, had its own separate requirements, the HEW (now HHS) procedures were the most developed and tended to be adopted by the other agencies (Reynolds, 1982, p. 104). **Institutional Review Boards** are research screening committees set up in colleges and universities to oversee the ethical propriety of research.

Institutional review boards

In a sense, the original HEW guidelines were comparable to a researcher's "Miranda warning"—basic information that must be assured with respect to the consent of research subjects. The original 1971 HEW guidelines contained six elements for obtaining informed consent (Code of Federal Regulations, 1975, pp. 11854–11858):

1. A fair explanation of the procedures to be followed, and their purposes, including identifications of any experimental procedures.
2. A description of any attendant discomforts and risks that can be expected.
3. A description of any benefits reasonably to be expected.
4. A disclosure of any appropriate alternative procedures that might be advantageous for the subject.
5. An offer to answer any inquiries concerning the procedures.
6. Instruction that the person is free to withdraw consent and discontinue participation at any time without prejudice to him or her.

Because HEW supported both physical (particularly biomedical) and social science research, these rules originally applied equally, and some critics suggested that this marriage produced unworkable requirements, particularly when applied to field research.

Informed consent

The requirement that sponsored research include provisions for making the subjects aware of the intentions of the study and sign **informed consent** forms obviously represented problems in field research of deviants. Weppner saw two problems that this raised for *Street Ethnography* (1977, p. 41). The first is the possible desire of subjects, if engaged in deviant or illegal activity, to remain anonymous; and second, the difficulty of gaining informed consent from others who turn up on-the-scene but are not the primary subjects of observation. He felt that a strict interpretation of HEW guidelines would make street ethnography impossible and the ability of subjects to withdraw might also destroy random samples in other types of research. O'Connor, in reviewing revised recommendations of HEW guidelines, also felt that, "If the recommendations of the Commission are accepted as they stand, the covert observation debate, long an issue of contention within social research, will have been settled" (1979, p. 253). The settlement would be a ban against such research. Talarico (1980, p. 207) views the issue as a two-edged sword in that important concerns for privacy may protect influential system officials from needed investigation. Should criminal justice become a subject that studies solely volunteers?

Assuming that the specter of criminal justice researchers as mad Nazi scientists is misplaced, and that professional investigators do not go out of their way to harm or threaten the well-being of respondents, some privacy invasion is necessary. Sometimes investigative research strategies involve deceit and infiltration as necessary approaches to studying hidden behavior. This intrusion is tolerable if potential harm to respondents is avoided and if the researcher takes adequate steps to assure that the respondents' identity is protected in any publications (Douglas, 1978). Such protection may include, as Denzin suggests, the decision to delete or not report certain portions temporarily until the subjects are out of harm's way. Publication is delayed until the subjects have left the scene, and thus the information is no longer threatening to their status (Denzin, 1989, p. 336).

Informed consent was viewed as applicable in controlled biomedical and psychological experimentation where researchers have definite plans for their subjects, but in fieldwork the issue was seen as less straightforward. Wax (1980, pp. 275–276) identifies six paradoxes of consent as applied to the practice of fieldwork:

1. Many people studied may be semiliterate and not accustomed to the legal argot of forms.
2. Many will distrust a situation requiring their endorsement of a piece of paper.
3. Consent of subjects is a continual process dependent on mutual learning and evolution.
4. Knowing nothing of ethnography, they have no basis upon which to decide to give or not to give consent.
5. Ethnography involves observation and discussion and not a rationalistic a priori analysis.
6. Fieldwork is an evolving process; thus the subjects of investigation are likely to shift during the course of study.

A related question is "Are all subjects equally deserving of informed consent?" Public figures and institutions can be observed by anyone and are less vulnerable than private citizens in private places (Thorne, 1980). The right to privacy may not apply to Hitler, Stalin, Ku Klux Klan (KKK), or Murder Incorporated, (Fichter and Kolb, 1953). Galliher very lucidly makes this point:

> While all people may be worthy of the same respect as human beings, it does not necessarily follow that their activities merit the same degree of protection

and respect. As indicated earlier, Lofland questioned possible prohibitions on the undercover study of fascist groups. It is questionable whether the files of the American Nazi Party are deserving of the same respect as any other data source; must one secure the active cooperation of the Ku Klux Klan, or for that matter of the Pentagon, before conducting research in their organizations or with their personnel? While doing research in South Africa, van den Berge concluded "From the outset, I decided that I should have no scruples in deceiving the government. . . ." The question is, how much honor is proper for the sociologist in studying the membership and organization of what he considers an essentially dishonorable, morally outrageous, and destructive enterprise? Is not the failure of sociology to uncover corrupt, illegitimate, covert practices of government or industry because of the supposed prohibitions of professional ethics tantamount to supporting such practices (Galliher, 1973, p. 96).

Application of the same rule intended to protect the powerless from powerful institutions is misdirected (Galliher, 1980, p. 305). Applications of HEW standards to Woodward and Bernstein's Watergate investigations would have changed the course of American history (O'Connor, 1979, p. 264).

The Belmont Report

Belmont
Report

Reaction to many of these concerns regarding written informed consent led to the National Research Act of 1974, which created the National Commission for the Protection of Human Subjects (NCPHS). NCPHS reviewed the HEW guidelines and developed revised guidelines, *The Belmont Report: Ethical Principles and Guidelines for the Protection of Human Subjects of Research,* in which it proposed altering the role of IRBs so as not to interfere with the investigator's freedom of research and recommended alteration of the informed consent in the case of field research (HEW, 1978). Chambers (1980, p. 331) indicates that a distinction is also made between biomedical and social science research, with the latter viewed as having lower potential risk and thus potentially subject to fewer restrictions in the review process.

Protection of
human
subjects

O'Connor (1979), in a review of the implications of The Belmont Report, claims that many of the same restrictions on medical research still bind internal review boards overseeing social science research. The Belmont Report (National Commission for the *Protection of Human Subjects,* 1978a) called for the recognition of *three basic principles:* respect for persons, beneficence, and justice. According to the *principle of respect for persons,* individuals are to be treated as autonomous agents and, if autonomy is diminished, they are entitled to protection. The principle of respect for persons is realized through informed consent. The *principle of beneficence* requires that research not harm subjects and that possible benefits be maximized and potential harm minimized. This is implemented through *risk-benefit assessment.* Finally, the *principle of justice* asks that both the benefits and burdens of research be distributed equitably through the selection of subjects (O'Connor, 1979, p. 229).

Perhaps the final resolution of the application of HEW regulations to social and behavioral research took place in January 1981 with the publication of new regulations by the Department of Health and Human Services. Taking into account most of the criticisms by social scientists of the original regulations, it virtually excludes most social science research from the regulations. The types of research excluded from the review requirements are survey or interview procedures, observations of public behavior, and the use of existing data if these are not linked to identifiers ("Regulations on the Protection of Human Subjects," 1981).

HHS Guidelines

HHS guidelines

In response to The Belmont Report as well as criticism by social scientists of strict federal regulations designed to regulate biomedical research, major changes in the *HHS guidelines* and federal regulation of research took place on January 26, 1981 (Federal Register 46, no. 16, 8366–8392). These changes reduced dramatically HHS review over most social science research and placed the actual decisions involving studies in the hands of IRBs (Institutional Review Boards)—committees at the researcher's home institution. Principal changes included the following:

The regulations apply only to research with human subjects conducted with HHS or supported fully or in part by HHS funds.

Most areas of social science and criminal justice research, for example most field studies, are exempt from the regulations.

Many projects (particularly routine biomedical research) are now qualified for "expedited" review, usually approval by only one member of the IRB.

The new federal regulations were viewed as minimal standards and local IRBs could require higher standards if they wished. The new guidelines acknowledge that HHS has no jurisdiction over research receiving no federal funding.

Research Activities Exempt from HHS Review

Research exempt from HHS review

Research activities exempt from HHS review include research in educational settings related to normal educational practices, such as curriculum strategies and instructional techniques. Also exempt is research using educational tests, as long as confidentiality is maintained. Most important to social science researchers is the general exemption for research involving survey or interview procedures, except where all of the following conditions exist:

Responses are recorded in such a manner that the human subjects can be identified, directly or through identifiers linked to subjects.

The subject's responses, if they became known outside the research, could reasonably place the subject at risk of criminal or civil liability or be damaging to the subject's financial standing or employability.
The research deals with sensitive aspects of the subject's own behavior such as illegal conduct, drug use, sexual behavior, or use of alcohol. All research involving survey or interview procedures is exempt, without exception, when the respondents are elected or appointed public officials or candidates for public office.

Similarly, research involving the observation (including observation by participants) of public behavior is exempt, except where all of the following conditions exist:

Observations are recorded in such a manner that the human subjects can be identified, directly or through identifiers linked to the subjects.
The observations recorded about the individual, if they became known outside the research, could reasonably place the subject at risk of criminal or civil liability or be damaging to the subject's financial standing or employability.
The research deals with sensitive aspects of the subject's own behavior such as illegal conduct, drug use, sexual behavior, or use of alcohol.

Research involving the study of existing data, documents, records, pathological specimens, or diagnostic specimens is exempt, if these sources are publicly available or if the information is recorded by the investigator in such a manner that subjects cannot be identified, directly or through identifiers linked to the subjects (*Federal Register* [January 26, 1981], 386–388).

The specific areas identified for expedited review had relevance primarily to biochemical rather than social science research, for example, the use of medical and dental diagnostic equipment. The one area that had some relevance was studies of perception, cognition, game theory, or test development in which there is little stress placed on or manipulation of subjects (*Federal Register* [January 26, 1981], 8392).

Projects that are not exempt still require full review, in which case the IRB must weigh the cost and benefits of such studies.

[T]he IRB is expected to consider the extent to which risks to the participants are minimized, the relationships between risks and anticipated benefits of research, and the importance of the knowledge to be developed. The IRB will also consider the equitable selection of subjects and the acquisition and documentation of informed consent, it will monitor participants when necessary to ensure their safety and make provisions for protecting their privacy. If participants are vulnerable to coercion (such as mental patients and children), additional safeguards should be considered (Reynolds, 1982, p.106).

The "Elements of Informed Consent" applicable to nonexempt programs detail specific guarantees to subjects required of all projects, additional requirements for more hazardous projects, exceptions for evaluations of existing public programs, and exceptions for "deceptive research" in which subjects are informed afterward so as not to destroy the scientific purposes of the project (*Federal Register* [January 26, 1981], 8389–8390). These are expanded requirements of the original HEW guidelines discussed previously; there are fewer objections by social researchers now, because most of their projects are exempt.

In reviewing federal regulation of research, the National Research Act of 1974 had created IRBs to monitor research, but ambiguous guidelines from the HEW and the utilization of biomedical guideposts created a storm of protests from social scientists. The revised regulations represent a victory for the social sciences.

> The major battle on the limits of power by IRBs on social science research has been completed. The issues were complex. Initially there was widespread misunderstanding of the nature and "risk" of social science research, based on misplaced similarities with biomedical research. In the long run, HHS was responsive to the criticisms which emerged from the inappropriate reviews which had occurred in the past by some IRBs. The final regulations do not treat all social science research as inherently involving risk. It narrows its attention by exclusion and thus focuses its attention on that which is relevant. It is quite possible that other problems might develop in the implementation of the new rules, but, as of now, that result is a considerable "victory" for the social sciences ("Final Research," 1981, p. 9).

Combining professionalism, ethical behavior, and informed consent issues, Sanders draws yet another analogy between detective work and sociological researchers, although the same holds for criminal justice research:

> Unlike the detective, the sociologist does not face legal constraints in gathering evidence. The sociologist's data will not be invalidated if he does not warn his subjects that what they say may be used against them, nor do defense lawyers instruct subjects not to speak to sociologists. However, sociologists do have an unwritten code by which they attempt to abide.
>
> Sociological researchers should not invade the privacy of others without their permission. For instance, even if they were legally able to do so, sociologists should not plant bugs in people's homes or locate themselves so that they can secretly observe others in private places. Similarly, sociologists should avoid lying, cheating, and stealing as resources for gathering data. Often it may seem that the only way to get information is by using techniques that are unethical and rationalizing their use in the name of sociology. Not only is such behavior unethical, but if sociologists began to engage regularly in these practices, they would soon lose their position of trust and would find it difficult to persuade informants to reveal information (Sanders, 1976, p. 9).

The withdrawal of government regulation over many areas of social research is a recognition that professional groups will regulate their own ethical conduct.

National Institute of Justice's Human Subject Protection Requirements

The National Institute of Justice (NIJ) utilizes the HHS guidelines as well as specifies the following:

> Research that examines individual traits and experiences plays a vital part in expanding our knowledge about criminal behavior. It is essential, however, that researchers protect subjects from needless risk of harm or embarrassment and proceed with their willing and informed cooperation. NIJ requires that investigators protect information identifiable to research participants. When information is safeguarded, it is protected by statute from being used in legal proceedings. "[S]uch information and copies thereof shall be immune from legal process, and shall not, without the consent of the person furnishing such information, be admitted as evidence or used for any purpose in any action, suit, or other judicial, legislative or administrative proceedings" (42 United States Code 3789g) (NIJ, 1994, p. 30).

Regulations on confidentiality

NIJ's Regulations on Confidentiality protect individuals by forbidding the use of any research or statistical information that might identify them. In addition, the Institute has adopted the HHS *Model Policy on Human Research Subjects.* This policy requires that each institution engaged in NIJ research provide written assurance that it will comply with these regulations as codified at 45 Code of Federal Regulations 46. Pursuant to that policy, each research project falling within the guidelines established by HHS must be approved by the recipient's IRB prior to initiation of the project. Approval by the IRB need not precede the submission of a proposal to NIJ but it must be obtained prior to the beginning of any research activity (NIJ, 1994). Applicants should file their plans to protect sensitive information as part of their proposal. Necessary safeguards are detailed in 28 Code of Federal Regulations (CFR) paragraph 22. A short "how-to" guideline for developing a privacy and confidentiality plan can be obtained from NIJ program managers.

In addition, the U.S. Department of Justice has adopted Human Subjects policies similar to those established by the U.S. Department of Health and Human Services. In general, these policies exempt most NIJ-supported research from Institutional Review Board (IRB) review. However, the Institute may find in certain instances that subjects or subject matters may require IRB review. These exemptions will be decided on an individual basis during application review. Researchers are encouraged to review 28 CFR 46, paragraph 46.101 to determine their individual project requirements (NIJ, 1994, p. 30).

Confidentiality of Criminal Justice Research

Regulations on the confidentiality of research and statistical data were enacted as part of the 1973 amendment to the Omnibus Crime Control and Safe Streets Act. Section 524(a) reads:

> Except as provided by Federal law other than this title, no officer or employee of the Federal Government, nor any recipient of assistance under the provisions of this title, shall use or reveal any research or statistical information furnished under this title by any person and identifiable to any specific private person for any purpose other than the purpose for which it was obtained in accordance with the title. Copies of such information shall be immune from legal process, and shall not, without consent of the person furnishing such information, be admitted as evidence or used for any purpose in any action, suit, or other judicial or administrative proceedings (LEAA, 1979, p. 1).

Shield laws

This law basically constitutes a "shield law" for researchers performing federally funded research. **Shield laws** constitute a governmental immunity from prosecution, a state-guaranteed right to confidentiality for researchers if they are subpoenaed. "All identifiable research or statistical information is with limited exceptions, immune from administrative or judicial process" (Dahmann and Sasfy, 1982, p. 13). Investigators may be encouraged to probe more sensitive topics because they are able to protect their data. This law also protects respondents by ensuring that the data they have provided will not be used to invade their privacy. Guidelines such as those of the HHS or NIJ are, of course, established, issued, and promulgated by federal agencies, that is, governmental bodies outside of the occupation. They are intended for data gathered under their auspices or sponsorship. Of primary concern is the fact that the Freedom of Information Act of 1976 makes it possible for individuals to obtain access to nonclassified information that is collected with public funds. This could include field data that could compromise confidentiality (Chambers, 1980, p. 332). Trend, for instance, describes a project in which he was involved where, after the fact, the General Accounting Office (GAO) requested "unrestricted access to certain records" he and others had gathered as part of a Housing and Urban Development project. They wanted the case files so that an audit could check family sizes and incomes as part of an eligibility study (Trend, 1980, p. 344). Eventually, a compromise was worked out that allowed a GAO audit while maintaining confidentiality. Trend, as a result of his experience, offers the following advice:

> Telling people to read the contract they sign, to know how far they're willing to go if pressed, and to not make promises they cannot keep all seems pretentious and sappy. . . . In the end, the best advice I can give is to not be gulled into thinking that your notes are sacrosanct and nobody can get to them no matter what. If you're sure of your contract, your client, and your own resolve, then promising confidentiality in writing may increase the chances that you can

maintain it. However, if none of those prerequisites obtain, then the time to stop and think is before you start the research (Trend, 1980, p. 348).

In addition to governmental regulations, more fully developed professions attempt to police themselves, to establish their own guideposts for ethical conduct. The Code of Ethics of the American Sociological Association (American Sociological Association, 1968, p.318), the Code of Professional Ethics and Practices of the American Association for Public Opinion Research (1978), the Code of Ethics of the American Psychological Association (APA), the Principles of Responsibility of the American Anthropological Association, and the Rules of Conduct of the American Political Science Association exemplify professional organizations with their own codes of ethics.

Based on examination of governmental agency guidelines for grant recipients such as HHS and NIJ, as well as the codes of ethics of professional organizations such as the American Sociological Association and a myriad of literature in the general social sciences[1] as well as criminal justice,[2] some general principles can be derived. Once again these are presented as suggestions rather than hard and fast rules because there is, as of this writing, no code of ethics in guiding research in criminal justice itself.

A Code of Ethics for Criminology/Criminal Justice Research

From what has been thus far indicated, there is no limit to ethical issues confronting criminal justice researchers (Adamitis and Haghighi, 1989). Although no code of ethics as such has been adopted in criminal justice research other than governmentally induced ones or guides borrowed from parent or adjacent disciplines, a detailing of the major features of a code is useful. Criminal justice researchers adhere to most of these principles as a matter of professionalism, although as we will see, rigid adherence to a checklist is simplistic and does a disservice to the complexity of the research experience. A code of ethics in criminal justice research would include that the criminal justice researcher take personal responsibility to:

Avoid procedures that may harm respondents
Honor commitments to respondents and respect reciprocity
Exercise objectivity and professional integrity in performing and reporting research
Protect confidentiality and privacy of respondents

[1]See, for instance, Diener and Crandall (1978), Duster, Matza, and Wellman (1979), Freund (1970), Katz (1972), National Commission for the Protection of Human Subjects (1976), Nejelski (1976), Reynolds (1979), and Rivlin and Timpane (1975).

[2]See, for instance, Bloomberg and Wilkins (1977), Holmes (1978), Inciardi (1977), Klockars (1977), Klockars and O'Connor (1979), Mitford (1978), Soloway and Walters (1977), and Wolfgang (1976).

Avoid Research That May Harm Respondents

Avoid harm   As a general rule, in the name of science, *researchers should not conduct studies that may be harmful to subjects,* particularly if the potential harm has not been explained to the subjects and their informed consent elicited. The National Advisory Committee on Criminal Justice Standards and Goals suggests that participants give their formal consent to serve as subjects, based on full knowledge of the experiment (National Advisory Committee, 1976, p. 38).

It is the researcher's duty to assume personal responsibility for all phases of the project as it may potentially impinge on the well-being of subjects. If, after considering the ethicality of research, problematic areas still exist, the investigator should seek out advice from university, professional, or governmental committees to ensure adequate safeguards. Failure of a researcher to obtain informed consent or give full disclosure of the study to respondents increases the need to safeguard confidentiality. Thus, when deception is necessary in a study, it becomes more incumbent on the people conducting the study to prevent harm and where appropriate debrief, reassure, and explain the project afterward to subjects (Homan, 1991; and Lee, 1993).

The informed consent issue is a complex one, particularly in correctional research. As experimentation entails unequal or different treatment of experimental and control groups, is the unequal treatment justified for research or scientific purposes? Geis (1967) points out some major difficulties regarding the issue of informed consent in prison research. Communication beforehand as to who is in the treatment and who is not creates "reactivity" or "Hawthorne effects." There are studies in which the aim is to hide the treatment in order not to arouse anxiety.

In her review of the legal and ethical issues in correctional research, Erez (1986) concluded that most such randomized field experiments in corrections were both legal and ethical. The use of only volunteers in a study certainly also presents potential bias and may handicap its generalizability.

Risk/benefit   The protection of human subject guidelines is also viewed as proposing a
ratio   **risk/benefit ratio,** wherein the potential benefits must outweigh the possible hazards to respondents. That is, some risks are justified as long as the scientific knowledge gained exceeds the potential harm. Douglas (1979, p. 30) perhaps correctly suggests that in the final analysis the attempt to rationalize a cost-benefit analysis of research borders on the simplistic in that the conclusion is almost always going to be ruled in favor of science. Such a decision-making process converts the researcher into a "moral administrator" who assumes the right to inflict harm on the subjects in the name of science, once again the mad scientist hangup (Reiman, 1979, p. 45). Although an interesting philosophical debate, the fact of the matter is that most criminal justice researchers simply have no interest in being Dr. Frankenstein. Obviously, any research that is likely to impose long-term harm on participants is anathema to ethical concepts of investigation. In the name of

research one should not espouse behavior that one would not normally find acceptable in normal interpersonal conduct. The exclusion of most social science research from review by HHS guidelines was a frank recognition that there has been little documented harm associated with such studies.

Honor Commitments to Respondents and Respect Reciprocity

Researchers have an ethical responsibility to keep any promises or agreements made with subjects during and after the course of study. The notion of **reciprocity** involves a mutual trust and obligation between researcher and subject. The researcher would have been unable to obtain information without the cooperation of participants who were willing to share of themselves in the belief that the investigator is obliged not to betray this trust by using the information in an inappropriate manner or one that may prove harmful or embarrassing to the subject. Klockars feels that simple researcher-subject models such as in biomedical research do not begin to capture the complexity of reciprocal obligations in field research.

Reciprocity

> Vincent was not only my subject but also my teacher, student, fence, friend and guide. Likewise to Vincent, I was not only researcher but biographer, confidant, customer, friend, and student. These roles, most of which involve multiple obligations and responsibilities and expectations, are potentially in conflict not only in the researcher-subject dimensions but in other dimensions as well. To speak of the working relationship between the life historian and his subject as a researcher-subject relationship simply misconstrues what happens in the context of life history work. The researcher who treats his friends as subjects will soon find that he has neither (Klockars, 1977, p. 218).

Exercise Objectivity and Professional Integrity in Performing and Reporting Research

Objectivity

Honesty, integrity, and **objectivity** are essential expectations of ethical professional conduct. The researcher should attempt to maintain a value-free, politically indifferent approach to the subject matter. Personal, subjective feelings should be kept separate from a disinterested scientific study of things as they are. The researcher first and foremost is an investigator, not a hustler, huckster, salesperson, or politician. Researchers should bar themselves from studying subjects or subject matter for which they feel they cannot properly control potential subjectivity, for example, a strong aversion or affinity toward the object of investigation.

It is important that researchers be frank and honest in conducting their affairs. Researchers should not misrepresent their research abilities or generalize beyond their data. The researcher, in addition to having a concern for accuracy, should avoid any statistical misrepresentations of findings or purposely choose techniques that are most likely to produce positive results. Unethical practices or sponsors who attempt to control the outcome should be avoided. Finally, the researcher has a responsibility to communicate results to professional audiences that are in the best position to judge the findings. Of course, the investigator should always give proper acknowledgment to others who assisted in the research.

Protect Confidentiality and Privacy of Respondents

Erikson takes a very rigid stand in suggesting that the criminal justice researcher should avoid deliberate misrepresentations of his or her identity when entering the private realm of subjects' lives which otherwise would be barred to the researcher. He feels that it is generally unethical to misrepresent the purpose of research (Erikson, 1978, p. 244). Although such an inflexible view is not always appropriate, its general applicability to much research is warranted. To give a personal example of naiveté regarding this matter, the author, while doing field research for a graduate thesis, ineptly handled this privacy matter and almost sabotaged a research project.

> In researching life in the early development of the new town of Columbia, Maryland, the author began attending many community meetings to get a feel of the temper of the pioneers in the young community. Having spotted an announcement in the local paper of a meeting of the "Informal Discussion Group," whose topic was to be the "Economics of New Towns," the author, after consulting with his research mentor, attended the meeting. As perhaps should have been surmised by the group's name, the meeting was very "informal" with less than ten people in attendance and conversation never got around to the scheduled topic. The main point of discussion revolved around griping by the residents about feeling like they were living in a glass bowl. Sightseers on weekends created traffic jams outside their homes; national news magazines had interviewed, at one time or another, nearly everyone in the room or members of their family. Worse yet, one person complained that he heard that the developer was bringing in his behavioral scientists to see if "us rats are running the maze properly." At this point the author began to feel very uncomfortable as I had failed to announce my purposes beforehand or ask permission to attend the session. Finally, since everyone but the author had participated in the discussion, one person indicated that he had not heard anything from me. I then proceeded to explain that I was a graduate student doing research, and he (a local councilman) took down my name and affiliation. Not surprisingly, the meeting ended almost immediately afterwards even though I tried to explain that I was a harmless researcher and not a spy for the developer. Needless to say I regretted my naiveté in not making known my presence from the beginning, and the feeling of having invaded one of the last privileged sanctuaries of the harassed residents was very much impressed upon me. The very next day a representative of the developer (who had obviously heard from the councilman) requested and had a meeting with the author and his mentor, and to his credit offered to assist in my research on the community as long as the data gathering would avoid direct participant observation. A study of the planning process was viewed as far less obtrusive under the circumstances (Hagan, 1968, p.128).

The folly of naively approaching the research setting without making one's presence known is certainly illustrated by this example. But what about secret observation (Menges, 1978)? Erikson's stance (1978) would exclude many subjects from inquiry. Roth (1962) suggests that in a sense, most research design in the social sciences involves a level of deceit, because the exact nature of the study is often hidden. The revelation of the true purpose would either bias the outcome or eliminate the possibility of research (Henslin, 1972, p. 48). To answer a question we asked earlier in this chapter, criminal justice should not restrict its research targets to volunteers.

Confidentiality

Confidentiality. All social science researchers, including criminal justice investigators, have a special obligation to protect the **confidentiality** of such information. The National Advisory Committee on Criminal Justice Standards and Goals (1976) recommends that:

> Data obtained by criminal justice researchers under explicit or implicit pledges of confidentiality require protection against improper or unauthorized use. In particular, when researchers assemble a data file that would be subject to the provisions of the Privacy Act if held by a Federal agency, they incur an implicit obligation to protect its confidentiality. When confidentiality of such data is unlikely to be protected, as in research conducted on behalf of a party in litigation, informed consent should include acknowledgment of the circumstances under which the data will be released (National Advisory Committee, 1976, pp. 41–42).

As indicated previously, confidentiality of government-sponsored research is guaranteed in Section 524(a) of the Omnibus Crime Control Act of 1973 as amended. In gaining access to confidential government data, the criminal justice researcher is generally interested in identification of subjects for sampling and follow-up purposes.

> Researchers rarely require records containing the direct identification of individuals or organizations except during the initial stages of a project when possible personal identifiers should be deleted or destroyed or if needed for follow-up *link files* (which match coder identifiers to personal identifiers) should be stored in a remote and secure location (National Advisory Committee, 1976, pp. 42–43).

Government sponsored research appears to provide safeguards to ensure confidentiality of data. What of the private researcher?

Ethical Problems

Ethical problems

Unlike priests, doctors, or other client-oriented practitioners, the independent criminal justice researcher has no legally recognized privilege of confidentiality. Such researchers are then potentially vulnerable to subpoena (Nejelski and Lerman, 1971). In that sense, social science researchers find themselves in a situation akin to the journalist in which they must decide whether they would be willing to go to jail rather than violate confidentiality. Soloway and Walters (1977), in examining Pennsylvania Penal Code and decisions on this matter, clarify some of the issues regarding researcher complicity or culpability. In most instances the researcher would actually have had to assist, aid, or abet the actual commission of a specific criminal act to be liable under statutes in that state. Soloway and Walters proclaimed this warning:

> Let us not bask too very long in this unaccustomed legal comfort, for, while such laws seem to relieve us of responsibility prior to a governmental investigation, they pertain very little after such an investigation has begun. Once a criminal investigation and/or prosecution has commenced, we are still absolved of a legal responsibility to come forward, of our own accord, with our information. Once summoned to so testify, however, we have no legal recourse but to divulge our information and its source under the threat and consequence of a contempt citation. This was made amply clear in the U.S. Supreme Court's landmark decision in 1972 against Paul Branzburg, a journalist investigating junkies in Kentucky, and Earl Caldwell, a journalist investigating the Black Panthers and other militant black organizations (Soloway and Walters, 1977, p. 175).

These decisions held basically that a journalist or investigator had no privilege to refuse appearance before a grand jury or to decline answering questions regarding sources or information received in confidence. James (1972, p. 139) is the only case Soloway and Walters could find that involved a scientific investigator being subpoenaed. In this case the subpoena was dropped when the investigator produced a previously signed agreement to safeguard the confidentiality of sources.

Wolfgang (1981, 1982) reports that in his cohort study (Wolfgang et al., 1972) four respondents admitted involvement in criminal homicide and seventy-five were involved in forcible rape for which none of them had been arrested. Members of the research staff could have theoretically been prosecuted for "misprison of a felony" (being accessories after the fact), which, although outdated in most states, is a federal offense.

Longmire (1983) in a survey of a sample of members of the American Society of Criminology found that 63 percent indicated having experienced one or more ethical dilemmas. With respect to ethical problems impacting on participants, the biggest problem was confidentiality problems, with 9 percent so indicating. Professional ethical issues were more of a problem, with 27 percent indicating that they had experienced pressure to engage in undesired research. This involves primarily academic institutions "twisting the arm" of researchers to pursue research in areas for which there is grant money.

Although vulnerability to subpoena is an ever-present threat to social science researchers, Reynolds (1979) was able to find fewer than a dozen such cases and most incidents seemed to involve newspersons.

In discussing the run-in with the law of Yablonsky (1968a), author of *The Hippie Trip*, Irwin states that:

> There has been some concern expressed over the danger of arrest while studying criminals, mainly because the researcher will have firsthand knowledge of felonies and misdemeanors. . . . To my knowledge the closest anybody ever came to having legal sanctions imposed on him because of his research was Lewis Yablonsky. . . . The judge asked him nine times if he had witnessed Gridley [one of his informants] smoking marijuana. Yablonsky refused to answer because of the rights guaranteed him in the Fifth Amendment of the United States Constitution. Although he did not actually receive any legal sanctioning, he stated that the incident was humiliating and suggested that researchers should have guarantees of immunity. Despite this case, I feel there is small risk of being prosecuted. If we keep our "heads straight" and avoid being sucked in or bowled over by the criminal world, and thereby do not slip or plunge into greater complicity than knowledge of crimes, we actually do have immunity (Irwin, 1972, pp. 128–129; see also Yablonsky, 1968b).

In 1979, political scientist Samuel Popkin became the first American professor incarcerated for defending his right to maintain confidentiality regarding *The Pentagon Papers.* Popkin had refused to reveal his sources to a federal grand jury and subsequently spent one week in jail until the jury was dismissed (Wolfgang, 1982, p. 395).

The Brajuha Case (Weinstein Decision)

In April of 1984, Judge Jack B. Weinstein of the U.S. Eastern District Court of New York ruled that:

> Serious scholars [Mario Brajuha] cannot be required to turn over their field-notes in a grand jury investigation when the government fails to establish a "substantial need" for them to do so. Weinstein's ruling establishes a "qualified privilege not to reveal documents or confidential sources" for social science researchers, akin to the privileges enjoyed by journalists. . . . According to Weinstein, "Serious scholars are entitled to no less protection than journalists" (Erikson, 1984).

Brajuha/
Weinstein
Case

The *Weinstein decision* cited as support the American Sociological Association's code of ethics, which indicates that "Confidential information provided by research participants must be treated as such by sociologists, even when this information enjoys no legal protection or privilege and legal force is applied" [Erikson, 1984].

The researcher in this case was Mario Brajuha, a sociology graduate student at SUNY—Stony Brook, who had been subpoenaed by a grand jury investigating a restaurant fire. He had been doing a participant observation study of the restaurant as a waiter for ten months prior to the fire and had collected data for his dissertation.

The Weinstein decision was appealed by the prosecutors and, in a directive issued by the court of appeals judge, a compromise of sorts was struck. Brajuha's defense attorney prepared an edited version of Brajuha's field notes, which was accepted as sufficient to satisfy the original subpoena and dismissed the case against him. As Brajuha's attorney explains:

> From the beginning, Mr. Brajuha was prepared to testify as to his observations and nonprivileged communications. . . . In the context of this case, a claim of privilege with respect to (his) observations was unnecessary. The issues in this litigation centered around the portions of the research journal which contained communications with privileged sources and matters of personal privacy, for example, opinions (Thaler, 1985, p. 1).

Pseudonyms
    A standard procedure for attempting to protect the identity of subjects, organizations, or communities is the use of **pseudonyms** (false names) in publications. "Doc," "Chic," "The Lupollo Family," "Deep Throat," "Wincanton," "Cornerville," "Slumtown," and "Middletown" are but a few of the many aliases given such subjects often to little avail. For instance, even the Trobriand islanders were aware of Malinowski's books and one even indicated that he did not understand their system of clans and chiefs (Barnes, 1970). Gans in *The Urban Villagers* (1962) noted that during an election in the same West End Boston area Whyte had studied, one of the candidates had received negative voter reaction based in part on Whyte's description of the individual years ago in *Streetcorner Society* (1955).

    Despite Klockars' efforts to protect his fence's identity, vanity won the day:

> I also told Vincent that I would not reveal his identity unless it meant that I was going to jail if I did not, and he told me that he really could not expect me to do more. These contingencies notwithstanding, Vincent just could not resist a little advance publicity.
>
>   He told everybody—judges, lawyers, politicians, prosecutors, thieves, hustlers, and most of his good customers. He started this word-of-mouth publicity campaign a full year before the book appeared in the *New York Times Book Review;* anyone who did not know who Vincent Swaggi really was was simply confessing that they were outsiders to the Philadelphia scene (Klockars, 1977, p. 214).

Vincent even sold and gave away autographed copies in his store, although he turned down offers to appear on national televised talk shows. Threats to researchers may come from many sources. In the Ofshe case the threat was from an organization he studied, whereas in the Hutchinson case it was from a member of Congress.

The Ofshe Case

Organizations or individuals may file lawsuits against researchers. In the 1960s, Synanon (a drug rehabilitation program headquarters in California) had received widespread, positive, national publicity. In the early 1970s Richard Ofshe, professor of sociology at the University of California, Berkeley, began an investigation of the organization and, along with journalist colleagues, began to uncover and expose patterns of extreme violence and intimidation employed by Synanon. In addition to scholarly works and an investigative newspaper series, Ofshe and colleagues published a book which was later the basis of a CBS television movie (Maldonado, 1987).

Since 1979, the Synanon foundation has filed three lawsuits charging Ofshe with libel and slander. Although the cases were eventually dismissed or charges were dropped by the Synanon litigants, Ofshe was fortunately assisted by the University of California, Berkeley, with defense legal costs, since the basis of the suits rested on his academic research. In 1987 Ofshe was awarded over $500,000 for costs of litigation by a Marin County, California, judge in connection with his fight against the Synanon suits. "Based on a preliminary review, the amount is believed to be one of the most substantial costs of litigation ever granted to an academic in a case involving pursuit of research and academic freedom" (Maldonado, 1987, p. 3). Ofshe is continuing to press his legal case, charging Synanon with malicious prosecution and hoping for a ruling that the suits were a form of harassment and attack on academic freedom.

The Hutchinson Case

During the 1950s the United States went through a period of "anti-Communist" hysteria led by Senator Joseph McCarthy of Wisconsin in which many people had their careers and lives ruined by innuendos that they were, or had been, associated with Communists. During this period intellectual debate was intimidated or closed as researchers and others retreated from controversial topics and the onslaught of political demagoguery. Beginning in the 1970s in the United States a new brand of McCarthyism presented itself, although this time the device was public ridicule and the charge against its targets was that federally funded researchers were "ripping off" the taxpayers' money on useless studies of "ridiculous" topics.

Ironically, one of the chief engineers of the new McCarthyism is the very man who took the senatorial seat of the late Joseph McCarthy, former Senator William Proxmire. Through his infamous "Golden Fleece of the Month Awards," Proxmire intended to call public attention to the waste of public tax money on research works whose titles sounded absurd. This ridicule of specific research at times impugned the integrity and motivation of the researchers themselves, such as Ronald Hutchinson. According to the Fund to Protect Scholars from Defamation (1980):

Possibly because of Proxmire's bias against social scientists, Ron's work was selected for an "award" and, although he has admitted the statement to be inaccurate, Proxmire issued a press release charging that Ron had personally received a half million dollars in research funds. Proxmire also charged that Ron had "made a fortune from his monkeys." Focusing ridicule on the fact that some of Ron's work involved jaw clenching as a measure of aggression, Proxmire accused him of taking a "bite out of the taxpayers and characterized seven years of scientific research as "monkey business," "transparently worthless," and "nonsense which had "made a monkey out of the American taxpayer. Representatives of agencies which funded the research, however, described it as "of particular importance," "well designed," "well executed," "valid," "sound," and a "moderate expenditure." ONR [Office of Naval Research] described the research as the first objective testing system for measuring and examining aggressive behavior. In addition to his written statements, Proxmire also ridiculed Ron's work in radio and television shows and either directed or permitted his aides to pressure agencies funding Ron's research to terminate funding.

The "Golden Fleece" was a disaster in Ron's life and those associated with him, as it has been in the lives of other recipients. In order to continue his work, Ron set up a laboratory at his own expense. In 1976–77 his salary was only 33% of what it had been in 1974–75. The scholarly work of a productive scientist was seriously disrupted. The effect was not limited to his professional life. As a result of the sarcastic and demeaning publicity, his children were embarrassed at school. Each press release brought with it still other invasions of his privacy in the form of phone calls and "hate" mail. Those of us who were close to him at the time know that he was subjected to extreme physical and emotional stress.

In a law suit finally brought before the Supreme Court, Hutchinson and Proxmire agreed to settle out of court. Besides a public apology on the floor of the Senate by Proxmire, payment was made to Hutchinson of $10,000 from Proxmire's own personal funds. While Hutchinson encumbered huge legal fees, the U.S. Senate paid Proxmire's legal bills of around $130,000 (Fund to Protect Scholars from Defamation, 1980).

Important in the Supreme Court's willingness to hear this case was its decision that research scientists could sue for defamation of character even if they were receiving federal research funds and that senatorial privilege did not extend to remarks made outside the Senate chamber.

Although the Hutchinson case represents the most glaring example of what has been characterized as the new McCarthyism, more subtle attacks certainly continue. A related concern is the possibility that criminal justice and other social science researchers will concentrate inquiry into fundable, safe, societally directed areas and thus avoid controversy or studies that may uncomfortably focus on "crime in the suites."

The issue of ethics in criminal justice research draws greater attention now than in the past. Ethical concerns in research gain complexity with revisions in federal laws regulating privacy, confidentiality, and freedom of information; and debates continue in the various professional disciplines involved in studying criminology and criminal justice. The desire to address these issues is reflected in the establishment of a specialized journal, *Criminal Justice Ethics.*[3]

Additional Ethical Concerns

The parent disciplines to criminology/criminal justice, such as sociology, psychology, political science, and anthropology, have both unique and common ethical concerns, as reflected in their codes of ethics. Because professions pride themselves on autonomy and self-regulation, these requirements are usually beyond any minimal standards set by government agencies. Some specific ethical considerations are incorporated by these codes. Although every effort may be made to preserve their anonymity, subjects should be made aware that they may unintentionally be compromised. A researcher's pseudonyms should not be indiscriminately revealed. Anthropologists indicate that, if secretive research is performed for a sponsor, such reports should also be released to the public and subjects. Researchers should be honest with sponsors regarding qualifications, capabilities, and harm, and open concerning the acknowledgment of sponsorship of research. Any government-supported research should be unclassified, and researchers should not use their research as a cover for government intelligence work.

If research has potential policy implications, it is even more imperative that investigators state the limitations of their findings. Relationships that may compromise objectivity or create a conflict of interest should be avoided. Psychologists insist on a high standard of competence, including use of the latest rules regarding validity and reliability of tests and measurements employed in research or practice. Political scientists have specific guidelines on involvement in the political arena, often a necessary part of the discipline. Sociologists mirror most of these same themes, but add that, regardless of work setting, sociologists are obligated to report findings fully and without omission of significant data. Also as an ethical matter, researchers are obligated to make their data available to other qualified social scientists at reasonable cost once they have completed their study.

Avoiding Ethical Problems

Reynolds (1982, p. 141) points out that concern with ethical issues should not cripple social research:

> Social scientists, individually and collectively, have a choice between studying important, critical, human and social phenomena that may involve moral

[3]Published by Institute for Criminal Justice Ethics, John Jay College of Criminal Justice, 444 West 56th Street, New York, NY 10102.

dilemmas, or focusing upon tangential, insignificant, safe issues. The more important the phenomenon, the greater likelihood that the research may involve a risk of negative effect, stress, or embarrassment for the participants. Investigators must then be diplomatic, imaginative, and conscientious in demonstrating respect for the participants' rights and welfare. They may take comfort from two facts: participants almost never experience lasting damage from social science research and seldom take offense when they are involved. Those choosing to pursue important phenomena may find themselves confronted with a series of moral dilemmas, there will be [no] obvious permanent solutions, only temporary compromises.

Because of the nature of the subject matter, ethical problems are likely to present themselves in many criminal justice research projects. One way of avoiding ethical problems is to *carefully consider alternate means of data gathering* that may not entail ethical problems. Some study designs pose less hazard than others. For example, perhaps existing data or some other unobtrusive method would make it unnecessary to collect new data. Rather than set up an experimental group and a control group in a prison, one could locate two similar prisons that already constitute natural experimental and control groups. Simulations, either human or computer, may enable one to address the same issue without as much of an ethics problem. One could seek conditions under which negative effects have already occurred (Bailey, 1987, pp. 407–410). Similarly, the use of samples or only low levels of the treatment may reduce the potential harm.

The reporting of aggregative rather than individual data with proper prior destruction of identifiers may ensure protection. Such simulations as "mock jury studies" may also avoid ethical problems with real populations.

In an earlier discussion of sample surveys it was pointed out that there is a potential growing "respondent revolt" against the increased requests to participate in studies. All research is to some extent an imposition on the lives or time of subjects. By the same token, research also poses, as we have seen in this chapter, potential unethical impacts on those involved in a study. Although the points set forth in this section can alert the investigator to broad guideposts, the actual research path is in the last analysis the sole responsibility of the researcher.

Summary

Ethical horror stories were reviewed in order to document some examples of unethical behavior in research. Accounts of biomedical research by Nazis, the Tuskegee Syphilis Study, experiments on prisoners, as well as secretive research sponsored by intelligence agencies preceded discussion of social science examples. The latter included Milgram's "obedience to authority" study, Zimbardo's "simulated prison study," and Humphreys' "Tearoom

Trade." Plagiarism and researcher fraud such as the Piltdown Tasaday hoaxes were also discussed as examples of scams and researcher misconduct.

As one of the social sciences, criminal justice must be concerned with many of the same issues of ethical behavior in conducting research on human activity. Potential role conflict exists for the investigator who has to balance the roles of researcher, criminal justice practitioner, citizen, and humanitarian. In mediating these roles it is essential that the researcher anticipate many of the possible points of friction beforehand, keeping in mind that *the researcher's primary role is that of scientist.*

Research targets in criminology and criminal justice include the criminal, the victim, the criminal justice system, practitioners, and the general public. Each research situation presents its own unique set of ethical problems, just as ethics itself is relative to the setting. Although science itself is ethically neutral, individual scientists cannot entirely avoid moral concerns in studying human groups or individuals. In aspiring for acceptance as professionals, criminal justice researchers attempt to demonstrate that on the basis of knowledge and ethical conduct they should be granted autonomy and high professional regard. Although this striving and establishment of ethical codes may be viewed as a smokescreen to gain monopolistic power, if a field fails to set its own standards, the government will set the standards for them. No universally accepted code of ethical conduct in research exists in criminal justice. The purpose of this chapter has been to call attention to key features. Rather than a rigid set of requirements, they might best be viewed as general principles that must be tailored to the unique features of individual research projects.

The most influential guidelines governing funded research in the United States are those of the Department of Health and Human Services, *Model Policy on Human Research Subjects.* Researchers involved in ethnography or field studies were critical of the attempted application of these informed consent guidelines to participant observation studies and felt that they would make such studies impossible. Fieldwork was viewed as different in kind than biomedical and experimental studies of controlled subjects. The National Commission for the Protection of Human Subjects (1978a) in The Belmont Report partially revised these guidelines, putting their interpretation in the hands of review boards and suggesting an alteration of informed consent in the case of field research. Revision of HHS guidelines in 1981 virtually excluded most social science and criminal justice/criminological research from required review.

In addition to government agency regulations regarding funded research, professional associations, for example, the American Sociological and Psychological associations, have their own codes of ethics governing research. Taking both governmental and other professions' codes of ethics, some *Ethical Principles in Criminal Justice Research* are presented as suggestive elements of consideration in investigations: (1) researchers should avoid procedures which may harm respondents; (2) one should honor commitments to respondents and respect reciprocity; (3) investigators should maintain objectivity and exercise professional integrity in performing and reporting research; and (4) investigators should protect the confidentiality and privacy of respondents. In addition, discussion was presented that criminal justice researchers should be alert to the fact that they enjoy no legally recognized privilege of confidentiality (except, of course, in some cases of funded research that are restrictive in coverage).

Some ethical problems experienced by researchers such as Brajuha, Ofshe, and Hutchinson were discussed. Finally, some means of avoiding ethical problems are the use of alternate methods that possess fewer ethical problems, study groups that possess characteristics or natural treatments, the use of samples instead of larger populations, the reporting of only aggregative data, the use of simulations, as well as exposure of groups to only low levels of treatment. In the last analysis, researchers must assume personal responsibility for the morality of their research.

Key Concepts

Research Fraud	HEW Guidelines for	Shield Laws
Plagiarism	Protection of Human	Risk/Benefit Ratio in
Role of Researcher	Subjects	Research
Research Targets in	Institutional Review	Reciprocity
Criminal Justice	Boards	Confidentiality
Professional Ethics	Informed Consent	Pseudonyms
Ethical Principles in	The Belmont Report	
Criminal Justice	NIJ's Regulations on	
Research	Confidentiality	

Review Questions

1. Research in criminal justice and criminology faces many ethical hazards. How concerned should researchers be with ethical conduct in research? What is the researcher's role and what constitutes appropriate conduct?
2. The regulation of ethically acceptable research conduct may take one of three forms. Discuss these and include your opinion as to which of these is most effective.
3. How did the new HHS guidelines resolve the principal objections of field researchers to the informed consent issue?
4. What are some elements of a code of ethics for criminology/criminal justice research?
5. Discuss some examples of researcher misconduct. Why does this occur and how can it be prevented?

CHAPTER

3 Research Design: The Experimental Model and Its Variations

Research design is the plan or blueprint for a study and includes the who, what, where, when, why, and how of an investigation. The research design should flow from the problem formulation and the critical issues that were identified for observation. Who is to be investigated—an individual, one group, many groups, organizations, or communities? What is to be investigated— attitudes, behavior, or records? Where is the study to be conducted? Do we wish to look at the past (after-the-fact, post hoc, or a posteriori studies) or the present or to predict the future? Do we want to look at a group once or over time? Why do we wish to do the investigation—to describe, explain, or predict? Finally, how do we design the study so that upon completion we are able to address the hypotheses and present findings that resolve in some manner the research problem?

Types of Research Design

The identification of types of research design varies in the social sciences, and there is no consensus regarding these types. The types to be presented are not necessarily mutually exclusive (pure and nonoverlapping) nor exhaustive of all the types identified by different writers (the reader may wish to consult other texts identified in the references to Chapter 1 for other examples). The types of research design identified by Isaac and Michael (1981, p. 41) include:

Historical	Causal-Comparative
Descriptive	True Experimental
Developmental	Quasi-Experimental
Case or Field	Action
Correlational	

Although each type will be described in detail in subsequent chapters from the standpoint of data-gathering procedures, a brief description will

Historical analysis

Descriptive research

Inferential studies

Developmental research

Case/field studies

Correlational studies

Causal-comparative designs

True experimental designs

Quasi-experimental designs

Action research

acquaint the reader with their differences in scope and purpose. *Historical analysis* examines the past in an attempt to objectively chronicle and explain these events. A study of crime during the Puritan times in New England would serve as an example. *Descriptive research* attempts to accurately describe or characterize an individual or group's attitudes, behaviors, or characteristics. Studies by the census bureau or public opinion surveys are often intended to catalogue or tally results without attempting to examine causal connections. Usually distinguished from descriptive studies are *inferential studies,* which are intended to generalize findings from a study group to a larger population. Victim sample surveys, which attempt to represent the entire nation, are such examples. It should be noted that historical, descriptive, and case study designs are nonexperimental in nature. *Developmental research* (sometimes called trend, longitudinal, cohort, or panel studies) analyzes growth or change in a group over time. Studies of delinquency in birth cohorts (for example, all boys born in 1945 and followed until their 18th birthday) serve as an illustration. *Case and field studies* are in-depth studies of an individual, group, institution, or community generally involving qualitative research. Field investigations of a professional criminal, a gang, a prison, or crime in a U.S. city are examples.

Correlational studies examine the extent to which changes in one variable are related to (associated with) variations in another variable(s). Studies that use statistics such as correlation coefficients will be discussed in Chapter 12. Correlational studies are the most commonly used type of research in the field of criminology and criminal justice (Holmes and Taggart, 1990). Studies that explore the relationship between unemployment rates and crime rates are an example of correlational studies. *Causal-comparative (ex post facto)* designs look at existing outcomes and after the fact attempt to trace back and determine what may have predicted these outcomes. Comparisons are made between groups that exhibit and do not exhibit the outcome. For example, a group of delinquents and a comparison (nondelinquent) group (one similar in age, sex, and so on) are examined with respect to background characteristics that may explain what caused delinquency. *True experimental designs* involve random assignment of groups to experimental (treated group) and control (untreated group) groups, and measurement occurs before and after exposure to treatment in order to determine the cause of any differences. An experiment in which inmates are randomly assigned to a rehabilitation program or not and measured before and after the program is illustrative.

Quasi-experimental designs are designs that attempt to approximate the true experimental design but lack random assignment to experimental and control groups. Most field experiments in natural settings, such as a foot patrol investigation, are of this type. Finally, *action research* (called policy analysis or evaluation research in Chapter 13) is applied research that is intended to resolve some immediate policy concern. For example, the results of an experiment with an employment program for released offenders may be intended as a demonstration project to decide whether to expand or eliminate such programs. All of these types of research designs can also be viewed as variations of the experimental model.

The Experimental Model

Some people view experiments as involving white-coated scientists with an impressive assortment of equipment tediously studying obscure phenomena in some isolated laboratory. Although such a picture may indeed be accurate in some instances, the experimental model contains many variations and need not be restricted to this stereotypical view. The experimental model will be treated in this chapter as the benchmark for comparison of all other research designs and methods. Most studies of an empirical nature in criminology and criminal justice can be viewed, for heuristic purposes, as variations of the experimental model (Campbell, 1977; Cook and Campbell, 1979; Weubben, Straits, and Shulman, 1974). The research design notation (X's and O's) used in this chapter may at first appear intimidating, but if you give it a chance, you will find it excellent shorthand for dissecting any research study. This chapter contains more "researchese" than any other chapter, but if you bear with it, you will be more than rewarded in becoming fluent in the language of research.

Research Design in a Nutshell

In learning something new such as swimming or driving, the initial lessons seem the most difficult; once the foreignness of this new experience is overcome, the rest is relatively easy. Unfortunately, learning research methods is similar. The language of research design in this chapter by its very nature has this same foreignness at first. One philosophy is to teach something by simply doing it, such as throwing the student in the deep end of the pool or the fast lane on the Capitol Beltway (which, incidentally, is where this writer learned to drive). Rather than following this practice and throwing you in the deep end, let us begin with a short lesson. Read Figure 3.1, even if you do not fully understand it. It gives the "guts" of the entire chapter. As you are reading or after completing the chapter, you may wish to reread it because, if you understand Figure 3.1, you have the underlying logic of research design.

X = treatment (independent variable), e.g., Foot Patrol
Y = outcome (dependent variable), e.g., Crime Rate
Z = any rival causal factor (other variables besides X that could really be causing a change in Y), e.g., history, selection bias, testing, etc.
O = observation (some measurement or assessment of dependent variable)
E = equivalence (randomization or matching)
1, 2 = time

Design 1: $O_1 X O_2$ (One Group Before–After Design)

- A precinct with a crime rate of 1,000 (O_1) is exposed to foot patrol (X) for one year and then has a crime rate of 500 (O_2).
- Problem: Other variables (Z) could actually have caused the decline in crime rate (Y) rather than foot patrol (X), e.g., History, Selection Bias, Testing Effects.
- Solution: A better research design (such as Design 2) to control or exclude these rival causal factors (or other variables).

Design 2: $EO_1 X O_2$
$EO_1\ \ O_2$ (Classic Experimental Design)

- Two precincts as similar as possible (E, matching) on relevant characteristics are studied.
    Both are observed (O_1) and have a crime rate of 1,000.
    One precinct receives foot patrol (X) and is the experimental group.
    The other precinct receives no treatment (control group).
    After one year, the experimental precinct has a crime rate of 500 while the control group has a crime rate of 1,000 (or no change). The decrease is attributed to foot patrol.
- Rival causal factors (Z) were controlled for (excluded) by the classic experimental design, for example,
    The change could not have been due to some historical event if we assume that both groups were similar and exposed to the same history.
    The change could not be due to selection bias because we purposely chose two similar or matched precincts (E) and their crime rates were the same from the beginning (O_1)
    If there were testing effects (citizens were not surveyed; we used police reports), both groups should have reacted the same to an awareness of being studied.
    Thus, the relationship between X and Y is not due to Z [we have gained internal validity (accuracy)].
- Problem: Can we generalize this finding (foot patrol reduces crime) to all police departments in the country? This is the problem of external validity.
- One Solution: Replications (repeat studies) in other settings with other police departments.

Figure 3.1 Research Design in a Nutshell.

Causality

Causality

The ultimate purpose of all scientific investigation is to isolate, define, and explain the relationship between key variables in order to predict and understand the underlying nature of reality. The problem of *causality* has been a subject of continuing philosophical discussion, but scientific investigation is based on the a priori assumption that the fundamental nature of reality can be known—that causation lies at the basis of reality.

Resolution of the Causality Problem

Resolution of Causality Problem

To approach this matter, scientific investigation entails basically *three essential* **Steps for Resolving the Causality Problem.** *The first step* involves the demonstration of a relationship or covariance between variables. That is, one variable is related, increases or decreases in value, in some predictable manner along with increases or decreases in the value of another variable. *The second step* consists of specifying or indicating the time sequence of the relationship. Which variable is the independent or predictor variable X, and which is the outcome or dependent variable Y? Generally, logic or knowledge of which variable comes first gives one the direction of causation. For instance, it usually would make more sense to assume that criminality of parents (X) would precede in time and possibly predict criminality in offspring (Y), rather than vice versa. In most instances one has little difficulty in identifying the outcome (Y) one is interested in predicting. It is usually the subject of the study. Although this process of causality resolution in research has been greatly oversimplified for presentation purposes, most studies of an empirical and predictive nature in criminal justice can be found to undergo essentially the first two steps that have been outlined. *The third step* is the stage where many studies bog down and where research

Rival causal factors

findings are subject to interminable debate. It involves the exclusion of **rival causal factors,** or the elimination of other variables that could conceivably explain away the original relationships the researcher had claimed. Other variables or rival causal factors may be responsible for the variations discovered (Hyman, 1995; Steffensmeier and Terry, 1975; Hirschi and Selvin, 1966; and Denzin, 1989).

Spuriousness

In excluding rival causal factors, researchers are attempting to demonstrate that the relationship between X and Y is nonspurious. A **spurious relationship** is a false relationship; that is, one that is not caused by the believed variables, but that can be explained by other variables. The presumed relationship between foot size (X) and intelligence (Y) may disappear (be demonstrated to be spurious) when controlled for age (Z). That is, among Thirty-year-olds there is no relationship between foot size and intelligence.

To summarize and clarify this process, once again, the *three essential steps in resolving the causality problem* are:

1. Demonstrate that a relationship exists between the key variables.
2. Specify the time order of the relationship.
3. Eliminate rival causal factors.

Suppose a researcher wanted to prove that a relationship exists between the increase in foot patrols in a precinct and a decline in crime. Assuming that foot patrols have been increased in the target precinct, the researcher looks at some measurement, for instance, precinct records of reported crime. If no relationship between increased foot patrols and crime is discovered, the entire process stops with step 1. There is little need to proceed if no relationship at all exists. If a decrease or for some reason an increase in crime is discovered, however, the researcher goes on to the next step. For our purposes we will assume that an increase in foot patrols is the predictor variable, X, and a decrease in reported crime is the outcome, Y. We assume that foot patrols affect crime rates, rather than vice versa. One could see, however, where a researcher might be interested in studying the latter; that is, high crime areas may more likely precipitate the deployment of foot patrols.

Finally, suppose a relationship was discovered and specified; namely, there was an increase in foot patrols and a decline in reported crime within the precinct. Does this then prove that increases in foot patrols will cause a decrease in crime as measured by crime reported to police? The answer to this question is, of course no. The most obvious reason, which will become clear in Chapter 12 when we discuss statistics, is that *correlation or relationship by no means implies or demonstrates causation.* Such a finding merely brings us to stage 1 or 2 of our steps in resolving the causality problem. If the prudent investigator has not already guessed, one's critics will very quickly point out that other things (variables) could have accounted for this relationship.

Rival Causal Factors

Rival causal factors are any variables other than X (the treatment) that may be responsible for the relationship. It is traditional in the social sciences, following the lead of Campbell and Stanley (1963), to discuss these other variables, or rival causal factors, as being of two general types: *internal factors* or other variables within the study itself that may tend to invalidate one's findings and conclusions, and *external factors* or elements outside of one's immediate study that may imperil the researcher's attempts to draw generalizations from the study and infer one's findings to be true of larger populations.

Internal factors

External factors

Validity

Validity

Validity refers to accuracy or correctness in research. Internal factors question the internal validity of research, whereas external factors impugn the external validity of findings. The former asks whether the observational process itself produced the findings; the latter is concerned with whether the results were unique and applicable only to the group or target studied. In checking **internal validity** one is concerned with whether a factor (variable) other than X (the treatment) may have produced a change in Y (the dependent variable). With **external validity** one asks what other factors (variables) may limit one's ability to generalize the findings in a study to larger populations or settings.

Internal validity

External validity

Internal Factors: Variables Related to Internal Validity

Internal factors

Campbell and Stanley's classic monograph, *Experimental and Quasi-Experimental Designs for Research* (1963), points to the following internal factors as possibly threatening the internal validity of a study:

History	Statistical Regression
Maturation	Selection Bias
Testing	Experimental Mortality
Instrumentation	Selection—Maturation Interaction

All of these are rival causal factors that could have been responsible for producing the results rather than the treatment assumed to be responsible. That is, although X and Y are related, the real reason for this relationship is Z, some other variable or rival causal factor.

History

History

History refers to other specific events that may have taken place during the course of the study and may have produced the results. For example, what events other than increased foot patrols may have occurred in the hypothetical precinct and accounted for the decrease in crimes reported? Perhaps the area was the target of a "Crime Watch" program that encouraged citizen vigilance and reporting, or a new employment program was initiated to hire unemployed youths, or urban renewal changed the nature of the popula-tion inhabiting the precinct. Social, seasonal, and other events may be responsible for changes in a study target. Garwood (1978) gives an example of a burglary reduction program using "operation identification" in which belongings are engraved to discourage burglars and fences. A northeastern experimental city received the treatment, operation identification, and, especially during January 1978, showed a dramatic decrease in reported burglaries. Can we assume that the X, operation identification, was responsible for bringing this about? No. On further investigation it was discovered that other cities without such a program, notably Buffalo, Detroit, and Boston, demonstrated equally impressive declines in burglary. What may have occurred in January 1978 to account for this? It was the winter of incredibly deep, record-breaking, crippling snows in the Northeast and thus bad weather, a historical hidden variable, was most likely responsible for the decline in burglary statistics. Similarly, a tough 1880 anti-horse theft law in New York City is not responsible for the virtual disappearance of such thieves a hundred years later; rather, it is the historical change in transportation.

In reviewing shortcomings of sentencing research, Farrington (1978) points out that because of the lack of premeasures and control groups, it is difficult to assume that any decrease in crime after a change in legal penalties or sentencing is due to these changes or other unmeasured social changes that may have taken place at the same time.

In the late 1970s a major problem in evaluating the success of DWI (driving while intoxicated) programs using one group before and one after measurement was the existence of rival historical factors such as growing fuel shortages and a new 55-mile-per-hour speed limit. Thus, fewer DWI arrests in areas with such programs may have resulted from these historical changes rather than the changed behavior of drunk drivers going through DWI programs (Charalampous and Skinner, 1977).

Maturation

Maturation

Maturation refers to biological or psychological changes in the respondents during the course of study that are not due to the experimental variable. "Time heals all wounds," according to the old medical dictum, referring to the phenomenon in medical research wherein a given number of patients can be expected to reveal improved conditions with or without treatment. Perhaps the precinct under investigation in our foot patrol example was in the process of change, either deterioration or upgrading, that brought about the change in crime reporting irrespective of foot patrol.

A hypothetical example may serve to illustrate maturation as a rival causal factor. An interesting controversy of the sixties was fluoridation of water in the United States. Opponents claimed that the addition of such chemicals was potentially harmful. Suppose an avid supporter of such a view were to state, "In 1850 Erie, Pennsylvania, was the first city to fluoridate its water and not a single citizen from that time is alive today." Quite obviously the demise of this population was due primarily to natural causes, maturation, rather than the assumed cause, fluoridation.

In a more serious vein, claims as to the long-term effectiveness of rehabilitation programs must certainly control for the fact that as a given age cohort matures, its crime commission in general tends to decrease; that is, there are very few eighty-year-old cat burglars. As a more detailed example will illustrate later in this chapter, all other things being equal, older delinquents can be expected to show lower crime commission over time than younger delinquents.

Testing

Testing

Testing (pretest bias) refers to the bias and foreknowledge introduced to respondents as a result of having been pretested. On a second testing the respondents are no longer naive regarding the subject matter and can make use of sensitivities, information, and attitudes garnered from the first testing. If one wanted to test a bank's reaction to a simulated robbery, the reaction of a bank that had been held up the previous day would probably not yield valid or typical results.

Instrumentation

Instrumentation

Instrumentation involves changes in the measuring instrument from the beginning or first period of evaluation to the second, later, or final evaluation. The measuring instrument may refer to observers, questionnaires, interviews, analyses of existing records, or any standard method of data gathering. Suppose, for instance, that in our foot patrol experiment, the method of recording citizen complaints was dramatically improved from what it had been at the beginning of the project. An increase in crimes reported to police at the end of the study could very well have resulted from instrumentation, a rival causal factor, rather than the assumed predictor variable—foot patrol. A major limitation of comparing crime rates of today with those of yesteryear relates to the continual improvement in record keeping so that an indeterminate proportion of the increase may simply be evidence of improved instrumentation. We will discuss this subject in detail in Chapter 4 in the section on the Uniform Crime Report. The crime rate of a city may show an increase of 100 percent over the previous year, not necessarily because of increased crime commission, but because of installation of a computer, a change in the manner in which crime is measured or recorded.

Statistical Regression

Statistical regression

Statistical regression is the tendency of groups that have been selected for study on the basis of extreme high or low scores to regress or move toward the mean or average on second testing. As in our example, if a precinct were selected for study on the basis of an extremely high or low volume of citizen complaints, it is expected, irrespective of the treatment variable, that the second reading will be closer to the average for all precincts or certainly less at the extreme.

It should not be surprising that extremely high or low scores would move toward more normal scores upon retest. Extremely tall people as a group are likely to have children shorter than themselves, just as extremely short people are likely to have children taller than themselves. Imagine taking the first examination in a class that you detest; after having had a bad night the night before (illness, an all-nighter), you flunk the test. As a member of the lowest group, you are then chosen for study. But before the second test you have a normal night's sleep, so we might expect your performance to improve. The point is that the improvement may not be due to any increase in intelligence, but that your first test performance was atypical.

In critiquing reported positive claims of a program involving diversion alternatives for youths who would otherwise have been incarcerated, Gordon et al. point out that regression effects had been overlooked. The juveniles studied were chosen on the basis of extremely high crime commission that could be expected to decrease upon second observation even without intervention. Not surprisingly, it was claimed that the most extreme delinquents demonstrated the greatest drop in recidivism as a result of a wilderness program. The most likely explanation, however, was an expected regression toward the mean on the basis of the initial choice of extreme cases (Gordon et al., 1978; Murray, 1978).

Selection Bias

Selection bias

Selection bias occurs when the researcher chooses nonequivalent groups for comparison. Studies that compare the attitudes or behavior of volunteers and nonvolunteers are often subject to selection bias. If in our foot patrol study the precinct chosen for the experiment was characterized by high levels of citizen involvement and reportage of crime, and these data were compared with those for another nonfoot patrol precinct with historically low levels of reported crime, the rival causal factor, selection bias, rather than foot patrol, might explain the differences in findings.

Similarly, comparison of an experimental group consisting of all model prisoners and a control group of incorrigible prisoners would hardly be fair. Many demonstration projects have been accused of "creaming clients"—taking the cream of the crop—or stacking the deck by assigning the best clients to the treatment and the dregs to the control group.

Experimental Mortality

Experimental mortality

In studying the same group over a period of time, an expected loss of subjects can be anticipated. This dropping out of respondents from the study group is referred to as **experimental mortality.** In our foot patrol experiment a decline in residential population as a result of urban renewal would certainly impinge on the number of crimes reported. In correctional research, long-term recidivism studies have been handicapped by the inability to follow all or most of the original respondents. Perhaps those who cannot be found are more likely to be successes or failures than those on which data are available.

In one study of drug use behavior of high school students, a 55 percent attrition of respondents took place from the time of the first survey until the second, two years later (Josephson and Rosen, 1978). Such loss rates, unless controlled for, can seriously undermine studies of groups over time.

One method of assessing possible bias as a result of the loss of respondents is to compare known characteristics of respondents with those of nonrespondents. Similarity in such demographic characteristics as sex, age, race, and income may lead one to suspect that nonrespondents do not differ much from respondents and therefore introduce little bias.

Selection—Maturation Interaction

Selection–maturation interaction

Obviously, factors within the experiment other than the assumed predictor variable may be responsible for the findings. Interaction or combination impacts of any or all of these variables may bring about the obtained results, for instance, interaction of selection bias and differential maturation of groups. **Selection–maturation interaction** was illustrated by Gordon et al. (1978) in their critique of a diversion program in which the researchers failed to control for age—selection bias—or to spot a potential maturation effect when older delinquents were placed in the wilderness programs that showed the greatest decline in recidivism. The latter can be viewed as a maturation effect in that as a group ages, its overall crime commission declines.

External Factors: Variables Related to External Validity

External factors

External factors refer to rival causal factors that negatively affect external validity or the representativeness or generalizability of study findings to larger populations beyond the group studied (Campbell and Stanley, 1963), and they include:

Testing effects
Selection bias
Reactivity or awareness of being studied
Multiple-treatment interference

Although a clever researcher may do much to control for the effects of rival causal factors within a study, this may not in any way enhance the ability to generalize beyond the group studied. The testing effects and selection bias previously discussed as affecting internal validity also affect external validity (reactive or interaction effects of pretesting).

Testing Effects

Testing effects

Testing effects point to the tendency of pretests to destroy the naiveté of respondents with respect to the variable(s) being studied and decrease or more predictably increase the subjects' awareness or sensitivity, thus complicating the ability to generalize their responses to a larger population that has not been pretested. For illustrative purposes let us alter the foot patrol example by adding a different dimension. Assume that the purpose of introducing walking beats was to enhance community relations and public attitudes toward the police. At the beginning of the study, residents of the precinct were questioned regarding these matters; then foot patrols were introduced, and the residents were questioned again. A more favorable attitude toward police would be assumed to have been produced by walking patrols; however, perhaps it was induced in part, or primarily, by the group having been pretested and thus having had time to reflect and consider their views. Furthermore, attitudes in this precinct could not be generalized to other even similar precincts, without some hazard, unless a similar pretest–posttest had occurred there also.

Selection Bias

Selection bias

Selection bias can have negative impacts on the ability to infer findings beyond the group studied. Nonrepresentative selection of a study group obviously invalidates any attempt to generalize to larger populations. For instance, the purposive selection of a precinct with high citizen vigilance in responding to crime as the setting for an experiment in police deployment would not be a fair test of how this same program would operate in more typical settings.

Reactivity or Awareness of Being Studied

Reactivity

Reactivity or respondent awareness of being studied tends to produce atypical or unnatural behavior on the part of subjects. Most people have had experience with previously announced inspections, visiting or guest teachers and the like, to realize that behavior observed during that day tends to be at times quite different from what normally occurs. Similarly, if the sample foot patrol precinct were announced and continually covered in the media during the course of the experiment, the residents' behavior, as well as the behavior of the police, would be different than usual.

This phenomenon is variously described as the "Hawthorne effect," "placebo effect," or "stooge effect," as we will see shortly. Thus, an awareness of being studied, rather than the experimental treatment, may become the major factor bringing about a particular outcome.

Multiple-Treatment Interferences

Multiple-treatment interference

Multiple-treatment interference occurs when more than one treatment or predictor variable is used on the same subjects. The outcome may be brought about by a specific sequence or combination of independent variables that can be uncovered only by more complicated research designs, as will be examined later in this chapter. If the foot patrol officers also wore blazers and did not carry guns and gave out free tickets to sports events, a more positive attitude may have been produced by any one or combination of variables, in addition to or irrespective of foot patrols.

Related Rival Causal Factors

Hawthorne Effect

Although not distinct from those already discussed, a number of other Hawthorne related terms for sources of invalidity can be identified. The **Hawthorne effect** serves as an example of reactivity or reactions resulting in atypical behavior or attitudes on the part of research subjects as a result of their awareness of being studied. This factor gets its name from a pioneering industrial study of a group of workers in the Hawthorne plant of the Western Electric Company in Chicago (Roethlisberger and Dixon, 1939; Carey, 1967). To the bemusement of the researchers, alterations in treatment designed to either increase or decrease worker efficiency consistently increased efficiency. Rather than reacting to the treatment variable, X, workers were reacting to a rival causal factor—the fact that they had been singled out for an important study. The workers reacted as they suspected the researchers wanted them to act, rather than as they would under normal circumstances. These acquiescent, "guinea pig," or "stooge" effects are likely in situations where the group being studied is aware that they are being studied.

Hawthorne effect

Halo Effect

Halo effect

The **halo effect** was coined by Thorndike (1920, p. 25), who noticed that when supervisors rated subordinates the ratings were all "higher than reality." It refers to observer bias in which observers, perhaps unconsciously, follow an initial tendency to rate certain objects or persons in a particular manner; this initial orientation carries over into all subsequent ratings. The less specified and discretionary the variable to be rated, the greater the danger of the halo effect (see Cooper, 1981).

Self-fulfilling prophecy

Related in part, but more subtle than the halo effect, is the carryover into research of a phenomenon first noted by sociologist W. I. Thomas. His basic maxim of "the definition of the situation," or what others refer to as *self-fulfilling prophecy,* has a major bearing upon the bias of the researcher. "If groups or individuals define a situation as real, it is real in its consequences" (Thomas and Swaine, 1928, pp. 571–572). A researcher's own hidden biases and expectations may influence his or her perception of events so as to bring about that which had been assumed. Selective perception may lead to one ignoring anything that does not fit one's preset cognitive map and thus presents us with an experimenter effect (Rosenthal, 1966).

Post Hoc Error

Post hoc error

Post hoc error comes from the Latin phrase "post hoc; ergo, propter hoc," literally, "after this; therefore because of it." It is a fallacy to argue that one variable is the cause of an outcome because it precedes that outcome in time. What is considered an effect is often only a subsequent event. An example would be to argue that because every morning when the rooster crows the sun rises, the crowing causes the sunrise. Another example can be found in the common claims made by police chiefs that crime (reported crime) declined in their city in the 1980s because of new and effective policies. More likely than not, what one was observing was the predicted "crime dip" of the 1980s, resulting in part from demographic shifts in what has been described as the post–World War II "baby boom."

Gelles (1977) gives an example of such fallacious reasoning in research on child abusers. Sometimes psychological conditions that are identified as being present after the abuse incident are viewed as the cause of the incident, for example, abusers may be found to be paranoid and depressed, conditions that may be results of the incident, rather than its cause.

Placebo Effect

Placebo effect

Complete enumeration of related tags or descriptions of rival causal factors would be endless and beyond our needs at this point. One final factor that often appears in the literature is the **placebo effect.** This involves, similar to the Hawthorne effect, the tendency of subjects to react to a known stimulus in the predicted manner (Loranger, Prout, and White, 1961). Commonly used in medical research, the "sugar pill" or a placebo or fake treatment with no known effects is administered to the study group to hide the real treatment group and also to control for the placebo effect. The actual effects of the true experimental pill can then be compared with effects induced in the control group by the sugar pill. Other terms used to refer to this same reactivity phenomenon are *evaluation apprehension* or *demand characteristics.* In the former, Rosenberg (1969) notes that subjects are apprehensive about participating in experiments, and this very anxiety may produce atypical behavior. "Was I a good subject?" is often the question asked by respondents who are willing to, in an acquiescent manner, elicit on demand characteristics they believe are sought by the researcher (Orne, 1969).

Double-blind experiment

To control for the "placebo," "Hawthorne," and "experimenter" effects, medical researchers have developed the **double-blind experiment,** a design in which neither subjects nor people administering the experiment are aware of which group is the experimental group (the one receiving "real" treatment) and which group is the control group (the one receiving "phony" treatment) (Glaser, 1976, p. 773).

Other Rival Causal Factors in Criminal Justice Field Experiments

In a revision of the original Campbell and Stanley classic, Cook and Campbell's *Quasi-Experimentation: Design and Analysis Issues for Field Research* (1979) adds some additional rival causal factors threatening the internal validity of experiments. These include:

Diffusion of treatment
Compensatory equalization of treatment
Local history

Diffusion of Treatment

Diffusion of
treatment

Diffusion of treatment occurs when the control group learns about and imitates the experimental group. In essence the control group inadvertently receives the treatment as well. "The experiment thus becomes invalid because there is no treatment or control group in any functional sense and the experimental–control differences at the end of the experiment will not reflect any real differences in the treatment experienced even if the treatment was very effective" (Schneider, 1978, pp. 2–9). Police officers in a control group precinct might hear about and borrow patrol tactics (treatment) of the experimental precinct. Isaac and Michael (1981, p. 86) call this the "John Henry effect" in which the control group, after learning about the treatment group, wants to outdo them or "show them a thing or two."

John Henry
effect

Compensatory Equalization of Treatment

Compensatory
equalization

Compensatory equalization of treatment occurs when members of the control group observe the administration of desirable services (treatment) to the experimental group and subsequently request the same treatment. Obviously, there is no longer a control group. Voters in a control neighborhood might demand the same youth summer jobs program (an antidelinquency treatment) that exists in an experimental neighborhood. The impact of jobs programs upon reducing delinquency would now be difficult to evaluate.

Local History

Local history

Local history is a special case of history (previously described) in which some event happens to either the experimental or control group, but not both. The latter would be called "global history." Suppose in our antidelinquency jobs program that either the experimental or the control group area experienced an outbreak of civil disorder. This would represent yet another, unplanned treatment that would confound our analysis. In addition to those elements of invalidity identified by Campbell and Stanley and related effects, Adams (1975) has identified other factors that may invalidate field experiments:

Masking effects
Contamination of data
"Erosion" of treatment effect
Criterion problems

Although Adams identified even other factors, they are more appropriate in our treatment of evaluation research in Chapter 13.

Masking Effects

Masking effects

Masking effects refer to the fact that "experimental treatments may have opposite effects upon different kinds of subjects" (Adams, 1975, p. 69). For instance, a new police patrol system may demonstrate no overall change in arrests; however, examining arrests by offense, we may discover that more arrests of serious criminals and fewer arrests of minor offenders may have hidden the substantively important effect—"more pinches of serious criminals." A better classification by type of subjects in terms of program outcome should unmask this problem. It becomes not a question of whether the treatment works but, rather, how well does it work with what types of subjects.

Contamination of Data

Contamination of data

Contamination of data takes place when unanticipated events or experiences differentially impact upon experimental or control groups, but not in the same way. This may occur when the control group does not follow the intended plan. Adams (1975, p. 70) cites the Los Angeles Group Guidance Project in which a partially treated gang performed more like the treated gang than the control gang; however, if considered merely a control gang, it would have obscured differences between treated and "untreated" gangs.

Erosion of Treatment Effect

Erosion of treatment

Erosion of treatment effect is the decline of treatment effect demonstrated by the experimental group after treatment, for example, when shortly after a study the experimental group shows superiority over the control group, but three months later there are no differences.

Criterion Problems

Criterion problems

Criterion problems involve the use of one measure rather than many measures of outcome criterion or similar problems of divergent or contradictory indicators of successful outcome. Adams (1975, p. 71) points out, for instance, that in the Silverlake Experiment (to be discussed later in this chapter), the community rehabilitation of juveniles showed no greater recidivism benefits but cost half as much as standard incarceration. If only the first criterion—recidivism—is reported, the program is a failure; however, on the second criterion—cost—it is a success. Although related factors such as these will be explored in Chapter 13 in the section on evaluation research, these rival factors must be controlled or accounted for in research design, as discussed next, or statistically controlled, as discussed in Chapter 12.

All of these rival causal factors are sources of potential error or invalidity in research. Other sources (to be discussed in Chapters 11 and 12) *include errors of a mechanical nature, human errors in data management and sampling error, and errors in estimating population parameters.* The sure way to avoid error in research is not to do any research. This is another way of reinforcing our point that error is ever present in even the best research. The skillful researcher, however, has at his disposal a number of procedures for eliminating or controlling for rival causal factors. One primary means is research design.

Experimental Designs

Research designs

Research designs are a major way of controlling for invalidity in research or, as in step 3, in resolving the causality problem, a means of excluding rival causal factors (Cresswell, 1994). Previously in this chapter we indicated that experiments may be viewed as the benchmark for comparison of all other research methods. The language of research design is heavily couched in that of experimental designs, and a mastery of this specialized jargon is helpful in developing a standard taxonomy by which to classify various forms of research.

Three general types of experimental designs are discussed in this section:

1. *Experimental designs* (sometimes called true experimental designs) are characterized by random assignment to treatment and control groups and include the classical, posttest-only control group, and Solomon four-group designs.
2. *Quasi-experimental designs* do not use random assignment of groups and instead employ matching or other means of obtaining equivalence of groups. Quasi-experimental designs include time-series and counterbalanced designs.
3. *Preexperimental designs* lack any equivalence of groups and include one- and two-group ex post facto and one-group before–after designs.

What we will describe as the classic experimental design is one of the most effective methods of controlling for internal rival causal variables before the fact. In that sense, the experiment becomes the point of departure for a comparison of all other research designs.

The Classic Experimental Design

Classic experimental design

The **classic experimental design,** which serves as a prototype for our discussion of all other research designs, *contains three key elements:*

Equivalence
Pretests and posttests
Experimental and control groups

Equivalence

Equivalence refers to the attempt on the part of the researcher to select and assign subjects to comparison groups in such a manner that they can be assumed to be alike in all major respects. The two methods by which equivalence of groups to be compared is gained are randomization and matching.

Randomization

Randomization is the random assignment of subjects from a similar population to one or the other group(s) to be compared in such a way that each individual has an equal probability of being chosen and an equal probability of being assigned to any of the groups to be compared. We discuss the process of randomization more thoroughly in Chapter 5, but at this point it will suffice to indicate that one of the principal means of accomplishing randomization is by use of simple random samples or some means of selection in which each case in the population has an equal probability of appearing.

Matching

Matching deals with assuring equivalence by selecting subjects for the second or other comparison groups on the basis of matching certain key characteristics such as age, sex, and race, so that the groups are similar or equivalent with respect to these characteristics. Matching and randomization can be combined. In the Cambridge–Somerville study (McCord and McCord, 1959), 325 pairs of boys were matched on delinquency potential and one member of each pair was randomly assigned to treatment (Farrington, 1983, p. 261).

Pretest/ posttest

Assuming that the groups are similar, both are exposed to a **pretest** or observation prior to exposure to treatment and a **posttest** or measurement after exposure to treatment. Finally, the group exposed to treatment is called

Experimental group

the **experimental group;** the group that is not exposed to the stimulus or predictor variable is the **control group.**

Control group

For heuristic purposes, we adapt the notation developed by Campbell and Stanley (1963) for schematically depicting the various research designs: X equals treatment, O symbolizes observations (some researchers use T instead of O), subscripts for O, such as O_1 and O_2, represent the first and second observations, respectively, and E stands for the equivalence of comparison groups. Please note that purists would be more conservative and insist that randomization (R) and not matching is necessary for a classic experimental design.

Classic Experimental Design

$$E \quad O_1 \quad X \quad O_2$$
$$E \quad O_1 \qquad O_2$$

E = equivalence
O = observation
X = treatment
1, 2 = time

Following our previous presentation of this design with our newly introduced notation, we find that the classic experimental design involves an equivalent assignment to experimental and control groups which are observed both before and after the experimental group receives treatment.

Using some of the rival causal factors affecting internal validity, we can now examine the point that experimental designs are effective in controlling for many of these sources of error before the fact. Suppose a classic experimental design had been employed for the foot patrol experiment discussed earlier. Two precincts alike in all possible respects would have been chosen for study (equivalence). The experimental precinct would have been pretested prior to the treatment (foot patrol), whereas the control precinct would have received no treatment (retained usual patrol practices). At the end of the study both groups would once again have been observed and any differences between them would be assumed to have been produced by the deployment of foot patrols. History and maturation would not be likely rival explanations for these differences, because both groups were similar and thus exposed to the same historical and maturation conditions. Both groups were exposed to a pretest; thus, the differences could not result from the pretest, or at least the extent to which the pretest influences results can be assessed because it will show up in both groups. If it is assumed that both groups received the same instrument, changes in the instrument would not account for differences as long as these changes were the same for both groups. Statistical regression should be the same for both groups. Equivalence assures no selection bias and experimental mortality should hopefully be the same.

Field experiment

Laboratory experiment

This hypothetical foot patrol study is an example of a *field experiment,* a type of experiment that is conducted in a natural (field) setting; a *laboratory experiment* is a type of experiment that takes place in contrived or researcher-created conditions. Our next examples illustrate field experiments. Because most of these studies employ matching rather than randomization as the means of assuring equivalence, purists might argue that they are not true experimental designs but rather quasi-experimental designs.

Some Criminal Justice Examples of the Classic Experimental Design

Candid Camera

In 1975 the Seattle Police Department installed hidden cameras in stereo speaker boxes in seventy-five commercial establishments identified as high-risk potential robbery victims. These businesses constituted the experimental group; a group of similar businesses received no treatment. The pretest for both groups consisted of gathering statistics on the percentage of robberies cleared by arrest and conviction rates prior to the study. If held up, a clerk triggered the camera by pulling a "trip" bill from the cash drawer. A special project director would make prints of the photograph of the robber available. A posttest comparing the two groups found that 55 percent of the robberies of experimental companies were cleared by arrest versus 25 percent of the control firms. Similarly, 48 percent of robbers at hidden camera sights were convicted, compared with 19 percent of the control group robbers ("Hidden Cameras Project," 1978).

Scared Straight

In the late seventies, claims of reduced recidivism among juveniles in trouble with the law in response to visits with prisoners were illustrated by the Rahway prison project portrayed in the film *Scared Straight.* The assumption was that much of the "glamor" attached to criminal life by juveniles on the road to more trouble could be nipped in the bud by blunt, heart-to-heart dialogue with specially selected prisoners. Many jurisdictions began to set up what appeared to be a new gimmick in corrections. Later evaluations, however, suggested that the benefits claimed were premature.

Yarborough conducted an evaluation of the JOLT (Juvenile Offenders Learn Truth) program at the State Prison of Southern Michigan at Jackson. Unlike some earlier programs, verbal attacks and obscenities were deemphasized. In 1978 subjects were randomly assigned to experimental and control groups and then measured at three- and six-month follow-up periods. All subjects were male, and arrested or petitioned for an offense that, had they been adults, would have been criminal. No significant differences were found between those who had attended the JOLT session and those who had not. There were no differences in the proportion having petitions filed nor in the types of offenses committed (*Scared Straight,* 1979).

In 1987, WOR TV (Secaucus, New Jersey, June 21, 9:00 P.M. EST) aired a documentary entitled *"Scared Straight:* Ten Years Later." This program presented a very positive picture of the experiment, relying primarily on interviews with people who had attended. Finckenauer (1982), in *Scared Straight! and the Panacea Phenomenon,* felt that the original documentary (1977) had misled the American public into thinking this was a miracle cure for juvenile crime. Despite many problems and lack of cooperation in attempting to evaluate the "Juvenile Awareness Program" or "Lifer's Program" (*Scared Straight* Program) at Rahway, Finckenauer found that his randomly assigned *Scared Straight* experimentals actually had higher seriousness delinquency scores afterward than the controls who did not attend the program. Similarly, many of the juveniles put through the program were not the hardened "junior criminals" the public had been led to believe. Exhibit 3.1 describes a field experiment in Kansas City that met with success.

Community Policing

Community policing has become a subject of much interest in law enforcement since the 1980s. The term broadly refers to a variety of strategies that attempt to get the police away from rapid response to service and closer to the community on a day-to-day basis. Order-maintenance, community crime prevention, problem solving, neighborhood safety, foot patrol, and a host of police–community relations strategies are all included under community policing (Mastrofski, 1992). Such efforts are reflected in other aspects of the criminal justice system such as community-based corrections and even community prosecution and crime prevention programs (Gramckow, 1995).

A variety of field experiments regarding the impact of neighborhood safety programs such as "neighborhood or block watch," "police storefronts," and "foot patrol" experiments have been undertaken. The Police Foundation's analysis of a neighborhood watch experiment in Houston found no noticeable reduction in crime compared with a similar area that had not received the program. Another Houston program established a police department storefront (a combination precinct station, social center, and community outreach center). Houston also experimented with personal-contact patrol in which officers attempted to stop and talk to as many citizens as possible. Despite problems in maintaining experimental conditions, some positive findings were obtained. The neighborhood watch and storefront programs had no noticeable impact upon crime reduction but an enormous impact upon reduction of citizen fear of crime. In addition to reducing fear, the personal-contact patrol reduced household victimizations by one-half and resulted in improving the attitudes of residents on community issues (Sherman, 1985; Wycoff et al., 1985a, 1985b).

A continuing subject of debate has been public dissatisfaction with anonymous, routine policing in automobiles and requests for foot patrols, even though most police managers until recently viewed such assignments as inefficient deployment of limited police personnel. During the late 1970s experiments with foot patrols were conducted in Newark, New Jersey, and Flint, Michigan (Police Foundation, 1981; Wilson and Kelling, 1982; Trojanowicz and Banas, 1985). The same findings were obtained in both studies (Kelling, 1985, p. 2): decreased fear of crime, greater citizen satisfaction, greater appreciation of neighborhood values by the police, and greater

EXHIBIT 3.1

The Kansas City Gun Experiment

The United States has both the highest violent crime and homicide rate of any developed country as well as the largest armed civilian population in the world. National attempts to significantly control firearms are effectively blocked by the powerful National Rifle Association. Given these contingencies, what can police do to try to control growing youth homicide rates? One possibility tested in the Kansas City gun experiment by Sherman, Shaw, and Rogan (1995) was that greater enforcement of existing laws against carrying concealed weapons could reduce gun crime. With a Bureau of Justice Assistance "Weed and Seed" program grant, the Kansas City Police Department selected a target patrol beat and a control beat. The target beat had a 1991 homicide rate of 177 per 100,000 persons, about twenty times the national average. The control beat had a similar violent crime rate. The research design involved a matched groups before–after design. The "hot spot" target area received increased proactive patrols.

The actual technique the officers used to find guns varied, from frisks and searches incident to arrest on other charges to safety frisks associated with car stops for traffic violations. Every arrest for carrying concealed weapons had to be approved for adequate articulable suspicion with a supervisory detective's signature (ibid., p. 6).

Figure 1 illustrates the differences between the target beat and the comparison beat during the one-year experiment.

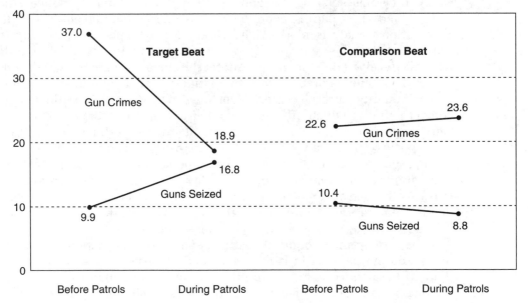

Figure 1   Kansas City Gun Experiment—Guns Seized Per 1,000 Persons. (*Source:* Sherman, Saw, and Rogan, 1995, p. 1.)

Gun crimes in the target beat decreased from 37 per 1,000 persons to 18.9, and guns seized increased from 9.9 to 16.8. The comparison beat showed little change in gun crime (22.6 to 23.6 per 1,000) and an actual decrease in guns seized (10.4 to 8.8 per 1,000). There was no displacement of gun crimes to surrounding areas. Drive-by shootings dropped from 7 to 1 in the target area, but doubled from 6 to 12 in the comparison area, again with no displacement effect. Figure 2 compares offenses by firearms.

Other positive findings were a decline in homicides in the target area, but not in the comparison area. Citizens in the target area were less fearful, but there was no change in fear in the comparison area. Two-thirds of those arrested for gun carrying in the target area were from outside the area.

Finally, only gun crimes were reduced by the directed patrols which had no effect on calls for service or reduction of other crimes. Further replications are underway as of this writing. Lawrence Sherman, the principal author of the report, is on leave from the University of Maryland and is serving as Criminologist to the Indianapolis Police Department in order to further test the program.

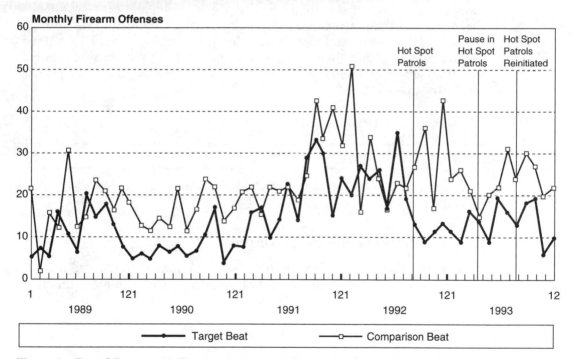

Figure 2 Total Offenses with Firearms by Month in Target and Comparison Beats (*Source:* Sherman, Shaw, and Rogan, 1995, p. 7.)

Source: Sherman, Lawrence W., James W. Shaw, and Dennis P. Rogan. "The Kansas City Gun Experiment." National Institute of Justice Research in Brief, January 1995. Document available from National Criminal Justice Reference Service, Box 6000, Rockville MD 20849-6000; call 1-800-851-3420 or lookncjrs@aspensys.com.

job satisfaction, less fear, and higher morale for officers who patrol on foot than for officers who patrol in automobiles. The Flint study showed a decrease in service calls via telephone of 40 percent and a modest reduction in crime, whereas the Newark program showed no crime reduction. More replications (repeats of the experiments) are under way. Foot patrols are obviously no panacea but have been found popular, particularly when selectively implemented in densely populated urban areas.

In the 1990s the National Institute of Justice has contracted a large number of studies of community policing ("Community Policing," 1992). For example, an evaluation of the Madison, Wisconsin, Police Department's "quality" policing program examined a community–oriented policing program with a new organizational design based on the work of management expert Edwards Deming. In comparing the experimental with the comparison police district it was found that in the experimental district the managers viewed themselves more as problem solvers and employee attitudes regarding their work and organization improved. In addition, citizen interaction improved and their perception of crime as a problem was reduced, and they also expressed a more positive attitude toward the police (Wycoff and Skogan, 1994).

Other Experimental Designs

Other experimental designs include the *posttest-only control group design* and the *Solomon four-group design.*

Posttest-Only Control Group Design

To assess the impact of consolidated police departments on public satisfaction with policing in their area, Ostrom, Parks, and Whitaker conducted a *posttest-only control group design* (1973).

Posttest-only
control group
design

$$E \quad X \quad O$$
$$E \quad \quad \; O$$

Three Indianapolis neighborhoods with a consolidated police department were matched with three communities with independent police departments. The researchers discovered higher public satisfaction in the communities with independent departments. Without a pretest it is unclear, however, whether this difference could not in fact have been caused by other rival factors; for example, perhaps even before police department consolidation, the Indianapolis neighborhoods had lower degrees of satisfaction with their policing.

Solomon Four-Group Design

The *Solomon four-group design* (Solomon, 1949) is viewed by some as the purest of research designs. Basically it combines the classic experimental design with the posttest-only design. The Solomon design has four groups, the first two resembling a classic design and the second two a posttest-only control group design.

$$
\begin{array}{cccc}
E & O_1 & X & O_2 \\
E & O_1 & & O_2 \\
E & & X & O_2 \\
E & & & O_2
\end{array}
$$

To illustrate the Solomon design let us hypothetically suppose, using the same Indianapolis example, that four areas could be chosen for study from evenly matched communities. The first two areas would both be measured with respect to public attitude toward the police. Only one of these would receive the treatment (consolidated policing) and both would be remeasured with respect to attitude. Two other areas would not receive the premeasure; that is, they would be measured only after one had received treatment (consolidated policing) and one had not. Such a design would assess the effect of testing effects as well as provide a premeasure lacking in the posttest-only control group design. The advantage of the posttest-only control group design is that it eliminates testing effects and possibly reactivity entirely, although it lacks a measure of where the groups stood prior to the treatment. The Solomon four-group design obviously has the advantage of having the premeasure and, by adding the second two groups, has the same advantage as the posttest-only control group design. It is, however, expensive and difficult to implement and, therefore, not practical in many research situations.

The classic Solomon and posttest-only control group designs are examples of experimental designs. Randomization, in which equivalence is obtained by random assignment of subjects to experimental and control groups, is the key distinguishing characteristic of experimental designs. Preexperimental designs lack equivalence of groups, and quasi-experimental designs rely on matching of subjects to achieve equivalence. In many field experiments such as the Indianapolis example randomization may be inappropriate or impossible; as long as equivalence is assured, it can be argued that these are true experiments.

Preexperimental Designs

Research designs that lack one or two of the three major elements of experimental designs—equivalence or experimental and control groups—are designated as preexperimental designs.

One-Group Ex Post Facto Design
X   O

One-Group Before–After Design
O   X   O

Two-Group Ex Post Facto Design
X   O
O

One-Group Ex Post Facto Design

One-group ex post facto design

All of these preexperimental designs fail to provide equivalence or any assurance that the group(s) being studied is representative in any way of some larger population(s). The *one-group ex post facto design,* or one–shot case study, is quite typical of many early criminal justice demonstration projects. Our original example of the precinct foot patrol experiment, if it contained no preobservation, would serve as an illustration. Unlike true experimental designs, one-group ex post facto (after the fact) studies are subject to many internal invalidity factors or errors. One simply has chosen for study a group that has already been exposed to a particular treatment. Obviously, things other than the treatment could explain the outcome. If one finds a precinct that had experimental foot patrols or an agency with low recidivism rates, without premeasures, equivalence, and control groups, one is on shaky ground in concluding that lower crime rates or lower recidivism are due to these factors. Many studies, particularly field studies in criminology and criminal justice, are of the one-shot case study variety. Cressey's (1957) study of incarcerated embezzlers, for instance, may have major problems with respect to selection bias and reactivity but, on the other hand, may be the only way of obtaining exploratory information on a little-known topic. What one-group ex post facto studies lose in terms of internal control of error may be gained in terms of studying groups in natural field conditions.

Early research on the XYY or "supermale syndrome" assumed, on the basis of studies of incarcerated violent offenders, that an extra male chromosome may have been responsible for violent crime (Witkin et al., 1978). Only later examination of the general population suggested that it may be as prevalent among the "noncriminal" male population. As mentioned previously, in lamenting the shortcomings of studies of sentencing behavior, Farrington (1978) points out that few studies use both before and after measures, or compare a sentenced group with an unsentenced group, thus making it difficult to know whether changes in behavior are due to sentences or penalties or other concurrent social changes.

In another example of a one-group ex post facto study, Heussenstamm (1971) reports on a field experiment in which subjects, none of whom had received traffic violations the previous twelve months, attached Black

Panther bumper stickers to their automobiles. They attracted so many traffic citations that the experiment had to be canceled. That Heussenstamm had knowledge of the fact that the subjects had not received citations before the treatment may qualify the study as being an example of the next type, the one-group before–after design.

One-Group Before–After Design

One-group
before–after
design

The *one-group before–after design,* or one-group pretest–posttest design, is an example of a longitudinal design. A group, which is not necessarily chosen on the basis of representativeness, is observed, exposed to treatment, and again observed. The primary advantage of this design over the one-group ex post facto design is, of course, the presence of a premeasure. This adds, however, the problem of testing effects, and has the same problem as the one-group ex post facto design in that one's findings cannot be compared with those for a similar control group not exposed to treatment.

An example of a one-group before–after design is Pierce and Bowers' (1979) analysis of the impact of the Massachusetts Bartley–Fox gun law, which carried a one-year minimum prison sentence for the unlicensed carrying of firearms. With the use of recorded crime statistics and observations both before and after passage of the law, the earliest part of a longitudinal design suggested a decrease in gun-related assaults, robberies, and homicides; however, this was offset by increases in nongun assaults and robberies using other weapons. Without a control group the same problem exists as in our previous burglary reduction program (Garwood, 1978)—other variables may be responsible for these findings.

Two-Group Ex Post Facto Design

Two-group ex
post facto
design

The *two-group ex post facto design* eliminates possible pretest reactivity by studying both an experimental and a control group after the experimental group has been exposed to some treatment. The primary problem with this design is that there is no way of being sure that the two groups were initially equivalent. Skillful selection of groups for comparison, however, may be the only option a researcher has in some instances. Brown et al. (1970) surveyed two groups of parolees: those who had succeeded and those who had failed at parole. After the fact, they were asked to identify factors in the institution and community that assisted or impeded their adjustment. Such two-group ex post facto designs were heavily utilized in early biological and psychological theories. These theories in criminology that claimed genetic or personality differences between criminals and noncriminals suffered

Dualistic
fallacy

from what Reid (1982, p. 657) describes as the *dualistic fallacy,* the assumption that prisoners (who are supposed to represent criminals) and groups from the general population (all of whom are assumed to be noncriminals) represent mutually exclusive groups (or are nonoverlapping).

Cross-Sectional and Longitudinal Designs

Cross-sectional
studies

Longitudinal
studies

Before going further, it is crucial to briefly introduce a general distinction used to describe research designs. *Cross-sectional designs* involve studies of one group at one time and usually refer to a representative sample of this group. *Longitudinal studies* are studies of the same group over a period of time and generally are studies of change (Menard, 1991).

Time-series designs involve variations of multiple observations of the same group at various times. Variations may include dividing the original group into equivalent groups and observing these portions longitudinally. In Chapters 5 and 6 we discuss the usefulness of panel designs in such surveys as the National Crime Survey in providing an in-depth view over time of the same study population. In a now classic criminological study, Wolfgang et al. (1972) used existing records to trace longitudinally the criminal or non-criminal careers of 9,945 boys born in Philadelphia in 1945.

In a replication that included females, Tracy, Wolfgang, and Figlio (1985) tracked the criminal history of males and females born in Philadelphia in 1958 who continued to live there from the age of 10 until adulthood. Both studies were instrumental in identifying the concept of serious career criminals, finding that approximately 6 percent of the 1945 group had been responsible for 53 percent of arrests for violent crime and 71 percent for robbery, whereas 7 percent of the 1958 group had committed 75 percent of all serious crime by this group. Farrington (1979) conducted a similar study in London begun in 1961 of boys eight to nine years old in state primary schools.

One of the earliest series of cohort analysis was done by the Gluecks, who studied 500 reformatory inmates over ten years and 1,000 juvenile delinquents for more than fifteen years (Glueck and Glueck, 1937, 1940). Such longitudinal designs are useful in giving us the long view as well as short-term variations over time. Another example of an ambitious longitudinal study was the Cambridge–Somerville Youth Study begun in 1937 and continuing with some interruption through 1945. Extensive data were gathered on each of the 650 boys who began the project including delinquency, neighborhood, family conditions, school behavior, intelligence, and personality. In 1955, the McCords (1959) reexamined the data and compared official and unofficial delinquents. Exhibit 3.2 examines a longitudinal study of child abuse and neglect victims.

Time-series
designs

Trend studies

Time-series designs and panel designs are other terms used to refer to types of longitudinal studies, as are cohort and trend studies which are also variations of longitudinal designs. **Time-series designs** involve measuring a single variable at successive points in time. In an *interrupted time-series design,* measurements are taken at time points prior to treatment and for an equivalent period after intervention. The rate of crime committed one year prior to treatment could be compared with the rate for the first year after treatment (Schneider and Wilson, 1978). *Trend studies* simply study

EXHIBIT 3.2

The Cycle of Violence and Victims of Child Abuse

In previous research Cathy Spatz Widom (1992) found that childhood abuse or neglect increased the odds of future delinquency and adult criminality by an overall 40 percent. The study consisted of a longitudinal study of 1,575 cases from childhood through young adulthood. A group of 908 cases of child abuse or neglect processed by the courts between 1967 and 1971 were tracked using official records for fifteen to twenty years. A comparison group of 667 was matched by age, sex, race, and family social class. The study concluded that:

> While most members of both groups had no juvenile or adult criminal record, being abused or neglected as a child increased the likelihood of arrest as a juvenile by 53 percent, as an adult by 38 percent, and for violent crime by 38 percent (ibid., p. 1).

Using these same cases, Widom (1995) also examined the relationship between childhood sexual abuse and later criminal behavior, particularly sexual offenses. The key finding was that:

> People who were sexually victimized during childhood are at higher risk of arrest for

committing crimes as adults, including sex crimes, than are people who did not suffer sexual or physical abuse or neglect during childhood. However, the risk of arrest for childhood sexual abuse victims as adults is no higher than for victims of other types of childhood abuse and neglect (ibid., p. 2).

Compared with victims of physical abuse, child abuse victims are more likely to be arrested for prostitution. Victims of physical abuse were more likely to commit rape and sodomy than were sexual abuse victims or the nonvictimized. The long-assumed relationship between childhood sexual abuse, running away, and prostitution was not borne out by the research.

All of these findings relied on official statistics for measuring the dependent variable of crime commission. Continuing research in this series is examining other sources. An attempt is being made to reinterview all 1,575 subjects in order to discover other consequences of child abuse including social, emotional, cognitive, psychiatric, and health outcomes. Also to be examined are factors which protect child abuse victims from later negative consequences.

Sources: Cathy Spatz, Widom, "The Cycle of Violence." National Institute of Justice Research in Brief, October 1992; Widom, Cathy Spatz. "Victims of Childhood Sexual Abuse—Later Criminal Consequences." National Institute of Justice Research in Brief, March 1995. Documents can be obtained from the National Criminal Justice Reference Service, Box 6000, Rockville MD 20849–6000; call 1-800-851-3420 or Internet lookncjrs@aspensys.com.

Cohort studies

Panel studies

different samples of the same general population longitudinally, whereas *cohort studies* analyze subgroups over time, although each time may consist of a sample of the cohort. *Panel studies* examine the same select group or sample over time, as we will see in the National Crime Surveys. The most ambitious longitudinal study ever conducted in the social sciences is discussed in Exhibit 3.3.

Although there has been some debate in the field of criminology regarding the overapplication of scarce federal research funds to expensive longitudinal studies, it is often the only way of sorting out many trends and causal relationships (Esbensen and Menard, 1990, p. 5). Tontodonato (1988)

EXHIBIT 3.3

The Project of Human Development: An Accelerated Longitudinal Design Using Nine Spaced–Age Cohorts

In the largest longitudinal study ever undertaken in criminal justice/criminology, NIJ's Project of Human Development in Chicago Neighborhoods is unprecedented in scope. It is examining a broad range of factors at the community, family, and individual level that are believed predictors of crime and deviance. A team of researchers headed by Albert Reiss, Jr. (Yale) and Felton Earls (Harvard) are conducting the study; and it will examine everything from gestation, infancy, and childhood to adulthood to age thirty-two. Such a prospective design would usually take thirty-two years; but the unique feature of the research design, an accelerated longitudinal design depicted in Figure 1, speeds up the timetable.

Between 1994 and 2002 the investigators will gather detailed data about 11,000 individuals and their communities. A preliminary five-year planning phase and the accelerated longitudinal design will provide data much more quickly than the standard longitudinal design. Overlapping age cohorts will be studied, each with five-year overlap periods, thus mimicking a thirty-two year longitudinal study. Figure 2 describes the key variable examined in the research.

Data collection began in Chicago in August 1994. For three years prior, exploratory studies of topics and methods took place and research protocols were pretested. Subjects and their families will be interviewed across the nine age cohorts. Support from a variety of community organizations is being solicited particularly in investigating mental health, child development, and substance. It is hoped that the multidisciplinary approach integrating community, family, school, peer, and individual characteristics will do much to advance our understanding of crime causation and in developing future crime control policy.

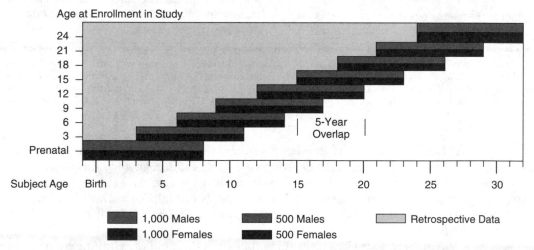

Figure 1　Project on Human Development, Accelerated Longitudinal Design 2002—Completion of Study. (*Source:* Visher, 1994, p. 13.)

The Community
Social, economic and demographic structure
Organizational/political structure
Community standards and norms
Informal social control
Crime, victimization and arrests
Social cohesion
Residential turnover
Level of involvement in drug and gang networks

The School
Academic achievement expectations
School policies regarding social control

School conflict
Teacher-student relationships
Strengths and weaknesses of the school environment

Peer Relationships
Composition and size of social network
Substance abuse and delinquency by peers
Deviant and prosocial attitudes of peers
Location of peer networks (school or community)
Changes in peer relationships over time

The Family
Family structure
Parent–child relationships

Parent disciplinary practices
Parent characteristics
Family mental health
Family history of criminal behavior and substance abuse

The Individual
Physical and mental health status
Impulse control and sensation-seeking traits
Cognitive and language development
Ethnic identity and acculturation
Leisure-time activities
Self-perception, attitude and values

Figure 2 Project on Human Development: The Contents and Factors to be Studied. (*Source:* Visher, 1994, p. 14.)

Source: Visher, Christy A. "Understanding the Roots of Crime: The Project on Human Development in Chicago Neighborhoods." National Institute of Justice Journal, November 1994: 9–15. Interim reports can be obtained from: The Project on Human Development in Chicago Neighborhoods, Harvard School of Public Health, Department of Maternal and Child Health, 677 Huntington Avenue, Boston MA 02115.

Event history analysis describes a variation of a longitudinal design called *event history analysis,* which involves "studying actions over time and their possible causes" (ibid., p. 456). This method makes possible the examination of the repeat occurrence of the same event or the appearance of a different event. For example, rather than speak simply of chronic offenders and offense specialization, event history analysis provides a model to explain the transition rate from one type of crime to another. Cross-sectional and longitudinal research need not be viewed as mutually exclusive entities; they can complement each other (Deschenes, 1990, pp. 163–164).

Quasi-Experimental Designs

There are many variations of the experimental design. In fact, as mentioned previously, almost all research in criminal justice can be described using the notation with which we have been working. Because quasi-experimental designs rely on matching—the use of "comparison groups" or means other than randomization to obtain equivalence—the value of using comparison groups depends upon how similar the groups are on key variables to the treatment group. Some quasi- or semiexperimental designs include single time-series, multiple time-series, and counterbalanced designs.

Time-Series Designs

Time-series designs   *Time-series designs* refer to the analysis of a single variable (for example, crime rate) at many successive time periods with some measures taken prior to treatment and other observations taken after the intervention. It is sometimes called an interrupted time series because the series of observations is interrupted by a treatment (X).

Interrupted Time-Series Designs
$$O \qquad O \qquad O \qquad O \qquad X \qquad O \qquad O \qquad O \qquad O$$

It is desirable to have at least ten preobservations and a bare minimum of two, but probably more, postobservations (Schneider et al., 1978, pp. 2–13). Such designs are widely used in criminal justice research in examining the impact of a new law or treatment upon trends in crime.

Interrupted time-series designs   *Interrupted time-series designs* then can be defined as an analysis of a single variable measured at many successive time points, with some measures taken prior to a treatment (interruption) and others taken after the treatment. Preproject observations are used as a basis for estimating the trend, and differences between this projected trend and the trend observed after treatment can be assessed to determine whether the treatment had an impact.

Figure 3.2 depicts time-series data for a problem-oriented policing program (the treatment) designed to reduce larcenies from automobiles. The overall reduction in trend lines can be noted from before to after the intervention.

Figure 3.3 demonstrates the advantage of time-series designs over simple pretest–posttest designs. In both instances simple analysis of the last point before and the first point after the intervention would have led to the conclusion of no significant change where, in fact, examination of trend lines showed significant change.

Monahan and Walker (1990, p. 66) give an illustration of the superiority of a time-series design over a before–after design in their analysis of the impact of the Community Mental Health Centers Act of 1963. This program's goal was the reduction of state mental hospitalization.

> In 1963, the year the act was passed, the resident population of state mental hospitals in the United States was approximately 500,000. In 1990, it was less than 150,000. These before–after figures have been used to persuade Congress of the effectiveness of the act. When a time-series with more than one mea-

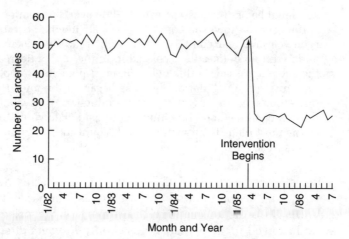

Figure 3.2 Time-Series Data for Larcenies from Automobiles in Newport News, Virginia. The Intervention (Treatment) Was a Problem-Oriented Policing Approach That Consisted of Special Tracking and Investigation of Crime Incidents. (*Source:* Spelman, William, and John E. Eck. "Problem-Oriented Policing." *Research in Brief.* National Institute of Justice [January 1987]:7)

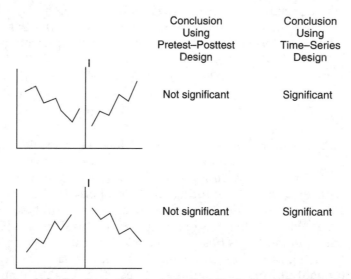

Figure 3.3 A Comparison of Pretest–Posttest Designs and Time-Series Designs. (*Source:* Schneider, Anne L., et al. *Handbook of Resources for Criminal Justice Evaluators.* Washington, D.C.: National Institute of Law Enforcement and Criminal Justice [1978]: 2–47.)

surement before the passage is used, however, the results seem quite different. A time-series shows the population of state mental hospitals to have increased each year from early in the century until 1955, and decreased each year thereafter, with no noticeable acceleration in the rate of decrease in 1963, the year the act was passed. In this light, the most plausible hypothesis is that the factor causing the population decrease began in the mid–1950's, and not in the mid–1960's. Many now view the introduction of psychotropic medication as the principal method of treating mental patients, which indeed began in 1955, as the most plausible hypothesis to account for the "deinstitutionalization" of mental hospitals.

In yet other variations of interrupted time-series designs, the impact of new prisons (experimental counties) was compared with matched/control counties in order to examine the impact of the prisons. Twenty variables were followed for two years before and two years after the prison openings (Smykla et al., 1984). The relationship between "War and Capital Punishment" was examined by studying the number of executions before, during, and after three war periods (Schneider and Smykla, 1990).

Multiple Interrupted Time-Series Designs

A distinction is also made between *single interrupted time-series designs,* which examine one group or site's preprogram and postprogram outcomes over time, and *multiple interrupted time-series designs,* which contrast one group's performance with that of relevant comparison groups.

Multiple interrupted time-series designs

Multiple Time-Series Designs

O	O	O	O	X	O	O	O	O
O	O	O	O		O	O	O	O

Although a single interrupted time-series design might examine the impact of the 55-mph speed limit upon vehicular deaths, a multiple interrupted time-series design would compare a state with the new speed limit with one without it during the same period. For example, Connecticut's 1955 crackdown on speeding reduced traffic fatalities, whereas neighboring states without this program experienced no decrease (Campbell and Ross, 1980). In the 1960s Boston and New York City had very restrictive handgun licensing laws but complained that their laws were defeated by guns brought in from nonrestrictive states. Zimring (1975) studied the impact of the Federal Gun Control Act of 1968 on interstate traffic in guns on homicide rates and found that handgun homicide rates actually grew faster in New York City and Boston (the restrictive cities) than the average trend for fifty-seven control cities. Such time-series designs are indispensable and widely used in criminological and criminal justice research because the subjects often require analysis of trends or long-range effects rather than short-term outcomes.

Counterbalanced Designs

Counter-
balanced
designs

Counterbalanced designs are intended to manage or control the problem of multiple-treatment inference in which X_1 refers to one treatment, X_2 a second, X_3 a third, and X_4 a fourth. By using four groups that are equivalent and exposing each group to all four treatments and observing after each combination of treatments, it becomes possible to isolate the treatment(s), combination of treatments, or sequence of treatments that produces the outcome. For example, in four precincts where the treatments were X_1—foot patrol, X_2—media campaign, X_3—police blazers, and X_4—unarmed police, perhaps the desired outcome is obtained only by X_3—police blazers and X_1—foot patrol in that sequence of introduction only. Such a design, although complex, is the only way to uncover such a relationship.

$$
\begin{array}{ccccc}
E & X_1O & X_2O & X_3O & X_4O \\
E & X_2O & X_3O & X_4O & X_1O \\
E & X_3O & X_4O & X_1O & X_2O \\
E & X_4O & X_1O & X_2O & X_3O \\
\end{array}
$$

There are many other variations of the experimental model. Familiarity with the notation and basic designs we have discussed enables one to conceptualize these other designs as offshoots of the basic ones.

Some Other Criminal Justice Examples of Variations of the Experimental Model

The Provo and Silverlake Experiments

Provo and
Silverlake
experiments

Empey and Erickson (1972) and Empey and Lubeck (1971) employed the classic experimental design to assess the effect of experimental community-based treatment programs in Provo (Utah) and Silverlake (Los Angeles). The subjects were all juveniles who were either serious and/or repeat offenders. All were ordinarily candidates for reformatories who were sentenced by a judge to probation or incarceration. All were male. None were seriously retarded or heroin addicts or had a history of serious assaultive violence.

Although both the Provo and Silverlake experiments are relatively complex in theoretical design and methodological execution, a brief review of two elements of the analysis will serve our purposes. One element in community resistance to community-based treatment programs has been the fear of crime perpetrated by those undergoing treatment. The Provo researchers, and later the Silverlake study, compared randomly assigned experimental and control groups from two disposition conditions. Our discussion is concerned primarily with the Provo Study, although the Silverlake experience is also briefly discussed.

Provo Research Design

Probation experimental group	*E*	*O*	*X*	*O*
Probation control group	*E*	*O*		*O*
Incarceration experimental group	*E*	*O*	*X*	*O*
Incarceration control group	*E*	*O*		*O*

Equivalence of groups was obtained by randomly assigning those given probation to the Provo program or regular probation, and similarly assigning those scheduled for incarceration to either the Provo treatment or actual incarceration. With the incarceration group, randomization broke down because the population was too small and the matched control group was selected using a state training school.

In evaluating arrest rates as an indicator of crime committed, the probation controls had a rate twice as high as the probation experimentals. Surprisingly, the arrest rate for "incarcerated" experimentals was almost as low as that for incarcerated controls. The latter were either on furloughs or escapees who, in addition, tended to commit more serious crimes. Similar findings were obtained in the Silverlake experiment, which added the variables of urban setting and race (20 percent Chicano or African-American, versus 100 percent Caucasian in the Provo study).

In analysis of yet another dependent variable, postprogram arrest rates, by means of a longitudinal follow-up four years after release, the experimental probation types were not greatly superior to regular probation control types (a 71 percent reduction in crime compared with the rate four years prior to the experiment, versus 66 percent for the regular probation group). The "incarcerated" experimental group showed a 49 percent reduction, whereas the incarcerated control group exhibited only a 25 percent reduction. Maturation or age did not affect these differences when controlled statistically; that is, these differences operated independently of age. Among some methodological problems introduced in the Provo experiment was a breakdown in equivalence, because the judge sentenced too few to the reformatory. Additionally, a possible Hawthorne effect was present, as suggested by the fact that the success rate for the control group given regular probation was higher than that for the same group before the experiment began. The probation officers' knowledge of the study may have had this impact (Hood and Sparks, 1971, p. 209).

Despite some problems, given the higher costs of incarceration, the Provo-Silverlake findings were a major demonstration of the utility of the community-based corrections movement. Exhibit 3.4 reports on evaluations of shock incarceration.

EXHIBIT 3.4

Evaluations of Shock Incarceration

With a burgeoning prison population in the eighties, intermediate sanctions such as electronic monitoring, intensive probation, and shock incarceration became popular, cost effective alternatives to overcrowding prisons. They turned out not to fit the role of a popular panacea. Often increased recidivism took place due to an increased "net of control" (Morris and Tonry, 1990) or increased technical violations due to greater surveillance during community supervision (Petersilia and Turner, 1990). While boot camp programs (shock incarceration) vary in content, most involve offenders participating in military-type training and variations of physical exercise, hard physical labor, ventilation therapy, substance abuse, and prerelease education. Doris Mackenzie and associates have examined a number of boot camp programs.

Examining a Louisiana boot camp (shock incarceration) program, Mackenzie and Shaw (1993) looked at shock incarceration releasees after two years of community supervision and compared these with similar offenders who had been given probation or parole. Four groups of offenders were compared: shock releases, probationers, parolees, and shock dropouts. These were contrasted with respect to technical violations (terms of supervision offenses), new crime arrests, and new crime convictions. The shock graduates had higher rates of technical violations and revocations than the probationers and parolees, lower rates of new convictions, and in some analyses lower rates of arrests and revocations for new crimes. There were no differences between shock alumnae and shock dropouts in the Louisiana study (ibid.). This study was an example of the utilization of a quasi-experimental design with comparison groups in which there was no random assignment of subjects. The shock experimentals were compared with offenders who had been eligible for shock incarceration but had received other treatments instead. Possible invalidities in such a design include selection bias (in that offenders were not randomly assigned) and the fact that shock offenders were more carefully scrutinized on release, which most likely accounted for the greater number of technical violations (ibid., p. 483).

Between 1982 and 1992 the number of shock programs had increased to forty-one programs. In an evaluation of eight shock incarceration programs in Florida, Georgia, Illinois, Louisiana, New York, Oklahoma, South Carolina, and Texas, Mackenzie and Souryal (1994) found recidivism rates similar to comparable offenders who did not go through boot camps. Where shock offenders had lower rates, this may have been due to selection bias (specially selected offenders for the program). It appears that boot camp experience itself does not reduce recidivism (Travis, 1994). Successful programs were followed by six-month intensive supervision in the community. Participants in boot camps gave higher ratings to their experience and felt safer.

Sources: Mackenzie, Doris L., and James W. Shaw. "The Impact of Shock Incarceration on Technical Violations and New Criminal Activities." *Justice Quarterly* 10 (September 1993): 462–488; Mackenzie, Doris L., and Claire Souryal. *Multisite Evaluation of Shock Incarceration.* Rockville, Md.: National Criminal Justice Reference Service, NCJ #150062, 1994; Travis, Jeremy. "Researchers Evaluate Eight Shock Incarceration Programs." National Institute of Justice Update, October 1994.

The Kansas City Preventive Patrol Experiment

Kansas City
experiment

Yet another variation of the classic experimental design was employed in the *Kansas City preventive patrol study* (Kelling et al., 1974).

Experimental Group I (Reactive Patrols)	E	O_1	X_1	O_2
Experimental Group II (Proactive Patrols)	E	O_1	X_2	O_2
Control Group (Usual Patrols)	E	O_1		O_2

A fifteen-beat area of the city was divided into three matched five-beat groups. The first group was reactive in patrol procedure; that is, officers responded only to calls for service and did not deploy preventive patrols. The second group was proactive, or increased preventive patrols up to three times the normal levels. Usual deployment, or preventive patrols at their normal levels, was assigned to the control group.

Outcome variables analyzed prior to the treatments, O_1, included reported crime and victimization surveys of citizens and businesses. Posttreatment outcomes in citizen and business victimization and perception of security and reported and unreported crime showed no statistically significant differences among the three types of patrol areas studied. Despite methodological criticisms such as the location of cars withdrawn from reactive patrol, small size of beats, and small numbers used in the survey, the study suggested that police administrators have greater leeway than they supposed in patrol deployment (Chaiken, 1976; Davis and Knowles, 1975; Kelling and Pate, 1975; Larson, 1975; Pate et al., 1975). Similar replications of the Kansas City experiment essentially confirmed the same findings (Albuquerque, 1979).

In a review of the Kansas City data, critics concluded that it was not likely that randomization had been used in beat assignments (Feinberg, Singer, and Tanur, 1985). Kelling, the principal director of the project, admitted that the police selected the beats on the basis of the department's needs (Fagan, 1990, p. 110). Research by Sykes (1984) further illustrates the need to measure different outcomes of increased enforcement efforts. In examining saturation patrol as a deterrent to drunk driving, he found that it did deter some types of deviant behavior but was not a "panacea."

The Minneapolis Domestic Violence Experiment

A 1977 Police Foundation (1977, p. iv) study in Kansas City found that in the two years preceding a case of domestic assault or domestic homicide, the police had been at the address of the incident five or more times in half of the cases. This suggested that the police had an opportunity to attempt to head off domestic violence. Beginning in the late 1960s the police had been encouraged to train their officers and utilize counseling and family crisis intervention strategies in domestic dispute cases. By the 1980s concern for the rights of female victims, possible lawsuits against police for failure to make arrests where subsequent violence occurred, and a more conservative punitive-policy orientation led to a questioning of this policy.

Minneapolis experiment   In 1983 the *Minneapolis Domestic Violence Experiment* (Sherman, 1985; Sherman and Berk, 1984a, 1984b) was undertaken to attempt to provide evidence as to the most effective strategy. The research design is similar to the Kansas City Preventive Patrol Experiment—that is, it contains three groups (two with different treatments and one control), or it could be described as having three different treatment groups. In Minneapolis, police officers volunteered to give up their discretion in handling simple (misdemeanor) domestic assaults and take whatever action was dictated by a random system: instructions written on a card and drawn from an envelope at the scene. Three different instructions were given: (1) *arrest* the suspect; (2) *separate* or remove the suspect from the scene for 8 hours; or (3) *advise* and mediate.

Minneapolis Domestic Violence Experiment

Arrest	E	O_1	X_1	O_2
Separate	E	O_1	X_2	O_2
Mediate[a]	E	O_1		O_2

After the police intervened, researchers attempted to interview the victims every two weeks for the next six months as well as monitor police records to check if there were any subsequent assaults. The results appeared to be dramatic: 37 percent of the "advised" subjects and 33 percent of the "separated" subjects had recidivated (committed new assaults within six months); however, only 19 percent of the "arrested" subjects were repeaters. This reduction was accomplished even though arrest usually entailed only a night in jail.

The Minneapolis experiment has been both the most widely accepted and the most influential policy experiment of recent years; no other policy experiment has had quite the same impact on criminal justice policy. The changes it has effected may be explained in part by the conservative tenor of the times, which emphasizes a law enforcement orientation for solving social problems; it may also be explained by the very aggressive dissemination of the study's findings (Binder and Meeker, 1991). Buzawa and Buzawa (1991) note that even though the research project was a modest pilot study with acknowledged limitations, extraordinary efforts to publicize the results in the national media resulted in premature police policy changes. In the first published replication of the study in Omaha, Nebraska, the researchers

---

[a]Mediation could be considered a third treatment or X_3

Dunford, Hiuzinga, and Elliott (1989, 1990) found that arrest alone did not have any greater impact than mediation or separation.

A critique   Binder and Meeker (1991) have provided the most thorough critique of the Minneapolis study. They cited several objections:

- The areas chosen for study were two Minneapolis precincts with the worst domestic violence rates.
- Officer participation in the study was not only voluntary, but poor. By study's end, about 28 percent of the cases were being processed by only three officers.
- Approximately 60 percent of the Minneapolis sample of victims and suspects were unemployed, whereas a similar study by Ray (1982) in the New York City area found that most were employed.
- Nearly 60 percent of the Minneapolis sample had previously been arrested, and only one–third had had husband–wife relationships. By comparison, in Ray's study (1982) only 10 percent had previous records, with two–thirds being married couples.
- The comparison treatments of separation or mediation by police officers without special training were not realistic comparison points.
- Other problems with the statistical analysis (Binder and Meeker, 1988) of prison crowding and of internal factors such as "officer interest in victim's story" raised further questions regarding the study's broad conclusions.

Further replications will tell us if we have too quickly embraced an "arrest panacea" for handling domestic disputes. Preliminary results from four of the completed six replications seem to suggest that arrest does not work more effectively in deterring domestic assault.

The point of all of this is to suggest that research is an ongoing process and one in which replication is essential; panaceas or simple solutions based on one study are suspect.

If you refused to be intimidated by the researchese in this chapter and learned your *X*'s and *O*'s and how research design is a powerful tool for controlling rival causal factors, you are now conversant in the language and actually have gotten through the worst part. In the following chapters we attempt to make you fluent in this language.

The Experiment as a Data-Gathering Strategy

We have thus far viewed experiments primarily from the standpoint of research design; however, the experiment obviously is also a data-gathering strategy. Through its three key features of assuring equivalence of groups, pre- and posttests, and experimental and control groups, the experiment is a powerful strategy for research.

As a research design strategy, the experiment consists of blueprints outlining the conduct of the study. Saying that the experiment is the benchmark of comparison for other designs suggests that by using the *X* and *O* notation scheme, we can depict a basic model of a research study and also the potential strengths and weaknesses of such a design or research plan. The experiment is also a tool for data gathering, a strategy for obtaining and analyzing data. As a data-gathering strategy, the experiment has many variations that are defined by the setting. These variations range from laboratory experiments to field experiments, the former having greatest control over experimental conditions (thus high internal validity); but because of the very controlled atmosphere, problems may exist in terms of artificiality or external validity. The latter have fewer internal controls but greater external validity. In discussing relative advantages and disadvantages of the experiment, it is difficult to distinguish whether critics are talking about a design or data-gathering strategy or whether they are critiquing laboratory and/or field experiments or both.

Advantages of Experiments

Advantages of experiments

The **advantages of experiments** are many. They offer the best control for factors that tend to affect the internal validity of studies. The researcher is able before the fact, by the very design of the study, to control for many of the rival causal factors that tend to invalidate findings. The experimenter can control for the effects of many variables by including them in or excluding them from the study design.

A second advantage of experiments is that they are *relatively quick* and *inexpensive.* In contrast to many of the other data-gathering strategies that we will examine in Chapters 4–8, an experiment generally produces the required data necessary for analysis rather quickly. Depending on the scope of the study and required staff, facilities, and equipment, the experiment may represent a bargain compared with the expense of surveys or field strategies.

Another advantage of the experiment is its *manageability,* because the researcher is able to call the shots by controlling the stimulus, the environment, the treatment time, and even the degree of subject exposure. The conditions and conduct of experiments are often so rigorously defined that they lend themselves to replication by which the design and methodology can be repeated by other investigators. This is a major advantage over some field studies and surveys where it may be more difficult to repeat all of the ingredients.

Experimental strategies can be applied to natural settings in which the researcher has the best of both worlds, rigorous control and a more natural setting. If conditions can be viewed as realistic by subjects, *experiments may be the only way of studying certain complex behaviors.* Additionally, "natural experiments," which "occur as part of a natural process, where neither the setting nor the randomization process are controlled" (Fagan, 1990,

p. 13), may present themselves without any intervention by the researcher. For example, a new treatment program might be implemented, but it might be applied to only half of the subjects due to funding shortages.

Disadvantages of Experiments

Despite the many advantages of experiments as a data-gathering strategy, there are potential disadvantages a researcher should take into account in whether experiments are the preferred strategy. The major **disadvantage of experiments** is their *artificiality*. In essence, the very controls imposed by the researcher to control for rival causal factors internal to an experiment may create artificial conditions that impede the ability to extrapolate to larger populations which are subject to natural conditions. In controlling for extraneous conditions, one may literally be creating a mere shadow of the former entity. This problem is more severe with laboratory than field experiments.

Disadvantages of experiments

In a typical critique of the contrived nature of some experiments, Field showed how many laboratory simulations of jury decision making using college students as jurors may be in error. Using randomly selected students and nonstudents in juror roles, Field (1978) found students to be significantly more lenient in their sentencing. Thus, experimental results have no assumed built-in validity. Some of the scorn with which some experimental researchers view data obtained by other social science and criminal justice researchers using field research methods is misplaced.

Other major problems relate to the general difficulty of doing experimental research in terms of obtaining human subjects or situations or conditions in which one can properly manipulate the variables to be investigated. Major ethical issues can be raised by experimental research. Luskin points out the difficulty of implementing experimental designs in court research. Court personnel may decline to experiment with new procedures or be unable to manipulate key variables (Luskin, 1978). Hackler suggests that in evaluations of delinquency prevention programs, traditional experimental–control group procedures are nearly impossible, create unnecessary stress for program staff, and may produce hostility toward the researcher. After-the-fact statistical analysis is in this instance viewed as far less obtrusive and more useful than precontrolled studies (Hackler, 1978). Most judges are unwilling to permit treatment decisions to be governed by pure random selection. In fact, one professor of criminal law indicated that such assignment could constitute a violation of the right to due process (Glaser, 1976, p. 775), although others point out that most randomized experiments are ethical and legal (Erez, 1986). *Experimenter effects* may also occur in experiments in which those conducting the research actually selectively observe that they wish to see or unconsciously give cues to the subjects as to the desired behavior or attitudes expected. Experiments provide an excellent method for controlling for factors regarding internal validity, but they are often weak with respect to external validity.

Experimenter effects

Summary

    Assumptions of causality rest at the basis of scientific investigation. Three essential steps are necessary to attempt to resolve the causality question: demonstration of relationship, specification of time order, and control for, or exclusion of, rival causal variables. The experimental model is one of the most powerful means of controlling for rival causal factors before the fact through the design of research. Rival causal factors may be treated as factors affecting internal validity and those affecting external validity. Although the former are errors introduced because of flaws within the study, the latter are factors that impinge on the generalizability of the study to larger populations. Factors affecting internal validity include history, maturation, testing, instrumentation, statistical regression, experimental mortality, and interaction effects such as selection–maturation interaction. Those impacting on external validity include testing effects, selection bias, reactivity, and multiple-treatment interference. Related invalidating factors include the Hawthorne effect, the placebo effect, the halo effect, and post hoc error.

    The classic experimental design is the benchmark or point of departure for all other research designs. That is, in a sense, all forms of research can be viewed as a variation of the experimental model. The three basic components of the classic experiment are pretest and posttest, experimental and control groups, and equivalence. In addition, familiarization with the notation of experimental designs is a useful heuristic device for breaking down the essentials of a research design. Classic experimental designs provide for the most rigorous before-the-fact control over factors of internal validity, and different variations enable control for rival causal factors. Illustration of the various designs with examples from criminal justice research provides the reader some familiarity with applications of these designs from the criminology and criminal justice literature.

    After this review and examination of examples of the experimental model and its variations, Chapter 4 will explore the relative advantages and disadvantages of alternatives to the experimental model in criminal justice and criminology.

    Experimental methods of gathering data have distinct *advantages* such as rigid control over rival factors within the experiment, the relative quick and inexpensive manner in which readily quantifiable data can be gathered, and overall manageability from the standpoint of the researcher. The *disadvantages* of experiments often outweigh their advantages, particularly in dealing with criminal justice subject matter. Major shortcomings of the experimental method include artificiality, which may hinder its generalizability to wider populations, and difficulty in applying the approach to human subjects and situations in criminal justice.

    Examples of the Kansas City Gun Experiment, Child Abuse Victims and Violence, Shock Incarceration and the Project of Human Development illustrated various research designs in this chapter.

Key Concepts

Steps for Resolving
  Causality Problem
Rival Causal Factors
Spurious Relationship
Internal Validity
External Validity
History
Maturation
Testing
Instrumentation
Statistical Regression
Selection Bias
Experimental Mortality
Selection–Maturation
  Interaction
Testing Effects

Reactivity
Multiple-Treatment
  Interference
Hawthorne Effect
Halo Effect
Post Hoc Error
Placebo Effect
Double-Blind
  Experiments
Diffusion of Treatment
Compensatory
  Equalization of
  Treatment
Local History
Masking Effects
Contamination of Data

Erosion of Treatment
  Effect
Criterion Problems
Classic Experimental
  Design
Equivalence
Randomization
Matching
Pretests/Posttests
Experimental Groups
Control Groups
Time-Series Designs
Advantages/
  Disadvantages of
  Experiments

Review Questions

1. How does research design control for rival causal factors? Describe for example how the classic experimental design controls for history and maturation.
2. Find a recent journal article that employs an experimental, preexperimental, or quasi-experimental design. Name, describe, and illustrate the design, and discuss any rival causal factors controlled for in this design.
3. Why are time-series designs particularly useful in criminal justice studies?
4. Design a hypothetical study, and discuss how your design controls for many rival causal factors.
5. Discuss the Kansas City Gun Experiment. What type of research design was employed and what were the major findings of the project?
6. Discuss the research design and particularly the accelerated longitudinal design features of the Project of Human Development.

An Introduction to Alternative Data-Gathering Strategies and the Special Case of Uniform Crime Reports

This chapter, in part, serves as an introduction to the next four chapters, which deal in detail with alternatives to the experiment as a data-gathering strategy. These alternatives include surveys, participant observation, case studies, and unobtrusive measures. A brief introduction to each of these strategies will be followed by an examination of the FBI Uniform Crime Reports (UCR). The UCR serves as a special case of a data source, and, for a time, it was about the only source of information consulted by researchers in examining crime and criminal behavior. Because most of our later discussion of sources, such as victim and self-report surveys, are contrasted with the UCR, it receives early and separate coverage in this chapter.

Alternative Data-Gathering Strategies

As has been indicated, the classic experimental design rests as a reference point with which to compare all other research strategies; however, this by no means suggests that the experiment as a method of data gathering is better or a more desirable strategy. This debate, or sometimes civil war, among social scientists, who disagree about which means of data gathering is best, illustrates the notion of *methodological narcissism* (discussed in Chapter 1), which causes individuals to become so committed to a particular research strategy that they consider all other approaches inferior. The final resolution of this issue will be discussed in Chapter 9 under triangulation, where we will argue that the best resolution of many of these issues is simply to employ multiple methodologies or a wide array of instruments. Arguments that suggest its superiority are misplaced in that the experiment, despite its obvious strengths with respect to internal controls, tends to have primary weaknesses that other techniques do not have with respect to external validity. Outside of captive prisoner research, many topics in criminal justice require "real world" strategies, or approaches that bring the researcher into the actual environment of naturally occurring events (Filstead, 1971). Researchers may wish to examine the controlled experiment as the ideal in this field and consider whether or not alternatives are more acceptable, if not more powerful (Carter and Wilkins, 1976, p. 763).

Glaser very lucidly describes what he calls "the elusive paradise of correctional research":

> In the long run, I believe the paradise lost is most likely to be regained by controlled experiments. In the past two decades we have had many evangelical movements, from Cambridge–Somerville to SIPU [Special Intensive Parole Unit in California] and beyond, vainly preaching salvation by experimentation. The earlier sects repeatedly assembled the faithful to await miracles—and then disappointed them. Many of the sins we have been ascribing to correctional research grew out of frustration from experimentation. Yet negative or inconclusive results are but trials by which these pilgrims to the shrines of science are tested. They still may progress toward grace if they recognize past sins and seek salvation through new research design (Glaser, 1978, p. 772).

Experiments are, therefore, by no means the most effective data-gathering strategy. Depending on one's subject matter a variety of techniques may be more appropriate or perhaps necessary, because not all subjects lend themselves to experimentation. Figure 4.1 is an attempt to illustrate the relative strengths and weaknesses of major data-gathering strategies. As has been indicated, experiments are an outstanding method by which the researcher can exercise great control over factors that may impair internal validity, as well as yield relatively quick and inexpensive quantitative data; however, such an approach trades such control for its chief limitation of artificiality.

As we proceed down the vertical arrows in our illustration, we discover that the subsequent techniques become in general less quantitative, and the research exercises less control over rival causal factors impacting on internal validity. On the other hand, as we move away from experimentation, the researcher gains external validity and moves closer to the natural environment in which behavior occurs (Bouchard, 1976). This scheme is intended as an "ideal type" that overgeneralizes to simplify presentation. The model

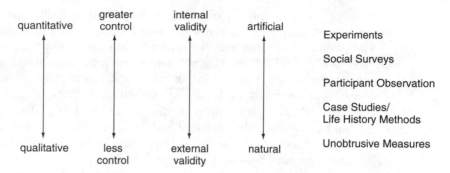

Figure 4.1 Alternative Data-Gathering Strategies in Criminal Justice: A Heuristic Model.

TABLE 4.1 Types of Data-Gathering Methods

Experiments	Surveys	Participant Observation	Unobtrusive Measures	Case Studies
Laboratory	Questionnaires	Complete participation	Physical trace analysis	Life histories
Field (includes Experimental, Quasi-experimental, and Preexperimental designs)	Interviews Structured Unstructured Depth (includes Mail, Self-administered, Telephone)	Participant as observer Observer as participant Complete observation	Existing data Observation Disguised observation Simulation	Oral histories

is not entirely true in all cases; for example, some unobtrusive methods can be very quantitative. In fact, our division of methods of data gathering is also somewhat arbitrary but hopefully it organizes these methods in a manner that clarifies their presentation. Table 4.1 outlines some of the subtypes of procedures within each of the types of data-gathering methods. The description of a study as being an example of one or the other of these methods is, however, somewhat arbitrary, because, in reality, a particular example may employ multiple methods or even a single method may be labeled differently. For example, a field experiment involving disguised observation and simulation could be an example of all three types. Although these techniques and their variations are treated in detail in Chapters 5–8, a brief overview at this point may further clarify the interrelationships.

Social Surveys

Social surveys

Social surveys are means of data gathering which involve asking a segment of the population their attitudes or reported behavior. Social surveys, although often associated with election polls, opinion polls, and marketing surveys, are also powerful tools for obtaining quantitative data for both descriptive and inferential studies and for addressing the issue of causality. The principal approaches to gathering data for surveys are questionnaires, interviews, or telephone contact. Many not familiar with recent advances in survey methodology still think of surveys as descriptive tallies and polls; in reality many surveys make use of statistical analysis to examine causation and, through statistical controls, to exclude rival causal factors. Following the lead of sociologists, criminal justice researchers are increasing their use of statistics as a tool for inferential and causal analysis (Hackler, 1978). Many researchers heavily indoctrinated in the experimental tradition fail to appreciate the power of survey research combined with statistical analysis in addressing social scientific research issues. In surveys, statistics are often used to control for rival causal factors after the fact at the analysis stage or after the data have been gathered. Such control may be as effective as pre-controls in the hands of a skillful researcher. Detailed discussion of victimization surveys in Chapter 6 will serve as an illustration of the potential contributions of surveys.

Surveys have been extensively used in criminal justice recently in assessing victimization, fear of crime, attitudes toward police, and the criminal justice system. Some other uses of survey methodology in criminology and criminal justice include self-report (admissions) of crime studies as well as crime severity (seriousness) studies. In the latter, respondents assign scores or seriousness weights to different crimes.

Participant Observation

Participant observation

Participant observation, the favorite tool of the anthropologist, involves a variety of strategies in data gathering in which the researcher observes a group by participating, to varying degrees, in the activities of the group. The degrees of participation or observation may vary in scope and, although some more observational-type studies are more quantitative, for the most part, the decision to employ participant observation as the primary means of data gathering generally entails a commitment to a more qualitative or "sensitizing" strategy. As an illustration, some of the most fascinating, enthralling, and important literature in criminal justice contains nothing more quantitative than page numbers. In-depth field studies of pool hustlers and con artists (Polsky, 1967), drug addicts (Yablonsky, 1965), the Guardian Angels (Albini, 1986), street corner gangs (Whyte, 1943), and the police (Reiss, 1971; Skolnick, 1966) serve as but a few examples of the many to be covered in more detail in Chapter 7.

Besides being a data-gathering strategy, participant observation also represents a commitment to a theory-generating activity, a grounded theory approach in which the investigator avoids rigid, preconceived hypotheses and attempts to focus on relevant theories as he or she becomes more sensitized to the scene (Glaser and Strauss, 1967).

For some of these subjects participant observation was the only visible data-gathering strategy. Although this method will be covered in detail in Chapter 6, let us pick up on the last point. In saying that for some subjects or situations participant observation may be the only viable strategy, we could infer an even more general, basic point—*none of these methodologies has inherently any superiority over any of the others. The consideration becomes one of matching the appropriate methodology(ies) with the appropriate subject.* The reverse procedure, matching a preferred methodology with a subject, although legitimate at times, borders on what was previously labeled *methodological narcissism* or perhaps *methodologism.* The latter represents an even narrower empirical approach assuming that "if I cannot measure it with my favorite methodology, it is probably not worth studying."

Life History and Case Studies

Life history/ case study   **Life histories** and **case studies** involve in-depth analysis of one or a few cases. These data-gathering strategies also represent a commitment to a qualitative or sensitizing strategy when approaching subject matter. Although more quantitative approaches aim to provide a more macrocriminological view or big picture of the subject matter, these methods provide a microcriminological or in-depth closeup of only one or a few subjects. The assumption is that by probing deeply into just one or a few cases, the researcher may gain a greater feel or "verstehen" (Weber, 1949) for the subject that might be missed in a more aggregate or group analysis.

Perhaps the classic illustration of the use of case studies is Sutherland's *The Professional Thief* (1937). Many other studies (discussed in Chapter 7) have been done in criminal justice, however, including Shaw's *The Jack-Roller* (1930), Snodgrass' follow-up of the Jack-Roller (1982), Klockars' *The Professional Fence* (1974), the Ianni's *A Family Business* (1972) (a study of an organized crime family), and Chambliss' study of a "box man" or safecracker (King and Chambliss, 1984).

Life history methods   *Life history methods* generally involve the analysis of diaries, letters, biographies, and autobiographies to obtain a detailed view of either a unique or a representative subject(s). Some examples from the popular literature of useful documents include Maas' *The Valachi Papers* (1968) or Teresa and Renner's *My Life in the Mafia* (1973). Further examples will be detailed in Chapter 7.

Unobtrusive Measures

Unobtrusive measures   **Unobtrusive measures** (nonreactive methods) refer to clandestine or nonreactive methods of data gathering (Webb et al., 1966). Although a variety of methods, including physical traces, observation, analysis of existing data, and archives, may be subsumed under unobtrusive methods, the key distinction is that *they refer to any methods of gathering data in which the subjects are not aware that they are being studied.* If the subjects are not aware of being analyzed, they do not react in an artificial or atypical manner and thus "stooge" and "Hawthorne effects" are avoided. Unobtrusive methods provide an attractive and often inexpensive alternative to many of the other strategies we have discussed. As we will see in Chapter 8, rather than assuming that they must always gather new data directly, researchers should be aware that many data already exist or can be cleverly and indirectly measured with oftentimes great savings in time, expense, and reactivity. Despite limitations, extensive analysis has been carried out in criminal justice using such data as official police statistics, private agency records (Clinard, 1952), or private agency statistics (Cameron, 1964). Under unobtrusive or nonreactive methods we will discuss (Chapter 8) the use of physical trace analysis, observation and disguised observation, existing data, and simulations.

Although each of the alternative data-gathering strategies will be explored in depth in Chapters 5 through 8 of this text, and the uses of available data will be discussed in Chapter 8 under unobtrusive methods, the Uniform Crime Report is discussed separately here. This is necessary because of the overreliance on these statistics, until recently, as the most widely used measure of crime in the United States. Other unobtrusive measures will be dealt with in Chapter 8.

The Special Case of Uniform Crime Reports

Uniform Crime Reports (UCR)

The **Uniform Crime Reports** is a special case in that, of all of the methodological sources to be discussed, it has traditionally been the most widely cited on crime in the United States. It is also used as a point of comparison for other data-gathering procedures, particularly victim surveys and self-reports.

Beginning in 1930, the U.S. Department of Justice instituted the compilation and publication of national crime statistics, the *Uniform Crime Reports* (UCR). Although participation in the program by police departments and reports to the Federal Bureau of Investigation (FBI), which assumed responsibility as a clearinghouse, was voluntary in nature, the number of departments and comprehensiveness of reports have continually improved over the years. Large metropolitan areas were the best participants.

Most newspaper and other media accounts are based on summaries presented in the UCR. In most instances, these are data presented in an uncritical and alarmist manner without supplying many of the qualifying problems with the official crime statistics reported. Being the major source of crime statistics in the United States until 1974, the UCR basically comprises crimes known to, and recorded by, local police departments. Figure 4.2 illustrates the relationship between crime committed and other sources of crime statistics including the UCR.

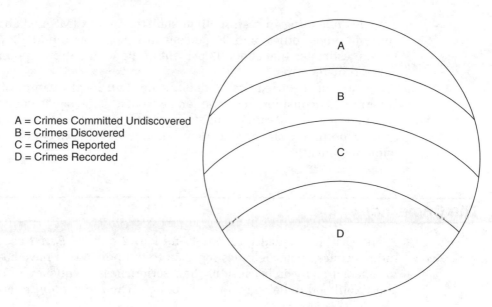

A = Crimes Committed Undiscovered
B = Crimes Discovered
C = Crimes Reported
D = Crimes Recorded

Figure 4.2   Theoretical Relationship between Crimes Committed and Official Statistics.

Although in Chapter 6 we will explore the usefulness of victimization surveys in estimating the number of crimes committed, it is unclear whether it is possible to obtain an accurate estimate of the volume of annual crime in American society. For various reasons, not all crimes committed are discovered; for instance, some crimes involve situations in which the victim is not aware of having been victimized or there is no identifiable victim. Not all crimes discovered are reported to the police and not all crimes reported to the police are recorded by the police. Although some may be concealed, a number of crimes reported are unfounded or defined by investigating officers as not constituting a criminal matter. Thus, even though crimes recorded by the police have an uncertain relationship to actual crimes committed, the UCR represented until 1974 the available statistics on crime in American society. The further removed statistics are from crime committed, the poorer the figures are as estimates of the true crime level. For instance, number of arrests, indictments, convictions, incarcerations, and other dispositions such as probation or parole are all inadequate in estimating the amount of crime in a society. They have much more to do with police efficiency or allocation to correctional systems or other societal policies toward crime. The researcher who chooses to utilize official statistics must become familiar with any shortcomings or sources of bias they may contain.

The FBI receives these data from local police departments. In the majority of states there are operational state UCR programs in which the states required local departments to report their data to the state and then share such data with the federal government. In the 1980s, 98 percent of the police agencies operating in metropolitan statistical areas (MSAs),[1] about 94 percent of "other" cities, and 90 percent in rural areas reported. The Census Bureau estimates that about 97 percent of the total national population was covered by the report.

Because of the tripartite—federal, state, and local—nature of American government, considerable variation exists in state penal codes regarding criminal offenses. Participating departments receive instruction in uniform crime reporting to standardize their crime reports into a comparable nationwide document.

The Crime Index

Index crime

The UCR is divided into Part 1 and Part 2 crimes. *Part 1* consists of the **index crimes,** major felonies reported to the police that have been selected for special analysis because of their seriousness, frequency of occurrence, and likelihood of being reported to police. The *index offenses* are:

Murder and nonnegligent Burglary
   manslaughter Larceny-theft
Forcible rape Motor vehicle theft
Robbery Arson[2]
Aggravated assault

Part 2 crimes are nonindex crimes such as simple assault, vandalism, gambling, and drunkenness. In all, twenty-two other crimes (twenty-one, excluding arson) are accounted for under Part 2 offenses. Although the FBI indicates that it cannot vouch for the validity of data received from individual police agencies, it attempts to examine all reports for accuracy, question any unusual changes in trends, undertake special inquiries if necessary, and eliminate, estimate, and otherwise control for at least the most crass errors.

Tables 4.2 and 4.3 illustrate typical data and trends reported using the crime index and the notion of crime rate.

Crime Rate

Crime rate

The **crime rate** is expressed as the number of crimes per unit of population, in this case per 100,000. Such a statistic enables control of population size and thus permits a fair comparison of different size units. The growth in crime one reads about in the paper is usually based on the crime rate for

---

[1]MSA includes central cities (over 50,000) and contiguous counties that are functionally integrated economically and socially with the core cities.
[2]In October of 1978, the U.S. Congress passed a law that required that arson be included as a Part 1 or index crime.

TABLE 4.2 The UCR Crime Index

Crime Index Offense	Number	Rate per 100,000
Murder and nonnegligent manslaughter	24,526	9.5
Forcible rape	104,806	40.6
Robbery	659,757	255.8
Aggravated assault	1,135,099	440.1
Burglary	2,834,808	1,099.2
Larceny-theft	7,820,909	3,032.4
Motor vehicle theft	1,561,047	605.3
Arson[1]	—	—
U.S. TOTAL[2]	14,140,952	5,482.9
Violent crime[3]	1,924,188	746.1
Property crime	12,216,764	4,730.0

[1]Although arson data are included, sufficient data are not available to estimate totals for this offense.
[2]Because of rounding, the offenses may not add to totals.
[3]Violent crimes are offenses of murder, forcible rape, robbery, and aggravated assault. Property crimes are offenses of burglary, larceny-theft, and motor vehicle theft. Data are not included for the property crime of arson.

Source: Modified from U.S. Department of Justice, FBI Uniform Crime Reports: Crime in the United States, 1993, Washington, D.C.: U.S. Government Printing Office, December, 1994, p. 59.

the index offenses (excluding arson). Although the notion of scales and indexes will be treated in Chapter 10, for the purposes of this chapter it is important to realize that the crime index is unweighted; that is, each offense is merely summed and in a sense given the same importance as all other offenses. The crime rate is the total number of seven original index crimes per 100,000 population.

$$\text{crime rate} = \frac{\text{number of index crimes}}{\text{population}} \times 100,000$$

Cautions in the Use of UCR Data

The following statement serves as a caution in using any official government statistics:

> The government is very keen on amassing statistics. They collect them, add them, raise them to *n*th power, take the cube root and prepare wonderful diagrams. But what you must never forget is that every one of these figures comes in the first instance from the *chowty dar* (village watchman), who puts down what he damn pleases (Stamp, 1929, pp. 258–259; cited in Webb et al., 1981, p. 89).

Although the UCR has been steadily improved and refined in its more than half a century of existence and can serve useful purposes, a researcher using these data for the analysis of crime must exercise caution and be aware

TABLE 4.3A Index of Crime, United States, 1993

Area	Population[1]	Crime Index Total	Modified Crime Index Total[2]	Violent Crime[1]	Property Crime[1]	Murder and Non-negligent Manslaughter	Forcible Rape	Robbery	Aggravated Assult	Burglary	Larceny-Theft	Motor Vehicle Theft	Arson[2]
United States total	**257,908,000**	**14,140,952**		**1,924,188**	**12,216,764**	**24,526**	**104,806**	**659,757**	**1,135,099**	**2,834,808**	**7,820,909**	**1,561,047**	
Rate per 100,000 inhabitants		5,482.9		746.1	4,736.9	9.5	40.6	255.8	440.1	1,099.2	3,032.4	605.3	
Metropolitan statistical area	**204,951,864**												
Area actually reporting[4]	96.6%	12,158,473		1,725,319	10,433,154	21,514	86,573	634,848	982,384	2,377,910	6,594,975	1,460,269	
Estimated totals	100.0%	12,389,557		1,746,540	10,643,017	21,712	88,611	639,413	996,804	2,423,097	6,741,385	1,478,535	
Rate per 100,000 inhabitants		6,045.1		852.2	5,192.9	10.6	43.2	312.0	486.4	1,182.3	3,289.3	721.4	
Cities outside metropolitan areas	**21,233,685**												
Area actually reporting[4]	85.8%	997,708		94,508	903,200	979	7,319	13,391	72,819	185,845	675,069	42,286	
Estimated totals	100.0%	1,126,113		107,112	1,019,001	1,117	8,297	15,137	82,561	210,809	760,531	47,661	
Rate per 100,000 inhabitants		5,303.4		504.4	4,799.0	5.3	39.1	71.3	388.8	992.8	3,581.7	224.5	
Rural counties	**31,718,451**												
Area actually reporting[4]	85.6%	561,222		62,093	499,129	1,470	7,141	4,576	48,906	179,631	288,150	31,348	
Estimated totals	100.0%	625,282		70,536	554,746	1,697	7,898	5,207	55,734	200,902	318,993	34,851	
Rate per 100,000 inhabitants		1,971.1		222.4	1,749.0	5.4	24.9	16.4	175.7	633.4	1,005.7	109.9	

[1]Populations are Bureau of the Census provisional estimates as of July 1, 1993, and are subject to change.

[2]Although arson data are included in the trend and clearance tables, sufficient data are not available to estimate totals for this offense.

[3]Violent crimes are offenses of murder, forcible rape, robbery, and aggravated assault. Property crimes are offenses of burglary, larceny-theft, and motor vehicle theft. Data are not included for the property crime of arson.

[4]The percentage representing area actually reporting will not coincide with the ratio between reported and estimated crime totals. since these data represent the sum of the calculations for individual states which have varying populations, portions reporting, and crime rates

Complete data were not available for 1993 for the states of Illinois and Kansas; therefore, it was necessary that their crime counts be estimated See "Offense Estimation," page 376 for details

Source: U.S. Department of Justice, FBI Uniform Crime Reports: Crime in the United States, 1993, Washington, D. C.: U.S. Government Printing Office, December, 1994, p. 59.

Table 4.3B Index of Crime, Regional Offense and Population Distribution, 1993

Region	Population	Crime Index Total	Modified Crime Index Total[1]	Violent Crime[2]	Property Crime[2]	Murder and Non-negligent Manslaughter	Forcible Rape	Robbery	Aggravated Assault	Burglary	Larceny-Theft	Motor Vehicle Theft	Arson[2]
United States Total[3]	100.0	100.0	100.0	100.0	100.0	100.0	100.0	100.0	100.0	100.0	100.0	100.0	100.0
Northeastern states	19.9	16.8		19.0	16.4	17.1	13.9	25.1	16.0	15.9	15.5	21.8	
Midwestern states	23.7	20.8		19.1	21.0	19.0	24.6	18.9	18.7	19.4	22.3	17.8	
Southern states	34.7	37.8		37.3	37.9	41.2	38.5	32.0	40.2	40.6	38.2	31.9	
Western states	21.7	24.7		24.6	24.7	22.7	22.9	24.1	25.1	24.1	24.1	28.5	

[1]Although arson data are included in the trend and clearance tables, sufficient data are not available to estimate totals for this offense.

[2]Violent crimes are offenses of murder, forcible rape, robbery, and aggravated assault. Property crimes are offenses of burglary, larceny-theft, and motor vehicle theft. Data are not included for the property crime of arson.

[3]Because of rounding, percentages may not add to total.

Complete data were not available for 1993 for the states of Illinois and Kansas; therefore, it was necessary that their crime counts be estimated. See "Offense Estimation," page 376 for details.

Source: U.S. Department of Justice, FBI Uniform Crime Reports: Crime in the United States, 1993, Washington, D.C.: U.S. Government Printing Office, December, 1994, p. 59.

of the limitations of these statistics. An impressive body of literature on the UCR has accumulated that point out these deficiencies.

Factors Affecting the UCR

Although no attempt will be made here to summarize the many fine critiques of the UCR[3] and many of the points to be elaborated overlap, some of the primary shortcomings of this source of crime data can be detailed:

- As previously suggested in Figure 4.2, recorded statistics represent only a portion of the true crime rate of a community. Although we will examine victim surveys in detail later, the Bureau of the Census victim surveys suggest that there is possibly twice as much crime committed as appears in the official statistics.
- The big increase in the crime rate beginning in the mid-1960s and extending through the 1970s was in part explained by better communication, more professional police departments, and better recording and reporting of crimes. Surprisingly, for instance, there appears to be a positive relationship between a larger, improved, and professionalized police establishment and rising crime rates. Higher urban crime rates are related in part to the fact that there is a higher proportion of formal policing and professional law enforcement in such areas. Increased urbanization itself also has its own impact.
- Increased citizen awareness of crime and a general change in public morality may have resulted in a larger proportion of crimes committed being reported to the police. The usual and expected Saturday night barroom brawl of fifty years ago is now regarded as a serious assault warranting police attention. In light of the success of the Civil Rights movement, many more ghetto residents report crimes to the police, expressing confidence in the greater willingness of the police to respond to ghetto crime.
- Generally, most federal cases, "victimless" crimes, and white-collar crimes are not contained in the UCR. Many of the analyses of age, sexual, and racial characteristics of those arrested, then, describe the inept and poor criminal or concentrate on "crime in the streets" rather than "crime in the suites."
- Changes in police administration, politics in the statistical tabulating process, and simply more attention to better record keeping have had a major impact on crimes recorded. Obvious inadequacies in statistics from a jurisdiction are checked out by the FBI. In 1949, for instance, the FBI refused to publish New York City Police Department statistics. With improved recording, the robbery rate jumped 800 percent. Other changes in police practices showed jumps of 61 percent in Chicago in

[3]See for example Black (1970), Kitsuse and Cicourel (1963), Lejins (1966), Savitz (1978), Seidman and Couzens (1974), Sellin (1957), Sherman and Glick (1984), Skogan (1974), and Wolfgang (1963). These represent only a sampling of the extensive literature on this subject.

1961 because of a change in chief, 202 percent in Kansas City in 1959 because of reforms, and 95 percent in Buffalo in the early 1960s (President's Commission, 1967, p. 25). Crime rates have a mysterious way of dropping if required for political purposes. Nixon's identification of the District of Columbia as a target of a crime busting program resulted in a dramatic drop in the crime rate that was more likely a matter of classifying crimes out of the index. Until 1973, grand larceny of $50 or more could simply be classified as under $50 and thus out of the index (Glaser, 1978, p. 58). An interesting example of statistical shenanigans occurred in the mid-seventies during police negotiations in Cleveland under the administration of Mayor Ralph Perk. The police were told that if they expected a 5 percent salary increase, they would have to demonstrate greater efficiency by dropping the crime rate by a similar amount. Predictably, the crime rate recorded a drop in index crimes.

Such "creative" work with crime statistics continued into the 1980s; the Chicago police department systematically underreported crime ("Burying Crime," 1983), and Sherman and Glick (1984) showed that local police departments were continuing to make consistent errors in their uniform crime reporting.

Limitation of crime index

- In addition to those factors already indicated, Savitz (1978) notes some **limitations of the crime index.** He summarizes a large number of elements that at the very least must be considered in using the index. *In interpreting UCR statistics one must keep in mind what arrest statistics do and do not include.* Arrests do not equal crimes solved or suspects found guilty. Many potential crimes are also unfounded by police. These are complaints that, on investigation by police, are determined not to be criminal matters.
- In cases of a multiple offense, only the most serious crime is recorded for statistical purposes. Most crimes that are committed are not index offenses. Questions have been raised that auto theft, a less serious crime with high reportability and clearance, artificially inflates the crime index and might best be dropped from the Part 1 designation (Savitz, 1978).
- Rhodes points out that inflation caused incidents like bicycle theft to become larceny, an index crime. In 1973 all larcenies were included as index offenses, thus sharply increasing the crime rate (Rhodes, 1977, p. 168). At the same time, greater insurance coverage of property crimes encourages their reporting.

Unweighted index

- To be explored later in Chapter 10 is the problem that *the crime index is an unweighted index;* that is, a murder counts the same or has the same weight as a bicycle theft. Imagine two cities each with a crime rate of 100 per 100,000 population. In City A, 100 murders were recorded, whereas in City B 100 joyrides were recorded. Somehow, these crime rates should not be regarded as the same. Most bodily injury crimes are "nonindex" or Part 2 crimes (Savitz, 1978).

- The existence of the "crime index" may cause police agencies to concentrate on these crimes at the expense of other crimes.
- Until 1957 the UCR crime rates were calculated not on the basis of annual census updates, but rather on the decennial census. Thus, crime rates for rapidly growing areas of the Southwest appeared worse, because the 1959 crimes were divided by a 1950 population base.
- Although in 1978 Congress required that arson be included as an index offense, it has never been included in the crime index because of the unreliability of arson offense information. Jackson (1988) compared UCR arson data with a national survey of 683 fire departments and found significant underreporting in the UCR. He explains that arson is unlike other index offenses since determining whether a fire was purposefully set or attempted requires a specific investigation.
- Raising yet another limitation, Wilbanks (1986) points out that despite the fact that the media are fond of ranking cities with respect to index crimes—for example, Dade County was number one in murder and violent crime in 1985—the UCR itself correctly cautions against comparing statistical data of individual reporting units from cities, counties, and states solely on the basis of their population coverage. Such features as population density, size of locality, age structure, population mobility, economic and cultural conditions, climate, strength of law enforcement agencies and their policies, politics, citizen attitudes, and reporting practices are all factors that complicate such comparisons.

Related UCR Issues

Crime dip

Although it does not speak to any inaccuracy in the UCR itself, demographic shifts may provide some explanation for rapidly rising or falling crime rates. Some criminologists had forecast the **crime dip** in the 1980s, a general stabilization or decline in the crime rate. Although other factors offset the decline, this prophecy was based on changes in population distribution. For UCR crime rates, the maximal age range of criminality is 15–19, or 20–24 if an adult cohort is considered. After World War II, the United States experienced an unprecedented "baby boom," a much larger than usual proportion of births beginning in 1946 and extending through the 1950s. This group at first overwhelmed the capacity of hospital nursery wards; later, elementary schools and high schools were hard pressed to meet the demands for space. In the late 1960s, colleges could not expand fast enough to accommodate demand. Today most of these sectors have either stabilized or declined in demand as the economy struggles to supply jobs and housing for the now mature "baby boom" group. Similarly, the criminal justice system was struggling to deal with the larger than normal group in the maximum crime-committing ages. As this group moves into middle age and a smaller proportion of the population will be found in the high-crime ages, the criminal justice system will hopefully find itself with a far more manageable situation. A counterbalance to this demographic shift is the relationship between arrest rates and race. If the birthrates and crime rates of minorities remain higher than the general population, we may not see much of a drop in the crime rate.

Other variables that may also explain this decline include a greater reliance on longer sentences, incarceration and incapacitation of serious offenders, a decline in the number of state UCR programs, and an almost unnoticed decline in the per capita number of police in the United States since 1978. The researcher who decides to make use of official statistics such as the UCR must become familiar with their inadequacies to avoid drawing inappropriate conclusions. Despite the shortcomings that have been identified, the UCR remains an excellent source of information on police operations.

UCR Redesign

UCR redesign   Beginning in 1977 the International Association of Chiefs of Police, as well as the National Sheriffs Association, called for a major redesign of the UCR system and, after more than ten years of effort by committees, task forces, and project staffs, the first major revision in the sixty-year history of the program was accomplished (Poggio et al., 1985; and Rovetch, Poggio, and Rossman, 1984). The lengthy process of the redesign study enabled redesign teams to take advantage of the decade's revolution in computer technology.

National Incident-Based Reporting System

The major change in the new UCR program was its conversion to a
NIBRS   **National Incident-Based Reporting System (NIBRS),** which involves a unit-record reporting system in which each local law enforcement agency reports on each individual crime incident and on each individual arrest. The original UCR only reported summary counts. The NIBRS uses fifty-two data elements to describe victims, offenders, arrestees, and circumstances of crimes. While the UCR focuses upon eight index crimes, NIBRS has twenty-two Group A offenses, including bribery, counterfeiting/forgery, drug and narcotic offenses, extortion/blackmail, fraud, kidnapping, pornography, non-forcible sex offenses, and firearms violations.

Participation by law enforcement agencies in the program depends upon a department's data processing resources. If an agency cannot meet full participation requirements, it may limit itself to reporting details of incidents involving the UCR's eight index crimes rather than the NIBRS's expanded list of twenty-two crimes (Dodenhoff, 1990, p. 10). NIBRS divides data collection into two levels. *Level I* covers all law enforcement agencies and requires basic Group A incident-based data on the twenty-two categories of offenses. *Level II* participation includes an additional eleven-category Group B list of lesser offenses, as well as more detail in submissions. Agencies serving populations in excess of 100,000 plus a sampling of 300 smaller agencies will participate in Level II. Exhibit 4.1 reports on features of the National Incident-Based Reporting System.

NIBRS versus UCR

NIBRS vs. UCR

Some key differences between the National Incident-Based Reporting System (NIBRS) and the Uniform Crime Reporting (UCR) program include (Dodenhoff, 1990, p. 11; and U.S. Department of Justice, 1991, pp. 4–6):

- *Incident-Based versus Summary Reporting.* The UCR reports Part I (index) offenses and Parts I and II arrest data in aggregate (summary) form. NIBRS, which requires detailed data on individual crime incidents and arrests, receives separate reports for each incident/arrest. These reports include fifty-two data elements describing the victims, offenders, arrestees, and circumstances of the crime.
- *Expanded Offense Reporting.* The UCR is a summary-based system and collects totals on criminal incidents in eight offense classifications within the Part I type. NIBRS receives detailed reports on twenty-two categories and forty-six offenses in the Group A list. It adds the following list to the original UCR Part I crimes: bribery, counterfeiting and forgery, vandalism, drug offenses, embezzlement, extortion and blackmail, fraud, gambling offenses, kidnapping, pornography, prostitution, nonforcible sexual offenses, weapons law violations, and stolen property offenses. In addition many of the Part I offenses have been expanded. For example, the forcible rape category now includes all forcible sexual offenses, such as forcible sodomy, sexual assault with an object, and forcible fondling.
- *New Offense Definitions.* In addition to expanding the original list of UCR offense categories, NIBRS revised the existing definitions of crime. Rape, for example, is defined as "the carnal knowledge of a person, forcibly and/or against that person's will; or, not forcibly or against a person's will where the victim is incapable of giving consent because of his/her temporary or permanent mental or physical incapacity" (Ibid.).

Hierarchy rule

- *Elimination of the Hierarchy Rule.* Under the UCR **"hierarchy rule,"** if multiple crimes took place within the same event, only the single most serious crime was reported. NIBRS eliminates the hierarchy rule and cites all crimes reported as offenses within the same incident.
- *Greater Specificity of Data.* Because it collects more specific information regarding criminal incidents, NIBRS data will eventually lead to more detailed crime analysis, criminal profiling, and crime reporting. NIBRS will also have the capability of providing breakdowns regarding

victims, cost, involvement of weapons, injuries, and the like, innovations that had not been possible in the past.

- *Crimes against Society.* Whereas the UCR distinguishes between "crimes against person" and "crimes against property," the addition of many new offense categories in NIBRS necessitated the creation of a new category—"crimes against society." This category includes crimes such as drug offenses, gambling violations, pornography, and prostitution.
- *Attempted versus Completed Crimes.* The UCR system reports many attempted crimes as completed ones. The NIBRS system will include a designation of each crime as either attempted or completed.
- *Designation of Computer Crime.* With NIBRS data of the future, it will be possible to determine whether a traditional crime, for example larceny, was committed by computer. But this specificity will not eliminate the traditional classifications that are important for historical trend analysis.
- *Better Statistical Analysis.* NIBRS will permit a greater opportunity for examining interrelationships between many variables such as offenses, property, victims, offenders, and arrestees.

These features represent the first major overhaul of the UCR system in more than 50 years.

EXHIBIT 4.1

The National Incident-Based Reporting System (NIBRS)

With 1991 data, the Uniform Crime Reports (UCR) program of the Federal Bureau of Investigation (FBI) began moving from summary counts to a more comprehensive and detailed reporting system known as the National Incident Based Reporting System (NIBRS). By 1982 the Bureau of Justice Statistics (BJS) had already provided over $11 million to States to establish centralized State level UCR programs. In a 1985 report, an FBI-BJS task force that BJS underwrote recommended an incident based system. When the Attorney General approved NIBRS, BJS allocated an additional $13 million to the States to implement the system.

NIBRS versus the Traditional UCR System

The traditional, summary-based UCR system counts incidents and arrests, with some expanded data on incidents of murder and nonnegligent manslaughter. NIBRS, which will eventually replace the traditional UCR as the source of official FBI counts of crimes reported to law enforcement agencies, is designed to go far beyond the summary-based UCR in terms of information about crime.

One important difference between the two systems is number of crime categories. The traditional UCR counts incidents and arrests for the 8 offenses of the FBI Crime Index and counts arrests for other offenses; NIBRS provides detailed incident information on 46 *Group A* offenses representing 22 categories of crimes (table A). NIBRS, unlike the traditional UCR, also makes a distinction between attempted and completed crimes.

In September 1982 a BJS-FBI task force undertook a study of improvements to the Uniform Crime Reporting Program, which was

Continued.

TABLE A. The NIBRS *Group A* Offenses

Arson	Negligent manslaughter
Assault offenses	Justifiable homicide
Aggravated assault	Kidnapping/abduction
Simple assault	Larceny/theft offenses
Intimidation	Pocket picking
Bribery	Purse snatching
Burglary/breaking and entering	Shoplifting
Counterfeiting/forgery	Theft from building
Destruction/damage/vandalism of property	Theft from coin-operated machines
Drug/narcotic offenses	Theft from motor vehicle
Drug/narcotic violations	Theft of motor vehicle parts/accessories
Drug equipment violations	All other larceny
Embezzlement	Motor vehicle theft
Extortion/blackmail	Pornography/obscene material
Fraud offenses	Prostitution offenses
False pretenses/swindle/confidence game	Prostitution
Credit card/ATM fraud	Assisting or promoting prostitution
Impersonation	Robbery
Welfare fraud	Sex offenses, forcible
Wire fraud	Forcible rape
Gambling offenses	Forcible sodomy
Betting/wagering	Sexual assault with an object
Operating/promoting/assisting gambling	Forcible fondling
Gambling equipment violations	Sex offenses, nonforcible
Sports tampering	Stolen property offenses
Homicide offenses	Weapon law violations
Murder/nonnegligent manslaughter	

created in 1930. Law enforcement organizations, State UCR program managers, and the research community strongly supported this effort. In January 1984 a conference considered various recommendations, and in 1985 BJS and the FBI released *Blueprint for the Future of the Uniform Crime Reporting Program.*

The resulting program, the National Incident-Based Reporting System, collected its first data in 1991. An estimated 40% of the Nation will report to NIBRS by the end of 1994. NIBRS represents a new way of thinking about crime, providing details about victims, offenders, and the environments in which they interact. This report on the first NIBRS data is a beginning step toward using the data for planning and evaluating law enforcement responses to crime. It also illustrates the close partnership among BJS, the FBI, and the more than 17,000 State and local law enforcement agencies.

NIBRS collects arrestee information on the 46 *Group A* offenses and an additional 11 *Group B* offenses (table B). Unlike the traditional UCR, NIBRS requires arrests as well as exceptional clearances to be linked to specific incidents.

In addition to expanded crime categories, NIBRS definitions of certain offenses are more inclusive than the traditional UCR definitions. For example, the NIBRS definition of rape has been expanded to include male victims.

In incidents where more than one offense occurs, the traditional UCR counts only the most serious of the offenses. NIBRS includes informa-

TABLE B. The NIBRS *Group B* Offenses

Bad checks	Drunkenness	Runaway
Curfew/loitering/vagrancy	Liquor law violations	Trespassing
Disorderly conduct	Nonviolent family offenses	All other offenses
Driving under the influence	Peeping Tom	

TABLE C. NIBRS Data Elements

Administrative segment:
1 ORI number
2 Incident number
3 Incident date/hour
4 Exceptional clearance indicator
5 Exceptional clearance date

Offense segment:
6 UCR offense code
7 Attempted/completed code
8 Alcohol/drug use by offender
9 Type of location
10 Number of premises entered
11 Method of entry
12 Type of criminal activity
13 Type of weapon/force used
14 Bias crime code

Property segment:
15 Type of property loss
16 Property description
17 Property value
18 Recovery date
19 Number of stolen motor vehicles
20 Number of recovered motor vehicles
21 Suspected drug type
22 Estimated drug quantity
23 Drug measurement unit

Victim segment:
24 Victim number
25 Victim UCR offense code

26 Type of victim
27 Age of victim
28 Sex of victim
29 Race of victim
30 Ethnicity of victim
31 Resident status of victim
32 Homicide/assault circumstances
33 Justifiable homicide circumstances
34 Type of injury
35 Related offender number
36 Relationship of victim to offender

Offender segment:
37 Offender number
38 Age of offender
39 Sex of offender
40 Race of offender

Arrestee segment:
41 Arrestee number
42 Transaction number
43 Arrest date
44 Type of arrest
45 Multiple clearance indicator
46 UCR arrest offense code
47 Arrestee armed indicator
48 Age of arrestee
49 Sex of arrestee
50 Race of arrestee
51 Ethnicity of arrestee
52 Resident status of arrestee
53 Disposition of arrestee under 18

tion about each of the different offenses (up to a maximum of 10) that may occur within a single incident. As a result, the NIBRS data can be used to study how often and under what circumstances certain offenses, such as burglary and rape, occur together.

The ability to link information about many aspects of a crime to the crime incident marks the most important difference between NIBRS and the traditional UCR. These various aspects of the crime incident are represented in NIBRS by a series of more than 50 data elements (table C).

Continued.

The NIBRS data elements are categorized in six segments: administrative, offense, property, victim, offender, and arrestee. NIBRS enables analysts to study how these data elements relate to each other for each type of offense.

Administrative segment includes the ORI (originating agency identifier) and incident numbers that uniquely identify each incident. These tie together all the records of a single incident. The administrative segment also includes the date and hour of the incident and if relevant, exceptional clearance information.

Offense segment includes the type of offense(s) reported, whether the offense was attempted or completed, whether the offender was suspected of using drugs or alcohol, the type of location where the offense occurred (such as a store or residence), the type of weapon or force used, and whether the offender was motivated by bias against the victim's race, religion, ethnicity, or sexual orientation. For certain offenses, the type of criminal activity (such as possessing, selling, or transporting) is indicated. For burglary incidents, the method of entry and the number of premises entered are included.

Property segment includes (for all property offenses, extortion, kidnaping, and a few other specified offenses) the type of property loss (burned, counterfeited, destroyed, seized, or stolen), the type of property involved (such as cash or jewelry), the value of the property, and, if recovered, the recovery date. For incidents of motor vehicle theft, special indicators for the number of stolen and recovered vehicles are included. For drug offenses, the type and quantity of illegal drug(s) seized are included.

Victim segment includes a victim identification number, the UCR code for offense(s) committed against the victim, and the victim's sex, age, race, ethnicity, and resident status. In cases where the victim is not an individual, codes are used to distinguish among businesses, financial institutions, governments, religious organizations, and society at large. For incidents of homicide or aggravated assault, codes describing the circumstances of the incident (such as an argument or drug deal) are provided. In incidents where the victim is injured, information describing the injury (such as fractures or lacerations) is included. Each victim is linked by an offender number to the offender(s) who committed an offense against him or her, and the nature of the victim's relationship (such as family member, acquaintance, or stranger) to each offender is reported.

Offender segment includes information on the age, sex, and race of the offender.

Arrestee segment includes information on persons arrested in connection with the incident, including the date of arrest, and the age, sex, race, ethnicity, and resident status of the arrestee.

An example of how those interested in the study of crime can tap the potentially rich source of new information represented by NIBRS is seen in the Supplementary Homicide Reports data published annually by the FBI in its *Crime in the United States* series. Cross tabulations of various incident based data elements are presented, including the age, sex, and race of victims and offenders, the types of weapon(s) used, the relationship of the victim to the offender, and the circumstances surrounding the incident (for example, whether the murder resulted from a robbery, rape, or argument). These data were provided to the FBI for about 87% of the 24,703 murders reported nationwide in 1991.

For other violent crimes such as rape and robbery, UCR data beyond the summary counts have generally been limited to a univariate distribution by month. With the advent of NIBRS, the supplemental data elements that were previously available only for murder incidents can now be used in the analysis of other violent crimes.

Of course, NIBRS also provides some data elements that were not previously available for any violent crimes, including murder. These new data elements include whether the offender was suspected of using alcohol or drugs shortly before or during the incident, the type of location of the crime, the resident status of the victim, and the nature of any injuries sustained by the victim.

For robbery incidents, NIBRS also provides previously unavailable data describing the property that was lost and its value. Using NIBRS, a researcher could study carjackings, for example, by selecting robbery incidents that included a vehicle as the property description.

Source: Reaves, Brian A. "Using NIBRS Data to Analyze Violent Crime." Bureau of Justice Statistics Technical Report, October, 1993.

Summary

Criminal-justice data gathering frequently requires real-world strategies as well as the use of alternative approaches, such as social surveys, participant observation, case study/life history methods, and unobtrusive measures. None of these methods is inherently superior to the others, although their relative strengths and weaknesses can be broken down with respect to quantitative/qualitative strength, greater or less control over rival factors, control over factors of internal/external validity, and artificiality/naturalness (see Figure 4.1). Each of these alternatives to experiments is briefly discussed as a prelude to detailed treatment in successive chapters.

The *Uniform Crime Report* (UCR) is given special treatment in this chapter so that it will not be lost in our discussion of other studies using available data or official statistics. Until recently, criminology and criminal justice in the United States have heavily relied on the UCR for research purposes. Most popular presentations on crime rates in the United States are usually taken uncritically from the UCR without a full appreciation of the limitations of these data. The UCR is published annually by the FBI and represents not crimes committed, but crimes reported to, and recorded by, the police. In general, the further from the actual offense commission, the poorer the official statistics are in providing an accurate picture of crime. The participation of local police departments in the UCR reporting system has improved over the years, with about 98 percent of the national population covered by 1978. The *Crime Index* consists of a simple summated index of seven (arson, added 1978, equals eight) crimes considered more serious, most likely reported, and most frequently occurring. The index offenses are murder and nonnegligent manslaughter, forcible rape, robbery, aggravated assault, burglary, larceny-theft, auto theft, and arson. The *crime rate* is the number of crimes per unit of population. Investigators using the UCR for research purposes should become familiar with its major limitations which make it a particularly hazardous statistic for comparing crime over time or measuring actual crime commission.

In 1985 a blueprint for a redesigned UCR program was developed, and by the early 1990s it had begun to be implemented. This program featured a National Incident-Based Recording System (NIBRS), which will eventually replace the traditional UCR. This comprehensive system provides far more detail than the previous summary-based one.

Key Concepts

Alternative Data- Gathering Strategies	Unobtrusive Measures	Limitations of the Crime Index
Social Surveys	Uniform Crime Report (UCR)	Crime Dip
Participant Observation	Index Crimes	UCR Redesign
Life History/Case Study Methods	Crime Rate	NIBRS
	Factors Affecting UCR	Hierarchy Rule

Review Questions

1. Some researchers feel that experiments represent the only and best means of data gathering. Discuss this issue with respect to the relative strengths and weaknesses of alternative data-gathering strategies.
2. Other than examples given in Chapter 4, discuss some other examples of research studies employing the alternative data-gathering strategies.
3. What is the UCR? What are its major components? What are the major components of the crime index? The calculation of crime rate? What have been some major identified shortcomings of the UCR?
4. Given the identified shortcomings of the UCR, read and then discuss how features of the redesigned UCR may eliminate some of these shortcomings.
5. Discuss the National Incident-Based Reporting System. What are some of its principal features as well as advantages over the traditional UCR?

CHAPTER

Sampling and Survey Research: Questionnaires

Sampling may be used with any of the data-gathering procedures we discuss. The fact that it is included here with surveys is simply a matter of editorial convenience. Some research involves a complete enumeration of the total population, households, or the target of study. Since 1790, for instance, the U.S. Census attempts to survey every household unit—man, woman, and child—in the United States every ten years. Similarly, city directories attempt to count and obtain information on all persons eighteen years of age or older who reside within their urban target areas.

Sampling

Rather than attempting to enumerate an entire population, most studies make use of sampling. **Sampling** is a procedure used in research by which a select subunit of a population is studied in order to analyze the entire population. Sampling enables an inexpensive, relatively quick assessment, by even small groups of researchers, of a population that is often so large that complete enumeration is prohibitive. The logic of sampling enables one to make inferences to a larger population (Kish, 1965).

Sampling frame

The initial step in selecting a sample is to develop a **sampling frame,** a complete list of the population (or universe) that one is interested in studying. For example, if one is interested in generalizing to all judges in California, a complete list of such judges would constitute the sampling frame.

Types of Sampling

The major types of sampling procedures follow.

Probability	*Nonprobability*
Simple Random	Quota
Stratified Random	Accidental
Cluster	Purposive
Systematic	Snowball
(Multistage)	

Probability Samples

Probability samples

Probability samples refer to samples that permit estimation of the likelihood of each element of the population being selected in the sample.

Simple random samples

Simple Random Samples. Simple random samples (SRSs) are samples in which each element of the population (or universe) has an equal probability of being selected. Sometimes the mnemonic device EPSEM samples is used to denote the key features of an SRS (Babbie, 1992, p. 197).

EPSEM

EPSEM, a means of sample selection, is an acronym that stands for Equal Probability of SElection Method. This method provides a way for selecting a sample in which each and every unit or person in the population has the same or equal chance of appearing in the sample. EPSEM or probability samples are very important in the field of statistics because the various calculations and estimations of statistics assume that the sample was chosen by some probability method. In describing samples that use an equal probability of selection method, we will use the shorthand acronym EPSEM.

If probability methods have been utilized in selection of the sample, the concept of sampling error enables researchers to assess confidence limits so that with a given degree of error, they can assume that what is true of the sample is true of the population, and that the sample mean approximates that of the population.

Procedure. To select a simple random sample, it is necessary to acquire a clear and complete list of all elements of the population because all elements must be independently and randomly chosen. Suppose there were thirty people in a room and a simple random sample of five were to be drawn. One could give each person a number, drop these numbers into a hat, scramble them, and then draw five, one at a time. State lottery daily numbers usually make use of an honest gambling device procedure that is essentially a simple random sample. What if, as in a large survey of the public, one wished to draw a simple random sample of adults from a city of a million. Obviously, one would not put numbers in a hat. To sample such large populations, researchers make use of a table of random numbers. Figure 5.1

Angelo, Gerald	Kozak, Dave	Thiel, Myrtle
Bell, Earl	Lewis, Ed	Thompson, Mary
Bender, Harry	Mack, Bob	Tierney, Estelle
Benekos, Peter	McGill, Bill	Unterwagner, Jim
Bethune, David	Morris, Tom	Vance, Lance
Bozo, Boris	Mucha, Fred	Vega, Terence
Bruno, Albert	Norris, Herb	Wahlen, John
Burns, Rich	Numa, Tod	Wayne, Mike
Buxton, Bob	Obernan, Stan	Weeks, Bary
Buzawa, Eve	Parker, Omar	Zeno, Mike
Clemons, Randy	Parks, Zeke	
Dammer, Harry	Penn, Wally	
Dutkowdky, Andrew	Quick, Bob	
Edsel, Earl	Rapp, Sean	
Erisman, Mike	Rasp, Doug	
Frederici, Mike	Ross, Joe	
Goblick, Al	Runt, Juan	
Hairbreath, Harry	Saxon, Sid	
Harlow, Joe	Simmons, Mary	
Johnson, Leroy	Simpson, Ted	

Table of Random Numbers[4]

07001	61569	08812	07344	92880	71728
43102	29751	87806	12031	56214	41387
61622	71481	20091	37658	99612	28143
50126	51296	07509	61483	25143	61974

Figure 5.1 Sampling Frame of Inmates of San Rocco Correctional Institution. (The table of random numbers is provided for illustration purposes only. For actual projects, consult Appendix B.)

[4]This Table of Random Numbers is provided for illustration purposes only. For actual projects, consult Appendix B.

illustrates a theoretical population and a hypothetical typical table of random numbers. Appendix B contains a larger table of random numbers.

To select a sample of ten inmates one would first number the list of inmates, then choose a random start, for example, the top left of Table of Random Numbers. As the entire population consists of fifty cases, numbers from 00 to 99, or two-digit numbers, would enable each name to have an equal probability of selection. Numbers from 51 to 99 are, of course, unusable; if these numbers are chosen, they should be skipped and the selection process continued until the next two-digit number between 01 and 50. According to Figure 5.1, the first number is 07—Albert Bruno, the second is 00—no case, the third is 16—Frank Fox, and so forth, until ten cases are chosen. If the same number is chosen twice, it is skipped because each respondent should appear only once in the sampling frame. For complex sampling, various computer programs are available that provide a simple random sample of a specified size (Norusis, 1988).

Advantages/Disadvantages. The chief advantage of the SRS is that it enables the use of statistical probabilities that are necessary in many statistical procedures. The primary disadvantages of the SRS, however, are that it *requires a complete list of the population to be sampled* and, if large numbers are involved, it *can become a rather tedious and cumbersome procedure,* although this can be offset by computer. The SRS *by no means guarantees a representative sample.* On the last point, by chance it is possible in our San Rocco sample to obtain a sample that is 50 percent female, even though females represent only 10 percent of the population. As we will see in our discussion of statistics in Chapter 12, the probability of this occurring is small, but it certainly is possible. Such a nonrepresentative sample certainly raises problems for a researcher attempting to infer to the larger population. Primarily for this reason, much survey research involving sampling utilizes stratified random samples.

Some examples of research employing simple random samples include a study of New York City drug laws by Japha (1978) in which he randomly selected cases from the Criminal Court of Manhattan of persons convicted for a nondrug felony who had been given a nonincarceration sentence. In addition, he drew random samples of cases entering court for arraignment, cases reduced or dismissed at first arraignment, clients in drug treatment programs, and males held on felony charges in Manhattan. Sparks (1982), in a study of Massachusetts statewide sentencing guidelines, constructed a random sample of 1,440 convicted criminals who had been sentenced in Massachusetts Superior Court during a 1-year period.

Stratified random sample

Stratified Random Samples. Stratified random samples rely on knowledge of the distribution or proportion of population characteristics to choose a sample that assures representativeness of these characteristics. Such characteristics are generally demographic in nature, such as age, sex, race, social class, or of pertinence to the study, such as area of residence, nature and type of criminal record, region, or some quality of importance in the analysis.

The general procedure involves dividing the population into strata or groups based on the variable(s) of stratification and then selecting the sample either proportionately or disproportionately, depending on the decision made in this regard. For **proportionate stratified samples** sample subjects are chosen in roughly the same ratio as exists in the population. For instance, suppose that in our San Rocco study of fifty inmates, we wanted to choose a proportionate stratified sample by sex of ten inmates. Because one of ten are female in the population, we must be certain that only one of the ten subjects in the sample is female. Such a procedure assures representativeness by sex, unlike the SRS in which half of the sample were females.

Proportionate stratified samples

Disproportionate stratified sampling involves oversampling—taking a larger than proportionate number of certain groups to assure the appearance of a sufficient number of cases for comparative purposes of a group that is small in the population. Again, returning to our example in Figure 5.1, suppose that we wished to investigate differences between male and female inmates at San Rocco. A SRS could result in a sample of all males, which would certainly destroy our ability to even conduct the study. A proportionate stratified sample would yield one female and nine males, a situation that would be quite hazardous because, on every variable of analysis, the 100 percent response of females would be referring to only one respondent. A disproportionate stratified sample might take all five female subjects and compare them with a sample of male respondents, for example, five males. *There is generally no problem in comparing males with females using a disproportionate stratified sample; however, if inferences were to be attempted from a sample that is overrepresentative of females to all inmates, the sample is obviously nonrepresentative. Weighting* of sample responses is a recommended procedure to adjust sample data to enable inference to the general population. Basically, weighting involves the differential assignment of adjustment factors to data to take into account the relative importance of that data.

Disproportionate stratified samples

Table 5.1 illustrates this process. The responses of the males in the sample would in actuality carry nine times more weight than those of females. That is, each response of males in the sample actually represents the response of nine males—the respondent and eight others—whereas the female respondent represents only herself. Thus, disproportionate stratified sampling permits comparisons between subgroups where at least one of the subgroups might otherwise be too small. In the early victimization surveys of select U.S. cities conducted by the U.S. Census Bureau on behalf of the

TABLE 5.1   San Rocco Correctional Institution: Weighting of Disproportionate Sample

	Population	Disproportionate Stratified Sample	Weight
Male	45	5	9 ×
Female	5	5	1 × or none

Department of Justice, the sampling frame was the complete housing inventory for the city as determined by the *1970 Census of Population and Housing.* To select a stratified sample, the city's housing units were categorized into 105 strata, for example, own or rent, occupied or unoccupied, and single-family or multiple-dwelling unit (Criminal Victimization Surveys in Milwaukee, 1977). Garofalo describes the sampling procedure utilized in the initial study of eight cities involved in LEAA's High Impact Crime Reduction Program:

> Supplemental samples were drawn from new construction permits issued in each city. Census Bureau interviewers visited the housing units selected and interviewed residents about personal and household victimizations suffered during the preceding 12 months. About 10,000 households or 22,000 individuals were interviewed in each city. . . . The samples were sufficiently large to make reliable estimates of what the attitude responses would have been if everyone in the city had been interviewed (Garofalo, 1977, p. 14).

The numbers in the victimization survey report are weighted estimates as if the entire population were surveyed. The history—the evolution of the operation of Bureau of Justice Statistics-sponsored victimization surveys—will be covered in depth in Chapter 6.

In an analysis of characteristics of high- and low-crime neighborhoods in Atlanta, Greenberg, Williams, and Rohe (1982) utilized a stratified random sample from three matched pairs of neighborhoods selected on the basis of crime, racial, and income characteristics. A study of the relationship between narcotics addiction and criminal activity in Baltimore by Nurco et al. (1985) involved a sample of 354 male narcotic addicts who were selected using a stratified random sample of a population of 6,149 known narcotics abusers who had been arrested or identified by the Baltimore Police Department between 1952 and 1976. The sample was selected not on the basis of criminality but by race and year of police contact.

Cluster
sampling **Cluster Sampling. Cluster sampling** is generally used in surveys that involve field interviews and is most useful in studies that involve widely dispersed subjects. The population to be surveyed is divided into clusters, for example, census tracts, blocks, and sections, and then a probability sample of clusters is selected for study. Such a sampling procedure is less time consuming and costly, particularly in terms of field staff. Once the clusters are chosen, other sampling procedures, such as a systematic sample of every *n*th house, may be employed. Cluster sampling is particularly useful as a means of reducing travel costs in field interviewing.

An example of the use of cluster sampling is provided by Schuerman and Kobrin's (1986) study of neighborhood change and criminal activity in Los Angeles. They drew a sample from census tract clusters in Los Angeles County that were defined as high-crime areas in 1970. They then used a statistical procedure to assemble contiguous census tracts into 192 clusters or neighborhoods and studied the impact of socioeconomic and demographic trends in these areas on crime rates. Sigler and Johnson (1986; see also Sigler and Haygood, 1987), in a study of public perceptions of sexual harrassment in Tuscaloosa, Alabama, employed a multistage, stratified cluster sample in which grids on city maps, blocks, and residences were the sampling units.

Systematic samples

Systematic Samples. In systematic samples every *n*th item in a list is included in the sample. (In the language of statistics, *n* represents every second, third, fourth, or *n*th case.) Purists insist that such a sample is a nonprobability sample, because various patterns, for example ethnic surnames, may exist in a list that would destroy its representativeness. If offenders or arrestees were listed in order of offense seriousness, the final sample may be biased. This writer has chosen to place systematic sampling in the probability group because the majority of researchers feel that it satisfies the EPSEM requirement and belongs in the probability group. To illustrate systematic sampling, let us return to Figure 5.1, the San Rocco example. Suppose we wished to select a sample of ten from a population of fifty. Assuming the names are already numbered, we would select first the proper sampling interval, in this case every fifth name. Sampling intervals are selected by the ratio of sample size to population size—in our example, ten of fifty or 1 of 5. By choosing every fifth, theoretically every name in the population list has an equal probability of being

Random start

chosen so long as one uses a *random start.* The choice of random start involves randomly choosing where the interval will begin within the first interval—in this case, 1 to 5. For example, if the number 3 were chosen from a table of random numbers, the sample selected with the every-fifth-sampling interval would be 3, 8, 13, 18, 23, 28, 33, 38, 43, and 48. As long as one suspects that there is no pattern in the population list and one uses the proper sampling interval and random start, such that each individual or unit has an equal probability of being chosen, then one most likely has a probability sample. The obvious advantage of systematic samples is their relative ease of selection, although it may become burdensome with large populations. In choosing a systematic sample from a uniformly spaced list of names, a simple procedure, once the random start is selected, is to mark off with a ruler or other measuring rod and proceed down the list until all cases are selected.

Multistage sampling

Multistage Sampling. Multistage sampling involves combinations of stratified and/or cluster and/or simple random samples or other sampling procedures. For example, a national survey of neighborhood crime might stratify first on the basis of region—north, east, south, west. Within regions, clusters are randomly selected, and within the selected regions, blocks are randomly selected for door-to-door household interviews.

Multistage sampling can become quite complex, as illustrated by the study by O'Keefe et al. (1984) of media crime prevention campaigns.

The population examined included a national sample of the noninstitutionalized civilian population of the United States age eighteen and over. A one-call quasi-probability sample design was employed, based upon the Roper Organization's master national probability sample of interviewing areas. First, 100 counties were chosen at random proportionate to population after all counties in the nation had been stratified by population size within geographic region. Second, cities and towns were randomly selected from the sample counties according to their population. Third, four blocks or segments were then drawn within each location. Quotas for sex and age, as well as for employed women, were set in order to assure proper representation of each group in the sample (O'Keefe et al., 1984, in Loftin, 1987, p. 100).

Nonprobability Samples

Any sampling procedure that violates the EPSEM (Equal Probability of SElection Method) is viewed as a nonprobability sample.

Quota
sampling

Quota Samples. Quota samples are nonprobability stratified samples. The researcher attempts to ensure that the sample proportions, for example, age, sex, and race, resemble those of the population, but does not fill these proportions or quotas on the basis of an EPSEM. Rather than attempting to ensure that each element of each quota has an equal chance of appearing in the sample, the researcher uses skilled judgment to select adequate numbers to fill each quota. The data are collected and analyzed on an ongoing basis until an adequate decision or prediction of outcome becomes possible. Quota sampling is the favorite technique of many private marketing and consumer survey organizations. Often at shopping malls, interviewers eyeball shoppers until someone appearing to fit the requirements of one of their quotas is identified—for example, a black male in his forties. At times the interviews are aborted when, on the basis of demographic information, it turns out that the interviewer guessed wrong on a characteristic and the individual is not needed in the quota.

An illustration of a quota sample is provided in a Philadelphia bail experiment conducted by Goldkamp and Gottfredson (1984). First, a sample of judges was selected from Philadelphia Municipal Court, and then cases from court files were selected according to a stratified quota sampling design by which cases were chosen on the basis of seriousness of charge and judge.

A quota sample was also used in a study of criminal victimization among the homeless in Birmingham, Alabama (Fitzpatrick, LaGory, and Ritchey, 1993). The researchers used a previous Birmingham Homeless Enumeration and Survey Project to construct sampling parameters and stratified on geographic site, gender, and race. They then conducted a quota sample survey of 150 homeless adults by randomly selecting persons from each homeless shelter or public site to match the proportions found in the previous enumeration. After determining the number of respondents required from the site, interviewers selected subjects on the basis of sex and race. The demographic characteristics of the sample matched those of previous studies in Texas and Tennessee.

Accidental
samples

Accidental Samples. Accidental samples are the favorite "person on the street" interviews where the "researcher" makes little attempt to ensure representativeness of the sample. This is well illustrated by many television

commercials, for example, "Nine out of ten doctors recommend _____."
Which nine of ten? An interview of the easiest and most accessible generally
will not yield data from which one could infer to larger populations.

Purposive
samples

Purposive Samples. Purposive (judgmental) **samples,** on the other hand,
represent the selection of an appropriate sample based on the researcher's
skill, judgment, and needs. This type of sampling is well used on election
nights when the major networks, based on sample precincts, are able to quite
accurately predict the likely outcome, often with a small margin of error with
only 2 percent of the votes cast. Marketing studies often use test areas that
possess characteristics quite similar to those of the nation. Both political

Focus groups

campaign planners and market analysts have made use of **focus groups.**
Organizers of these focus groups bring together purposively selected volunteers in order to measure reactions to or attitudes about products, candidate
speeches, and the like (Krueger, 1994; Morgan, 1993; and Stewart and

Criminal
profiling

Shamdasani, 1990). **Criminal profiling** refers to attempts to construct typical
characteristics of certain types of criminals. Holmes (1989) used a purposive
sample and corresponded with and talked to offenders, asking them questions about their crimes, motivations, and crime scenes. This technique is
used by researchers—for example, by those in the FBI's Behavioral Research
Unit—for forecasting purposes and to aid in the investigation of certain types
of criminals, for instance, serial murderers. In a criminal profiling of forty-
one convicted serial rapists, 76 percent were found to have been sexually
abused as children. This same profile found that the majority of serial rapes
had not been reported to authorities (Hazlewood and Warren, 1989).

Although purposive samples are not probability samples, their usefulness
is judged on the basis of whether they work in predicting future behavior or
attitudes of the target population, for example, voting patterns and consumer behavior.

The following caveat was issued by Sheley and Wright (1993, p. 3) in their
study of juvenile possession of firearms by selecting purposive samples of
835 male serious offenders incarcerated in six juvenile facilities in four states
and 785 male students in ten inner-city high schools near these facilities:

> It should be stressed that these findings are technically not generalizable to
> other settings and populations. The four states serving as research sites for this
> study were not a probability sample of States. Moreover, to maximize percent-
> ages of respondents involved in the behavior of interest, the study purposely
> focused on serious juvenile offenders and on students from especially prob-
> lematic inner-city schools. Therefore, the 6 correctional facilities and 10 high
> schools (and by virtue of the voluntary nature of participation in the study, the
> respondents in those institutions) serving as research sites were not probabil-
> ity samples of their respective universes.
>
> Nonetheless, comparison of inmate respondents' profiles with those known
> through studies of youth in similar institutions indicates that the present sam-
> ple was not dissimilar to samples of State maximum-security wards serving as
> subjects of other studies. Moreover, a 1984 study of inner-city high school stu-
> dents' criminal activity employed data collected from randomly selected high

school students from inner-city, high-crime neighborhoods in four cities and indicated age and race breakdowns very similar to those found among the student respondents.

A large number of evaluation studies in criminal justice employ purposive sampling as illustrated by the following. To assess the impact of determinate sentencing on institutional climate and prison administration, Goodstein et al. (1984) studied three states that had recently implemented determinate sentencing and purposely chose states that differed in the types of determinate sentencing enacted. In an age cohort analysis of arrest rates, Greenberg and Larkin (1985) chose twenty-five large cities for study on the basis of geographic representativeness. The detailed planning in choosing a purposive sample can be illustrated in Jacob's (1984) study of ten city governments' responses to crime from 1948 to 1978. The cities were chosen on the basis of fiscal strength, type of city government, region, quality of urban life, possession of sufficient research capabilities, accessibility (cooperativeness in the past) to research, availability of prior research, and program initiativeness (had received federal grants in the past). Pate et al. (1986) studied fear of crime in Houston and Newark, the former representing a new, growing city with low population density and the latter a mature, high-population-density city with declining economic resources. Toborg's (1981) choice of sites in her study of pretrial release practices in nine jurisdictions was based on very practical reasons, which probably exist in most purposive samples: geographic diversity, wide range of (release) types, accurate and accessible records, and a willingness of agencies to cooperate with the study. Agency contacts and cooperation are essential in such studies because, without such "hospitality," suspicion will very likely undermine the project.

Snowball sampling

Snowball Sampling. Snowball sampling is a type of strategy employed particularly in exploratory studies of little-known or hard-to-obtain subjects (Goodman, 1969; and Biernacki and Waldorf, 1981). It basically entails obtaining a first subject and, on the basis of this subject, obtaining an entrée and introduction to a second subject and then a third and so forth. Gradually, as many subjects as practicable are accumulated. Polsky (1967) employed this strategy in studying uncaught criminals, as did Solomey (1979) in his study of undercover police. Alex (1969) also employed this strategy in order to study black police officers in New York City. Such a sampling procedure may be the only means of obtaining data on little-known or secretive subject matter. In order to study "The Social Organization of Drug Use and Drug Dealing Among Urban Gangs," Fagan (1989) used a snowball sample of gang member respondents. Initial subjects were recruited through neighborhood agencies, and gang members who were recruited later were nominated by these first respondents. All participants received payment for their cooperation in the form of caps, T-shirts, or coupons to record stores.

In contrasting a history of Asian gangs in San Francisco, Toy (1992) interviewed sixty-four active gang members as well as nine respondents for historical purposes. Utilizing a snowball sampling technique subjects were initially recruited through neighborhood social service agencies and then asked to refer other gang members. Respondents were paid $50 and another $40 for each successful referral.

The selection of the sample and instrument to be used for data collection is always governed by time, cost, and staff available to collect and analyze the data. Unless selection probabilities can be estimated, statistical inference to larger populations is hazardous. In the hands of skillful researchers, however, and for specific research problems, nonprobability samples may be preferred.

Sample Size

There is no simple answer to the question: "What is an appropriate size sample to choose?" It depends on a number of considerations, and there is no predetermined appropriate sample size for all conditions. The choice of sample size can depend on the degree of accuracy required, the funds available, the expected frequency (or rarity) of the characteristic to be observed, and the anticipated subclassification of the variables. It's important to note that without a representative sample, sample size becomes irrelevant. A small representative sample would yield a better estimate of the population than a much larger, unrepresentative sample.

The size of the sample is statistically determined by the size of the sampling error to be tolerated rather than the total size of the population (Kish, 1965; Loether and McTavish, 1980). The larger the sample size, the smaller the sampling error or extent to which the sampling values can be expected to differ from population values. Depending on available funds, researchers should attempt to obtain as large a sample as is practical. Statistical tables for determination of sample sizes are available in standard statistical texts (Isaac and Michael, 1981, p.193; Bogue, 1981, pp. 212–214). For instance, for the 95 percent probability that a sample will have less than a plus or minus 5 percent error in estimating the population, a population of 500 would require a sample of 217, a population of 1,000 needs a sample of 286, a population of 10,000 requires 370, and a population over 100,000 must have a sample of roughly 400.

The sample size also depends on the expected frequency (or rarity) of the characteristic to be observed in the population. For example, in the discussion of victim surveys in Chapter 6, it will be indicated that a sample of 60,000 households is used for the National Crime Survey of the entire U.S. population. A similar number was required for each city surveyed as part of the original central city surveys. Why are such large samples required in victim surveys when similar public opinion surveys are sometimes conducted with only a few hundred in the sample? Because nearly everyone has an opinion, whereas victimization for a specific crime may be rare, thus requiring a large sample in order to obtain a few cases.

Related to the last point is the fact that too small samples may provide too few cases for analysis once the sample is subclassified. For example, if the study entailed comparison of three race categories by ten different crime victimizations, some of the subclassifications (e.g., Asians who have been burglarized) may yield too few cases for statistical analysis. In such cases larger samples are required than minimums expressed in statistical tables.

The reader is advised to examine statistical texts on sampling for more technical detail on this subject (Kish, 1965; Loether and McTavish, 1980), as well as to consult journal articles and examine sample sizes employed in similar studies.

Survey Research

Survey research, an area that is emerging as a strength in criminal justice research, is an excellent tool for primary data gathering.

In Indiana, legislative hearings dealing with the death penalty for juveniles ended with the following statement (Hamm, 1989, p. 224):

> We have debated capital punishment for juveniles today and have come to various conclusions. Yet one thing we know for sure. Never fill out a questionnaire from a criminologist again.

Criminologist Mark Hamm was told this by the press and by other persons associated with the legislature. He was also told that his research "struck too close to the bone." Beginning in the fall of 1986, he received survey responses from eighty-five legislators (85 percent of the General Assembly). He was relatively certain that many of the legislators had filled out the survey themselves rather than relegating it to their staffs because, he said, (ibid., p. 223):

> in my testimony on the juvenile death penalty before the Indiana General Assembly, a number of legislators indicated a familiarity with the substantive content of the survey. Indeed the survey became a heated topic of debate during these proceedings. My testimony—one among some 30 given before the General Assembly—was the only one terminated by the Legislature. It was cut short on the grounds that it was inappropriate to discuss statistical reasons why some legislators might favor the execution of juveniles and why others might not.

The fact that, as in this example, participants in a legislative hearing were threatened by the results of a survey certainly illustrates the power and potential usefulness of such an instrument.

In this chapter we examine mail questionnaire and self-report studies whose features illustrate well many of the opportunities and pitfalls of survey methods. Other major data-gathering approaches, such as interviews, victim surveys, and telephone surveys, will be the subject of Chapter 6.

Surveys have been often misunderstood by some researchers who have been socialized in the experimental tradition. Many times hostility appears between some theoreticians and some practitioners with respect to the strong emphasis placed on the experimental tradition as an ideal in social science research. Part of this methodological argument may result from a lack of full appreciation of the nature of survey research methods and their potential as tools in investigating many important questions facing the criminal justice system. The notion of a survey connotes images of a poll or simple tally (count of opinion), but survey research has many purposes and can address

Descriptive survey research

Analytic survey research

many scientific problems beyond a simple count of opinion. *Descriptive survey research* may use statistical probability theory to assess sampling error (Is what is true of the sample true of the population?), whereas *analytic survey research* attempts to explore questions of cause and effect similar to traditional experimental research. The experimenter utilizes research design *before* the fact to remove the effects of rival causal factors, whereas the survey researcher tries to remove these rival factors *after* the fact (after the data have been collected) through the use of statistical analysis.

A basic quality of survey research that is at times forgotten and is responsible for much potential error in interpretation of findings is that in most instances *surveys record either expressed attitude or claimed behavior and seldom the behavior itself.* In Chapter 7 we will detail potential errors in surveys in which the full importance of this statement will be explained, but at this stage, acceptance of this point as an article of faith will suffice. Previously we indicated that surveys are not just useful for political and consumer polls, but are also effective means of addressing scientific questions and the causality problem. Rather than control for rival causal factors prior to the fact by means of research design, surveys generally employ quantitative methods and statistical procedures post hoc to control for extraneous variables and sources of invalidity, because natural field settings make the control of sources of invalidity more problematic.

Survey research may employ a variety of data-gathering methods ranging from the administration of structured questionnaires to captive audiences such as all sections of Introduction to American Criminal Justice at a college or university, to mail questionnaires, field interviews, telephone surveys, and their variations. In this chapter we concentrate on the mail questionnaire. It is widely used and offers the possibility to discuss many issues that occur in the other types of survey approaches. We will first examine some guidelines for questionnaire construction.

Some Guidelines for Questionnaire Construction

Although it would be foolish for anyone to claim that there is one and only one way of constructing an effective questionnaire, a number of procedures have been established by practitioners through trial and error and custom.

The most crucial and most underestimated step in questionnaire construction involves clearly formulating the research problem and the data required to speak directly to the research problem (Lazarsfeld, 1954). A common method of specifying the relationship between research issues and data is creation of a *variables list which is keyed to questionnaire items and dummy tables.*

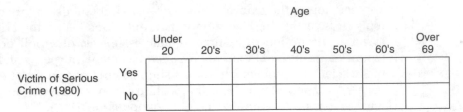

Figure 5.2 A Dummy Table for the Relationship between Victimization and Age.

Variables list

A **variables list** is constructed after the initial rough draft of the questionnaire. The concepts or variables to be measured are listed along with the numbers of the questions that purport to measure them. By rigorously reviewing a questionnaire in this manner, duplicative items, unmeasured concepts, or an emphasis that is undesirable may be discovered. This procedure will be detailed in Chapter 11.

Dummy tables

Dummy tables are preliminary blank tables constructed prior to data gathering that suggest the type of data needed, as well as the type of data analysis. Figure 5.2 illustrates the use of a dummy table to call attention to data that will be needed for a two-variable cross-tabulation.

Assuming that such a tabular analysis is planned, the researcher is now alerted to the need to check the data-gathering instrument to see if the questions for these two variables have been asked in a manner that would render itself to the type of categorization in the dummy table. The real utility of a dummy table is realized when the researcher discovers that he or she has failed to ask a question necessary to the study. Although variables lists and dummy tables may strike those anxious to get on with a study as ritualism, they act to ensure that the data needed are obtained before the fact, rather than after the fact when it may be too late. A basic maxim of research is no more data should be gathered than needed; however, blind application of this dictum is myopic. A study should be viewed as a research opportunity, one in which the basic needs of the present research enterprise as well as "riders," (related research questions that may be analyzed once the main project is completed) are present. For instance, in the course of a federally funded project on attrition among rehabilitation counselors, data gathered on professionalism can later be analyzed to address the issue of professional developments in the field (Hagan, Haug, and Sussman, 1975).

Questionnaire Wording

Sudman and Bradburn's *Asking Questions* (1982) is a gold mine of suggestions on questionnaire wording and construction. They caution you to resist writing questions until you have carefully thought through the research questions or problems. It is also quite useful to collect and borrow successful questions from other researchers. This may even enable the comparison of questions across studies (ibid., p. 14).

The language used in questionnaires must be geared to the target population. If the study group is a specialized one, for example, forensic pathologists, then the use of occupational argot and technical language would be preferred. In fact, pretests of the instrument with members of this occupation may suggest appropriate terminology. On the other hand, if the general population is to be surveyed, a more common language should be used. If the target group includes significant non-English-speaking populations, it may be necessary to employ bilingual strategies such as dual-language instruments. Faculty of foreign language departments at local colleges often prove to be invaluable consultants in this regard. Similarity of respondent understanding of language is particularly problematic in cross-cultural research. Anyone with exposure to foreign languages realizes that certain ideas, idioms, and jargon are not readily translated into another language. The same holds true across cultures with similar languages. Asking if a person has ever been mugged may puzzle others who may confuse the term with kissing or being served a drink.

Care must also be taken to identity clearly who should answer the questions, for example, head of the household or any adult member of the household. This writer was once the subject of a shopping mall marketing survey and, as part of an apparent quota sample, was asked his opinions regarding some sample cereal box covers. The covers featured pictures of sports figures and, after the completion of a fairly long interview, my wife asked me when was the last time I purchased cereal? One could just imagine supermarkets loaded with cereal boxes picturing hockey players while consumers purchase those featuring smiling children.

Some of the following *suggestions on questionnaire wording and construction* are not intended to be either exhaustive or mutually exclusive:

- *Avoid biased or leading questions.* The classic example is, "Do you still beat your spouse?" No matter how respondents answer that question, they are admitting spousal abuse.
- *Avoid double-barreled questions.* Such questions ask two questions in one. Do not ask something like, "Do you walk to work or carry your lunch?"
- *Do not ask questions in an objectionable manner.* "Did you exercise your duty as a citizen and report this incident to the police?" Respondents would feel unpatriotic if they answered no.
- *Avoid assuming prior information on the part of the respondent.* One might ask, "Do you support the Miranda decision?"—only to discover too late that half of the respondents thought Miranda was a shortstop with the Pittsburgh Pirates.
- *Avoid vague wording.* Use language with as much common meaning as possible.
- *Do not ask more than you need to know.*
- *Avoid "response set" patterns by using reversal questions.* Do not word all questions so that a positive or negative answer is the most desirable;

otherwise, respondents may answer the first few and then check off the remainder in a similar fashion without even reading them.

Barton (1958, p. 67) gives humorous examples of many of the techniques that have been used as a means of asking threatening questions (cited in Sudman and Bradburn, 1982, pp. 54–55). In this case we want to ask, "Did you kill your wife?"

"Did you kill your wife?"

- *The Casual Approach:* "Do you happen to have murdered your wife?"
- *The Numbered Card:* "Would you please read off the number on this card which corresponds to what became of your wife?" (Hand card to respondent.)
  1. Natural death
  2. I killed her.
  3. Other (What?)
     (Get the card back from respondent before proceeding.)
- *The Everybody Approach:* "As you know, many people have been killing their wives these days. Do you happened to have killed yours?"
- *The "Other People" Approach:*
  (a) "Do you know any people who have murdered their wives?"
  (b) "How about yourself?"
- *The Sealed Ballot Technique:* In this version you explain that the survey respects people's rights to anonymity in respect to their marital relations and that they themselves are to fill out the answer to the question, seal it in an envelope, and drop it in a box conspicuously labeled, "Sealed Ballot Box" which is carried by the interviewer.
- *The Kinsey Technique:* Stare firmly into respondent's eyes and ask in simple, clear-cut language, such as that to which the respondent is accustomed, and with an air of assuming everyone has done everything, "Did you ever kill your wife?" Put the question at the end of the interview.

Although Barton's wife-killing example involves a preposterous topic, the techniques used to ask threatening questions are quite common and useful in survey research.

Researchers must also decide whether open-ended (unstructured) or closed-ended (structured) questions will yield the necessary information:

Open: Some people feel that certain parts of the criminal justice system do not work. Do you agree? If so, what parts?

Closed: Some people feel that certain parts of the criminal justice system do not work. Is this belief _____ True, _____ False, _____ Don't Know. If true, what parts? _____ Police, _____ Courts, _____ Corrections, _____ Other Specify _____

Although open-ended questions may provide greater detail and permit respondents to express in-depth their attitudes, such responses pose difficulty as we will see in our discussion of coding in Chapter 11. Closed–ended (structured) questions, although they ease the coding process and are easier for respondents, may not give respondents an opportunity to explain fully their views.

To illustrate some question ambiguity in even professionally designed surveys, the following illustrations were drawn from the presentation on analytical issues in victim surveys by the Crime Statistics Analysis Staff to the Panel for the Evaluation of Crime Surveys (Panel for the Evaluation of Crime Surveys, 1976, pp. 167–176):

Question:	Were the police informed of this incident in any way? **1.** ☐ No **2.** ☐ Don't Know—Skip to Check Item G. Yes—Who told them? **3.** ☐ Household member **4.** ☐ Someone else **5.** ☐ Police on scene
Some Problems:	The use of the term "informed" is a potentially suggestive one. The possibility may be ruled out that the police were on the scene or happened on-the-scene or may have been called without the respondent being aware.

Question:	**8a.** What were the injuries you suffered, if any?
	    1. ☐ None—Skip to 10a.
	    2. ☐ Raped
	    3. ☐ Attempted rape
	    4. ☐ Knife or gunshot wounds
	    5. ☐ Broken bones or teeth knocked out
	    6. ☐ Internal injuries, knocked unconscious
	    7. ☐ Bruises, black eye, cuts, scratches, swelling
	    8. ☐ Other—Specify _____
	b. Were you injured to the extent that you needed medical attention after the attack?
	    1. ☐ No—Skip to 10a.
	    2. ☐ Yes.
	c. Did you receive any treatment at a hospital?
	    1. ☐ No
	    2. ☐ Emergency room treatment only
	    3. ☐ Stayed overnight or longer
	        How many days?

Problems:	Question 8b may be subject to varying interpretations. The interviewer training manual defines "need" as actually securing aid from a trained medical professional. However, to a respondent, "need" could be based on a conception of the seriousness of the injury. Because the

interviewer may not always provide the official interpretation of "need," responses may reflect different
interpretations of the meaning of the question. Question
8a responses 2 ("Raped") and 3 ("Attempted rape") were
to be interpreted as determinants of physical injury, but
attempted rape may involve only verbal threats. That is,
the inclusion of attempted physical injury may cause
distortions in data on physical injury.

Question 8c, in obtaining data on hospital care only,
fails to identify other types of medical care, professional
or nonprofessional, or institutional or otherwise.

Question: 2. About what time did this (most recent) incident
happen?
1. ☐ Don't know
2. ☐ During the day (6:00 A.M. to 6 P.M.)
3. ☐ 6:00 P.M. to midnight
4. ☐ Midnight to 6:00 A.M.
5. ☐ Don't know

Problem: Noncomparable categories of time provide too broad a
category for daytime which could be subdivided to
6:00 A.M. to noon and noon to 6:00 P.M.

Question: 11b. How old would you say the person (offender) was?
1. ☐ Under 12
2. ☐ 12–14
3. ☐ 15–17
4. ☐ 18–20
5. ☐ 21 or over
6. ☐ Don't know

Problem: Category 5, "21 or over," is too broad and should be
subdivided.

In asking opinion questions, *do not assume that the respondents have all
the information necessary to make a meaningful or informed decision.* For
instance, a researcher could ask, "Do you support the current interpretation
of the Miranda decision?" Perhaps 60 percent of the respondents may say
"yes," however, not having asked the respondents if they had any idea what
the Miranda decision was, it may turn out that 90 percent of the subjects did
not know what it was but were too embarrassed to say so.

Pretest

Although formulation of dummy tables and a variables list and adherence
to general points discussed so far will assist the researcher in the development

Pretest

of a potentially useful instrument, prior to using the questionnaire with target respondents a pretest of the instrument is a must. A **pretest** is a reconnaissance operation or exploratory testing of the instrument using subjects who are similar to the group to be studied. The pretest subjects are asked to critique the instrument, pointing out confusions or misunderstandings and perhaps suggesting more proper wording or issues to be explored.

Organization of the Questionnaire

The order of questions may influence the willingness of subjects to respond to the survey. A common error in surveys is to begin with the demographic items such as age, sex, and race. Although these questions are an important part of any survey, they also are routine and boring for most respondents. Such questions are better asked later or even last in the instrument (see Schuman and Presser, 1981). A good rule of thumb is "first impressions last." *A questionnaire is best begun with items that arouse interest and gain the respondent's attention.* The beginning of the survey is also not the appropriate place for sensitive items, as one would not ask a person he or she had just met extremely personal questions. The following illustrates what not to ask in the beginning of questionnaires:

> *A Guaranteed Low-Response Questionnaire*
> What is your name?
> How old are you?
> What is your sex?
> How much money do you earn?
> Do you cheat on your income tax?
> How is your sex life?
> When was the last time you committed a crime?

Perhaps for good measure one could throw in, "Do you still beat your spouse?" and "Do you walk to work or carry your lunch?"

The questions should be arranged in a logical sequence that is readable, interesting, and easy to respond to. In mail surveys, open-ended questions should be kept to a minimum.

Mail Surveys

Most readers of this book are probably already familiar with the properties of mail questionnaires because it is becoming a common cultural phenomenon in North America and other developed countries to participate in such surveys. The most common type of **mail survey** is the self-administered, mail-back variety in which a return stamped and addressed envelope is enclosed.

Mail survey

The mail survey is a popular instrument for research because it promises, at a minimum of time and expense, to deliver fairly wide coverage for a study. The subjects that creative researchers have studied have been as diverse as victimization (Koenig et al., 1983), international crime rates (Archer and Gartner, 1984), public ratings of crime seriousness (Cullen, 1983), and even self-admissions of criminality (Wallerstein and Wyle, 1947), to mention a few. Perhaps this asset of the mail questionnaire has made it the favorite instrument of a variety of organizations selling products, soliciting opinions, collecting charitable donations, and those attempting to conduct social, scientific, or criminal justice research. In the seventies a special conference of the American Statistical Association addressed itself to the growing concern of nonresponse in such surveys. It appeared as if the potential respondents were becoming overburdened. In the mid-1960s, large private research organizations could expect roughly a 75 percent response rate in mail surveys; by the mid-1970s this figure had dropped to 60–65 percent. This is assuming even a number of follow-up inquiries to solicit participation (American Statistical Association, 1974).

In *The Phantom Respondent,* John Brehm (1993) notes some alarming trends about the growing nonresponse problem in polls and surveys such as the National Election Studies, (NES) based at the University of Michigan and the General Social Survey (GSS) at the University of Chicago. The former is done every federal election year since 1954 and the latter every year since 1972 (Morin, 1993). While the NES averaged nonresponse of less than 10 percent in the 1950s, by the 1990s it had the same 20 to 30 percent nonresponse as the GSS. The major media polls have 30–50 percent nonresponse (ibid.). The key question is whether the nonrespondents differ significantly from respondents, and the answer is: yes. Overrepresented in surveys are the elderly, blacks, women, the poor, and the less educated. Men, young people, whites, and the wealthy are underrepresented.

Those considering using mail surveys as their means of data collection should consider the fact that they are competitors for the time of respondents who are becoming increasingly more difficult to interest in participating. A prudent researcher should, prior to deciding to employ mail surveys, carefully consider the relative advantages and disadvantages as well as alternative data-gathering strategies that might make it unnecessary to collect new data. The definitive source on mail survey and related survey research is the journal *Public Opinion Quarterly,* a publication of the American Public Opinion Association, an organization that sets standards in the field and to which most reputable private research organizations belong. One practice of such organizations, for instance, is a 5 percent verification check on surveyed subjects to assure accuracy of data; that is, 5 percent of those already questioned are questioned again to certify their responses.

Although the problems and prospects raised by a particular survey vary from study to study, a presentation on general disadvantages and advantages of mail surveys may help one decide whether it is the appropriate data-gathering method for a study.

Advantages of Mail Surveys

As previously suggested, one important attractive feature of mail surveys is that they *afford wide geographical and perhaps more representative samples at a reasonable cost, effort, and time.* Compared with the personal interview (discussed in Chapter 6), the mail survey *requires no field staff,* thus eliminating transportation and other costs. By the same token, it *eliminates interviewer bias effects,* because there are no interviewers. Surveys by mail may tend to *afford the respondents greater privacy* as well as an opportunity to think out their responses, leading to *more considered answers.* This is particularly the case for a survey attempting to obtain detailed information that may require checking records, files, historical documents, and the like. For example, in a survey of presidents of professions related to rehabilitation, this author asked questions such as the following (Hagan, 1975):

Question: What was the average budget of your organization from 1970 through 1973? (If it would be easier, you may wish to supply the information yearly.)

Average Income _____

Average Expenditures _____

Total Assets _____

Net Assets _____

Optional: 1970 1971 1972 1973

Question: Below are a series of events that are believed relevant by some writers in the field to the history of the development of occupations and their professional associations. Please supply estimates and answers.

Event	*Estimated Date*	*Comments (For instance, where, if applicable?)*
1. At what time did work in your field emerge as a full-time occupation?	_____	_____
2. When was the first training school established?	_____	_____
3. When was the first state licensing law in your field established (if any)?	_____	_____
4. When was the first formal professional "code of ethics" adopted?	_____	_____

Obviously, such questions are most appropriately asked in a mail survey, which enables the respondent to devote adequate time to look things up, rather than in an on-the-spot interview.

Disadvantages of Mail Surveys

The chief problem with many mail surveys is *nonresponse.* Inexperienced researchers without sponsorship may be fortunate to obtain a 20 percent rate in first-wave mailings, that is, a one-time-only survey without follow-up (Miller, 1991, p. 77). Even with fairly high rates of return, the researcher is still faced with the problem of *possible differences between respondents and nonrespondents* with respect to the issue being investigated. Other potential problems may exist with respect to a *lack of uniformity in response, slowness of response to follow-up attempts, the possibility that a number of respondents may misinterpret the questions, and escalating costs if several follow-ups are required.* Although these and other problems create difficulties, they are by no means insurmountable, as demonstrated later in this chapter. Still, these disadvantages must be seriously considered by the researcher and addressed in some fashion by means of planning, prior to the first canvass.

Ways of Eliminating Disadvantages in Mail Surveys

An entire arsenal of techniques is at the disposal of the clever researcher to attempt to outmaneuver many of the problematic elements of the mail survey. The nonresponse problem can be broken down into two groups, those who have yet to respond and those who refuse to cooperate in the survey. It is standard practice in research, unlike encyclopedia sales, to honor a potential subject's right to refuse to participate in a study. So long as this rate is small, less than 1 percent for instance, it is an expected loss in surveys. Further pleas to the respondent to participate, such as "We do hope you will reconsider," stretch a delicate boundary and may be conceived as harassment on the part of the respondent. If high refusal rates are expected, a far better strategy is oversampling to create a replacement pool. Although this introduces some potential error in that the replacement subjects may not match the subjects they replace, at least the study can continue with a filled sampling frame. The researcher must acknowledge this potential source of error.

Ways of increasing responses in mail surveys

Some **ways of increasing responses in mail surveys** include, but are not limited to, the following:

Follow-up	Endorsements
Offering remuneration	Personalization
Altruistic appeals	Shortened format

Use of attractive format   Good timing
Sponsorship

Follow-up

The use of techniques to increase response in surveys is limited only by the imagination and perhaps the time and finances of the researcher. Of major importance in most surveys is the *follow-up* with respondents. Continued efforts to solicit response may include renewed mailing(s) of the original questionnaire, mailings of shortened versions of the instrument, postcards, telephone calls, interviews, telegrams, mailgrams, and their combinations (Heberlein and Baumgartner, 1978). Some researchers mail a "reminder/ thank you" postcard three days after the initial mailing to encourage response. An interesting procedure sometimes followed is enclosure of an identifying postcard with an anonymous survey form so that the respondents can, at the time they return the form, register that they have responded and should not receive further reminders (Dillman, 1972, 1976). In general, special delivery and certified delivery are superior to first-class mail which, in return, is superior to second- and third-class mail. Certified mail can yield a return receipt verifying delivery. If first-class letters are marked "address correction requested," postal authorities will notify the sender of the filed forwarding address to which the letter has been redirected.

A common practice for determining proper timing for the follow-up is illustrated by a hypothetical study (Figure 5.3).

Beginning on June 1, 1,000 residents of Millvale were mailed questionnaires. Returns began to arrive on June 4. The daily number of returns peaked on June 16. By June 23 the replies, encouraged by the second mailing (or first follow-up), began to arrive and peaked around July 15. At that time a second follow-up was undertaken, the results of which tailed off in late August, when a third request was mailed to respondents. The third followup had little impact on encouraging more responses and, because the

Follow-up

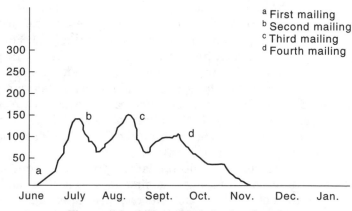

ᵃ First mailing
ᵇ Second mailing
ᶜ Third mailing
ᵈ Fourth mailing

Figure 5.3   Millvale Victimization Survey.

end of the targeted period for data gathering was nearing, no further follow-up probes were assumed necessary.

Offering Remuneration

Offering
remuneration

Offering remuneration involves offering rewards or incentives to survey participants. It may, depending on subject and type of respondents, increase response. Some researchers actually enclose, rather than just promise, payment on the assumption that people will feel guilty about keeping the money and not answering the survey. A variation of inducement is the offer to share a summary or copy of the report with interested respondents. A word of caution—financial offerings may be out of order with some subjects; for example, a one-dollar offer might insult wealthy or influential subjects, or an offer of coupons for free chocolate bars would be in poor taste in a survey dealing with hunger and starvation. In the latter instance, *altruistic appeals* to the respondents' concern for science and humanity would be more effective.

Attractive Format

Attractive
format

An *attractive format* for the instrument may impress on the respondent the important nature of the study. Although cost limitations may determine the ultimate *appearance of a questionnaire,* a ditto reproduction is less desirable than a mimeograph, which again is inferior to a lithograph or a good print job. Other possibilities include colored paper and print, photographs, illustrations, and booklets. Anything that can attract interest in the survey may enhance response.

Sponsorship and Endorsements

Sponsorship/
endorsements

Sponsorship and *endorsements* are excellent means of enhancing the potential prestige and legitimacy of the survey in the eyes of respondents. Generally, *the greater the public visibility and reputation of the organization sponsoring or conducting the survey, the greater the potential response.* Unattached researchers or students generally can expect poorer response than known persons or organizations in the field. For students, letters from professors bearing the college insignia and urging response would be more effective than the student's own cover letter. *Endorsement cover letters from prominent individuals,* for example, presidents of national organizations of which the respondents are members, may increase response. A survey of police officers may yield better response if the questionnaire is accompanied by letters urging response from the Chief of Police and the president of the local Fraternal Order of Police.

In a mail survey of the 100 largest police departments in the United States regarding police undercover practices, Hamilton and Smykla (1994) were able to achieve an 87 percent response rate. This high response may have been achieved in part due to the fact that the cover letter came from the

New York Attorney General's Office and one of the authors was a known practitioner in the law enforcement community.

Personalization

Personalization

Personalization of survey instruments is the attempt to make less impersonal the appearance of the survey package or follow-up probes. Because all good mail surveys should contain preaddressed, stamped return envelopes, some feel the attachment of colorful commemorative stamps to the envelopes adds more personalization than bureaucratic and impersonal postage meters. Better yet, commemorative stamps that deal with topics related to the subject matter of the survey may call additional attention to the survey. A criminal justice survey featuring a stamp with Justinia, the blind goddess of justice, would certainly be eyecatching. More research needs to be undertaken in this regard, however, for Heberlein and Baumgartner (1978) found the highest response rates for government-sponsored studies in which a franked or metered postage was used. This was apparently assumed to lend an "official" air to the project.

A handwritten "P.S." on the cover letter urging response has been claimed to increase response, as does personalization of the cover letter by use of the respondent's name (Dillman and Frey, 1974). In one survey of presidents of national professional associations, this writer stumbled upon a gimmick which, although prohibitive in larger surveys, ensured a last-resort response from a few remaining important respondents. After four unsuccessful follow-up probes that included requesting professionals from these fields to look them up at national conventions and urge response, a personal touch worked. A visit to a local museum of art yielded some occasional cards that featured a colorful reproduction of a famous masterpiece. Through sheer luck the campus post office was selling commemorative stamps with famous paintings, one of which matched the cards. The combined visual impact, along with a handwritten final request for participation on the card, elicited cooperation (Hagan, 1975).

Shortened Format

Shortened format

Shortened format of follow-up instruments may encourage response from those who were previously hesitant because of the length of the original instrument. Although a "reminder/thank you" postcard sent a few days after an initial mailing is likely to result in a higher response rate, a last-resort postcard featuring the minimum essential questions will at least salvage information on key items, as well as give some reading of how a group that would have been nonrespondents differs from respondents. In a review of the literature on methods of improving response rates in mail surveys, Heberlein and Baumgartner (1978) claim that longer survey forms were perceived as more important than shorter forms, and, all other things being equal, were associated with greater response.

Good Timing

Good timing for survey mailing includes avoiding competitive seasons or other historical events that may impede response. Vacation periods should be avoided. Household questionnaires should arrive near the end of the week, whereas business surveys are likely to fare better at the beginning of the week. Other gimmicks have been developed by imaginative researchers. *The Public Opinion Quarterly* is an excellent source of such "trade secrets."

Despite valiant efforts, because of time, cost, and other factors most surveys do not expect 100 percent response rates. One way to assess the impact of nonresponse bias on results is to compare characteristics of the survey respondents with known characteristics of the general population. For instance, even though we may have a 60 percent response rate and no way of knowing for sure how the 40 percent nonrespondents differ from those cooperating in the survey, knowledge that the respondents were representative of the population with respect to age, sex, race, income, and other key characteristics may give us greater confidence in these findings. Table 5.2 illustrates a comparison of the proportional distribution of sample survey respondents as compared with the general population from which they were drawn. The basic conclusion suggests representativeness at least by region (Hagan, Haug, and Sussman, 1975, p. 8).

In a survey of victims in which only 125 of 450 questionnaires were returned and the prosecutor's office prohibited follow-up mailings to victims, the researchers (Erez and Tontodonato, 1992) assessed the representativeness of the sample by comparing respondents with nonrespondents, finding that the former were more serious cases but were similar on other relevant variables.

In an imaginative combination of research strategies Sigler and Johnson (1986), studying a sample of the general population of Tuscaloosa, Alabama,

TABLE 5.2 Comparison of Survey Data and Population Data by School RSA Region

Region	Survey %	Population %
I	6.3	5.3
II	11.2	13.8
III	15.4	13.8
IV	18.0	17.1
V	18.8	20.1
VI	8.3	8.3
VII	5.1	5.5
VIII	3.8	3.1
IX	10.4	10.5
X	2.4	2.6
Total	99.9	99.9
N	791	1,241

Source: Hagan, Frank E., Marie R. Haug, and Marvin B. Sussman. *Comparative Profiles of the Rehabilitation Counseling Graduate: 1965 and 1972.* 2d series, Working Paper No. 5. Cleveland: Case Western Reverse University, Institute on the Family and the Bureaucratic Society, 1975, p. 8.

first sent a postcard to households indicating that they had been selected for study. Then three days later, Johnson personally delivered the self-administered questionnaire by hand to each adult in residence and arranged a time for retrieval. Of 300 delivered to 170 households, 174 were retrieved with 30 refusals, netting 144 usable questionnaires.

Self-Reported Measures of Crime

Self-reports   **Self-report surveys** are data-gathering methods which involve asking respondents to admit to various behavior. In an attempt to overcome some of the inadequacies of official measurements of crime, such as the Uniform Crime Reports discussed in Chapter 4, criminologists have developed surveys in which subjects are asked to admit to the commission of various crimes and deviant acts, particularly delinquent ones. Nettler (1978, pp. 97–113) provides an excellent review of such studies which he breaks down into the following types:

> Anonymous questionnaires
> Anonymous questionnaires in which respondent is identifiable and
>   response can be validated by later interviews or police records
> Signed questionnaires validated against police records
> Anonymous questionnaires identified by number and validated by fol-
>   lowup interviews and threat of polygraph (lie-detector test)
> Interviews
> Interviews validated against official records

In addition to those indicated by Nettler, other researchers have employed peers (Gold, 1966) and detached workers (Short and Strodtbeck, 1965) as informants.

Most self-report surveys have been conducted in the United States with the primary subjects being either schoolchildren, high school students or college students (Hood and Sparks, 1971, p. 19; Glaser, 1978, p. 72). Such studies have not been limited, however, to youths. In an early study by Wallerstein and Wyle (1947) of adults from all walks of life using a mailed self-report method, 99 percent of the respondents admitted that they had committed at least one offense. In another early study, Porterfield (1946) found a similar rate of admitted delinquency among Texas college students as existed among officially processed delinquents.

In a unique study, Greenwood and Abrahamse (1982) studied 2,000 inmates' self-reports of past conduct and utilized these data to construct a parole prediction scale. Previous parole prediction scales had been based entirely on objective records and other criteria. Studies of crime admissions by incarcerated ex-addicts (Inciardi, 1979) and career offense admissions (Petersilia, Greenwood, and Lavin, 1977) have been useful in complementing official statistics. Adult populations have been studied, through self-reports, by Tittle and Villemez (1977), who sampled adults in three states, and by O'Donnell et al. (1976), who conducted a nationwide survey of drug use.

Major recent self-report surveys using national probability samples include work by Gold (Gold and Reimer, 1974); the "Youth in Transition" studies of Bachman and associates (Bachman, O'Malley, and Johnston, 1978); and the "Monitoring the Future" surveys which involve an annual survey of high school seniors (Bachman, 1987; and Osgood et al., 1989). The

National Youth Survey best known of these recent self-report surveys is the *National Youth Survey* (NYS). The NYS included a multicohort design, a national probability sample of youth born in the period from 1959 to 1965. The survey began with 11–17-year-olds in 1976, and it followed up with four consecutive surveys of the same group plus a sixth one in 1984 (Jackson, 1990, pp. 39–40).

The NYS was found to yield valid and reliable data, indicating delinquency/ crime levels much higher than in the National Crime Survey (victim surveys) or in UCR (Huizinga and Elliot, 1984). Table 5.3 illustrates an example of the National Youth Survey self-report instrument.

A particularly innovative research program sponsored by the National Institute of Justice is the Drug Use Forecasting Program (DUF). This program will be described in detail in Chapter 9 as an illustration of validation of self-reports. Basically, arrestees are asked questions regarding their drug use behavior and are then asked to provide urine specimens which can be tested for drug use. Such a program provides an ingenious way for estimating drug usage among criminal populations; it also provides a barometer on the impact of various policies on drug use.

Some Problems with Self-Report Surveys

Nettler (1978, p. 107) states the matter succinctly by pointing out that "asking people questions about their behavior is a poor way of observing it." In specifying difficulties in the accuracy of self-reports on other types of behavior such as voting and medical treatment (LaPiere, 1934; Deutscher, 1966; Levine, 1976), critics wonder why we should expect respondents to be

Problems with self-report surveys accurate and honest in admitting deviant behavior. The **major problems with self-report surveys** relate to inaccurate reporting, use of poor or inconsistent instruments, deficient research designs, and poor choice of settings or study subjects (Nettler, 1978, p. 107).

Hood and Sparks describe how American studies of self-reported crime include items that may not be regarded as delinquent.

> In most studies of schoolchildren in the United States (where the definition of "delinquency" is extremely wide and not, as in Europe, a synonym for crime committed by the young), the lists of offences include such items as "had fist fight with one person," "defied parent's authority," "taken things you didn't want," "hurt someone to see them squirm" (Short and Nye), "took things that belonged to others" (Slocum and Stone), "took articles less than $2," "defying people other than parents" (Empey and Erickson). Without a detailed

TABLE 5.3 Self-Reported Delinquency and Drug-Use Items as Employed in the National Youth Survey

How many times in the last year have you

1. *purposely damaged or destroyed property belonging to your parents or* other family *members.*
2. purposely damaged or destroyed property belonging to a *school.*
3. purposely damaged or destroyed *other property* that did not belong to you (not counting family or school property).
4. stolen (or tried to steal) a *motor vehicle,* such as a car or motorcycle.
5. stolen (or tried to steal) something worth more than $50.
6. knowingly bought, sold, or held stolen goods (or tried to do any of these things).
7. Thrown objects (such as rocks, snowballs, or bottles) at cars or people.
8. run away from home.
9. lied about your age to gain entrance or to purchase something; for example, lying about your age to buy liquor or get into a movie.
10. carried a hidden weapon other than a plain pocket knife.
11. stolen (or tried to steal) things worth $5 or less.
12. attacked someone with the idea of seriously hurting or killing/him.
13. been paid for having sexual relations with someone.
14. had sexual intercourse with a person of the opposite sex other than your wife/husband.
15. been involved in gang fights.
16. sold marijuana or hashish ("pot," "grass," "hash").
17. cheated on school tests.
18. hitchhiked where it was illegal to do so.
19. stolen money or other things from *your parents* or *other members of your family.*
20. hit (or threatened to hit) a *teacher* or other adult at school.
21. hit (or threatened to hit) one of your *parents.*
22. hit (or threatened to hit) other *students.*
23. been loud, rowdy, or unruly in a public place (disorderly conduct).
24. sold hard drugs, such as heroin, cocaine, and LSD.
25. taken a vehicle for a ride (drive) without the owner's permission.
26. bought or provided liquor for a minor.
27. had (or tried to have) sexual relations with someone against their will.
28. used force (strong-arm methods) to get money or things from other *students.*
29. used force (strong-arm methods) to get money or things from a *teacher* or other adult at school.
30. used force (strong-arm methods) to get money or things from *other people* (not students or teachers).
31. avoided paying for such things as movies, bus or subway rides, and food.
32. been drunk in a public place.
33. stolen (or tried to steal) things worth between $5 and $50.
34. stolen (or tried to steal) something at school, such as someone's coat from a classroom, locker, or cafeteria, or a book from the library.
35. broken into a building or vehicle (or tried to break in) to steal something or just to look around.
36. begged for money or things from strangers.
37. skipped classes without an excuse.
38. failed to return extra change that a cashier gave you by mistake.
39. been suspended from school.
40. made obscene telephone calls, such as calling someone and saying dirty things.

How often in the past year have you used

41. alcoholic beverages (beer, wine and hard liquor).
42. marijuana or hashish ("grass," "pot," "hash").
43. hallucinogens ("LSD," "Mescaline," "Peyote," "Acid").
44. amphetamines ("Uppers," "Speed," "Whites").
45. barbiturates ("Downers," "Reds").
46. heroin ("Horse," "Smack").
47. cocaine ("Coke")

Source: Elliot, Delbert S., and Suzanne S. Ageton. "Reconciling Race and Class Differences in Self-reported and Official Estimates of Delinquency." *American Sociological Review* 45 (February 1980): 108-109. Reproduced by permission.

investigation of the situations in which such acts took place—who was the "victim" and what was the relationship between the respondent and victim— it is difficult to know whether these actions can properly be classified as delinquent (Hood and Sparks, 1971, p. 65).

The often small and nonrepresentative nature of some of the samples used may limit their generalizability. Many samples, for example, had poor representation of blacks. In addition to possible difficulties presented by the lack of complete anonymity in some surveys, self-report studies may be subject to lying, poor memory, and telescoping, or the moving of past incidents into the time frame being studied (Elliott and Ageton, 1980, p. 96). Many studies fail to provide a time reference during which the claimed offenses were to have taken place.

Until recently, self-report surveys have been plagued by lack of replication and overreliance on one-shot case studies often of atypical populations. They had not been conducted in a standardized fashion; often as many different instruments as studies were employed with little comparability of settings or populations (see Brantingham and Brantingham, 1984, pp. 60–61).

Strengths of Self-Report Surveys

Strengths of self-report surveys

Despite the preceding criticisms, an impressive body of research has accumulated that highlights the **strengths of self-report surveys.** Both the validity and the reliability of this method and utilization of the method have steadily improved.

Reliability

Nettler (1978, pp. 108–109) reviewed a number of measures of reliability in self-report surveys. Hirschi (1969, p. 56) found only moderate correlations in admissions of the six kinds of crimes he measured. Clark and Tifft (1966) found about an 82 percent reliability for subjects who were retested regarding self-admissions when they were threatened with a lie detector the second time. Dentler and Monroe (1961) found a 96 percent concordance between first and second self-reporters, and Kulik et al. (1968) found a 98 percent agreement with little difference if the questionnaire is anonymous or signed.

Contrary evidence is provided by Farrington (1973). He had English boys respond to thirty-eight crimes listed on separate cards and place them into piles as to whether they did or did not commit these acts. On retest two years later, only 75 percent of the original crimes were readmitted and half of these were more serious crimes. Gertz and Talarico (1980) point out an important and often overlooked source of unreliability—clerical carelessness and coding error.

Validity

Validity of self-reports

The validity of self-report surveys rests on whether people tell the truth or can accurately recollect past crimes or incidents of deviant behavior. Some means of attempting to get at the *validity of such studies are:*

Validity checks using official or other data
Checks using other observers (peers)

Use or threat of polygraph
"Known group" approach
"Lie scales"
Measures of internal consistency
Recheck reports using interviews

Use of Other Data

Use of other
data

Self-report data can sometimes be checked against official police records, school records, and other sources or criteria. Nettler (1978, p. 111) correctly points out the paradox of the critics of official statistics using these same statistics to validate what is claimed to be a superior self-report instrument. Given our previous discussion of problems with official statistics, it is unclear what type of overall relationship would be desired.

A significant number of studies have been conducted employing *checks against official statistics.* Some of these have been discussed in part in our previous analysis of self-report surveys. In interviews with boys in Utah, Erickson and Empey (1963) found that a check of court records indicated that none of the boys lied about having been in court or failed to describe the offense. Voss (1963) found a strong relationship between admissions and official police records in his Hawaiian sample. Farrington (1973) also found agreement, concluding that self-reported delinquents were quite similar to official delinquents. Hirschi (1969) had mixed feelings, with general under-reporting among his sample. McCandless et al. (1972) found even a poorer matchup between admissions and police records. On the other hand, Hardt and Hardt (1977) found a strong correspondence between self-reported violations and police statistics; based on this correspondence as well as other checks they made on their data, they concluded that many of the conflicting reports in previous surveys may have resulted from the use of inadequate instruments. Hirschi (1969) also checked other records such as truancy reports and admitted school suspensions.

Use of Other Observers

Use of other
observers

Checks using other informants, peers, or people who might be able to speak to the respondents' behavior constitute yet another way of obtaining some validation. Gold (1966) interviewed associates of the respondent to check whether the person was either told about or observed the acts claimed by the respondent. Short and Strodtbeck (1965) used confirming reports of detached workers.

Use of Polygraph

Use of
polygraph

The use of, or threat of, polygraph validation was employed by Clark and Tifft (1966). They found less than 20 percent changed their initial responses when threatened with a "lie detector" test.

"Known-Group" Validation

Known-group validation

In **known-group validation** (Nye and Short, 1957; Voss, 1963) groups whose official transgressions are already a matter of record are studied and their self-admissions are compared to this same behavior. Hardt and Hardt (1977) used, as part of their sample, those who had been previously identified through official arrest statistics. They concluded that such groups yielded valid responses. Nye and Short, as well as Voss, found significant differences between "known delinquents" and others. Nettler points out that there is an essential problem in attempting to validate an instrument with a criterion, in this case official statistics, which itself is of questionable validity. As a possible explanation, Hardt and Hardt (1977) found that the majority of boys ranking high on the self-report scale did not have an official police record. Comparing initial with later responses, however, they found that most respondents changed something, and most of these changes were in the direction of admitting more deviance. Although minor offenses like truancy and stealing tended to be underreported, major offenses like violence and sex offenses were overreported. The greatest inaccuracy was found among items replicated from Short and Nye (1958) and Dentler and Monroe (1961).

Use of Lie Scales

Lie scales

Another useful tool for checking the validity of responses is the employment of **lie scales** or "truth scales," a series of questions that measure truthfulness of respondents in answering a survey. Previously, we discussed the tendency of respondents in experiments and surveys to be agreeable or to give the researcher what they think is desired. "Lie scales" attempt to assess this, usually by asking the respondents to admit to a type of behavior that—it is assumed—no one person would have performed or by trying to crossup the respondents by having them give inconsistent responses. Some other procedures involve having the respondent deny behavior that—it is reasonably assumed—everyone would perform. Such questions are usually weaved among other attitudinal questions in the survey. Figure 5.4 gives typical "lie scales" based in part on those used by Hardt and Hardt (1977) and Gross (1962).

In scoring "lie scales," researchers set a limit for the number of "incorrect" answers to questions they are willing to tolerate before questioning the truthfulness of the respondent and thus calling into question all other

---

1. I always tell the truth.
2. Sometimes I tell lies.
3. Once in a while I get angry.
4. I never feel sad.
5. Sometimes I do things I am not supposed to do.
6. I have never taken anything that did not belong to me.
7. I have never kept anyone waiting for an appointment.

Figure 5.4 Examples of a Lie Scale.

responses of that individual. These cases would be dropped from the analysis. Such procedures are quite commonly used in standard personality inventories such as the Minnesota Multiphasic Inventory.

Measures of Internal Consistency

Internal consistency

Related to "lie scales" is the measurement of the **internal consistency** of an individual's response by using interlocking items. This involves the repetition of similar items, sometimes expressing them first in a positive and then a negative manner. For example, one might say, "I always tell the truth," and then later in the survey say, "I never tell a lie." Hardt and Hardt (1977) in their self-report survey asked first whether the respondent had ever been warned or questioned by police, and later whether the subject had ever been arrested or ticketed by the police. It was assumed that a positive response to the latter would require a positive answer to the former question; if not, the subject's responses were considered inconsistent. In combination with the "lie scale" this measure of inconsistency was used as the means of discarding questionable respondents. The use of reversals, stating some of the questions in a negative manner, is a means of checking response sets. The latter refers to the tendency of subjects to answer all of the items, often without reading many of them, on the basis of their answers to the initial questions. That is, if the respondents strongly agreed with the first few items, then they might simply check off this same response for the remainder. This is also a partial check on socially desirable response patterns (Edwards, 1957).

Use of Interviews

Reinterviews

Subsequent interviewing of subjects permits probing regarding the details and context of the acts. For example, claims of the respondent can be questioned and the criminal intent of the acts can be established (Hood and Sparks, 1971, p. 68). Primary disadvantages of this approach are that anonymity of subjects is lost (Gold, 1966) and there may be a tendency for concealment of offenses depending on the characteristics of the interviewer (Coleman, 1961, pp. 16–17).

Various sources of error in self-report surveys have been presented previously. Although some researchers have become so disillusioned with these errors in self-report surveys that they at times have called for their abandonment (Dentler and Monroe, 1961), others suggest that the problem is not with the method itself but with the particular scales employed (Clark and Tifft, 1966), as well as the lack of carefully employed validity checks.

Although self-report surveys have their limitations, they do provide another measure of criminality in addition to official statistics. Particularly when combined with victim surveys, they offer another means of assessing unreported crime. Chilton (1993, pp. 6–7) even suggests that it might be time for criminologists to propose the creation of a National Self Report Survey. Such a representative survey would most likely face serious political and methodological problems, but would certainly give us a broader picture of crime. Requests for such serious data are almost certain to be "inconvenient for someone's party position on crime and its causes" (ibid., p. 8).

Summary

Sampling involves scientifically selecting a microcosm of a larger population to which one wishes to infer, usually at great savings in time and cost. There are two major types of sampling: probability samples and nonprobability samples. In probability samples, which consist of simple random, stratified, cluster, and systematic samples, an equal probability of selection method (EPSEM) is employed. Each type has relative advantages or disadvantages over the others that must be considered prior to the decision to employ one. Nonprobability samples do not make use of an EPSEM procedure, and thus make hazardous the employment of statistical techniques that assume this. They also make problematic any generalization to the larger population from which the sample was drawn. The major types of nonprobability samples are quota, accidental, purposive, and snowball. Even though these do not employ EPSEM procedures, careful use of nonprobability samples can be an effective tool in gaining information regarding larger populations. Because of its increasing use as a data-gathering strategy in criminal justice, survey research is presented in two chapters in this text. This chapter concentrated on sampling, mail questionnaires, and questionnaire construction, as well as self-report surveys of crime. Chapter 6 will cover major interviewing procedures.

Focus groups are purposively selected groups brought together to measure reactions to some stimuli. *Criminal profiling* is an attempt to construct typical characteristics of certain types of criminals.

It is most important to remember that surveys, for the most part, measure respondent attitude and not behavior.

Characteristics and qualities of mail surveys have been described in detail because many of their features are similar to those of other data-gathering strategies in criminal justice survey research. The chief disadvantages of the mail survey include nonresponse, unpredictable uniformity in response, slow replies, possible misinterpretation of questions, and costly follow-up. To be weighed against these are the many advantages of mail surveys, including wide geographical coverage with a minimum of time, minimal cost and effort, no field staff required, no interviewer bias, greater privacy, and the opportunity for more considered replies.

Some possible ways of reducing nonresponse in mail surveys are followup, payment or altruistic appeals, attractive format, sponsorship, endorsements, personalization, shortened format, and good timing.

Some guidelines exist for questionnaire construction. First, there should be a clear notion of what is to be measured and a certainty that the instrument can address this. The use of variables lists and dummy tables are intermediary steps. Among the suggestions discussed were the use of language appropriate to respondents; clear specification of respondents; avoidance of biased, leading, or objectionable questions; and the types of questions to use. A pretest, or trial run, of the instrument is an absolute necessity. The questionnaire should begin with the most interesting questions; biographical items should appear later or last.

Self-report surveys involve asking, usually anonymous respondents, to admit to a variety of offenses they had committed in the past. Keeping in mind our early injunction that reported behavior does not necessarily equal actual behavior, these surveys have been criticized for inaccurate reporting, poor use of instruments and research designs, and inadequate settings or study subjects. Despite these shortcomings, defenders of the technique have demonstrated accuracy and reliability by employing known-group comparisons and record checks, as well as "lie scales" and other methodological devices. Certainly, self-report surveys present the criminal justice researcher with another tool with which to measure crime.

Key Concepts

Sampling	Purposive Sample	Ways of Increasing
Sampling Frame	Focus Groups	Response in Mail
Probability Samples	Criminal Profiling	Surveys
Simple Random Sample	Snowball Sample	Self-Report Surveys
Stratified Random	Guidelines for	Problems with Self
Sample	Questionnaire	Report Surveys
Proportionate Stratified	Construction	Strengths of Self-Report
Sample	Variables List	Surveys
Disproportionate	Dummy Tables	Known-Group Validation
Stratified Sample	Pretest	Lie Scales
Cluster Sample	Mail Surveys	Internal Consistency
Systematic Sample	Advantages/	
Multistage Sample	Disadvantages of Mail	
Quota Sample	Surveys	
Accidental Sample		

Review Questions

1. Discuss the various types of sampling and when it would be most appropriate to use each one.
2. For what is weighting used in disproportionate stratified sampling, and why would samples be disproportionately drawn in the first place?
3. What are some disadvantages of mail surveys? Discuss ways of eliminating them.
4. Suppose a student group planning on conducting a questionnaire survey discovered that you had taken a research course and asked you for some specific suggestions. What are some general recommendations that you would give?
5. What are some problems as well as benefits of self-report surveys as a data gathering strategy?

CHAPTER

6 | # Survey Research: Interviews and Telephone Surveys

Interviewing can refer to a variety of face-to-face situations in which the researcher orally solicits responses. These range from in-depth, lengthy interviews of one or a few subjects to fairly structured surveys of large groups. As with the other techniques of data gathering discussed, the advantages and disadvantages of interviewing as a means of obtaining information should be carefully considered along with other techniques before the decision is made to proceed.

Types of Interviews

Researchers use different terms to denote interviews. There are three basic forms:

Structured interviews
Unstructured interviews
Depth interviews

Although other types of interviews exist, such as the investigative interview used in journalism (Douglas, 1976) or the preliminary interview employed prior to a larger study, elements of these are contained in these three principal types.

Structured interviews

Structured interviews, sometimes called closed interview schedules, usually consist of check-off responses to questions that are either factual or to which most responses easily fit an expectable pattern.

Question: Compared with last year, what type of job do you feel the local police are performing in preventing crime in your neighborhood?

_____ Much better
_____ Somewhat better
_____ About the same
_____ Somewhat worse
_____ Much worse

Question: In which of the following income ranges did your combined family income fall this past year?

_____ Under $10,000
_____ $10,000–$20,000
_____ $20,001–$30,000
_____ $30,001–$40,000
_____ $40,001–$50,000
_____ Over $50,000

In structured interviews the interviewer should avoid soliciting additional comments but, when they occur, record them verbatim (Institute on the Family, 1974). The principal disadvantage of closed-ended questions is that they generally elicit only limited response patterns; their advantages are easy administration and data processing as will be seen later.

Unstructured interviews have many variations depending on the purpose. Sometimes referred to as focused, clinical, or nondirective interviews, they generally provide for open-ended responses to questions. That is, unlike the closed interviews, no predetermined response categories are provided. To use an example with which all of us have had experience, the structured interview is comparable to an objective educational test consisting of multiple-choice and true-and-false items, whereas the unstructured interview is similar to essay tests or tests in which a person is asked to define or explain the topics being tested. Examples of open-ended response questions are:

Question: Do you think the police are better or worse in preventing crime in your local neighborhood than last year? _____

_____

Question: Why do you feel this way? _____

_____

Question: If you were personally the victim of a crime since January 1 of this year, could you explain the circumstances surrounding this incident? _____

_____

In comparing the relative advantages and disadvantages of the unstructured questionnaire vis-à-vis the structured, the previous test question example is a useful touchstone for analogy purposes. The closed-ended items (for example, the analogy to true and false) are excellent for recording simple items in which likely categories of response can be predetermined. Such questions make codification and tabulation easy, but may not provide the depth and quality of response needed. Open-ended items may present a tabulation nightmare, but provide the qualitative detail and complexity of response that may be required, particularly if the subject of study is little known.

The **depth interview** is a more intensive and detailed interview, usually of fewer subjects than is the case in a standard survey, and is particularly useful in life histories or case studies. In a depth interview, the researcher has a general list of topics to be explored, but exercises great discretion and flexibility in the manner, timing, and direction of questioning. Such interviews are excellent for hypothesis-generating or exploratory research (Merton, Fiske, and Kendall, 1956).

Smykla (1987), with the approval of a state Department of Corrections, wrote to death row inmates and later, through further correspondence and visitation, requested from them names, addresses, and telephone numbers of family members. He was able to arrange interviews with forty family members and describe what he called their "distorted grief reactions." Classic examples of the use of depth interviews can be found in many case studies and oral histories (to be discussed in detail in the next chapter), such as Sutherland's *The Professional Thief* (1937), the result of in-depth interviews with a professional thief, or Laub's *Criminology in the Making* (1983), an oral history of American criminology based on interviews with leading criminologists. Cressey's *Other People's Money* (1953), which involved extensive interviews with 133 incarcerated embezzlers, also serves as an example.

Advantages of Interviews

One chief attraction of the interview is the opportunity it provides for personal *contact between the researcher and the subject.* Such a situation presents many possibilities. Because of the face-to-face relationship, interviews generally bring about a *higher response rate* than mail surveys. Being on the scene, the interviewer can *clear up any misunderstandings or confusions* the respondent may have in interpreting questions. Additionally, the interviewer can also *act as an observer,* and not only record verbal responses, but also make note of his or her own impressions regarding the respondents and their environment. For example, in a survey of rural elderly respondents one of the interviewers recorded the following impressions or observations (Hagan, 1972, p. 10):

> I spoke with two spinster sisters, one 80 and the other 84 years of age. The 80-year-old reads the Bible everyday and talked of the will of the Lord, saying that for everything that happens in the world there is a reason, and that God will take care of the ill. While she spoke, I noticed that the kitchen ceiling was patched with pieces of cardboard. I also learned that their roof leaks; the house is in need of general repairs; they have no house, fire or health insurance and the 84-year-old hasn't had teeth for years. Despite these poor circumstances, they were able to speak of God as something good and right.

Interviewers can also read questions to those with literacy problems and thus obtain a more representative sample.

Interviews provide an opportunity for the interviewer to make use of cards, charts, and other *audiovisual aids.* In asking individuals about their income, for instance, the researcher can hand the respondents a card with a list of income ranges and ask them to identify the range within which household income falls. Having greater flexibility, the interviewer can make return visits if necessary and pitch the language to the level of the respondent. Perhaps less deliberated responses reflect the respondents' true attitudes, and the nature of the interviewing process taps this. Unlike researchers who mail questionnaires, interviewers can determine the actual individual who is responding and can use *their discretion* as to the appropriate time at which to ask the more sensitive questions. With guarded or suspicious respondents, questions regarding income and the like can be saved for last,

Audiovisual aids

so as not to prematurely abort answers to the other questions; or such questions can be asked at a point in the interview when the subject appears most cooperative. Interviews are more flexible, may elicit more spontaneous responses, and can utilize more complex lines of questioning than is often possible in mail surveys.

Feminist researchers challenge what they call "malestream" (mainstream male) approaches to empirical criminal justice research (McDermott, 1992) for not incorporating feminist views. One researcher used in-depth interviews as a way of getting at women's experiences that are obscured in standard surveys (Stanko, 1990).

Disadvantages of Interviews

Disadvantages of interviews

Interviewer effect

Field interviews

Despite the many advantages of interviews they possess obvious problems. Some principal **disadvantages of field interviews** are that they may be very time consuming and costly. Although these problems can be offset in part by cluster sampling, covering widely dispersed households in person can be a problem. **Interviewer effect** or *bias* may be responsible for distorted results. Similarly, the *interviewer may make mistakes* in asking questions or recording information. Because of these problems the use of even a few interviewers requires supervision, training, and monitoring. In assigning and coordinating *field interviews,* the supervisor should be aware of the need for weekend and evening interviews to obtain representative responses. Interviewing becomes a particularly difficult strategy when attempting to obtain information from hard-to-reach populations, although by way of trade-offs respondents who do not own telephones can be reached.

Interviews may be problematic for respondents if factual data that must be looked up are requested. They are sometimes less convenient to the respondent and afford less anonymity than mail surveys. Perhaps the chief potential problems rest in the quality, integrity, and skill of the interviewers, factors that may be uneven in interview surveys.

Question wording in interviews can alter response. Exhibit 6.1 gives some examples from public opinion polls.

One must weigh these advantages and disadvantages of interviewing and compare them with those of other data-gathering strategies before deciding on the means of data collection.

Interviewing Aids and Variations

Although most standard interviews are recorded more or less on the spot by the interviewer, using either an interview schedule, a structured interview protocol, or, in the case of depth interviews, notes that can be reconstructed into finished form immediately after the interview, a variety of mechanical

EXHIBIT 6.1

Public Opinion Polls

Survey research organizations such as Gallup, Roper, and Yankelovich play a critical role in taking the pulse of the American public's opinion regarding public policy. In 1994, 27 percent of the American public named crime as the most important problem. Surprisingly, only 3 percent had done so the previous year. Even though the official crime rate had actually declined from the previous year, 58 percent of those surveyed said crime in their community had gotten worse in the past year and 73 percent said crime in the country had worsened (Morin, 1994c).

Often the very wording of survey questions can produce differing results. In 1992 the American Jewish Committee was shocked when a poll they had commissioned by the Roper organization discovered that about one-third of those polled felt it was possible that the Holocaust either never happened or they were not sure. The actual question asked was (Morin, 1994a):

As you know, the term Holocaust usually refers to the killing of millions of Jews in Nazi death camps during World War II. Does it seem possible or does it seem impossible to you that the Nazi extermination of the Jews never happened?

In April 1994 Roper simplified the question to read:

Does it seem possible to you that the Nazi extermination of the Jews never happened?

Only 1 percent said it was possible that it never happened and only 8 percent were unsure. In thirteen different polls the Holocaust doubters varied from 1 to 46 percent. Why? Question wording. The high group had questions that were ambiguous or even contained double negatives, as in our first example. When questioned specifically as to whether the Holocaust happened, 98 percent of the "doubters" changed their position and said it did happen (ibid.).

In one final example, Richard Morin (1994b), chief of polling for *The Washington Post*, points out how the wording of presidential approval questions produce skewed results. Most of the media polls such as *The Washington Post* and ABC News ask:

Do you approve or disapprove of the job that Bill Clinton is doing as President? Is that strongly or somewhat approve or disapprove?

The Washington Post tested whether a simpler response scale might produce a different response. They did a splitballot test in which half of the respondents were asked the old questions (above) and half were asked:

Do you strongly approve, somewhat approve, somewhat disapprove, or strongly disapprove of the job Bill Clinton is doing as President?

While the first version produced 58 percent favorable, 38 percent unfavorable and 4 percent no opinion, the second version yielded 62 percent approving, 32 percent disapproving, and 6 percent undecided. These illustrations clearly describe the critical importance of questionnaire construction and wording in not just measuring attitudes, but in some cases creating them.

Sources: Morin, Richard. "From Confusing Questions, Confusing Answers." *Washington Post National Weekly Edition.* 18–24 July 1994a p. 37; Morin, Richard. "Ask and You Might Deceive." *Washington Post National Weekly Edition.* 6–12 December 1994b, p. 37; and Morin, Richard. "When the Method Becomes the Message." *Washington Post National Weekly Edition.* 19–25 December 1994c, p. 33.

aids exist that lend even greater versatility and accuracy. In a small number of important interviews, *videotapes* may be used. With the decrease in cost and wider availability of these units their usage is likely to become more commonplace in the future.

The *recording of interviews by means of cassette tapes* releases interviewers from the task of taking on-the-spot notes and enables them to concentrate on conducting the interview. Dictaphone transcription enables verbatim reconstruction of interviews and, although it produces an enormous amount of material, presents the researcher with the raw material to digest after the fact, rather than at the time of the interview. To illustrate that data gathering is limited only by imagination, Albini (1971), in *The American Mafia: Genesis of a Legend,* reported great success with mail interviews using cassettes. To cut expenses, time, and travel in interviewing police officials, organized criminals, and experts on organized crime, he mailed his interview protocol—list of questions—along with blank cassettes and was able to secure interviews with individuals who otherwise would not have been interviewed. In an extension of the oral history technique, Mutchnick (1986) conducted a videotaped interview through public television of Sir Leon Radzinowicz, a prominent British criminologist.

Although we will discuss the brief, structured telephone interview survey, the telephone interview can be expanded under special circumstances by tape recording interviews (Bucher, Fritz, and Quarantelli, 1956). An inexpensive electronic patch can be purchased at any electronics store and easily attached to a telephone to permit verbatim cassette recording of interviews. Unless one is involved in secretive measurement, an issue to be discussed in detail in Chapters 7 and 12, it is standard procedure to ask, prior to beginning an interview, the respondent's permission to record. Obviously, problems are raised with respect to the assurance of anonymity and respondent candor. These problems can sometimes be circumvented by agreeing beforehand to shut off the recorder for more sensitive items that may be identified as "off-the-record."

Pictorials, photographs, and motion pictures have all been successfully utilized to enhance studies involving interviews (Selltiz et al., 1976, p. 274). For such sensitive items as income, respondents can be handed a card that contains income ranges and asked to specify the general range. Individuals can be asked to rank their preferences for various items listed on a card.

Randomized response technique

Another method for coping with resistance to sensitive questions is the **randomized response technique** (Liu and Chow, 1976; Tracy and Fox, 1981). The technique, originally developed by Warner (1965), basically uses indeterminate questions; that is, the actual question answered is known only to the respondent and is unknown by the researcher. The interviewer is blind or unaware of the actual question a respondent is answering. The randomized response technique (RRT) is rather complicated to explain, but basically it uses known probabilities in order to estimate unknown proportions. Neuman (1991, p. 237) provides an example of one variation:

Here is how RRT works. An interviewer gives the respondent two questions. One is threatening (e.g., "Do you use heroin?"), the other not threatening (e.g., "Were you born in September?"). A random method (e.g., toss of coin) is used to select the question to answer. The interviewer does not see which question was chosen but records the respondent's answer. The researcher uses knowledge about the probability of the random outcome and the frequency of the nonthreatening behavior to estimate the frequency of the sensitive behavior.

In Tracy and Fox's (1981) example, 100 married men are brought together in a room and each is asked to flip a coin. Next, they are asked to raise their hand if they either get a head on the coin or if they have abused their wives. If sixty hands are raised, we can assume ten wife abusers among those with heads on the coin, because fifty heads would be expected by chance. Additionally, ten of the fifty with tails would also be assumed to be abusers for a total of twenty estimated abusers. In an actual interview situation, a single respondent would be asked to respond to "anonymous" sensitive questions in the same manner. Despite some possible shortcomings, randomized response procedures have been found to yield more accurate results than direct questioning methods on sensitive items (Fox and Tracy, 1986). A variety of randomization procedures are employed. For example, Guerts, Andrus, and Reinmuth (1976) posed questions to subjects in pairs, one sensitive and one innocuous. The question answered is determined by a coin flip. They used the technique to analyze shoplifting, destruction, price altering, and other consumer violations. This technique has also been utilized to study abortion and fertility control, drug use, child abuse, drunk driving, sexual behavior, illegal gambling, and shoplifting (Klockars, 1982, p. 454).

General Procedures in Interviews

Much of this discussion on procedures in interviewing is applicable primarily to large, standardized field surveys; however, most of the specific suggestions have been derived from the experience of both survey research organizations and individual researchers and is appropriate advice even for individual projects.

Training and Orientation Session

For interview surveys, an adequate amount of time must be spent on training interviewers. These training sessions, which may last anywhere from a day to a week depending on the complexity of the study, should familiarize the interviewers with the organization carrying out the survey as well as the study's purposes. Details of the project should be provided to make the interviewers feel that they are an important part of the study and to prepare them to answer any questions regarding the intent of the survey. Hoinville, Jowell, et al. (1978, p. 117) indicate that an effective manner of impressing the importance of confidentiality of responses on interviewers is to ask them to sign a declaration of confidentiality promising not to disclose any information in their possession. Depending on the sampling plan, either a preliminary letter is mailed or a telephone call is made to schedule an appointment for the interview.

Although detailed policies are too lengthy for presentation for our purposes, some excellent sources exist (Institute on the Family, 1974; Survey Research Center, 1969; Converse and Schuman, 1974; Selltiz et al., 1976; Gordon, 1969).

Arranging the Interview

Interviewers conducting household surveys should not arrive too early or too late, generally no earlier than 10:00 A.M. or no later than 8:00 P.M. Surveyors should be furnished with, possess at all times, and present identification to avoid being taken for door-to-door salespersons. A prominently displayed name tag featuring the official project name and a picture of the interviewer is frequently useful. On arrival be sure that the proper person to be interviewed within the household is located. At this point the interviewer should not ask if the respondent wishes to be interviewed now, but rather matter-of-factly indicate that the respondent had received a letter about the survey and that the interviewer is there to conduct it.

If the interviewer is unsuccessful in scheduling a meeting with the respondent, he or she should keep written track of callbacks and avoid recalls on the same days or same times.

Demeanor of Interviewer

Advice to interviewers can be as simple as beware of dogs, carry change for telephones in case of emergency, and dress appropriately for audience and weather (Sanders, 1976, p. 273). Where possible, the field surveyors should match, as closely as possible, the subjects with respect to age, sex, race, social class, and dress. Attire should be comfortable, but the interviewer should be neither overdressed nor underdressed for the occasion. Interviewers should have experienced a few practice interviews beforehand so that they become familiar with the flow of the instrument to be employed. The interviewer's language style should also be adapted to the group being studied .

In addition to assuring the respondents that their responses will be held in strictest confidence, the interviewer should attempt to build up rapport with the subjects by being friendly and diplomatic, as well as convincing, regarding the importance of the study. The interviewer should attempt to give the impression that the interview will be a pleasant, interesting, and rewarding experience (Payne, 1951). Casual conversation can be effective in building rapport with clients. The weather, children, appearance of the home or grounds, sports, and the like are useful topics. Interviewers should try to communicate an air of acceptance of respondents' statements, but must maintain their neutrality (Survey Research Center, 1969). In addition to being a sympathetic *diplomat,* the interviewer must be prepared to be a persistent *boor,* a person willing to ask the types of sensitive questions that generally are considered "nosey" in nature (Converse and Schuman, 1974).

Administration of the Structured Interview

In structured interviews, it is important for interviewers to become familiar with the flow of the questionnaire. The instrument should contain good transition statements that in a conversational style help the respondent to anticipate what comes next. It should be administered in an easy, informal, friendly manner to avoid the appearance of an inquisition. For this reason, at no time should the study be referred to as an investigation. The purpose of a structured questionnaire is to standardize the manner in which responses are obtained (Survey Research Center, 1969). Therefore, interviewers should be instructed not to reword or change in any way the questions.

Although procedures may vary depending on the nature and type of interview survey, in general, questions should be asked in the order listed on the questionnaire. If clarification is necessary, the interviewer should mark down and list such necessary comments on the questionnaire itself (Institute on the Family, 1974, p. 8).

If the person being interviewed resists answering sensitive questions, explain that the study is interested in a group picture of people of different incomes, ages, and backgrounds, and this information is important to the purposes of the study. In addition, the interviewer must assure the respondent that the information will be held in strictest confidence and no individuals will be identified in the final report.

Probing

Probing

Often the answer to a question does not provide enough information for the purposes of the study and it therefore becomes necessary for the interviewer to probe. **Probing** involves asking follow-up question(s) to focus, expand, clarify, or further explain the response given. The interviewer should be familiar with what response is needed to each question to know when a probe is necessary. Given the following hypothetical example, it is obvious that a probe is necessary:

Question: Do you think the police in this community are doing an adequate job in protecting the community?

Answer: Yeah, I guess so.

Probe: What do you mean by that? In what way?

Of possible assistance in the probe is the interviewer's informal mood and responsiveness to the answers provided by the respondent. The probe should not appear to be a cross-examination, but a natural extension of the interview. Conversation can be stimulated by frequent "uh-huh"'s and "I see"'s and by repetition of the respondent's answer while recording it. Occasional silence, although uncomfortable at times, may encourage more thoughtful and considered responses. Silence may also indicate, similar to police interrogations, that the interviewer is not going to accept that response. It is almost like saying "You are going to have to come up with something better or provide an improved explanation" (Sanders, 1976).

Most beginning interviewers have cold feet and fear hostile respondents. Such respondents are few; however, a problem can also be raised by the overly friendly respondent. Because the interviewer has imposed on the respondent's time and good will, a reasonably friendly socializing is usually required at the end of the session. What, however, of respondents who, during or after the interview, account in detail their life history, stories of the big war, or the perils of lumbago? If this occurs during the interview, some tolerance may be in order to permit the respondent a break from the demands of the interview schedule (Converse and Schuman, 1974). The digression can be reoriented by a polite interruption indicating that there is a question directly relating to that later. Demonstrating inattention such as putting down one's pencil or closing the interview schedule may also work. If the digression takes place after the interview, a polite excuse such as another appointment will usually work.

The Exit

As indicated, once the interview is completed the interviewer should carry on light conversation and be alert for any additional comments that the respondent may then offer. Such relevant remarks should be added to the interview notes as soon as possible after leaving the premises. Finally, the interviewer should thank the subjects for their time and hospitality and should clear up any concerns or doubts the respondent may have regarding the survey before leaving. Informal discussions after the interview can often lead to important "off-the-record" information. The interviewer can elicit such information by asking in an easy manner, "What do you think?" or "Is there anything else?" or similar open-ended questions.

Berg (1995, pp. 57–58) neatly summarizes some of the rules and advice for good interviewing in his ten commandments of interviewing:

1. Never begin an interview cold.
2. Remember your purpose.
3. Present a natural front.
4. Demonstrate aware hearing.
5. Think about appearance.
6. Interview in a comfortable place.
7. Don't be satisfied with monosyllabic answers.
8. Be respectful.
9. Practice, practice, and practice some more.
10. Be cordial and appreciative.

If you think about it, this constitutes pretty sound advice for a date, job interview, or life in general.

Recording the Interview

Although the actual mechanics of data tabulation will be examined in Chapter 11 under Data Management, a few customary interview procedures bear presentation. Interviewers should be instructed to write legibly, in pencil, as much of the relevant substance of the interview as possible. An inexpensive clipboard provides the necessary hard writing surface. The interviewer should distinguish personal observations from the actual interview by using parentheses. **Editing** entails reviewing the interview schedule after completion of the interview, and cleaning it up and preparing it for analysis. The completed interview schedule should be self-explanatory.

Editing the interview

The interviewer should have covered each item in the schedule. Unanswered questions should be marked NA for not applicable or simply X to indicate inappropriate. Where personal observations are included, it may help the coder (the person charged with assigning numerical values to the responses) if the interviewer cross-referenced any relevant items. For example, if an observation has an impact on understanding of another question, some notation such as (see Q. 10 for further explanation) would be in order.

The interviewer should attempt to record as much as possible during the interview. Because it is often impossible to record such information verbatim, the jotting down of key passages for later expansion is helpful. Interviewers should avoid summarizing or paraphrasing responses, but rather try to use the respondent's own words (Institute on the Family, 1974, p. 19). Paraphrasing requires interpretation and may change the color and gusto of the real remarks. The interviewer need not ask obvious questions such as the sex of the respondent. Personal observations can be added at any point they appear pertinent to an understanding of the response, for example: (the respondent appeared very fearful and shaken when relating this incident). Finally, the end-of-the-interview protocol should include an opportunity for the interviewer to discuss any other observations that may lead to a fuller understanding of the context of the interview.

Field interview designers should make use of the face-to-face nature of such encounters to employ audiovisual and other materials that make the interview more interesting, as well as aid in the data-gathering process, particularly for overcoming reluctance to answer sensitive questions.

If the research project can afford the luxury of two interviewers per respondent, then much of the difficulty of recording and conducting an interview can be split, with one interviewer asking the questions and the other concentrating solely on recording responses.

Telephone Surveys

Although the interview ensures a high response rate and possesses many distinct advantages, the cost, size of staff, and time required often make it prohibitive for many surveys. If use is made of the widespread ownership of telephones, however, certain advantages of interviews can be gained without the need for a large field staff and at a fraction of the cost.

Advantages and Prospects of Telephone Surveys

The advantages of telephone surveys include not only the *elimination of a field staff,* but *simpler monitoring of interviewer bias,* because the supervisor can be present at the time interviews are conducted by listening to the interviewers or listening in on calls. Thus, potential bias or patterns can be caught early and corrected. Although even lengthy interviews can be obtained through inexpensive electronic patches between telephone and tape recorder, the primary intent of telephone surveys is to obtain wide and representative samples. Such surveys are *inexpensive and quick, generally yield a low nonresponse rate, and provide easy and inexpensive follow-up.* The growing tendency of organizations to obtain WATS lines—flat rate charges that permit fairly unlimited long-distance calls—has made national telephone surveys more of an economic possibility.

Sudman suggests that phone surveys are more effective in obtaining hard-to-locate respondents than person-to-person interviews. The potential for high refusals can be circumvented, particularly if short "yes" or "no" answers are used (Sudman, 1980; Glasser and Metzger, 1972).

Disadvantages of Telephone Surveys

Telephone interviews may have *difficulty in obtaining in-depth responses* or considered answers over the telephone. There may be some loss of the qualitative detail provided by face-to-face interviews. In the past, a major objection to telephone surveys has been that they tended to *exclude* those who do not own telephones or who have unlisted or new telephone numbers. In some large metropolitan areas a considerable proportion of the numbers are unlisted. Also, high mobility in developed societies may add a large portion of new numbers, and the poor and transient may not own phones. Although household telephone ownership overall is estimated by the Census Bureau at approximately 92 percent, it is less than this for African American and minority groups. Ownership for Hispanics in areas of the Southwest is as low as 65 percent.

Additional, but not insurmountable, difficulties with telephone surveys include possible *high refusal rates.* This is related in part to problems in employing sensitive **screening questions.** These are initial queries made by the interviewer to determine whether the person who has answered the telephone fits the target population, for example, income and occupation.

Screening questions

Computers in Survey Research

The first wave of computer usage in the social sciences involved data management and statistical analysis. The second wave has involved the development of software that has enhanced data collection. A variety of possibilities exist. In a variation of the standard questionnaire, respondents can be asked to use a computer terminal and input their responses to items on the computer screen. In **CAPI (Computer Assisted Programmed Interviewing)** the researcher uses a laptop computer instead of a clipboard. The interview protocol appears on the screen, and the interviewer enters the responses. Inexpensive computers can be placed in respondent homes for longitudinal research. In one project, on completion of the study the respondents were given the computers as an incentive for having participated (Vasu and Garson, 1990). Computerized interviews may even have advantages over standard interviews in eliminating interviewer bias, obtaining more standardized responses, assuring anonymity, and reducing coding error (Monette, Sullivan, and DeJong, 1994, p. 114).

CAPI

Focus group research is particularly suitable for **CART (Continuous Audience Response Technology).** Such purposely selected groups are brought together to measure some stimuli. Respondents observe various video presentations and give their reactions on a continuous basis by means of a hand-held keypad (similar to a remote control device) by pressing appropriate buttons. For example, the buttons might represent 0 (negative reaction) to 5 (neutral reaction) to 10 (positive reaction). Group and individual responses can be instantaneously recorded, calculated, plotted, displayed on the video screen, and played back and reanalyzed; and all of this is on videotape for future analysis.

CART

Phone surveys can be done quickly and they can make maximum use of computerization through **CATI (Computer Assisted Telephone Interviews).**

CATI

Software packages exist to promote CATI systems. The computer flashes the question to be asked on the monitor, the interviewer keys in the answer, and the program chooses the next question to be asked. This is particularly useful for contingency questions, ones in which the interviewer is instructed to skip to different sequences of questions contingent upon the answer to others. The computer immediately stores the response, can track inconsistencies in response, and can even track interviewer performance.

Random Digit Dialing

Random digit dialing

Random digit dialing is a sampling procedure that enables the researcher to overcome a major shortcoming of telephone surveys—new or unlisted telephone numbers. The basic procedure can be summarized:

1. Find the universe of exchanges for the area to be surveyed. Some telephone books conveniently list these in the first few pages of the directory. The complete list of such numbers constitutes the universe (population) to be surveyed.
2. Use some randomized scheme to select the numbers. For example, take every nth name on a page selected by means of a table of random numbers and use that telephone number. (Suppose 864–0681 is chosen.)
3. Retain the first four digits (in this instance, 8640) and, using a table of random numbers to complete the number, be careful not to go beyond the range of the universe as determined earlier. By this procedure, persons with unlisted and new numbers are included in the sample, although those who do not own telephones are not (Sudman, 1976, p. 65). Such random numbers can also be generated one at a time by a CATI (Computer Assisted Telephone Interviewing) system.

In a study commissioned by the Police Foundation, Tuchfarber and Klecka indicate that for only a quarter of the cost of personal interview survey techniques, police departments can obtain equally effective victimization and public opinion survey data in their communities. Data regarding crime trends, neighborhood safety, and police performance showed no difference between face-to-face and telephone surveys, whereas victimization rates for households were higher in the telephone surveys (Tuchfarber and Klecka, 1976; Tuchfarber et al., 1976). The differences that appear between face-to-face interviews and telephone surveys may be more of a result of the actual interviewers involved than differences in the methods. The skills required in a telephone interview may be quite different from those involved in direct personal interviews (Groves and Kahn, 1979).

The utilization of random digit dialing procedures is illustrated in a study of citizen participation and community crime prevention in the Chicago area (Lavrakis, 1984; Skogan and Maxfield, 1981) and described in the following manner:

> A modified random digit dialing procedure was used to generate a total of 5,346 prospective sample numbers. A total of 1,803 interviews were completed. Within households respondents were adults (age 19 or older) stratified by sex and age. For analytic purposes, the sample of 1,803 completed interviews was weighted by the inverse of the number of different telephone numbers in each household, in order to correct for the probability of reaching a household with multiple phones (in Loftin, 1987, p. 84).
>
> Note the concern for accuracy in taking into account multiple telephone ownership, which certainly would not have been an issue only a few years ago (Lavrakis, 1993).

Techniques Employed in Telephone Surveys

A number of procedures used in telephone surveys enable, in part, the overcoming of some of the limitations of this technique. Sensitive items such as income can be handled by a line of questioning employing a **branching procedure** in which income is narrowed down to broad estimates as in Figure 6.1. Such a procedure has been found to take no more time than the method of handing the respondent a card with income ranges used in face-to-face surveys (Sudman, 1980).

The likelihood of refusals is greatest during the first minute of the telephone conversation. The interviewer should avoid screening respondents

Branching procedure

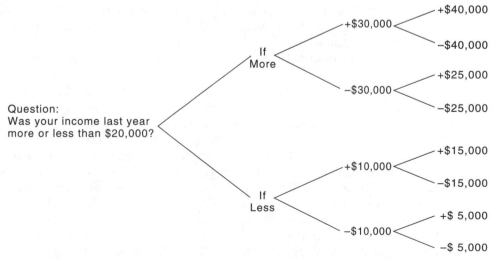

Figure 6.1 Branching Procedure Employed to Estimate Income in a Telephone Survey.

with threatening or sensitive questions or questions that easily permit the subject to refuse. For example, the question "Is there anyone there who earns under $20,000 a year?" makes it easy for the respondent to say no, even if it is not true, realizing that such a response will abort the interview. It would be similar to a door-to-door encyclopedia salesperson beginning with the question "Do you own any encyclopedias?" (Sudman, 1980).

Even questions requiring scaled responses rather than simply "yes" or "no" answers can be answered over the telephone. For example, respondents can be asked about their attitudes or ratings of a subject by being requested to respond by picturing a thermometer ranging from very cold, cold, mild, warm, and very hot. Telephone dials or buttons themselves can be utilized to measure degrees of response ranging, for instance, from 0 (the lowest rating) to 9 (the highest rating) (Sudman, 1980).

More in-depth questions can be undertaken through the randomization of questions so that fewer but more detailed questions can be asked of each respondent. In this procedure, more of the respondents are asked the entire set of questions. The order of questions can also be randomized. For additional information on telephone surveys, consult Frey (1989); Groves et al. (1988); and Lavrakis (1993).

Victim Surveys in Criminal Justice

In Chapter 4 we discussed major limitations of the use of official statistics such as the Uniform Crime Report as an indicator of the overall crime problem of a society. Unrecorded crime, or the ***dark figure of crime,*** as it was referred to by early European criminologists, has always escaped such official statistics. **Victim surveys** involve questioning a representative sample of the population to obtain an estimate of victimization, a portion of which is not reported to the police.

Dark figure of crime

Victim surveys

Even though Clinard (1978, p. 22) traces victim surveys as early as 1720 Denmark, surprisingly, it was not until the late 1960s that victim surveys were conducted on a large-scale basis to measure crime. In 1966 in the United States, the President's Commission on Law Enforcement and the Administration of Justice commissioned studies by Biderman et al. (1967) in Washington, D.C., and a pilot national survey of 10,000 households conducted by the National Opinion Research Center (Ennis, 1967), as well as other surveys carried out in Boston, Chicago, and Washington, D.C. (Reiss, 1967). The chief overall finding was that about twice as much crime was reported to the interviewers than was accounted for in official statistics (for a historical overview, see Lehnen and Skogan [1981]).

On the basis of the results of these surveys, a major victim survey effort was begun not only in the United States, but also in Belgium, Canada, Denmark, England, Holland, Norway, Sweden, Switzerland, and West

Germany (Sparks, Genn, and Dodd, 1977, p. 3; Nettler, 1978, pp. 94–95; Mackay and Hagan, 1978). Among both private and government-sponsored surveys, by far the most ambitious and sustained effort has been conducted in the United States by the Department of Justice's Bureau of Justice Statistics (BJS), which utilizes the U.S. Census Bureau as the data-gathering agent. The BJS was created by an act of Congress to coordinate the crime data generated by separate local, state, and federal agencies.

Other pilot surveys conducted by the Law Enforcement Assistance Administration (LEAA) in the early 1970s were invaluable in identifying major methodological issues to be addressed in later, larger BJS surveys. Such issues as recall periods, reverse validity checks (police records compared with survey reports), problems of under- and overreporting, credibility of respondents, and sampling questions were noted and had the benefit of a trial run (Panel for the Evaluation of Crime Surveys, 1976, pp. 33–48).

National Crime Victimization Survey

On the basis of the success of these studies, the National Crime Surveys were initiated in July 1972. Originally, the National Crime Surveys comprised the National Crime Panel Surveys and the Central City Surveys. Now, only the National Crime Panel studies are conducted and these are referred to as the National Crime Victimization Surveys. According to the National Academy of Sciences panel responsible for evaluating these surveys, the survey design, sampling, and estimating schemes were among the most complex ever employed on such a large scale in the social sciences (Panel for the Evaluation of Crime Surveys, 1976, p. 8).

These surveys began as a collaboration between the U.S. Department of Justice (DOJ) and the U.S. Census Bureau. In 1969, LEAA, which had been created as a branch of DOJ in 1968, evolved a subbranch, the National Criminal Justice Information and Statistics Service (NCJISS) that became involved in the early surveys. Since 1980, NCJISS has become BJS.

Sampling

The surviving set of surveys of the National Crime Victimization Survey (the national crime panel) consists of national surveys of housing units. Since 1991 the National Crime Survey has been known as the National Crime Victimization Survey. The national household survey is based on a sample of about 50,000 households, which were interviewed at six-month intervals (Bachman and Taylor, 1994, p. 501). These households contain about 101,000 individuals. This sample is subdivided into 10,000 households, each of which is interviewed every month. A housing unit remains in the sample for three years. The subsamples are designed so that every six months one group of 10,000 is rotated out of the sample and replaced by a new group. Rotation (reinterviews and replacement of panel subunits) enables the crime panel to remain fresh and representative. Without it the panel would eventually grow old and unrepresentative. The first and fifth interviews are conducted in person, while the others are via telephone.

Stratified multistage cluster sample

The NCVS is conducted using a complex *stratified multistage cluster sample* (Panel for the Evaluation of Crime Surveys, 1976, pp. 10–11), and is described in the original language so that the reader may appreciate the sampling design:

1. A national sampling frame is developed in which about 2,000 Primary Sampling Units (PSUs) are defined as either a Standard Metropolitan Statistical Area (SMSA), a county, or a small group of contiguous counties.
2. These clusters are then stratified on the basis of size, density, population mobility, and other relevant socioeconomic criteria into 376 strata.
3. In the first stage, one PSU is chosen from each stratum with a proportionate probability with respect to population size.
4. In the next stages within each sample, PSU clusters of roughly four adjacent neighboring housing units are selected systematically so that each housing unit in the country has an equal probability of being selected.

Panel Design

Crime panel

Bounding

The National Crime Survey consists of a crime panel. The **crime panel** repeats interviews every six months to bound or provide a benchmark for crime reports. **Bounding** involves using a pretest or initial interview to set a reference point for the survey reporting period. The initial interview sets a boundary or time period with which to compare future victimizations. In addition to general demographic information, these interviews probe such variables as victim–offender relationships, injury or loss suffered, the time and place of the incident(s), the time the crime is reported to the police, and other criminal justice matters.

Each subgroup of the crime panel is interviewed every six months for three years and then is rotated out of the panel and replaced by a new bounded subgroup.

The NCS is conducted for the BJS by the Census Bureau. Initially, face-to-face interviews are attempted with a household informant (any competent adult eighteen years of age or older). The core survey averages approximately thirty minutes per household; previous pilot studies suggest that longer interview times increase refusal rates. The survey has two parts: screening questions and incident reports. Questions regarding personal victimizations are asked of each household member twelve years of age or older

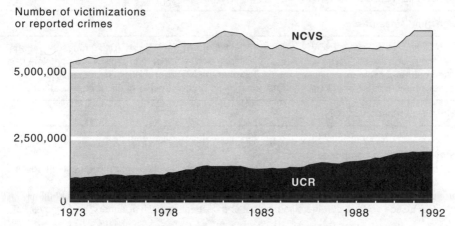

Violent crimes measured by NCVS and UCR*

*includes NCVS violent crimes of rape, robbery, aggravated assault, and simple assault; and UCR violent crimes of murder and nonnegligent manslaughter, forcible rape, robbery, and aggravated assault.

Figure 6.2 NCVS Provides Information on Both Reported and Unreported Crime. (*Source:* Bureau of Justice Statistics. *Highlights from 20 Years of Surveying Crime Victims: The National Crime Victimization Survey, 1973–92.* Washington, D.C.: Government Printing Office, October 1993, p. 6, NCJ-144525.)

(if the person victimized is hospitalized, incompetent, or temporarily absent, proxy respondents are accepted). If victimization is claimed in the screening instrument (see Figure 6.2), then the "incident reports" instrument is used to follow up on such details as clarification of the incident, determination of whether the incident was a crime, and information on offenders, offense, victim actions, economic loss, and the like. Subsequent interviews are obtained through a combination of personal and telephone interviews.

A Comparison of UCR, NCVS, and Self-Report Data

Menard (1987) examined five- to ten-year trends in crime and juvenile delinquency using Uniform Crime Reports (official police data), the National Crime Victimization Survey (victimization data), and the National Youth Survey (NYS) (self-reported delinquency). While the UCR showed steadily increasing rates of crime, the NCVS and NYS indicated stable or decreasing rates. Although the increase in the official statistics in the face of relatively stable crime commission rates might be taken as a positive sign of increased reporting and police effectiveness, it may also reflect an increased reliance upon formal legal controls and police professionalization. Table 6.1 compares the NCVS with the UCR.

TABLE 6.1 The NCVS versus the UCR

The Nation's Two Crime Measures

The National Crime Victimization Survey (NCVS) and the FBI's Uniform Crime Reports (UCR) measure various aspects of crime at the national level. These complementary series each contribute to providing a complete picture about the extent and nature of crime in the United States. Together the NCVS and UCR provide a more comprehensive assessment of crime in the United States than could be obtained from either statistical series alone.

The National Crime Victimization Survey

Using stable data collection methods since 1973, the NCVS has the following strengths:

- It measures both reported and unreported crimes.
- It is not affected by changes in the extent to which people report crime to police or improvements in police record-keeping technology.
- It collects information that is not available when the initial police report is made including contacts the victim has with the criminal justice system after the crime, extent and costs of medical treatment, and recovery of property.
- It collects detailed information about victims and characteristics of the victimization including who the victims are, what their relationship is to the offender, whether the crime was part of a series of crimes occuring over a 6-month period, what self-protective measures were used and how the victims assess their effectiveness, and what the victim was doing when victimized.
- On occasion, it includes special supplements about particular topics such as school crime and the severity of crime.

The Uniform Crime Reports

The UCR program measures police workload and activity. Local police departments voluntarily report information to the Federal Bureau of Investigation (FBI) including the numbers of crimes reported to police, arrests made by police and other administrative information. The UCR program has the following strengths:

- It can provide local data about States, counties, cities and towns.
- It measures crimes affecting children under age 12, a segment of the population that experts agree cannot be reliably interviewed in the NCVS.
- It includes crimes against commercial establishments.
- It collects information about the number of arrests and who was arrested.
- It counts the number of homicides (murders and nonnegligent manslaughters), crimes that cannot be counted in a survey that interviews victims. UCR also collects detailed information about the circumstances surrounding homicides and the characteristics of homicide victims.

Source: Bureau of Justice Statistics, 1993, p. 6.

Some Problems in Victim Surveys

From the initial pilot surveys of the late 1960s to the more recent ones, the Census Bureau and Bureau of Justice statistics researchers have been aware of a variety of shortcomings in surveys of victims and have tried to deal with them in various ways. Some potential **problems in victim surveys** are:

Cost of large samples	Sampling bias
False reporting	Overreporting and/or
Mistaken interpretation of incidents	underreporting

Memory failure, decay,
and telescoping

Interviewer effects
Coding and mechanical error
Problems measuring certain crimes

Although this list by no means covers all the difficulties encountered in conducting and interpreting victim surveys, it does enumerate the major ones.

Cost of Large Samples

Cost of samples

In the discussion of sampling in Chapter 5, it was indicated that most large-scale public opinion surveys in the United States are conducted with sample sizes of less than a thousand or two. Victim surveys require such large samples because of the need to ensure the appearance of rare events. For example, in that the vast majority of respondents are not likely to have been victimized in the past year or six months, it becomes necessary to interview large numbers to obtain only a few victims. Glaser explains that by using official statistics one must survey ten respondents to obtain one victim. For more rare victimizations such as rape, even larger numbers are needed to obtain a few cases. Also, because sampling error is proportionate to the size of the sample instead of the size of the population being sampled, one often needs as large a sample to estimate victimizations in small or large cities as would be necessary for the entire nation (Glaser, 1978, p. 63).

False Reports

False reports

False reports on the part of respondents may produce erroneous victim data. Some falsity in victim reports should be expected according to Levine (1976, p. 98), who found that respondents were inaccurate in disclosing behavior with respect to voting, finances, business practices, sexual behavior, academic performance, and other activities. Certainly, one would be overoptimistic in assuming greater accuracy in recall of criminal victimization.

Mistaken Reporting

Mistaken reporting

Mistaken reporting is another source of error in victim surveys. Thomas' "definition of the situation" holds that, if individuals inaccurately feel that a situation is real, it is nevertheless real in its consequences (Thomas and Swaine, 1928, pp. 571–572). A person who has lost something may inaccurately, but honestly, believe it was stolen. Perhaps the neighborhood paranoids do in fact believe people have been attempting to break into their house, when no such incidents ever took place. In addition, many respondents are ignorant of the complexities of legal definitions of criminal events and may report incidents that are not really crimes. Such incidents often tend to be regarded, even by respondents, as trivial, hardly worth the effort, or not really a police matter. Many of these events would most likely have been labeled "unfounded" by police, had a request been made for police investigation.

Poor Memory

Poor memory

Poor memory on the part of those surveyed is another potential difficulty in surveying possible victims of crime. Memory failure, or *recall decay,* refers to the phenomenon of progressive memory loss as the distance increases between the time of the event and the time of the interview concerning the event. For example, a crime that took place last week is more likely to be recalled as well as reported than a crime that occurred last month or last year (Panel for Evaluation, 1976, p. 21; Gottfredson and Hindelang, 1977).

Telescoping

Telescoping

A principal type of memory fading in victim surveys is **telescoping**—the tendency of respondents to move forward and report as having occurred events that actually took place before the reference period. That is, a crime that happened two years ago is mistakenly reported as having taken place within the last six months. In a pretest in the District of Columbia, the U.S. Bureau of Census (1970, p. 9) performed a *reverse record check* in which known crime victims were interviewed after the fact. About 20 percent of the victimizations in police records recorded as having occurred before the reference period were reported by the survey sample as having taken place within the reference period. Similarly, the Dayton–San Jose surveys showing greater victimization reported in the first half of the year are a likely case of forward telescoping (U.S. Department of Justice, 1974b, p. 37). Biderman (1970) suggests that some subjects may unconsciously telescope events to please interviewers; thus **demand characteristics** or overagreeableness on the part of those surveyed is a related problem in surveys of public victimization.

Reverse record checks

Demand characteristics

Sampling Bias

Sampling bias is a thorny problem in much survey research including victim surveys. Even the decennial U.S. Census of Population underenumerates the young, males, and members of minority groups. As Skogan (1978, p. 17) aptly points out, "Males, African Americans and youths are much more likely than others to fall victim to most crimes, but they are less likely to be found and questioned." Although the Census Bureau estimates and attempts to correct for such nonresponse bias, it still remains a problem.

Overreporting and Underreporting

Over/ underreporting

Overreporting in victimization surveys may be accounted for by the fact that when asked, respondents will report to interviewers acts that they ordinarily would regard as too trivial or unimportant to warrant police attention.

Much of the deep, dark figure of crime consists of minor property crime, a good proportion of which would most likely have been "unfounded" by police (Black, 1970). While many critics of victim surveys have assailed their tendency to overreport certain categories of crime (Levine, 1976; Singer, 1978), these surveys also contain some of the same shortcomings of the UCR and other official police statistics in underreporting certain crimes. Victim surveys tend to *underreport* crimes and because certain crimes are not reported or queried victims do not tend to report crimes in which the perpetrator was a friend, relative, or family member. As with the UCR, victim surveys do not concern themselves particularly with corporate, occupational, organized, professional, political, and public order crime.

An additional concern in contrasting official police statistics with surveys of victims relates to different bases of comparison. Police statistics are based on the number of incidents, whereas victim surveys are based on individual victims. Glaser (1978, p. 64) gives the following example: Ten people from ten households were robbed in one holdup, and only one person was robbed in another. This was recorded as only two robberies in police statistics; however potential victimizations are tallied in a survey of victims. Most victim surveys exclude nonresidents and foreign visitors, a serious underestimate of crime particularly in tourist cities and/or cities with large commuter populations.

Interviewer Effects

Interviewer effects

Any survey involving interviewers contains the potential for interviewer bias. Although outright deception and exaggeration are possibilities, more likely to occur are subjective bias on the part of the interviewer and the artificiality introduced by the interview situation. Levine (1976) suggests that interviewer self-interest may impact on the results in that the enumeration of many crimes may be thought to ensure more surveys and thus continued employment. Additionally, potential reactivity of respondents who are continually reinterviewed as part of the national panel may impact on their attitudes or reported victimizations (National Advisory Committee, 1976, p. 147). Panel fatigue or other response effects have been demonstrated to occur in the National Crime Panels (Lehnen and Reiss, 1978).

Coding Unreliability and Mechanical Error

Coding error

Mechanical error

In addition to all of the previously mentioned sources of possible error, *human mistakes in coding,* keypunching, and analyzing may account for significant inaccuracy. Sussman and Haug (1967) have pointed out the serious degree of unchecked *mechanical errors* in coding and keypunching in general large-scale surveys.

Because of the concern over potential errors in the NCVS, its suspension was seriously considered in the late 1970s. Fortunately, this did not take place, and the NCVS has become institutionalized. Once viewed as a novel adjunct crime count, it is now perceived as an important social indicator, as noted more recently by adoption of its design principles by the United Nations.

Problems Measuring Certain Crimes

The NCVS obviously does not interview victims of murder, but Helen Eigenberg (1990) points out that the data on rape has been inadequate because it never asked respondents directly whether they had been raped. Although she feels the new screening questions are an improvement over the old ones because they ask whether the subject has ever been assaulted, she thinks that "researchers must note that the NCVS has traditionally operationalized rape poorly" (ibid., p. 655).

The NCVS rate does, however, appear to be a better measure of the true rate of rape over time than the UCR. The latter reflects trends in organization and management of rape victimizations (Jensen and Karpos, 1993). Improved operationalization of rape and domestic violence in the redesigned NCVS was implemented in 100 percent of the samples beginning July 1993 (Bachman and Taylor, 1994). In August 1995 the NCVS released the first report on rape data from the newly designed survey and doubled their estimate of the number of rapes. The new estimates asked specifically whether respondents were raped or sexually assaulted, whereas the previous protocol asked only about attacks of any kind without mentioning rape or sexual assault.

Benefits of Victim Surveys

Despite some methodological problems, many of which can be controlled as will be elaborated, victim surveys hold much promise:

1. They have become a model spurring international imitation.
2. Such studies present an opportunity to obtain a picture of victims and their characteristics.
3. Because of nonreporting in official statistics, victim surveys may be a more accurate estimate for commission of such crimes as rape and assault (National Advisory Committee, 1976, p. 145).
4. The potential exists, using telephone surveys (as discussed in this chapter), for local jurisdictions to conduct their own victim surveys to gauge, plan, and evaluate elements of police services.
5. Victim surveys are additionally useful for measuring crime costs with respect to injuries, insurance, and crime prevention programs (Skogan, 1978, p. 2).
6. They also assist in obtaining better descriptions of criminals and their methods of operation.

7. Such surveys also assess such issues as fear of crime, satisfaction with police services, attitude toward the police, and reasons for not reporting crimes to the police.

A Defense of Victim Surveys

Despite the shortcomings of victim surveys that have been elaborated, it should once again be pointed out that no method of data gathering is perfect. Many of these sources of error are not the sole province of victim surveys, but may apply equally to some of the other techniques of data gathering. Victim surveys are a relatively young endeavor in criminal justice. Much has already been learned. And much has yet to be learned in future methodological analyses.

BJS is constantly monitoring and attempting to update the methodological accuracy of the NCVS. In 1985 a panel of experts in criminology—The National Crime Consortium—was charged with the task of devising better screening questions to obtain better control over forgotten as well as sensitive items. Redesign of the NCVS reflects this effort.

Controlling for Error in Victim Surveys

Some common means of controlling for error in victim surveys, some of which have already been mentioned, are:

Use of panels
Bounding of target groups
Evaluations of coding
Reverse record check surveys of known groups
Reinterviews of the same group
Interviews with significant others

Bounding

The use of panels in the National Crime Victimization Survey permits the researcher to achieve *bounding.* The first interview with residents results in a panel that can then be followed up five times every six months before being dropped out of the sample. At each six-month interview, respondents

Bounding   are asked about events since the last interview. *Bounding* is made possible beginning with the initial interview during which the *boundary, or time period during which events were recalled as having taken place,* can be established. Any events recalled later can be tracked since the previous interview, thus eliminating telescoping of reports.

Simple coding procedures—the assignment of responses to categories—have high degrees of measurement error and intercoder discrepancies (Crittenden and Hill, 1971; Sussman and Haug, 1967). The utilization of different coders to classify the same data enables assessment of coding error (Ennis, 1967, p. 93).

Reverse Record Checks

Reverse record checks

Reverse record checks involve validation of reported behavior on the basis of studying a group whose behavior is already known. Pilot studies of known victims who had reported their incidents to police were conducted in Washington, D.C., Baltimore, and San Jose (Panel for the Evaluation of Crime Surveys, 1976, p. 33). The surveys found that recall deteriorates more quickly after six months, and particularly forgotten are crimes committed by close acquaintances. In the San Jose survey, 52 percent of assaults known to police were not reported in victim surveys (National Advisory Committee, 1976, p. 146). Reiss interviewed a sample of respondents who had reported crimes to the police the month before and discovered that one out of five failed to report to interviewers crimes they had reported to police the previous month (Reiss, 1967).

Reinterviews

Reinterview of the same group enables an assessment of potential bias and interviewer bias. Results obtained by the initial interviewer can be compared with those obtained by the second interviewer. Such information can then be reconciled or resolved through agreement (Panel for the Evaluation of Crime Surveys, 1976, p. 63).

Interviews with significant others, peers, teachers, and the like provide a cross-check on claimed behavior.

Victim Surveys: A Balanced View

In 1974, when LEAA released the findings from its thirteen central city surveys, Donald Santarelli, then head of the organization, was quoted as having remarked "For the first time in history, we now have an accurate measure of crime in America—at least in these 13 cities" (Burnham, 1974, pp. 1, 51). Other popular reviews pointed to how victim surveys, in covering the dark figure of crime, showed that there was actually twice as much crime as appears in official police statistics. After review of the advantages and disadvantages of victim surveys it seems fair to conclude that:

1. For the types of personal and household crimes, both victim surveys and the UCR measure, the true rate is most likely somewhere between victim surveys, which overestimate crime, and the UCR, which underestimates crime.

2. For other types of crimes such as occupational, corporate, and public order crime, both measures underestimate crime.

3. Despite shortcomings, victim surveys present a needed separate and independent assessment of crime and other criminal justice matters of importance.

The problems encountered with most methods of data gathering are not inherent to the nature of the method; rather, the problems arise because the method is used as the sole means of assessment.

Redesign of the National Crime Victimization Survey

National Crime Survey redesign

In 1974, in response to an evaluation by the National Academy of Sciences and an internal review by a predecessor of the BJS, a project was begun to evaluate and redesign the National Crime Victimization Survey. The evaluation was put together by a consortium of universities and private research firms and by the staff from BJS and the Census Bureau. Implementation of some of these redesign plans was begun in 1986; others were phased in later (Taylor, 1989, p. 1).

The first changes, those which would have minimal impact on NCVS victimization rates, were introduced in July 1986. Most of these items related to the expanded list of questions, those that were added to the questionnaire which had remained fundamentally unchanged since 1972. These new questions related to: drug and alcohol use by offenders, self-protective measures taken by victims, police actions, victim contact with the justice system, location of crime, victim's activity, and expansion of several existing questions (Whitaker, 1989, p. 2). Among other changes was the decision to use *CATI technology* (computer-assisted telephone interviewing). With this CATI technology questionnaire items can be flashed on a video monitor, and then interviewers can immediately enter responses on the keyboard. The redesigned NCVS program is also considering but has not implemented **CAPI technology** (computer-assisted programmed interviewing), which makes possible the use of portable laptop computers in field interviews. Although the proposed changes involve too many details for our presentation, it is worth noting some other modifications. These modifications include altering the scope of crimes measured or adding new topical supplements to the NCVS on a regular basis. Special questions will be periodically added to deal with timely topics, such as school crime or victim risk (Bureau of Justice Statistics, 1989).

Efforts were made in redesigning the NCVS to avoid disrupting the integrity of its longitudinal design. The new survey instrument was phased into the NCVS so as not to compromise trend data (Bachman and Taylor, 1994, p. 502). Exhibit 6.2 details the Redesigned National Crime Victimization Survey.

EXHIBIT 6.2

The Redesigned National Crime Victimization Survey

Additional details about the redesign of the National Crime Victimization Survey

The redesign of the NCVS

In the mid-1970's the National Academy of Sciences evaluated the NCVS for accuracy and usefulness. While the survey was found to be an effective instrument for measuring crime, reviewers identified aspects of the methodology and scope of the NCVS that could be improved. They proposed research to investigate the following:

- an enhanced screening section that would better stimulate respondents' recall of victimizations
- screening questions that would sharpen the concepts of criminal victimization and diminish the effects of subjective interpretations of the survey questions
- additional questions on the nature and consequences of victimizations that would yield useful data for analysis
- enhanced questions and inquiries about domestic violence, rape, and sexual attack to get better estimates of these hard-to-measure victimizations.

The redesign has improved the measurement of domestic violence

Respondents may be reluctant to report acts of domestic violence as crimes, particularly if the offender is present during the interview. In addition, victims may not perceive domestic violence as discrete criminal acts but as a pattern of abuse. Though these issues still pose measurement problems, the redesigned screening section includes explicit questions about incidents involving family members, friends, and acquaintances. Screening questions also include multiple references to acts of domestic violence to encourage respondents to report such incidents even if they do not define these acts as crimes. The survey staff review these reported incidents using standardized definitions of crimes. Thus, within the categories of violent crime measured by the NCVS, the redesign will produce fuller reporting of

those incidents that involved intimates or other family members.

A comparison of the old and new questionnaire illustrates the expanded cues that help a respondent recall an incident

New

2. People often don't think of incidents committed by someone they know. Did you have something stolen from you OR were you attacked or threatened by—
   a. Someone at work or school—
   b. A neighbor or friend—
   c. A relative or family member—
   d. Any other person you've met or known?
3. Did you call the police to report something that happened to YOU which you thought was a crime?
4. Did anything happen to you which you thought was a crime, but did NOT report to the police?

Old

2. Did you call the police to report something that happened to YOU which you thought was a crime?
3. Did anything happen to YOU which you thought was a crime, but did NOT report to the police?

The new NCVS has resulted in more victimizations being reported than when the old instrument was used. The survey now includes improved questions and cues that help victims to remember victimizations. Interviewers now ask more explicit questions about sexual victimizations. Victim advocates have also been instrumental in encouraging victims to talk more openly about these experiences (National Crime Victimization . . . , 1994).

Reasons for differences in violent crime rates because of the new and old screener questions

The new screener questions provide more specific cues regarding kinds of items used as weapons and kinds of offender actions that better define the in-scope crimes of violence for the NCVS. In particular, the explicit cuing of rape and other sexual assaults has been added to the new screener. A side-by-side comparison of the new and old screener questions is provided.

Furthermore, two frames of reference have been added or more explicitly defined in the new screener. The first relates to crimes being committed by someone the respondent knows. The second relates to the possible location of a crime or activities the respondent may have been involved in. This screener question takes the few sporadically mentioned cues of location/activity in the old screener questions and creates another specific frame of reference with a greatly expanded list of location/activity cues.

Violent crime screener questions

New

1. Has anyone attacked or threatened you in any of these ways—
   a. With any weapon, for instance, a gun or knife—
   b. With anything like a baseball bat, frying pan, scissors, or stick—
   c. By something thrown, such as a rock or bottle—
   d. Include any grabbing, punching, or choking,
   e. Any rape, attempted rape or other type of sexual attack—
   f. Any face to face threats—
   OR
   g. Any attack or threat or use of force by anyone at all? Please mention it even if you are not certain it was a crime.

2. Incidents involving forced or unwanted sexual acts are often difficult to talk about. Have you been forced or coerced to engage in unwanted sexual activity by—
   a. someone you didn't know before
   b. a casual acquaintance OR
   c. someone you know well?

Old

1. Did anyone take something directly from you by using force, such as by a stickup, mugging or threat?

2. Did anyone TRY to rob you by using force or threatening to harm you?
3. Did anyone beat you up, attack you or hit you with something, such as a rock or bottle?
4. Were you knifed, shot at, or attacked with some other weapon by anyone at all?
5. Did anyone THREATEN to beat you up or THREATEN you with a knife, gun, or some other weapon, NOT including telephone threats?
6. Did anyone TRY to attack you in some other way?

All types of crimes screener questions

New

1. Were you attacked or threatened OR did you have something stolen from you—
   a. At home including the porch or yard—
   b. At or near a friend's, relative's, or neighbor's home—
   c. At work or school—
   d. In places such as a storage shed or laundry room, a shopping mall, restaurant, bank or airport—
   e. While riding in any vehicle—
   f. On the street or in a parking lot—
   g. At such places as a party, theater, gym, picnic area, bowling lanes, or while fishing or hunting—
   OR
   h. Did anyone ATTEMPT to attack or attempt to steal anything belonging to you from any of these places?
2. People often don't think of incidents committed by someone they know. Did you have something stolen from you OR were you attacked or threatened by—
   a. Someone at work or school—
   b. A neighbor or friend—
   c. A relative or family member—
   d. Any other person you've met or known?
3. Did you call the police to report something that happened to YOU which you thought was a crime?
4. Did anything happen to you which you thought was a crime, but did NOT report to the police?

Continued.

Old

1. Was anything stolen from you while you were away from home, for instance, at work, in a theater or restaurant, or while traveling?
2. Did you call the police to report something that happened to YOU which you thought was a crime?
3. Did anything happen to YOU which you thought was a crime, but did NOT report to the police?

Reasons for differences in burglary rates because of the new and old screener questions

In general, the same frame of reference is established for burglary in the new and old screener. However, the new screener has several more specific cues. These additional cues relate to how the offender might have gotten into or attempted to get into the respondent's home and/or other types of buildings that may be on the respondent's property.

Burglary screener questions

New

1. Has somebody—
   a. Broken in or ATTEMPTED to break into your home by forcing a door or window, pushing past someone, jimmying a lock, cutting a screen, or entering through an open door or window?
   b. Has anyone illegally gotten in or tried to get into a garage, shed or storage room?
   OR
   c. Illegally gotten in or tried to get into a hotel or motel room or vacation home where you were staying?

Old

1. Did anyone break into or somehow illegally get into your home, garage, or another building on your property?
2. Did you find a door jimmied, a lock forced, or any other signs of an ATTEMPTED break in?
3. Did anyone take something belonging to you or any member of this household, from a friend's or relative's home, a hotel or motel, or vacation home?

Motor vehicle theft rates

There is no significant difference in motor vehicle theft rates between the new and old methods. One reason is that the new and old screener questions are very similar. Another reason is that motor vehicle thefts are highly salient events (demonstrated by the fact that they have the highest percent reported to police), suggesting little room for improvement in their measurement. Similar results were observed in the Computer-Assisted Telephone Interviewing (CATI) research. While CATI increased ratios for most types of crime, it had no significant effect on motor vehicle theft rates.

Motor vehicle theft screener questions

New

1. Was it—
   a. Stolen or used without permission?
   b. Did anyone ATTEMPT to steal any vehicles?

Old

1. Did anyone steal, TRY to steal, or use it without permission?

Redesign of type of crime classification scheme

A major reclassification scheme has shifted most of what were previously categorized as personal crimes of theft into property crimes of theft. Under the old scheme, theft was characterized as a personal or household crime based on location of the incident. If an item were stolen from the grounds of a home, it was considered a household theft; if the same item were stolen from someplace away from the home it was considered a personal theft. This distinction was rather arbitrary and unwieldy, since many items are jointly owned by members of a household. The redesigned NCVS classifies all thefts as household thefts unless there was contact between victim and offender. Personal thefts with contact (purse snatching and pocket picking) are now the only types of theft that are categorized as personal theft. Table 4 compares the old and new type of crime classification scheme.

Overlap between the old and new NCVS methods

As discussed previously, an integral part of the planned transition from the old methods to the new methods of conducting the NCVS was to include a substantial overlap period in which both methods were implemented concurrently. Besides being used for comparing crime estimates, the overlap data can be used to extend earlier time trends data. Statistical models will be developed to adjust for the effects of the new methods on victimization reporting. Adjustment factors will be estimated at least for the major crime categories and possibly for other important variables if reliable differences are found.

TABLE 4. Changes in Totals Reflect the Headings under Which Offenses Are Counted

Type of Crime (Old Classification)	1992 Crime Rate	Type of Crime (New Classification)	1992 Crime Rate
Personal crimes	126.8	Personal crimes	51.1
Crimes of violence	49.3	Crimes of violence	49.3
Rape/other sexual assault	2.9	Rape/other sexual assault	2.9
Robbery	6.2	Robbery	6.2
Completed	4.1	Completed	4.1
Attempted	2.1	Attempted	2.1
Assault	40.2	Assault	40.2
Aggravated	11.1	Aggravated	11.1
Simple	29.1	Simple	29.1
Crimes of theft	77.5	Purse snatching/pocket picking	1.8
Household crimes	180.8	Property crimes	325.3
Burglary	58.7	Burglary	58.7
Household larceny	103.5		
Motor vehicle theft	18.6	Motor vehicle theft	18.6
		Theft*	248.0

*The theft category is a new crime category. It includes those crimes that were previously classified in two other crime categories: *Household larceny* and *personal larceny without contact* (a subcategory of *crimes of theft*). (*Source:* Bureau of Justice Statistics, 1994a, p.10.)

Summary

Although many of the issues regarding survey research discussed in Chapter 5 are also applicable to this chapter, the purpose of this chapter has been to explore major elements of the interview, particularly as it is used in criminal justice research. Interviewing, which basically involves face-to-face interaction between the interviewer and the respondent, has many variations depending on the purpose of the interview. Principal among these are structured (closed response), unstructured (open-end response), and depth (focus) interviews.

Some general advantages of the interview method are personal contact, which affords observation, clarification of misunderstandings and control over respondents, and the opportunity to employ visual aids, make return visits, and gear language to the level of the respondent. Interviews are also more flexible than mail questionnaires. Disadvantages of interviews include their sometimes time-consuming and costly nature, potential interviewer bias and mistakes, need for field supervision, and difficulty in reaching certain respondents. Also, question wording in public opinion polls has been shown to radically alter response.

Some interview situations may lend themselves to the use of various electronic recording equipment or other aids which can be a considerable bonus. The randomized response technique, in which the interviewer is blind to the specific item (either a sensitive one or probability one) being answered, may assist in overcoming respondent reactivity to sensitive questions.

Some appropriate procedures in conducting interviews have been detailed. The interviewer should receive an orientation and training session to be made aware of the organization and the survey and to practice interviewing and become familiar with the instrument to be employed. Arrangement of the interview, proper protocol, demeanor of interviewers, and administration of the questionnaire, including probing and exiting, were detailed. Interviewers should follow established procedures in recording and editing their survey schedules.

The use of the telephone survey to assess victimization holds promise as a means of reducing the cost of victim surveys. Phone surveys have such limitations as reduced scope, less in-depth responses, high refusal rates, and exclusion of disproportions of certain populations, particularly the poor and minorities. On the other hand, they have the advantages of no field staff, simple checks on interview bias, inexpensiveness, quickness, and easy follow-up.

Computer software such as CART (Continuous Audience Response Technology) has greatly expanded the versatility of the interview. Random digit dialing enables the coverage of unlisted numbers, a previous shortcoming of phone surveys of victims. The use of more careful screening questions and branching procedures for sensitive items may reduce nonresponse. Clever procedures have been developed to ask even attitudinal scale questions by telephone.

Victim surveys have been surprisingly ignored as a means of measuring crime until relatively recently. As the result of pilot studies in the late 1960s, LEAA, in cooperation with the Census Bureau, began two major types of surveys that involved direct questioning of persons as to whether they had been victims of crime. The first type, the National Crime Victimization Surveys, collected information from both central city households and commercial establishments. The second type, called the National Crime Panels, consisted of a national stratified multistage cluster sample of households and a two-stage probability sample of businesses. The unique characteristics of the crime panels were bounding of panels and reinterviews of respondents every six months until they were rotated out of the sample and replaced by a new unit.

Victim surveys are not without their problems. Principal among these are high cost, false reports, mistaken interpretation of incidents as crimes, memory failure and decay, sampling bias, over- and/or underreporting, telescoping, interviewer effects, and coding and mechanical error. In defense of surveys of victims, many of their shortcomings are also present in other techniques; and many of the problems identified are in part controllable through the use of panels, bounding, quality control, overcoding, reverse record checks, studies of known victim groups, reinterviews, and interviews of persons who know the victim. As was the case with self-report surveys, victim surveys provide a valuable additional assessment of crime.

Beginning in 1986, redesign of the NCVS began to be implemented. This redesign included plans to use CATI (computer-assisted telephone interviewing) and, in the future, possibly CAPI (computer-assisted programmed interviewing). The redesigned NCVS improved particularly the measurement of domestic violence.

Key Concepts

Structured Interviews
Unstructured Interviews
Depth Interviews
Advantages/
  Disadvantages of
  Interviews
Interviewer Effect
Randomized Response
  Technique
Probing
Editing the Interview
Telephone Surveys

Advantages/
  Disadvantages of
  Telephone Surveys
Screening Questions
CATI
Random Digit Dialing
Branching Procedure
Dark Figure of Crime
Victim Surveys
CART
NCVS

Crime Panels
Bounding
Some Problems in Victim
  Surveys
Telescoping
Demand Characteristics
Benefits of Victim
  Surveys
Reverse Record Check
CAPI

Review Questions

1. What are some distinct advantages of interviewing as a data-gathering strategy? Discuss some interviewing aids which further enhance this technique.
2. Suppose you were the director of a research project and assigned the task of running a short training program for the interviewers. What are some specific points you would present?
3. Compare the NCS with the UCR as measures of crime in the United States.
4. What are some methodological problems in victim surveys as well as some means of controlling for them?
5. What are some techniques employed in telephone surveys, particularly in those that are designed to overcome identified shortcomings of telephone surveys?
6. What impact does the wording of questions have on response in surveys, public opinion polls, and victim surveys?
7. Discuss some redesign features of the NCVS particularly as it relates to the measurement of domestic violence.

Participant Observation and Case Studies

Who are Chic Conwell, Doc, Long John, Vince Swaggi, Harry King, and Stanley the "Jack-Roller"? They are pseudonyms of legendary subjects of social science field studies and "native guides" to the criminal "turf" as well as to some of the most fascinating literature in criminology. In this chapter you will meet Chic Conwell, Sutherland's *The Professional Thief* (1937); Doc and Long John, members of Whyte's *Street Corner Society* (1943); Vince Swaggi, Klockars' *The Professional Fence* (1974); Harry King, Chambliss' safecracker in *The Box Man* (1975); and Stanley, a mugger in Shaw's *The Jack-Roller* (1930) and Snodgrass' *The JackRoller at Seventy* (1982).

A Critique of Experiments and Surveys

Some researchers feel that social science and criminal justice research have been overdependent on the artificial elements of questionnaires, interviews, and experimental settings. Such data-gathering approaches are viewed as creating, as well as measuring, attitudes and bringing about atypical roles and responses (Webb et al., 1966). Such strategies intrude into a setting as foreign elements, are limited to cooperative and obtainable populations, and tend to elicit stooge effects or response sets, particularly with much of the early corrections research.

Whyte (1981) laments the recent ascendancy of quantitative methods and decline of qualitative field work and says that if a history of the current period of sociology were to be written, one of the chapters would have to be "Captured by Computer."

Verbal Reports versus Behavior

Criticism of quantitative methods

Critics of such quantitative research suggest that little relationship exists between attitude and behavior, and that more "sensitizing" strategies involving field studies contain greater accuracy (Deutscher, 1966; Phillips, 1971). Such writers typically cite a classic study to illustrate their point of nonconvergence of attitude and behavior—LaPiere's "Restaurant Study" (LaPiere, 1934). LaPiere traveled with a Chinese couple to a large number of restaurants on the West Coast and observed the treatment they received. Only one of 251 establishments refused them service. Later, he sent the same establishments a questionnaire; more than 90 percent replied that they would deny service. The disparity between what people say (attitudes) and what people do (deeds) illustrates the hazards of attitudinal measurement of behavioral items.

Although Chapter 9 will discuss in detail the validity of verbal reports, Levine cites a number of studies of various subjects in which respondents misreported known behavior that could be checked. People were inaccurate in reporting voting behavior, time of vaccination of children, money in savings accounts, level of loan debt, sexual activity, class attendance, and school grades. Studies of known crime victims found that a significant number failed to report to interviewers victimizations that they had already reported to the police (Levine, 1976).

Error of measurement

In Chapter 3 it was suggested that error is ever present, even in the best research. Critics of more quantitative and artificial means of measurement indicate that instead of speaking of error in measurement, it would be more accurate to speak of the *error of measurement* (Deming, 1944; Phillips, 1971). These errors in surveys and experimental studies include variability in response as a result of the noncomparability of studies and differences caused by the methodologies employed. For example, telephone surveys may turn up greater victimization than face-to-face interviews. The degree and kind of canvass will impact on results. Interviewer bias, if unchecked, may produce error. In doing a study of rural elderly using five interviewing teams, this writer was startled to discover in a preliminary analysis the high level of fear of crime in what was assumed to be a pastoral setting. A quick check, however, revealed that one interview team produced the majority of cases in which crime was a perceived problem. During our weekly staff meeting it came to light that one of the interviewers, an elderly woman, had recently been victimized and unconsciously led her respondents into seeing crime as a primary problem. Fortunately, this was caught and corrected before it did major harm to the study results (Hagan, 1972).

Bias

Bias of auspices or sponsorship may compromise the results of many studies. For this very reason many criminal justice programs bring in outside, objective evaluators to analyze program outcomes. Certainly, a study of the benefits of a product would be more suspect if conducted by the manufacturer of a product, rather than by an independent laboratory.

Design imperfections

Design imperfections, in either the instrument or the analysis, can produce inaccurate results. Failure to account for nonrespondents may compromise the results of surveys. Nonrespondents may differ considerably from those who cooperate in a survey. Much survey research, although planned and designed by professionals, is conducted by "hired hands," individuals who may have little interest in the accuracy or are unaware of idiosyncracies and subtleties in data. Sussman and Haug (1967) point out that unchecked mechanical errors in coding and keypunching may be more serious in survey data than many suppose. Sampling errors and nonrepresentative samples may lead to error, as might errors in interpretation of findings on the part of the researchers.

Orne found that subjects in his experiments were willing to put up with boring, uncomfortable, painful, and ridiculous tasks if asked to do so by the experimenter. In fact, he was unsuccessful in finding experimental tasks that the subjects would refuse to perform. Most would yield to any request because "it's an experiment" (Orne, 1974). In one attempt to assign an obnoxious task, respondents were asked to perform serial additions of rows of digits and then tear up their answers and start all over again. The subjects so eagerly continued this dull and senseless task without refusal that the experimenter finally gave up (Orne, 1974, p. 142).

For these and other reasons, some critics feel that findings based on surveys and experiments are questionable, that much "artificial" research is really measurement error or the "error of measurement"; therefore, more natural methods of data gathering should be employed.

A Defense of Quantitative Research

Defense of quantitative research

In defense of quantitative methods, it should be reiterated from the third chapter that error is ever present in all research. Many of these errors are not the exclusive problem of surveys and experiments alone, but can be found in the very methods advocated by the critics. *The only perfect research is no research.* Also, many errors are not additive in their effect and may cancel each other, just as many of these potential errors are not inevitable but can be controlled before the fact, through research design, or after the fact, through statistical analysis.

Chapter 9 will illustrate that no data-gathering methodology alone has any guaranteed inherent superiority over another. So, although the problems with surveys and experiments may have been overstated, these criticisms remain the major reasons why some prefer more natural field methods, ethnographic or qualitative measures, such as participant observation.

Participant Observation

Participant observation has long been the favorite tool of the anthropologist in studying preliterate tribes (Bernard, 1994). This is so much the case that in jest it has been suggested that the typical Navajo family consists of a grandparent, mother, father, three children, and an anthropologist.

Participant observation

Participant observation refers to a variety of strategies in which the researcher studies a group in its natural setting by observing its activities and, to varying degrees, participating in its activities.

A very moving call for field studies in an unpublished statement by Robert Park in the 1920s was recorded by Howard Becker, one of Park's students at the time:

> You have been told to go grubbing in the library, thereby accumulating a mass of notes and a liberal coating of grime. You have been told to choose problems wherever you can find musty stacks of routine records based on trivial schedules prepared by tired bureaucrats and filled out by reluctant applicants for aid or fussy do-gooders or indifferent clerks. This is called "getting your hands dirty in real research." Those who thus counsel you are wise and honorable; the reasons they offer are of great value. But one thing more is needful: first hand observation. Go and sit in the lounges of the luxury hotels and on the doorsteps of the flophouses; sit on the Gold Coast settees and on the slum shakedowns; sit in Orchestra Hall and in the Star and Garter Burlesk. In short, gentlemen, go get the seat of your pants dirty in real research (McKinney, 1966, p. 71).

The Chicago School of Sociology in the 1920s not only got the seat of their pants dirty, but positively wore them out, along with shoes and pens. Much of the early ethnographic work in criminology was pioneered by the students of this school. Perhaps with the demise of the funded "golden age of criminal justice research" (the 1970s), researchers may return to the qualitative methods and people-oriented Chicago School style research (Reichel, 1985).

The target populations of criminal justice research—the public, victims, criminals, and criminal justice functionaries—have been subject to a variety of methodological analyses. Although some fine examples of the use of participant observation exist in the field, it has been viewed as a neglected and underused technique in criminal justice. Despite this belief and police suspicion, clandestineness, and resistance to researchers, a disproportionate number of police studies have utilized participant observation as the major means of data gathering (Manning and Van Maanen, 1979; Manning, 1972; Sanders, 1977).

Contrary to advice offered by writers of leading criminology textbooks such as Sutherland and Cressey (1978), Polsky suggests that it is not unwise or impossible to study criminals in their natural environment. In his book, *Hustlers, Beats and Others,* Polsky (1967) describes how he successfully employed participant observation in studying uncaught organized criminals, pool hustlers, drug dealers, and con artists. Advocates of participant observation such as Polsky feel that we have been too dependent on studies of imprisoned criminals in an unnatural environment or on unquestioned use of official statistics, and that this has led to an inaccurate view of criminals and criminal behavior.

Previously the point was made that all research may be viewed as a variation of the experimental model; Douglas (1972, 1976) suggests that similarly, *participant observation may be viewed as the beginning point of all other research.* Before one can design a survey or experiment, one must observe the subject of the investigation sufficiently to know the proper areas to probe. As we have indicated, participant observation has been most heavily used in anthropology where it was often the only way of studying preindustrial groups without a written language, by employing methods other than questionnaires or other standard methods. It represents a commitment to a more inductive or sensitizing strategy. Weber (1949) referred to such strategies as

Verstehen approach illustrative of a **verstehen approach,** one in which the researcher purposefully attempts to understand phenomena from the standpoint of the actors or to gain critical insight through an understanding of the entire context and frame of reference of the subjects under study. Ethnography, ethnomethodology, and field studies are other labels for techniques similar to, if not the same as, participant observation (Garfinkel, 1967; Denzin and Lincoln, 1993).

Grounded theory Glaser and Strauss (1967) call for a *grounded theory approach,* by which a theory is developed during the data gathering, thus grounding it in the real world, rather than artificially predetermining which hypotheses will be looked at.

Types of Participant Observation

Previously, participant observation was defined in terms of the degree to which participation and observation may vary. Figure 7.1 suggests how each of the following items may vary (Gold, 1958): complete participation, participant as observer, observer as participant, and complete observation.

Complete participation *Complete participation* takes place when the researcher not only joins in, but actually begins to manipulate the direction of, group activity. Such a strategy is rare and tends to violate an essential element of good participant

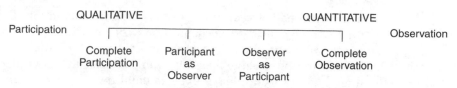

Figure 7.1 Types of Participant Observation.

observation, that the researcher attempt to avoid influencing the attitudes or behavior of the subjects under study. Another way of viewing complete participation is to label it "disguised observation," a subject to be treated in detail in Chapter 8.

The most frequently cited example of complete participation in the social science literature is the case of a group of researchers who joined a small doomsday cult *When Prophecy Fails* (Festinger, Riecken, and Schachter, 1956). Because the group was small, questions were raised as to the extent to which the researchers brought about the behavior they wished to investigate.

Describing his research strategy as "complete participation," Marquart (1986) worked as a prison guard for nineteen months while collecting data on prison life. He was able to enter into more sensitive aspects of guard work, particularly after he established his credibility by successfully defending himself against an attack by an inmate. Complete participation is very similar to, if not the same as, disguised observation, a topic which will be discussed in the next chapter.

Participant as observer

The *participant as observer* is the type that most people identify as constituting participant observation. The researcher usually makes his presence known and, although attempting not to influence situations, tries to objectively observe the activities of the group. Most of our discussion in this chapter will relate to this type.

Observer as participant

The *observer as participant* describes the one-visit interview. Even though the interviewers may not think so, they are also short-term participant observers. Holzman and Pines (1979) employed in-depth interviews of thirty primarily white, middle-class "johns" and were unable to find support for the "pathology-ridden depictions of the clients of prostitutes." Other examples involving in-depth interviews include Cressey's (1953) *Other People's Money,* which involved interviews with 133 incarcerated embezzlers; Klein and Montague's (1977) interviews with imprisoned, retired, and uncaught check forgers; and Letkemann's (1973) study of forty-five bank robbers and burglars. The last study provided much of what criminologists know regarding "casing" (looking over) of banks and the bank robber's dependence on uniformity of bank design, as well as handy parking. Experimental and unobtrusive measures may be viewed as a type of partic-

Complete observation

ipant observation that stresses *complete observation.* Stein (1974), employing one-way mirrors, was able to secretly observe and record hundreds of sessions between prostitutes and their clients. In reality, specific studies seldom fall into any one of these categories, or "ideal types," and might better be viewed as falling along a continuum, as in Figure 7.1.

Henceforth, our discussion of participant observation will focus on the participant-as-observer type. It should be noted at this point that descriptions of and distinctions between types of participant observation, field interviews, and unobtrusive measures become somewhat arbitrary at times and that what one writer might call participant observation another might view as a type of interview or unobtrusive measure. Some studies are examples of more than one method, for example, an experimental design may be employed to conduct a simulation that involves disguised observation in which subjects are interviewed.

Characteristics of Participant Observation

Perhaps the most distinctive qualities of participant observation are its *demands on time and personal cost.* Cost here refers not to financial obligations, but to personal involvement. As a general rule, the researcher is committed to studying a group for a considerable period, ranging from several weeks or months to several years. Participant observers hope to understand the frame of reference of the group they are studying. This is done by joining the group in their normal activities to experience things as they do. In doing so, the researcher may temporarily become a "different person" (Weinberg and Williams, 1972, p. 165).

The observer must attempt to operate mentally on two different levels: becoming an insider while remaining an outsider. The observer cannot be so far "inside," or socialized into the group, that everything seems so normal as not to be worth reporting. By the same token, the observer must be able to report patterns of behavior and interrelationships objectively and without moral bias. The role of "outsider" can be very valuable in that subjects may be willing to share important information because she or he is an outsider. Informants may be more willing to open up to neutral, reliable outsiders (Trice, 1970; Plate, 1975).

The researcher must avoid *oversocialization,* or *going native.* Some become so enamored by the new lifestyle of the group they are studying that they pass into a new identity and become too much a part of the group. Polsky, for instance, describes how some of the "uncaught criminals" he was studying told him that he would make a fine "wheelman" (driver of a getaway car) or "steer-horse" (accomplice who fingers the score in a con game) (Polsky, 1967). In doing his participant observation study of vice squads, Skolnick was asked to play a "john" (prostitute's customer), drive a stakeout van, surveil a bar for suspects, and offer advice on the legality of an arrest (Skolnick, 1966; National Advisory Committee, 1976, p. 131).

Objectivity in Research

The researcher must avoid not only overidentification with the study group, but also aversion to it. The ability of social scientists to remain objective despite personal subjective bias is illustrated by the work of anthropologists. They occasionally find some of the attitudes, beliefs, and behaviors of the societies they study repugnant and immoral; however, they are trained not to judge, but rather to determine objectively and record the meaning of these behavior patterns to the people who practice them. Famous anthropologist Malinowski, author of *Crime and Custom in Savage Society* (1926), *Argonauts of the Western Pacific* (1922), and other fine early studies of the Trobriand islanders, has been pointed to as a model of objectivity. Social scientists and others were shocked in the late 1960s when Malinowski's personal posthumous memoirs, *A Diary in the Strict Sense of the Word* (1967), were released. Although personally he found the group revolting, this bias was controlled and cannot be detected in his scholarly writings. This reflects an interesting debate in criminal justice research wherein Yablonsky, author of such field studies as *Synanon* (1965a) and *The Violent Gang* (1962), criticizes Polsky's view that the field researcher in criminal justice should avoid moralistic stances. Yablonsky (1965b) feels that such a posture is going too far, whereas Polsky claims that such a position is necessary to gain a full picture of group activity:

> Until the criminologist learns to suspend his personal distaste for the values and lifestyles of the untamed savages, until he goes out in the field to the cannibals and headhunters and observes them without trying either to civilize them or turn them over to colonial officials, he will be only a veranda anthropologist. That is, he will be only a jailhouse or courthouse sociologist, unable to produce anything like a genuinely scientific picture of crime (Polsky, 1967, p. 147).

Manning looks at this same issue from the other side of the fence, in "Observing the Police":

> Does the observation, if it occurs, of brutality, harassment, incompetence, or malfeasance *obligate* the researcher to reveal immediately to the policeman's superiors, or should he overlook them and pussyfoot in the interest of completing the study? Will a complete study have an even greater cumulative impact on the organization than revelation of instances of wrongdoing? (Manning, 1972, p. 258).

On this same general issue, some researchers take the stance that participant observation is obnoxious manipulation and immoral (Shils, 1961), or "psychological espionage," or necessary deception in order to obtain needed data (Gans, 1968). Becker perhaps best stated the argument supportive of Polsky's view of a nonmoralistic stance:

> In spite of the romantic yearnings of researchers and the earnest ideological assurance of some deviants, scientific requirements do not force us to join in deviant actions. But our scientific purposes often require us to hear about and on occasion to observe activities we may personally disapprove of. I think it equally indisputable that one cannot study deviants without foregoing a simple-minded moralism that requires us to denounce openly any such activity on every occasion. Indeed the researcher should cultivate a deliberately tolerant attitude, attempting to understand the point of view from which his subjects

undertake the activities he finds distasteful. Amoralism that forecloses empirical investigation by deciding questions of fact *a priori* is scientifically immoral (Becker, 1978a, p. 99).

"Going Native"

Soloway and Walters, in discussing ethnographic fieldwork, state the point succinctly: "Approaches must be found to avoid the dilemmas and pitfalls of a facile and unconstructive 'hipness' on the one hand and stagnating righteousness on the other" (Soloway and Walters, 1977, p. 176).

Perhaps an even more common outlook resulting from close contact with a new group over a sustained period is the *tendency of observers to over-identify with groups.* There are examples in the literature of an anthropologist who married a cannibal chief and of other individuals who, without being aware of it, have taken on the mannerisms of the groups they have studied. **Going native** is a situation in which the researcher identifies with and becomes a member of the study group, and in the process abandons his or her role as an objective researcher. Toby (1986, p. 2) attacked criminologist John Irwin for a speech he gave before the American Society of Criminology, accusing him of romanticizing criminals:

"Going Native"

> Irwin talks about prisoners as though all of them are victims of an oppressive society. And, in an aside to emphasize his point, he alluded to his personal history. (As is well known in the profession, Irwin served a prison term before becoming a criminologist.)
>
> Of course, John Irwin is not alone among criminologists in romanticizing criminals, in seeing virtue rather than moral flaws in offenders. And I can well understand that a person who has himself served time in prison is aware of decent people, who, through adverse circumstances, committed crimes, were convicted and were sentenced to incarceration. I can even understand criminologists, who, like Edwin Sutherland, get to know and become quite attached to professional criminals. However, loving the man and hating the fault is quite different from denying the existence of the fault because criminals are human beings . . . .
>
> I think of criminology as a discipline. By "discipline" I mean more than subject matter. I mean that we ought to restrain impulses, including benign impulses, that prevent us from seeing the world realistically. Just as anthropologists cannot be trusted (intellectually) when they go native to the extent that they glorify rather than study their preliterate societies, so a criminologist who has gone native cannot be trusted to tell us what criminals are like.

A parallel to research objectivity could be drawn with police undercover operations and issues such as entrapment. Certainly in the act of investigating for prosecution purposes, the individual should not be responsible for precipitating the behavior to be observed, because it may not otherwise have occurred. An interesting, related example is the "case of Tommy the Traveler," in the late 1960s. At a small college in upstate New York, Hobart College, a paid undercover informant (Tommy the Traveler), who had been placed to gather information on potential student radicals, became the leader of a mob that temporarily took over a portion of the campus, destroying property, including police cars. In such a situation, whether it be research or police investigation, the individual conducting the probe should not so influence the course of events as to destroy the ability to assess the subjects' true behavior.

General Procedures in Participant Observation

There is no one and only method of participant observation. There exists continual debate among field researchers themselves regarding specific operations (Lofland, 1971; Wolff, 1960); however, a core of customary procedures have accumulated with which researchers would not radically disagree, although they may on specific points.

McLuhan (1989, p. 167) whimsically stated that "the last person to ask how the water is is a fish." This is his way of suggesting that *it is generally not a good idea to attempt to study a group in which one has been a lifelong member.* First, the researcher is too far immersed in the culture to maintain objectivity. Second, the members of the group get to know the researcher too well and may often be unwilling to treat him or her as a researcher. The old speaker's rule of thumb holds that one must travel at least 100 miles from home grounds to be regarded as an expert.

Field Notes

Field notes

One important practice that is essential in field studies is the *keeping of extensive and detailed field notes or diaries.* Webb et al. (1966, p. 196) state that "the palest ink is clearer than the best memory." Initial participant observation is often exploratory and presumably the researcher does not fully understand the culture of the group. Thus, it is necessary to take complete notes on as many details as possible, even those that appear trivial, because it may be these very "unimportant details" that later provide the key to some important facet of the study. A good investigator records observations as often as possible and does not rely upon memory. As much importance and time should be allotted to recording observations as to participating, observing, and gathering such information. The participant observer, unlike the vacationer, cannot tell the reader that "you just had to be there to appreciate what I am telling you."

Berg claims that there is a 4:1 ratio of field-note writing to time in the field (Berg, 1995, p. 110). Novice field researchers in particular may wish to limit their initial time spent in actual fieldwork in order to assure that they will have the time and energy to put together quality field notes.

"Word crunching" (Dennis, 1984), the use of computers in qualitative analysis, has increased tremendously. Software programs such as Ethnograph (Tesch, 1990 and 1991) is quite popular as is the adaptation of standard software packages such as Lotus 1-2-3, Gofer, HyperCard, WordStar, and WordPerfect (Berg, 1995, pp. 195–196). Word searches in WordPerfect, for example, can be utilized for content analysis purposes (Fielding and Lee, 1991).

Mnemonics

Often it is unwise or impossible to record notes on the spot. It may, however, be crucial that one be able to reconstruct in exacting detail much of what has taken place. Skilled researchers train themselves in an ancient art used by preliterate tribes to pass down word for word their traditions. Most are familiar with the closing chapter of Alex Haley's *Roots* (1976) in which Haley, after asking the tribal elder whether a Kunta Kinte ever lived in this village, received no direct answer. Instead he had to listen hour upon hour to an oral recitation of the chronological history of the tribe until the wise

Mnemonics   one mentioned the sought-for information. Using **mnemonics,** a system of memorizing, the elder was merely using his mind as a vast computer memory bank and effortlessly providing an extensive oral printout of information. We have all used *mnemonic devices.* In elementary school, "ROYGBIV" for the color spectrum, "*every good boy does fine,*" and "FACE" for the musical scale, and poems to remember spelling or calendars—all provide useful tools for remembering. Anagrams (words or names), first letters of important lists, caricatures, and mental associations all permit later recall, reconstruction, and recording of important information.

The recording of detailed notes on a dictaphone and their later transcription can be effective, although this method may prevent the researcher from thinking through the material and may yield huge transcripts that must be boiled down.

Caution in Use of Other Recording Methods

Sanders (1977), in a participant observation study of detectives, quickly realized that taking notes made his subjects nervous. He cut down on this practice and began to leave the notebook open in the detectives' offices when he left each evening to show he had nothing to hide. Later he ceased taking notes on the spot altogether, and used the time for relaxed observation to improve rapport. Sanders also took *photographs* to improve recall. These acted as a second type of field notes (Sanders, 1977, p. 200). Certainly, in the proper circumstances, tape recorders, videotapes, films, and other mechanical aids can greatly improve recall. Nevertheless, such devices must certainly be used with caution or perhaps not at all if the subject matter is criminal activity, although they have successfully been employed with this group also (Klockars, 1977, p. 210; Sherizen, 1976).

Whether the researcher is aware of it or not, a newcomer to a group is assigned a role by the old members. He or she is viewed as a potential, if not actual, disturbance. *Generally, it takes some time before the newcomer is accepted to the degree that the group becomes less suspicious and begins to act more naturally.* Usually, the smaller the group, the greater the potential disturbance introduced by the researcher; however, the longer the participant is present, the less the disturbance over time because he or she is eventually accepted by the respondents.

Tips on Participant Observation

In a classic statement on participant observation in criminology, Polsky (1967) offers some tips on studying criminals in their natural environment. He suggests that one should keep in mind that the *subject is in greater jeopardy as a result of being studied in the field* than is someone in jail. The researcher is more of an intruder and the subjects are certainly freer not to cooperate. In studying criminals on their "turf," researchers should *avoid taking notes on the spot,* and using standard data-gathering tools such as questionnaires or tape recorders. *Initially they should spend their time observing and listening, and avoid asking a lot of questions* (Spradley, 1970). The researcher's middle-class language styles and probing may prove irritating to subjects. William Foote Whyte, in his *Streetcorner Society,* was never able to do an entirely successful analysis of the rackets in Cornerville because he blew an opportunity with a racketeer to whom he had been introduced (Whyte, 1943; see also McCall, 1978; McCall and Simmons, 1969):

> One has to learn when to question and when not to question as well as what questions to ask.
>
> I learned this lesson one night in the early months when I was with Doc in Chichi's gambling joint. A man from another part of the city was regaling us with a tale of the organization of gambling activity. l had been told that he had once been a very big gambling operator, and he talked knowingly about many interesting matters. He did most of the talking, but the others asked questions and threw in comments, so at length I began to feel that I must say something in order to be part of the group. l said: "I suppose the cops were all paid off?"
>
> The gambler's jaw dropped. He glared at me. Then he denied vehemently that any policemen had been paid off and immediately switched the conversation to another subject. For the rest of the evening I felt very uncomfortable.
>
> The next day Doc explained the lesson of the previous evening. "Go easy on that 'who,' 'what,' 'why,' 'when,' 'where' stuff, Bill. You ask those questions, and people will clam up on you. If people accept you, you can just hang around and you'll learn the answers in the long run without even having to ask the questions" (Whyte, 1943, p. 303).

These suggestions need not be limited to studying deviants, but apply to much field research in general. As an American Fulbright scholar in Uruguay, Smykla (1989, p. 29) described how his initial involvement entailed "inoffensive social interaction." This wins the subjects' confidence, identifies important contacts and who has the most prestige and insight, and permits the researcher to learn the words and symbols that will elicit response without forcing the researcher's own agenda and preconceptions.

(margin note:) Participant observation of criminals

Gaining Access

Polsky advises that one *learn the "argot"* (specialized jargon) of the group being studied, but avoid overusing it or trying too hard to be an insider. Initial introductions to criminals in the field may be gained by frequenting their haunts or sharing other common recreational interests. Becker (1963) recommends cabdrivers, reporters, bartenders, and cops as good sources of information on deviant hangouts, although his avenue to studying drug users was his performance in a jazz band. Polsky (1967) was very adept at playing pool, whereas Bryan (1965) was a counselor and gained access to other prostitutes through one of his clients who was in the trade. Some criminals spend a lot of time in court. Talese was successful in establishing contact with Bill Bonanno during a trial recess. Initially, he simply indicated that "Someday, months or years from now, I would like to sit down with him and discuss the possibility of writing a book about his boyhood" (Talese, 1971, p. 13). After many months Talese began to establish contact with young Bill and his family, although at first the family was suspicious and skeptical:

> Nor did I question them: I was sensitive to the situation and at this juncture I was more interested in the domestic atmosphere and the style of the people than in specific information. I was content to observe, pleased to be accepted. At night, after I returned home I recorded (Talese, 1971, p. 501).

Becker (1978a) suggests various strategies for studying deviants. If previous status provides access to deviant groups, it should be taken advantage of. Ianni was able to gain cooperation on the basis of mutual ethnic identity (Ianni and Ianni, 1972).

If access is totally lacking, begin with incarcerated individuals. If the type of deviance being studied is prevalent, subjects may be obtained from larger samples of the population. Steffensmeier (1986, p. 1) describes how he first decided to undertake his study of The Fence, "Sam Goodman":

> I first met Sam Goodman, a white male, nearly sixty years of age, through the recommendation of several burglars I had been interviewing as part of a research project on the topic of female criminality. "Talk to Sam," they advised, "He's an 'old head,' knows his way around if anybody does." I did interview Sam—in January of 1980 in the Midstate Penitentiary where he was serving a three year term for stolen property. During this interview, in questioning Sam about the types of crimes women commit and the criminal roles they play, I found my interest shifting to questions about Sam himself, his life and his colorful criminal career. Since then, I have regularly interviewed and studied Sam, even after his release from prison in the summer of 1981 and on into the present time. (In 1994, Sam passed away, but not before contacting Steffensmeier and having him visit.)

Advertising for subjects in periodicals geared to their interests has been successfully employed (Lee, 1969). Finally, the offering of services that deviants need or cannot readily obtain elsewhere may induce them to reveal themselves. Bryan, for instance, offered counseling services to prostitutes (Bryan, 1965; Becker, 1978a; Johnson, 1990). Exhibit 7.1 describes gaining access in a study of skinheads.

EXHIBIT 7.1

American Skinheads: The Criminology and Control of Hate Crime

Entering the world of violence, hate, and racial paranoia of skinhead subculture, "idiots with ideology," contains more than the usual challenge to field researchers. Similar to other field investigators (Thompson, 1967; Yablonsky, 1962) Mark Hamm's attempts were on one occasion greeted with violence. He was attacked by members of the American Front at the corner of Haight and Ashbury in San Francisco. Kicked in the shins with a pair of steel-toed Doc Martens was his punishment for having been seen conversing with an Indonesian prostitute.

Hamm (1993, pp. 100–101) describes his method:

I began to systematically collect data on the American skinheads in the fall of 1989. Drawing from the native field study approach, I started the investigation by visiting various U.S. cities where I tracked down skinheads in their natural habitat (street corners, bars, coffee shops, record stores, survivalist outlets, rock concerts, and motorcycle shops). These subjects were not hard to identify. They had shaved heads and wore white power and/or Nazi regalia. Two skinheads, for example, were tattooed in the middle of their foreheads with the mark of the swastika. To gain a broader context for the research, I used the same methods to interview skinheads on the streets of Montreal, Vancouver, London, Amsterdam and Berlin.

He simply approached these youths and asked if they would consent to an interview in a research project that was attempting to "set the record straight on skinheads." No electronic devices were used. Hamm offered $10 for a completed interview. Another technique involved getting membership lists from the underground teen press and Tom Metzger's publication *WAR* (*White Aryan Resistance*).

After sending letters to twenty-six skinhead leaders promising $25 for a collect call telephone interview, Hamm obtained nine interviews plus an unexpected dividend. Three additional unsolicited leaders heard about the research, called, and were interviewed. Nonrespondents were sent five copies of a questionnaire and asked to fill one out and pass the others to four other members and they would be paid $10. This produced eight additional usable questionnaires. Using Internet, Hamm next logged onto the *WAR* board. He identified himself as a sociologist with no axe to grind and offered $10 to any skinhead who came online and conversed. This yielded two responses. Finally, Hamm used the prison field methods approach, and with the cooperation of authorities was able to interview incarcerated skinheads in four states. Hamm (1993, pp. 102–103) concludes:

In summary, then, I conducted thirty-six original skinhead interviews using native field methods, clandestine community agency techniques, and prison field study strategies. I controlled for paranoia by primarily focusing on subcultural leaders—or core members who are likely to display the highest rates and severity of hate crime violence—and by presenting myself as a sociologist operating independent of law enforcement and community service agencies. The early Haight street assault notwithstanding, I experienced no life-threatening violence.

Source: Hamm, Mark S. *American Skinheads: The Criminology and Control of Hate Crime.* Westport, Conn.: Praeger, 1993.

Gatekeepers

Gatekeeper

Of major assistance to gaining access to a new social world is an *introduction to a gatekeeper, leader, or person who is willing to accept the purpose of the study and vouch for the researcher's presence.* A community worker's introduction of Whyte to Doc, leader of the Norton Street Gang, made access to Cornerville possible because Doc told everyone that Whyte was his friend (Whyte, 1943). Agar (1977, p. 145) indicates that transfer to the street with a trusted "native" has several advantages:

1. You have a guide to the territory. You quickly learn the social spaces in the neighborhood and the kinds of persons and activities that occupy each.
2. You have an introduction into at least some groups on-the-scene. The importance of this cannot be overemphasized. A straight outsider is often a "mark" just waiting for a disaster to occur. An introduction from a trusted insider immediately establishes an openness together with certain rights and obligations as so-and-so's friend.

Walker and Lidz (1977) suggest the employment of "indigenous observers," paid researchers from the ranks of those to be studied. Such remuneration is viewed as tangible reciprocity, or evidence of respect; such employment helps some to improve their circumstances; however, researchers must be certain that they are not eliciting demand characteristics or the creation of work as a result of the pay offer.

Announcement of Intentions

Announce intentions

Polsky (1967) suggests that if researchers gain access on the basis of some common interest, for instance, gambling or drinking, they should very early on *indicate their true purpose:* "do not pretend to be one of them." Most subjects will accept the simple explanation that the researcher is writing a book on the subject, although Orenstein and Phillips (1978, p. 312) correctly recommend that a far more detailed explanation be given to the leaders, sponsors, or contact who must answer for the investigator's presence.

Sampling

Because of the very nature of most participant observational studies in criminal justice, particularly of sensitive subjects, the use of standard sampling procedures is inappropriate. Chapter 5 discusses *snowball sampling* as a much used technique in field studies, in which the investigator builds subjects on the basis of faith and the introductions of former subjects. This further reinforces the necessity of being "up front" with key contacts.

Reciprocity and Protection of Identity

Reciprocity

Reciprocity involves a system of mutual obligations. The research subjects help the investigator; now what is owed them?

Reciprocity would entail that the researcher permit the subjects to study him or her as well by answering questions they may ask. Of great importance in participant observation, particularly of criminals in the field, is *protection of the identity of informants.* Most researchers use *pseudonyms* (*aliases*) to shroud the actual names of the subjects. Some of these pseudonyms have now become legend in criminology and criminal justice: Sutherland's professional thief "Chic" Conwell (1937), the Iannis' Lupollo organized crime family (1972), and Klockars' professional fence Vincent Swaggi (1974). Related to this issue is the need for researchers to *decide beforehand the degree to which they wish to be privy to criminal activity.* Klockars (1977, p. 214) struck a deal with Vincent: "I also told Vincent that I would not reveal his identity unless it meant that I was going to jail if I did not, and he told me that he really could not expect me to do more." In speaking further to this hazard Klockars suggests:

Pseudonyms

> The risks were known to Vincent, and he accepted them freely. I considered those risks justifiable because of the potential benefits of my research:
> 1. Criminology, before *The Professional Fence,* knew very little about the trade in stolen property. My work promises to guide law enforcement and legislative efforts in the reduction of property theft and the prosecution of a type of criminal essential to it.
> 2. Moreover, I defend the risks that I took and the right of researchers like myself to take similar risks in the pursuit of knowledge which may benefit mankind, and I would claim this right even if *The Professional Fence,* as a single effort in the work of scientists, proved fruitless (Klockars, 1977, p. 224).

Polsky (1967) tells us that although a researcher should not pretend to be "one of them," he or she should also not stick out like a sore thumb. For instance, Polsky wore short-sleeved shirts and an expensive watch in studying heroin use and trafficking.

Finally, as we will discuss later in this chapter, not everyone should attempt to gather data by means of this technique. First, long hours of boredom may make huge demands on time before the few things the researcher wishes to observe occur. Second, there is *danger;* for instance, Bill Bonanno was concerned with Talese's welfare during the "Banana Wars" in New York (Talese, 1971). Polsky (1967, p. 141) tells us that "most of the danger for the field worker comes not from the cannibals or headhunters, but from colonial "officials."

Concern for Accuracy

Participant observers should, where possible, employ other methods as well to further validate findings (Irwin, 1972). The Iannis developed a pecking order or scale that they used to assign validity to the data they gathered (from highest to lowest):

1. Data gathered by direct observation where we were participants.
2. Data gathered by direct observation where we were not direct participants.
3. Interviews which can be checked out against documented sources, for example, records of arrest or business ownership.
4. Data corroborated by more than one informant.
5. Lowest priority is assigned to data gathered from only one source.

In addition, informants were graded from "always reliable" to "unreliable" (Ianni and Ianni, 1972, pp. 188–189).

Similarly, Steffensmeier, in *The Fence: In the Shadow of Two Worlds* (1986, pp. 4–6), indicates the following validity checks:

1. The interview format provided a cross check, i.e., did the second, third and fourth interviews all say the same thing? Some interviews were also tape recorded and some were checked by Sam Goodman (the subject) himself.
2. Documents, e.g., newspapers, personal documents, court records, letters, sales receipts, advertising, and the like were examined.
3. Observations of Sam at work were supplemented with interviews and meetings with customers, friends, and dealers.
4. Consultation took place with police and legal officials.
5. The data were consistent with biographies and autobiographies of thieves.

Examples of Participant Observation

This writer's personal interest in participant observation may be related to the fact that I was an unknowing subject in a journalistic field study by James Gittings (1966) entitled *Life Without Living: People of the Inner City,* a series of studies he conducted in the Pittsburgh and New York City areas. Part of his study of Millvale (near Pittsburgh) was a description of a corner gang—"the bridge boys"—with whom I occasionally had contact. From my youth, I recall a man (who, in retrospect, I now assume was working under the cover of a caretaker at a local private girls' high school) who would strike up conversations with us. In his book Gittings described quite accurately local political corruption, gambling operations, and a gang war that occurred while I was away at college. The competing sides in the battle ironically consisted of boys this writer had grown up with in his old neighborhood (in Pittsburgh) versus "the bridge boys" and others in his new neighborhood.

Although we have discussed a number of participant observation studies, some further examples demonstrate the versatility of such studies. Having previously conducted a participant observation study of a chapter of the Guardian Angels in Detroit, Albini (1986) conducted a field study in

1983–1984 of all Guardian Angels chapters in the United States and Canada. He underwent training, became a member of the organization, and patrolled with every chapter, concluding that they were not vigilantes as some had charged. Taylor (1984) in *In the Underworld* performed a two-year field study of uncaught professional criminals in the London underworld, whereas the Adlers in *Wheeling and Dealing* (1985) interviewed and observed for six years upper-level cocaine and marijuana dealers and smugglers. Sullivan (1989) spent more than four years studying youth gangs and crime on the streets of Brooklyn, while Sanchez Jankowski (1991) spent over ten years studying gangs in three cities (see Exhibit 7.2). Eleanor Miller (1986) did field research interviewing sixty-four prostitutes in Milwaukee, Marquart (1986) worked as a prison guard, and Hopper (1991) studied outlaw motorcycle gangs.

EXHIBIT 7.2

Islands in the Streets

From 1978 to 1989 Martin Sanchez Jankowski conducted a participant observation study of about thirty-seven gangs in Boston, New York, and Los Angeles. The gangs were African-American, Jamaican, Puerto Rican, Dominican, Chicano, Central American, and Irish as well as gangs of mixed ethnic origins. Jankowski's entree required two steps. First he contacted community individuals or agencies that worked with these gangs and arranged introductions and subsequent meetings with gang leaders. He simply explained to the leaders that he was a professor and wanted to write a book, the idea of which many found interesting. Despite a Polish last name from his adopted father, Jankowski's Latino ancestry eased his cooperation from Latino and African-American gangs.

Next, the gangs presented Jankowski with two tests. To test whether he was an informant, they committed illegal acts to see if he would turn them in to authorities. He was on one occasion falsely accused and physically attacked. The second test (for all gangs but the Irish) involved what other gang observers call a "beat down" or initiation rite. Jankowski would have to demonstrate how tough he was when other members would start a fight with him. Despite his training in Karate, this test created much anxiety. In the ten years of research he was only seriously injured twice.

After the initial period of suspicion, the gangs tended to forget or no longer care that he was conducting research. He was often with them during some risky situations and apparently handled himself up to their expectations. Perhaps the ultimate compliment was, "You don't look like a professor," and/or, "You don't act like one" (p. 13). Jankowski explains:

In sum, I participated in nearly all the things they did. I ate where they ate, I slept where they slept, I stayed with their families, I traveled where they went, and in certain situations where I could not remain neutral, I fought with them. The only things I did not participate in were those activities that were illegal. As part of our mutual understanding, it was agreed that I did not have to participate in any activity (including taking drugs) that was illegal (ibid.).

Jankowski carried two notebooks, a small pad and a larger 8 ½ by 11 inch pad. He would record notes on both of these as well as use two tape recorders, one regular size and the other pocket size. The latter was used to record notes during the day. All of this was done, of course, with the gangs' permission.

Source: Jankowski, Martin Sanchez. *Islands in the Streets.* Berkeley: University of California Press, 1991.

In addition to participant observation studies of criminals and the public by Polsky (1967), Whyte (1943), Thrasher (1927), and Humphreys (1970), a variety of such studies have been done with the police as subjects. Kirkham (1976) in *Signal Zero* was a professor who became a police officer. Reiss (1971) and Skolnick (1966) did field studies of police operations. Numerous other examples exist in the literature, including case studies that concentrate on fewer subjects. The sometimes humorous subjects of participant observation are represented in such titles as "The Milkman and His Customer: A Cultivated Relationship" (Bigus, 1978) or "The Cabdriver and His Fare: Facets of a Fleeting Relationship" (Davis, 1959).

Other unusual subjects of participant observation have been Skipper's "Stripteasers" (1979), Weinberg's "Sexual Modesty: Social Meanings and the Nudist Camp" (1968), and Cavan's *Liquor License* (1966), a study of mating behavior in singles bars. It is incumbent on the researcher using participant observation to consider some of the relative advantages and disadvantages of the technique over other means available for gathering data.

Advantages of Participant Observation

Participant observation represents a commitment to a sensitizing or "verstehen" strategy in which the researcher attempts to actually experience the life conditions of the study group. Such an approach generally produces *less prejudgments,* is *less disturbing* to respondents than experiments, and is *more flexible* and natural than more artificial means of data gathering. Contradictions between attitude and behavior become apparent. Being on-the-scene, the researcher can double-check assumptions regarding the meaning of observations. It is an excellent means of gathering detailed *qualitative data,* particularly on subjects about which little information may exist. All of this takes place in *more natural settings* in which the subjects normally carry out their activities. Participant observation has produced some of the most fascinating, informative, and readable literature in criminology and criminal justice. In addition a full picture of criminal behavior should incorporate the offender's perspective (Wright and Bennett, 1990, p. 149).

Disadvantages of Participant Observation

A principal disadvantage of participant observation is its *very time-consuming nature.* Commitments of several months or even years are not uncommon (Schwartz and Schwartz, 1955). This may take precedence over one's previous lifestyle. It certainly is not the easiest way of performing a study, nor is it the preferred method for most. Carey describes such problems in studying "speed freaks" (those who inject massive quantities of amphetamines):

> The peculiar round of life . . . posed enormous practical difficulties. . . . Our conventional commitments . . . had to be put aside. . . . We were continually reassured by our medical collaborators that the possibility of contracting hepatitis was extremely remote. . . . It caused constant concern while in the field, however, for every vague malaise was interpreted as the onset of hepatitis. . . . Our middleclass notions of hygiene led to feelings of revulsion at the physical conditions in one flash house where most of our observations were conducted (Carey, 1972, p. 82).

The observer is often not in a position to control the action and must often wait for the activities of interest to occur. In studying criminal groups, for instance, researchers may have to spend hours or days in what some may regard as boring activities, for example, marathon card games or drinking bouts before something noteworthy happens. As discussed previously, *over-identification or dislike of the group being studied can be problematic.*

Participant observation poses the *problem of gaining entry into and acceptance by a group.* It is perhaps the *most personally demanding technique.* Whyte voted numerous times in the same local election, Humphreys broke the law, Becker performed in a jazz band, and others have faked symptoms of mental illness (Caudill, 1958; Goffman, 1961).

Ethical
dilemmas

Ethical dilemmas are sometimes raised by this technique, particularly if uncaught criminals are the subject of study. Reciprocity indicates that because the subjects have given of themselves, they are owed something. On the other hand, where does one draw the line between the role as researcher and the role as responsible citizen? Those studying "deviant groups" may have to decide between participating in immoral or illegal conduct and blowing months of work.

There is a difference, however, between knowing about something illegal and actually doing it. This is the "it takes one to know one fallacy," the false belief that to understand a phenomenon one must have actively participated in it. Whyte (1943), having illegally voted numerous times, later expressed regret for having done so, finding it to be a foolish risk that did not increase insight. Certainly one would not have argued that Jonas Salk have polio to discover a cure or that Durkheim commit suicide to fully appreciate it. Although a researcher should avoid deceiving respondents, he or she must also avoid being deceived by the study group. The level of mutual cooperation is described by Sanders: "Instead of doing research 'on' detectives, the activity would be more accurately characterized as doing research 'with' detectives. In a way, the relationship was something like a master and an apprentice, with the researcher as the apprentice" (1977, p. 202).

Some researchers view deception as a necessary ploy to obtain information that cannot be gained in any other manner (Gans, 1968). Deception will be examined in greater detail in Chapter 8.

Participant observers must make major attempts to control their biases which may heavily influence what they observe, record, and interpret. Liebow (1967), a white anthropologist studying lower-class black street-corner men in the early 1960s, apparently had fewer problems than a middleclass black researcher doing a similar study as part of the same project.

Fujisaka and Grayzel (1978), in an ethnographic prison study report on *observer bias* or "subjectivity," obtained different results in the same setting because of differences in their own social backgrounds.

A major challenge to participant observation is the fact that it generally *yields nonquantitative data* and thus may require greater literary and analytic skill at the write-up stage.

Case Studies

Case studies   *Case study methods* are in-depth, qualitative studies of one or a few illustrative cases (Becker, 1978b). The types of studies included as examples of the case study approach vary greatly, from general field studies to studies of one individual. Because no consensus exists, we take the more general approach to case studies in this discussion.

Wheeler (1970, 1978) claims that most case studies have been restricted to delinquency research and that there have been fewer than a couple of dozen such studies that examine adult criminals. Travis (1983, p. 47), however, says that case studies abound in the literature:

> The case study approach involves the identification of one or more exemplary instances of the phenomenon under study and an in-depth analysis of the phenomenon and related factors . . . a research strategy which seeks to explain the occurrence of a phenomenon in its natural setting. . . . Researchers have investigated crime causation in general and for specific types of crime through the intensive study of one or more criminals' life histories.

Travis (1983, p. 46) has noted a decline in coverage of the case study approach in criminology and criminal justice texts and attributes this to its eclipse by quantitative methods and the unfortunate labeling of any case study as an example of a "one-shot case study" by Campbell and Stanley (1963).

Life History/Oral History

Life histories and oral histories are some methodologies employed in case
Oral/life   studies. *Oral and life histories* are "recounts of events by participants"
histories   (Laub, 1983, p. 226). Journalists use the term *autobiography,* whereas historians and social scientists use *documentary expression* or *oral history.* Laub (1983), in *Criminology in the Making: An Oral History,* examines the history of criminology by means of in-depth interviews with major criminologists. Such research can be used to test theories and generate hypotheses for future research, as well as sensitize researchers to important questions (Laub, 1984). In addition, many subjects are not susceptible to more quantitative treatment, and case studies can provide insight into the subjective elements of institutional processes (Kobrin, 1982; Bennett, 1981; Bertaux, 1981). The

versatility of the oral history can be expanded by means of videotaped interviews, as demonstrated by Mutchnick (1986) in an interview with Sir Leon Radzinowicz, one of the foremost British criminologists.

Some Examples of Case Studies

Concentrating on single individuals, groups, or communities and employing life history documents, oral histories, in-depth interviews, as well as participant observation (Yin, 1994), the case study is quite versatile and has generated some fascinating literature. The classic example of a landmark case study in criminology was Sutherland's (1937) *The Professional Thief,* in which his informant, Chic Conwell, described the world of the professional thief. Some other examples from the academic literature are the Iannis' (1972) study of the Lupollo family in *A Family Business: Kinship and Social Control in Organized Crime* and Shaw's *The Jack-Roller* (1930), *Brothers in Crime* (1938), and *The Natural History of a Delinquent Career* (1931). Shaw's "Jack-Roller" (mugger), "Stanley," was followed up by Snodgrass (1982) in *The Jack-Roller at Seventy: A Fifty-Year Follow-up.* Klockars' *The Professional Fence* (1974) (a dealer in stolen property), given the pseudonym "Vince Swaggi," has his counterpart in Steffensmeier's *The Fence* (1986) and "Sam Goodman." *Box Man* (1975), a case study of a professional safecracker, has since been updated and entitled *Harry King: A Professional Thiefs Journal* (King and Chambliss, 1984).

Many other case studies too numerous to detail have been employed in criminology and criminal justice and include studies of chronic alcoholics (Spradley, 1970), an armed robber (Allen, 1977), vice lords (Keiser, 1969), heroin addicts (Agar, 1973; Rettig, Torres, and Garrett, 1977), a jewel thief (Abadinsky, 1983), a "wise guy" (organized crime member) (Abadinsky, 1983), and an organized crime family (Anderson, 1979). Case studies of communities are illustrated by the President's Crime Commission study of "Wincanton" (Reading, Pa.) (Gardiner and Olson, 1968) and Blok's (1975) study of the Mafia in a Sicilian village. Travis (1983) cites many one-time studies of such agencies as the police, corrections officers, and courts as representative of the numerous case studies in the field.

Journalistic Field Studies

A discussion of case studies would not be complete without mention of the many fine works by investigative journalists. A foremost sociological field researcher, William Foote Whyte (Fox, 1980, p. 2) acknowledges his debt to the writings of turn-of-the-century journalist Lincoln Steffens, author of *The Shame of the Cities* (1904), for having inspired him to undertake participant observation. Investigative journalists (similar to their television counterparts on "60 Minutes," "20/20," and "48 Hours") are interested in documenting and exposing social conditions and are generally less interested in theoretically incorporating their findings into the social science literature.

In *Paper Lion,* George Plimpton (1965) participated in the training camp of the Detroit Lions football team. In later investigations he performed with a philharmonic orchestra and in a circus as a trapeze artist; played professional tennis; entered the entertainment industry; and was a photographer for *Playboy,* a professional hockey player, and a stand-up comic at Caesar's Palace (Plimpton, 1985). Thompson (1967) rode with the Hell's Angels motorcycle gang, whereas Talese (1971) studied the Bonanno organized crime family and also visited and worked in massage parlors (Talese, 1979). Terkel (1970, 1974, 1980, 1984) has made excellent use of first-person oral histories in describing historical events, such as the Depression and World War II, from the viewpoint of average people. Mills (1986) in *The Underground Empire* conducted a five-year field study of international drug trafficking organizations and concluded that the United States was fighting a two-faced war on drugs, one with phony rhetoric on the six o'clock news and the other with secret deals and tolerance of politically connected conspirators and countries in the name of foreign policy. Other collections of personal accounts and investigations (Jackson, 1972; Denfield, 1974; Plate, 1975) enable us to view the illegal world in the words of, and from the perspective of, the deviant.

The major advantage of the case study is its in-depth, qualitative view of a few subjects; the major problems associated with such methods are possible researcher bias and atypicality of the cases chosen for analysis.

The use of case study and life history material will be explored in further detail in our discussion of unobtrusive measures in Chapter 8, particularly in the discussion of biographies and autobiographies.

Single-Subject Designs

Single-subject designs

Not all case studies are qualitative. **Single-subject designs** are quantitative case studies that involve the longitudinal measurement of a dependent variable on a single subject or case. While time-series designs measure groups, single-subject designs measure populations in which $N = 1$. In such designs the time interval is usually divided into a baseline period (A), an intervention period (B), and any number of additional variations.

Figure 7.2 depicts three types of single-subject designs (see Kazdin, 1982; or Tawney and Gast, 1984, for more detail). *AB* is the *basic design,* while *ABA* or *ABAB* are examples of reversal designs. In the first such reversal design (*ABA*), treatment is withdrawn (*A*) after a baseline period (*A*) and a treatment period (*B*); in the last such design (*ABAB*), after the treatment is withdrawn (*A*), it is once again reintroduced (*B*). *ABACA* is an example of a multiple-treatment design, where *C* represents a new treatment or one different from treatment *B* (Hagan, 1989).

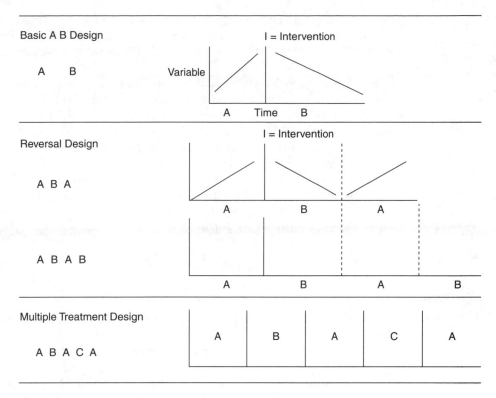

Legend

    A = Baseline Phase or Period of Treatment Withdrawal

    B = Treatment Phase

    C, D = Additional Treatment Phase or Phases

Figure 7.2 Single Subject Designs. (*Source:* Hagan, Frank E. "Single Subject Designs: A Strategy for Quantitative Case Studies." Paper presented at Academy of Criminal Justice Sciences Meeting, Washington, D.C., March 31, 1989.)

By way of example, using the basic *AB* design, suppose that for the baseline period *A* we had plotted line *A,* measuring monthly levels of psychological depression of an inmate. The intervention (*I*) would entail starting the inmate in a counseling program, and line *B* would represent the measurement of monthly decreases in depression.

Traditional social science research utilizing group designs (*X*'s and *O*'s) is often inapplicable to case studies and practitioner needs. Hurwitz (1984, p. 41) contributed one of the few articles devoted to single-subject designs in the criminal justice literature. In it he noted that relying on group designs (nomothetic) to measure the success of crime control programs blurs the individual cases of success or failure by using average achievement scores. As a result of this weakness in group designs, process evaluation models using time-series designs have become more popular; so too has the single-subject (idiographic) model, which assesses the intervention process with individual clients. The treatment may work for most individuals, but not all. "The treatment goals and desired direction of change for one individual may be counter to those of the overall group" (Robinson, Bronson, and Blythe, 1988, p. 38).

The single-subject technique is viewed as promoting research by practitioners simply because clinical service providers find it to be more practical than group designs. Such research provides hard evidence of a client's progress (Monette, Sullivan, and DeJong, 1994 p. 330). As with any case studies, single-subject designs do face the problem of generalizability—that is, can we generalize from this single case study to all such cases? However, replication is one means of addressing this concern. In the final analysis single-subject designs appear to provide yet another useful methodological tool which is particularly applicable to practice settings where group designs may not always be feasible.

Summary

Field study methods such as participant observation and case studies are viewed by their proponents as an *important alternative to more quantitative methods of data gathering* such as experiments and surveys. *Critics* of experiments and surveys point to a myriad of shortcomings, including artificiality, assumption of a connection between attitude and behavior, and the tendency of the findings to be a result of the method used rather than real findings. Type of canvass, instrument used, interviewer effects, biased sponsorship, nonresponse bias, mechanical errors, and demand characteristics of respondents are a few of the many rival causal factors that the critics feel invalidate many of the results of such studies. None of these problems is unique to more quantitative methods or is uncontrollable; thus, these criticisms do not inherently destroy the utility of such methods.

Participant observation is a strategy by which the researcher studies a group by, to varying degrees, participating in and observing their activities. Participant observation is a very useful technique in criminal justice and criminology and can be successfully employed to study uncaught, "successful" criminals, a much needed approach in the field. In the past, criminal justice has been overreliant on studies using official statistics and incarcerated populations. Utilization of participant observation represents a commitment to a "verstehen," qualitative or sensitizing orientation, and renders in-depth descriptions of selected subjects.

Some *general characteristics* of these studies are their demanding nature (time and personal cost), simultaneous existence as an insider and an outsider, avoidance of overidentification as well as aversion, and maintenance of objectivity. Ethical issues related to such techniques are possible knowledge of illegal activities, confidentiality, privacy, and reciprocity.

General procedures in participant observation relate to the choice of study population, the need to keep a field diary, and mnemonic or other techniques for recalling events. *Suggestions for conducting field studies of criminals* are offered by those who have conducted such studies. Such topics as gaining access, acceptance, gatekeepers, proper conduct, gathering subjects, reciprocity, confidentiality, danger, and accuracy are discussed. *Single-subject designs* are described as quantitative case studies that involve longitudinal measurement of a variable dependent on a single subject or case.

Investigators considering the use of participant observation, in addition to considering the utilization of other techniques, should weigh the relative advantages and disadvantages of participant observation carefully before deciding to use it as the principal data-gathering device. *Major advantages* are fewer prejudgments, less disturbance, greater flexibility, more natural settings, and the sensitizing, qualitative nature of such studies. *Leading shortcomings* are the very demanding nature of such research as well as such problems as gaining acceptance, maintaining objectivity, facing ethical dilemmas, avoiding oversocialization or aversion, and the nonquantitative nature of such information. Finally, *case studies* are briefly discussed as a form of participant observation that concentrates on one or a few illustrative examples. Examples of Hamm's skinheads study and Jankowski's *Islands in the Streets* were used to illustrate participant observation/field studies.

Key Concepts

Critique of Experiments and Surveys
Verbal Reports versus Behavior
Defense of Quantitative Research
Participant Observation
"Verstehen" Approach
Types of Participant Observation

Characteristics of Participant Observation
"Going Native"
Objectivity
General Procedures in Participant Observation
Field Notes
Mnemonics

Participant Observation of Criminals
Advantages/ Disadvantages of Participant Observation
Single-Subject Design

Review Questions

1. What are some distinctive advantages of a qualitative strategy for data gathering, such as participant observation, over more quantitative approaches?
2. What are some specific procedures followed by those conducting participant observation studies?
3. Discuss some of the special considerations participant observers must be aware of when studying criminals in field settings.
4. Of what importance have case studies been in criminological/criminal justice research? Provide examples that have used this approach.
5. Using Hamm's Skinheads and Jankowski's gang studies discuss some of the potential dangers as well as prospects of studying deviant groups on their turf.

CHAPTER

Unobtrusive Measures, Secondary Analysis, and the Uses of Official Statistics

Unobtrusive measures

Unobtrusive measures are nonreactive methods of gathering data, that is, means of obtaining information in which subjects are not aware of being studied (Bouchard, 1976; Sechrest, 1980; Webb et al., 1966). The subject's lack of awareness of being studied eliminates reactivity or stooge effects. Sanders, in *The Sociologist as Detective* (1976), gives an excellent illustration of the use of unobtrusive measures by means of Conan Doyle's fictional master detective, Sherlock Holmes. Holmes, much like the social scientist, attempted to gather information to answer the research problem "Who killed the lord of the manor?" Through careful observation, questioning of respondents (suspects and witnesses), and collection and evaluation of evidence, he is able to speak of the plausibility of several rival hypotheses. Did the butler do it, or was it the rejected brother, or perhaps the victim committed suicide? If the family dog did not bark the evening of the murder, perhaps the culprit was a friend or family member. Does one of the suspects develop a nervous tic when questioned? Other evidence is gathered through crime scene investigation or the analysis of physical evidence. Did the murderer leave any clues? Thus, by combining various methods of data gathering including unobtrusive measures, Holmes is able to make a reasonable guess as to which of the hypotheses to reject or not to reject (Truzzi, 1976).

Webb et al., in *Unobtrusive Measures: Nonreactive Research in the Social Sciences* (1966) and in their revised edition entitled *Nonreactive Measures in the Social Sciences* (1981), describe these techniques as nonreactive methods in which undisturbed subjects are observed in natural or manipulated settings. Nonreactive methods usually involve clandestine, novel, and often "oddball" observations of existing situations. The observer is removed from the actual events and the subject is not aware of being observed; therefore, the act of being studied tends not to elicit artificial behavior or "stooge effects."

An analogy can be drawn between unobtrusive methods and surveillance by security personnel in a commercial setting. Security people do not simply ask people "Have you stolen anything?" and expect to be effective. Although uniformed personnel can discourage pilferage, clandestine methods (disguised shoppers, mirrors, cameras) are far more effective in secretly observing the actual behavior.

Major Types of Unobtrusive Methods

The major types of unobtrusive methods are:

Physical trace analysis
Archival, existing data, and autobiographies
Simple observation
Disguised observation
Simulation

Physical trace analysis

Physical trace analysis is the study of deposits, accretion of matter, and other indirect substances produced by previous human interaction. Much like the archeologist or crime scene detective, the criminal justice researcher attempts to reconstruct, after the fact, the substance of the phenomenon.

Archival records

Archival records, memoirs, diaries, and historical documents contain much information that can provide a historical overview of criminological issues. The *analyses of available data* comprise not only the analysis of official statistics and records, but also procedures such as content analysis and secondary analysis.

Content analysis

Content analysis is the systematic classification and study of the content of mass media, for example, newspapers and magazines (Holsti, 1969).

Secondary analysis

Secondary analysis entails the reanalysis of data that were previously gathered for other purposes (Hyman, 1972).

Observation

Observation (similar to our discussion of complete observation in Chapter 7) involves strategies

Disguised
observation

Simulation

in which the researcher's participation with the subjects is kept at a minimum and the investigator carefully records activities of the subjects. In **disguised observation** the analyst covertly studies groups or individuals by
temporarily misrepresenting his or her role. **Simulation** entails a variety of
gaming strategies that attempt to imitate a more complex social reality.

Given many of the shortcomings of data-gathering methods discussed previously, such as increasing nonresponse and respondent hostility, it is imperative that the wise researcher ask "Do these data already exist, or is there
some way of gathering this information without bothering respondents?"

As mentioned previously, the pure classification of research as unobtrusive measures or case studies or interviews is not mutually exclusive, and
there is much overlap. Some examples could fit into a number of categories.
To provide a picture of the diversity and flavor of unobtrusive measurement,
a large number of examples from the general social science literature is presented, along with criminal justice examples, as the imaginative researcher
could certainly employ many of these same techniques and apply them to
criminal justice subjects. As a student reading all of them, it should be sufficient for you to know a couple of examples of each type of unobtrusive
measurement.

Physical Trace Analysis

Physical trace analysis is well illustrated in the fields of criminalistics and
crime scene investigation. The detective's search for clues and circumstan-
tial evidence is analogous to the indirect research indicators attempted by
the social researcher using physical trace analysis as the means of unobtrusive measurement. An example may be found in the method police patrols
use to spot stolen cars—they look for dirty license plates on clean cars, or
clean plates on dirty cars, assuming that the thieves switch plates. Borrow-
ing from a technique used by "snoopy" superintendents for years, an investigator wishing to discover the level of whiskey consumption in a town that
is officially dry did so by counting empty bottles in trash cans (Sawyer,
1961). In 1979, after a police raid on mobster Joseph "Joe Bananas" Bonanno's
home, from which the manuscript for his memoirs was confiscated for intelligence purposes, the FBI revealed that for years they had been collecting
Bonanno's garbage. As is common practice in many American communities,
on the evening for trash pickup, the Bonannos would deposit their trash
bags at curbside for pickup. Prior to the actual pickup, federal agents would
swap lookalike trash bags and sift through Bonanno's trash. Information garnered was enough to precipitate the raid to get the actual manuscript ("Not
So Quietly Flows the Don," 1979) which was later published as *A Man of
Honor* (Bonanno, 1983).

A classic example in the social sciences is the case of "the hatching chick
exhibit" at Chicago's Museum of Science and Industry. In an attempt to determine the popularity of various exhibits, the curators discovered that the

selective erosion of floor tiles—their replacement rate—could serve as a rough index of visitor interest. Although the tiles in some parts of the museum had not been replaced for years, those surrounding the hatching chick exhibit required replacement every six weeks (Webb et al., 1966, p. 2). Care must be taken, however, in generalizing from indirect evidence. A similar museum that used to pride itself on having one of the largest volumes of public usage in the United States discovered that its attendance dropped dramatically when a building with large public restrooms was constructed next door (Wallis and Roberts, 1966, p. 160). Apparently, the large attendance figures were in reality, a result of people using the restrooms. The level of vandalism in a community may serve as a measure not only of lawbreaking, but also of affluence, as vandalism is primarily the product of affluent societies; in poorer societies, what little exists of value is carefully guarded (Clinard and Quinney, 1979, p. 59). In the early days of television, monitors at the Dayton, Ohio, Water Department were amused to discover that water pressure dropped considerably during commercials as people used bathrooms and sinks. This indirect index of program and commercial popularity has come to be referred to as the "Dayton Water Survey" (Simon, 1989, p. 60). In an interesting variation, a radio reporter, in what was called the "Royal Flush" experiment, conducted a political poll of sorts by broadcasting from atop the community water tower and asking listeners to register their preference for various political candidates by flushing their toilets as each name was announced. The drop in water level was used as a barometer and produced results closely matching the later vote (Webb et al., 1981, p. 2).

One researcher estimated the readership level of a printed advertisement by counting the number of different fingerprints on the page (Webb et al., 1981, p. 12). The size of attendance at a social event can be estimated by the amount of trash left behind (Webb et al., 1981, p. 19). Studies of graffiti (scrawlings or messages written on the walls of public facilities) have been done by Mockridge in *The Scrawl of the Wild* (1968). Others have found variation by sex, age, and education in which female graffiti had romantic themes whereas male scribblings were erotic. Sales of burglar alarms or firearms in a community might be taken as an indirect index of fear of crime (Sechrest and Olson, 1971). Graffiti can also be studied as an indicator of social environmental atmosphere and subcultures. Klofas and Cutshall (1985), for instance, studied graffiti from the walls of an abandoned juvenile correctional facility.

Use of Available Data and Archives

The National Institute of Justice was the pioneer among federal agencies in requiring that data sets from funded research be given to the agency upon completion of the project. In 1985 the National Academy of Sciences described this policy as "remarkable and a model for other research funding agencies," and in 1986 the National Science Foundation adopted a data resource policy similar to the NIJ policy that had been in existence since 1979.

In describing the importance of encouraging *secondary analysis* of such research data, then director of NIJ, James Stewart (1987, p. iii), indicated:

> Original data collection is expensive and time consuming. Often, researchers can devote only a limited time to analyzing the data they have collected. Rarely can original data collectors explore all the policy questions that their data permit. Archiving data offers several important benefits. It permits original findings to be validated by independent investigators. It also allows alternative approaches to be explored at a fraction of the original data collection costs and in considerably shorter time.
>
> Secondary analysis is a vital aspect of contemporary public policy research. The reuse and reexamination of these data resources permit relatively economical exploration of important policy issues. They bring the analytical talents of a large number of researchers to bear on questions of concern to criminal justice practitioners. To the extent that secondary data analysis confirms the findings of the original research, policymakers can have greater confidence in using research findings to inform policy. Clearly, the scientific endeavor necessary to generate a fully documented data set is comparable to the contribution made by published research findings.

Secondary Analysis

Secondary
analysis

Secondary analysis, or the reanalysis of data that were originally gathered or compiled for other purposes, is an excellent economizer of researcher time in data gathering, is nonreactive, and is a resourceful use of the mountains of data generated in modern society (see Hyman, 1972; D. Stewart, 1984). Reanalysis of historical records, precinct and court records, and such documents as the Uniform Crime Reports, given certain recognized limitations, can make excellent use of data that, although gathered for other purposes, can be used to address research concerns in criminology and criminal justice.

Primary data
sources

Secondary
data sources

Many second-hand stores have names like "Trash 'n Treasures," referring to the phenomenon that one person's trash (or discarded material) is another's treasure (something they find usable). Our industrial society has generated so much material to be discarded that our trash sites are nearly filled to capacity. Similarly, our current postindustrial society generates information and data at considerable expense that, once they serve agency or organizational purposes, are often confined to the equivalent of a trash dump site. Some of these data consist of both **primary data sources,** which refer to raw data unaccompanied by any analysis or interpretation, and **secondary data sources,** which consist of analyses, syntheses, and evaluations of the information (Lutzker and Ferrall, 1986). Thus, the UCR itself would constitute a primary data source, whereas an existing research study that used the UCR and other sources to predict crime trends would be a secondary source. Such available data, consisting of both primary and secondary sources, represent a "goldmine" of information waiting to be exploited.

Primary records such as letters, diaries, and memoirs may provide insight into events or research issues long after they have occurred (Gottschalk, Kluckhohn, and Angell, 1945).

Personal Documents and Biographies

The use of personal documents in social research was pioneered by Thomas and Znaniecki in their classic sociological work *The Polish Peasant in Europe and America* (Thomas and Znaniecki, 1918). They made particularly good use of diaries and personal letters to provide in-depth, personal views of their subjects.

Diaries kept by subjects have also been used as a source of information on drug subcultures (Zimmerman and Wieder, 1974). In the latter, individuals may keep intimate journals, memoirs, and logs (Denzin, 1989). The diary method involves investigators commissioning individuals to maintain a record of activities for a specified period of time (Courtright, 1995). In addition to combatting memory decay, respondents are better able to reflect on their performances and have greater flexibility in recording events and their meaning than in a standard retrospective interview. This technique has been used to measure behavior such as television viewing, lifestyles, alcohol consumption, sexual behavior, and anxiety in children. Some variations of the method have included using the diary method in conjunction with follow-up interviews as well as questionnaires and "experience sampling methods," in which systematic self-reports are provided at random occasions. The latter may involve respondents carrying "beepers" (electronic pagers) which signal times for diary entries (ibid.). A computer-based anonymous group diary called the "electronic group diary" was used as a feminist research method to record incidents of sexism within an academic department (Reinharz, 1992). Pocket computers have been used to have respondents record answers at specified times (Taylor et al., 1990). The provision of payment for training as well as recording devices such as tape recorders have all enhanced the diary method (Courtright, 1995).

Within many autobiographies and biographies of criminals exist useful insights that, when viewed with scrutiny and caution by a researcher, can be highly useful in analyzing crime, criminals, and criminal justice. Sanyika Shakur (Kody Scott), in *Monster: The Autobiography of an L.A. Gang Member* (1993), provides an autobiographical account of his violent life as a Crip gang member in south central Los Angeles.

The first criminal autobiographical life history in America appeared in 1807 with the publication of Henry Tufts' *The Autobiography of a Criminal* (Pearson, 1930). Tufts' description of his career as a thief, imposter, swindler, Indian doctor, and Revolutionary soldier began a long tradition of such works, many of questionable validity. The widespread interest on the part of criminals in such activities is illustrated by New York State's passage of the "Son of Sam" law to prevent serial murderer David Berkowitz and other criminals from profiting from any books, and by statements by

Watergate conspirator John Dean—"I wish I could write a book and not have to make a living"—and Arthur Bremer (who attempted to assassinate George Wallace)—"How much do you think I'll get for my autobiography?" (Hagan, 1990, p. 110).

In the case of Maas' *The Valachi Papers* (1968), Joseph Valachi, former Mafia member and federal informant, was asked by federal authorities to set down on paper his recollections. It was hoped these remembrances would help fill in the holes in his testimony before the McClellan Commission, as well as provide some information that may not have turned up in earlier questioning. In editing and making more intelligible Valachi's story, Maas interviewed Valachi directly, interviewed past associates, and analyzed interrogation transcripts as well as other official sources and documents (Maas, 1968).

Another federal informer, Vincent Teresa (*My Life in the Mafia,* 1973), had his autobiography at first recorded on tape by Renner. Renner conducted these sessions while Teresa was under federal guard and they took place in secret meeting locations. Former associates of crime figures have been instrumental in biographies. Wolf, one of the authors of *Frank Costello: Prime Minister of the Underworld,* had been Costello's personal lawyer for thirty years (Wolf and DiMona, 1975). The behind-the-scenes quality of such literature can be illustrated by some of the incidents described in Pileggi's *Wiseguy: Life in a Mafia Family* (1985), which is the life story of Henry Hill, a career criminal who literally grew up in the mob. Hill gives his account of the Paul Vario organized crime family, the Lufthansa robbery at Kennedy Airport (until 1983 the most successful cash robbery in U.S. history, scoring $5 million in cash), the Sindona scandal which nearly collapsed the Vatican bank, and the Boston College basketball point-shaving scandal.

In their study of *A Family Business,* discussed in Chapter 7, the Iannis developed organized crime family charts on the basis of files of the U.S. Justice Department (Ianni and Ianni, 1972, p.185). The potential usefulness of such official data is illustrated by the case of the DeCavalcante tapes. In the late 1960s, as a result of a trial of New Jersey organized crime figure Sam "The Plumber" DeCavalcante, more than 2,300 pages of tape logs were made available to the public by the U.S. Justice Department. The FBI had bugged DeCavalcante's plumbing and heating company office for almost four years, providing us with a rare glimpse of the inside day-to-day operations of the mob (Volz and Bridge, 1969).

In a revealing pseudo-autobiography Charles "Lucky" Luciano reveals the "true" story behind the mob's believed cooperation with the Allied effort during World War II (Gosch and Hammer, 1974). To create an incident that would require their assistance in waterfront vigilance against sabotage and hopefully secure Luciano's freedom from prison, the mob firebombed the soon-to-be-converted troopship, the French luxury liner *Normandie.* Although much credit was given to him for smoothing the Allied invasion of Sicily through Mafia underground contacts, Luciano claims that he never denied the acclaim, but had absolutely no contacts on the island with which to provide assistance. Luciano was given credit for securing the docks and assisting the invasion until he finally denied both in his autobiography. The hazards of using such information are pointed out by Abadinsky (1993), who claims that the Gosch and Hammer work on Luciano has been discredited and might best be cited as a possible example of fraud.

The hazards of using existing data and so-called "insider books" are illustrated by the numerous autobiographical accounts by major figures involved in the Watergate event. So much self-serving and contradictory information was presented by this group that the works might better be put in the fiction rather than nonfiction category. Taking a related illustration, publication of *The Brethren: Inside the Supreme Court* provided one of the first inside looks at a previously secretive and sacrosanct institution (Woodward and Armstrong, 1979). The authors, relying much on information supplied by 170 present and former clerks and staffers of the high bench, claim to have validated their data by checking at least three or four confirming sources. They made use of interviews, internal memorandums, letters, and conference notes, as well as diaries. Despite these efforts, legal experts and other well-informed court observers have been highly critical of its accuracy ("Sharp Blows at the High Bench," 1980).

Examples of Secondary Analysis

Criminologists have made quite imaginative use of official statistics and other existing public documents to generate some very useful studies. The following examples represent only a fraction of the many such studies, but they should help the reader appreciate the goldmine of data awaiting imaginative research prospectors eager to stake a claim. Glaser and Zeigler (1974) used official statistics to examine the relationship between homicide rates, death penalty, and sentencing policy in various states. Similarly, Erickson and Gibbs (1976) used official statistics such as the UCR and Bureau of Prisons statistics and discovered an inverse relationship between crime rate and certainty of imprisonment, but not with length of imprisonment.

In "Danger to Police During Domestic Encounters: Assaults on Baltimore County Police," Uchida, Brooks, and Kopers (1987) questioned recent research and police academy practice, both of which tend to underestimate the potential dangers to police who are mediating domestic encounters. Using five sources of existing information—Baltimore County Police Department records on police assaults, police personnel records, calls for service data, Census Bureau demographic data, and the FBI's count of the number of law enforcement officers killed or assaulted—they found that domestic (household) disturbances put police at great risk. In another example using two sources of existing data—Interpol and WHO homicide data—Messner (1989) was able to support the hypothesis that economic discrimination was highly related to high homicide rates.

In order to study women who kill in domestic encounters, Mann (1988) drew a randomly selected sample of 296 cleared homicide cases in Chicago,

Houston, Atlanta, Los Angeles, New York City, and Baltimore for the 1979 to 1983 period; in each case the perpetrator was a female. Mann traveled to each city to examine these cases and explains (Mann, 1988, p. 35):

> The completed homicide files of the sample cases for 1979–1983, some of which included photographs and autopsy reports and any other police record sources such as arrest and fingerprint files and FBI reports were examined minutely. I recorded information from these documents on previously designed research schedules after I had assigned each case a code number to insure confidentiality.

Sampson and Laub (1992) discovered sixty cartons of data that had been stored in the Harvard Law School basement. They recoded and computerized the data. In this secondary analysis of an existing longitudinal data set, they reanalyzed a classic study by Sheldon and Eleanor Glueck (1968), which they had conducted from 1940 to 1965. The study followed 500 delinquent and 500 matched nondelinquents for over a 25-year period (Laub, Sampson, and Kiger, 1990).

Lieber and Sherin (1972) studied the influence of lunar cycles on homicides by analyzing both UCR data and meteorological data during a fifteen-year period in Dade County, Florida, and a thirteen-year period in Cuyahoga County, Ohio. Wolfgang, Figlio, and Sellin (1972) analyzed the delinquent records of a birth cohort—every boy born in 1945 who lived in Philadelphia between his tenth and eighteenth birthdays. This retrospective longitudinal study analyzed nearly 10,000 boys. In a replication of this study Tracy, Wolfgang, and Figlio (1985) followed the criminal histories of boys born in Philadelphia in 1958 who lived there from the age of ten until adulthood.

Sutherland's *White Collar Crime* (1949) used the records of regulatory agencies, courts, and commissions to study the seventy largest American industrial and mercantile corporations and their violations over a forty-year period of laws regulating such things as false advertising, patent abuse, wartime trade violations, price-fixing, fraud, and intended manufacturing and sale of faulty goods.

Imaginative use of the official files of U.S. federal regulatory agencies has been made by Nader's Raiders. As part of this group's Center for the Study of Responsive Law, investigatory groups have published reports on air pollution (Esposito and Silverman, 1970), the Federal Trade Commission (Cox, Fellmeth, and Schulz, 1969), food and drug regulatory activities (Turner, 1970), antitrust activity (Green et al., 1973), and occupational safety violations (Page and O'Brien, 1973).

Clinard and Yeager's *Illegal Corporate Behavior* (1979) and *Corporate Crime* (1980) represent landmarks in the investigation of white-collar crime, superseding Sutherland's pioneering and more modest effort. In the first large-scale, comprehensive investigation of corporate crime, they conducted an analysis of administrative, civil, and criminal actions by twenty-five federal agencies against 477 of the largest American manufacturing corporations during 1975–1976. They also employed regulatory agency records to examine 105 Af the largest wholesale, retail, and service corporations. Chapter Appendix 8.1 provides an example of the use of police records to map gang turf in Chicago.

The analysis of documents, statistical and nonstatistical records of agencies, is fertile ground for research. Clinard's study, *The Black Market: A Study of White Collar Crime* (1952), dealt with wartime pricing and rationing violations using the official records of federal agencies.

The records of store detectives were used by Cameron in her key study of shoplifting, *The Booster and the Snitch: Department Store Shoplifting* (1964). Certainly Durkheim's (1951) analysis of suicide statistics in different European countries provides an excellent example of one of the earliest uses of existing data in social science research.

Miller, as part of a twelve-city survey of gang violence, analyzed newspaper reports as one source to validate his findings that since the end of World War II there has been an increase in gang victimization of nongang members and more killings as a result of increased availability of firearms (Miller, 1975). In *Anatomy of a Scam: A Case Study of a Planned Bankruptcy by Organized Crime,* DeFranco (1973) relied exclusively on public records such as transcripts of court proceedings and Senate hearings.

In an attempt to measure the concept of "professionalization" in different occupations, this writer (Hagan, 1975, 1976) examined a variety of existing sources in addition to gathering primary data. Included in the author's analysis were an obtrusive method (a survey of presidents of national professional associations) and unobtrusive methods, including a reanalysis of data previously gathered in a national survey of practitioners, literature supplied by national officers of the professional associations, data obtained in a literature review, and data from sourcebooks and from the *Encyclopedia of Associations.*

In an imaginative use of mass media, Phillips (1977, 1978) examined the impact of news media reports of suicides of famous people like Marilyn Monroe or fictional suicides in television soap operas on suicide rates and found that suicides increased after both. He also studied and discovered that homicides increase after professional boxing matches and decrease after executions. Using FBI and other police intelligence files, Anderson (1979) studied the "Benguerra" organized crime family (believed to be a pseudonym for the Angelo Bruno family in Philadelphia). Using New York City Police Department "rap sheets" (records of past offenses) of narcotics violators and their associates, Lupscha (1982) analyzed the "New Purple Gang" in New York.

Finally, mention should be made of the growing interest in comparative-international research in criminal justice (see Brantingham and Brantingham, 1984). Examination of one landmark work of this type is illustrative of the usefulness as well as the difficulty of such research. Archer and Gartner's *Violence and Crime in Cross-National Perspective* (1984) constructed a set of crime data, which they call the "Comparative Crime Data File" and which consists of recorded patterns of crime and violence in 110 nations and forty-four major international cities. Having begun a small project to locate and use an existing comparative data file to investigate the effect of wars on domestic crime rates and finding that none existed, they undertook their study with no idea that the archive would reach its final size. Four years later, their method of data collection consisted of:

1. Correspondence with national and metropolitan government sources in virtually all nations in the world
2. A painstaking search through annual statistical reports and other official documents of those nations that have (at least at some time) published annual crime data
3. Secondary examination of the records kept by various national and international agencies (Archer and Gartner, 1984, p. 12)

Their final product was one of the best cross-cultural databases on criminal violence ever compiled.

Limitations of Official Data

In addition to the problems in using UCR data for research purposes detailed in Chapter 4, official data may contain any or most of the same shortcomings. The investigator must remember that the data have been gathered for agency purposes and therefore may not contain the degree of accuracy or operationalization the researcher desires. Data may be deliberately "fudged" to give a favorable impression of the organization. Studies over time are hazardous because of instrumentation or changes in the recordkeeping procedures of the agency. Of great dismay to the researcher is the realization that the variables have not been measured in the manner that the investigator had hoped. These are all obstacles, but not always insurmountable ones. They might better be viewed as challenges to the imagination and cleverness of the researcher to see what she or he can tease out of official data.

Cross-national research in criminal justice and criminology is particularly hazardous. Carol Kalish (1989), Director of International Programs, Bureau of Justice Statistics, points out:

> Often the statistics are out of date; usually the statistics are incomplete; and occasionally the statistics are incomprehensible. Many countries do not report consistently from one year to the next; many countries do not report for every year; many countries do not report at all.

She also notes that, despite these problems, recent efforts by the United Nations and Interpol to gather more accurate data should persist. The UCR's experience can serve as an example of what can be accomplished. Because the statistics compiled by the fifty states have steadily improved, the UCR has been able to gather more accurate data. Bennett and Lynch (1990), for their part, compared four international sources of crime statistics (Interpol,

World Health Organization, U.N., and the Comparative Crime Data File) and found that similar problems existed in all the sources but that the homicide and theft statistics were comparable (see also Huang and Wellford, 1989).

Measuring Hidden Populations

In questioning often uncritically cited figures on how many heroin addicts there are and the amount they steal in New York City, Singer (1971) demonstrated that by taking numbers seriously, and checking them against other sources and available demographic information, the likely figure is much less than usually stated. Singer shows how a skillful researcher using available data can avoid accepting the same erroneous data that are picked up and passed on as fact, even by responsible research organizations.

Ecologists, among others, have a keen interest in estimating wildlife populations in given areas. Using such techniques as *mark–recapture* or removal, they are able to obtain a fairly accurate count of inhabitants. Utilizing capture statistics, for example arrest rates, adaptations of such techniques are viewed as having potential in criminal justice (Burnham, 1980). Procedures have been proposed for estimating juvenile recidivism from aggregated official data (Wanat and Burke, 1980), the size of drug user populations (Demaree, 1980), and income unreported on individual income tax returns (Kenadjian, 1980).

Webb et al. (1981, p. 23) describe a case in which the IRS attempted to estimate whether a barber, who kept few records, was paying sufficient taxes. They attempted to estimate his income on the basis of the number of towels he used. The tax court, while accepting the IRS estimate, disallowed IRS claims that the barber sometimes used the same towels twice and also indicated that the IRS estimate of three towels per haircut did not account for the fact that the barber occasionally gave free trims.

Historical and Archival Data

A potentially hazardous and relatively neglected area of criminal justice research has been the primary use of historical and archival data. Much of this omission of historical data has been due to the tendency of sociologists and social scientists to view history as a mere chronicle of unique events, part myth, allegory, and fiction (Inciardi, Block, and Hallowell, 1977, p. 9).

In an analysis of crime and punishment in the nineteenth century, Graff (1977) indicated that a great number of records on criminals, particularly jail registers, held promise for the history of criminals. Monkkonen (1979), in an article critical of Graff's position, indicates that great care must be taken in using such data, and he argues that consideration must be given to the original methodology and rationale under which such data were collected. With this warning in mind, neglected sources include annual reports of city, county, and state criminal justice agencies, as well as U.S. Bureau of Census data on state and local agencies (Monkkonen, 1979). At a minimum, such records complement aggregate data in providing more personal examples of criminal activity of the past (Graff, 1979). One must, of course, attempt to carefully weigh, double-check, and verify with other sources any information obtained through this method (Davies, 1956; Wheeler, 1970). In 1990 Monkkonen (1990) served as editor of a sixteen-volume series on *Crime and Justice in American History,* which represents an encyclopedic *tour de force* in historical criminology.

Many examples of the use of historical data exist. K. Erickson (1966), for example, used official statistics to analyze deviance and immorality in *Wayward Puritans,* an analysis of Puritan New England. In tracing the genesis of the legend of the Mafia in Sicily, Albini (1971) consulted records, maps, and other government reports of the Italian Military Archives, to refute certain myths regarding the Mafia's origin. Chappell and Walsh use a historical case study of infamous London fence Jonathan Wild to shed light on professional fences (Chappell and Walsh, 1974; Howson, 1970). In order to examine the impact of death penalty–execution publicity on homicide rates, Bailey (1990) used Vanderbilt University's television news archives, which abstracts ABC, CBS, and NBC news programs. He looked at television publicity devoted to executions and monthly homicide rates from 1976 to 1987. His findings neither supported deterrence theory (since executions did not decrease homicides) nor brutalization theory (since executions did not increase killings).

In *American Assassins: The Darker Side of Politics,* Clarke (1982) attempted to address the "pathological myth" about assassins, the belief that most had suffered and were motivated by some mental sickness, insanity, or derangement. He felt that most analyses of assassins' pathology committed post hoc error, the false assumption that because one variable or outcome follows another in time, it is the cause of that outcome. For example, assassins may act mentally abnormal after the fact because they have been caught and processed, not because they have a long-term condition that caused them to become assassins. Clarke evolved a list of different types including sane and politically motivated assassins by examining materials from the National Archives, Library of Congress, FBI, Secret Service, government agencies, and court hearings and investigations, trial transcripts, diaries, autobiographies, medical records, newspaper clippings, tapes, and other biographical and historical documents.

Using the private archives of an American-Jewish self-defense organization in *East Side–West Side,* Block (1979) conducted a historiographical analysis of the cocaine trade in New York City from 1910 to 1918. Historiography involves the application of empirical social scientific methods to the analysis of history. The user of historical data should weigh carefully the validity of the sources used, asking such questions as "How reliable is the author?" "Do other sources agree?" "Does it make logical sense?" (Inciardi, Block, and Hallowell, 1977, p. 25). The potential uses of available data in criminal justice and criminology have only begun to be tapped.

Content Analysis

Content
analysis

    Another important method of analyzing existing data is through *content analysis,* the systematic analysis and selective classification of the contents of mass communication. This technique is excellent for comparative and historical studies or for discerning trends in existing phenomena. It is often used, for instance, by intelligence agencies to uncover potential changes in international diplomacy. Olson describes the process of content analysis in one study:

> These categories and subcategories were devised in discussions among those who eventually coded the material. After initially reading many of the books, trial runs with various alternative categories were made. Following progressive refinement, the scheme was "frozen" for the complete study. This initial period of discussion provided not only a more refined scheme but also developed intimate knowledge of the scheme's meaning among those recording their observations (Olson, 1976, p. 161).

The basic procedure in content analysis involves:

- The selection of categories and subjects to be analyzed
- The rigorous establishment of criteria for inclusion, a feature which ensures that the study can be replicated by others
- Carefully following the preestablished classification scheme
- Statistically analyzing the results (Berelson, 1952; Pool, 1959)

    The best test of the usefulness of a content analysis scheme is its replicability—that is, a different group, using the scoring system and instructions assigned, should be able to come up with the same categorizations.

    A number of imaginative subjects have been examined using content analysis. Davis (1952) studied the amount of space devoted to crime in select newspapers and related this to the local crime rates. Many forms of mass media such as newspapers, magazines, television, and movies contain subject matter that can be used for an analysis of popular stereotypes of deviants or shifts in public propaganda about crime. As part of a larger study of the fear of crime in four American cities, Bielby and Berk (1980) did a content analysis of accounts of crime and column inches devoted to the subject in large city newspapers. In a study of government response to crime, Jacob, Lineberry, and Heinz (Jacob et al., 1980) examined and reanalyzed a wide variety of available data, such as changes in local ordinances and state criminal codes, changes in amount and distribution of police manpower, court decisions, inmate populations, court and correctional expenditures, type and shifts of city government, and mayorality election year and their relationship to UCR data. They also examined newspapers. The sample comprised nine city newspapers over a thirty-one-year period, using randomly selected proportions of weeks. Page one articles (or articles on the first three pages of tabloids) and letters to the editor were examined and classified.

In another study of how the news production process, both print and electronic, affected the presentation of crime in the media, Chermak (1994) did a content analysis of nine newspapers and three evening television newscasts. He coded nine newspapers for content every fifth day for the first six months of 1990 and an additional eighteen days for a three-month period in 1991 of the *Cleveland Plain Dealer*. Also coded were local evening broadcasts in Albany, Cleveland, and Dallas for seven nights a week for an eight-week period in 1991. He followed this up with ethnographic observations of news rooms as well as with forty interviews of people in the news trade.

Researchers have done content analysis of:

- Newspaper reports of gang activity (W. Miller, 1975)
- Popular articles about marijuana using them to measure the effectiveness of propaganda campaigns designed to assist in the passage of stricter drug laws (Becker, 1970)
- Jokes, comic strips, and popular culture regarding mental illness and insanity (Scheff, 1966)
- The history of the stereotype of assassins and hashish usage (Mandel, 1966)

Wolfgang, Figlio, and Thornberry (1978) used content analysis as well as other techniques to examine the scientific status of the field of criminology. Part of the analysis involved reading, classifying, coding, and rating 4,417 works. The raters used a scale from seven for the highest to one for the lowest evaluation of scientific merit.

As part of an attempt to develop a model of professionalization, this author did a content analysis of thirty-seven major writers on the subject and identified twenty-nine different criteria (Hagan, 1975). Similarly, Table 8.1 shows a content analysis by this writer (Hagan, 1983) of major dimensions of selected writers' definitions of the concept "organized crime." Although many of these writers discussed the issue, a large number never bothered to define the concept; among those that did, there was no consensus on all elements, although the majority seemed to agree on certain elements of organizations—use of force or threats of force, profit from provision of illicit services that are in public demand, and assurance of immunity of operation.

There has been a large growth in computer software which supports the analysis of qualitative data (Miles and Huberman, 1994).

Content Analysis by Computer

Inexpensive optical scanners make it possible to create text files from raw printed material. Such text files can then be searched, classified, and categorized using computer software designed for such purposes. Hypersearch, which is designed for Macintosh computers, is one such example. Word search capabilities of standard computer software such as Wordperfect or Word for Windows can also be utilized to perform some of the classification and identification functions.

TABLE 8.1 A Content Analysis of Dimensions of Selected Writers' Definitions of Organized Crime*

Dimension	Abadinsky (1981)	Albini (1971)	Barlow (1981)	Clinard and Quinney (1973)	Conklin (1981)	Cressey (1969)	Haskell and Yablonski (1974)	Inciardi (1975)	Mack (1975)	Maltz (1976)	Organized Crime Task Force (1967)	Sutherland and Cressey (1974)	Vetter and Silverman (1978)
Nonideological	X	X	X	X	X		X	X	X	X	X		X
Organized hierarchy continuing	X	X		X	X	X	X	X	X	X	X	X	X
Violence (force or threat of force)	X										X		
Restricted membership	X					X					X		
Rational profit through illegal activities		X	X	X	X	X			X	X		X	X
Public demand		X	X	X	X		X	X	X			X	
Corruption (immunity)			X	X	X	X	X	X	X	X		X	X
Monopoly						X		X				X	
Specialization					X								
Code of secrecy			X										
Extensive planning							X				X		

*Many writers, including those of textbooks, fail to supply explicit definitions of organized crime.

Source: Hagan, Frank E. "The Organized Crime Continuum: A Further Specification of a New Conceptual Model." *Criminal Justice Review* 8 (Fall 1983:53) Reprinted with permission.

Meta-Analysis

Meta-analysis   The term **meta-analysis** was coined by Gene Glass (1976) and refers to quantitative analysis that reviews, combines, and summarizes the results of many different studies dealing with the same research question. It could be described as a transcending "analysis of analysis." Whereas a literature review qualitatively summarizes and analyzes, meta-analysis could be viewed as "quantitative reviewing" (Green and Hall, 1984). Furthermore, whereas secondary analysis reanalyzes an original data set, meta-analysis involves summarizing and comparing the statistical results of multiple data sets.

Wells (1991, p. 1) indicates:

> Most studies end with a call for more research and more elaborate analysis. But perhaps the task is to make better use of the data and studies we already have, adopting analytic procedures that are more deliberately cumulative and integrative. . . . [T]he technique of *meta-analysis* provides an explicit strategy for summing and synthesizing results across multiple separate studies to produce cumulative conclusions.

Smith and Glass (1977, p. 760) suggest that:

> [s]cholars and clinicians are in the embarrassing position of knowing less than has been proven, because knowledge, atomized and sprayed across a vast landscape of journals, books and reports, has not been accessible. Extracting knowledge from accumulated studies is a complex and important methodological problem which deserves further attention.

Traditional qualitative literature reviews may be turning into an inappropriate means of summarizing empirical literature (Wells, 1991, p. 2). While the basic steps involved in meta-analysis are little different from a good research review, its emphasis on quantification maximizes precision and replicability. There is even computer software available to assist with this task (ibid., p. 10).

Steps in   Wells (1991, p. 4) tells us that the *steps in meta-analysis* are little differ-
meta-analysis   ent from those of any good research review. These steps involve:

- Conceptualizing and specifying clearly the content of the research problem and its basic terms
- Searching the literature and selecting a representative set of studies relevant to the review
- Building a base of relevant data for the review by summarizing, describing, and coding the features of separate studies and translating them into comparable categories and terms
- Analyzing the database of studies for patterns of significant effects and for theoretically meaningful correlations
- Providing a summary description of the results and some evaluation

In one example, Smith and Glass (1977) analyzed 375 studies of psychotherapy and counseling and concluded that there were only negligible differences in the effects produced by different therapy types; they also determined that the typical therapy client was better off than 75 percent of the untreated subjects. Rosenthal (1976, 1978) used meta-analysis to examine the frequency of recording errors in observational studies and found that, although only one percent of all observations were in error, about two-thirds of the errors favored the hypothesis of the observer.

Although meta-analysis has been employed in hundreds of studies in the field of psychology, it is used relatively infrequently in criminal justice. In his own search of the literature, Wells (1991, p. 11) found only sixteen examples in criminal justice since 1980; in the vast majority of these cases meta-analysis was used to evaluate the effectiveness of treatment rather than to analyze theoretical propositions. Tittle, Villemez, and Smith (1978) performed a meta-analysis on empirical studies examining the relationship between social class and criminality. Loeber and Stouthamer-Loeber (1986) did a meta-analysis of family factors and delinquency, while Whitehead and Lab (1989) meta-analyzed correctional treatments. Finally, Wells and Rankin (1991) did a meta-analysis of the literature on broken homes and delinquency.

Sources of Existing Data

Also classified under unobtrusive methods is the usefulness of literature reviews or review of the results of studies by others to assess and develop one's own research problem. Services such as those provided by the National Criminal Justice Reference Service in this regard replace hours of tedious library searches with computer searches and the provision of annotated bibliographies.

A thorough literature review of existing books, articles, journals, and other publications is, in reality, as important a part of data gathering as the primary collection of data. The National Advisory Committee on Criminal Justice Standards and Goals (NACCJSG) encourages researchers to utilize available data:

> Criminal justice agencies have been overwhelmed with data collection efforts, and much of the information already collected remains unused by researchers. The difficulty of knowing what data exist, the geographical dispersion of resources, problems of access, and questions of validity and suitability for research all lead to a continued preference by researchers to collect new data for each project (National Advisory Committee, 1976, p. 55).

Some sources of criminal justice statistics are the UCR, the *National Crime Survey,* and *National Prisoner Statistics* (formerly *Prisoners in State and Federal Prisons and Reformatories*) published by the U.S. Department of Justice, and *Federal Prisons* released by the Federal Bureau of Prisons. Various federal agencies, for example, the Treasury Department and the Drug Enforcement Agency, publish annual reports of the trends and numbers of violations under their jurisdiction.

The Department of Justice, through its Bureau of Justice Statistics and particularly the National Criminal Justice Reference Service (NCJRS), provides indispensible services to users. The NCJRS compiles and disseminates information through Selective Notification of Information (SNI), which is mailed to users and provides updated annotated listings of publications, computer search services for those eligible, free microfiche, and a literature loan program. The Bureau of Justice Statistics publishes the *Sourcebook of Criminal Justice Statistics* annually. In 1979, the NCJRS made available *The Document Retrieval Index* (DRI), a reference volume that includes bibliographical citations, annotations, and availability information on documents in their collection. The microfiche DRI provided access to approximately 40,000 documents beginning in 1979 and is supplemented annually.

Offender-based transaction statistics

Offender-Based Transaction Statistics (OBTS) collect felony arrest records from those participating states that detail such cases from booking to final-disposition. Such processing begins with fingerprinting and ends either when the case is dismissed or when the arrested person is acquitted or convicted and sentenced. Local criminal justice agencies record arrest data on disposition documents and fingerprint cards, and these records are then forwarded to the state's criminal information repository, which updates appropriate master records. OBTS receives data from these repositories. BJS regularly solicits states to extract and submit such data following OBTS guidelines (Bureau of Justice Statistics, 1989).

Researchers can also obtain original data from agencies or other researchers and reanalyze the data for their own purposes. Problems in using such data relate to its location, permission or access, the validity and reliability of such data, possible misinterpretation of codes, and other nuances in the data that may not have been of concern to the original researcher. Incomplete data and, in some cases, inadequate form of the data may also be problematic.

Researchers interested in currently classified government information can file under the federal Freedom of Information Act (see Sherick, 1980) and, unless the data are viewed as essential to national security, they should be made available for legitimate scholarly or investigative research. The National Archives and Federal Records Administration and Library of Congress have mountains of such historical and declassified documents. As an example, in 1987, a researcher discovered a handwritten draft of the Bill of Rights in the National Archives that no one knew existed. Some declassified FBI files that are available are investigative case files of the Bureau of Investigation (the FBI's predecessor), 1908–1922; the file on the Black Panther Party, North Carolina, 1968–1976; "Communist Infiltration of the Southern Christian Leadership Conference" investigative files; the Martin Luther King, Jr., assassination file; Malcolm X FBI surveillance file; Cointelpro: Counterintelligence Program file; the firebomb and shooting at Kent State file; Watergate investigation file; HUAC—House Un-American Activities Committee file; and the Albert Einstein file.[1]

Imagine that in doing research you would be able to do all of the following:

Have a computer search done of as many as 100 different data banks on your topic and identify and supply short (roughly 500 word) summaries (annotated bibliographies) of what each article, book, or source contains.

Have any of the items that you are interested in that are not available at your library made available either in full document or microfiche form within a couple of weeks.

Be able, if you have any questions, to call toll free experts on your topic for further advice on sources.

Be able to purchase (at a fraction of the cost of the original study) the raw data files with codebooks (guides to what the data mean) for your own reanalysis.

Be able to use sophisticated prewritten (canned) computer programs to analyze these data.

All of these services are currently available and used by criminological and criminal justice researchers.

Computer searches
In *computer searches* a computer's retrieval system is used to search its data bank for sources that a user identifies by key words. On-line searches (done on the spot) give instant returns, but are more expensive, whereas off-line searches (where data are later mailed to the client) cost less but, of course, take more time. DIALOG, one of the largest search systems, comprises more than 100 databases including NCJRS, PAIS (Public Affairs Information Service), and ERIC (Educational Resources Information Center). NCJRS alone had a document collection in 1987 of over 85,000 sources. Those considering such searches should consult their local reference librarian. As the cost of such searches continues to decrease, we can expect their greater utilization in the future.[2]

Data archives
Data Archives (or data libraries) are institutes or organizations that store data resources (raw data) from previous studies. The world's largest repository of computer-readable social science data is the Interuniversity Consortium for Political and Social Research (ICPSR) at the Institute for Social Research, Ann Arbor, Michigan. Since 1978, within the ICPSR, the Bureau of Justice Statistics has funded the creation of the National Archive of Criminal Justice Data (formerly CJAIN, the *Criminal Justice Archive* and *Information Network*) to encourage the sharing of data resources.[3] Data (from

---

[1]Such data are sold in microfilm form by Scholarly Resources, Inc., 104 Greenhill Avenue, Wilmington, DE 19805.

[2]For information on NCJRS search services call toll free (800) 851-3420 or write to Users Service, NCJRS, Box 6000, Rockville, MD 20850.

[3]Call 1–800–999–0960 or write to National Archive of Criminal Justice Data, P.O. Box 1248, Ann Arbor, MI 48106.

EXHIBIT 8.1

Violence Research Data from the National Archive of Criminal Justice Data

In 1994 the Inter-university Consortium for Political and Social Research (ICPSR) issued a compact disc entitled "Violence Research Data" (NCJ–151523), which contained the primary (raw) data plus codebooks for fifty-nine studies/data sets.* This included on one CD some of the most celebrated empirical studies ever conducted in the field and constitutes a gold mine for researcher prospectors. Included are:

James Alan Fox: *Uniform Crime Reports: Supplemental Homicide Reports 1976–1992*

Marvin Wolfgang, Robert Figlio, and Thorsten Sellin: *Delinquency in a Birth Cohort in Philadelphia, Pennsylvania, 1945–1963*

Murray Straus and Richard Gelles: *Physical Violence in American Families, 1985*

Alfred Blumstein and Jacqueline Cohen: *Adult Criminal Careers, Michigan, 1974–1977*

James Wright and Peter Rossi: *Armed Criminals in America: A Survey of Incarcerated Felons, 1983*

Malcolm Klein, Cheryl Maxson, and Margaret Gordon: *Police Response to Street Gang Violence in California, 1985*

Delbert Elliott: *National Youth Survey: Wave V, 1983*

Robert Figlio, Paul Tracy, and Marvin Wolfgang: *Delinquency in a Birth Cohort II: Philadelphia, Pennsylvania, 1958–1988*

Cathy Spatz Widom: *Child Abuse, Neglect, and Violent Criminal Behavior in a Midwest Metropolitan Area of the United States, 1967–1988*

Richard Berk and Lawrence Sherman: *Specific Deterrent Effects of Arrest for Domestic Assault: Minneapolis, Minnesota, 1981–1982*

Dane Archer and Rosemary Gartner: *Violence and Crime in Cross-National Perspective, 1900–1974*

John H. Laub and Robert J. Sampson: *Criminal Careers and Crime Control in Massachusetts (The Glueck Study): A Matched-Sample Longitudinal Research Design, Phase 1, 1939–1963*

*Available for $25 from National Archive of Criminal Justice Data, P.O. Box 1248, Ann Arbor, MI 48106-1248, (800)999-0960.

original studies) are disseminated to the researchers on magnetic computer tape supplied by the user (person requesting the data). Although space prohibits a detailing of the rich possibilities of data available, Exhibit 8.1 presents a glimpse.

Observation

Observation   *Observation* is a strategy of data collection in which the investigator attempts to examine the activity of subjects while keeping her or his presence either secret or to a minimum, so as not to interfere. This may take the form of laboratory observations or more "naturalistic" field observations. Returning to our sleuth Holmes, he not only questioned suspects, but carefully observed exterior body and physical signs, expressive movements or "body language," the "silent language" of the eye, and facial movements.

Cavoir and Howard (1973) had raters assign attractiveness ratings to pictures of juvenile offenders and to members of a control group of nondelinquent high school graduates. The delinquents received poor ratings. Applying an observational strategy in an actual setting, Stewart examined the "Defendant's Attractiveness as a Factor in the Outcome of Criminal Trials" (1979). All other things being equal, he found that less attractive defendants were more likely to receive heavier sentences than more attractive defendants. Both of these examples involved observation as an unobtrusive means of data gathering.

An important study that well illustrates the controversy surrounding observational studies in the field is the "Chicago jury study." A group of researchers had received permission to "bug" actual jury deliberations. Despite the fact that great pains were taken to ensure that any names or other identifying elements would be eliminated and screened by the overseeing judicial officials, legislators felt that the potential scientific merit of such a study was outweighed by the need to secure the sanctity of the jury room. Finally, federal legislation was passed to prohibit the study, as well as any future similar studies, making it a federal crime to record such deliberations (Vaughn, 1967). Similar controversy was raised by other studies. Stewart and Cannon's (1977) study of bystander reactions to "simulated theft," using stooges or accomplices as thieves to speed up the action, raised controversy that abbreviated the study. They describe how their "simulated thefts" were abruptly brought to a halt:

> The investigators took pains to make sure that the study was safe and sought the advice of local security firms, a professor of law enforcement who was also a former FBI agent, and a local businessmen's association. All of these individuals and groups gave the authors their support and advice.
>
> However, a local newspaper, without consulting the senior author, printed distorted accounts of the investigator's intention to stage robberies to study people." Because of the external pressures resulting from this biased and largely misleading publicity, experiments II and III, which were to be sequels of the present one, were cancelled. No reporters at any stage attempted to contact either of the investigators, nor was any mention made of the fact that the so-called "robberies" did not involve violence in any way, nor that a local merchants' organization had advocated a need for such research. In addition, a local security firm gave the authors its full support and backing (Stewart and Cannon, 1977, p. 322).

Manning (1976), in an excellent review of methodologies used in studies of police, identified a number of studies that employed observational strategies. He distinguishes between "active role" observers, where participation was emphasized, and "passive role" observers, where the primary emphasis was placed on observation. In all of the passive role observations of police work he described, the observer's presence was made known to the subjects (see, for instance, Banton, 1964; Buckner, 1967; Black, 1968; Reiss, 1968). Because the observer's presence is known, such studies are not fully unobtrusive in nature, although the true purpose of the observation may be hidden from the subjects. Black (1970), in a systematic observation of police-citizen transactions in Boston, told the officers that his research was concerned with citizen behavior rather than police behavior, whereas it involved both.

Purists would insist that if a person's presence is known, the method is no longer unobtrusive; however, if the true purpose of one's presence is unknown, such as in disguised observation, the mere act of being on-the-scene may not elicit reactivity.

An indirect measure of sexual or occupational bias could be measured by having groups rate written or videotaped presentations or speeches in which only the name or occupation assigned is changed. In a study of the impact of the stigma of ex-convict status on subsequent employment, Schwartz and Skolnick (1962) sent prospective employers resumés in which only the criminal record varied. They discovered that as the criminal record condition changed—from no record or acquitted (with a letter from the judge) to acquitted (with no letter) to convicted—there was a steady decline in job offers.

Lost letter technique

To measure the popularity of various organizations, Milgram (1969) cleverly introduced the *lost letter technique,* in which letters addressed and stamped, but unposted, were "lost" in specified areas. The addresses varied; for example, "The American Nazi Party," "Ku Klux Klan," and the like. On the basis of the percentage returned, some indication of the relative unacceptability of these organizations was gained. The technique obviously yields only an indirect measure, but it certainly represents an imaginative means of assessment. The hazards of such research are illustrated by the case of a criminologist who was arrested while attempting to conduct such a study at a shopping mall. Variations of the lost letter technique include a study in which wallets containing cash in an envelope (Tucker et al., 1977) or lost letters containing cash (Farrington and Knight, 1979; and Knox and McTiernan, 1973) were left on the street.

Disguised Observation

Another dimension is added to observation when the investigator assumes a clandestine role. In Chapter 7 we mentioned Stein's (1974) study of prostitute–customer relations by employing one-way mirrors and secretly observing and recording hundreds of sessions. Humphreys' (1970) study of male homosexual behavior in public restrooms raised considerable debate regarding the issue of disguised observation versus invasion of privacy. He pretended to be a "peeper" (voyeur) or lookout for males participating in homosexual activity in public restrooms. He secretly recorded license numbers of participants. Later, after tracing their licenses, and under a different guise and disguise, he interviewed these men in their homes. Although he claimed to take great pains to protect the privacy and identity of respondents, without their permission, Humphreys certainly placed the subjects in a situation of potential harm and possible blackmail were the data to fall into the wrong hands.

Disguised
observation

Disguised observation involves any type of research in which the researcher hides his or her presence or purpose for interacting with a group (Roth, 1962). As in our discussion of participant observation, researchers who conduct such investigations do so without the subject's prior approval. Some view such behavior as privacy invasion, voyeurism, or snooping (Von Hoffman, 1970); others view such deception as necessary to conduct social scientific studies of many forms of behavior that could not be observed appropriately in any other manner (Stricker, 1967). To study difficult subjects in the field, researchers have posed as "thieves and victims" (Stewart and Cannon, 1977), a "watch queen" (Humphreys, 1970), a "mental patient" (Caudill et al., 1952), "Black Panther supporters" (Heussenstamm, 1971), "naive international tourists" (Feldman, 1968), and a "caretaker" (Sherif and Sherif, 1966), to mention a few.

Steffensmeier and Terry (1973) and Steffensmeier and Steffensmeier (1976) found that shoplifters (role-playing students) dressed as hippies were more likely to be reported than those dressed conventionally.

Feldman (1968) used disguised observation to study the honesty of the French, Greeks, and Americans given the opportunity to cheat in transactions in which either a fluent stranger or foreigner asked directions, overpaid cashiers and taxi-cab drivers, or the like. On this same subject of dishonesty, one of the earliest series of consumer investigations of this sort was conducted by *The Reader's Digest* in the 1940s. They brought previously checked out products to establishments for repair. On the basis of their investigations, they concluded that sixty-three percent of the garages, sixty-four percent of the radio repair shops, and forty-nine percent of the sample watch repair shops were dishonest (Riis, 1941a, 1941b, 1941c). A rival causal factor, of course, would be incompetence. In a more recent study of insurance fraud in the auto-body repair business, Tracy and Fox (1989) borrowed damaged cars from a car rental company and then approached a sampling of Massachusetts repair shops for estimates for repair work. If the estimators were told that the car was covered by insurance, the estimates were nearly one-third higher.

In defense of covert research, Douglas describes how early doctors were accused of ghoulish crimes in their attempts to study the human body scientifically:

> As doctors, lawyers, and other professionals have done over the centuries, sociologists must work purposefully to carve out a special *moral niche*. . . . Exceptions to important social rules, such as those concerning privacy and intimacy, must be made only when the research need is clear and the potential

contributions of the findings to general human welfare are believed to be great enough to counterbalance the risks. If we can agree that these factors are present . . . then we should have the courage to try to change the morals of our society and to do the research with as little invasion of privacy as possible (Douglas, 1972, pp. 8–9).

One major problem with observational studies is the potentially long period of waiting for that which one wishes to observe to occur. Allen Funt, director of the popular television program *Candid Camera,* discovered that large amounts of time had to be expended waiting for something to happen (Webb et al., 1966, pp. 156–158). Finally, in later programming formats, Funt Confederates relied on **confederates** (persons planted to facilitate that which is to be observed) to speed up the action. One could imagine, for instance, attempting to observe the willingness of bystanders to come to the aid of a victim by means of a hidden camera. Years may pass before even one observational case would present itself. To illustrate how the use of confederates produces cases, let us examine Stewart and Cannon's "simulated theft" study once again:

> Each subject was selected by the criterion that he or she be seated at a bench and engaged in no activities other than relaxing. . . . After a subject was selected, the victim (confederate) walked to within three meters of the subject, clearly in his or her line of sight. The victim would then produce a cigarette, and would begin his search for a match. Upon finding no match, the victim would make sure that the subject was observing him before any other manipulation took place (Stewart and Cannon, 1977, pp. 318–319).

Next, the authors varied the stimulus by having the confederate ask the subject to watch his bag while he ran into a store or by simply, in a preoccupied manner, leaving the bag and also going into the store. About two minutes later, another confederate dressed as either a working person, a business executive, or a priest would steal the bag. As soon as the subject reacted by any movement or utterance, he or she was immediately approached by an assistant to the researchers and the debriefing process was begun (Stewart and Cannon, 1977).

Perhaps the classic example of disguised observation using confederates is Asch's (1951) study of group pressure. Experimental confederates were instructed to choose the wrong answer in a series of perceptual processes in which the correct answer was obvious, for example, "Which of these lines is the shortest?" The naive subject responded after the others had done so incorrectly, and the willingness of the subject to comply with the group, or exercise correct independent judgment, was assessed.

Rosenhan (1973), in "On Being Sane in Insane Places," had himself and several associates placed into a mental hospital as fake patients. They pretended to have the symptoms of schizophrenia and from the vantage point of patients, and unbeknownst to the staff, they were able to record the real world of the mental institution. Once diagnosed as mentally ill, the patients had a difficult time escaping this definition of the situation and in convincing the doctors that they were not disturbed. With the average stay of nineteen days, each was eventually released with the diagnosis of being schizophrenics in remission.

Formby and Smykla (1981, 1984) assigned students in a criminal justice simulation class to perform disguised observations to examine whether passersby would assist drunks (role-playing students) in unlocking their car doors to drive home and, in a separate study, whether passersby would intervene to prevent burglars (role-playing students) from attempting to break into automobiles. For the burglary study each group consisted of a car, a driver, a thief, and two observers; the "crime" was committed in a variety of high-pedestrian-traffic locations. Of sixteen incidents of auto burglary, only two instances of overt citizen awareness took place, neither of which produced sufficient intervention to end the burglary or to call the police. The latter, of course, had already been alerted to the study's existence. In the drunk driving study (Formby and Smykla, 1984) students were assigned the roles of drunk, observer, safety person, and police officer (the latter were actual police officers who were students in the class). "Students assigned the role of drunks were splashed with whiskey and vigorously applied it to their hands, neck and face. Drunks practiced their roles and benefited from the critique of instructor and students in modeling the drunk behavior." Sixty-two percent of the eighty-five pedestrians helped the drunk open the car door.

In an Urban Institute study of racial bias against black jobseekers, selected pairs of black and white men applied for 476 entry-level jobs. Even though each pair was equally qualified, blacks were three times as likely as whites to face discrimination.

> Ten pairs of men between nineteen and twenty-four years old were dispatched to respond to randomly chosen help-wanted ads published last summer [1990] in the Washington Post and Chicago Tribune. The men were paired to be similar in appearance and manner. One team, for instance, consisted of a 6-foot-4 inch bearded white and a 6-foot-2 inch bearded black. Each team memorized similar biographies and practiced interviews to minimize differences. Nearly all the help-wanted ads were for retail, hotel, restaurant or other service jobs (Wessel, 1991, A9).

Blacks fared worse than whites far more often in Washington, D.C., than in Chicago. In Washington, D.C., 60 percent of blacks versus 16 percent of whites were treated less favorably than their counterparts. This less favorable treatment entailed waiting longer or having a shorter interview or receiving discouraging comments from interviewers.

As a final example, in order to examine questionable sales practices of "junk bond" mutual funds, Donald Anspach posed as a "pseudo-client" (pretend client) and let the sales people make their sales pitches while he carefully recorded the deceptive and misleading proposals (Anspach, 1990).

Observational studies can be considerably enhanced through voice telegraphy validation, polygraph validation, videotaping, motion pictures, photography (including infrared photography), and other mechanical aids to data gathering.

Simulations

Simulation

One way of avoiding problems of unobtrusive measurement in the field is through the use of simulations. A *simulation* is a *situation or game that attempts to mimic, or imitate, key features of reality*. They may range from very simple, relatively nonserious play activities or games to highly complex computer simulations of the world economy or international diplomacy (Haney, 1976; Guetzkow, 1962). As was the case in the Chicago jury study discussed earlier, it is often impossible to study the actual subjects in real life situations. Even though the subjects studied in a simulation may differ from real subjects, it may be the only choice in some circumstances. Simulated jury studies, although they have been criticized for artificiality, overreliance on volunteers or college undergraduates, and the like, have been predictive of actual jury deliberations (discussed in part in Chapter 3) (Colasanto and Sanders, 1978; Landy and Aronson, 1969).

Two well-known and controversial studies that illuminate some key issues of research through simulation are Haney, Banks, and Zimbardo's "Simulated Prison Study" (1973) and Milgram's *Obedience to Authority* experiment (1974). Haney, Banks, and Zimbardo (1973) created a "mock prison" and used undergraduates to play the roles of prisoner and guard. The overzealous undergraduates, particularly the guards, carried away with their roles, became more aggressive and even violent; at the same time, the prisoners became increasingly more hostile and passive. In the end, the experiment had to be prematurely brought to a halt for fear of danger to the participants.

Milgram's simulations with *Obedience to Authority: An Experimental View* (1974) attempt to address conditions under which people will "follow orders" when told to do so by what appear to be competent authorities, even if these activities appear immoral or harmful to others. Using volunteers from a variety of backgrounds and without explaining the true purpose of the exercise, Milgram and researchers told the subjects that they were involved in a study regarding learning. The subjects were introduced to other subjects (actually confederates in the experiment) who were identified as pupils in the experiment. The subject-teachers were shown a shock-generating machine with which it was explained they were to deliver jolts to pupils who would be behind a screen attempting to answer questions. If the answer was wrong, the subject-teachers were instructed to flick a succession of switches marked with various labels from small voltage up to "XXX." None of the subjects refused to flick at least one switch and a large proportion administered even the highest voltage when reassured to do so by the researcher, despite screams and cries of protest from the confederates. Although the simulation could certainly be criticized for artificiality and "demand characteristics," Milgram claims the experiment was real to the participants, many of whom claimed to have suffered some psychological problems after the experiment, after reflecting on what they had done. Fortunately, follow-up inquiries found no lasting impacts.

Not all simulations contain the potential ethical problems of the Milgram studies. Most do not involve hidden or manipulative processes, and most elicit the informed consent of subjects, but all simulations or disguised experimentation should involve the *debriefing of subjects* to reassure them and explain the full purposes of the study.

Debriefing

Simulations such as "mock trials," in which participants play the roles of principal actors in a courtroom, may be used for research as well as teaching or training purposes. Such training can be quite realistic, serious, and hopefully preparative to actual situations. As part of a larger study of plea bargaining, Miller, McDonald, and Cramer (1980) administered a simulation to 136 prosecutors and 104 defense attorneys, and McDonald and Cramer (1980), in a quasi-experimental design, manipulated such variables as prior record of defendant and strength of case. Computer simulations of complex social processes can be utilized to trace alterations in systems introduced as a result of changes in specific variables. Assuming that the simulation model is accurate, such theoretically introduced changes can be assessed before they are attempted in the real world, at great savings in cost and potential error.

Advantages of Unobtrusive Measures

Nonreactivity

The chief advantage of unobtrusive methods of data gathering is their **nonreactivity.** If the subjects are unaware that they are being studied, then it might be assumed that the behavior or attitudes observed are *more natural,* unhampered by reactive effects to testing or artificial experimental arrangements. Nonreactive measures are also a means of *avoiding the overreliance on attitudinal data,* or verbal descriptions by respondents, about their behavior.

Mechanical aids, both audio and visual, greatly enhance the data-gathering process in unobtrusive measurement. The use of *recording hardware can increase accuracy,* is often better than a human observer, and provides a permanent record for later analysis. Such gadgets as voice-activated tapes require little monitoring and relieve the boredom of observing nonactivity.

The collection of physical evidence is *inconspicuous and grants anonymity.* Archival records enable the *study of phenomena over time.* Observational studies have the advantages of *gaining information firsthand* and taking into account nuance and context of the behavior. If it is behavior that is the object of interest, its actual observation is *superior to survey claims.* A major consideration is the fact that *nonreactive measures may be the only means of studying some research problems.*

To overcome the often time-consuming nature of this technique, *researchers can employ accomplices* to precipitate the type of behavior they wish to investigate. By making use of data already gathered by others, the researcher can conduct large-scale and even international analysis *quickly and inexpensively.* Such data exist in large quantity and await clever investigators to tease out appropriate and useful analyses. No claim is made for the superiority of unobtrusive measures over other means of gathering data, but they are highly useful, particularly when combined with other methods.

Disadvantages of Unobtrusive Measures

The leading disadvantages in employing secretive means of gathering data are ethical questions, particularly that of *privacy invasion.* Because the permission of respondents to participate or be observed has not been requested, the researcher is in a sense an uninvited snooper; and because the subjects are not on guard, the behavior or attitudes they display may relate to private or intimate behavior that may prove embarrassing, or even dangerous to the subjects, were the information to fall into the wrong hands.

Right of confidentiality

Criminal justice researchers, unlike some practitioners, have *no state-granted right to confidentiality* or recognized entitlement to privileged communication. They can be subpoenaed for information and be jailed for obstruction of justice. Possessing confidential information with the consent of subjects would be hazardous enough in such circumstances, but without their prior approval, such information would certainly put the subjects potentially in harm's way.

Some other possible difficulties with clandestine methods relate to the representativeness of the subject(s). They *may be atypical and therefore not generalizable* to larger similar groups. In most instances, the purpose of the investigation is to infer to this larger group. For instance, the National Institute of Justice may sponsor a study in Cleveland, Ohio, not because they are interested in Cleveland per se, but because they hope to generalize to other similar cities.

Unobtrusive measurement can also be a *very time-consuming enterprise,* although accomplices can be employed to speed up the action. Such approaches are also subject to *possible observer bias,* unless carefully monitored by the research field director. Unlike participant observation, in which the researcher can test out interpretations of attitude as it intersects with behavior, unobtrusive studies concentrate primarily on behavior and thus may be removed from the subjective meanings attached to this behavior by the actors involved.

The use of available data or public observations may, of course, overcome some of the disadvantages we have elaborated. Existing records and archival data may have been previously contaminated by reactive biases or subject to selective deposit (what remains is not typical) or selective survival (what survives is not typical). The major problem with nonreactive methods is their accuracy when they are used as the only measure of some phenomenon.

Summary

Unobtrusive measures are secretive, or nonreactive, means of gathering data. They refer to a variety of methods in which the subjects are not aware they are being studied and thus are less likely to act artificially. The *major types of unobtrusive measures* are physical trace analysis; archives, existing data, and autobiographies; simple and disguised observation; and simulation. *Physical trace analysis* is analysis of deposits, accretions, or other indirect signs of human activity. Some principal methods of analyzing available data are content analysis and secondary analysis. *Content analysis* is systematic classification and analysis of the subject matter of human communication, such as publications and mass media. *Secondary analysis* is the reanalysis of data that had been previously gathered by someone else. Personal documents, biographies, autobiographies, and existing official data represent fertile sources for the analysis of available data. The use of sources of existing data in criminal justice has been considerably augmented by organizations such as the National Criminal Justice Reference Service.

Observation makes use of a strategy in which the analyst minimizes interaction with the subjects to carefully record and examine their behavior. In *disguised observation,* the researcher covertly enters the research scene without the knowledge or permission of the subjects. This technique often makes use of *confederates* or accomplices who facilitate the desired activity to be observed, as well as *debriefing sessions* in which the true purposes of the deception are explained to the subjects and any anxiety introduced is hopefully allayed. *Simulation* strategies involve attempts to imitate more complex realities by means of games or controlled experiments or computer models.

Numerous examples of criminal justice and criminological research attempting to utilize elements of these approaches are presented. The relative advantages and disadvantages of unobtrusive measure are detailed. Chief advantages of *unobtrusive methods* are that they are more natural, are nonreactive, depend less on verbal reports, and make excellent use of available data. Among some of the disadvantages are ethical and privacy invasion issues, lack of license to confidentiality, nonrepresentativeness of groups studied, possible time-consuming nature of the procedure, and observer bias.

The use of unobtrusive measurement in criminal justice research presents an opportunity to observe groups naturally and is limited only by ethics and the imagination and creativity of the investigator.

Key Concepts

Unobtrusive Measures	Primary Sources	Debriefing
Physical Trace Analysis	Secondary Sources	Advantages of
Archival Records	Meta-Analysis	Unobtrusive Measures
Content Analysis	Sources of Existing Data	Nonreactivity
Secondary Analysis	Disguised Observation	Disadvantages of
Simulation	Confederates	Unobtrusive Measures

Review Questions

1. What are the major types of unobtrusive methods? Give an example of each from studies in criminology and criminal justice.
2. What are some advantages and examples of the use of secondary analysis in criminology and criminal justice?
3. What are data archives, and of what use are they in research?
4. What are the relative advantages and disadvantages of unobtrusive measures as a strategy of research?
5. Discuss how the Blocks utilized existing data in order to investigate gangs in Chicago.

CHAPTER APPENDIX 8.1

Street Gang Crime in Chicago

Issues and Findings

Discussed in the brief: A study supported by the National Institute of Justice of street gang-motivated violence in one major U.S. city—Chicago. Analysis of police homicide records over twenty-six years and gang-motivated incident records over three years revealed the street gang affiliation of every offender and the location of each offense, which gives a detailed picture of gang activity and the relationships of individual, gang, and neighborhood characteristics.

Key issues: Gangs—and gang-related violence and drug trafficking—are growing problems across the country. Street gangs and the crimes in which they engage cannot be viewed as monolithic. One neighborhood may be unaffected, while nearby; another is the marketplace for a gang's drug operation or the center of lethal turf battles. Bursts of gang-related violence appear among specific gangs and suddenly stop.

Key findings: For a 3-year period, 1987–1990, the study results included the following:

- Gang-related, high-crime neighborhoods can be classified into three types: turf hot spots, where gangs fight over territory control; drug hot spots, where gang motivated drug offenses concentrate; and turf and drug hot spots, where gang-motivated crimes relate to both.
- Gang involvement in violence and homicide is more often turf-related than drug-related. Only eight of 288 gang-motivated homicides were related to drugs.
- The city's four largest street gangs were identified with most of the street gang crime. Representing 51 percent of all street gang members, they accounted for 69 percent of recorded criminal incidents.
- The rate of street gang-motivated crime in the two most dangerous areas was seventy-six times that of the two safest.

- A gun was the lethal weapon used in almost all gang-motivated homicides. Use of high-caliber, automatic, or semiautomatic weapons dramatically increased.

These and other findings of the research have policy implications for formulating intervention strategies.

- Programs to reduce nonlethal street gang violence must be targeted to the specific street gang problems In each neighborhood.
- Effective intervention strategies must be built on continuously updated information.

Street gang activity—legal and illegal, violent and nonviolent, lethal and nonlethal—occurs disproportionately among neighborhoods and population groups. Types of incidents tend to cluster and increase in bursts in specific neighborhoods and among specific gangs.

Neighborhoods often differ sharply in the predominant type of street gang-motivated incidents they experience. For example, one city neighborhood may be unaffected by street gang activity, while another close by may be a marketplace for a street gang's drug operation, and yet a third may be plagued by frequent and lethal turf battles.

In addition, the chief criminal activities of one street gang often differ from those of another. For example, one outbreak of lethal street gang violence may be characterized by escalating retribution and revenge, while another may be associated with expansion of a drug business into new territory. Consequently, street gangs and the crimes in which they engage cannot be viewed as monolithic in nature.

This Research in Brief describes these and other patterns of street gang-related violence in a major U.S. city—Chicago. All available information, including Chicago police records of illegal street gang-motivated activity—from vandalism to drug offenses to violent offenses (both lethal and nonlethal—was examined across time, neighborhood, and street gang affiliation. Individual, gang-level,

Continued.

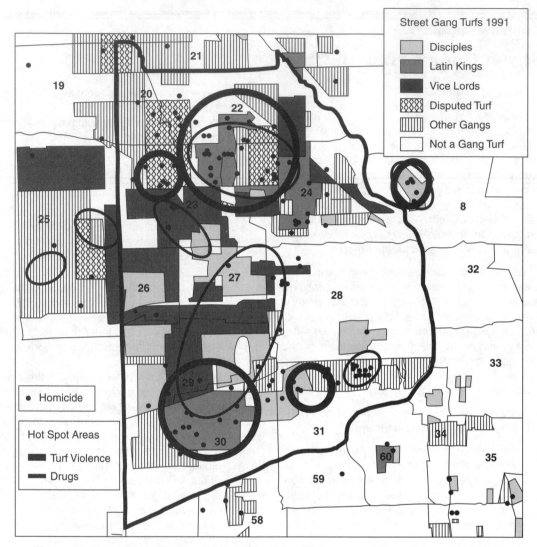

Figure 1 Street Gang-Motivated Homicide, Other Violence, and Drug Crime, 1987–1990. (*Source:* Chicago Police Department).

and neighborhood level characteristics were also analyzed to determine the relationships among these three factors. The results of the analysis give one of the most complete pictures of street gang crime available today.

Study Methodology

Researchers examined Chicago gang homicide data over a 26-year period, from 1965 through 1990, and detailed information on other gang-related crime from 1987 to 1990. Two methods of analysis were used to determine the extent to which neighborhoods differed in the type and concentration of street gang activity and to examine the neighborhood characteristics that were associated with high levels of lethal and nonlethal street gang activity. The information analyzed was primarily from Chicago Police Department (CPD) records, which were organized into three sets of data on Chicago homicides, street gang-motivated offenses, and street gang territories. Neighborhood characteristics and population data for rate calculation were obtained from the U.S. Bureau of the Census. This information was gathered by tract and aggregated into the seventy-seven Chicago community areas.

Researchers geocoded the address of each homicide and street gang-motivated incident. Boundaries of the community areas were mapped, geocoded offenses were aggregated by community area, and offenses were analyzed in relation to population and other community characteristics. Finally, the densest concentrations (hot spot areas) of individual addresses of street gang-related incidents were identified regardless of arbitrary boundaries and related to gang turfs, gang activity, and community characteristics.

Data on homicides. One of the largest and most detailed data sets on violence ever collected in the United States, the Chicago homicide data set contains information on every homicide in police records from 1965 to 1990. More than 200 variables were collected for the 19,323 homicides in this data set. The crime analysis unit of the Chicago Police Department has maintained a summary—Murder Analysis Report (MAR)—of each homicide over the 26-year period. On the basis of these reports, 1,311 homicides were classified as street gang-motivated.

Data on street gang-motivated offenses. This data set included information on 17,085 criminal offenses that occurred from 1987 to 1990 that were classified by the police as street gang-related. These offenses were categorized as follows:

- 288 homicides.
- 8,828 nonlethal violent offenses (aggravated and simple assault and battery).
- 5,888 drug offenses (violations related to possession or sale of hard or soft drugs).
- 2,081 other offenses (includes more than 100 specific crimes ranging from liquor law violations to intimidation, mob action, vandalism, robbery, and weapons law violations).

Data on street gang territory boundaries. This data set included the location of street gang territory boundaries in early 1991. These boundaries were based on maps drawn by street gang officers in Chicago's twenty-six districts, who identified the territories of forty-five street gangs—both major and minor—and noted areas that were in dispute between one or more street gangs.

Defining gang affiliation. These three data sets included several possible aspects of street gang affiliation for each incident—for example, the street gang affiliation of the offender or offenders, the affiliation of the victim or victims (if any), and the location of the incident within the boundaries of a gang's turf. In this study researchers classified street gang-motivated criminal incidents according to the affiliation of the offender(s).

Source: Block, Carolyn Rebecca, and Richard Block. *Street Gang Crime in Chicago.* National Institute of Justice Research in Brief, December 1993, NCJ 144782.

Validity, Reliability, and Triangulated Strategies

Much of the preceding text has concentrated on the weaknesses of individual data-gathering strategies. This chapter explores the issue of measurement, and it specifies operational procedures for attacking problems of validity and reliability in research, with emphases on multimethod strategies.

Levels of Measurement

Variables may be measured on four levels:

Nominal   Interval
Ordinal   Ratio

Nominal
variables **Nominal level variables** represent the simplest level of measurement. Objects are usually placed into mutually exclusive categories or types, and there is often no necessary quantitative or statistical meaning to numbers assigned to these categories, except as a convenience in distinguishing groups. Thus, any numbers assigned are merely qualitative descriptions, or labels, that enable us to keep track of differences. Demographic variables such as sex, race, religion, and city are examples of nominal variables. Values might be assigned, such as 1 to Protestant, 2 to Catholic, 3 to Jewish, and 4 to other. Three Protestants, however, do not equal one Jewish. The numbers merely assist in categorizing qualitative distinctions. Many variables that should take on higher scale value may be treated as nominal level, although information is lost as a result. In criminal justice, numbers could be arbitrarily assigned to different types of crimes in order to categorize them, for instance:

1. Homicide
2. Assault
3. Robbery
4. Burglary

Obviously, as in the previous example, the actual numbers assigned have no mathematical meaning. That is, a homicide (1) plus a robbery (3) does not equal a burglary (4), nor do four homicides equal one burglary. Other qualitative or nominal categories to which numbers are assigned are telephone numbers, social security numbers, room numbers, addresses, and officer badge numbers. Any reduction in the level of measurement of a variable from higher level to nominal measurement involves a loss of precision or detail. Similarly, any increase in the level of measurement to ordinal, interval, or ratio involves an increase in information, or precision, over the previous categories.

Table 9.1 ranks data on violent criminal victimization. In a representation of the same data using only nominal level information, the cities would be classified as either Eastern or Western, for example:

1. Eastern cities 8
2. Western cities 5

Another nominal means of assigning values to the data in Table 9.1 would be to consider scores above fifty-four as high, and assign them a value of 1, and scores of fifty-four or below as low, and assign them a value of 2.

For instance, weight, which could be measured in pounds and inches, could be reduced to simply heavy and light. Similarly, "sentence imposed," which could be measured in months, might be reduced to simply "long" and "short. "

Ordinal variables

Ordinal level variables contain all the properties of nominal variables, but they also enable the placement of objects into ranks, that is, highest to lowest. In Table 9.1, the city with the highest victim rate was assigned a rank of 1, the city with the second highest a rank of 2, and so forth to 13 for the lowest. For cities that were tied, the average of the ranks that would have been assigned is given to each of the tied values. Most attitudinal scales used in the social sciences and criminal justice are ordinal in nature. They enable

TABLE 9.1 Violent Criminal Victimization Rates in Thirteen Selected Cities (per 1,000 Residents 12 and Older)

		Rank	Location
Detroit	68	1	Eastern
Denver	67	2	Western
Philadelphia	63	3	Eastern
Portland	59	4	Western
Baltimore	56	5.5	Eastern
Chicago	56	5.5	Eastern
Cleveland	54	7	Eastern
Los Angeles	53	8	Western
Atlanta	48	9	Eastern
Dallas	43	10	Western
Newark	42	11.5	Eastern
St. Louis	42	11.5	Western
New York	36	13	Eastern

Source: National Crime Panel Surveys. Law Enforcement Assistance Administration, 1974.

us to rank respondents, but they must not be mistaken for real numbers. For example, a person whose attitudinal scale score is 50 is higher than a person who scored 30, which is again higher than one who scored 10. Thus, we know that each is higher than the next. We do not know by how much each is higher; the ranks are not comparable to meters or dollars. As another example, although we know that a student with a 3.6 quality point average in college is .6 higher than one with a 3.0, we would have no idea of the unit differences in points among students who ranked first, fifth, and tenth unless the actual averages were provided.

Interval
variables

Interval level variables contain all the elements of nominal and ordinal data and also assume equal distance or interval between objects on a scale. It not only provides a ranking of objects, but also reflects equal intervals or a standard unit between scale scores. Thus, the distance between scores 2 and 4 is exactly the same as the distance between 8 and 10. Using our victimization rate example from Table 9.1, the assignment of nominal level measurement to the data merely resulted in mutually exclusive categories of east–west or high–low, whereas ordinal assignment ranked the cities from highest to lowest. Interval level data, the actual rates, give us this same information plus the unit differences between each value. That is, we now know not only which city ranks higher or lower, but how much higher or lower. Interval level measurement also contains an arbitrary zero point.

Ratio variables

Ratio level variables not only assume the interval quality of data, but they also have a fixed meaningful zero point. Such data enable one to show how many times greater one value is than another. Some examples of ratio variables are variables such as age, weight, income, education, number of children, and frequency of crime commission. Although it is possible to have zero income or education, one would not have zero IQ or attitude toward crime. Each scale is more complex and takes on the properties of the preceding.

Error in Research

Error is another term for invalidity, and sources of potential error or invalidity are ever present, even in some of the best research. In fact, as we have reiterated throughout this book, the only perfect research is no research. By way of example of this truism, Walters and White in "Heredity and Crime: Bad Genes or Bad Research" (1989) point to many methodological flaws in such genetic studies. Particularly problematic in such studies has been the question of operationalizing zygosity, that is, of determining whether twins were monozygotic (identical) or dizygotic (fraternal). Walters and White note that contrary to popular belief, monozygotic twins are not always identical-looking; nor are all identical-looking twins monozygotic. Advances such as blood and serum typing provide for more valid measurement.

In lamenting the lack of validity in much of the research on physical child abuse, Mash and Wolfe (1991, p. 10) note:

> Research into [child] abuse has been plagued by such interrelated methodological problems as a lack of a priori predictions; a narrow research focus on physical injuries; an insensitivity to important child development parameters; poorly defined independent and dependent variables; confounded variables; inadequate and/or biased sampling; lack of adequate demographic descriptions; no or poorly matched comparison groups; the use of inappropriate measures of unknown or inadequate reliability and validity; the use of nonblind experimenters and coders; inappropriate analysis and illegitimate inferences and interpretations .

Validity

Reliability

The question of validity, as we will see, logically precedes that of reliability. **Validity** asks "Does my measuring instrument in fact measure what it claims to measure?" Is it an accurate or true measure of the phenomenon under study? **Reliability,** on the other hand, concerns the stability and consistency of measurement. If the study were repeated, would the instrument yield stable and uniform measures? Before consideration of the consistency of measurement, accuracy should be assumed. A consistent inaccurate measurement of a phenomenon is one that is predictably wrong and therefore not very useful.

In Chapters 3–8 we reviewed the many sources of error and critiques of the validity and reliability of much of the quantitative research conducted in the social sciences and, specifically, criminal justice. W. Bailey (1971), for instance, in a review of a sample of 100 correctional outcome reports, concluded that much of the research was invalid, unreliable, and based on poor research design. Generally, the more rigorous the design, the less the likeli-hood that significant outcomes in treatment will be claimed. In their review of criminological research, Hood and Sparks (1971, p. 9) were led to the following conclusion: "Yet the unhappy fact is that much criminological research—even in recent years—is so defective methodologically as to be virtually worthless; and many other studies are so limited in this respect that very little weight can be put on their conclusions." Although later modifying his views and admitting that perhaps he had been too methodologically narcissistic, Martinson (1974) blasted correctional research in his now famous "nothing works" criticism. He felt that there was little evidence of significant programs in corrections that had any important impact on reducing recidivism.

Reasons for Lack of Validation Studies in Criminal Justice

As part of its recommendations regarding research designs, the National Advisory Committee on Criminal Justice Standards and Goals (1976, p. 53) indicated that "Descriptions of proposed research designs should include in at least rudimentary form, a comparison of the selected design with possible alternatives and, where applicable, an indication of the methods to be used to overcome the inherent weaknesses of the selected design." In this same assessment of *Criminal Justice Research and Development* the advisory committee noted that despite the great need for validation and replication of studies in criminal justice, few have been conducted. *Some reasons for the lack of validation studies in criminal justice are:*

Little professional esteem in replication
Lack of complexity in technique
Design faults in original study
Unfavorable climate
Interjurisdictional disputes
Tradition

It is unfortunate that *less professional prestige* is assigned to replication studies. Often, professional journals are not interested in publishing such results, considering it old news. Unlike laboratory experiments in the physical sciences, which are easily replicable, much criminal justice research may be of a nontechnical quality, making exact replication more difficult. *Design faults* in original studies, often called attention to by the researcher to bring about improvements in future studies, make exact replication of studies unlikely. Any change makes the validation study different than the original; thus, any differences found may be the result of instrumentation rather than flaws in the initial study.

The *unfavorable climate* for validation research is due to the human nature of organizational findings. Most organizations simply have little interest in objective findings that may shed negative light on the agency, particularly at budget time. If the initial study had positive results, then the point of view might be why restudy the obvious, particularly when funding for existing programs is needed. If the results were negative, there would not likely to be a warm reception for yet another study.

[margin notes] Reasons for lack of validity studies

Design faults

Interjurisdictional and agency differences are so large that even several studies of agencies in different jurisdictions may still be viewed by officials in criminal justice agencies in other states or domains as inapplicable to the differing conditions in their province.

Finally, the *lack of a research tradition* that would support validation studies in criminal justice research may create a self-fulfilling prophecy in that researchers tend not to view the need to carefully outline their methodology so as to permit replication and possible future validation. To encourage such a tradition, the National Advisory Committee called for expeditious federal funding of small-scale unsolicited proposals that involve inexpensive validation studies. In this same mode, comparative international research was viewed as an additional and important source of assessing the validity and reliability of criminal justice research.

In concluding the section on validation, the National Advisory Committee on Criminal Justice Standards and Goals recommended that:

> Research projects intended to validate previous research play an important role in the advancement of knowledge. Validation studies should be encouraged as initial steps of larger studies and should be funded as separate projects in greater numbers than in the past. Validations should be carefully designed and reviewed, however, to determine whether there are serious obstacles to successful completion. When few obstacles are present, as in small-scale validations, procedures should be available for funding and publishing such studies expeditiously.
>
> 1. In order to facilitate validation studies, R&D [Research and Development] funding agencies could require that R&D projects be documented in a form that permits validation.
> 2. Data used in a research project could be made available to other researchers, within existing confidentiality constraints (National Advisory Committee, 1976, p. 54).

Ways of Determining Validity

Let us examine appropriate procedures with which to determine the reliability and validity of measuring instruments. Table 9.2 provides a summary of the types of validity and reliability.

Types of validity

The *types of validity* include:

Face validity
Content validity
Construct validity
Pragmatic validity
Convergent–discriminant validity

TABLE 9.2 Types of Validity and Reliability

Types of Validity

Face	Does the measuring instrument appear "at face value" to be measuring what I am attempting to measure?
Content	Does each item or the content of the instrument measure the concept in question?
Construct	Does the instrument in fact measure the concept in question?
Pragmatic	Does the instrument work in practically distinguishing current status (concurrent validity) or future outcomes (predictive validity) of the concept being measured?
Convergent– discriminant	Does use of different methods or measures (triangulation) of the concept yield similar results, while use of the same method to measure different concepts produces different (discriminate) results?

Types of Reliability

Test–retest	When the same instrument is administered at least twice to the same group, are the results or scores the same (or stable)?
Multiple forms	Does the administration of a disguised or alternate version of the same instrument to the same group result in the same (stable) scores?
Split-half technique	In the administration of the instrument to one group at one time, are separate halves of the instrument similar in response (are they consistent?)

Face Validity

Face validity **Face validity** is the simplest measurement and asks, "Does the measuring instrument appear, at face value, to be measuring what I am attempting to measure?" Such an approach to establishing validity is very judgmental and does not rest particularly on any empirical grounds. It simply looks good, or strikes informed judges as a reasonable attempt to measure the point in question. Hardt and Hardt (1977) were satisfied with the face validity of a self-report scale they administered to a group of high school students. They noted that the prosocial behavior item, "helping parents," received the highest endorsement as expected, as did two more trivial antisocial items, "fist fighting" and "smoking." Again, as anticipated, the least frequently reported items were more serious ones such as "joyriding" and "drug experimenting."

To explain all of the types of validity, we use an example to which most students should relate very well: a midterm examination in research methods. The concept that the instrument (the exam) is supposed to be measuring is "student knowledge of research methods." Suppose your class, which I am sure is very bright, took the examination, and most of you flunked despite the fact that all of you have given the class reasonable effort and are Dean's List students in other classes. Arguments with the professor are going nowhere, until one student questions the face validity of the examination. The instructor checks and, sure enough, realizes that he or she had asked the department secretary to type a four-year-old test based on different books and entitled "Research Methods in Psychology."

Content Validity

Content validity

    Content validity entails examining each item—the content of an instrument—to judge whether each element measures the concept in question. Similar to face validity, content validity is also judgmental and usually nonempirical in nature; however, an item analysis may be employed to eliminate nondiscriminatory items. Using our midterm examination once again, although students may have been relatively satisfied with their general performance, all of them missed questions 40 and 56 and all of them had questions 1 and 2 correct. All of these questions tap a constant; the concept being measured does not vary because everyone gets them correct or incorrect. Although no student will argue about the easy questions, one student indicates that questions 40 and 56 deal with subject matter that is covered later in the text and is not part of the assigned material. Such items should be eliminated from the scoring.

Construct Validity

Construct validity

    Construct validity (sometimes called concept validity) is perhaps the most theoretical and philosophically basic question. It asks whether the instrument in question does, in fact, measure what it has been designated to measure (Cronbach and Meehl, 1955). The problem may be with the label given to the scale rather than the instrument itself. Perhaps an excellent measurement is obtained of something other than what the instrument was claimed to measure. Construct validation involves skillful reasoning rather than measurement per se, because there seldom exists any criterion against which the measure may be compared. Selltiz et al. (1959, p. 160) indicate that if the predictions are not borne out, it may not be clear whether the problem lies with the measuring instrument itself or in the concept it is believed to represent. One more rigorous manner of approaching the issue of construct validity, "convergent-discriminant validation," will be discussed shortly. Construct validity, then, refers to the fit between theoretical and operational definitions of terms (Maltz and McCleary, 1977). In discussing methodological inadequacies of psychological research on prisoners, Reppucci and Clingempeel (1978) identified poor construct validity as a chief limitation. Those engaged in personality research with prisoners should use multiple measures, including natural treatments, behaviors, and settings, together with unobtrusive measures.

    Returning to our midterm test example, suppose that the test is an objective test in which the questions are phrased in very sophisticated, esoteric language. The score on the test may be highly related to possession of an English major or high verbal SAT scores rather than a knowledge of research methods. This midterm test in research methods tended to be a better measure of knowledge of the English language. One of the major criticisms of some IQ tests is that they measure middle-class background more than intelligence.

Pragmatic Validity

The types of validation discussed so far entail theoretical or judgmental procedures, whereas **pragmatic validity** asks, "Does it work?" There are *two types of pragmatic validity:* concurrent validity and predictive validity. **Concurrent validity** concerns itself with whether the measure enhances the ability to gauge present characteristics of the item in question. The ability to accurately forecast future events or conditions defines **predictive validity.** Both concurrent validity and predictive validity are sometimes referred to as examples of criterion validation because both seek outside criteria as means to assess the accuracy of measurement. Use is made of some outside checks that could in no way be influenced by the measure under question. Sources of primary validation include files of juvenile and criminal courts, clinic records, data on income, education, and marital status, school records, and the like.

In concurrent validation of a recidivism scale, crime commission of those who score as high or low risk on parole would be examined for differences.

A predictive validation of a recidivism scale would entail checking, for example, five years later, to see whether the index worked as predicted.

One problem in the attempt to demonstrate pragmatic validity is that for many abstract concepts employed in the social sciences and criminal justice, appropriate indicators may not be readily available or may be of questionable validity. For instance, concurrent or predictive validation of fear, cynicism, witness perception, or police morale might be quite difficult compared with checking reported age or education.

Schlesinger (1978), in assessing predictions of the dangerousness of 122 juveniles one year after release from a clinic, discovered that the variables used for diagnosis of juveniles undergoing treatment had very poor predictive ability. Some problems in performing predictive validation studies with such subjects are the uncertain reliability of many of the variables, the bias of a sample based on juvenile offenders, and inaccurate offender records. The latter entails the frequent problem of finding adequate criteria with which to assess the validity of measures.

Concurrent validation of our midterm exam might ask whether scores of the midterm agree with the performance of students on other assignments and quizzes that had been given so far. For example, if everyone had been doing above-average work until then, why did everyone flunk the midterm? Something is wrong, and that something could be the validity or appropriateness of the test. Predictive validity might ask whether performance on this midterm exam predicts a student's final grade in the course.

In a final example, in "A Longitudinal Validation Study of Correctional Officer Job Performance as Predicted by the IPI and MMPI," Shusman and Inwald (1991) explored the predictive validity of two personality tests, the Minnesota Multi-Phasic Inventory (MMPI) and the Inwald Personality Inventory (IPI). Could these two tests forecast correctional officer job performance an average of three and one-half years into the future? Using data

Pragmatic validity

Concurrent validity

Predictive validity

on absences, tardiness, disciplinary actions, and supervisors' reports, they found that the IPI was a better predictor.

Convergent–Discriminant Validation/Triangulation

Convergent–discriminant validation

Convergent–discriminant validation involves the use of multiple methods to measure multiple traits (Campbell and Fiske, 1959). The logic of convergent–discriminant validation holds that by "using different methods (interview, questionnaire, experiment, observation) of measuring a construct, the results should be similar, whereas the same method measuring different things should yield dissimilar results" (ibid, p. 81). Thus, the use of different techniques to measure the same concept should yield the same findings (*convergence*), whereas the use of one technique to measure different things should yield different results (*discrimination*) (see Figure 9.1). The use of multiple methods to measure the same phenomenon is also referred to as **triangulation** (Campbell and Fiske, 1959; Webb et al., 1966).

Triangulation

Triangulation methods assume that it is relatively hopeless to attempt to demonstrate the validity or reliability of one measurement using only one method. The use of multiple methods enables the introduction of "methods used" as a variable or rival causal factor. If there is no difference in findings despite the use of different methods, then any one method, for example experimenter or interviewer effects, could not be responsible for producing the findings.

Although measurements of a concept (alienation) using different methods should yield the same results, measurements of different concepts with the same method should yield different results. If a student's midterm, final, and term paper scores are all F's, there is convergence; however, if every time Professor Jones gives an objective midterm in any course everyone receives an F, the problem is the method. The problem is not the inadequacy of a particular method; it is that the method is used alone. It is fruitless to be concerned with the validity or reliability of the measurement of one concept, at one time, using only one measure. Chilton and Spielberger (1972, p. 74) indicate the serious disadvantage of using any single measure of crime alone.

Trait	Experiments	Surveys	Unobtrusive Measures
Alienation	X	X	X
Anomie	–	–	–
Authoritarianism	–	–	–

Figure 9.1 Convergent–Discrimination Validation: *X*, Similar Findings; –, Dissimilar Findings.

In order to study decision making in jury trials, Reed observed actual jury trials, recording jury selection proceedings, the length and nature of the testimony, legal objections and rulings, and other measures. Next, interviews were conducted with attorneys and jurors in cases where a verdict was returned. Finally, an experimental jury simulation study was conducted to analyze many of these same issues. Reed claims that among the advantages of combining research methodologies were gaining access into the legal milieu, obtaining active cooperation of the presiding judge, and gaining 100 percent cooperation from attorneys and 74 percent cooperation from jurors. In addition, the simulation was able to contain variables with applied value (Reed, 1976).

In our previous discussion of participant observation (Chapter 7) we described how Clarke (1982) utilized multiple sources to construct his typology of assassins. Similarly, we saw how journalists, such as Maas (1968) in *The Valachi Papers,* do not rely only on the testimony of an informant, but carefully use other independent sources to verify this information. Lupscha (1982) identifies the following sources of information that may be triangulated to obtain valid, convergent data on organized crime: informers, congressional hearings and investigations, court trial transcripts and depositions, articles in newspapers and popular periodicals, investigative reporting, wire surveillance transcripts, memoirs/biographies/autobiographies, government reports and releases, National Institute of Justice-assisted research, archival/historical documents, and in-depth interviews. Field studies could also be added to this list. The point is that the larger the number of independent sources that say the same thing, the greater the confidence attached to the findings. An analogy can be drawn to a criminal trial in the United States, where the prosecution is responsible for convincing a judge and jury of the guilt of a defendant who has pleaded innocence. The prosecution may present evidence, witnesses, and expert testimony, question and cross-examine, and bring to bear as many independent sources of information as possible to make the case. The state, however, must "prove" its case "beyond a reasonable doubt"; that is, it may never be able to make the case absolutely that the individual is guilty. Similarly, researchers seldom absolutely "prove" the validity of their findings; rather, they eliminate rival causal factors and errors to the point at which a sufficient number of independent, objective sources have been brought to bear that there is a high probability (but not absolute certainty) that the conclusions are valid.

By introducing, as a variable, different observers, interviewers, or methods of data collection, the researcher is able to control for invalidity of the method. The greater the number of diverse, converging measures on a phenomenon, the greater the confidence in the validity of the measure (Brewer and Hunter, 1983).

To validate scales measuring police probity, personal integrity, departmental anticorruption policy, and peer support for corrupt practices, Fishman (1978) compared the survey results with prior knowledge of the departments by an advisory board of an anticorruption management project. In addition, other sources of validation included the evaluation of the corruption level of the departments by a panel of experts, an examination of departmental records, a study of newspaper articles in each city covering a two-year period, as well as in-depth interviews with departmental brass and officers. On the basis of these pieces of corroborating evidence, Fishman found that responses to the instrument significantly differentiated corrupt from noncorrupt organizations and claims that the questionnaire is useful in aiding police administrators in evaluating the moral climate of their departments.

Some additional examples of triangulation methodology are the use of court records, in-court observations, and a simulation game in a study of plea bargaining (Miller, McDonald, and Cramer, 1980) and the use of court records, observations of conferences, and interviews of participants in a study of pretrial settlement conferences (Kerstetter and Heinz, 1979).

Pretests   *Researchers should use pretests to measure the validity and reliability of instruments prior to their use in a study.* Pretests or pilot studies are preliminary studies conducted with a few subjects to test the instrument and uncover any obvious problems before administering it to the study population. This is similar to a firedrill or test run of a racing car. A piece of computer slang to remember in this regard is "GIGO" (garbage in—garbage out), which indicates that inadequately measured concepts, which have been assigned numbers and which often have been subjected to sophisticated analysis, are no better than the initial operationalization decision.

In the long run, validity is never entirely demonstrated or proven; rather, invalidity is lessened, or researchers are able to express greater degrees of confidence in their data. (For further detail on validity, see House [1980] and Thorndike and Hagen [1977].)

Reliability

Reliability   *Reliability* is demonstrated through stable and consistent replication of findings on repeated measurement. Thus, there are two types of reliability: stability and consistency.

Stability   *Stability* of measurement is determined by whether, assuming that conditions (rival causal factors) have not changed, a respondent will give the same answer to the same question on second testing. A different score on second testing may not be caused by the unreliability of the measurement, but rather by some other variable (for example, history). This type of reliability is most important for analyzing events and behavior data.

Consistency   *Consistency* of measurement is determined by whether the set of items used to measure some phenomenon are highly related (associated with each other) and measuring the same concept. Schneider et al. (1978, pp. 2–50) explain:

> In attitude measurement it is frequently assumed that a fairly complex phenomenon is under investigation such as alienation and multiple items are required to operationalize the concept. Since each of the items is designed to

measure the same concept (with slightly different aspects of the concept being dealt with by specific items), it is assumed that a reliable set of items will have a relatively high average inter-item correlation.

Statistics (Kuder–Richardson tests or Cronbach's alpha) are generally used to assess this type of reliability (Kuder and Richardson, 1967; Traub, 1994). *Three primary methods are used to demonstrate reliability:*

Three types of reliability

Test–retest
Multiple forms
Split-half techniques

All three assessments basically involve comparison of the instrument with itself to evaluate consistency.

Test–Retest

Test–retest

In the **test–retest method** of determining reliability the same instrument is administered twice to the same population and, if the results are the same, stability of measurement is assumed.

A strong relationship between the two measures is assumed to indicate reliability. A reliability coefficient (correlation or alpha) of .80 is the most accepted indicator (Carmines and Zeller, 1979). Ideally, continued repeated measures of the same population with the same instrument would provide a means of assessing reliability. Such repeated measures are likely to be regarded as annoying to respondents if the purpose is not explained, and, if it were explained, the responses would most likely be invalid because of reactivity.

In measuring "fear of crime" for instance, a scale should yield the same measurement or score for individuals if applied at different times. If it does not, either an actual change may have taken place in the individual's attitude (for example, having been victimized recently), or the scale is not a good measuring instrument. Assuming no change in attitude, if the first administration of the scale indicates that an individual is very fearful and a subsequent administration indicates little fear, then the scale may be questioned as being unreliable.

Pretest bias

The fundamental problem with this method of demonstrating reliability relates to our discussion in Chapter 3 of rival causal factors. Having already experienced the pretest the subjects are no longer naive regarding the subject of measurement and therefore are liable to "testing effects" on second measurement. That is, the scores may differ in the posttest, not because the instrument is unreliable, but because the subjects were affected by pretesting.

Another way of attempting to resolve this reactivity problem is to wait longer before giving the second test. This, however, also presents problems, because it is more likely that an actual change in attitude will occur the longer the period between tests. A quasi-experimental model similar to those discussed in Chapter 3 can in part measure this. Randomly assigned, the experimental group could receive the pretest/posttest, and the control group only the posttest (Orenstein and Phillips, 1978, p. 272). Additionally, other rival causal factors such as history and maturation may also pose problems. For these reasons, researchers attempt to masquerade the nature of the retest by changing its appearance.

Multiple Forms

Multiple forms

Multiple forms involve the administration of alternate forms of the instrument to the same group. This actually is a disguised test–retest in which, hopefully, the subjects do not realize they are being retested. As in the test-retest, a strong relationship between the two administrations is indicative of reliability or stability. Despite the charade, the possibility remains that the subjects may be aware of the similarity of the pretest and posttest; thus, multiple forms could be subject to the same shortcomings as the test–retest approach. For this reason, the most popular and widely used technique for demonstrating reliability is the split-half technique.

Split-Half Technique

Split-half reliability

Thus far, the demonstration of reliability has involved temporal stability, in which two different administrations of basically the same instrument to the same group should correlate highly. **Split-half reliability** does not involve retesting and substitutes the assessment of internal consistency for temporal consistency; each half of a scale is analyzed as if it were a separate scale (Crano and Brewer, 1973, pp. 228–229). If a respondent were to receive the same score on even-numbered items as on odd-numbered items, then the scale would be assumed to be internally consistent or reliable.

The split-half technique administers only one measure to one group at one time. After the data are gathered the instrument is randomly divided in half and each half is treated as if it were a separate test or instrument. For example, the even-numbered items might be correlated with the odd items or the random halves compared; and if they are highly correlated, reliability would be supposed. The logic of the split-half approach is that, if an instrument is reliable, it should be consistent throughout. Such an approach removes the problem of testing effects or, for that matter, any other internal rival causal factor that would have been introduced with a posttest. Generally, a coefficient of reliability or equivalence, alpha (Cronbach, 1951), where high correlation is taken to indicate reliability, is used. A correlation of at least .80 is assumed to be indicative of internal consistency or reliability. A problem with both multiple forms and split-half techniques is the concern as to whether the two forms or halves really are equivalent.

For statistical calculations on reliability, see Slavin (1984), Cronbach (1970), or Guilford and Fruchter (1978).

Mythical Numbers

Mythical
numbers   All of us, including trained criminologists and criminal justice researchers, are at times "taken in" by estimates of events or behavior without a clear notion of who provided such guesswork. In a classic article entitled "The Vitality of Mythical Numbers," Singer (1971) questioned the often uncritically cited figures on how many heroin addicts there are and how much they steal. As discussed in Chapter 8, he demonstrated that by using other available data, one could avoid accepting the same incorrect data that are picked up and passed on as fact, even by responsible research organizations. As part of a war on drugs in the early 1970s, government agencies estimating the amount of street crime committed by addicts practiced statistical overkill. Estimates such as $18 billion were much greater than the total dollar amount of all property stolen in the country according to the UCR data for the same year.

Phantom Army of Addicts

Epstein (1977) used "The Phantom Army of Addicts" to describe a "statistical" epidemic of heroin addicts created by the Bureau of Narcotics and Dangerous Drugs (BNDD) in the early 1970s. In 1969, using such traditional measures as data from police and medical authorities, BNDD estimated the number of addicts at 68,088. By 1970 the estimate was 315,000, and by 1971, it was 559,000, an apparent "epidemic" in the making. The epidemic was a statistical one, however, and more a product of government statisticians than of heroin smugglers. Epstein (1977) explains that until 1970, official estimates were based on the official register, whereas the 1970 and 1971 figures were based on a new estimating formula—"the mark–recapture technique." Previously, in our discussion of unobtrusive measures, we examined attempts to estimate such hidden entities as the amount of tax evasion or crime by drug addicts in the population. We mentioned various methods employed by ecologists to estimate, for example, the number of fish in a Mark–
recapture
technique pond. The *mark–recapture technique* uses tagged (marked) samples to estimate the size of an unknown population. To estimate the number of fish in a pond, several fish (sample) are caught, tagged, and released. Then, a second sample of fish are caught from the same pond and the total fish population is estimated. If, for instance, one in ten of the second sample of fish have tags, then the entire population of the pond would be assumed to be ten times the number of fish in the first sample. Suppose fifty fish were tagged in the first sample and released. Then fifty more were caught, five of which bore tags. The fish population would be estimated as 10 x 50, or 500.

With this estimating procedure, BNDD compared the names on the 1970 register ("been tagged") and counted the number of recidivists as tagged addicts. The 1969 estimate was multiplied by the calculated ratio of repeaters providing an estimate of 315,000 for 1970, a classic example of "instrumentation," that is, the increased numbers are due to changes in the measuring instrument. As a validity check, U.S. Army draftees' records at the time indicated no change and treatment centers actually showed a decrease in new addicts for several years (Epstein, 1977, p. 177).

Despite the attention called to the danger of these "mythical numbers" by Singer (1971), Reuter (1984, p. 136) indicates that in the thirteen years (at the time of his writing) since the appearance of Singer's article there has been "a strong interest in keeping the number high and none in keeping it correct." Estimates of addict crime, as well as the size of the illegal drug market, remain problematic (Chaiken and Chaiken, 1982; Ball et al., 1982).

Drug Use Forecasting (DUF)

Drug Use
Forecasting
(DUF)

An excellent case illustration of the effectiveness of using urine tests to validate self-reported drug usage is provided by the Drug Use Forecasting Program. **Drug Use Forecasting (DUF),** a research program sponsored by the National Institute of Justice, asks volunteers from a population of arrestees in various cities to provide urine specimens that are then tested for illicit drugs. Since 1987 arrestees in as many as twenty-three cities have first been asked questions regarding their drug usage; then they have been asked to submit to urine tests. The data are used only for research purposes and anonymity is assured. Exhibit 9.1 describes the DUF program.

EXHIBIT 9.1

The Drug Use Forecasting Program

Methodology

DUF data and urine specimens are collected in selected booking facilities throughout the United States. For about 2 weeks each quarter, trained local staff obtain voluntary and anonymous urine specimens and interviews from samples of booked arrestees who have been in facilities less than 48 hours. At each site, approximately 225 males are interviewed each quarter. In all except 3 sites, approximately 100 females are also sampled. Response rates are consistently high; more than 90 percent of the arrestees who are approached agree to be interviewed. Approximately 80 percent of those interviewed provided urine specimens.

Arrestees are not selected for the survey on a random or probability basis. Rather, male arrest-

ees are selected at the discretion of site personnel, who are guided by a target sample size and crime charge priority system. To obtain samples of male arrestees with a sufficient distribution of serious arrest charges, DUF interviewers, where possible, place a priority on felony arrestees and those arrested for offenses other than the sale or possession of drugs. Analyses have shown that those arrested for drug offenses are more likely than other arrestees to be using drugs; as a result, DUF statistics are likely minimum estimates of drug use among the population of those arrested for serious offenses. With the exception of Omaha, males charged with driving offenses generally are excluded from the sample due to DUF's emphasis on more serious crimes. (In Omaha, all male

Continued.

arrestees brought to the booking facility are included in the DUF sample to obtain a sample of sufficient size.) Because they are fewer in number, all adult female arrestees brought to the booking center during the data collection period are included in the DUF sample, regardless of charge.

In ten sites, Atlanta, Chicago, Cleveland, Denver, Detroit, Houston, Omaha, Philadelphia, St. Louis, and Washington, D.C., the catchment area is the entire city. In Dallas, Ft. Lauderdale, Indianapolis, Manhattan, Miami, New Orleans, Phoenix, Portland, San Antonio, and San Jose, the catchment area is the entire county or parish. The catchment area for Los Angeles includes part of the city and part of the county, and in Birmingham and San Diego the catchment area includes the city and part of the county.

All urine specimens are sent to a central laboratory for analysis. The specimens are analyzed by EMIT™ for 10 drugs: cocaine, opiates, marijuana, PCP, methaqualone, benzodiazepines, methadone, propoxyphene, barbiturates, and amphetamines. All positive results for amphetamines are confirmed by gas chromatography to eliminate positives that may be caused by over-the-counter drugs. The urine test can usually detect drug use within the previous 2 to 3 days. The exceptions are marijuana and PCP, which can sometimes be detected several weeks after use.

TABLE A.   Drug Use by Booked Arrestees, Drug Use Forecasting Program

Site	Male	Female
Atlanta	72%	74%
Birmingham	68	55
Chicago	81	*
Cleveland	64	77
Dallas	62	61
Denver	64	66
Detroit	63	76
Ft. Lauderdale	61	60
Houston	59	53
Indianapolis	60	58
Los Angeles	66	77
Manhattan	78	83
Miami	70	*
New Orleans	62	47
Omaha	54	*
Philadelphia	76	79
Phoenix	62	62
Portland	63	74
St. Louis	68	69
San Antonio	55	42
San Diego	78	78
San Jose	54	51
Washington, D.C.	60	71

*Females were not tested at this site.

Source: *Drug Use Forecasting, 1993, Annual Report on Adult Arrestees. Washington,* D.C.: National Institute of Justice, November 1994, NCJ 147411.

In examining various "Federal Drug Data for National Policy," Collins and Zawitz (1990, p. 8) conclude:

> The major limitation of DUF is the absence of a probability sampling plan permitting generalization of results to the total arrestee populations in the participating cities and in the United States. On the other hand, evidence from several DUF cities demonstrated considerable agreement between DUF sample estimates of drug use and estimates derived from larger samples from the same cities.

Other Examples of Research Validation

In the development of a police career index Dunnette and associates (Bownas and Dunnette, 1975) employed a number of means of validating the final instrument. The intent was to develop a scale that was tested in both the field and in simulations. The goal was a predictive scale for measuring job performance of police officers. In addition to completed tests and inventories, job ratings were collected and matched for several hundred officers in nine cities. On the basis of observational studies of actual police performance, a variety of simulations was developed. A number of police psychologists and officials reviewed and rated these. A series of tests were administered that solicited personal and biographical information and opinion and self-description inventory to tap personality dimensions, as well as various cognitive performance tests. A group of senior police officers then discarded those items for which there was a low correlation between raters' scores and the instruments. The raters provided criterion or concurrent validation.

In our earlier discussion of errors in surveys, we mentioned that an important source of invalidity may be introduced by coding, the process of assigning numbers to and scoring responses. To control for this, Dunnette and associates employed cross-validation. They randomly split the sample of respondents into two groups and then developed scoring keys separately for each. Each key was separately applied to the other subsample to estimate its validity. Additional scaling procedures such as item analysis and factor analysis were also employed.

Hood and Sparks (1971, pp. 30–31) discuss the use of validity checks on victim surveys in which research assistants determine whether a crime has been committed. The assistants agreed that about one quarter of all incidents reported to them by respondents were not crimes and excluded these along with doubtful cases. A sample of the retained victimizations were examined by a group of criminal lawyers and police officers who agreed that about two thirds of the retained incidents recorded as crimes by the assistants were not crimes at all.

Issues of validity and reliability in criminal justice research are not limited to quantitative studies, as much of our discussion suggests, but are also applicable to more qualitative findings (Kirk and Miller, 1986). No area of criminology contains a literature as nonscientific as that of the study of organized crime. The subject has been much the province of sensationalistic tabloids, with much fiction confused for fact. In a great deal of the literature, statements of fact are made without supporting documentation. Albini (1971) found this to be the case for theories regarding the origin of the term *mafia*. On the basis of an examination of historical archives, painstaking literature review, field visits, and interviews, he was able to dispute many theories that had been unquestioningly presented by others. Block (1978) indicates that much of the early history of the American Mafia is based on the testimony of informants Valachi and Reles (Maas, 1968; Turkus and Feder, 1951). Valachi's account of the Castellammarese wars in New York City claimed fifty to ninety gangland slayings, whereas later in Senate testimony he indicated only four or five victims. Block's (1978) search of newspapers of the period found only four possible gangland slayings during that time. Similar "myths" may have been accepted with respect to "La Cosa Nostra," "omerta," and other legends regarding the Mafia.

Brantingham and Brantingham (1984, p. 91) point out the numerous sources utilized by Shaw and McKay (1931) in their classic studies of delinquency in Chicago. They skillfully combined ecological analysis of group rates by mapped areas with in-depth case studies of individuals living in these areas. Some of the sources they utilized were criminal justice records of crime and delinquency distribution by area; personal memoirs of delinquents; interviews with parents, siblings, friends, and significant others; analysis of friendship patterns; and clinical analysis of physical, mental, and social health.

Summary

The question of error unreliability and invalidity is central to criminal justice research. Validity refers to the accuracy of findings, whereas reliability is concerned with consistency and predictability of research. In its assessment of the state of *Criminal Justice Research and Development,* the National Advisory Committee on Criminal Justice Standards and Goals partly explains why there has been a lack of validation studies in criminal justice. These include little professional self-esteem in replication, lack of complexity in technique, design faults in the original study, unfavorable research climate, interjurisdictional disputes, and lack of a research tradition that emphasizes such studies.

The principal measures of validity are face validity, content validity, construct validity, pragmatic validity (which includes concurrent and predictive validity), and convergent–discriminant validity (triangulation). Face validation involves simply the judgment that the instrument appears to be measuring that which it is intended to measure. Content validity is concerned with the examination of each item to assess whether the instrument is measuring what it is intended to measure. Construct (or concept) validity questions the tag or concept assigned to the scale. Pragmatic validity simply asks, "Does it work?" and comprises concurrent validity, which asks whether the scale predicts present events, and predictive validity, which asks whether it predicts future events. Triangulation is the use of multiple methods to measure the same phenomenon and is also referred to as convergent validity. Discriminant validation suggests that use of the same method to measure different things yields different findings. The use of different methods (triangulation) to measure the same thing should yield similar results (convergence). The validity of any one measure at one time is relatively inconsequential. Triangulation is the logical method to assessing validity.

Reliability is usually approached through test–retest, multiple forms, and split-half techniques. In test–retest the instrument is administered at two different times to the same population and the results are compared. The multiple forms technique is similar to the test–retest, except the retest is disguised by rearranging the items or hiding them as part of a larger questionnaire. Both of these techniques may be subject to testing effects; however, the split-half procedure involves one administration with random halves of the scale intercorrelated. If the correlation is sufficiently high, internal consistency of reliability is assumed.

The chapter concluded with illustrations of triangulated studies—and particularly the Drug Use Forecasting Program.

Key Concepts

Nominal Scales	Content Validity	Triangulation
Ordinal Scales	Construct Validity	Test–Retest
Interval Scales	Pragmatic Validity	Multiple Forms
Ratio Scales	Concurrent Validity	Split-Half Techniques
Validity	Predictive Validity	Mythical Numbers
Reliability	Convergent–Discriminant	DUF
Face Validity	Validation	

Review Questions

1. Why has there been a lack of validation studies in criminal justice? What is the importance of developing a tradition of such studies in the field?
2. Discuss the various ways of determining the validity of a particular measure. Of what importance is triangulation in resolving the issue of validity?
3. Discuss the three means of demonstrating reliability of measurement.
4. What is the "mark-recapture technique" and how might it raise problems in being employed to measure hidden human populations such as the addict population?
5. Using various examples from this chapter describe how researchers attempt to approach the issues of reliability and validity in their studies.
6. Discuss the methodology of the DUF program. How does this program benefit criminal justice research?

10 | Scaling and Index Construction

On arising in the morning, a typical American may "hit the scales" and discover that he or she has gained three pounds. While reading the morning newspaper they discover that the Gross Domestic Product has increased by only 2 percent, whereas the Dow Jones Industrial Average is up three points, the Consumer Price Index is 1.2 percent for the previous month, and the FBI reports that the crime rate for the first six months is up 6 percent. In addition, the pollution index is 65 (which is in the fair range), and an earthquake in California registered 3.6 on the Richter scale. Without realizing it, most of us are quite familiar with the use of scales to measure degrees of change in factors affecting our lives.

Chapter 1 pointed out how meaningful concepts or abstractions of reality are created to provide insight and useful tags with which to manipulate and understand reality. Previously, variables were described as operationalized concepts, or concepts that vary or take on various values. Scales reflect levels of measurement or various degrees of quantitative value that a variable can take on. As we shall see in this chapter, each level of measurement has appropriate corresponding statistical measures.

Scaling Procedures

The purpose of measurement is to make connections between concepts and numbers. Mere observation, measurement, and assignment of numbers to responses are not the same as a proper measure. Scales can be viewed as calibrated instruments with which to interrogate concepts (Wright, 1980). Thus, there is a difference between scaling and scoring of test items. The level of measurement of a variable is very important in the utilization of various statistical procedures, as we will discuss in Chapter 12. Many statistical procedures, for instance, require interval variables and are inappropriate if used with nominal or ordinal variables.

Although many of the scaling procedures discussed in this chapter can be calculated by hand, the increased availability of inexpensive computer hardware and "canned" or prewritten computer programs makes these procedures easier to perform (Norusis, 1988).

Scaling   **Scaling** procedures involve attempts to increase the complexity of the level of measurement of variables from nominal to at least ordinal and hopefully interval/ratio. They build more complex, composite indicators of phenomena. A great many well-constructed scales already exist and should be consulted and analyzed before construction of a new scale. Established scales may be used as they are, or modified to fit the special needs of a specific study. Such scales have an established track record.

Various excellent handbooks that catalog scales exist. These not only classify scales by the concept to be measured, but report reliability, validity, previous studies that employed the scale where one could obtain the instrument, as well as usual sample items from the scale.[1] Strong consideration of previously developed scales is important because *replication,* the repetition of measures with different populations, enables establishment of a comparative and universal social science.

Although some writers attempt to make major distinctions between scales and indexes, in reality they are referred to quite interchangeably. One distinction is that a scale is generally concerned with only one attribute of a concept, whereas an index involves many dimensions or scales. With an index the researcher combines or averages the results for more than one phenomenon. It is this writer's preference to view the terms *scale* and *index* as synonyms.

Scales are useful for a number of reasons, but primarily because they avoid reliance on any single response alone as an indicator. For example, the response to any single item may be an error, may be misclassified or misinterpreted by subjects, or may not adequately tap the full dimension of the idea being measured (Orenstein and Phillips, 1978, pp. 258–259).

---

[1]Some examples of excellent reference handbooks for scales include: Delbert C. Miller, ed. *Handbook of Research Design and Social Measurement,* 5th ed. New York: Longman, 1991; Stanley Brodsky and O'Neal Smitherman, eds. *Handbook of Scales for Research in Crime and Delinquency.* New York: Plenum Press, 1983; and J.P. Robinson, P.R. Shaver, and L.S. Wrightsman, eds. *Measures of Personality and Social Psychological Attitudes.* San Diego: Academic Press, 1991.

Income (Annual)		*Education*		*Occupation* (Using U.S. Census Ratings)	
$40,000 and over	= 5	College Graduate	= 5	Higher Professional, Managerial	= 5
$30,000–$39,999	= 4	Some College	= 4	Less Professional, Managerial, Technical & Sales	= 4
$20,000–$29,999	= 3	High School Grad.	= 3	Services	= 3
$10,000–$19,999	= 2	Some High School	= 2	Skilled Labor	= 2
Under $10,000	= 1	Grade School or Less	= 1	Unskilled Labor	= 1

Figure 10.1 An Arbitrary Social Class Scale.

Arbitrary Scales

Arbitrary scales

Arbitrary scales are developed by the researcher and are based primarily on face validity (the scale appears to be measuring what one intends to measure) and professional judgment. They are intended to measure relative degrees of a concept or provide a rough estimate. A simple way of developing arbitrary scales is to begin with ordinal or interval scales of phenomena that lend themselves readily to accepted measurement, for example, income, education, and attendance. Figure 10.1 presents a hypothetical example of the construction of a social class index using three subscales—income, education, and occupation. In reality, it would make far better sense to utilize an existing, well-accepted social class scale from one of the handbooks discussed previously than to construct a new scale.

It might be quite misleading for a researcher to use one of the three subscales alone as a measure of social class; however, use of an index that takes into account all three measures overcomes this. But how might an index be constructed using this arbitrary scale of social class? Suppose we have a respondent who earns $40,000, is a college graduate, and is in sales. Such a case would score 14 out of a possible 15 on our scale. One might arbitrarily decide that scores of 1–5 represent lower class, 6–10 middle class, and 11–15 upper class. Thus, according to our operationalization of social class, our respondent would be upper class.

Because the construction of arbitrary scales rests primarily on the judgment of the researcher, they are easily criticized. For this reason attitudinal scaling procedures have been developed that permit logical and methodological defenses for scale operationalization.

The Uniform Crime Report as an Arbitrary Scale

UCR index

A lengthy exposition of the UCR was presented in Chapter 4. Using the original UCR, a simple summation of the eight index offenses is made. The *UCR index offenses* are those crimes that are considered serious and that the police feel are fairly accurately reported and uniformly measured:

Homicide   Larceny
Forcible rape   Car theft

Robbery   Burglary
Aggravated assault   Arson (not actually calculated in index due to
                              unreliability of measurement)

Although arson is listed as part of the index, the unreliability of such data prevents it from being included in any calculations. As discussed in Chapter 4, the crime index is the total number of such offenses recorded by police per 100,000 population. Table 10.1 presents a typical UCR crime index summary. In addition to all of the shortcomings presented in Chapter 4, a principal difficulty with the UCR as an index of crime in the United States is that it is an unweighted index. That is, each crime incident, whether homicide or auto theft, is added to the total index without any consideration of its relative seriousness. No monetary or differential psychological value is attached. A city with fifty burglaries per 100,000 and a city with fifty homicides per 100,000 would actually have the same UCR crime index. Similar problems exist with unweighted victimization rates. Later in this chapter we discuss attempts to develop crime seriousness scales to measure not only the quantity, but also the severity of crime.

Attitude Scales

Three major types of attitude scales that have been developed in the social sciences are used in criminology and criminal justice:

Thurstone scales
Likert scales
Guttman scales

TABLE 10.1 The UCR Crime Index[a]

Offense	Number
Murder and nonnegligent manslaughter	23,400
Forcible rape	102,560
Robbery	639,270
Aggravated assault	1,054,860
Burglary	3,073,900
Larceny-theft	7,945,700
Motor vehicle theft	1,635,900
Arson	–
Index total	14,475,600
Index rate	5,820.3 (per 100,000)

[a]Offenses may not add to index total because of rounding.

Source: U.S. Department of Justice. *FBI Uniform Crime Reports: Crime in the United States,* 1990. Washington, D.C.: U.S. Government Printing Office, August 11, 1991, p. 50.

Thurstone Scales

Thurstone scales

Thurstone scales were the first to be developed (Thurstone and Chave, 1929). Thurstone had actually devised various techniques for developing scales, but all shared in common the *use of judges to select items.* Judges are individuals whose expertise is respected and who might be in a position to help in the determination of the most useful items.

The earliest method developed by Thurstone was the *method of paired comparisons.* A number of judges are presented with all possible pairs of items to be used in a scale. Items or questions are then rated by the judges as to which of each pair is more favorable to the issue in question. Such a procedure tends to be quite tedious and time consuming.

Thurstone's
equal
appearing
intervals

As a judgmental technique, Thurstone's method of **equal appearing intervals** is superior to the paired comparisons method in that it requires only one judgment per item. Each judge is required to sort the items into a predetermined number of categories so that the intervals between them are subjectively equal. Figure 10.2 illustrates the rating of three items by five different judges using an 11-point scale in which 1 indicates that the item is a positive measure of the entity being measured, and 11 indicates a negative measure.

The ratings for item 1 by five judges were 9, 10, 10, 11, and 11; that is, the judges generally agreed that the item was a negative measure of the entity in question. On item 2 the judges were in basic agreement that the item was positive, whereas they disagreed on item 3. According to Thurstone's procedure, the third item would be eliminated because of the conflicting interpretations of the judges. Sometimes investigators assign weights to the items on the basis of the median scores of the values assigned by the judges. The logic of *weighting* assumes that responses to the first item carry a more negative meaning (a weight of 10) than those to item 2 (a weight of only 3). The final form of the scale is made up of those agreed-upon items that provide even intervals on the scale from high to low.

An interesting application that partly involved Thurstone methods was the development of police assessment centers (Dunnette and Motowidlo, 1976). As part of the procedure to develop a police career index that would permit police departments to predict likely successful candidates for both hiring and promotion, a group of psychologists and senior police officials reviewed a series of items, including simulations that had been constructed

Judge No.	Item 1	Item 2	Item 3
1	9	2	2
2	10	3	3
Median 3	10	3	9
4	11	3	10
5	11	4	11

Figure 10.2 Method of Equal-Appearing Intervals: Five Judges Assign an 11-Point Scale to Three Items.

by the researcher. Those items deemed most promising and on which there was the greatest agreement were then pretested.

Summary of Thurstone procedure

The following is a *summary of the Thurstone scaling procedure:*

A large number of questions believed to be related to the concept under investigation are constructed.

A number of judges are asked to assign weight to each item using a pre-determined scale ranging from favorable to unfavorable.

The median (midpoint) of the values assigned to each item is taken as its score or weight.

Those items on which there was significant disagreement by the judges are eliminated.

Selected items with weights spread at intervals along the scale are retained for the final scale which can now be administered to respondents (Miller, 1991, p. 88).

Likert Scales

Likert scales

Likert scales, the scales most commonly used in attitudinal research, are named for Rensis Likert who developed the procedure (Likert, 1932). Figure 10.3 illustrates a typical Likert scale. **Likert scales** consist of a simple summation of usually a 5-point bipolar response ranging from strongly agree to strongly disagree. Figure 10.4 portrays the scoring key for Figure 10.3, the

---

For each of the following questions circle the response that best represents your attitude:

		Strongly Agree	Agree	Don't Know	Disagree	Strongly Disagree
1.	The best way to handle people is to tell them what they want to hear.	SA	(A)	DK	D	SD
2.	When you ask someone to do something for you, it is best to give the real reasons for wanting it rather than giving reasons which might carry more weight.	SA	A	DK	(D)	SD
3.	It is hard to get ahead without cutting corners here and there.	(SA)	A	DK	D	SD
4.	Barnum was wrong when he said, "There's a sucker born every minute."	SA	A	DK	(D)	SD
5.	It is wise to flatter important people.	SA	A	(DK)	D	SD
6.	All in all, it is better to be humble and honest than important and dishonest.	SA	A	DK	(D)	SD

Note: Those circled represent hypothetical response.

Figure 10.3 A Likert Scale: Adaptation of the Machiavellianism Scale. (*Source:* Christie, R., and F. L. Geis. *Studies in Machiavellianism.* New York: Academic Press, 1970.)

		SA	A	DK	D	SD
1.	"Handle People"	+5	(+4)	+3	+2	+1
2.	"Give Real Reasons"	+1	+2	+3	(+4)	+5
3.	"Cut Corners"	(+5)	+4	+3	+2	+1
4.	"Barnum"	+1	+2	+3	(+4)	+5
5.	"Flatter"	+5	+4	(+3)	+2	+1
6.	"Better To Be Honest"	+1	+2	+3	(+4)	+5

Figure 10.4 Scoring for a Likert Scale: the Machiavellianism Scale in Figure 10.3 (hypothetical response).

six Machiavellianism[2] items in which the more manipulative orientation is given the higher score or + 5.

According to the scoring system in Figure 10.4, our hypothetical respondent scored 24 on a scale that ranged from 6 (low Machiavellianism) to 30 (high Machiavellianism). The low or high numbers are arbitrarily assigned by the researcher. Low scores could have been assigned to high orientations or vice versa, as long as the investigator remembers the assignment for later

Reversal items   analysis. The even items, questions 2, 4, and 6, are examples of *reversal items,* in which the substance of the question is worded in a negative fashion relative to the orientation being measured; that is, strong agreement is assigned a low score or denotes low *Machiavellianism.* Such reversals are

Response set   standard in Likert scales to avoid *response sets*—patterns of consistent responses in which the respondent reads only the first few items and, on the basis of these responses, merely circles the remaining responses in a similar pattern. Such response sets can be spotted by noting straight vertical patterns or widely inconsistent extreme responses that are highly unlikely. If response sets appear despite reversals, the analyst may decide to discard the case entirely because the subject did not act in good faith by providing his or her true feelings. Standardized examinations such as the Scholastic Aptitude Test or Graduate Record Exam discourage test takers from merely guessing the answers to questions as time runs out by deducting two points for incorrect items, while giving only one point for correct ones.

The Thurstone procedure for discarding weak questions was based on the disagreement by the judges on the scoring weight to be assigned. Likert procedures skip this step of using judges and accomplish the same thing by analyzing the responses after the fact. In the Likert method the respondents do the job that the judges do in the Thurstone procedure. Basically, item analysis asks whether both high and low scorers answered particular items the same way. If so, these items are considered nondiscriminating and therefore are eliminated from the scale. By nondiscriminating we mean that the responses to these questions add nothing to the final scale measurement because they do not distinguish between high and low scores. For example,

[2]Machiavellianism takes its name from the thirteenth-century Italian philosopher Niccoló Machiavelli, whose classic work *The Prince* (1952) has often been described as a "handbook for dictators" in its espousal of the "end justifies the means" in obtaining power. Socially, Machiavellianism refers to a manipulative orientation toward others.

if both high Machiavellians (say, scores over 20) and low Machiavellians (scores under 20) agreed that "There's a sucker born every minute," then perhaps that question is not measuring manipulative orientations and should be eliminated from the scale. It would be as if everyone got a question correct or incorrect on a competitive test; such items do nothing to predict who will do well or poorly and therefore should be eliminated. The final scale then would consist of only those items that appeared to have variability or distinguish between high and low scores.

In the process of developing a scale, researchers begin with a much larger number of items than they expect to employ in the final score. On the basis of elimination, the final scale is trimmed down to the most useful items. Table 10.2 illustrates a hypothetical item analysis.

Taking the first item in Table 10.2 we find that the highest scorers (those that fell into the top 25 percent of all respondents) scored 3.6, whereas the lowest scorers (bottom 25 percent) scored 3.2. Little difference was exhibited between high and low scorers and therefore this item is dropped from the final scale. Items 2 and 3 show large differences between high and low scorers and thus are discriminating items to be retained. Item 4 shows little ability to distinguish high from low scorers and is also eliminated.

A major shortcoming of Likert scaling is that on the basis of the total scale score it is impossible to predict the exact endorsement of each individual item. Suppose a person's Machiavellianism score from Figure 10.4 was 20. On the basis of this score, can we predict how the individual responded to item 4, "Barnum was very wrong when he said, 'There's a sucker born every minute'"? No, such a total score could be obtained with a person circling any of the response categories supplied.

Summary of Likert procedure

The following is a summary of Likert scaling procedures.

A large number of items are selected and about evenly expressed as either positive or negative statements regarding the subject of investigation.

For each item the respondent is asked to respond using usually a 5-point scale (strongly agree, agree, don't know, disagree, and strongly disagree).

The total score for each individual is the simple sum of all items although the researcher should exercise caution in identifying and scoring appropriate reversals or items that were negative.

TABLE 10.2 Hypothetical Item Analysis

Item	Average Score of Top Quartile	Average Score of Low Quartile
1	3.6	3.2
2	4.1	1.7
3	3.9	1.2
4	2.6	2.2

Items that lack variability or fail to distinguish between high and low
   scores are eliminated from the final scale.
Only those items retained in the final index are scored and used in the
   final analysis.

Missing data **Handling Missing Data in Likert Scale Construction.** Even with the provision of "don't know" categories, some respondents may answer all but a
few items in a scale. If a large number of respondents fail to answer a particular item, then that item should be eliminated from the scale. If the missing item is one of a series of measures of the same basic dimension, we could
assign to that item the average score for the items answered. For example, if
an individual answers nine of ten questions on the same subject and the
nine scores average 2.5, then a score of 2.5 can be assumed for the missing
response. Obviously, if too many nonresponses exist, it may be necessary to
drop the respondent from analysis. Although there is no universal rule, it
would seem reasonable that if more than three of ten responses are not ascer-
tained, the individual's responses for the entire set of scale items should be
dropped from the analysis. Another alternative to substituting the average
score from the items answered is to assign an intermediate score to missing
responses (Orenstein and Phillips, 1978, p. 268). For instance, if the scoring
for the item ranges from 1 to 5, a 3 would be assigned. Although simpler
than the other procedure, such assignment tends to reduce or inflate the
total scores of high and low scorers.

Guttman Scales

   Guttman scales were developed as one outcome of a research series conducted by social scientists during World War II (Guttman, 1944, 1950).
Sometimes referred to as scalogram analysis, but more often referred to by
Guttman scale the name of its developer, Louis Guttman, **Guttman scaling** insists that an
Unidimensionality attitudinal scale be based on *unidimensionality;* that is, it should measure
one and only one dimension or concept. In our Machiavellianism exam-
ple, it may appear that the items are measuring things other than Machiavellianism, for instance, cynicism, honesty, practical judgment. Guttman
procedures provide a quantitative procedure by which to approach this
issue.

   The major advantage of Guttman scaling over Likert scaling is that from
the final scale score one should be able to predict the exact pattern of item
endorsement. As in our previous example, a score of 20 on the Machiavellianism scale (Figure 10.5) would enable a fairly accurate prediction that a
person scored, let us say, 2 on the "Barnum" question. Before going into the
quantitative aspects of the Guttman procedure, let us first provide some
examples and follow the logic of the procedure. Figure 10.6 presents two
hypothetical examples.

   In examining each of the scales in Figure 10.5 note that the items are pro-
gressively more difficult. Additionally, endorsement of the more difficult

Mathematical Ability Scale	Spelling Ability Scale
1. Can you *add* and *subtract*?	1. Can you spell *CAT*?
YES NO	YES NO
2. Can you do *long division*?	2. Can you spell *CATTLE*?
YES NO	YES NO
3. Can you *solve equations* with one unknown?	3. Can you spell *CATASTROPHE*?
YES NO	YES NO

Figure 10.5 Hypothetical Guttman Scales. (*Source:* The Mathematical Ability Scale is from Cole [1972, p. 52].)

Theft Scale
Have you ever taken:

1. Things of little value?	YES	NO
2. Things of moderate value?	YES	NO
3. Things of large value?	YES	NO

Fear of Crime Scale
Are you afraid:

In the city?	YES	NO
Down the block?	YES	NO
Outside own house?	YES	NO
Inside own house?	YES	NO

Figure 10.6 Hypothetical Guttman Scales. (*Source:* The Theft Scale is from Hirshi and Selvin [1973, p. 64] and the Fear of Crime Scale was suggested by Baumer and Rosenbaum [1980].)

		Question #1 (Add & Subtract) (Cat)	*Question #2* (Long Division) (Cattle)	*Question #3* (Simple Equation) (Catastrophe)
	1.	+	+	+
	2.	+	+	−
	3.	+	−	+
Response	4.	+	−	−
Patterns	5.	−	+	+
	6.	−	+	−
	7.	−	−	+
	8.	−	−	−

Figure 10.7 Possible Response Patterns in the Guttman Scales: +, Ability to Perform; −, Inability to Perform.

items almost presupposes that one would have affirmatively answered the previous items. Figure 10.7 presents a Guttman analysis of the possible response patterns for these scales. There are eight possible combinations of responses to these items. Assume that these scales measure spelling or mathematical ability, and that anyone who can do the more difficult problems can do the less difficult ones and that the opposite is seldom true. Which response patterns are unlikely? Patterns 3, 5, 6, and 7 are unlikely or are considered errors in the predictability of the scales. Because no scale can be completely accurate, Guttman suggests that a 90 percent coefficient of reproducibility is the minimum acceptable level of accuracy and, if achieved, is indicative of scalability. It is this quality, a cumulative nature of scoring, that Guttman attempted to build into his scaling procedure.

Coefficient of reproducibility

The *coefficient of reproducibility* is calculated in the following manner:

$$\text{reproducibility} = 1 - \frac{\text{numbers of errors}}{\text{number of responses}}$$

That is, on the basis of the scale score one should be able to predict the exact pattern of response, although as much as 10 percent of the time one could be in error in doing so. The "Spelling Ability Scale" in Figure 10.7 ranges from 0 (no spelling ability) to 3 (very good spelling ability). Although a score of 2 could be obtained by means of response patterns 2, 3, and 5, only response pattern 2 (ability to spell "cat" and "cattle") is acceptable. Rarely would an individual be able to spell "cat" and "catastrophe" but not "cattle," as in response 3, or be able to spell the latter two without knowing how to spell "cat," as in response 5. Thus, if the scale is unidimensional, a score of 2 should enable you to predict with at least 90 percent accuracy that the individual endorsed items 1 and 2 but not 3. If greater than 10 percent error were introduced by anomalies with regard to item 2, "cattle," the scale would need to be reconstructed with "cattle" dropped in favor of a more workable substitute.

Although Guttman scaling has a distinct advantage over Likert scales in that it provides the facility to predict a fairly precise pattern of response to each item given the final scale score, its insistence on unidimensionality may be too rigid a demand. Many concepts, particularly abstract ones, may be multidimensional in nature and therefore not amenable to Guttman scaling.

A different series of complex traits may feed together to provide similar composite scores. For example, perhaps in a scale measuring counselor effectiveness it is discovered that people scoring above average on a hypothetical scale are most effective; however, such a score could be obtained by those rated excellent in knowledge but average in empathy, as well as those rated only average in knowledge but excellent in empathy. An insistence on unidimensionality in this instance would be inappropriate. Many important concepts are multidimensional. The insistence on Guttman scaling procedures may become a "fetish" (Hirschi and Selvin, 1973, p. 209) similar to the misuse of some statistical tests of significance to be discussed in Chapter 12.

Summary of Guttman procedure

The following is a *summary of Guttman scaling procedures:*

Construct a large number of items that appear on face validity to measure the concept.

Pretest the instrument by administering it to a sample of people.

Any item with greater than 80 percent agreement or disagreement should be discarded from the analysis and final scale.

Order respondents from highest score (most responding "yes" to each
item) to lowest score (fewest "yes" responses).
Also order items from left to right from most favorable to least favorable
responses.
After discarding those items that fail to discriminate between high and
low scorers, calculate the coefficient of reproducibility where errors
are defined as those responses that are out of the predictable pattern.
If the coefficient of reproducibility equals .90 or higher, then scalability
or unidimensionality is assumed.
The respondent's final score is calculated by simply summing the number of favorable items (Miller, 1991, p. 90).

Some examples of the use of Guttman scales in criminal justice research
are found in Scott (1959), Arnold (1965), Nye and Short (1957), and Dentler
and Monroe (1961). One of the earliest pieces of research in the social sciences that exhibited cumulative qualities was Bogardus' "Social Distance
Scale" (1933). Each respondent was asked to indicate the closeness of relationship they were willing to accept with a variety of ethnic groups. The
response categories were:

1. Would exclude from my country
2. As visitors only to my country
3. To citizenship in my country
4. To employment in my occupation
5. To my street as neighbors
6. To my club as personal chums
7. To close kinship by marriage

With 7 indicating highest acceptance or least social distance and 1 indicating the converse, index scores could be devised to rate the relative acceptance of various groups. Similar criminal justice applications in which types
of criminals are substituted for ethnic groups seem possible.

In their excellent review of delinquency research, Hirschi and Selvin
(1973) indicate an element of Guttman scaling that may be overlooked by
those analyzing self-report data. Guttman scaling of items such as Figure
10.6 is appropriate only if the period during which the acts could have taken
place is relatively long. If the time span were short, it would be possible that
an individual committed a more serious act and not less serious ones, during the specified period, thus making a Guttman scale inapplicable (see also
Dentler and Monroe, 1961). In measuring delinquent acts it makes more
sense to concentrate on more recent acts rather than acts over an extended
time period. "Suppose the boy with three delinquent acts committed all of
them within the preceding year, while the boy with five delinquent acts
committed none in that period. At the time of the study, which boy is more
delinquent?" (Hirschi and Selvin, 1973, p. 65). A more valid measurement
would be gained by restricting the time period and thus not using Guttman

scaling because it makes sense to concentrate on more recent acts, rather than those that may have occurred at any time.

Other Scaling Procedures

The three types of attitude scales that we have discussed—Thurstone, Likert, and Guttman—are the key generic classifications of such scales; most others can be viewed as variations.

Q Sort

Q Sort   **Q sort methodology** is a newer variation of the Thurstone process; the respondents rather than the judges place a series of statements into previously predetermined categories (Stephenson, 1953). The individual's sorting is scored and summed into an index. Farrington (1973) had a group of English juveniles place thirty-eight cards on which various crimes were printed in two different piles—"have done it" and "have not done it." In investigating attractiveness and juvenile delinquency, Cavior and Howard (1973) had a group of college students sort pictures of delinquents and nondelinquents into five categories ranging from 1 (very attractive) to 5 (very unattractive).

Semantic Differential

Semantic differential   The **semantic differential** usually consists of a 7- or 9-point bipolar rating scale in which individuals are asked to indicate their perception of a tag or description that is provided. Originally developed in the field of linguistics as a nondirective means of measuring the subjective meaning of words to respondents (Snider and Osgood, 1969; Osgood et al., 1957), it has been found to be an exceptionally versatile tool in attitudinal research. In particular, the semantic differential has been found to be useful in cross-cultural research and with a wide cross section of the population with broad ranges in education and vocabulary level. An illustration of the use of the semantic differential in research related to criminal justice would be an examination of labeling theory—seeing whether people are viewed as being what they do. That is, a person who has an alcohol problem is viewed as an alcoholic, or one with a drug problem as a drug addict. Figure 10.8 illustrates a typical semantic differential scale.

Suppose our sample scale were to be used in this study: Subjects would be asked to respond to their interpretation of the term *heroin* using the scale, and then *heroin addicts* using a second page containing the same scale. Subjects asked to fill out a semantic differential scale typically say "What is it that I am to do?" or "I do not see where some of the things we are to rate are applicable to the subject." The monitor should merely reply "Do the best you can."

1.	painful	:___:___:___:___:___:___:___:	pleasurable
2.	orderly	:___:___:___:___:___:___:___:	disorderly
3.	trivial	:___:___:___:___:___:___:___:	important
4.	masculine	:___:___:___:___:___:___:___:	feminine
5.	popular	:___:___:___:___:___:___:___:	lonely
6.	poor	:___:___:___:___:___:___:___:	wealthy
7.	individualistic	:___:___:___:___:___:___:___:	conformist
8.	mature	:___:___:___:___:___:___:___:	childish
9.	right	:___:___:___:___:___:___:___:	wrong
10.	lonely	:___:___:___:___:___:___:___:	well liked

Figure 10.8 Semantic Differential Scale.

Each respondent checks off the point on the scale for each item that corresponds to their reaction to that concept. One obvious advantage of the semantic differential is that the researcher need not tediously prepare a large series of statements, but rather merely add the concept to be rated to a previously constructed scale as in Figure 10.8. Obviously, the bipolar descriptors must be altered so that they are appropriate for the evaluation of the concept under analysis.

In an interesting use of the semantic differential scale, Thielbar and Feldman (1978) had subjects rate different forms of deviant behavior and those who perform such activities on an 11-point scale featuring twenty-four bipolar adjectives for each type, such as kind–cruel, good–bad, and honest–dishonest. Of the eleven types of behavior evaluated, rapists and child molesters were the most negatively regarded and welfare recipients and marijuana smokers the least negatively regarded.

In a Chicago study, Short and Strodtbeck (1965) asked black and white gangs to rate various forms of conduct by means of the semantic differential. They found that gang boys tended to rate such middle-class values as school, saving, and reading as high, as did nongang middle-class boys; however, these same gang boys tended to rate pimping, fighting, and similar behavior higher than did the nondelinquent nongang boys. Nevertheless, that nongang nondelinquent and gang boys gave the same ratings to middle-class values has important implications with respect to some leading subcultural theories of juvenile delinquency (Cohen, 1955; Cloward and Ohlin, 1961).

Other Variations

There are perhaps an infinite variety of scales depending on subject matter. In addition to consulting handbooks that review scales used in previous studies, researchers should examine useful literature that discusses scaling procedures (Edwards, 1957; Maranell, 1974; Oppenheim, 1966; Shaw and Wright, 1967; Torgerson, 1958; Summers, 1970). Appendix H describes factor analysis, which is a statistical procedure by which underlying patterns, factors, or dimensions are identified among a series of scale items. It is a means of identifying subscales (see Appendix H).

Brodsky and Smitherman, in their *Handbook of Scales for Research in Crime and Delinquency* (1983), have performed a real service for researchers in criminology and criminal justice by collating hundreds of scales and indexes applicable to these fields. This handbook outlines the scales available to measure a particular concept, describes their development and scoring, generally assesses their reliability (consistency/stability) and validity (accuracy). The scales are organized by topical area, and references to sources are provided. In some cases, actual scale items are included. The scales are also classified by target and purpose. The *research targets* of criminal justice scales are law enforcement/police, courts/the law, corrections, delinquency, offenders, crime/criminality, and general scales/citizens. *Scale purposes* include attitudes, behavior ratings, personality assessment, milieu ratings, prediction, and description. The following list is a sample of the scales described:

Niederhoffer Cynicism Scale
Police Job Stress Interview
Attitude Toward Law Scale
Competency Screening Test
Judicial Role Perception Scale
Attitude Toward Death Penalty
Prison Adjustment Index
Prisoner–Therapist Q Sort
Parole Adjustment Scale
Recidivism Prediction Scale
Prison Guard Job Perception
Delinquency Attitude Scale
Nye and Short Self-reported
   Delinquency Scale
Compulsive Masculinity Scale
Rokeach Dogmatism Scale

Delinquency Proneness Scale
Teenage Slang Test
Differential Association
   Questionnaires
Sellin–Wolfgang Delinquency Index
Severity of Offense Scale
Criminally Insane Attitude Scale
Inmate Personality Survey
I-Level Classification
Perception of Addicts Scale
Attitude Toward Violence Scale
Legal Dangerousness Scale
Crime Seriousness Ratings
Authoritarianism Scale
F Scale (Fascism)
Alienation Scale

Instead of developing their own measurements, researchers should review available measures and, unless theirs are clearly superior, consider using or modifying an existing index. By utilizing an available measure, a researcher is also replicating findings, an important feature of maturing sciences.

Crime Seriousness Scales

Previous criticism of the UCR crime index indicated that one of its major shortcomings is that it represents an unweighted index. No consideration is given to the type of crime; that is, a homicide and a petty theft have equal weight. **Crime seriousness scales** attempt to assign weight to crimes in terms of their relative severity.

Sellin–Wolfgang Index

Despite early work by Thurstone (1929), the pioneering work in the area of crime seriousness ratings was performed by Sellin and Wolfgang (1966), who had a group of respondents (police officers, juvenile court judges, and college students) rate descriptions of criminal incidents on the basis of amount stolen, method of intimidation, and degree of harm inflicted. They actually employed two different types of measures: an 11-point rating scale and a magnitude scale (to be discussed shortly). On the basis of a relatively complex methodology (see their book for greater detail), they were able to develop a crime seriousness scale or weighting system for crime based on bodily injury, property theft, and damage. This **Sellin–Wolfgang index** tries to account for both the quality (seriousness) and the quantity of an act. For example, a robbery involving no injury but a loss of $5 because of verbal intimidation would receive a crime seriousness score of 3: no points for lack of injury, 1 point for economic loss of $5, and 2 points for verbal intimidation. These scores were arrived at on the basis of analysis of respondents' previous seriousness ratings of descriptions of various crimes. The following are some of the scores (weights) produced by the Sellin–Wolfgang index:

Sellin–
Wolfgang
index

Assault (death)	26
Forcible rape	11
Robbery (weapon)	5
Larceny $5,000	4
Auto theft (no damage)	2
Larceny $5	1
Assault (minor)	1

An extensive literature has since developed on crime seriousness measures and, although some cross-cultural and subcultural differences have been found (Akman et al., 1967; Hsu, 1973), various replications have demonstrated striking similarities (Rossi and Henry, 1980). Blumstein (1974) assigned similar seriousness weights to UCR data and came up with results similar to the Sellin–Wolfgang index, and the index was found useful in a Prosecutor's Management Information System (PROMIS) in which prosecutors set prosecution priorities on the basis of various factors including crime seriousness (Jacoby, 1975).

Types of Crime Seriousness Scales

There are two basic types of crime seriousness (severity) scales: simple rating scales and magnitude scales. Simple rating scales of crime seriousness ask respondents to rate crime usually on a scale ranging from 9 (extremely serious) to 1 (not serious at all). In surveys of residents of Baltimore, Maryland (Rossi et al., 1974; Rossi and Henry, 1980), and Macomb, Illinois (Cullen, Link, and Polanzi, 1982), respondents were asked to rate roughly 140

Simple rating
scales

descriptions of crime using the 9-point scale. The average score for each crime is used as the measure of crime seriousness. Strong relative agreement is found among the Rossi and Cullen studies and similar studies. Some examples of scores (rounded) from Cullen, Link, and Polanzi (1982, p. 88–90)

Planned killing for a fee	8.9
Forcible rape of a neighbor	8.4
Armed bank robbery	8.2
Child battering	8.0
Armed robbery $200	7.6
Loitering in public place	3.5

Such simple rating scales are ordinal (result in relative rankings) and are unable to take into account the magnitude of the differences between scale scores. For example, is a planned killing only about three times more serious than loitering? They cannot be used to weight crime seriousness, although they are useful in examining relative changes in public ratings (rankings of crime seriousness) over time. This problem becomes apparent when almost all of the 140 crimes rated were given scores above the theoretical midpoint of 5.

Magnitude scales

Magnitude scales measure public rankings of the degrees of relative seriousness of various crimes. They are an attempt to develop interval/ratio level scores that can be assigned to various criminal acts. Our description of the Sellin–Wolfgang index was such an example. Another is the following case of the *National Survey of Crime Severity,* which was designed by Wolfgang et al. (1985) and conducted in 1977 as a supplement to the NCS. As you may recall, the NCS surveys 60,000 households and thus is the *largest crime seriousness study ever conducted.* Similar to the methodology employed in the Sellin–Wolfgang index, respondents were

each given a description of a crime, "A person steals a bicycle parked on the street," and told that the seriousness of this crime was "10." They were then given a list of other crimes and told to compare them in seriousness to the bicycle theft. If a crime seemed to be twice as serious, they were to rate it at 20. If it were four times as serious, they were to rate it 50, and so on. Each person rated 25 crimes, but not everyone had the same 25. Overall, 204 items, each of which was illegal in at least one state, were rated.

Combining the ratings given by each of the 60,000 respondents, a single severity score was developed for each of the 284 items (crimes). (Klaus and Kalish, 1984, p. 2).

Table 10.3 reports some of the scores of the 204 events measured in the NCS crime seriousness study.

The present emphasis on "just deserts"—"let the punishment fit the crime"—suggests that research on crime seriousness scales and other attempts to quantify dangerousness and career criminals will continue.

TABLE 10.3   The National Survey of Crime Severity: How People Rank the Severity of Crime[a]

Severity Score	Offense
72.1	A person plants a bomb in a public building. (highest score)
52.8	A man forcibly rapes a woman. As a result of physical injury, she dies.
47.8	A parent beats his young child with his fists. As a result, the child dies.
33.8	A person runs a narcotics ring.
30.0	A man forcibly rapes a woman. Her physical injuries require hospitalization.
21.2	A person kidnaps a victim.
18.3	A man beats his wife with his fists. She requires hospitalization.
16.9	A legislator takes a bribe of $10,000 from a company to vote for a law favoring the company.
14.6	A person, using force, robs a victim of $10. The victim is hurt and requires hospitalization.
9.0	A person, armed with a lead pipe, robs a victim of $1,000. No physical harm occurs.
6.2	An employee embezzles $1,000 from his/her employer.
3.1	A person breaks into a home and steals $100.
1.6	A person is a customer in a house of prostitution.
0.8	A person under 16 years old runs away from home.
0.8	A person is drunk in public.
0.5	A person takes part in a dice game.
0.2	A person under 16 years old plays hooky from school.

[a]This represents only a selection of 204 items rated.

Source: Wolfgang, Marvin E. et al. *The National Survey of Crime Severity.* Washington, D.C.: U.S. Department of Justice, 1985, pp. vi–x.

Prediction Scales

Prediction scales

A rich tradition exists in the field of corrections of attempting to develop **prediction scales,** or experience tables, as they are sometimes called. Such scales attempt to assign scores that hopefully predict the likelihood of an individual committing crime or being a success or failure on probation or parole (Hood and Sparks, 1971, pp. 171–192; Simon, 1971, p. 1015; Gottfredson and Ballard, 1966). Some of the earliest work in this area was performed by the Gluecks (1960) and Mannheim and Wilkins (1955). The Gluecks attempted to develop a Social Prediction Table that would forecast the risk of a child becoming delinquent. An index was developed based on the scores assigned to such items as family togetherness, parental love, disciplinary policies, and supervision (Glueck and Glueck, 1950). Mannheim and Wilkins developed statistical prediction tables attempting to forecast parole success. These are often referred to as experience tables or base expectancy tables, because they are based on the experience of those who have already undergone treatment. Risk groups are usually developed on the basis of past probabilities of failure using items such as past record of offenses, seriousness of offenses, family conditions, age, and work record. Mannheim and Wilkins used techniques such as multiple regression (discussed in Chapter 12) to choose the most predictive variables and the relative weights to be assigned to each. Wilkins also assisted the California Department of Corrections in developing similar "base expectancy tables" (Hood and Sparks, 1971, p. 183). Ohlin (1951) developed parole prediction scales based on case records, personality assessments, and more traditional items.

In criminal justice, prediction scales may be employed to assess probation/ parole risk, to establish sentencing guidelines, to predict "dangerousness," and to establish a scoring system for targeting and incapacitating "career criminals."

Statistical predictions are based on the behavior patterns of an individual compared with others of similar background. This is common in insurance or actuarial predictions. *Clinical predictions,* on the other hand, are based on professional evaluation of individual behavior. Farrington and Tarling (1983) indicate that actuarial predictions of human behavior have been more successful than the individualized clinical element.

The Salient Factor Score

Salient factor score

The **Salient Factor Score** has been used by the U.S. Parole Commission since the early 1970s to objectively assess the likelihood of a prisoner's recidivism on parole. Six items are used to construct a 10-point scale, which ranges from 0 (poor risk) to 10 (very good risk) (Hoffman, 1985):

1. The offender's prior criminal convictions
2. The offender's prior criminal commitments for longer than thirty days
3. The offender's age at the time of the new offense
4. How long the offender was at liberty since the last commitment
5. Whether the prisoner was on probation, parole, or escape status at the time of the most recent offense
6. Whether the prisoner has a record of heroin dependence

The Salient Factor Score is combined with the seriousness of the current offense in a grid to establish a guideline range for sentencing (see Table 10.4). The example in Table 10.4 shows that an offender with a very low Salient Factor Score may serve a sentence two or three times as long for the same offense as an offender with a high score. Although problems exist with any prediction efforts (see Hoffman, 1984, 1985), the Salient Factor Score has demonstrated clear differences in recidivism rates between categories, although perfect prediction within categories is perhaps impossible.

Greenwood's "Rand Seven-Factor Index"

Rand seven-factor index

Greenwood's "Rand Seven-Factor Index" was aimed at *selective incapacitation,* individualization of sentences on the basis of predictions that particular offenders are likely to commit serious crimes at a high rate if not incarcerated (Blumstein et al., 1986; Cohen, 1983a, p. 1). A self-report survey of inmates in which robbers and burglars admitted crime commission during the two years preceding incarceration yielded an index that came up with

TABLE 10.4 Salient Factor Score Grid[a]

Offense Severity Category	Example	Salient Factor Score			
		Very Good (10–8)	Good (7–6)	Fair (5–4)	Poor (3–0)
1 Low	Minor theft	6–10	8–12	10–14	12–14
2 Low/moderate	Forgery/fraud (under $1,000)	8–12	12–16	16–20	20–25
3 Moderate	Motor vehicle theft	12–16	16–20	20–24	24–30
4 High	Robbery (no weapon)	16–20	10–16	26–32	32–38
5 Very High	Robbery (weapon)	24–36	36–48	48–60	60–72
5 Greatest	Willful homicide	(scores vary because of extreme variations in cases)			

[a]This is a compilation and abridgement for illustration purposes, as the Salient Factor Scores undergoes revision over time and may not reflect current sentencing guidelines. (All figures are months for a given sentencing guideline range.)

Source: Compilation of Peter Hoffman, "Predicting Criminality." *Crime File Series.* Washington, D.C.: National Institute of Justice, 1985; and Peter Hoffman, "Screening for Risk: A Revised Salient Factor Score." *Journal of Criminal Justice* 11(1984):539–547.

predictive results quite similar to those of the Salient Factor Score (Hoffman, 1985, p. 3; Greenwood and Abrahamse, 1982). Seven variables were selected to form a simple additive scale from 0 (low risk) to 7 (high risk):

1. Prior conviction for same charge
2. Incarcerated more than 50 percent of preceding two years
3. Convicted before age sixteen
4. Served time in state juvenile facility
5. Drug use in preceding two years
6. Drug use as a juvenile
7. Employed less than 50 percent of preceding two years

True positives

False positives

Although space prohibits a full detailing of such predictive efforts (see Cohen, 1983b), the forecasts of such scales are probabilistic, that is, not 100 percent accurate for each score. The Greenwood scale had a 45 percent rate of "true positives" (sometimes called "hits") or correctly identified that percentage of high-rate offenders; however, the "false-positive" ("misses" or inaccurate prediction) rate was 55 percent, which was similar to findings by Monahan (1981) who analyzed scales that attempt to predict potential violence or dangerousness. Kratcoski (1985) points out that in the use of such instruments to decide probation supervision, it should not be assumed that recidivism will be reduced at all supervision levels; instead, these instruments should be used to ensure efficiency and productive allocation of resources within supervision levels. Vito (1986) points out that in using different measures of the success of such efforts, multiple outcomes of success must be employed: "The goals of intensive supervision must be clearly specified and measured so that we avoid the premature crucifixion of intensive supervision upon the cross of recidivism" (p. 24).

Career Criminal Programs

The police have had much less experience in using prediction devices to target police resources on "repeat offenders" or "career criminals." The ROP (Repeat Offenders Project, pronounced "rope") of the Washington, D.C., Metropolitan Police uses criminal informants and other sources of information on criminals to concentrate police efforts on those most active in crime (Sherman, 1985; Martin and Sherman, 1985). A similar program in Minneapolis combines formal and informal methods reviewing "nominations" (of criminals to target) from many sources and extensive information and established criteria in focusing on a small group of active criminals. Validation of the criteria employed in both programs is incomplete, but the evaluation of the ROP targets by the Police Foundation noted that all had criminal histories, all had been arrested the previous year, and, as a result of the program, all were five times more likely to be arrested than were those randomly assigned to a control group (Sherman, 1985). Officers assigned to the ROP program had a smaller number of arrests, but more "quality arrests" of more serious, active criminals with records. The Police Foundation study was not able to determine the impact of the program on reducing crime in the District of Columbia.

Prediction criteria employed by prosecutors (district attorneys) tend to be more formal than those used by the police. A system employed in Charlotte, North Carolina, assigns weight to such factors as alcohol or drug abuse, age, and length of criminal career to create a scale for deciding which cases are most likely to be successfully prosecuted (Sherman, 1985).

An important caution in the utilization of prediction tables is that the administrator should be careful that the group to be rated does not differ significantly in experience from the group on which the base expectancy table was calculated. It is important that the table be validated or tested on samples other than the original on whose experience it was developed (Simon, 1971; Wilkins, 1969).

Related to the prediction table tradition are numerous psychological studies that use personality inventories and scales to discover a distinctive criminal personality. Tennenbaum (1977), in an update of earlier reviews by Scheussler and Cressey (1950) and Waldo and Dinitz (1967), reviewed studies employing various personality scales that attempt to distinguish criminal from noncriminal personalities. Although 80 percent of the studies claimed to have found personality differences, they failed to identify the complex, multidimensional nature of these differences. The majority had greater variation within groups than between groups, and thus no significant differences can be claimed (Tennenbaum, 1977, p. 19).

Advantages of Scales

The development of scale measurement *enables more exact measurement of phenomena* from simple nominal to ordinal or interval level. Rather than vaguely suggesting that City A has a bigger problem than City B, one could indicate that, according to the 1980 victimization index for eight specific crimes, the rate of crime was 30.6 per 1,000 in City A and 21.2 per 1,000 in City B. Thus, more quantitatively precise measurement can be obtained by means of scales.

Scales lend themselves to replication and the longitudinal measurement of even small changes in the phenomena under investigation. For example, the index offense crime rate may increase from 30.6 to 30.8 per 1,000. The construction of scaled measurement *forces more rigorous thinking* in that the researcher is involved in a systematic approach to operationalization.

Disadvantages of Scales

A principal critique of the use of scales is a philosophical one and relates to an antiquantitative approach to research. Those who oppose the scaling tradition question whether it really measures what it is claimed to measure or *whether a person's true attitude or behavior can be measured on a 5- or 7-point scale.* In the same light, there may be little relationship between a scaled measurement and the entity being measured. Some antiempiricists feel that rather than speak of errors in measurement we should speak of the *"error of measurement."* As with any measurement, scales are subject to problems of unreliability and invalidity.

Despite these and other criticisms, scaling is widely used in the social sciences and criminal justice and has been found useful in measuring a variety of concepts such as personality, occupational aptitude, authoritarianism, self-concept, cost of living, urbanization, industrialization, anomie, alienation, social class, crime, marital satisfaction, and job satisfaction.

These problems are not by any means exclusive to the development of scales in criminal justice. In the field of economics the widely used Consumer Price Index (CPI) has been under attack despite the fact that it is generally considered one of the best price measures in the world. This index represents the composite average increase in prices consumers pay for such items as shelter, food, utilities, clothing, furnishings, upkeep, transportation, health, and entertainment. With the double-digit inflation of the early eighties being fired primarily by high housing, interest, and gasoline prices, critics charged that the CPI tended to exaggerate the inflation rate for those consumers whose spending pattern differed from the average pattern. That is, consumers who already owned their home or car in that given year may have been unaffected by as much as 40 percent of the rise in the inflation rate (Fritz, 1980, p. 86; Samuelson, 1974, pp. 34–35).

There is no mysterious, magical, mechanized process that will ensure adequate indicators for concepts. In this sense, scaling procedures and methodological wizardry are no substitute for creative, logical, and sensitive theoretical conceptualization.

Summary

Scaling is the process of attempting to develop composite measurement or ranked or unit measurement of phenomena. The *levels of measurement* are nominal, ordinal, interval, and ratio. *Nominal* measurement is the simple placement of objects into categories in which the actual numbers assigned have no mathematical meaning. *Ordinal* measurement entails the ability to assign ranks, higher to lower. *Interval* measurement assumes equal units or distances between the scores. *Ratio* measurement assumes, in addition to equal units, a meaningful zero point.

Arbitrary scales are constructed on the basis of the judgment of the researcher. The Uniform Crime Report (UCR) is an arbitrary scale that, in the opinion of those who constructed it, reflects most serious crimes as well as those crimes for which police departments generally have the best records. A major limitation of the UCR is that it fails to take into account the relative seriousness of the crimes, which are simply summated into an index.

There are *three major types of attitude scales:* Thurstone, Likert, and Guttman. Other scaling procedures covered in this chapter are Q sort, semantic differential, factor analysis, and prediction scales. *Thurstone scales* make use of a series of judges to decide on appropriate scale items. A *Likert scale* is a simple summated scale of items usually containing a 5-point response category ranging from "strongly agree" to "strongly disagree." Likert scales typically make use of reversal items to eliminate response sets. In addition, item analysis is employed to eliminate nondiscriminating items. *Guttman scales* insist on unidimensionality—that one and only one dimension be measured by a particular scale. The cumulative nature of such a scaling procedure ensures a reasonable (if proper reproducibility) ability to predict the exact pattern of responses on the basis of an individual's scale score.

Q sort methodology is a variation of the Thurstone procedure in which the respondents place statements written on cards into assigned scale categories. The *semantic differential scale,* originally developed in the field of linguistics, is a 7- or 9-point bipolar rating system in which respondents are asked to indicate their perception of a concept or subject. *Factor analysis* is a procedure that identifies underlying dimensions among a series of scale items. Because many concepts are multidimensional, factor analysis not only is useful in identifying subscales, but also assigns factor loadings or weights to items. Thus, the relative importance of each item is taken into account in calculating scale scores.

Crime seriousness scales attempt to measure the gravity, or seriousness, of crime by means of public ratings using either simple rating scales (e.g., a 0-to-9 scale) or magnitude ratings (e.g., the Sellin–Wolfgang index or National Survey of Crime Severity). *Prediction scales,* sometimes called experience or base expectancy scales, are constructed on the basis of past experience to predict future performance usually in probation and parole.

The *Salient Factor Score* is used by the U.S. Parole Commission in assessing the likelihood of prisoner recidivism and in the determination of sentencing. The Rand Seven-Factor index and career criminal programs represent similar prediction efforts.

The relative *advantages* of using scales is that they provide more composite and exact measurement. They lend themselves to longitudinal assessment and replication studies, and they force more rigorous thinking on the part of the investigator. Disadvantages, on the other hand, point to the artificiality of such measurement and the question as to whether people really think in scale patterns. Scaling is by no means a substitute for good theoretical and substantive knowledge of the subject under investigation.

Key Concepts

Scales	Guttman Scales	Prediction Scales
Arbitrary Scales	Unidimensionality	Salient Factor Score
Thurstone Scales	Q Sort	Advantages/
Equal Appearing	Semantic Differential	Disadvantages
Intervals	Crime Seriousness Scales	of Scales
Likert Scales	Sellin–Wolfgang Index	Item Analysis

Review Questions

1. Discuss the three major types of attitude scales. What are the unique features of each?
2. In a recent journal, find an example of a study employing a scale. Describe the characteristics, scoring, reliability, and validity of this measure.
3. What are the two types of crime seriousness scales and of what utility are they in criminal justice research?
4. Discuss and give examples of the use of prediction scales in criminology and criminal justice.

Data Analysis: Coding, Tabulation, and Simple Data Presentation

It is hoped that earlier decisions in the research process have paved the way for the researcher in data analysis, data summarization, and presentation. Most novice researchers, however, are seldom prepared for the massive problem of efficient data management. Months of painstaking effort in problem formulation, research design, and data gathering can be wasted by inefficient and poorly thought out data analysis and presentation.

Data analysis should be planned at the beginning of a project rather than at the end. Recall, for instance, our description of the use of dummy tables as an exercise to check for the inclusion of necessary items for analysis. For very small studies that involve fewer than 100 subjects and only a few variables, it is possible to simply page through and tally data directly from the questionnaire. Most studies, however, are simply too large to permit such simple analysis; and even though deliberate planning for later analysis may at times appear to be a ritualistic obstacle in the project, it is absolutely essential.

Variables List

Variables list

A **variables list** keyed to questionnaire items enables the identification and examination of questionnaire content to ensure proper coverage, balance, and nonduplication of items. Such a variables list of questionnaire items justifies the inclusion of questions in the study. Figure 11.1 illustrates a typical variables list; each variable is identified and keyed to a hypothetical question number. On the basis of construction and review of a variables list the researcher may discard or add items.

1. *Demographic Variables*
   Sex—34a, Race—34b, Age—34c, Marital Status—34d,
   Dependents—34e
   Education—34f, Training—34g (Type)—34h,
   Hometown—34i, Job History—35, Parents' Background—36a–d,
   Spouse's Background—36e, f,
   Experience With Disability—8

2. *Professional–Paraprofessional Roles*
   Professional Roles—
   Paraprofessional—17, 22
   Appropriate Activities—23
   Professionalism—24, 25
   Rating of Profession—26, Professionalization Attitude—27,
   New Careers—28

3. Recruitment to Rehabilitation Work
   Individual Recruitment—2, 3
   Career Choice—5a, b, 6
   Agency Recruitment Policies—20, 21

4. *Utilization*
   Present Employment—1a, Type of Agency—1b
   Supervisory Responsibility 4a, b,
   Job Satisfaction—7a, b
   Duties—9, 10, 11
   Suggested Changes—12
   Training Since Employed—13
   Desired occupational Mobility—14, 15
   Job Satisfaction—16
   Promotion—18
   Characteristics of Work—29
   Important Tasks—31, 32
   Agency Climate—33

5. *Additional Areas of Investigation*
   Agency Change—19, 39
   Client Preference—30
   Agency Mission—37
   Severely Disabled—38

Figure 11.1 Variables List.

To construct a variables list, the researcher simply goes through the questionnaire that has been constructed and identifies the concept or variable that each question was design to measure. For example, Figure 11.1, section 2, deals with professional-paraprofessional roles, with questions 17 and 22 addressing paraprofessional roles, item 23 measuring appropriate activities, items 24 and 25 dealing with professionalism, and so forth. By means of such a list, the researcher is able to check, before the fact, for omission of important items, duplication of items, and similar content problems to ensure that the instrument is addressing all of the issues necessary for later analysis.

Computers

For much of this discussion, possession of basic computer literacy is assumed, because the computer is now used for all but the most simple data analysis. Those who are computer illiterate are at a disadvantage in today's information society. Computers are merely handy tools for research that offer numerous possibilities of analysis once the data have been properly entered. Before data are input into a computer for storage, analysis, and retrieval, they must first be coded so that they can be read by the computer. An orientation tour of your local computer center will acquaint you with the available equipment, which may vary from terminals connected to a large mainframe computer to self-sustained minicomputers and microcomputers (similar to personal computers).

No extensive knowledge of computers or computer programming is required in most instances, as a number of user-friendly, canned statistical packages (software), which calculate most statistics, are available. The most widely used computer packages in the social sciences are SPSS-X (Norusis, 1990), BMDP (Dixon et al., 1981), and SAS (SAS, 1982). Our presentation will focus on SPSS-X, which is the most common, although the others contain some features that have advantages over SPSS-X. SPSS stands for Statistical Package for the Social Sciences; the "X" signifies that the package is the latest version of this software. Appendix B explains analysis with SPSS-PC in detail, but will be more understandable after the reader completes this chapter and the next. The PC version of SPSS is now able to perform personal computer analyses, which at one time could only be performed on a main-frame computer.

Although this discussion will concentrate on the statistical capabilities of computer software, these programs also have many other data management capabilities, which are invaluable to the criminal justice researcher. These programs manage data files (sorting, merging, and saving files), manage data (sampling, selecting, and recording), and produce graphics and reports (pie charts, bar graphs, and tables). The microcomputer (PC or personal computer) has become very powerful and, in addition to statistical and data management functions, can perform functions such as client record management, business applications, word processing, desktop publishing, and decision support systems such as evaluation research (Monette, Sullivan, and DeJong, 1994, pp. 357–360).

Data Management

Data management

Data management, in the context of this chapter, is concerned with the process by which the raw data gathered by some instrument or measurement are converted into numbers for analysis purposes. Figure 11.2 outlines the *steps in the data management process:* collecting the information with the *data-gathering instrument* and, using a *codebook,* transferring this information onto a *codesheet.* The numerical data on the codesheet are used to create a *data file* (data decks, if cards are used). This data file may be created by *data entry* using a *computer keyboard* (or keypunch, if cards are used). *Data files* should also be cleaned (edited/verified) to ensure the accuracy of the data.

Editing

Editing

Prior to the actual coding, the questionnaires must be *edited.* Members of the research staff should check each questionnaire to be certain that the field interviewer or respondent completed each item accurately. Although most questions, particularly closed or structured questions, were probably precoded, codes may have to be developed for the open-ended items on the basis of a sampling of the initial returns.

In Chapter 5 we mentioned that researchers must decide whether to ask open-ended or closed questions. Although open-ended questions give respondents the opportunity to provide responses not limited to response categories, such questions raise greater difficulties with respect to coding. A useful *procedure in developing codes for open-ended items* is to read through a sufficient number of responses and create a preliminary code on the basis of these responses. Such a code, as any preliminary code, may require revision once the remaining responses are coded. According to a rule of thumb a code may require revision when 10 percent or more of the responses are classified as "other," or as not fitting any of the categories. It is thus useful to keep **"other" sheets** on which coders record the case

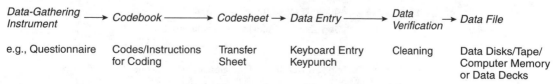

Figure 11.2 Steps in the Data Management Process.

number, the variable number, and a shortened version of the actual response recorded as "other." Patterns of "other" responses are thereby quickly noted and the recoding process is hastened. Generally, if more than 10 percent of the responses fall into "other," the code needs to be revised in order to include many of these responses.

Coding errors can be a major source of errors in surveys. The bulk of survey research work, particularly in large research organizations, is conducted by those who have the least training and often the least commitment to the scientific goals of research. Roth (1966) and Sussman and Haug (1967) speak of the perils of "hired hand research" and discovered that mechanical errors in such procedures as coding account for a significant level of error in survey research.

Coding

Coding   **Coding** is the assignment of numerical values to responses (information) gathered by a research instrument. As soon as or even before the data are gathered, the researcher can begin to construct a code for each item to be measured. Such codes are compiled into a *codebook,* which guides the numerical classification of questions to be coded. Figure 11.3 lists some typical questionnaire items. Figure 11.4 is a sample codebook for these same questions. The responses of a hypothetical respondent have been added for illustrative purposes.

The general purpose of the conversion of questionnaire information into numerical data is that, once this process is completed, the researcher can basically store the questionnaires and work from the summarized information—numbers. This can be particularly appreciated when a large number of cases and a large number of questions are asked. It becomes unmanageable to attempt to work directly from the original instrument.

Codebook   To summarize, coding is development of a code for each question in the questionnaire. This is called a **codebook.** All relevant questions are coded using the codebook as a guide, and these numbers are assigned to appropriate cells or columns on a codesheet (Figure 11.5).

Background Information

Please circle or fill in the correct information about yourself.

1. Sex: (circle one)   Male   (Female)
2. Race: (circle one)   Black   (White)   Other _____
                                                (specify)
3. Religious background in your home: (circle one)
    (Catholic)   Jewish   Protestant   Other _____
                                                (specify)
4. Present marital status: (circle one)
    Married   Single, never married   (Separated or divorced)   Widowed
5. When were you born? ____6____   ____42____
                       (month)   (year)

Figure 11.3 Sample Survey Instrument.

Question	Item	Column	Code
–	Study Number	1	As assigned
–	Case Number	2–4	As assigned
–	Coder Identification	5–6	As assigned
1.	Sex	7	1. Male
			2. Female
			9. Not ascertained
2.	Race	8	1. Black
			2. White
			3. Other
			9. Not ascertained
3.	Religious Background	9	0. None
			1. Catholic
			2. Jewish
			3. Protestant
			4. Other
			9. Not ascertained
4.	Present Marital Status	10	1. Married
			2. Single, never married
			3. Separated or divorced
			4. Widowed
			5. Not ascertained
5.	Age	11–12	Code last two digits of year respondent was born. If born in 1899 or before, code 00. 99. Not ascertained

Figure 11.4 Sample Codebook.

1	2	3	4	5	6	7	8	9	10
1	0	1	6	1	4	2	2		

11	12	13	14	15	16	17	18	19	20

21	22	23	24	25	26	27	28	29	30

31	32	33	34	35	36	37	38	39	40

41	42	43	44	45	46	47	48	49	50

51	52	53	54	55	56	57	58	59	60

61	62	63	64	65	66	67	68	69	70

71	72	73	74	75	76	77	78	79	80

Figure 11.5 Sample Codesheet. Codes Assigned to Cells 1–8 Refer to the Coding of the Survey Instrument (Figure 11.3) Using the Codebook (Figure 11.4).

Throughout this process the code or codebook is used as a guide in reading the numerical information. The codebook may require revision during the course of the coding procedure, particularly for open-ended items that may call for considerable judgment on the part of the coder.

Each column in our codebook (Figure 11.4) represents a box or cell on the **codesheet** (or transfer sheet) (Figure 11.5). Coding may be handled in a variety of ways, depending on the nature of the data-gathering instrument and the resources available. In addition to use of a separate codesheet, researchers may employ self-coding (similar to the pencil-in answer sheets used in machine-scored tests) or edge coding (in which the margins of the questionnaire itself are used for coding, thus eliminating the need for separate coding sheets). Self-coding instruments are automatically key punched[1] by an optical scanning sensor device, whereas edge-coded questionnaires can be designed so that they are precoded and can be directly keyboard entered. Such instruments are usually limited to closed or structured response questions.

The number of cells (columns) assigned to each variable depends on the largest expected number of digits for that variable. For example, if a variable ranges in value from 9 to 99, we would need two columns; if it ranged from 1 to 100, we would require three columns. For most software programs, blanks should be avoided; the computer generally reads these as zeros, which could be problematic if zero is a legitimate value. Unknown or missing values could be assigned a code value of 9, for example.

Let us illustrate the coding procedure by means of the hypothetical responses in the sample survey instrument (Figure 11.3) and our sample codebook (Figure 11.4). According to the codebook we first must assign a "study number" to this project. This item does not refer to any question number in the instrument and is assigned by the researcher. Because this is our first hypothetical study, we will call it study 1. Code 1 is assigned to cell 1 on the codesheet. If only one study is being analyzed, creation of a computer file name may eliminate the necessity for a study number for each case. The next item in the codebook is the "case number" that is assigned to the respondent. Assume that the top of the questionnaire indicated that this was case 16. Because cells 2, 3, and 4 have been reserved to record respondent case numbers, it appears that more than 100 and fewer than 999 subjects were expected to participate in the study. Recording case number 16 in cells 2 and 3 would result in its being read as $16X$ (X being 0–9). Instead, 016 should be coded in cells 2, 3, and 4 respectively. The next item in the code is the "coder identification." In larger studies, each coder is given a coder number beforehand. Our hypothetical coder is number 14; therefore, we enter 14 in columns 5 and 6.

Codesheet

[1] A keypunch machine, although still used, represents an older technology. It resembles a typewriter with characters such as numbers punched onto computer cards. The keyboard entry method replaces this technology for most purposes.

Finally, we begin coding actual substantive items in the sample survey instrument with question 1—sex. The respondent indicated that she was female which, using our code, is a 2. This is entered in column 7 on the codesheet. Question 2—race finds the response is "white," which is also a 2 in the code and is entered in column 8. Proceeding in similar fashion, 1—"Catholic" is entered in column 9, and 3 for "separated or divorced" is marked in column 10. Finally, a two-digit code was necessary to accommodate the last two digits in year of birth. In this case the numbers 4 and 2 were coded in columns 11 and 12, respectively. Although our sample codebook was a simple one for illustrative purposes, the same basic procedure is followed for all relevant items in longer instruments.

Coder Monitoring

Coder
monitoring

Coder monitoring involves checking the work of coders for accuracy. Coder monitoring is necessary to ensure quality control in research. One procedure used at a large university research institute[2] involves coder *verification and reconciliation* procedures as essential quality-control checks on mechanical error. Each questionnaire is double-coded; that is, two different coders independently code the same questionnaire. Next, disagreements are identified. Reconciliation involves the coders coming to an agreement on the proper code. Such a procedure not only eliminates outright errors in coding, but also results in greater uniformity and consistency. Such a process can also be supplemented with computer edit programs, which identify by column the incorrect values (those not defined by the codebook as proper values). Unfortunately, unchecked mechanical errors may be the true rival causal factor in many pieces of reported research. Thus, the results of a survey may not be due to accurate measurement; rather, they may simply be due to miscoding, mispunching, and other human and mechanical mistakes. In some instances, precision and care in earlier stages of a project are disregarded once the "boring" routine of "number crunching" is begun.

Keyboard Entry

Keyboard entry

The **keyboard entry** technique is the most widely used means of inputting data. The data typed on the keyboard are displayed on a video terminal. The terminal displays case 1, variable name 1, and prompts (asks for information) for case 1. Once these data are input, the screen prompts for the data for case 2; eventually, all of the data are entered. The computer can save the data (as a file in its memory) or output the data onto some medium, for example, paper (printout), magnetic tape, or diskettes, for later use. The printout is produced by a printer, which is similar to a typewriter. Data stored in memory or on tape or a disk are referred to as a completed *data file.*

[2]Institute on the Family and the Bureaucratic Society, Case Western Reserve University.

Data Verification

Data verification

Data verification or *cleaning* involves double-checking the data file in search of errors, many of which are inevitable despite the conscientiousness of workers. Code entries can be checked by computer programs themselves, as well as by checking data columns for inaccuracies. A simple frequency distribution run for each variable will identify unauthorized values, for example:

Sex	N
1. Male	48
2. Female	47
5.	2
6.	1
9. Unknown	2
	100

In this example, values 5 and 6 were not authorized in our code and are errors. Software packages generally further assist by identifying the case numbers of these unauthorized values, which can then be checked by examining whether the data were incorrectly entered (e.g., a column skipped). One can check the coding by going back to the original questionnaire. Some computer programs identify all unauthorized (not identified in codebook) values before doing any analysis. Ultimately, despite painstaking efforts, some errors are likely to remain; if a reasonable effort is made to clean the data, these errors should be minor. Once the data file has been cleaned to the satisfaction of the researcher, it is ready for analysis.

Simple Data Presentation

Marginal run

Simple data presentation involves summarizing and using univariate statistics. The initial step in data analysis is a **marginal run.** It is called "running the marginals" because it consists of single variable tabulations of the type of data that appear in the margins of tables to be constructed later. Table 11.1 depicts a standard marginal run which usually reports both the number and the percentage of cases. Such information is usually reported in the descriptive parts of a writeup. For inexperienced researchers, little thought is given to going beyond such tallying, although in reality the work has just begun. Such information as number of people victimized, number of people afraid of crime, or age, sex, and race characteristics of the population surveyed may be useful; but researchers are generally also interested in how victimization or fear might be affected by the age, sex, or race of respondents.

We have all been victims of the folly of asking a person about their summer vacation and then listening to a chronology of minute details. Although slides, postcards, and other graphic portrayals of the account sometimes make it more interesting or more tolerable, most people are simply interested

TABLE 11.1   Example of a One-Variable Table: Demographic Characteristics of Student Panels

Characteristic	% 1965	% 1972	Characteristic	% 1965	% 1972
Sex			*High School Location*		
Male	67.9	60.2	Metropolitan, population 1,000,000+	21.7	17.2
Female	32.1	39.8	Metropolitan—suburban	15.5	16.8
Total %	100.0	100.0	Urban, population 50,000 to 999,999	21.7	20.8
N	324	739	Urban—suburban	7.7	12.4
			Small town or rural	33.4	32.6
Race			Total %	100.0	99.8
Caucasian	93.1	94.9	N	323	690
Black	5.6	4.1			
Oriental	1.2	.9	*Index—Family Social Class*		
Total %*	99.9	99.9	Class I (upper)	11.4	14.5
N[a]	321	730	Class II (upper middle)	19.9	16.6
			Class III (middle)	25.6	28.6
			Class IV (lower middle)	27.2	28.9
Age			Class V (lower)	15.8	11.3
Under 25	26.0	28.9	Total %	99.9	99.9
25–29	31.0	37.3	N	316	723
30–34	16.7	15.7			
35–39	13.6	7.2	*Experience with Disability prior to*		
40–44	7.1	5.7	*Training*[b]		
45 or over	5.6	5.2	Personal disability	22.8	15.4
Total %	100.0	100.0	Parent or sibling	21.0	27.9
N	323	738	Spouse or children	6.2	4.9
			Other relatives	17.9	21.8
			Nonrelated persons only	23.1	20.0
			No experience with disability	27.8	27.7
			Total %[c]	118.8	117.7
			N	324	739

[a]In this and subsequent tables, variations below an *N* of 324 or 739 are due to missing data, and variations from 100% are due to rounding error.

[b]Differences between the two student groups exceeded those expected by chance, $\chi^2 = 9.59$, 2 *df*, $\rho < .01$ level when data were grouped by personal disability, *N*'s = 74 and 114, some experience with disability other than personal, *N*'s = 160 and 420, and no experience with disability, *N*'s = 90 and 205.

[c]Totals exceed 100% because of multiple responses. All percentages are computed on bases of 324 and 739.

Source: Hagan, Frank E., Marie R. Haug, and Marvin B. Sussman. *Comparative Profiles of the Rehabilitation Counseling Graduate: 1965 and 1972.* Working Paper No. 5, 2d series. Cleveland: Case Western Reserve University, Institute on the Family and the Bureaucratic Society, 1975, p. 10.

in the highlights—noteworthy incidents or unexpected developments. Although a scientific report does not have as its major purpose entertainment, it also need not be a cure for insomnia. Such reports must contain sufficient detail to enable the reader to assess the logic and validity of the procedures used; however, they certainly should not burden the reader with huge amounts of raw data or routine information. *Through the use of rates, statistics, tables, graphic displays, frequency distributions, and other summarizing procedures,* it should be possible to communicate the significant findings in as understandable and painless a fashion as possible.

Rates

Rates   *Rates,* proportions, percentages, and ratios are meaningful ways of standardizing data so that useful comparisons can be made between unequal populations. A rate expresses the number of cases of the criterion variable per unit of population, for example, per 1,000. These measures also summarize raw data in a form that is easier to read and understand. Suppose City A with a population of 1,500,000 had 400 serious index crimes in a given year, and City B with a population of 900,000 had 250. Which city had the worse crime problem is not readily apparent.

	City A	*City B*
Crimes	400	250
Population	1,500,000	900,000

Crime rate   The **crime rate** could be calculated with the following formula:

$$\text{Crime Rate} = \frac{\text{number of crimes}}{\text{population}} \times 100,000$$

For our data we would calculate

$$\text{(City A) crime rate} = \frac{400}{1,500,000} \times 100,000 = 26.7$$

$$\text{(City B) crime rate} = \frac{250}{900,000} \times 100,000 = 27.7$$

A more meaningful standardized comparison can now be made. Although City A has more crime, this is in part expected because it also has a larger population than City B. If the crime rate is expressed per 100,000 population, City A actually has a slightly smaller crime rate (26.7) than City B (27.7). This same information can be expressed using other summary devices.

Proportions

Proportions   **Proportions** express the number of cases of the criterion variable as part of the total population:

$$\text{proportion} = \frac{\text{frequency of criterion variable}}{N}$$

In our example of two cities we calculate

$$\text{(City A) proportion} = \frac{400}{1,500,000} = .00026$$

$$\text{(City B) proportion} = \frac{250}{900,000} = .00027$$

Proportions are obviously less useful in examples such as ours in which the criterion variable is a relatively rare event. In such cases, rate is a far more useful summary statistic.

Percentages

Percentages

Percentages are calculated by dividing a frequency by the total N and multiplying the result by 100. Percentages can be calculated quite easily from proportions:

$$\text{percentage} = 100 \frac{\text{frequency}}{N}$$

For our example the calculations would be

$$\text{(City A) percentage} = (100) \frac{400}{1,500,000} = .026$$

$$\text{(City B) percentage} = (100) \frac{250}{900,000} = .027$$

In both cities less than 1 percent of the citizens were victimized.

Ratios

Ratios

To illustrate the calculation of a ratio, we use a new example that provides more useful data for the purposes of this statistic. A **ratio** simply compares the number of cases in one category with the number in another. For example, suppose that in a given city 200 crimes were recorded, forty of which were committed by females. The ratio of male to female criminals could be obtained using the following formula:

$$\text{ratio} = \frac{\text{frequency 1}}{\text{frequency 2}}$$

$$\text{ratio (males to females)} = \frac{160}{40} = \frac{4}{1} \text{ or } 4:1$$

The ratio of male to female criminals is 4 to 1.

Often, in expressing ratios of criminals by sex, a demographic calculation called the sex ratio is made

$$\text{sex ratio} = \frac{\text{frequency males}}{\text{frequency females}} \times 100$$

In our example

$$\text{sex ratio} = \frac{160}{40} \times 100 = 400$$

A sex ratio of 400 indicates that for every 100 female criminals there are 400 male criminals.

The Frequency Distribution

In addition to the calculation of summary statistics such as those just discussed, it is standard procedure for researchers to summarize and group data into a form that is more easily interpreted by the reader. Suppose, for example, we had the following *victimization rates for thirty American cities:*

16	12	22
5	30	18
19	28	27
4	13	4
2	17	5
8	6	12
10	16	20
12	1	4
1	9	8
4	12	2

Frequency
distribution

Simple scrutiny of the data does not provide a very neat picture of the relative distribution of crime in these cities. A **frequency distribution** is a procedure in which the data are arranged in a more meaningful summary table.

There are a number of unwritten rules regarding the construction of a frequency distribution. First, the analyst must decide on the number of categories (classes) into which the data will be grouped. Generally, selection of too few (less than five) or too many (say fifteen or so) groups defeats the purpose of categorizing—the former because it fails to distinguish the data, and the latter because it is unwieldy and hard to read. Second, the groupings should be mutually exclusive; that is, it should be possible to assign each case to one and only one group. Finally, the groups should cover the entire distribution, with the within-group intervals as equal in size as possible. The major exception to the last rule would be the use of *over* or *under* categories for extreme cases. For example, the age group ninety and over would include the rare person who is 127 years old. Given unordered victimization rates for thirty cities, Table 11.2 illustrates a typical frequency distribution for such data.

The data were organized into six equal categories with both the frequency and percentage reported. Note that the percentages do not total to 100. This was due to rounding error and will be discussed in greater detail later in this chapter in the presentation on table construction.

Despite the report writer's time-consuming attempts to make sense out of data and present them in a most appropriate and simple manner, many readers are quite frankly bored by statistical presentations.

TABLE 11.2 Frequency Distribution for Victimization Rates in Thirty Cities (Hypothetical)

Victimization Rate[a]	N	Percentage
0–5	8	26.7
6–10	5	16.7
11–15	7	23.3
16–20	5	16.7
21–25	2	6.7
26–30	3	10.0
Total	30	100.1

[a]Per 100,000 population.

Graphic Presentations

Graphics

Graphs or **pictorial presentations** of data are an attractive means of capturing the reader's attention as well as of summarizing data, particularly information from frequency distributions. Because "a picture is worth a thousand words," pictorials may similarly provide a useful way of presenting complex data. Among graphic presentation techniques are:

Pie charts
Bar graphs
Frequency polygons

In addition to these, there are other devices used, particularly in criminal justice, such as crime clocks.

Pie Charts

Pie charts

Pie charts are simply circles (pies) whose pieces represent proportions of some phenomenon and total 100 percent. Figure 11.6 presents a typical pie chart. With crime index offenses from the Uniform Crime Reports, the relative percentages of each index offense are presented as pieces of a pie. The appeal of pie charts is their obvious simplicity of interpretation. In this instance it is easy to note that larcency-theft made up more than half of the index offenses, and together with burglary it accounted for more than three-fourths of index crimes.

Bar Graphs

Bar graphs

Bar graphs consist of rectangles. The width often represents the class intervals (not depicted here); and the height represents quantity or amount (Figure 11.7). There are a number of rules for constructing and reading bar graphs and frequency polygons:

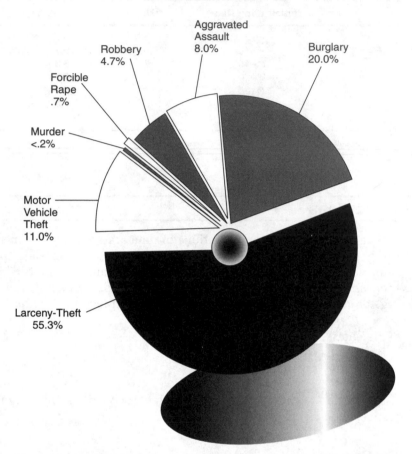

Figure 11.6 Pie Chart: Crime Index Offenses. (*Source:* U.S. Department of Justice. *FBI Uniform Crime Report: Crime in the United States, 1993.* Washington, D.C.: U.S. Government Printing Office, December 1994, p. 8.)

Score values are usually arranged along the horizontal dimension (across) and amounts such as frequencies and percentages are plot-ted vertically (upward or downward).

Appropriate labels should be used so that the graph is self-explanatory. The horizontal line, for example, could include name of city, type of crime, and so forth; for the vertical line, some calibration of amounts, percentages, or N's should appear.

Zero points should begin at the far left, and ascending values upward and to the right.

Figure 11.7 shows the percent variation from the monthly average for murder using Uniform Crime Reports data. The highest positive variation

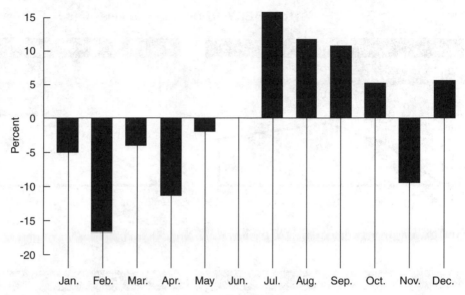

Figure 11.7 Murder by Month 1990, Variation from Monthly Average. (*Source:* U.S. Department of Justice. *FBI Uniform Crime Reports: Crime in the United States, 1990.* Washington, D.C.: U.S. Government Printing Office, August 11, 1991, p. 10.)

was during July, while the highest negative (below average) variation was in February.

Frequency Polygons (Line Charts)

Frequency polygon

In **frequency polygons** (or line charts), the frequency or percentages of the midpoint of each score value are plotted and connected by a straight line that begins and ends at the baseline. Figure 11.8 presents some typical frequency polygons, in this case from the Uniform Crime Reports. The horizontal axis contains the years 1986–1990, and the vertical axis contains percentage changes over the base year of 1986, which is recorded as zero. Note the dip below zero representing the decline in reported crime. Similarly, the actual horizontal axis is raised above the base to permit delineation of negative percentages that fall below the base zero line. In discussing the importance of graphic displays, Tracy (1990, p. 76) notes:

> Tables are effective when more than one statistical measure is being reported or when sets of exact scores should be given. On the other hand, figures, such as histograms and bar charts, are very effective for displaying descriptive measures when the interest is in highlighting particular relationships, especially comparative differences across groups. Line charts are essential in depicting data trends over time.

The easy availability of sophisticated statistical software packages has encouraged the use of statistical analysis, which is well and good. However,

ROBBERY Percent Change from 1989

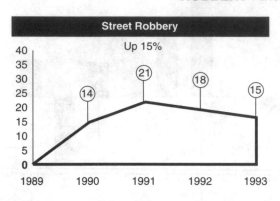

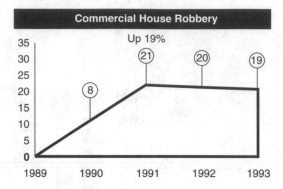

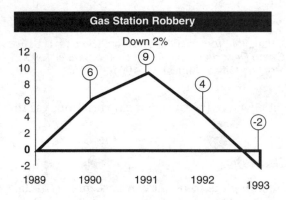

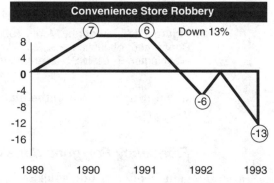

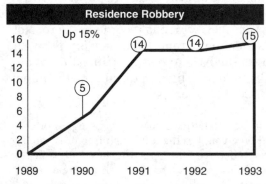

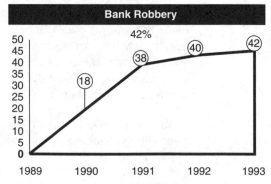

Figure 11.8 Frequency Polygons. (*Source:* U.S. Department of Justice. *FBI Uniform Crime Reports: Crime in the United States, 1993.* Washington, D.C.: U.S. Government Printing Office, December 1994, p. 30.)

this has led some report writers to ignore the use of tables and figures in describing their data. "The most simple analyses, effectively displayed, are often the most convincing and communicative to the reader" (ibid). The same software packages can generate terrific graphic displays.

Figure 11.9 is a comparative frequency polygon in which two different distributions are plotted on the same grid. Note how the frequency polygon better captures the similarity between the two groups, representing one group by a solid line and the other by a dashed (broken) line. A variety of other means of graphically depicting data exist. For more detailed information, see Huff (1954) and Zeisel (1957). Various three-dimensional and other appealing graphic figures attractively depict data. Figure 11.10, for instance, is a three-dimensional pictogram that dramatically illuminates the major types of larceny-theft.

Crime Clocks

Crime clocks

Despite its words of caution to the public (see box in Figure 11.11), the FBI publishes figures called *crime clocks* as part of the annual Uniform Crime Reports. Figure 11.11 shows "Crime Clock, 1990," which indicates that one crime index offense occurred every two seconds and that one violent crime occurred every seventeen seconds.

In such circumstances we could have the same proportion or even a relative decline in crime relative to population growth, but the crime clock would misleadingly show a consistent increase. A simple example may illustrate this point. Suppose that a given city in 1980 had 356 serious crimes for its population of one million. Ten years later the city had 712 serious crimes, but now a population of two million. The crime clock approach would suggest that crime doubled during the second period, whereas by controlling for population we find that the crime rate is actually the same.

The misleading feature of the crime clock is that it fails to control for population growth and uses a constant, fixed unit of comparison time. Although the FBI acknowledges this feature as misleading, it continues to publish the clock year after year.

If you have learned anything at all about crime clocks, please do this writer and many others in the criminology/criminal justice field a favor and ten years from now, when you are the director of some agency and asked to give a speech on crime to some civic club, do not begin your speech with a trite recitation of crime clock statistics, as so many unfamiliar with the inadequacy of such graphic displays are fond of doing. Better yet, if you hear such a speech, ask the speaker how the crime rate compares with these statistics over the past few years.

The sometimes tedious prospect of constructing figures has been in part alleviated by the fact that most computer packages will provide graphic displays of data suitable for presentation in a report or professional article. The reading and construction of graphic figures requires, at a simpler level, many of the same skills that are necessary in interpreting or building tables.

Relative Professionalism Level of Rehabilitation Counseling
As Perceived by Student Panels

Professionalism of Rehabilitation Counseling		1965 %	1972 %
low	−0	5.7	5.8
	1	5.1	8.6
to	2	18.2	16.1
	3	28.0	27.9
low-marginal	−4	27.4	28.7
high-marginal	−5	7.6	5.9
to	7	2.2	.7
high	−8	2.5	1.3
Total %		99.9	99.9
N		314	707

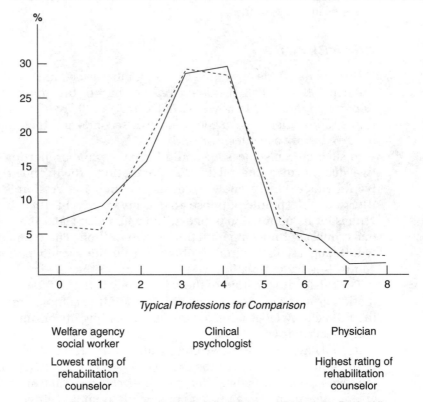

Typical Professions for Comparison

Welfare agency social worker	Clinical psychologist	Physician
Lowest rating of rehabilitation counselor		Highest rating of rehabilitation counselor

Note: Figure represents the plotted distributions of Table data. Dashed line equals 1965 cohort; solid line equals 1972 cohort. As suggested by the spread of ranks, differences between the two groups is not statistically significant, Kolmogorov-Smirnov, D = .0358, p > .05.

Figure 11.9 Relative Professionalism Level of Rehabilitation Counseling as Perceived by Student Panels. The Graph Comprises Plotted Distribution of the Data in the Table: —, 1965 cohort; —, 1972 cohort. As Suggested by the Spread of Ranks, Differences between the Two Groups Are Not Statistically Significant: Kolmogorov–Smirnov *D* = 0.358, *p* > .05. (*Source:* Hagan, Frank E., Marie R. Haug, and Marvin B. Sussman. *Comparative Profiles of the Rehabilitation Counseling Graduate: 1965 and 1972.* 2d series, Working Paper No. 5. Cleveland: Case Western Reserve University, Institute on the Family and the Bureaucratic Society, 1975, pp. 50–51.)

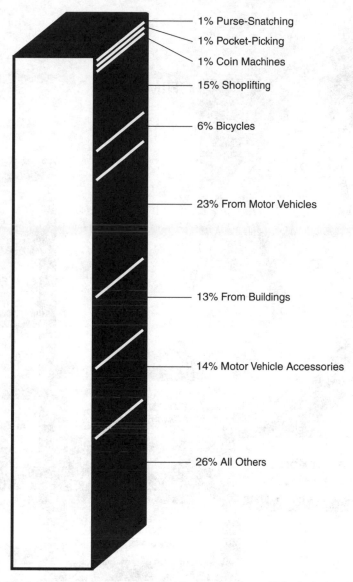

1% Purse-Snatching
1% Pocket-Picking
1% Coin Machines
15% Shoplifting
6% Bicycles
23% From Motor Vehicles
13% From Buildings
14% Motor Vehicle Accessories
26% All Others

Figure 11.10 Larceny-Theft—Percent Distribution by Type of Theft, 1993. (*Source:* U.S. Department of Justice. *FBI Uniform Crime Reports: Crime in the United States, 1993.* Washington, D.C.: U.S. Government Printing Office, 1994, p. 47.)

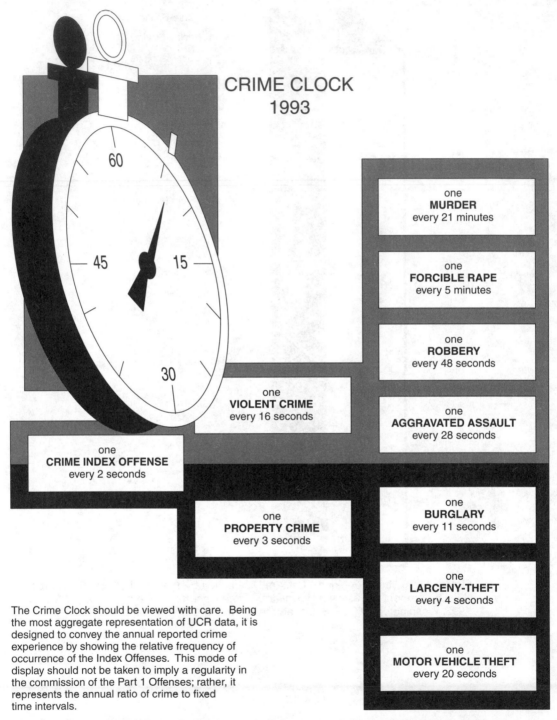

CRIME CLOCK
1993

one
MURDER
every 21 minutes

one
FORCIBLE RAPE
every 5 minutes

one
ROBBERY
every 48 seconds

one
VIOLENT CRIME
every 16 seconds

one
AGGRAVATED ASSAULT
every 28 seconds

one
CRIME INDEX OFFENSE
every 2 seconds

one
BURGLARY
every 11 seconds

one
PROPERTY CRIME
every 3 seconds

one
LARCENY-THEFT
every 4 seconds

The Crime Clock should be viewed with care. Being the most aggregate representation of UCR data, it is designed to convey the annual reported crime experience by showing the relative frequency of occurrence of the Index Offenses. This mode of display should not be taken to imply a regularity in the commission of the Part 1 Offenses; rather, it represents the annual ratio of crime to fixed time intervals.

one
MOTOR VEHICLE THEFT
every 20 seconds

Figure 11.11 Crime Clock 1993. (*Source:* U.S. Department of Justice. *FBI Uniform Crime Reports: Crime in the United States, 1993.* Washington, D.C.: U.S. Government Printing Office, 1994, p. 47.)

Table Reading

Table reading   *Tables* are presentations of quantitative data in a summary or uniform fashion. Many standardized tests such as civil service exams, the Graduate Record Exam, and professional tests feature a section on table reading. Individuals who are bored or panicked by such tables under normal conditions are very likely to do poorly in such testing situations. This is unfortunate because the mastery of some rather elementary procedures is likely to improve one's scores considerably. Table reading and construction in this presentation involve at least a 2 × 2 table in which percentaging and standard statistical procedures, to be discussed in detail later in Chapter 12, are performed.

A cross tabulation (or contingency table) examines one variable in terms of another (or other) variable(s). A 2 × 2 table is a cross tabulation that looks at two values of the first variable and two values of the second variable at the same time. For example, in tabulating or counting responses we would tally four (2 × 2) categories, let us say Male and Female and Criminals and Noncriminals. This procedure will be explained in more detail in the section on Presentation of Complex Data.

Why Bother with Tables?

Many people find tables boring and skip them when reading journal articles or reports; at the same time they may spend an hour reading verbal reports of what the author claims a table shows (Wallis and Roberts, 1956, pp. 270–271). The mastery of table reading can result in a great economy of effort, tantamount to speedreading. Readers may find themselves skipping the written portions of reports and reading the tables, gaining much of the needed information in much less time. In addition to being a useful skill, table reading and construction are valuable scientific and administrative tools, essential for summarizing and analyzing figures.

What to Look for in a Table

Table 11.3 is a typical table one might find in criminal justice or criminology. Let us ransack this table and systematically draw out some major points one should examine in a table.

There are a number of essential characteristics of most tables that a patient and systematic reader can look for which can be overlooked by a less methodical approach (Wallis and Roberts, 1956; Broom and Selznick, 1979, pp. 12–14; Cole, 1972, pp. 28–37).

TABLE 11.3 Personal Crime, 1992. Victimization Rates for Persons Age 12 and Over, by Race and Age of Victims and Type of Crime.

Race and Age	Total Population	Crimes of Violence	Completed Violent Crimes	Attempted Violent Crimes	Rate per 1,000 Persons in Each Age Group					Assault	
					Rape	Robbery					
						Total	With Injury	Without Injury	Total	Aggravated	Simple
White											
12–15	11,304,360	75.0	28.8	46.2	1.1*	10.8	2.3*	8.5	63.1	17.4	45.7
16–19	10,896,950	70.5	22.9	47.6	2.0*	10.2	4.2	6.1	58.3	20.2	38.0
20–24	15,131,160	67.5	23.9	43.7	2.6*	7.8	3.6	4.2	57.1	16.8	40.3
25–34	34,815,850	35.7	13.3	22.3	0.3*	6.4	2.2	4.2	28.9	9.0	19.9
35–49	40,013,130	21.0	7.0	14.0	0.3*	3.3	0.9	2.4	17.4	6.3	11.1
50–64	28,847,500	9.4	2.2	7.2	0.1*	2.2	0.9*	1.3*	7.1	2.1	5.0
65 and over	27,605,090	4.3	1.2*	3.0	0.3*	0.9*	0.0*	0.9*	3.1	1.3*	1.8
Black											
12–15	2,219,000	83.3	23.9	59.4	1.5*	5.3*	4.1*	1.3*	76.5	35.7	40.7
16–19	2,039,150	125.5	59.4	66.1	0.0*	46.7	11.1*	35.6	78.8	59.0	19.8
20–24	2,446,270	102.4	40.5	61.9	3.7*	34.5	6.0*	28.5	64.2	30.1	34.2
25–34	5,259,930	51.5	22.7	28.8	1.7*	17.3	10.9	6.4*	32.6	12.3	20.2
35–49	6,144,400	25.8	11.7	14.1	1.4*	7.2	3.4*	3.8*	17.1	13.1	4.1*
50–64	3,258,690	17.0	10.5*	6.5*	0.0*	8.2*	4.0*	4.2*	8.8*	4.8*	4.0*
65 and over	2,504,830	10.7*	5.3*	5.3*	0.0*	7.6*	4.0*	3.6*	3.0*	1.4*	1.6*

Note: Detail may not add to total shown because of rounding.

*Estimate is based on about 10 or fewer sample cases.

Source: U.S. Department of Justice. *Criminal Victimization in the United States, 1992: A National Crime Victimization Survey Report.* Washington, D.C.: Bureau of Justice Statistics, March 1994, p. 28.

Steps in Reading a Table

Read the title   The first step in systematically reading a table is to *carefully read the title.* A good title will inform the reader of exactly what is being presented. Table 11.3, for instance, tells us that we are examining personal crimes as opposed to crimes committed against commercial establishments. A properly constructed title will also usually list the dependent variable first and then the independent variable(s). In Table 11.3, for instance, victimization rates are the dependent variable; race and age are the independent variables. *The general rule, then, is dependent variable (victimization rate) by independent variable(s) (age and race).* In addition, the title of Table 11.3 indicates that the data are for persons age twelve and over and that the data presented will be broken down by the type of crime. The title also indicates that the data are for the year 1989.

Read headnote   Next, the *headnote*—section appearing in parentheses below the title—should be examined. This explains exactly what the numbers we are looking at represent. In this case, we are reading the rate per 1,000 population in each age group. This is important to note because sometimes readers are not sure whether they are interpreting raw numbers, percentages, or whatever. Be sure to note *what units* are being used in a table.

Note the source   Another very important item for the reader to note is *the source* from which the data in the table were drawn. In this case the original source was the U.S. Department of Justice National Crime Victimization Survey, which was conducted in 1992. Those familiar with this survey from our previous discussion are aware that it is conducted by the U.S. Bureau of Census on behalf of the United States Bureau of Justice Statistics and is a model of its kind. The data are based on a stratified multistage cluster sample that is representative of households in the United States. Of course, the statistics reported are claimed victimizations of the survey sample rather than official police records. One reason for noting the source is to obtain a relative evaluation of the reliability of the data. In this case, given known limitations, this source is generally regarded as one of the very best of its type.

Read footnotes   *Footnotes* contain additional information that may be of importance in judging the data presented in the tables. In this case the footnote mentions that the detail (data breakdowns) may not sum to the total shown in parentheses because of rounding. The numbers in the second column refer to the total national population in that group. The latter is important because it indicates that the sample data have been inferred to the national population and we are reading national statistics as if everyone in the United States had been surveyed. Finally, the footnote asterisk which refers to a few of the figures in the table states that these estimates may be unreliable because they are based on roughly ten or fewer sample cases. Thus, for instance, statistics on the rape rate are based on too few cases to be reliable.

Read subheads   *Read the subheads,* or stubs, as a guide to the information in the columns and rows. Similar to columns in a building, table columns run vertically while rows run horizontally. The subhead for rows appears in the far upper left-hand corner and each subcategory runs down the left-hand side of the table. In this case the rows refer to different age groups and races. The column subheads identify various types of crimes. Because the race-specific age groups are of unequal size, the only fair comparison would be to percentage or establish rates within each independent variable (age-race cohorts). As will be explained later, we wish to know *what proportion of the independent variable (race-specific age cohorts) is a category of the dependent (have been victimized).* Thus, proper percentaging or rate calculations are read across or within each category of the independent variable(s). Reading the first cell, 75 per 1,000 whites who were 12–15 years of age ($N = 11,304,360$) were victimized.

Find average   Another useful statistic to *look for* is the general *overall average and range* (variation from high to low) in the data. In this case Table 11.3 fails to provide any figures on overall rates for total, whites, blacks, or all ages. We can, however, obtain a picture of the general variation in the data. Although unreliable because of small sample *N*'s, the lowest victimizations, estimated at zero, were for rape among blacks age 16–19 and 50 or over and among whites age 25 and over. By contrast the highest rates, 125.5 per 1,000, were for blacks age 16–19 who were victims of crimes of violence. The highest specific victimization rate, 59 per 1,000, was for aggravated assault for blacks age 16–19.

Next, one should *examine the fluctuation of this range and/or average* within each category of the dependent variable (type of victimization). For crimes of violence, which include adjacent subcategories of rape, robbery and assault, the most victimized group was blacks age 16–19 (125.5 per 1,000); by contrast the least victimized group was whites age 65 or over (only, 4.3 per 1,000). In other words blacks in their late teens were about 31 times more likely to be victimized than whites over the age of 65.

Examine marginals   *Examination of marginals* or column and row totals is useful in obtaining a general overview of effects. Unfortunately, this table does not possess such figures and this will be illustrated with a later example. *For each independent variable, examine the overall effects.* With a total variation of 4.3 to 125.5 for crimes of violence, how do these rates vary by age and race? With only some exceptions for particular crimes, in general, the older the age cohort, the less likely the respondents indicated having been victimized. Also, blacks were more likely to be victimized by crime than whites.

Finally, those reading tables should examine each cell and look for inconsistent elements. Are there any countertrends or rates that go against the grain? In this table there did not appear to be any noteworthy anomalies.

Summary of Table 11.3

A summary of Table 11.3 would, of course, be much more brief than our detailed account. It would read that among victims of personal crimes age twelve and over in the United States in 1992:

Violent victimization ranged from a high of 125.5 per 1,000 among blacks age 16–19 to a low of 4.3 among elderly whites age 65 and over.

Although there was considerable variation within each age-race category for most crimes, there was a decrease in victimization by age.

If the race of the victim were considered, blacks were more likely to be victims of crime in almost all age cohorts for assault, rape, and robbery.

Much of the procedure for reading tables is, of course, also applicable to the reading of figures and other graphic presentations discussed earlier in this chapter. Careful reading of the title, units, source, headnotes, footnotes, and the like will assist in mastery of the data. Of course, researchers should attempt to make explicit all of these elements in tables and figures they are developing.

To illustrate the usefulness of reading marginal totals of a table, a feature that was missing in our previous example, Table 11.4 is presented. Ignoring for the time the footnote that describes statistical procedures, which will be analyzed in Chapter 12, the marginal totals are values below and to the side of the cells and serve as benchmarks with which to compare the intercellular values. For instance, the total marginals for rows (across the side) would indicate that 64 percent of all defendants were jailed. Comparing this with each category we discover that 79 percent of the "unattractive," compared with 54 percent of the "attractive," were incarcerated—a significant difference. Given knowledge of the marginals, proportion of total incarcerated gives us some basis on which to examine differences within categories of the independent variable, in this case, attractiveness or unattractiveness.

How to Construct Tables

Table 11.4 was the simplest type of table, the one-variable (univariate) table, which reports the type of data that ordinarily appear as marginal totals of more complex tables. For example, tabular presentation of the data from Stewart's study (1979) of incarceration by attractiveness of defendant would result in Table 11.5.

TABLE 11.4 Incarceration by Attractiveness (All Figures Are Percentages)[a]

| | Attractiveness | | | |
| | Below Average | Above Average | Total N | % |
Incarcerated				
Yes	79	54	45	(64)
No	20	46	25	(36)
Total N	29	41	70	(100)

[a]All figures are percentages. $\chi^2 = 4.87$, 1 *df*, $p < .05$.

Source: Adapted from John E. Stewart. "Defendant's Attractiveness as a Factor in the Outcome of Criminal Trials: An Observational Study." Paper presented at the Southeastern Psychological Association Convention, New Orleans, La., 1979. Reproduced by permission of the author.

TABLE 11.5   One-Variable Tables

	N	%
Defendant Disposition in Criminal Trials		
Incarcerated	45	64
Not incarcerated	25	36
Total	70	100
Rated Attractiveness of Defendants in Criminal Trials		
Attractive	41	59
Unattractive	29	41
Total	70	100

Source: Adapted from John E. Stewart. "Defendant's Attractiveness as a Factor in the Outcome of Criminal Trials: An Observational Study." Paper presented at the Southeastern Psychological Association Convention, New Orleans, La., 1979. Reproduced by permission of the author.

Presentation of Complex Data

One-variable tables are only the first and simplest step in reporting research findings. The next step is more analytic and attempts to discover which independent variables are most predictive of the outcome of the dependent variable(s). This may take the form of bivariate tables, to be presented in this chapter, or multivariate analysis to be discussed in Chapter 12 on statistical procedures. Because of the emergence of canned statistical programs (computer software) that perform sophisticated analysis more quickly and efficiently, some feel that tabular analysis may be outmoded, an antique. Hirschi and Selvin (1973, pp. 171–172) point out, however, that despite its obvious limitations, tabular analysis is still an excellent means of reporting the final results of a more complicated analysis in a form that is more easily understood by both professionals and the lay reader. A thorough grounding in tabular analysis also assists in better understanding the basic logic of more complex statistical procedures.

Bivariate tables   *Bivariate tables,* or those in which there is a two-variable cross tabulation, examine how one variable influences the other. To adapt an example from Cole (1972, p. 29), it would be as if we had a room full of defendants in a criminal trial and were to ask all those who are not to be incarcerated to move to the front of the room and all those who are to be incarcerated to the back. Next, we would ask all those who are not attractive (ugly) to move to the left and all those who are attractive to move to the right. The room would now look like this:

(Back)

Ugly Incarcerateds (23)   Attractive Incarcerateds (22)
Ugly Nonincarcerateds (6)   Attractive Nonincarcerateds (19)

(Front)

TABLE 11.6

| Number | Attractiveness | |
Incarcerated	Below Average	Above Average
Yes	23	22
No	6	19
Total	29	41

Statistically, this is exactly what Stewart (1979) did with his data in Table 11.5. This is presented in a two-variable table of these data in Table 11.6.

Usually, a two-variable table such as Table 11.6 is not very useful in its raw or original form. Such tables are usually percentaged and it is here that many errors in analysis as well as interpretation are made.

General Rules for Percentaging a Table

Although this presentation may be overly simplistic, there is often a virtue in simplicity that, if ignored, may lead to error. Many readers of this text may possess an intuitive logic that enables them without blundering to percentage tables correctly. If any doubt exists, utilization of the following rules may be of assistance:

Rules for percentaging a table

1. *Choose a title for the table* on the basis of knowledge of the dependent variable (denoted by Y) and independent variable(s) (denoted by X). Recall that the dependent variable is the outcome the researcher wishes to predict, whereas the independent variable(s) is the predictor. The title should read:
   (*Dependent Variable by Independent Variable(s)*
   [Y by X]. Although not pertinent to our concern with percentaging, the table should also contain as much additional information as is necessary to enable the reader to understand the source of data, units being measured, and the like.)
2. Keep in mind the need for fair comparisons if uneven-size groups are to be contrasted. The larger group is likely to exhibit the greatest amount of any condition and the smallest group the least amount, unless the comparison is made within rather than between groups.
3. Always percentage within the independent variable rather than the dependent variable. This controls for problems created by comparing unequal-size groups.
4. When doubt exists regarding the direction of proper percentaging, filling in the appropriate variables in the following question may be of assistance:

What percentage of the independent variable _____ is a category of the dependent variable _____ ? (Cole, 1972, p. 30)

Zeisel (1957) says simply to percentage in the causal and representative direction. Whether the independent or dependent variable should be listed at the top of the table or the side, and whether tables should be percentaged across or down, are questions more of style. The emerging preference is to list the independent variable on top and the dependent on the side. One then *percentages down* and *reads the table across.* The important thing to remember is to always percentage within categories of the independent variable; then, if you percentage down, read across, or, if you percentage across, read down (Babbie, 1992, p. 399). Unknowns should be eliminated from the base total in percentaging a table, and this should be stated in a footnote. It is generally good form to indicate in this same footnote the original N, prior to elimination of the unknowns. Also note if, because of rounding, percentages do not sum to 100. Figure 11.12, "How to Percentage a Table," schematically depicts one means of doing so.

How to
percentage
Prior to exploring the utility of these rules in examining and constructing tables, a very brief refresher example on percentaging may prove useful. To obtain a percentage as in "What percentage of 200 is 40?" one divides 40 by 200 and obtains 20 percent. If the question is "What is 20 percent of 200?" simply multiply 200 by .20 to get 40. Percentages are usually rounded to the nearest whole number; for example, 70.7 is rounded to 71. If the percentage is .5 always round to the nearest whole number.

Now, using this information our discussion returns to the raw data in Table 11.6. Seldom are such data presented in such a form in reports. In most cases the data would be displayed in percentage form. Table 11.7 presents the same data in the properly percentaged form. Note that the percentaging took place within each category of the independent variable, attractive/unattractive, and was intended to address the question "What percentage of the independent variable (of 41 attractive and 29 unattractive defendants) was a category of the dependent, incarcerated or not (23 of 29 = 79 percent and 22 of 41 = 54 percent)?"

In many research reports, these data are usually presented in summary form as in Table 11.8. Thus, 79 percent of unattractive defendants were incarcerated, whereas only 54 percent of the attractive ones were jailed. In reading summary tables the number in parentheses always refers to the total number of cases of the independent variable on which calculation of the percentage was based. In other words 79 percent (29) does not mean that 79 percent equal an N of 29, but that 79 percent of 29 cases, or 23 cases, were unattractive and incarcerated. The negative condition, not incarcerated, can easily be obtained by subtracting the percentage from 100 percent.

Improper Percentaging

It is not unusual to find errors in the presentation of data caused by the improper percentaging of raw information. Table 11.9, for instance, is an

Given: A bivariate table which looks at the relationship between Sex of Respondent and Crime Commission

1. Choose a Title: Dependent Variable by Independent Variable
   Y (Crime)   by X (Sex)

   Crime is the dependent variable since it is more logical to assume that a person's sex might influence crime commission rather than crime commission influencing a person's sex.

2.   Independent Variable
                            Sex (X)
                       Male   Female

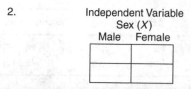

3.   Dependent
     Variable

   Crime
   Commission (Y)

4. Percentage Within or Down Independent Variable
                    Sex (X)

5. Read Across Dependent Variable

   (Y)

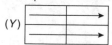

6. Answer the Question: What percentage of the independent variable (<u>in this case of males or females</u>) is a category of the dependent variable (<u>committed crime</u>)?

Figure 11.12 How to Percentage a Table.

TABLE 11.7

Percent Incarcerated	Attractive		Total N
	No	Yes	
Yes	79	54	45
No	21	46	25
Total N	29	41	70

TABLE 11.8

Attractive	Percent Incarcerated
No	79 (29)[a]
Yes	54 (41)

[a]Total number of cases is given in parentheses.

TABLE 11.9

Attractive	Percent Incarcerated
No	76 (25)[a]
Yes	49 (45)

[a]Total number of cases is given in parentheses.

TABLE 11.10 Personal Crimes of Violence, 1983: Percent Distribution of Single-Offender Victimizations by Race of Victims and Perceived Race of Offender[a]

Race of Victim[b]	Perceived Race of Offender				Total
	White	Black	Other	Unknown	
White (3,518,920)	77.8	16.4	4.0	1.9	100
Black (537,380)	11.0	87.1	0.7	1.3	100

[a]These data are abridged and constitute only a portion of a much larger table that gives breakdowns for other crimes as well.

[b]Figures are percentages and may not total 100% because of rounding.

Source: Bureau of Statistics. *Criminal Victimization in the United States, 1993.* Washington, D.C.: U.S. Department of Justice, 1984.

example of improper percentaging of the information in Table 11.6. The percentaging in Table 11.9 fails to address the correct research question. It answers the question "Does incarceration affect attractiveness?" rather than the more logical concern "Does attractiveness influence incarceration?" In short, it makes attractiveness rather than incarceration the dependent variable. Recall that the condition we are attempting to predict is always the dependent variable, whereas the independent variable is usually something like age, sex, race, or in this case appearance, which is uninfluenced, given, or precedes in time the outcome variable.

An Example of Table Percentaging

Wilbanks (1985) questioned a long-held assumption that (with the exception of robbery) violent crime is intraracial (that is, blacks victimize blacks and whites victimize whites). The National Crime Survey for 1983 (Bureau of Justice Statistics, 1984) had included only one percentaged table (Table 11.10) to analyze this assumption and basically addressed the issue to what extent black or white victims had been victimized by white or black offenders.

TABLE 11.11   Personal Crimes of Violence, 1983: (Repercentaged)

Race of Victim[b]	Perceived Race of Offender			
	White	**Black**	**Other**	**Unknown**
White	97.9	55.2	97.6	90.3
Black	2.1	44.8	2.4	9.7
	2,796,010	1,044,150	143,370	72,760

According to our rules, the NCS analyzed "offender" (dependent variable) by "victim" (independent variable), or that victimization caused the offender. Note that it percentaged across victims (incorrectly, according to our rules). This shows that violent crime is intraracial (occurs within races, because roughly 78 percent of whites were victimized by whites and approximately 87 percent of blacks were victimized by blacks). Wilbanks argued that the table should also be percentaged vertically (down) to determine "to what extent white or black offenders choose white or black victims," that is, according to our rules, "Victim by Offender," in which one percentages within offender. In response to his criticism, the NCS format was altered and another percentaged table of these same data was added to the 1983 report and all subsequent reports. Table 11.11 is an abbreviated version of this table. Thus, by percentaging these same data to answer the question to what extent do black or white offenders choose black or white victims, we find that violent crime is interracial (occurs between races)—blacks being more likely to commit violent crime against whites (roughly 55%) than against blacks (about 45%). This presentation has been oversimplified for presentation purposes, and readers are referred to Wilbanks (1985, 1986) for a more detailed explanation.

Although our detailed discussion of table reading may have struck you as unnecessarily tedious, the Wilbanks example illustrates its importance, particularly in an era in which computers can analyze and crank out data. Without a basic understanding of the logic of what we are attempting to address, we could end up with the correct data but the wrong interpretations or conclusions.

Elaboration

Elaboration   **Elaboration** refers to the process of introducing or controlling for third variables (control or test factors) by subclassifying original tables. In discussing the resolution of the causality problem in Chapter 3, we described three steps:

1. Demonstrate a relationship between the variables
2. Specify the time order (which is X [independent variable] and which is Y [dependent variable])
3. Control for or exclude rival causal factors

One way of controlling for such other factors is before-the-fact—that is, through research design. Another way is statistically through the subclassification of tables (elaboration) and through various statistical procedures such as partial correlation and multiple correlation and regression (to be discussed in Chapter 12). Elaboration enables us to introduce statistical or tabular controls after-the-fact. Here we will be discussing five basic results of elaboration, which are depicted in Figure 11.13.

Replication

Replication takes place when the partial tables replicate or reproduce the relationship in the original table. In controlling for a rival causal factor (Z), for example, the original relationship between X and Y should hold. Hypothetically, let us say that a researcher examined the relationship between sex (X) and delinquency (Y) and found a strong relationship—that is, that males are more delinquent than females. In this case controlling for social class (Z) did not alter this relationship. Tracy (1990) gives another hypothetical

Replication — The partial tables replicate (reproduce) the original table; the control variable (Z) has no effect upon original relationship between X and Y.

75	25
25	75

75	25
25	75

75	25
25	75

Specification — The partial tables do not replicate the original table or relationship, e.g., one partial table shows a stronger relationship and the other no relationship. The control variable specifies the conditions under which the relationship holds.

75	25
25	75

90	10
10	90

50	50
50	50

Explanation – Interpretation — The relationship that existed in the original table disappears (is shown to be spurious) in the partial tables. If the time order of Z is before X (antecedent), this is called explanation. If the time order of Z is after X, it is called an intervening variable and the process is called interpretation.

75	25
25	75

50	50
50	50

50	50
50	50

Suppression — Although there is little or no relationship in the original table, relationships appear in the partial tables when the control variable is introduced.

50	50
50	50

75	25
25	75

25	75
75	25

Figure 11.13 Types of Elaboration (All Figures Represent Percentages).

example: An individual's level of education might be used to predict prejudice even when controlling for age, race, or religion.

Specification

Specification specifies the conditions under which the original relationship holds. The elaboration or subclassification of tables might produce very
different partial tables—for example, one with weaker and one with stronger
relationships than in the original table. The third variable (Z), for example,
could be antecedent or intervening. Consider another hypothetical example
examining the relationship between sex (X) and delinquency (Y). Does a
positive relationship exist between these two variables? Not in a case that
controls for social class (Z). Such a case could show (specify) that although
there is a strong relationship between sex and delinquency among the lower-
class adolescents, there is no such relationship among middle- and upper-
class groups.

Explanation

Explanation occurs when the relationship observed in the original bivariate table weakens or disappears in the partial tables. If this third variable (Z)
is antecedent and logically precedes the independent variable (X), then this
is called *explanation*. If it logically occurs as an intervening variable, then it

Interpretation

is an example of **interpretation.** Thus, although in *interpretation* the partial
table relationships also weaken or disappear, the control variable is an intervening one or occurs between X and Y.

As an example of explanation, consider the case of a researcher who
claimed to have made the astounding discovery that there is a positive relationship between foot size (X) and intelligence (Y). But it turns out that
upon controlling for a third "antecedent" variable—age (Z)—the original
relationship disappears. That is, the third variable is the critical factor:
Adults are bigger than children and are smarter. Controlling for age—that is,
among adults or among children—causes the relationship to disappear.

Interpretation can be illustrated by the following hypothetical example. A
researcher suspects that a hypothetically strong relationship exists between
broken homes (X) and delinquency (Y). In controlling for social class (Z),
however, he or she finds that the relationship disappears—that is, among
both lower-class and upper-class individuals, there are no differences by
family type in delinquency. Lower-class groups do tend to have higher
delinquency rates overall, but this rate does not vary by family type.

Suppression

Suppression takes place when relationships occur in the partial tables
even though there is no original bivariate relationship. Suppose the original
table shows no relationship between broken homes (X) and delinquency
(Y); however, when we control for social class (Z), lowerclass broken homes
are found to produce higher delinquency rates than non-lower-class broken
homes.

The elaboration model could be used to control for rival causal factors by
dividing our original bivariate table into subtables based upon control variables, but doing this could be an interminable process. This task is aided by
computer software that can perform crosstabs (crossbreaks) very quickly.
Although much multivariate analysis relies upon more sophisticated statistical procedures, the elaboration model gives one a thorough grounding in

what Rosenberg called *The Logic of Survey Analysis* (1968), and such tabular analysis is also far more readily understandable to the lay reader of quantitative reports. Readers are referred to Lazarsfeld, Pasanella, and Rosenberg (1972), Rosenberg (1968), Hirschi and Selvin (1973), and Zeisel (1957) for more details regarding elaboration.

Lying with Statistics

Lying with statistics

Huff (1954) describes *How to Lie with Statistics* and particularly illustrates the misuse of graphic displays that exaggerate or underplay statistical findings by drawing figures out of scale or using calibrations of the horizontal or vertical axes that are misleading. He advises readers on "how to talk back to statistics" and, by addressing the following issues, to avoid "learning a remarkable lot that isn't so" (Huff, 1954, pp. 122–142):

Who Says So?

Look for bias such as "the laboratory with something to prove for the sake of a theory, a reputation, or a fee; the newspaper whose aim is a good story; labor or management with a wage level at stake."

How Does He or She Know?

Is the sample large enough to permit any reliable conclusion? You won't always be told how many cases. If percentages are given, make sure the raw figures are also present.

Did Somebody Change the Subject?

It is all reminiscent of the way that Lincoln Steffens and Jacob A. Riis (in the early 1900s), as New York newspapermen, once created a crime wave. Crime cases in the papers reached such proportions, both in numbers and in space and big type given to them, that the public demanded action. Theodore Roosevelt, as president of the reform Police Board, was seriously embarrassed. He put an end to the crime wave by simply asking Steffens and Riis to lay off. It had all come about simply because the reporters, led by those two, had got into competition as to who could dig up the most burglaries and whatnot. The official police record showed no increase at all (Huff, 1954, p. 131).

Is It a Real Conclusion?

Beware of a switch somewhere between the raw figures and the conclusion, in which one thing is reported as another. For example, more reported cases is not the same thing as actual cases, just as a voter's poll is not the same thing as voter turnout.

Does It Make Sense?

Many statistics defy our best judgment, but manage to get by "only because the magic of numbers brings about a suspension of common sense." Beware of impressively precise figures: $40.13 sounds more precise than "about $40." Beware of long-term trend predictions, as seldom are "all other things equal" (that is, other variables that are not taken into account).

Summary

In this chapter we have attempted to explore some of the major decisions and approaches involved in the initial analysis of data. Many important decisions related to this stage are made prior to the collection of data. A *variables list* keyed to questionnaire items is quite useful in ensuring that the instrument covers the elements that the researcher wishes to investigate. *Coding* is the assignment of numerical values to questionnaire items. A code is developed for each question and entered in a *codebook.* Each question is coded in the appropriate cell on a codesheet. The *codesheet* information is keyboard entered into a computer, with each cell corresponding to a column on the card. These data are then edited, and analysis begins.

Simple data presentation begins with the reporting of one-variable frequencies, tallies, or marginals. Various summarizing devices are available for reporting this information in an attractive and succinct format. These include the calculation of rates, ratios, proportions, and percentages, as well as the use of frequency distributions, graphic displays, and tables. Calculation of statistics, such as crime rates, is a useful way of standardizing information to fairly compare unequal-size groups. Frequency distributions serve to order, group, and percentage data into tables that are easier to read and understand. *Graphic or pictorial presentations include* pie charts, bar graphs, and frequency polygons. Often, readers who are bored by frequency distributions and tables are attracted by the pictorial appeal of graphic displays. Among other types of graphics, *crime clocks* were described as a misleading manner of comparing changes in crime over time, because they fail to control for population growth, while using time as the constant base for comparison. The same care must be taken in constructing graphs that is taken in preparing tables: categories must be similar in size and mutually exclusive, and appropriate labels must be supplied to make the figure self-explanatory. Another form of data presentation is the bivariate or multivariate table. Guidelines on both the reading and the construction of tables were given. Following carefully the presentation on things to look for in tables will help individuals in constructing their own tables. Note some *general rules for percentaging a table:*

1. Give the table a proper title, generally "dependent by independent variable(s)."
2. Keep in mind fair comparisons.
3. Always percentage within categories of the independent variable.
4. When in doubt, ask "What percentage of the independent variable is a category of the dependent variable?"

Three-variable tables involve the introduction of a third (control) variable to assess its impact (elaborate) on the original relationship. Such statistical controls instituted after the fact, through the subclassification of tables, constitute an alternative to precontrols developed during research design.

Elaboration refers to the process of introducing or controlling for third variables by subclassifying tables (creating partial tables). The *major types of elaboration are: replication, specification, explanation, interpretation, and suppression.* In *replication* the partial tables replicate (reproduce) the original table, for example, the relationship holds when controlling for a third variable. In *specification* the relationship is specified and may or may not remain when the original table is subclassified. One partial table may show a stronger or weaker relationship than the original table. Suppose the original relationship disappears (was spurious). This is called *explanation;* if Z (the control variable) occurs before X; if after X, it is called an intervening variable and *interpretation. Suppression* occurs when little or no relationship in the original table produces a relationship in the partial tables.

Key Concepts

A Variables List	Percentages	General Rules in
"Other" Sheets	Ratios	Percentaging a Table
Coding	Frequency Distribution	Elaboration
Codebook	Graphic Presentations	Replication
Codesheet	Pie Charts	Specification
Coder Monitoring	Bar Graphs	Explanation
Keyboard Entry	Frequency Polygons	Interpretation
Marginals Run	Crime Clocks	Suppression
Crime Rate	Steps in Reading	Lying with Statistics
Proportions	a Table	

Review Questions

1. Describe the "steps in the data management process." How does each step build on the others in producing valid data for analysis?
2. Graphic displays have sometimes been employed to "lie with statistics." How is this done, and how might readers avoid being mislead by such displays?
3. What are some useful hints in reading a table? Although it is certainly not exciting, why is table reading an important subject? How was this illustrated by Wilbanks' examination of interracial crime in the NCS?
4. What does the process of elaboration involve? How does such a process enable one to take account (or control for) rival causal factors?

12 | Data Analysis: A User's Guide to Statistics

Mention the word *statistics* and many people, particularly those in non-mathematical fields such as criminal justice and other social sciences, "turn off." These same individuals, however, may have at one point in their lives been able to rattle off batting averages, league standings, engine r.p.m.'s, or other such statistics that they found important. Statistics for most nonstatisticians are not interesting in themselves, but become so when they are relevant to an issue of substantive concern.

The purpose of this chapter is to provide a succinct computational and interpretive orientation to the typical statistics a criminal justice professional may expect to find in the literature in their field. This presentation will provide the reader with an overview of the various methods and also a reference to the most commonly used statistical devices. Statistics are essentially tools or summarizing devices. One need not have extensive statistical training to acquire a basic knowledge of how to interpret reported statistical findings. Although this chapter consists primarily of illustrations, computational examples, and "how to" interpretation suggestions for the most commonly used statistics, it should not be used as a crutch, and is not intended as a substitute for solid statistics courses for the more serious student. Even for the serious student, however, it serves as a handy refresher or quick reference guide to other sources of "need-to-know" information.

Why Study Statistics?

Although many people view studies that use many esoteric statistical techniques as an attempt by the writers to intimidate, impress, or intellectually bully readers, there are many very good reasons for becoming familiar with statistics. It is almost impossible to read most published literature in criminal justice and the social sciences without some familiarity with statistics. Most research published today is quantitative in nature and such data require statistical analysis. Electronic calculators and minicomputers are the toys of the next generation, making access to statistical thinking more widespread in developed societies. Furthermore, a survey of 172 criminal justice programs in the United States by Robertson and Fields (1986) indicated that the majority of four-year undergraduate programs required a statistics course.

Statistics summarize data. Once a few symbols are mastered, a mountain of data can be succinctly presented, as well as read and understood. Statistics enable us to discover patterns in data, to design useful research, to simply describe large amounts of information, and to infer to larger populations. The study of statistics provides us with a standard universal language with which to communicate research findings. Statistics should not be used to impress, confuse, or sanctify hollow data. Statesman Benjamin Disraeli is reported to have cynically remarked that there are "lies, damn lies and statistics." And although statistics are neutral, they can be misused—to "lie with statistics" (Huff, 1966); however, individuals who have a basic familiarity with statistics are in a much better position to avoid being duped. Even though "figures don't lie, liars can figure."

Readers of research reports or journal articles are very likely to run across information similar to the following:

$$\chi^2 = 4.67, 1 \ df, \ p < .05$$
$$r = .71, \ p < .01$$

$$\text{Gamma} = .32, \text{n.s.}$$
$$\overline{X} = 3.6 \; \sigma = 1.2$$
$$z = 3.01, \, p < .01$$

Many readers skip such statistical accounts and rely on the author(s) to describe what these things mean. If one cannot speak the language, one is obviously at the mercy of the judgment, honesty, and analytic skill of others.

If you recall, in the first chapter of this book we asked the question "Sprechen Sie Researchese?" ("Do you speak the language of research?"). Although one's response to some of the above figures might be "It's Greek to me!" (which in fact it is, as some of the mathematical symbols used in statistics are Greek letters), without a simple understanding of statistics the researcher is at a critical disadvantage when exposed to these simple research findings. The simple object of this chapter is to enable the reader to be able to interpret and have some idea regarding the meaning of these statistics. For a more thorough understanding of these and other statistics, the reader will be continuously referred to more detailed presentations in standard statistics textbooks.

Types of Statistics

Descriptive
statistics

Generally, statistics can be classified into two types: descriptive statistics and inferential statistics. **Descriptive statistics** are intended to summarize or describe data or show relationships between variables. Correlational measures actually do more than describe data, but are included under descriptive statistics for simplicity of presentation. We begin by discussing the simplest descriptive statistics—measures of central tendency and dispersion.

Inferential
statistics

Inferential statistics enable generalization or inference of sample findings to larger populations, or assessment of the probability of certain findings. We briefly discuss some of the more common inferential statistics such as chi-square, *t, z,* and *F* tests. Rather than burden you with too much information all at once, we further discuss the nature and types of statistics later in the chapter. First, let us become acquainted with a few statistics.

Measures of Central Tendency for a Simple Distribution

Measures of
central
tendency

Measures of central tendency are summary statistics that describe the "typical," "middle," or "average" of a distribution of scores. The three most commonly used **measures of central tendency** are:

Mean
Median
Mode

Mode

Mode

The **mode** is the simplest measure of central tendency and is simply the most frequently occurring score. Although the mode can be used with any of the levels of data discussed earlier (nominal, ordinal, interval, or ratio), it is the only one that is appropriate for nominal level data.

In most instances with a simple distribution the mode can be obtained simply by looking at the data for the following distribution:

$$1 \quad 3 \quad 4 \quad 5 \quad 3 \quad 4 \quad 4 \quad 2 \quad 6$$

Without even ordering or grouping the data it is simple to obtain the mode of 4. What about the following distribution?

$$1 \quad 3 \quad 4 \quad 5 \quad 3 \quad 1 \quad 4 \quad 5 \quad 4 \quad 2 \quad 2 \quad 3$$

We now have what is called a bimodal distribution, or a distribution with two modes, scores 3 and 4. When plotted, a bimodal distribution of scores would show two peaks rather than just one. Those familiar with criminological theory will recall Reckless' (1967) theory regarding the bimodal distribution of crime commission in the United States wherein crime is highest among the lower and upper classes.

Median

Median

The **median** (or midpoint) is a measure of central tendency that is applicable to ordinal (ranked) data. It is the score that divides the distribution in half, so that 50 percent of the scores are above the median, and 50 percent below. The median is calculated as follows:

1. Arrange all scores into an ordered array, that is, from highest to lowest or vice versa.
2. Calculate the median position by means of the formula

$$\text{position of median} = (N + 1)/2$$

where N equals the number of cases.
3. Now locate the median by counting up or down the distribution until the score that is in the median position is located.

Calculate the median for the following scores.

$$1 \quad 3 \quad 4 \quad 5 \quad 7 \quad 9 \quad 10$$

The median position is obtained $(7 + 1) \div 2$, or the case in the fourth position or the score 5. Again calculate the median for the following scores:

$$6 \quad 1 \quad 2 \quad 9 \quad 7 \quad 8 \quad 3 \quad 4$$

The data must first be reordered in an array: 1, 2, 3, 4, 6, 7, 8, 9. Calculating the median position, $8 + 1 \div 2 = 4.5$th position, or the score midway between 4 and 6, or the median = 5.

Mean

Mean   The **mean** (average) is the most familiar measure of central tendency and simply involves dividing the total score by the total N (or number of cases). It is most appropriate for interval or ratio level data. For simple distributions it is calculated by means of the formula

$$\overline{X} = \Sigma X/N$$

where

$\overline{X}$ = mean
Σ = sum of (letter is capital sigma)
X = raw scores
N = total number of cases

Using data from our last example in discussing the median (6, 1, 2, 9, 7, 8, 3, 4),

$$\overline{X} = 40/8 = 5$$

The mean, expressed as $\overline{X}$ (pronounced "X bar") is simply the sum of the scores divided by the number of scores. A variation of this formula for data that have been put into a simple frequency distribution is $\overline{X} = \Sigma fX/N$ where f equals the frequency of a score, for example:

Score	Frequency	fX
1	2	2
2	1	2
3	3	9
4	2	8
	$N = 8$	$\Sigma fX = 21$

$$\overline{X} = \Sigma fX/N = 21/8 = 2.6$$

These measures of central tendency were calculated for a simple distribution as in Example A on page 344. If, however, the data are grouped, as in Example B, different calculations must be performed. Calculations and explanations of the measures of central tendency for grouped frequency distributions are presented in Appendix D.

Example A	Example B	
Simple Distribution	Grouped Frequency Distribution	
Score	Score	*f*
2	76–100	4
2	51–75	8
5	26–50	16
6	1–25	10
10		

If you can answer the following questions correctly, you have enough of an understanding of what we have covered to proceed.

POP QUIZ 12.1[1]

For example A, calculate the following:
1. Mode = ____
2. Median = ____
3. $\overline{X}$ = ____

Measures of Dispersion

In addition to measuring the central tendency of a distribution, it is also standard to report the dispersion variability, or spread of a distribution. The simple reporting of the average score does not tell us whether this average was representative of the particular scores. Figure 12.1 illustrates three different curved frequency distributions, all of which have the same average. Note that for each group the average score was the same; however, the distribution of scores was not. In Example A we have a bimodal distribution of scores with most of the cases scoring around 50 and 90. In Example B, we have very little spread, with all of the cases scoring between 50 and 90. In the last example we have great variability, with the mean, median, and mode at 70, but the scores ranging from 0 to 100. Although there are three major measures of dispersion—range, average deviation, and standard deviation—we concentrate on the range and standard deviation because these are the most useful and the most commonly used.

Range

Range   The **range** is the simplest measure of dispersion and represents either the highest and lowest scores or the distance between the highest and lowest scores in a distribution. The range is calculated by subtracting the true upper limits of a distribution from the true lower limits. For example, to find the range of scores in the interval 1–10, we calculate

[1]Answers to Pop Quizzes are given in Appendix E.

Example A:

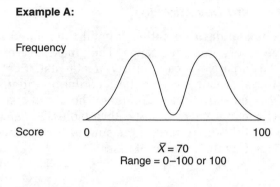

Frequency

Score   0   100

$\bar{X} = 70$
Range = 0–100 or 100

Example B:

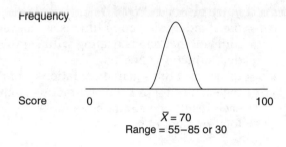

Frequency

Score   0   100

$\bar{X} = 70$
Range = 55–85 or 30

Example C:

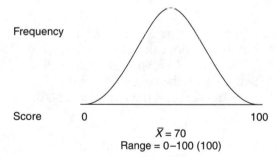

Frequency

Score   0   100

$\bar{X} = 70$
Range = 0–100 (100)

Figure 12.1 Hypothetical Scores on Police Promotion Tests.

range = true upper limit−true lower limit
range = 10.5 − 0.5 = 10

Had we, as some suggest, merely subtracted the highest from the lowest score 10–1, we would have identified only 9 units from 1 to 10, whereas there really are 10 (1, 2, 3, 4, 5, 6, 7, 8, 9, 10).

The range is not a very useful calculation because it is based on extreme scores. It ignores other information regarding distribution. A far more useful statistic is the standard deviation.

Standard Deviation (σ)

The **standard deviation** (σ) and the related statistic variance (σ²) are far more useful than the range. They make use of information regarding each score and are of greater utility in later statistical analysis. In fact, knowledge of these measures is essential in order to understand the basis of many more advanced statistical techniques. The use of standard deviation assumes that we have internal or ratio-level variables. To calculate the standard deviation, obtain the square root of the sum of the squared deviations from the mean divided by the number of cases:

$$\sigma = \sqrt{\Sigma x^2 / N}$$

where

σ = the standard deviation (this is sometimes represented as small s to indicate that one is dealing with sample data). If calculating s, the denominator is $N - 1$.

Σx^2 = the sum of the squared deviations from the mean obtained by taking each score (X) and subtracting from ($\overline{X}$) score and squaring each result and summing them

N = total number of cases

The basic steps in calculating the standard deviation for a simple distribution are

1. Calculate the mean, $\overline{X} = \Sigma X/N$.
2. For each score calculate the deviation score (x), where $x = X - \overline{X}$; that is, the mean is subtracted from each raw score.
3. Square each deviation score (x^2).
4. Sum the squared deviation scores, divide by N, and obtain the square root.

It is much easier using a calculator to employ the raw score formula for obtaining the standard deviation:

$$\sigma = \sqrt{(\Sigma X^2 / N) - \overline{X}^2}$$

For our data in Tables 12.1A and 12.1B

$$\sigma = \sqrt{(160/7) - (5.4)^2}$$
$$= \sqrt{37.54 - 29.16}$$
$$= \sqrt{7.979}$$
$$= 2.8$$

TABLE 12.1A   Standard Deviation Using the Deviation Score Formula for a Simple Distribution

X	x	x^2
9	+3.6	12.96
8	+2.6	6.76
7	+1.6	2.56
6	+ .6	.36
5	− .4	.16
2	−3.4	11.56
1	−4.4	19.36
$\Sigma X = 38$		$\Sigma x^2 = 53.72$
$N = 7$		
$X = 5.4$		

$$\sigma = \sqrt{53.72/7} = \sqrt{7.7} = 2.8$$

TABLE 12.1B   Calculation of Standard Deviation Using the Raw Score Formula for a Simple Distribution

X	X^2
9	81
8	64
7	49
6	36
5	25
2	4
1	1
$N = 7$	$\Sigma X^2 = 260$

In addition to the formulas that we have presented, there are others that are appropriate for group frequency distributions. Space, however, does not permit detailed coverage of each of these, and the reader can find further treatment of standard deviation for a grouped frequency distribution in Appendix D.

Interpreting Standard Deviation. The standard deviation has a great many uses beyond simply measuring dispersion of scores about the mean. The standard deviation squared is a measure of variance, a statistic whose importance will become apparent particularly in our later discussion of analysis of variance. To explain the meaning and interpretation of a standard deviation score, it is necessary to introduce a basic notion in statistics, the **Normal distribution** **normal distribution.** According to Gauss' law, most scores bunch around the mean; the remainder decline gradually as they reach the extremes of the distribution. If these scores are plotted, they form a bell-shaped curve—the normal distribution. Scientists have discovered that, when plotted, a variety of naturally occurring phenomena, such as height, IQ, and standardized test scores, fall into this distribution. Figure 12.2 illustrates standard deviation units and the areas of the normal curve each covers.

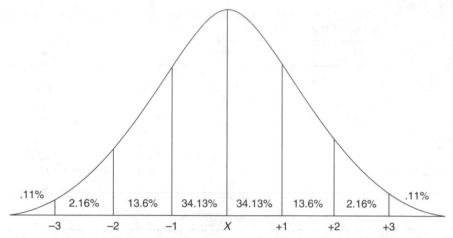

Figure 12.2 Standard Deviation Units and Areas of the Normal Curve.

One standard deviation unit, plus and minus, covers approximately 68 percent of the area of the normal curve. If the mean score on a test were 75 and the standard deviation were 5, then we would know that roughly 68 percent of those taking the test scored between 70 and 80. About 95 percent of a distribution is covered by plus and minus two standard deviation units or, in our example, around 95 percent of the cases would have scored between 65 and 85. Finally, nearly all cases (99.78 percent) would fall within plus and minus three standard deviation units or, in our example, scores of 60 to 90.

Suppose we knew that an individual scored 80 on this exam. What percentage of cases did this individual beat? This can be computed quite easily by examining Figure 12.2. As half of the distribution is below the mean of 75, we already know that half of the distribution lies below this score, plus an additional 34 percent. Thus, roughly 84 percent of the scores fell below 80.

Many readers may regard the standard deviation as an illustration of statistical legerdemain, wondering why, for instance, one standard deviation unit (plus and minus) always covers 68 percent of the area[2] or why scores distribute as a normal curve. It is best simply accepted on faith similar to π (pi) in geometry which always equals 3.1416. Many of us accept the operations of the internal combustion engine without any idea of how it works.

POP QUIZ 12.2

1. If $\overline{X}$ = 75 and σ = 5 for an examination, 68 percent of the students scored between _____ and _____.
2. If $\overline{X}$ = 72 and σ = 6, then 68 percent of the students scored between _____ and _____.
3. Using either the raw score or deviation score formula, calculate the $\overline{X}$, median, mode, and σ:

[2]Mathematically, it is the point where the slope of the curve changes from convex to concave, or where it changes its sign.

$$X$$
$$1$$
$$1 \qquad \overline{X} = \text{\_\_\_\_}$$
$$3 \qquad \text{Median} = \text{\_\_\_\_}$$
$$5 \qquad \text{Mode} = \text{\_\_\_\_}$$
$$\underline{5} \qquad \sigma = \text{\_\_\_\_}$$

Standard Deviation Units (*Z* Scores)

Returning to our test example, it is possible, given knowledge of the mean, the standard deviation, and the areas of the normal curve, to calculate the position of any score in a series of scores provided they are normally distributed. **Standard deviation units, or *Z* scores, measure the deviation** from the mean relative to the standard deviation. Each score is converted into a *Z* score, or standard deviation unit. In other words, the *Z* score measures the distance of a raw score from the mean and expresses this in standard deviation units. The formula for obtaining a *Z* score is

$$Z = x/\sigma$$

where $x = X - \overline{X}$ or the score minus the mean of the distribution. In Figure 11.2, it was pointed out that one standard deviation, plus and minus, covers roughly 68 percent of the curve. Similarly, one *Z* score, plus and minus, covers 68 percent. A *Z* score of ± 1.96 covers about 95 percent of the curve, whereas a *Z* of ± 2.58 covers 99 percent.

Using a table of *Z* values from Appendix F and our previous example of tests with a mean of 75 and standard deviation of 5, let us calculate the *Z* scores for each and obtain the percentile (proportion) of the distribution a given score is higher than:

Score	*Z Score*	*Percentile*
80	+1.0	84.13
75	0.0	50.00
70	−1.0	15.87
87	+2.4	99.18

Assume, for example, that you received an 80 percent on an examination where the class average was 75 and the standard deviation was 5. Your *Z* score would equal $X(80) - \overline{X}(75) \div \sigma(5) = + 1.0Z$. Appendix F reports that the area between $\overline{X}$ and a *Z* of 1.0 is .3413, or roughly 34 percent of the area above the mean. Because 50 percent of the normal curve is below the mean of 75, your percentile score would be approximately 50 percent + 34 percent = 84 percent. Only 16 percent performed better than you on the test. Similarly, a score of 75 yields a *Z* score of 0 (exactly at the mean), which beats 50 percent of the scores below the mean. Note that Appendix F reports proportions for only half of the curve (a Z score of 4.0 covering nearly .50 or 50 percent). Calculation of percentile calls for some logic on the student's part. One must picture a normal curve as in Figure 11.2 and, if the Z score is positive, the area proportion is added to .50 (the other part of the curve) and, if Z is negative, the area proportion is subtracted from .50.

Illustrating the procedure by means of our last score of 87,

$$Z = (87 - 75)/5 = 12/5 = 2.4$$

Using the standard Z table in Appendix F we find that a Z score of +2.4 covers 49.18 percent of the positive half of the curve, as well as automatically 50 percent of the negative portion of the curve, or 99.18 percent. In addition to being useful for calculating percentile areas, Z scores are also very important in assessing probability levels as we will see later in this discussion.

So far, we have examined only descriptive statistics, those that simply summarize or describe information. We will now look at an inferential statistic, which attempts to generalize or infer to a larger population, or to assess whether the findings are due to chance or sampling error.

POP QUIZ 12.3

Given $\overline{X} = 10$ and $\sigma = 3$, calculate Z scores for the following scores and identify the percentile such a score occupies on a normal curve:

	X score	*Z score*	*Percentile*
1.	13	____	____
2.	7	____	____
3.	8	____	____
4.	12	____	____

Chi-Square (χ^2)

Chi-square   **Chi-square** (symbolized by the Greek letter chi, squared, χ^2) is a test of the independence of the relationship between nominal or categorical variables. It asks whether the two variables are independent, exhibit no relationship or an association due to chance, or are dependent where the relationship is real and would seldom occur due to chance alone. Table 12.2 illustrates the notion of independence/dependence.

Inspection of Table 12.2(*a*) shows that there is no relationship between sex and fear of crime; that is, 30 percent of both sexes are afraid. Fear of crime can be said to be independent of the sex of the individual. In Table 12.2(*b*), however, there appears to be some relationship between fear of crime and sex because 40 percent of the males and only 10 percent of the females are afraid of crime. Chi-square does not measure the degree of association, although we will discuss measurements based upon chi-square later; it measures the significance of a relationship if one exists.

TABLE 12.2 Fear of Crime by Sex

	Afraid	Male	Female	
(a)	Yes	30	30	60
	No	70	70	140
		100	100	200
(b)	Yes	40	10	50
	No	60	90	150
		100	100	200

TABLE 12.3 Fear of Crime by Sex (Hypothetical)

Afraid	Male	Female	
Yes	40(25)[a]	10(25)	50
No	60(75)	90(75)	150
	100	100	200

[a]Values in parentheses are expected values.

Calculation of Chi-Square

Basically, the chi-square statistic compares observed cell frequencies with expected cell frequencies (or values that could be expected by chance, given table marginals); then, use of the chi-square formula assesses the probability of obtaining such a value by chance using a table of expected chi-square values from any statistical textbook. A formula for calculating chi-square is

$$\chi^2 = \Sigma[(f_0 - f_e)^2/f_e]$$

where

f_0 = frequency observed (the actual cell values)
f_e = frequency expected (values that would be expected by chance based on cell values)
Σ = "the sum of" (in this case for each cell value)

Utilizing the data in Table 12.2(*b*), the following procedure will result in the calculations presented in Table 12.3. Follow these steps to calculate chi-square:

1. Cross-tabulate the data into a table with observed cells and marginals.
2. To obtain the f_e (expected frequencies) for each cell use the formula

$$f_e = \frac{\text{(row total)(column total)}}{\text{total } N}$$

For example, for the *top left cell* of Table 11.2(*b*)

$$f_e = \frac{(50)(100)}{200} = 25$$

For the *bottom right cell*

$$f_e = \frac{(150)(100)}{200} = 75$$

3. Now, applying the formula for each cell, calculate the chi-square statistic.

$$\chi^2 = \frac{(40-25)^2}{25} + \frac{(10-25)^2}{25} + \frac{(60-75)^2}{75} + \frac{(90-75)^2}{75}$$

$$= \frac{225}{25} + \frac{225}{25} + \frac{225}{75} + \frac{225}{75}$$

$$= 24$$

4. Assess the significance of chi-square by consulting Appendix G, a table of expected chi-square values. The calculated value must be the same as or larger than the table value to be significant at a particular chosen level. This notion of "statistical significance" is described in detail in the next section.

5. Calculate the appropriate degrees of freedom (*df*)

$$df = (R - 1)(C - 1)$$

where

$$R = \text{rows}$$
$$C = \text{columns}$$

Degrees of freedom

Degrees of freedom refer to the number of cells that are free to vary; that is, once the value of certain cells are fixed, the others are no longer free to vary. In our example, if one cell was set at 20, the other cell values are determined by subtracting from the marginals.

In our example, the degrees of freedom equal (2 − 1)(2 − 1) or 1. For a 3 × 2 table, *df* = 2, and for a 3 × 3 table, *df* = 4, and so forth. For our example, chi-square = 24, 1 *df*, and is greater than the expected table value (statistically significant) at both the .05 level (3.8) and the .01 level (6.6). The latter means that only one time in 100 could such a relationship between sex and fear of crime be caused by sampling error (chance variation). Had this example been reported in a journal article, the author would have written: $\chi^2 = 24$, 1 *df*, *p* < .01; that is, a chi-square of 24, with one degree of freedom, is "statistically significant" at the .01 level of probability. Only one time in 100 could such a result have been obtained solely because of sampling error. Had the calculated value not exceeded the expected value, it would have been described as "n.s." (not significant at the .05 level).

Cautions

Chi-square can accommodate any number of cells, although with a large number of cells the likelihood increases that there may be few values in some cells, a situation that distorts the chi-square statistic. In such cases it is recommended that the number of cells be collapsed or combined. Chi-square is also unstable in the 2×2 case and especially if any of the expected cell frequencies are less than 10. In such circumstances one should employ the Yates correction in which .5 is deducted from the observed-minus-expected frequencies in each cell. Space does not permit an explanation, but readers should be alert to this limitation and consult more detailed coverage in any standard statistics test when its use appears warranted. Similarly, if any of the expected cell frequencies are less than 5, readers should apply Fisher's exact test (Siegel, 1956).

POP QUIZ 12.4

1. What do the following mean?
   a. $\chi^2 = 1.6$, 1 *df*, n.s.
   b. $\chi^2 = 6.4$, 2 *df*, $p < .05$
2. What are the appropriate degrees of freedom for the following size tables?
   a. 2×2
   b. 4×3
   c. 5×4
3. Do the following chi-square values exceed or not exceed the expected table values at the .05 probability level?
   a. $\chi^2 = 4.8$, 1 *df* _____
   b. $\chi^2 = 4.2$, 2 *df* _____
   c. $\chi^2 = 2.6$, 1 *df* _____

Chi-Square-Based Measures of Association

The concept of relationship (or association) of variables is explored in detail later in the chapter. At this point it is sufficient to know that, if variables are related, it means that they vary together (as one increases, so does the other). This may be a positive relationship where as one increases in value, so does the other; for example, years of education and lifetime income are positively related. There may be no relationship between variables, such as height and musical ability, or there may be a negative (inverse) relationship, where as one variable increases in value (e.g., education) the other decreases in value (e.g., prejudice).

As indicated previously, chi-square is not a measure of relationship. There are, however, a number of nominal measures of association based on the chi-square statistic. Despite certain limitations with respect to interpretation, they are appealing in that, once the chi-square statistic is obtained, only relatively simple modification of this statistic is required to calculate chi-square-based measures of association.

Phi Coefficient (φ) and Phi-Square (φ²)

Phi coefficient

For 2 × 2 tables, the **phi coefficient** or **phi-square** can be utilized. They are calculated in the following manner:

$$\phi = \sqrt{\chi^2 / N}$$
$$\phi^2 = \chi^2 / N$$

Using the chi-square value from our previous example of fear of crime by sex, phi-square can be calculated:

$$\phi^2 = 24/200 = .12$$
$$\phi = \sqrt{24/200} = \sqrt{.12} = .34$$

The phi coefficient takes on values between zero (no relationship) and one (perfect relationship), although positive or negative signs are meaningless. Its chief limitation is that it cannot be applied to tables larger than 2 × 2. A phi coefficient of .34 indicates only a very negligible relationship.

Phi-square
PRE

Phi-square is a very useful statistic in that it contains a highly preferred feature. It is a *PRE (proportional reduction in error)* measure that has a direct operational interpretation; given knowledge of one variable, for example sex, we can reduce the error in predicting or explaining a given proportion of the other variable, fear of crime. In our example, only about 12 percent of the variance in fear of crime is explained by a respondent's sex.

Contingency Coefficient (C)

Contingency
coefficient

The **contingency coefficient** (*C*) is calculated in the following manner:

$$C = \sqrt{\chi^2 / (N + \chi^2)}$$

This is a less useful chi-square-based measure of association in that a *C* of zero is interpreted as no relationship, but the upper limit is less than 1.00 and its value depends on the number of rows or columns.

Cramer's V

Cramer's V   **Cramer's V** is useful for contingency tables that are larger than 2×2. The formula for calculating V is

$$V = \sqrt{\chi^2 / [N(K-1)]}$$

where K is the smaller of either rows or columns. V is more useful than C in that its upper value is not determined by the size of the table. It varies between 0 and 1.0, from no relationship to perfect relationship.

POP QUIZ 12.5

1. $\chi^2 = 5.0$ and $N = 10$, calculate phi square (ϕ^2): _____
2. What does this value indicate?

Nature and Types of Statistics

Rather than expose you to too many statistical distinctions at the beginning of the chapter, you have been shown a few statistics (measures of central tendency, dispersion, chi-square, and chi-square-based measures) to "get your feet wet." Hopefully, you have gained a little confidence as well. Before we continue, some important further distinctions regarding statistics must be made.

Nonparametric Statistics

We have already discussed the difference between *descriptive statistics* (which summarize data or describe relationships) and *inferential statistics* (which generalize data to larger populations). Another important distinction

Parametric statistics   that can be made between types of statistics is that between **parametric** and **nonparametric statistics.** Generally, parametric statistics assume some interval level measurement and that the sample was representatively drawn from

Nonparametric statistics   a normal or bell-shaped population distribution. *Nonparametric measures* (see Siegel, 1956) are appropriate for ordinal and nominal data and are often referred to as "distribution-free statistics"; that is, statistics in which few assumptions need to be made regarding the normality of the distribution. In this chapter we assume the prevailing conservative view of basic assumptions that are necessary to use various statistical tests. Many of these statistics are, however, quite robust (versatile). Binder (1984) maintains that in a majority of cases in the social sciences, and particularly in criminal justice

TABLE 12.4 Types of Statistics

	Descriptive	Inferential
Parametric	Correlation coefficient X σ	ANOVA (F) t Z
Nonparametric	Median Mode Phi C V Gamma r_a	Chi-square

^aThis is an abbreviated table classifying statistics by function. For a more detailed classification, including level of measurement, see any standard statistics text.

and criminology, researchers may use statistics without so rigorous a concern or anxiety regarding assumptions about scale (nominal, ordinal, interval, etc.) properties. Table 12.4 depicts various statistics we have discussed or will discuss in terms of these qualities.

Thus, gamma and Spearman's rho (r_S), which, as we will see, are appropriate for ordinal data, are nonparametric alternatives to Pearson's *r*, and chi-square is used for nominal data instead of *Z*, *t*, or *F* tests, which require higher level assumptions regarding the nature of the data.

Null Hypothesis

In conducting inferential studies, or studies in which the objective is generalization to larger populations, researchers generally employ

The null hypothesis
The research hypothesis

Null hypothesis

Research hypothesis

The **null hypothesis,** symbolized by H_0, generally states that there is no difference between the groups being compared, or that there is no relationship in the general population, or that any observed differences are due to random error. The *research hypothesis* is the relationship or finding that the researcher is attempting to demonstrate, for example, that some independent variable or treatment had an impact on the dependent variable. In our earlier example, the null hypothesis would state that there are no differences between the sexes with respect to crime. The alternative or research hypothesis could be nondirective (there are differences between the sexes) or directive (males are more afraid). Researchers approach this issue in what might appear as a roundabout manner. Generally, one tests the null hypothesis and either rejects or fails to reject it. If the null hypothesis is rejected, one can then assume that the research hypothesis is probably correct.

Tests of Significance

Tests of
significance

Similar to the procedure we followed in assessing the significance of a calculated chi-square, investigators utilize **tests of significance** to assess whether the differences observed could be due to chance (sampling error), or that it is highly improbable that they have been due to sampling error and thus are considered statistically significant at a given probability level. Suppose, as in our previous chi-square analysis of fear of crime by sex, that there are actually no differences in the population. Using even random sampling methods it is possible by chance to obtain an unusual number of fearful males and fearless females such that the samples (due to atypical samples or sampling error) show a relationship that does not in fact exist in the population. Rather than prove his or her hypothesis, the researcher estimates the likelihood of the assumption being correct, given a certain probability of error. Further theoretical detail on hypothesis testing is beyond the scope of our presentation. One final point, however, is required before continuing with our overview of selected statistical measures.

Level of
significance

The *level of statistical significance* is set by the investigator in terms of the amount of risk or willingness to be in error in rejecting the null hypothesis (assuming a significant relationship). Statisticians speak of Type I error (mistakenly rejecting a true null hypothesis) or Type II error (mistakenly accepting a false null hypothesis). Customarily, researchers use the .05 probability level ($p < .05$; sometimes also symbolized as a [alpha]) as the minimum acceptance level for statistical significance. This means that we are 95 percent confident that the relationship is a real one; however, we are willing to accept being in error 5 times out of 100. That is, 5 in 100 times the results may be due to sampling error rather than real differences in the population. A .01 probability level ($p < .01$) indicates that only 1 time in 100 could the results have occurred by chance. The reader is once again referred to any good standard statistics text for a more detailed discussion (see, for instance, Loether and McTavish, 1980). Most statistical measures of association have corresponding tests of significance that involve comparing a calculated statistic with an appropriate table of probabilities. Most statistics textbooks provide needed detail on how to use such tables.

The *t* Test (Difference of Means Test)

t test

A test of significance that often appears in the criminal justice literature is the *t* **test** (Student's *t*). Many people assume that the name "Student" is associated with the *t* test because it was developed for the benefit of students. The actual origin is far more interesting as well as illustrative of the usefulness of the *t* statistic. "Student's" *t*, which could be regarded as "the beer drinker's statistic," was the pen name of a W. S. Gosset, who at one time worked for a brewery. In planning each formula for brewing, he had the problem of having to adjust for different quality of grains. He developed statistics that would enable him, with given degrees of error, to predict the most useful mixtures. One product of this investigation was the development of the *t* test and, incidentally, some excellent beer.

The *t* test is generally used to compare the sample means of two groups. If they are sufficiently different, the *t* test will be significant, thus enabling the researcher to reject the null hypothesis of no difference (or that the samples are from the same population). Failure to obtain a *t* statistic sufficiently high enough to exceed expected table values of *t* (see any standard statistics text) means that any differences could have been caused by sampling error alone. To use the *t* test and the *Z* score, which was discussed earlier but can also be used as a test of significance as we will see, certain assumptions must be met:

1. Although the assumption can be violated for some data with little apparent harm (see Binder, 1984), generally, interval level measurement of data is required. Thus, the use of such tests with ordinal data is questionable. For nominal data, it is impossible, because means cannot be calculated. For example, what is the mean of the following data?

		N
a.	Homicides	20
b.	Rapes	16
c.	Burglaries	42

A mean cannot be calculated with nominal data.
2. Some type of random or probability sampling is assumed.
3. The variables being sampled come from populations that are normally distributed.

Types of t Tests

A full explication of *t* tests requires at least a full chapter in a standard statistics text and will not be attempted here. We examine the most common types and refer you to statistics texts for detail on the others (Loether and McTavish, 1980). There are *three types of t tests:*

1. *t test for large samples* ($N = 30 +$ for both samples). In this case, *t* is the same as *Z* (standard deviation scores previously discussed).

Group 1	Group 2
$N_1 = 50$	$N_2 = 40$
$\overline{X}_1 = 10$	$\overline{X}_2 = 12$
$\sigma_1 = 3.6$	$\sigma_2 = 4.2$

2. *t test for small samples* (if either group is less than 30). An adjusted formula is required.

	Group 1	**Group 2**
	$N_1 = 10$	$N_2 = 20$
	$\overline{X}_1 = 110$	$\overline{X}_2 = 105$
	$\sigma_1 = 10$	$\sigma_2 = 12$

3. *t test tor correlated samples* (pre- and posttests of same group).

	Before	**After**	
	$\overline{X}_1 = 74$	$\overline{X}_2 = 82$	$N = 6$

The *t test for large samples* can be calculated using our example from type 1 and the formula

$$t = \frac{\overline{X}_1 - \overline{X}_2}{\sqrt{(\sigma_1^2 / n_1) + (\sigma_2^2 / n_2)}}$$

$$= \frac{10 - 12}{\sqrt{((3.6)^2 / 50) + ((4.2)^2 / 40)}}$$

$$= \frac{-2}{\sqrt{(12.96/50) + (17.64/40)}}$$

$$= \frac{-2}{\sqrt{.2592 + .441}}$$

$$= \frac{-2}{\sqrt{.7002}}$$

$$= \frac{-2}{.8368}$$

$$t = -2.39$$

For samples containing 30 or more, the calculation of t *is the same as that of* Z.

There are alternate formulas that must be used for *t* if sample sizes are below 30, are of unequal size, or if matched samples (before–after) are being compared. Detailed treatment of these are beyond the purposes of this presentation but are obtainable in any standard statistics text. Our primary interest is in providing the reader with a general ability to interpret and understand reports using such tests.

Interpretation of Z *and* t *tests of significance* is dependent first on a full understanding of figures such as the following:

$$Z = 1.86, \text{ one-tailed}, p < .05$$
$$Z = 2.48, \text{ two-tailed}, .01 < p < .05$$
$$t = 2.60, \text{ two-tailed}, p < .01$$

Using appropriate tables of probability (t or Z), the calculated values exceeded the expected values at the given levels. A one-tailed test makes use of only one half of the probability curve (shown in Figure 12.2) and reflects a directional hypothesis, comparable to predicting males will be more afraid of crime than females. A two-tailed test is a nondirectional hypothesis and simply states that there will be differences by sex in fear of crime. Our first example says that Z predicting direction was significant at the 5 percent level. Our second nondirectional Z was significant at the .05, but not the .01 level, while our t was nondirectional and significant at the .01 level.

In our example calculation $t = -2.39$ is significant (two-tailed at the .05 level requires a value of at least 1.96). Thus a difference in sample means of between 10 and 12 is sufficiently large to permit us to assume that differences exist in the population from which the samples were drawn.

POP QUIZ 12.6

For the following data, calculate t and test its significance at the .05 probability level, two-tailed (table value with significance = 1.96).

$$\overline{X}_1 = 10 \qquad \overline{X}_2 = 5$$
$$\sigma_1 = 2 \qquad \sigma_2 = 2$$
$$n_1 = 30 \qquad n_2 = 40$$
$$t = \underline{\hspace{1cm}}$$

ANOVA (Analysis of Variance)

In our discussion of t and Z we examined statistics that measured the statistical significance between two means. But often researchers are confronted with comparing three or more groups. They could simply compute t tests for each combination which would require 3 t tests for 3 groups, 6 t tests for 4 groups, and 10 t tests for 5 groups. Such computations would become unmanageable and with a large number of such tests a given proportion, for example, 5 in 100, are bound to be significant by chance, in this case at the .05 level. **Analysis of variance (ANOVA)** is used in comparing three or more sample means. One-way ANOVA (the type we will briefly discuss) involves three or more categories of an independent variable, such as a comparison of three different income groups with respect to some fear of crime scale score. There is such a thing as two-way ANOVA in which two independent predictors are examined. For a detailed presentation on the latter, see any more advanced statistical text.

ANOVA

The basic logic of ANOVA is that in comparing groups, types, or categories, there should be much greater variation between groups than within groups. If, for example, we were comparing three departments with respect to professionalism of the officers, where a score of 1 equals low professionalism and 10 equals high professionalism, then the high professionalism

TABLE 12.5 Professionalism in Three Police Departments[a]

	High	Medium	Low
	10	9	5
	9	7	3
	8	5	3
	7	3	3
	6	1	1
$\overline{X}$	8	5	3

[a]1 = low professionalism, 10 = high professionalism.

department should have more professional members than the medium or low departments. Table 12.5 illustrates this notion.

In Table 12.5, a sample of five officers from the three departments suggests that, although lower professionalism departments have some officers with higher professionalism ratings than some higher professionalism departments, in general it appears that the characterizations are useful types. ANOVA goes beyond such a judgmental approach and examines this question statistically, particularly because we are asking whether the differences that do exist do so by chance (sampling error).

Calculation of ANOVA

The basic idea of ANOVA is to have large variance between groups and small variance within groups. ANOVA uses the F statistic (which, similar to t and Z, has a table of probabilities with which the calculated statistic is compared). ANOVA is a fairly complex process and is summarized below simply to acquaint the reader with how the F statistic is obtained. It is not expected from this brief presentation that the student be able to perform ANOVA.

ANOVA can be viewed as a series of steps that lead to completion of the following chart:

Source	Sum of Squares	Degrees of Freedom	Variance (S²)
Between	(2)	(4) $K - 1$	(5)$\dfrac{(2)}{(4)}$
Within	(3)	(4) $N - K$	(5)$\dfrac{(3)}{(4)}$
Total	(1)	(4) $N - 1$	

With $= F$ at the right of the Between/Within rows.

1. Calculate the sum of squares for the total (SS_{total}). This is given in our example, but is detailed in Appendix D. $SS_T = 121.33$.

2. Calculate the sum of squares for between groups ($SS_{between}$). This is also given in our example and detailed in Appendix D. $SS_B = 63.33$.

3. Calculate the sum of squares for within groups (SS_{within}).

$$SS_{within} = SS_{total} - SS_{between}$$
$$= 121.33 - 63.33$$
$$= 58$$

4. Calculate the degrees of freedom (df).

$$df_{between} = K - 1$$

where K is the number of groups or categories being compared.

$$df_{between} = 3 - 1$$
$$= 2$$
$$df_{within} = N_{total} - K$$
$$= 15 - 3$$
$$= 12$$
$$df_{total} = N_{total} - 1$$
$$= 15 - 1$$
$$= 14$$

5. Calculate the variance between groups (S_B^2) and within groups (S_W^2).

$$S_B^2 = SS_{between}/df_{between}$$
$$= 63.33/2$$
$$= 31.67$$
$$S_W^2 = SS_{within}/df_{within}$$
$$= 58/12$$
$$= 4.83$$

6. Calculate the F ratio (test of significance).

$$F = S_{between}^2/S_{within}^2$$
$$= 31.67/4.83$$
$$= 6.56.$$

7. Compare it with the F table of probabilities at appropriate degrees of freedom [reading first $df_{between}$ ($K - 1$) and second df_{within} ($N - K$)].

$F = 6.56, 2, 12 \ df$ Table value significant at .05 level (3.88) but not .01 level (6.93). Reject null hypothesis.

Table 12.6 plugs the values we have calculated into the chart.

TABLE 12.6 ANOVA Calculations

Source	Sum of Squares	Degrees of Freedom	Variance (S^2)
Between	63.33	2	31.67/4.83 = F
Within	58	12	
Total	121.33	14	

A table of F distributions is available in any statistics text. On the basis of our analysis, our initial judgment is borne out. There was, in fact, sufficient similarity within groups and difference between groups to enable us to conclude that there are real differences between the three police departments with respect to professionalism. Five in one hundred times, however, this could be caused by sampling error, although a 95 percent chance of being correct seems a reasonable risk of being wrong.

As with other statistics, certain assumptions regarding the nature of the data must be reached before justifying their usage. The assumptions required for using ANOVA are:

Interval data
Random sampling
Sample drawn from a normal distribution.

POP QUIZ 12.7

What is indicated by the following values?

$$F = 7.61, 12, 4 \ df, p < .05$$

Other Measures of Relationship

The Concept of Relationship

Previously we explored chi-square-based measures of relationship for nominal level data. Discussion will now focus on measures of association appropriate for higher level data such as ordinal and interval scale information.

The notion of relationship or association is central to scientific investigation and was identified in Chapter 3 as the first essential step in resolution
Relationship of the causality problem. The idea of relationship assumes that, if one variable enables prediction of the values of a second variable, the variables are related. Perhaps a simple illustration will serve to explain this idea (Table 12.7).

TABLE 12.7[a]

	Case A		Case B		Case C	
	X	Y	X	Y	X	Y
	1	1	1	4	1	1
	2	2	2	3	2	1
	3	3	3	2	3	1
	4	4	4	1	4	1
	Positive relationship		Negative relationship		No relationship	

[a]1 = low, 4 = high.

Case A (Table 12.7) illustrates a perfect **positive relationship.** As variable X increases in value, so does variable Y; or, given knowledge of the value of variable X, the value of variable Y can be predicted exactly. Case B (Table 12.7) demonstrates a perfect **negative** (or inverse) **relationship.** As values of X increase, values of Y decrease proportionately. In Case C (Table 12.7), there is no relationship between X and Y. Changes in the value of X have no impact on Y, which maintains the same constant score.

Correlation Coefficient (Pearson's *r*)

Pearson's correlation

The Pearson product moment correlation coefficient (**Pearson's r**) is an interval level measure of relationship. To employ Pearson's *r*, three assumptions must be met with respect to the data:

1. They must be of interval level measurement.
2. If the joint frequency distribution were to be plotted, the relationship would be linear or resemble a straight line. If the relationship is non-linear, such as curvilinear, then other statistical measures must be used.
3. The deviations of points from this line must be relatively uniform (homoscedastic) or demonstrate equal variance.

Interpretation of Pearson's r

Values of the correlation coefficient (*r*) range from 0 (no relationship) to + or − 1.00 (a perfect relationship). A negative relationship is indicated by a minus sign and a positive relationship by a plus sign. In interpreting a correlation coefficient, the closer to zero it is, the weaker or lower the relationship, and the closer to 1.0 it is, the higher or stronger correlation is closer to 1.0. As a general rule of thumb, the following scale of correlation coefficients can be used:

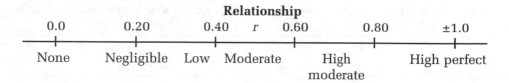

Of particular importance is the fact that r^2 (Pearson's r, squared) is a PRE measure (a proportional reduction in error measure) and can be interpreted as variance explained. For example, if the relationship between education and income is $r = .50$, $r^2 = (.50)(.50)$ or $.25$, or 25 percent of the variation in income is explained by education.

Calculation of Pearson's r

Uur discussion would be enhanced at this point by illustrating the computation of Pearson's r for a simple distribution. Two alternate formulas can be used to calculate the correlation coefficient; one uses raw data and the other makes use of deviation scores. The formula for calculating Pearson's r using raw scores for a simple distribution is

$$r = \frac{N\Sigma XY - \Sigma X \Sigma Y}{\sqrt{[N\Sigma X^2 - (\Sigma X)^2][N\Sigma Y^2 - (\Sigma Y)^2]}}$$

The formula for calculating Pearson's r using deviation score for a simple distribution is

$$r = \frac{\Sigma xy}{\sqrt{\Sigma x^2 \Sigma y^2}}$$

Table 12.8 is actually three tables. The first table (a) contains the original data, the second table (b) contains the calculation required to use the raw score formula, and the third table (c) illustrates the deviation score formula.

Using the data in Table 12.8 (b), the steps in calculating Pearson's r using the raw data formula are

1. Obtain the ΣX (sum of X) and ΣY (sum of Y). Simply add down each column. In our example, $\Sigma X = 15$ and $\Sigma Y = 30$.
2. Calculate X^2 (X square) and Y^2 (Y square) for each score and sum these to obtain ΣX^2 (the sum of X square) and ΣY^2 (the sum of Y square). In our example, $\Sigma X^2 = 65$ and $\Sigma Y^2 = 190$.
3. Calculate the cross-product or XY for each case. The ΣXY (sum of X times Y) equals 104 for our example.
4. Plug these values into the raw score formula:

TABLE 12.8 Scores of Five Correctional Officer Recruits on Mathematical (*X*) and Verbal (*Y*) Ability

(a)	X	Y			
	0	4			
	2	5			
	3	6			
	4	7			
	6	8			
Total	15	30			

(b)	X	Y	X^2	Y^2	XY
	0	4	0	16	0
	2	5	4	25	10
	3	6	9	36	18
	4	7	16	49	28
	6	8	36	64	48
Total	15	30	65	190	104

(c)	X	Y	x	y	x^2	y^2	xy
	0	4	−3	−2	9	4	6
	2	5	−1	−1	1	1	1
	3	6	0	0	0	0	0
	4	7	+1	+1	1	1	1
	6	8	+3	+2	9	4	6
Total	15	30			20	10	14

$\overline{X} = 3$, $\overline{Y} = 6$

$$r = \frac{5(104) - (15)(30)}{\sqrt{[5(65) - (15)^2][5(190) - (30)^2]}}$$

$$= \frac{520 - 450}{\sqrt{[325 - 225][950 - 900]}}$$

$$= \frac{70}{\sqrt{5000}}$$

$$= \frac{70}{70.71}$$

$$= .99$$

With use of the data in Table 12.8 (*c*), the formula for calculating Pearson's *r* for a simple distribution using deviation scores is

1. Calculate the mean for *X* and *Y*. $\overline{X}$ (mean of *X*) equals 3 and $\overline{Y}$ (mean of *Y*) equals 6.
2. Now convert each raw score into a deviation score—*x* (little *x*); this is obtained by subtracting the mean ($\overline{X}$) from each raw score (*X*) or ($X - \overline{X} = x$). Do the same for the *Y* distribution.
3. Obtain the cross product (Σxy) of the deviation scores for each score by multiplying *x* by *y* and summing.

4. Plug these values into the formula for obtaining Pearson's *r* for a simple distribution using deviation scores:

$$r = 14/\sqrt{(20)(10)}$$
$$= 14/14.14$$
$$= .99$$

Statistical Significance of Pearson's r

In general, in line with our earlier suggested interpretations of the meaning of correlation coefficients, low *r*'s are not likely to be significant. If the *r* is above .7, it is almost always statistically significant. Similar to other statistical tests we have discussed, statisticians have calculated expected values of *r* given specific sample sizes. These tables are available in any standard statistical text. For our computed *r* of .99, the expected table value of .88 for an *N* of 5 is exceeded ($\alpha = .01$, two-tailed); therefore, we are able to reject the null hypothesis and conclude that math scores (*X*) are very much related to verbal scores (*Y*). Previously we indicated that r^2 (variance explained) is a very meaningful statistic. For our example, $.99^2$ equals .98, or 98 percent of the variance in verbal scores is explained given knowledge of the mathematical score.

POP QUIZ 12.8

1. What do the following values mean and what percent of the variance is explained?

$$r = .70, p < .05$$

2. For the following data, calculate Pearson's *r*:

X	Y
1	3
3	3
5	6

Regression

The correlation coefficient not only tells us the strength of a relationship but also provides us with the raw data, enabling calculation of a **regression equation.** With the regression equation, we are able to predict, on the basis of the value of one variable, a person's score on a second variable. The formula for calculating a regression line is

Regression

$$Y' = \quad a \quad + bX$$
$$(\text{predicted } Y) = (Y \text{ intercept}) + (\text{slope } X)$$

where

> Y' = refers to a predicted score of Y (in our case, verbal scores)
> a = the Y intercept or place where the regression line crosses the Y axis (see Figure 12.3)
> b = the slope of the line (slope coefficient)

The formulas for calculating the regression equation for the raw data in Table 12.8 are presented in Appendix D.

Figure 12.3 plots the values of X and Y for the five correctional officers we have been examining, and by using the same calculations from our correlation example, we are able to obtain a formula for a regression line that predicts values of Y if we are given values of X.

$$Y' = 3.9 + .7X$$

Using this formula, if a new recruit had a score of 8 in verbal ability, we would predict a score of 9.5 on the math portion $[X = 3.9 + .7(8) = 9.5]$. In criminal justice such prediction formulas would serve many needs in estimating future outcomes from known data. This is particularly the case with multiple correlation and regression techniques, which we will discuss later in this chapter. But first, because many of the data we work with in criminal justice are of an ordinal rather than interval nature, let us examine some ordinal level measures of relationship.

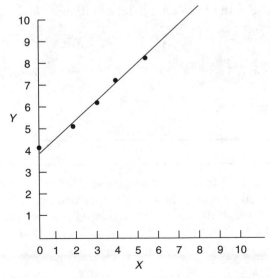

Figure 12.3 Regression Line for Scores of Five Correctional Officer Recruits on Mathematical (X) and Verbal (Y) Ability.

POP QUIZ 12.9

1. What does the following equation mean:

$$Y' = a + bX$$

2. With the formula for predicting correctional officer recruits, calculate the predicted values of Y (verbal ability) for new recruits with the following math scores (X):

   a. 10 _____

   b. 5 _____

$$Y' = 3.9 + 7X$$

Ordinal Level Measures of Relationship

There are a number of useful ordinal level measures of relationship. We will restrict our coverage to only two of these: Spearman's rho and gamma.

Spearman's Rho (r_s)

Spearman's rho *Spearman's rho* (symbolized by r sub s), or Spearman's rank order correlation coefficient, is an appropriate measure of relationship for ordinal level data. In previous discussion of ordinal data it was indicated that ordinal level measurement supplies only information regarding rank or higher or lower properties, and the actual scores do not contain any meaningful interval units between scores. Suppose, for instance, we wanted, similar to police assessment exercises, to measure the relationship between a sample of scores received at the police academy (X) and subsequent supervisor ratings of officer effectiveness (Y). Table 12.9 presents such fictitious data. Using the data in Table 12.9 we will illustrate the steps in calculating Spearman's rho:

1. Assign ranks to each score. Begin with the lowest score in column X and assign it the lowest rank of 1; then rank the next lowest and so forth to the highest score which is assigned the highest rank. (In case of tied ranks, assign the average of the ranks that would have been assigned.) If scores were tied for third and fourth place, they would each be assigned the rank of 3.5. The ranking of scores could be reversed assigning the lower ranks to higher scores, as long as each variable is ranked similarly.
2. Follow this same procedure for converting Y scores into Y rank scores.
3. Calculate D (difference in rank scores) by subtracting for each case the Y rank score from the X rank score.
4. Obtain D^2 by squaring each D value and calculate the ΣD^2.

TABLE 12.9 A Sample of Ten Officer Effectiveness Scores (Y) and Police Academy Scores (X)[a]

Officer	X	Y
A	71	20
B	78	31
C	79	32
D	80	28
E	83	42
F	85	81
G	89	72
H	90	84
I	92	96
J	98	99

[a]Academy scores ranged from 70 (pass) to 100 (excellent). Officer scores ranged from 1 (ineffective) to 100 (most effective).

TABLE 12.10

Officer	X	Rank X	Y	Rank Y	D	D²
A	71	1	20	1	0	0
B	78	2	31	3	−1	1
C	79	3	32	4	−1	1
D	80	4	28	2	2	4
E	83	5	42	5	0	0
F	85	6	81	7	−1	1
G	89	7	72	6	1	1
H	90	8	84	8	0	0
I	92	9	96	9	0	0
J	98	10	99	10	0	0
						$\Sigma D^2 = 8$

5. Plug these values into the formula for Spearman's rho (r_s):

$$r_s = 1 - \frac{6 \, \Sigma D^2}{N[(N)^2 - 1]}$$

Table 12.10 contains the calculations for r_s using the data from our example.

$$r_s = 1 - \frac{6(8)}{10(100 - 1)}$$

$$= 1 - \frac{48}{990}$$

$$= 1 - .04$$

$$= +.95$$

Interpretation of Rho

Similar to Pearson's *r*, rho requires assumptions regarding linearity (a straight-line relationship if plotted) and random sampling from the population. Unlike *r*, r_s is appropriate for ordinal data. Spearman's rho can be interpreted in the same manner as Pearson's *r*, with a 0.0 indicative of no relationship and a + 1.0 or − 1.0 indicating a perfect, either positive or negative relationship. Our example of a + .95 is indicative of a very high positive relationship.

Similar to other statistics that we have discussed, tables of expected probabilities for r_s exist in standard statistical texts in which the statistical significance of r_s values can be assessed. Our calculated value of .95 for an *N* of 10 exceeds the value at the .05 probability level (.65) as well as the .01 level (.79) for two-tailed tests. Thus in only one in one hundred samples could such a result have taken place by chance or sampling error.

PRE measure   Of even greater significance is the fact that r_s^2 (rho squared) is a **PRE (proportional reduction in error measure)** or a measurement of the proportion of variance explained. In our example $(.95)^2$ equals .90, or 90 percent of the performance ratings of officers can be predicted on the basis of academy scores.

Gamma

Gamma   **Goodman and Kruskal's gamma** (G) is another measure of relationship for ordinal data that requires the same assumptions as Spearman's rho: linearity, random samples, and ordinal data. The values of gamma also vary between 0.0 (no relationship—or no reduction in error in predicting the dependent variable, given knowledge of the independent variable) to + 1.0 or − 1.0 (perfect relationship—total predictability). Gamma is a PRE measure and the calculated statistic can be interpreted directly as variance explained. Yule's *Q* is a special case of gamma applicable to 2 × 2 tables only and can be interpreted in the same manner as gamma. We explore the calculation of gamma using data that have been placed in a contingency table (Table 12.11).

TABLE 12.11 Attrition among Professionals in Rehabilitation by Membership in Professional Associations[a]

Membership	Attrition In					Out	N
In	58	77	25	9	24	3	196
Out	1	3	5	1	17	2	29
							225

[a]Attrition refers to the act of leaving the occupation for which one was trained. Measurement was by means of a fairly complex two-level judgmental scale which is described in detail in the original source.

Variation from *N* of 243 is due to the elimination of unknowns. There is a positive relationship between membership in organizations in or related to the field of training and retention, gamma = .76, *p* <.001.

Source: Sussman, Marvin B., Marie R. Haug, Frank E. Hagan, and Gay C. Kitson. *Staying Power in Rehabilitation: The Impact of Rehabilitation Services Administration Support in Nine Occupations.* Cleveland: Institute on the Family and the Bureaucratic Society, Case Western Reserve University, 1975, p. 64.

The formula for calculating gamma is

$$G = (A - D)/(A + D)$$

where

> A = agreements or cases in predicted direction
> D = disagreements or cases not in predicted direction

Agreements and disagreements can be best explained by illustration. The steps in calculating gamma are

1. First, arrange the data from high to low (as in our example in Table 12.11). Both values of each variable should decrease in value as they move from the upper left cell.
2. Obtain the agreements by multiplying each value, beginning with the upper left cell, and by the sum of all cells below and to the right. Total the resulting values.

$$A = 58(3 + 5 + 1 + 17 + 2) + 77(5 + 1 + 17 + 2)$$
$$+ 25(1 + 17 + 2)$$
$$= 9(17 + 2) + 24(2)$$
$$A = 4{,}268$$

3. Now calculate the disagreements (D) beginning with the upper right one by multiplying each cell value by the sum of all values below and to the left.

$$D = 3(17 + 1 + 5 + 3 + 1) + 24(1 + 5 + 3 + 1)$$
$$+ 9(5 + 3 + 1) + 25(3 + 1) + 77(1)$$
$$= 579$$

4. Plug these values into our calculating formula to obtain gamma.

$$G = \frac{4{,}268 - 579}{5{,}268 + 579}$$
$$G = .76$$

A gamma of .76 is indicative of a relatively high relationship between membership in professional associations and remaining in one's field of training. Similar to other statistical techniques, there is a test of significance for gamma. In this case, a formula (see Appendix F) is used to convert gamma into a Z score that is compared with a table of expected Z scores. Our gamma was equivalent to a Z of 4.75, $p < .001$.

POP QUIZ 12.10

1. Calculate gamma for the following data:

Education	Income High		Low
High	10	5	10
Low	5	5	10

2. Calculate Spearman's rho (r_s) for the following data. Note that the data are *already ranked:*

X	Y
1	3
2	2
4	1
3	2

In most cases the criminal justice researcher does not calculate most of the statistical procedures that we have discussed by hand but rather uses "canned" (prewritten) computer packages such as SPSS-X (Statistical Package for the Social Sciences) (see Appendix C). With these packages, the researcher's primary concerns are employing the proper statistics with respect to the nature of and assumptions regarding the data to be analyzed and interpreting the meaning of the calculations performed by the computer. The purpose of our more detailed presentation of specific statistics is to acquaint the reader with some general methods. These are intended to provide a general overview or introduction so that the reader could then consult more in-depth treatment in statistical texts once the appropriate or required measure for their purposes is chosen. General familiarity with these statistics assists in understanding the description and discussion of other statistics.

In Chapter 3 we discussed the three steps essential to resolution of the causality problem: demonstration that a relationship exists, specification of the time order of this relationship, and exclusion of or control for other variables that may be the actual cause of the relationship. We have examined the demonstration of two-variable relationships such as chi-square-based measures, gamma, and the correlation coefficient. Specification of the time order or direction of causality took place with our identification of the independent (predictor) variable and dependent (outcome) variable. Also in Chapter 3, we discussed how researchers can attempt to control for rival causal factors through research design. We also indicated that often research topics do not lend themselves to such prior controls and that investigators can accomplish much the same thing through statistical controls, after the fact. Multivariate statistical analysis enables the statistical control of rival causal factors.

Multivariate Analysis

A variety of statistical techniques attempts to control for other variables. Subclassification of tables, partial correlation, two-way analysis of variance, multiple correlation and regression, and other procedures enable the investigator to statistically control for the effects of other variables. Detailed coverage of each of these is beyond the intended scope of what is essentially a research methods text; however, brief exposure to partial correlation and multiple correlation and regression will serve to illustrate multivariate techniques.

Partial Correlation

Partial correlation

We have already examined bivariate correlation in our discussion of simple Pearson's *r*. **Partial correlation** looks at the relationship between two variables while controlling for (taking into account) the effects of one or more other variables. In reporting correlation coefficients, it is standard procedure to list subscripts, as in r_{xy}. This indicates that we are looking at the relationship between variables X and Y. Such a simple correlation does not have any controls for other variables and is referred to as a zero-order correlation coefficient. A dot after the first two subscripted variables indicates that the partial correlation coefficient has controlled for other variables. If one variable follows the dot, then this is called a first-order partial correlation coefficient. If two variables follow the dot, then we have a second-order partial correlation coefficient. Examine the following partial correlations:

$$r_{XY}$$
$$r_{XX.ZAB}$$
$$r_{XY.1}$$

Our first example is of a zero-order correlation coefficient (no controls). The second case shows a third-order partial r with the relationship between X and Y controlled for (or taking into account the effects of variables Z, A, and B). Finally, our third correlation is a first-order partial r controlling for only one variable labeled 1. Multiple correlation and regression are generally regarded as more useful than partial correlations because they can simultaneously examine and control for multiple intercorrelations.

The reader is once again referred to statistics texts for detailed treatment of partial r, our purposes being met in providing a familiarity with the technique.

Multiple Correlation and Regression

An understanding of multiple correlation and regression is an extension of what we have discussed so far with respect to simple correlation and regression. Correlation measures the strength of the relationship and a

Multiple
correlation and
regression

regression line provides an equation with which to predict values of the dependent variable. **Multiple correlation** is symbolized by R and has its counterpart in **multiple regression,** which involves predicting Y (the dependent variable) on the basis of multiple predictors. Multiple regression has the general formula

$$Y' = a + b_1X_1 + b_2X_2 + \ldots b_KX_K + e$$

where

Y' = estimated value of Y
a = the Y intercept (or point where the regression line crosses the Y axis)
b = partial slope coefficient
e = a residual error term (this is usually ignored once the predictive equation is calculated)

Subscript 1 stands for variable 1, subscript 2 for variable 2, to subscript K for the total number of additional variables.

The interpretation of both multiple correlation and regression is analogous to our previous discussion of simple correlation and regression. Thus, R^2 equals variance explained and the regression equation enables us to predict Y given knowledge of multiple predictors. For example, in our multiple regression formula, Y could represent likely parole outcome, and X_1 previous record, X_2 length of incarceration, and so forth. The necessary computations for multiple R and regression are most ordinarily performed by computer and are far too involved for our purposes.

FINAL QUIZ

For the final quiz, describe what the statistical terms with which we began this chapter mean.

1. $\chi^2 = 4.67$, 1 *df*, $p < .05$
2. $r = .71$, $p < .01$
3. Gamma $= .32$, n.s.
4. $\overline{X} = 3.6$, $\alpha = 1.2$
5. $Z = 3.01$, $p < .01$

There are a large number of statistical techniques. Some feel that the field of criminal justice, because of the ready availability of funding beginning in the seventies, has been under an avalanche of such esoteric techniques. Given a basic knowledge of some of the techniques we have discussed, it is hoped that the reader will have the confidence to realize that, if one runs across an unknown technique, it is often a variation of one of those we have discussed and that it can be looked up and generally understood without the need for detailed mathematical explanations.

It is hoped that our discussion of the presentation of statistical findings will assist the reader in developing a healthy disrespectful confidence in approaching such data. Rather than intimidation, a brief exposure to the interpretive approach we have discussed should inspire some confidence. Throughout this chapter the reader has frequently been referred to standard statistics textbooks for more detailed analysis. Some that you might want to consult are Dometrius (1992); Elzey (1987); Kanji (1993); Fox and Levin (1994); Loether and McTavish (1980); Mueller, Schuessler, and Costner (1970); Siegel (1956); Vito and Latessa (1989); and Vogt (1993).

Statistical Software

The role of computers in research made its earliest impact in creating data files, managing these data, and particularly in the analysis of data by means of sophisticated software programs such as SPSS-X, SAS, BMDP, MICRO-CASE, and MINITAB (Brent and Anderson, 1990; Dometrius, 1992; Fox, 1992). The advent of such computerized statistical analysis has eliminated much of the drudgery from "numbers crunching" by hand or calculator, but still requires that the researcher have a good basic knowledge of statistics, assumptions regarding their usage, appropriate levels of measurement, and the interpretation of statistics. The ability of computer programs to quickly perform sophisticated analysis does not prevent the inappropriate use and interpretation of such statistics.

The emergence of "expert systems" and "artificial intelligence" such as Statistical Navigator Professional (Malcolm, 1992) can assist in such statistical decision-making. Similar to a "help" menu common in many computer programs, Statistical Navigator Professional contains a menu and series of questions that enable the user to narrow down his or her choices of appropriate statistics from 200 statistical procedures. The program also identifies appropriate statistical software and provides a brief tutorial on the statistics that have been chosen. Of particular note is the fact that much of this software, which at one time required a mainframe computer, is available on personal computers (see Appendix C for a description of SPSS-PC+).

Caveat Emptor

Caveat emptor   One excellent primer on statistics saw fit to entitle the last chapter "*Caveat Emptor*" ("*let the buyer beware*") (Franzblau, 1958, pp. 129–132). This is quite apt advice, particularly to those whose primary role will be a consumer of research and statistical information. The field of criminal justice, particularly because of the ready availability of research funds beginning in the seventies, has at times been awash in a sea of sometimes inappropriate mathematical wizardry. Sophisticated statistical analysis of inappropriate data can often lead to unfounded conclusions. More dangerous is the fact that the very intimidating nature of the apparent complexity of these techniques may hide faulty judgment. With the ready availability of computer packages, it becomes a simple technical matter to run statistical tests sometimes without paying proper attention to logic, substantive issues, and the many potential sources of error we have discussed throughout this text. It is hoped that the general overview of statistics in this chapter will begin to prepare the reader to become a more alert and vigilant consumer. The consumer of statistical findings should pay special attention to the following:

1. Statistical significance should by no means be taken as indicative of substantive significance. One might find a highly statistically significant relationship between foot size and intelligence, but not place any meaningful or important value on such findings.
2. Beware of statistics of convenience or types of analyses that may have been chosen by the researcher on the basis that they would most likely shed the best possible light on the data.
3. Be wary of discussion and generalization that goes far beyond the limited statistical findings. Sometimes studies that are done on one atypical group suddenly are assumed to be generalizable to larger populations. For example, Kinsey's study of *Sexual Behavior in the Human Female* (1953) was primarily a purposive sample of white American females. Niederhoffer's (1967) conclusions regarding the nature of cynicism among police, which was subtitled "The Police in Urban Society," was a study of the New York City Police Department.
4. Readers should be particularly vigilant regarding the misapplication of statistical techniques to data that do not meet such required assumptions as normal distributions, random samples, interval measurement, and the like.

The Ecological Fallacy

The "ecological fallacy" appears to have been noted independently in psychology (Thorndike, 1929) and in statistics (Yule and Kendall, 1950), but it was Robinson's (1950) paper on the subject that attracted the most attention and has the greatest relevance to criminal justice research. The **ecological fallacy** is the error of assuming that relationships based on groups (aggregate, ecological, or areal data) can be validly assumed to be true of individual correlations. A correlation coefficient (r) is a measure of relationship that ranges from -1.0 (a perfect negative or inverse association), to 0.0 (no relationship), to $+1.0$ (a perfect positive relationship). Robinson demonstrated his point by showing that the relationships between illiteracy and being foreign-born and between illiteracy and race varied greatly depending on the unit of analysis (Table 12.12).

Ecological
fallacy

When the data on illiteracy and being foreign-born were grouped by nine census areas, there was a moderate negative relationship ($-.62$); when these

TABLE 12.12 Relationship between Ecological Correlations and Individual Correlations

Unit of Analysis	Illiteracy by Foreign-Born	Illiteracy by Race (Black)
Nine census areas	$r_e = -.62$	$r_e = .95$
48 states	$r_e = -.53$	$r_e = .78$
Individuals	$r = .12$	$r = .20$

Source: Robinson, W. S. "Ecological Correlations and the Behavior of Individuals." *American Sociological Review* 15 (June 15, 1950): 351–357.

same data were regrouped by 48 states, there was a slightly smaller negative relationship (– .53). Finally, when the data were ungrouped, the individual correlation was a very small positive one (.12).

Similarly, when the relationship between illiteracy and race (black) was grouped by nine census areas, the relationship was a very high positive one (.95); clustered by 48 states the relationship was reduced but still high positive (.77); and when ungrouped, the association was only a small one (.20). Although individual correlations use persons as the unit of analysis, ecological correlations use groups of persons. In our previous tabular analyses it would be similar to using only the marginal totals to obtain ecological correlations, while individual correlations make use of the internal cell frequencies.

Much research in criminal justice, particularly the early literature in criminology and juvenile delinquency, has been plagued by shifts in these units of analysis which often lead to confusion. In their review of such research Hirschi and Selvin (1973, p. 269) indicate that "the researcher should analyze and present his data so as to avoid suggesting that the relations he observes are stronger than they actually are. One way of avoiding such suggestions is to distinguish carefully between properties of individuals and properties of the distribution of individual traits over a group or class." Particularly, the researcher should be cautious and make sure that, if the units of analysis are individuals, then the results of data aggregated into groups are not likely to reflect the real relationships.

Summary

The purpose of this chapter has been to provide the student of criminal justice with an overview of the primary types of statistical techniques one confronts in the literature today. Statistics are simply tools, means of summarizing and analyzing data. One need not have extensive training in statistics to be able to generally interpret reported statistical findings. Without such a capacity, it is becoming increasingly more difficult to read most of the latest literature in the field which is more and more quantitative in nature.

There are two basic types of statistics: descriptive and inferential. Descriptive statistics are intended to summarize, describe, or show relationships between data; inferential statistics infer or generalize sample findings to larger populations. Basic descriptive techniques such as measures of central tendency (mean, median, and mode) were illustrated, as were measures of dispersion such as the range and standard deviation. Z scores, or standard deviation scores, are quite useful in assessing probability so long as we can assume the data are normally distributed. Chi-square was presented as an inferential technique (test of independence) appropriate for nominal level data. As with other tests of significance, a calculated value is compared at appropriate degrees of freedom with a calculated table of expected values. If a calculated value exceeds the expected value at the .05 probability level ($p < .05$), this means that in fewer than five of one hundred trials could such a result be caused by sampling error. Chi-square is not a measure of relationship, although there are a number of chi-square-based measures of association such as phi, phi-square, contingency coefficient, and Cramer's V. Of these, phi-square is of the greatest utility in that it is a PRE measure. A PRE (proportional reduction in error) measure is most useful in that it has in common with other such statistics a direct operational interpretation—variance explained.

In addition to having descriptive or inferential functions, statistics can also be either parametric or nonparametric in nature. Parametric statistics assume interval level measurement, normal distributions, and linearity. Nonparametric statistics are "distribution free"; that is, they make few assumptions regarding the distribution of the population. Pearson's r, Z, and F tests (ANOVA) are examples of parametric statistics, whereas gamma, Spearman's rho, and chi-square are examples of nonparametric statistics.

In inferential statistics, researchers do not directly test the research hypothesis or relationship they are attempting to demonstrate, but instead statistically assess the null hypothesis, a statement of nonrelationship. Tests of significance measure whether results are due to chance or are so highly improbable of resulting from chance that they are significant at given levels of probability. The t test is a test of significance that compares sample means where the N of either sample is less than 30. For larger samples the Z test is more appropriate.

ANOVA (analysis of variance) is appropriate for testing, by means of the F ratio, three or more samples. It assumes that the variance between groups should be large, and the variance within groups small. At appropriate degrees of freedom, the F ratio is compared with a table of expected values to test statistical significance. All of the statistical procedures that have been discussed in this chapter are applicable to only certain types of data, and the researcher is advised to check these assumptions carefully prior to choice of the statistical measure.

Central to much scientific investigation is the notion of relationship. A positive relationship indicates that, as one variable increases, the other increases; a negative relationship (inverse) indicates that, as one variable increases, the other decreases in value. Finally, if one variable has absolutely no impact on another, this is indicative of no relationship. Pearson's correlation coefficient (r) is one of the most widely used measures of relationship. It is appropriate for interval level data that exhibit linearity and varies from

– 1.00 (perfect inverse relationship) to + 1.00 (perfect positive relationship). The square of r (r^2) is a PRE measure and indicates variance explained. A regression equation enables one to predict values of one variable (Y), given knowledge of a predictor variable (X).

Some measures of relationship that are alternatives to Pearson's r when working with ordinal (ranked) data are Spearman's rho and gamma. Both calculations can have PRE interpretation. Multivariate analysis includes partial correlation, in which controls for a third or more variables exist, as well as multiple correlation and regression. Multiple correlation (R) looks at the impact of multiple predictors (independent variables) on the dependent variable. Multiple regression provides a formula that enables the calculation of predicted values of the dependent variable, given values of independent variables.

Finally, the reader is urged to follow the maxim "caveat emptor" ("let the buyer beware") in reading statistical findings. Be wary of assumptions regarding the meaning of statistical significance, the misuse of statistical techniques, overgeneralizations beyond the data in discussions, and overlooked assumptions that are required in appropriately utilizing statistical measures.

Ecological fallacy is the error that occurs when the researcher's target is individuals, but the analysis is of groups. If the units of an analysis are individuals, then data aggregated into groups are not likely to reflect the real relationship.

Key Concepts

Descriptive Statistics	Chi-Square	Positive Relationship
Inferential Statistics	Degrees of Freedom	Negative Relationship
Measures of Central Tendency	Phi Coefficient	Pearson's r
	Phi-Square	Regression
Mode	Contingency Coefficient	Spearman's Rho
Median	Cramer's V	PRE measures
Mean	Parametric Statistics	Gamma
Measures of Dispersion	Nonparametric Statistics	SPSS
Range	Null Hypothesis	Partial Correlation
Standard Deviation	Tests of Significance	Multiple Correlation
Normal Distribution	t test	Multiple Regression
Z Scores	ANOVA	Ecological Fallacy

Review Questions

1. The types of statistics can be classified as descriptive or inferential and parametric or nonparametric. Discuss each of these and provide examples.
2. What is the notion of "normal curve" in statistics, and of what use is it in statistical tests?
3. What is the purpose of a test of significance? What, for instance, does $p < .05$ indicate?
4. "Caveat emptor"—what are some suggestions for consumers of statistical findings to guard against being misled?

13 Policy Analysis, Evaluation Research, and Proposal Writing

In the introductory chapter we addressed the criticism that much criminological and criminal justice research is either common sense or impractical. This chapter focuses on the latter concern: "So what; of what practical use are these research findings?" We will apply what we have learned to the tasks of policy analysis, evaluation research, as well as proposal writing—the cutting edge of government-sponsored criminal justice research today.

Policy Analysis

Policy analysis

Policy analysis is the "study of whatever governments choose to do or not to do," "the description and explanation of the causes and consequences of government behavior" (Dye, 1995, pp. 3–4). Jones (1977, p. 4) views policy analysis as the study of proposals (specified means for achieving goals), programs (authorized means for achieving goals), decisions (specified actions taken to implement programs), and effects (the measurable impacts of programs). Policy analysis is an applied subfield of economics, political science, public administration, sociology, law, and statistics. It involves the identification and description of social problems, the development of public policies that may alleviate these problems, and determination of whether these policies work (Dye, 1995, p. 17). Although there are many models, perspectives, or approaches to policy analysis, the policy process could be viewed as a series of political activities consisting of (Dye, 1995 p. 21) the following:

Identifying Problems	Demands are expressed for government action.
Formulating Policy Proposals	Agenda is set for public discussion. Development of program proposals to resolve problem.
Legitimating Policies	Selecting a proposal. Building political support for it. Enacting it as a law.
Implementing Policies	Organizing bureaucracies. Providing payments or services. Levying taxes.
Evaluating Policies	Studying programs. Reporting "outputs" of government programs. Evaluating "impacts" of programs on target and nontarget groups in society. Suggesting changes and adjustments.

Thus the policy process involves identification, formulation, legitimation, implementation, and evaluation.

Evaluation Research

Evaluation research is the last stage of the policy process, in which questions such as the following are asked:

Do the programs work?
Do they produce the desired result?
Do they provide enough benefits to justify their costs?
Are there better ways to attack these problems?
Should the programs be maintained, improved, or eliminated?

Evaluation research
Evaluation research is an applied branch of social science that is intended to supply scientifically valid information with which to guide

public policy. Historically, research in the social sciences had its origins in the physical sciences and was oriented toward development of theories and utilization of the experimental model to test these theories. Its concern was much more akin to pure or basic research discussed in Chapter 1—the acquiring and testing of new knowledge.

Evaluation research as a type of applied research has different roots as well as intentions. It evolved from the world of technology rather than science and emphasizes mission or goal accomplishment and product/service delivery rather than theory formation. Evaluation research aims to provide feedback to policymakers in concrete, measurable terms. Although such an approach has existed informally since early times, the introduction of computer technology in the 1950s and its successful application to "defense systems" and "space systems" have led to the application of evaluation research to "social systems" such as the "criminal justice system." Much of this thinking grew out of the "Planning, Programming, Budgeting Systems" (PPBS) approach originally employed by the U.S. Department of Defense in the 1960s, a method of policy evaluation widely adopted by other government agencies. PPBS attempts to specify (by clearly defining program objectives) and quantify (by developing measures of accomplishments) the output of a government program and to analyze the relative costs and benefits of the program (see Hudzik and Cordner, 1983; Rossi and Freeman, 1993; and Shanahan, 1985).

As billions of dollars were poured into social programs in the 1960s, the following questions were increasingly asked: Do the programs work or make a difference? Are they cost effective? Are they the most efficient manner of providing services? With fewer funds available in the 1990s the same questions are still relevant: How can the best use be made of limited resources to accomplish maximum program benefits (Vito, 1983)?

Other than its very practical bent and some relatively esoteric techniques such as cost–benefit analysis, many of the methodological procedures employed in evaluation research have already been covered earlier in this text in Chapters 1–12. Thus, rather than viewing it as a different type of research, readers can confidently assume that they can master the essentials of evaluation research on the basis of knowledge of many of the issues we have already described. Quite simply, *evaluation research can be defined as measurement of the effects of a program in terms of its specific goals, outcomes, or particular program criteria.* Weiss (1972, p. 4) states that the purpose of evaluation research is "to measure the effects of a program against the goals it set out to accomplish as a means of contributing to subsequent decision making about the program and improving future programming." It is essential to this purpose that the research methodology we have discussed be used to measure program outcomes in terms of specifically identified criteria in order to accomplish an applied or practical research objective—better programs. Similar to a scientific experiment, the research methodology is applied to evaluate social action programs to accomplish more efficient programs (Schwarz, 1980).

The National Advisory Committee on Criminal Justice Standards and Goals feels very strongly about the importance of evaluation research:

A high quality evaluation is expensive and time-consuming. Indeed, it may be many times more expensive than the operational program it is designed to test. Viewed in the context of that single program, such an expenditure may appear absurd. But in the context of advancement of knowledge, this type of concentration of funds is more likely to be fruitful than the same expenditure on a large number of inadequate evaluations would be. Progress does not depend on every program being evaluated; in fact, with limited resources for evaluation, it may be retarded by such a practice (National Advisory Committee, 1976, p. 52).

Some workers involved in administering applied or action programs in criminal justice may have either little understanding of evaluation, past exposure to poor evaluations, or perhaps little regard for the necessity of evaluation as they are already committed to a particular programmatic strategy. The logic of the National Advisory Committee statement would argue that a few expensive, well-designed evaluations are in the long run more cost-effective in revising or eliminating unnecessary treatments or procedures. The last point—elimination—is perhaps at the crux of the resistance to evaluations. Similar to early applications of social, scientific, and management studies in industry, many of those to be studied obviously have an understandably vested interest in maintaining a favorable image of the current procedures, practices, and staffing of their organizations.

Policy Experiments

Policy experiments

A close link between experimental methods and the assessment of public policy programs has increased dramatically since 1970 (Fagan, 1990, p. 108). **Policy experiments** are applied field experiments that address themselves to immediate practical policy questions. The National Research Council's Committee on Research on Law Enforcement and the Administration of Justice summarized the following steps in designing policy experiments (Garner and Visher, 1988, pp. 7–8):

Steps in policy experiments

1. Choose an interesting problem—a policy question that people really care about or an existing procedure that clearly needs improvement.
2. Do some creative thinking to solve legal and ethical issues that may arise.
3. Rigorously maintain the random assignment of persons, cases, or other units into treatment and control groups throughout the experiment.
4. Choose a design and methods of investigation that are appropriate both to the questions to be answered and to the available data.
5. Adopt a team approach between researchers and practitioners and keep working in close cooperation.
6. Put as much into your experiment as you want to get out of it.
7. Use an experiment to inform policy, not to make policy.
8. Understand and confront the political risks an experiment may involve.
9. Insofar as possible, see that the experiment is replicated in a variety of settings before encouraging widespread adoption of experimentally successful treatments.

Before exploring evaluation research more thoroughly, let us first provide an example of a policy analysis program that utilizes evaluation research.

Policy Analysis: The Case of the National Institute of Justice Research Program

NIJ research program

Although policy analysis and evaluation research in criminology and criminal justice are not restricted solely to government-funded research of primarily government-funded projects and NIJ is not the only agency sponsoring criminal justice research, NIJ does utilize the largest, most ambitious policy-oriented program of its type and has been heralded by the National Academy of Sciences as a pioneer and model for other programs. For this reason we explore the philosophy, aims, and research program plan of the National Institute of Justice.

NIJ Mission Statement

The National Institute of Justice is a research branch of the U.S. Department of Justice. The Institute's mission is to develop knowledge about crime, its causes, and control. Priority is given to policy-relevant research that can yield approaches and information that state and local agencies can use in preventing and reducing crime. The decisions made by criminal justice practitioners and policymakers affect millions of citizens, and crime affects almost all our public institutions and the private sector as well. Targeting resources, assuring their effective allocation, and developing new means of cooperation between the public and private sector are some of the emerging issues in law enforcement and criminal justice that research can help illuminate.

Carrying out the mandate assigned by Congress in the Justice Assistance Act of 1984, the National Institute of Justice aims to:

- Sponsor research and development to improve and strengthen the nation's system of justice with a balanced program of basic and applied research.
- Evaluate the effectiveness of criminal justice and law enforcement programs and identify those that merit application elsewhere.
- Support technological advances applicable to criminal justice.
- Test and demonstrate new and improved approaches to strengthen the justice system.
- Disseminate information from research, development, demonstrations, and evaluations (NIJ, 1994, p. 1).

In establishing its research agenda, the Institute is guided by the priorities of the Attorney General and the needs of the criminal justice field. The Institute actively solicits the views of police, courts, and corrections practitioners as well as the private sector to identify the most critical problems and to plan research that can help resolve them. Recent priorities include:

- Reduce violent crime
- Reduce drug and alcohol-related crime
- Reduce the consequences of crime
- Improve the effectiveness of crime prevention programs
- Improve law enforcement and the criminal justice system
- Develop new technology for law enforcement and the criminal justice system

Studies that involve the use of randomized experimental designs are encouraged, as are multiple strategies for data collection and well-controlled, quasi-experimental designs and equivalent comparison group designs. Qualitative studies, including ethnographic data collection, are also encouraged (NIJ, 1994, p. 2).

NIJ Research Priorities

The research priorities of NIJ in 1995–1996 are detailed in *NIJ Research Plan:* 1995–96 (NIJ, 1994). Among the selected topics targeted in those years were:

Studies of violent offenders/offenses
Violent situations
Firearms violence
Response to violent offenders
Violence against women
Substance abuse and criminal behavior
Substance abuse prevention
Drug use forecasting
Drug enforcement
Victim needs
Impact of crime on business
Prevention programs for high-risk youth
Community crime prevention partnerships
Crime and offender behavior
Sentencing
Illegal aliens
White-collar and organized crime (NIJ, 1994)

A Systems Model of Evaluation Research

Although a variety of terms and competing models of evaluation research exist, the "systems model" is presented here to acquaint the reader with a

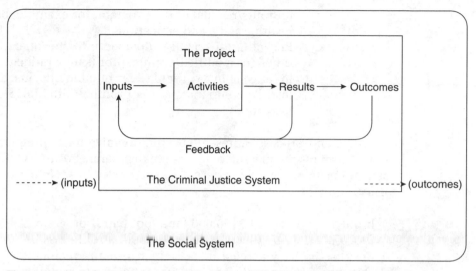

Figure 13.1 A Systems Model of Evaluation Research: System and Project Components. (*Source:* Schneider, Anne L. et al. *Handbook of Resources for Criminal Justice Evaluators.* Washington, D.C.: U.S. Department of Justice, 1978, pp. 3–24.)

A model

Systems model of evaluation

general evaluation approach. A *model* is a simplified schema that outlines the essential points of a theory. As a scheme a **systems model** assumes that all parts of an organism, organization, or program are interrelated and could be represented in basic computer language as a system of inputs into an existing system, processing of these inputs, and subsequent outputs (or outcomes). Figure 13.1 presents a systems model for evaluating programs in the criminal justice system. The project components to be evaluated in this model are inputs, activities, results, outcomes, and feedback (Schneider, 1978, pp. 3,23–3,31):

Inputs   Resources, guidelines, rules, and operating procedures provided for a program, for example, funds for personnel, equipment, operating costs, and authorization to introduce new policies (often an experimental treatment)

Activities   What is done in the project with these inputs (resources), for example, services provided, staffing patterns, and use of materials and human and physical resources (called "process" in many models)

Results   *Specific* consequences of the project activities or the specific objectives of the program, for example, amount of services provided, work completed, production accomplished, or cases closed or cleared (called "output" or "products" in many models)

Outcomes   Accomplishment of broader-range societal goals; these are general consequences of the specific accomplishments (outputs/results) of the program, for example, better justice, health, safety, and education

Feedback   Recycling of results/outcomes into the operation as additional (or modified) inputs; profits may induce a corporation to reinvest in a particularly profitable line, just as losses may lead it to eliminate a less profitable line (also called "feedback loop")

Inputs and process represent specific organizational/program *efforts* and outputs represent specific organizational/program *results*. Outcomes represent impacts on general, external societal activities. Note this *very* simple illustration:

Input	Grant of $100,000 for a foot patrol program
Process	Two officers assigned to foot patrol in Precinct A for one year
Results	Fifty percent increase in arrests in Precinct A
Outcome	Crime rate declines 10% and fear of crime declines 40%
Feedback	Allocate $1,000,000 and twenty officers to expanded foot patrol program

To summarize Figure 13.1,

> In this scheme, a criminal justice project is conceived of as a system consisting of *inputs* (resources, guidelines, and operating procedures); *activities* (those things the project and its personnel do); *results* (the initial consequences of the activities); and *outcomes* (the long-range, socially relevant consequence of the project). The system should contain a *feedback* loop through which the results and outcomes of a project impact upon the operation of the project and act as additional inputs (Schneider et al., 1976, pp. 3–8).

Types of Evaluation Research

With the evolution and growth of evaluation research as a field has come a whole lexicon of descriptive tags. Franklin and Thrasher (1976), for instance, mention a variety of research approaches as they relate to evaluation: continuous-versus-one-shot evaluations, "hip pocket"-versus-formal evaluations, policy research, applied research, decision-oriented research, social audits, action research, operations research, discipline-related research, basic research, front-line evaluations utilization reviews, and continuous monitoring and quality control. Unfortunately, many of these terms are used interchangeably by various writers and there is no consistent agreement on their meaning in the field. Even the terms *policy analysis* and *evaluation research* are often used as synonyms.

Evaluation research is different from other types of applied research in that the data are used to make a decision(s) regarding a specific program, rather than simply to represent findings of theoretical interest (Cochran, 1978). Although numerous types have been identified, there are *two general types of evaluation research:* process evaluation and impact evaluation. In most instances it is the latter term by which "evaluation research" is most often described in references. **Process evaluation** establishes causal relationships between results (such as an increase in arrests) and project inputs and activities (see Figure 13.2). **Impact evaluation** establishes causal relationships between outcomes (such as crime reduction) and inputs, activities, and results of programs.

Evaluation research is often confused with two related information gathering activities: assessment and monitoring. **Assessment** (sometimes called needs assessment) is the enumeration of some activity or resource, for instance, the need for a particular service in some target area. "It is a method of finding service delivery gaps and substantiating unmet needs in a community and is used to establish priorities for addressing problems" (Office of Juvenile Justice, 1978, p. 2). **Monitoring** is assessment of whether the plans for a project have in fact been realized: Are the activities related to the inputs? Monitoring is similar to an audit, an assessment of program accountability: Is the program doing what it is supposed to be doing (Waller et al., 1975)? A certain portion of the operating budget of an organization might be set aside to fund such a monitoring task.

Evaluation research need not be restricted to solely an analysis of output; it can involve any systematic assessment of various aspects of program review (Suchman, 1967). Effort, efficiency, operation, effectiveness of performance, adequacy of performance, and the like can all be subject to evaluation (Office of Juvenile Justice, 1978, p. 3). *Before an evaluation is undertaken,* it is important that it be decided whether an evaluation can and

Margin notes: Process evaluation · Impact evaluation · Assessment · Monitoring

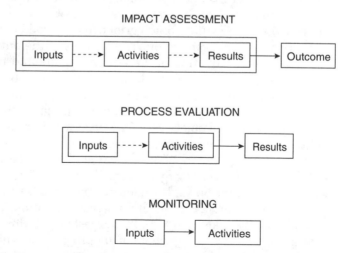

Figure 13.2 Types of evaluation. (*Source:* Schneider, Anne L. et al. *Handbook of Resources for Criminal Justice Evaluators.* Washington, D.C.: U.S. Department of Justice, 1978, pp. 3–33.)

should be done. According to the Office of Juvenile Justice and Delinquency Prevention (1978, p. 508) *three crucial questions must be answered:*

Will the findings be used?
Is the project evaluable?
Who can do this work?

Will the Findings Be Used?

Evaluation research has an applied quality to it that *requires the active support and cooperation of the agency or program to be evaluated.* Levine, Musheno, and Palumbo (1980, p. 551) put the matter succinctly: "The program administrator's desire to reaffirm his or her position with favorable program evaluations may conflict with the social scientist's desire to acquire an objective appraisal of a program's impact. The end result may be either a research design with low scientific credibility and tainted results, or a credible study that never receives a public hearing because the administrator does not like the results" (Levine, Musheno, and Palumbo, 1980, p. 551). Unless a sincere need for the research has been expressed by the agency administrators and the effort is viewed as something other than a public relations plume, evaluation research may become nothing more than a sham.

Is the Project Evaluable?

In asking *whether the project is capable of being evaluated,* the researcher is concerned with the existing design, defined objectives, and other programmatic elements that enable the measurement and assessment of specified criteria. For instance, if the purpose of the program is simply defined as "to do good" and no objectives, records, or other evaluable materials are kept by the organization, much grief can be saved by avoiding an evaluation of this particular organization. The success of the entire evaluation process hinges on the motivation of the administrators and organization in calling for an evaluation in the first place (Schulberg and Baker, 1977).

It should be possible to locate specific organizational objectives that are measurable. "The key assumptions of the program must be stated in a form which can be tested objectively. That is, not only must the outcome be definable, but also the process used to achieve it must be specifiable" (Office of Juvenile Justice, 1978, p. 7). If proper data for evaluation are absent and clear outcomes or criteria of organizational "success" are absent, then a proper evaluation cannot be undertaken. Rutman (1977) refers to this process as "formative research," a reconnaissance operation to determine program evaluability. Wholey (1977, 1983) suggests the following steps in evaluability assessment (assessing whether the program is evaluable):

1. Bounding the problem or program or determining what the objectives of the program are and where it fits in the service picture

2. Collecting program information that defines its activities, objectives, and assumptions
3. Modeling of the program and the interrelationships of program activities
4. Analyzing plans or determining whether the model and activities are measurable
5. Presenting to management (intended user) or reporting results of evaluation assessment and determination of the next steps to be taken

Rabow (1964, p. 69), in speaking specifically to corrections research, suggests that before any results are attributed to a particular treatment, the evaluation should address important questions, as outlined in the three stages of Rabow's research model.

Stage I is concerned with the population of offenders from which treatment and control groups will be selected.

1. How is the population of offenders from which groups will be selected defined with respect to age, record of offenses, geographical location, or any social or personality characteristics thought to be important?
2. How is selection carried out in order to eliminate bias—by random means or some matching process?
3. When and by whom is selection carried out? What are the mechanics?
4. What steps are taken to demonstrate the lack of bias in selection?

Stage II is concerned with the treatment process and the need to understand what is involved in it.

1. What is the theory of causation upon which treatment is proceeding?
2. What is the intervention strategy utilized in the treatment by which the causation variables will be modified?
3. Can a logical relationship between causation variables and intervention strategy be demonstrated?
4. Can it be demonstrated that the treater is fulfilling role requirements specified by the intervention strategy?
5. Assuming that treatment role requirements are being fulfilled, can it be demonstrated that variables cited in the theory of causation are being modified?
6. How shall any change in the variables be measured?

Stage III involves actual comparisons of groups subsequent to treatment.

1. What are the goals of treatment; that is, how shall success be defined— in terms of recidivism, attitudinal change, new social relationships, personality modification?
2. How is the measurement of these characteristics carried out?
3. Over what period of time are comparisons to continue?
4. How is the cooperation of subjects outlined?

Who Can Do This Work?

Who can do
this work?

In asking "Who can do this work?" one must decide on internal or external evaluators. If the evaluation is to be "in-house," that is, to be conducted by the internal staff of the agency to be evaluated, then adequate time and manpower must be allocated to permit a careful and hopefully objective evaluation. Outside evaluators may lend greater objectivity to the evaluation task but, as we will discuss later, require orientation to, and cooperation of, the agency to address the relevant objectives and goals from a policy perspective.

Steps in Evaluation Research

Steps in
evaluation
research

The actual *steps in evaluation research* do not differ significantly from the basic steps in the research process that were identified in Chapter 1:

Problem formulation
Design of instruments
Research design (evaluation model)
Data collection
Data analysis
Findings and conclusions
Utilization

Only in the last step does evaluation research differ significantly from other research processes. There are, of course, a variety of ways of slicing a pie; but most alternative listing of steps one way or another includes the key elements we have identified above. For instance, Albright et al. (1973), in *Criminal Justice Research: Evaluation in Criminal Justice Programs: Guidelines and Examples,* an evaluator's manual prepared on behalf of the National Institute of Law Enforcement and Criminal Justice (now National Institute of Justice), focus primarily on the data collection and analysis stages. They outline five essential **steps in evaluation planning** (Albright et al., 1973, p. 5):

Steps in
evaluation
planning

Quantify the objectives and goals
Determine a quantifiable objective/goal relationship
Develop evaluation measures
Develop data needs considering requirements, constraints, and reporting
Determine methods of analysis

These steps would be assumed or included in the design of instruments, research design, data collection, and data analysis stages that we have discussed throughout this text.

Problem Formulation

Problem
formulation

Just as in the other types of research we have discussed, evaluation researchers are also often in a hurry to get on with the task without thoroughly grounding the evaluation in the major theoretical issues in the field. Glaser (1974) feels that evaluation research in criminal justice would be more useful were it to differentiate offenses and offenders utilizing causal theory. Without this theoretical grounding, familiarization with past and current literature, and valid operationalization of concepts, many evaluation studies can easily deteriorate into glorious exercises in social accounting.

Glaser (1973) comments on how much of what is regarded as in-house evaluations in correctional agencies has been co-opted and is little more than head counting or the production of tables for annual reports.

The problem formulation stage, to reiterate a point that has been emphasized throughout this text, is the most crucial stage of research.

Design of Instruments

Design of
instruments

On the basis of problem formulation, review of the relevant literature, and program reconnaissance, a most important element in evaluation research is the identification and operationalization of key components of the program to be analyzed. The National Advisory Committee on Criminal Justice Standards and Goals (1976, p. 113) suggests that professional associations be commissioned to establish standardized definitions based on the following:

> A major problem in research on criminal justice organizations is the absence of standardized definitions for such basic terms as dangerousness, recidivism, discretion, disparity, equity, proportionality, uniformity, individualization, commitment sentence, probation, parole and length of follow-up. The confusion over definitions has not only impeded communication among researchers and, more importantly, between researchers and practitioners, but also has hindered comparisons and replications of research studies. R&D-funding agencies, such as the National Institute of Law Enforcement and Criminal Justice and the National Institute of Mental Health, should be sensitive to the way in which the terminology is used in the research studies being supported. Where appropriate, the use of common definitions can facilitate the direct comparison of research findings and, hence, the aggregation of research knowledge. For example, the development of standardized definitions has already occurred in the use of some identically worded questions in victimization surveys.

The greater use of replication of instruments employed by others can contribute to more confidence in the reality and validity of evaluation methodologies, as well as to more useful cross-site comparisons.

Research Design

Research
design

Ideally, researchers would prefer control over treatment and a classic experimental design, with random assignment of cases to experimental and control groups. Seldom does the evaluation researcher enjoy such a luxury in analyzing ongoing programs. Despite arguments to the contrary (see Boruch, 1976), in many instances it is very difficult to find organizations that would be willing to undergo experimentation, particularly if it involves the denial of certain treatments (control group) to some clients. Cook, Cook, and Mark (1977) describe some *problems related to the attempt to use randomized designs in field evaluations:*

1. The program planners and staff may resist randomization as a means of allocating treatments, arguing for assignment based on need or merit.
2. The design may not be correctly carried out, resulting in nonequivalent experimental and control groups.
3. The design may break down as some people refuse to participate or drop out of different treatment groups (experimental mortality).
4. Some feel that randomized designs create focused inequity because some groups receive treatment others desire and thus can cause reactions that could be confused with treatments.

Strasser and Deniston (1978) distinguish between preplanned and postplanned evaluations. Although the former may interfere with ongoing program functioning, the latter is less costly, involves less interference in the organization, and is less threatening to the personnel being evaluated. As per our discussion in Chapter 12, statistical analysis and postcontrols can substitute for experimental controls. Much of the bemoaning concerning the inadequacy of research design in evaluation methodology in criminal justice has arisen because of an overcommitment to experimental designs, and a deficient appreciation of the utility of post hoc controls by means of multivariate statistical techniques (see, for instance, Cain, 1975; Posavec and Carey, 1992).

Logan (1980, p. 36) agrees with this point when he states:

> It may be that more rapid progress can be made in the evaluation of preventive or correctional programs if research designs are based on statistical rather than experimental model. It was noted, above, that one major difficulty in evaluation research is in procuring adequate control groups. Modern statistical techniques can provide a means of resolving this problem by substituting statistical for experimental methods of control.

Data Collection

Data collection

One principal shortcoming of much evaluation research has been its overreliance on questionnaires as the primary means of *data gathering.* The use of a triangulated strategy of data collection employing multiple methodologies would assure greater confidence in the validity of findings (see, for instance, Fry, 1973). Where possible, agencies' records as outcome measures should be cross-checked against other data sources. Many of the issues discussed previously in this text are, of course, also appropriate to evaluation research. All of the sources of error, particularly in data collection, must be continually checked, to ensure that the findings are true findings and not the result of measurement error. Schwarz (1980, p. 14) presents the issue succinctly:

> In practice, the cup seldom reaches the lip intact. Designs must be compromised. There are mishaps in the field. Expecting both valid results and an impeccable process is overly optimistic. The most that can be expected is that the findings will be valid despite compromise and mishaps. Flaws cannot be avoided.

Although program supporters will jump on methodological or procedural problems in any evaluation that comes to a "negative" conclusion, Schwarz echoes a theme that has been emphasized throughout this text: There is no such thing as research without error. The only way to avoid error is to do no research at all.

MacKenzie and McCarthy (1990, p. 6) indicate that Criminal Justice researchers should not ignore secondary analysis; nor should they be afraid to reanalyze data previously collected by someone else. Two particularly important sources for such data are the National Archive of Criminal Justice Data (formerly the Criminal Justice Archive and Information Network [CJAIN]) and the National Center for Juvenile Justice (NCJJ). National Archive of Criminal Justice Data databases include many classic and well-known criminal justice studies, as well as data from recent National Institute of Justice-sponsored studies. NCJJ archives data on juvenile justice system transactions in about half of the states.

Data Analysis

Data analysis   As detailed in Chapter 12, the choice of appropriate statistical analysis must be based on whether the data meet the assumptions necessary for each technique to be employed. An important additional consideration is pointed out by Glaser (1976, p. 771):

> Some research reports from correctional agencies are not suppressed, but might as well be, for few officials—or even researchers—can understand them. Most notable among such reports are those which describe the use of various types of multiple correlation or multiple association statistical analysis of case data in administrative records to find guides for correctional operations. These reports are submitted to correctional officials who do not understand the statistical terminology and who feel no urgency to learn to understand it since the researchers share with the operations officials the impression that this statistical analysis has little or no practical value at present. Thus these researchers operate in a separate world, inadequately linked either with the university social system which seems to be their reference group, or with the leaders of the correctional system, which they are presumed to serve.

What might be excellent choices of statistical analysis for professional or academic purposes may not be appropriate in form for presentation to a lay audience. Recall in the first chapter of this text the point that, unlike the chemist or physicist, the criminologists must compete with "commonsensi-cal" views and explanations and, unfortunately, must often pitch their evidence toward the lowest common denominator. How, then, can the evaluation researcher in criminal justice resolve this dilemma of treating data with the most appropriate and rigorous statistical methodology they require, however esoteric, yet attempting to communicate these findings so that even politicians would understand? A useful practice is to perform the evaluation and write a report geared for a professional audience and then issue a *report for laypeo-ple,* in which the crucial findings are simplified, summarized, and understood by nonresearch professionals. In writing such reports the researcher may take license in generalizing findings, but it is exactly this succinct presentation that is usually viewed as most useful by the consumer. Instead of the results of stepwise multiple regressions and intercorrelation matrices, the critical relationships or statistically significant findings could be presented in simple bivariate tables, which are more easily understood by more people. An interesting exercise is boiling down the entire evaluation report to a two-page summary, the type that might be released as a press report. Although, of course, such a brief document does not do justice to the complexity of the analysis, anyone desiring the details can consult the full report.

Utilization

Utilization

Previous points, particularly with respect to data analysis, have a direct bearing on the *utilization of evaluation findings.*

Sharply critical of the state of the art in evaluation research, Abt (1976) claims that there is only about $2 million worth of effective evaluations of the $200 million spent annually to assess the more than $200 billion spent annually in the United States on social programs. Much of this waste, according to Abt, is due to passive bias and censorship within the field itself, which prevent the publication of weaker, less scientific findings, and to misplaced client loyalty (if the evaluator fails to be loyal to the clients, they will more than likely not be the recipients of additional contracts). Similar to our discussion of methodological narcissism in Chapter 1, many of the nonlongitudinal case studies are ignored as inferior specimens.

In discussing the "politicization of evaluation research," Maida and Faucett (1978) point out the increasing political nature of evaluations as they are increasingly used to decide the future of programs. Adams describes the dilemma of the agency administrator who is to be evaluated:

> Part of the administrator's concern about evaluative research comes from the dilemma that research creates for him. The evaluation process casts him in contradictory roles. On the one hand, he is the key person in the agency, and the success of its various operations, including evaluation, depends on his knowledge and involvement. On the other hand, evaluation carries the potentiality of discrediting an administratively sponsored program or of undermining a position the administrator has taken (Adams, 1975, p. 19).

Factors that limit the utilization of evaluation research findings in criminal justice are much the same obstacles that prevent effective evaluation research.

Obstacles to Evaluation Research

Pitfalls in
evaluation
research

In its first annual review volume of criminal justice evaluation, the National Criminal Justice Reference Service (NCJRS, 1979) surveyed most of the authors whose works appeared in the volume, members of the editorial board of the volume, as well as a companion volume, *Crime and Justice: An Annual Review of Research* (Morris and Tonry, 1979). In the order of perceived importance, the following dangerous pitfalls were identified by this group of evaluation experts (NCJRS, 1070, p. 370):

Poorly done evaluation design and methodology
Unsound and/or poorly done data analysis
Unethical evaluations
Naive and unprepared evaluation staff
Poor relationships between evaluation and program staff
Co-optation of evaluation staff and/or design
Poor quality data
Poorly done literature reviews of subject area
Focusing on the method not the process

Even the best laid evaluation plans can "bite the dust" in the "high noon" of political reality, illustrated by our next example.

Murphy's Law in Evaluation Research

Murphy's Law
in evaluation
research

A leading advocate of policy analysis and evaluation research, James Q. Wilson (1973, pp. 132–134), although denying his cynicism in doing so, suggests two laws of program policy research:

Wilson's First Law	All policy interventions in social problems produce the intended effect—if the research is carried out by those implementing the policy or their friends.
Wilson's Second Law	No policy intervention in social problems produces the intended effect—if the research is carried out by independent third parties, especially those skeptical of the policy.

Many evaluators, as illustrated by some of the points we have covered in this chapter, feel that they are victims of the whimsical Murphy's Law: "If anything can go wrong, it will." Some principal corollaries of this law hold that:

Left to themselves, things go from bad to worse.
If there is a possibility of several things going wrong, the one that will is the one that will do the most damage.
If everything appears to be going well, you have obviously overlooked something.

Garwood (1978, pp. 17–21) has humorously applied these maxims of Murphy to evaluation research:

A. Evaluation Design
   1. In any given cost or manpower estimate, the resources needed to complete the evaluation will exceed the original projection by a factor of two.
   2. After an evaluation design has been completed and is believed to control for all relevant (dependent and independent) variables, others will be discovered and rival hypotheses will multiply geometrically.
   3. The necessity of making a major decision change increases as the evaluation project nears completion.
B. Evaluation Management
   1. The probability of a breakdown in cooperation between the evaluation project and an operational agency is directly proportional to the trouble it can cause.
   2. If staying on schedule is dependent on a number of activities which may be completed before or after an allotted time interval, the total time needed will accumulate in the direction of becoming further and further behind schedule.
C. Data Collection
   1. The availability of a data element is inversely proportional to the need for that element.
   2. Historical baseline data will be recorded in units or by criteria other than present or future records.
   3. None of the available self-report formats will work as well as you expect.
D. Data Analysis and Interpretation
   1. In a mathematical calculation, any error that can creep in, will. It will accumulate in the direction that will do the most damage to the results of the calculation.
   2. In any given calculation, the figure that is most obviously correct will be the source of error.
   3. If an analysis matrix requires "n" data elements to make the analysis easy and logical, there will always be "$n - 1$" available.
   4. When tabulating data, the line totals and the column totals should add up to the grand total; they won't.
E. Presentation of Evaluation Findings
   1. The more extensive and thorough the evaluation the less likely the findings will be used by decision makers.

Although these applications of Murphy's Law to evaluation research are obviously of a tongue-in-cheek nature, they do call attention to some of the problems an evaluator can anticipate.

Weiss (1970) describes the unfortunate tendency of negative evaluation findings to stifle otherwise innovative programs. To avoid this outcome, she suggests that less stress be placed on evaluation of the general impact and more on variable conditions within programs. Greater use of systems approaches and avoidance of premature evaluations of organizations may also be helpful. As in all of the research methodologies we have discussed, evaluation research must also consider potential ethical problems.

Researchers and Host Agencies

Host agencies

The National Advisory Committee (1976, p. 133) suggests the following guidelines with respect to relationships between those performing evaluation research and the *host agencies:*

> R&D funding agencies that support studies of criminal justice organizations should be sure that researchers who conduct such studies are sensitive to the needs of the organizations that are part of the study. Such sensitivity will increase the likelihood of completing the project to the satisfaction of the funding agency, the organization that is part of the study (host agency), and the research team.
>
> 1. Before the research begins, clear agreements should be reached between the researcher and the host agency on such issues as: the purposes of the research, duration of effort, data to be collected, plans for protecting confidentiality of sensitive information, resources required of the host agency, extent to which the host agency may be identified by name in publications, form and timing of public disclosure of the results of the study, and any other topic of mutual concern.
> 2. Funding agencies should assist researchers in establishing favorable relationships with host agencies by:
>   a. Assuring that the research design does not necessarily interfere with the host agency's normal operations.
>   b. Arranging for host agencies to receive timely feedback on research progress or results.
>   c. Considering the reimbursement of expense incurred by the host agency in cooperating with the research project.
> 3. Existing educational programs for researchers could be broadened to include relevant courses, on-site projects conducted in cooperation with an operating agency, internships, and exchange programs to make researchers more cognizant of procedures that may improve their relations with criminal justice organizations. These programs should stress the necessity of developing a viable partnership with the host agency during the planning, conduct, and follow-up of a research study.

Exhibit 13.1 provides an example of a national evaluation of intensive supervision probation/parole.

EXHIBIT 13.1

Evaluating Intensive Supervision Probation/Parole: Results of a Nationwide Experiment

Intensive supervision probation/parole is a form of release into the community that emphasizes close monitoring of convicted offenders and imposes rigorous conditions on that release. Most ISP's call for:

- Some combination of multiple weekly contacts with a supervising officer.
- Random and unannounced drug testing.
- Stringent enforcement of probation/parole conditions.
- A requirement to participate in relevant treatment, hold a job, and perhaps perform community service.

Interest in ISP's has been generated in part by the increased proportion of serious offenders among the probation population, a group whose needs and problems may not be effectively addressed by routine probation. Another reason for interest in ISP's is the greater flexibility in sentencing options that they permit. They are better able than the traditional alternatives—prison or probation—to fit the punishment to the crime.

Intensive supervision probation and parole (ISP), the focus of this *Research in Brief,* is a type of intermediate sanction that has attracted widespread attention. By the mid-1980's, ISP's were still largely untested. To find out how they were working, the National Institute of Justice and the Bureau of Justice Assistance supported a nationwide ISP demonstration and evaluation program, conducted by RAND.

The researchers' findings suggest that the programs were more successful in achieving some goals than others. The most singular success lay in the area of control—ISP's include more surveillance and other restrictions that curtail the freedom of the offender. These successes suggest that continued development of ISP's is warranted. In meeting other goals, the programs were either not as successful or the results were inconclusive. Still in the testing stage, the ISP model needs to be further refined. One way, as the researchers suggest, is to select offenders for ISP earlier in their criminal careers. The deterrent and rehabilitative potential of ISP's might be more fully realized for offenders who are not as committed to a criminal lifestyle.

Study Methods [11]

Program Design

All jurisdictions selected by the Bureau of Justice Assistance for participation in the demonstration and evaluation were asked to design and implement an ISP program that was to be funded for 18 to 24 months. The jurisdictions also were required to receive training and technical assistance; both provided by outside consultants.[12] In addition, they took part in the independent evaluation, which required their gathering data about the program.

The population studied consisted of approximately 2,000 adult offenders, who were not currently convicted of a violent crime (homicide, rape,

Contra Costa County, California	Santa Fe, New Mexico
Los Angeles County, California	Des Moines, Iowa
Seattle, Washington	Winchester, Virginia
Ventura County, California	Dallas, Texas
Atlanta, Georgia	Houston, Texas
Macon, Georgia	Marion County, Oregon
Waycross, Georgia	Milwaukee, Wisconsin

Figure 1. The 14 Demonstration/Evaluation Sites

robbery, and assault). The vast majority of the offenders were men in their late 20's and early 30's, and most had long criminal records. In other respects, sites varied. Some, for example, chose offenders with more serious prison records than others. The nature of their offenses varied, as did their racial composition. The proportion of offenders who had prison records varied by site. For example, 86 percent of the offenders in Dallas had served a prison term, while for Contra Costa the figure was only 5 percent.

Because each site was allowed to design its own ISP, no two programs were identical. They adopted whatever components of the general ISP model they wished (such as random urine testing, curfews, electronic monitoring, and treatment referrals).

Close supervision of offenders was one of the few required program components. It consisted of weekly contacts with the officers, unscheduled drug testing, and stricter enforcement of probation/parole conditions.

Random Assignment

The study was conducted as a randomized experiment. Indeed, the study may well be the largest randomized experiment in corrections ever undertaken in the United States. At each site, along with the experimental group, a control group of offenders was set up to serve as a comparison. The offenders in the control group were not part of the program but instead were given a different sanction (either prison or routine probation or parole, for example).[13] After the jurisdictions selected the pool of offenders they deemed eligible for ISP programs, the researchers assigned them randomly to one or the other of the two groups.

Having a control group with which to compare findings ensured that the results were the product of the manipulated variables of the ISP program rather than of differences among the offenders in the two groups. Previous ISP evaluations lacked matching comparison groups.

Data Collection

For each offender, in both the experimental and the control groups, data collection forms were completed by the participating agency in the

respective jurisdictions. A *background assessment* recorded demographic information, prior criminal record, drug dependence status, and similar information. The other forms—*six and twelve month reviews*—recorded probation and parole services received, participation in treatment and work programs, and recidivism during the 1-year followup. Also recorded on this form were the number of drug tests ordered and taken, the types of drugs for which the offender tested positive, and the sanction imposed.

Measuring Program Effects

Separate calculations were devised for estimating costs and for measuring program implementation, the effect of ISP's on recidivism, and the effect on social adjustment (percentage of offenders who attended counseling, participated in training, were employed, and the like).

Effectiveness of ISP's

The demonstration was intended to answer the question of how participation in an ISP affected offenders' subsequent criminal behavior (that is, its effect on recidivism). The evaluation was intended to bring to light information about cost-effectiveness and extent of offender participation in counseling, work, and training programs. The effect of ISP's on prison crowding was not a study aim, but it has been a major policy interest in all ISP programs. The participating sites had their own objectives and interests. Most wanted to learn whether ISP's are an effective intermediate sanction, in which probation and parole conditions are monitored and enforced more credibly.

Overall, the results revealed what *cannot* be expected of ISP's as much as what *can* be. Most notably, they suggest that the assumptions about the ability of ISP's to meet certain practical goals—reduce prison crowding, save money, and decrease recidivism—may not have been well-founded and that jurisdictions interested in adopting ISP's should define their goals carefully. Other study findings indicate that ISP's were most successful as an intermediate punishment, in providing closer supervision of offenders and in offering a range of sentencing options between prison and routine probation and parole.

Source: Petersilia, Joan, and Susan Turner. "Evaluating Intensive Supervision Probation/Parole: Results of a Nationwide Experiment." *National Institute of Justice Research in Brief,* May 1993.

Proposal Writing

Funding Agencies

Funding agencies

Prior to World War II most government research funds were awarded to universities rather than to individuals. During World War II the Navy and later the other branches of the armed forces began to award projects directly to individual faculty members. This funded research had a great payoff in the scientific developments of post–World War II America. Creation of the National Science Foundation and scientific competition with the Soviet Union encouraged funded research. In addition to the federal grants which are channeled through the Department of Justice (National Institute of Justice) and other federal agencies, state agencies and private philanthropic organizations support criminal justice research on a competitive grants basis (MacKenzie and McCarthy, 1990, pp. 1–2). Grants-program offices publish announcements (program plans or research solicitations) to attract proposals, and federal agencies advertise these proposals in the *Federal Register.* As an example, the National Institute of Justice research plan will be discussed shortly.

Grantsmanship

Grantsmanship

Grantsmanship (proposal writing) is defined by MacKenzie and McCarthy (1990, p. 1) as "an art form, which requires faculty members [any grant writer] to combine hard work and creativity in their efforts to define and communicate their research objectives and strategy." Portions of the following discussion will draw from MacKenzie and McCarthy's *How to Prepare a Competitive Grant Proposal* (1990), a publication of the Academy of Criminal Justice Sciences. They view grantsmanship as a "means to achieve the study of salient and tractable research"—where *salient* problems are defined as those which are significant and worthwhile and *tractable* problems are defined as those which are manageable or feasible (ibid). Grantsmanship involves the interplay between choosing an issue that is significant and one that is also manageable. A good practice is for the proposal writer to concisely outline elements to be included in each section of the proposal and then to attempt to establish logical connections between these parts (Sponsored Programs, 1990, p. 3).

Individuals skilled in grantsmanship, proposal writing, and fund raising are now indispensable members of most organizations, even small ones. The art of proposal writing is best learned by doing. The exact components of proposals are usually specified by the funding agency, organization, foundation, or academic department. Here, we outline the core elements of a proposal. As was the case with evaluation research, many of the steps in proposal writing incorporate the basic steps in research that we discussed in Chapter 1 and detailed throughout this book. *The following outline, then, would be used only if a required form is not obtained from the organization to which the proposal is to be submitted.* Those submitting a thesis or dissertation proposal should certainly obtain the specific guidelines of the department or university (Locke, Spirduso, and Silverman, 1993; Rudestam and Newton, 1992).

Basic Elements of a Proposal

Elements of a proposal

The **basic elements of a proposal** (Office of Research Administration, 1971) are:

Title page
Abstract or summary
Table of contents
Introduction (including problem formulation)
Description of proposed study
    Statement of past work
    Statement of proposed work
    Methodology
    Significance of objectives
    Facilities
    Personnel
    List of references
    Bibliography
    Appendixes
    Guarantees of confidentiality (where relevant)
    Budget

Title page

The *title page* should contain brief but essential information such as title of the study; names, titles, and affiliations of principal investigators; date of submission; and purpose of the proposal. The purpose may be indicated simply by the agency, RFP number, or appropriate project category, such as thesis proposal.

Abstract

In addition to a good descriptive title, a *brief and well-written abstract* is most influential in informing busy reviewers of proposals of the project's intentions. An abstract is a brief statement of the purpose, design, methodology, and planned outcome of a project. In preparing a proposal the writer must keep in mind that reviewers are usually pressed for time in reading a large number of proposals. Reviewers rely very heavily upon the abstract, so it should be clear and concise and it should express the key features of the proposed project. Although the abstract appears first in the proposal, it is best compiled after the proposal has been completed (Sponsored Programs, 1990, p. 6).

Table of contents

A *table of contents* listing all major subheads of the proposal is desirable, particularly for longer proposals. Tables, illustrations, and the like should also be listed. Readers should consult standard handbooks such as that by Turabian (1973) for form and style.

Introduction   The *introduction* should cover those areas that we earlier described as issues related to problem formulation, including a brief review of relevant literature, an explication of the significance of the research problem, and an assessment of the need for such research. From this introduction, the writer(s) should derive a specific "angle" or "twist"; that is, what uniquely is it that the researchers are going to do? Is it a replication, a new approach, an attack on the shortcomings of previous studies, or what? The introduction should not concentrate solely on the content of the proposed program, but should also describe the applicant's or organization's ability to conduct such research.

Proposed study   The *description of the proposed study* is the heart of the proposal. Here the writer addresses the traditional questions of who, what, where, when, how, and why. This description should contain a *statement of past work* that has bearing on the proposed study and a *statement of proposed work.* The proposed research should be described succinctly, but in sufficient detail to permit reviewers to judge the scope and intent of the project.

A good literature review is an essential part of the problem formulation stage and involves more than a lengthy abstract or summary of findings. It involves analytic commentary, a search for common themes, as well as a quest for dilemmas or contradictions. It also identifies unresolved issues. It should include any preliminary data that may have been collected, and it should describe unique aspects of the study, as well as document the need for the study (MacKenzie and McCarthy, 1990, p. 15). It is essential that the literature review be as current as possible. If one relies upon books and official documents, one might already be two years out of date. Writing or visiting other professionals in your field and asking for reprints of published articles or copies of papers is a useful idea. MacKenzie and McCarthy (1990, p. 17) suggest:

> Make sure you have done a complete job on the literature review, both scientifically and politically. Include any likely panel member's best work if it is relevant at all; overdoing it won't hurt here. Give a complete citation, spelling out the title and all author's names.

Topic selection   In selecting and developing a research problem the investigator should become thoroughly grounded in the existing literature on the subject, and he or she should be familiar with the names of the major contributors to this state of knowledge, as well as with the current assessment of the state of this body of knowledge. *MacKenzie and McCarthy (1990, pp. 7–8) very succinctly provide advice for selecting a topic with "stay away froms" and "go fors":*

- Stay away from minor problems or research areas that no one else cares about.
- Stay away from old or "mined out" topics unless you can convincingly indicate some new angle which will solve past methodological problems.
- Stay away from foreign travel, especially if it might strike proposal reviewers as pleasurable.

- Go for "hot" topics, e.g., current examples are AIDS, shock incarceration, and violent crime.
- Go for topics of general interest to science rather than those of just particular concern to only a small handful of scholars.
- Go for publications by choosing a topic that has fertile prospects.
- Go for the new, but document background and experience that would speak to one's ability to complete the undertaking.
- Go for cooperation and collaboration, rather than lone efforts, to enhance the proposal.
- Go for generalizable information, that which can apply to other topics or problems.

Funding agencies are attracted to significant, researchable topics. They also find it particularly useful and impressive if the proposal includes preliminary data analysis (ibid., p. 9). Preliminary data supplied through pilot studies speak very effectively for the feasibility of the proposed project. Of particular usefulness in literature reviews are computerized data retrieval systems such as the National Criminal Justice Reference Service.

Methodology

The *methodology section* should detail exactly how the research is to be conducted. What research design is to be employed—experimental, quasi-experimental, cross-sectional, or longitudinal? How are the data to be gathered and operationalized? Are the data to be obtained by means of an experiment, survey, participant observation, or case study, or are unobtrusive measures such as the use of existing data to be employed? Sampling and other procedures should be detailed, as should the specification of instruments. Because proposals are often limited to a certain length, an extended discussion of methodology can be reserved for the appendixes. Various time frames within which completion of the proposed work is expected (Figure 13.3) should also be included, as should plans for analysis (e.g., anticipated statistical procedures) and for final presentation of data.

Research design should logically flow from the problem formulation and literature review. MacKenzie and McCarthy (1990, p. 10) summarize some of the issues to be addressed in research design and data collection:

> State clearly the definitions and measurements of the independent and dependent variables. Note any well-established measurement problems. Describe the data, sample size, sampling technique, and sources, including evidence of the cooperativeness of agencies providing access to the data. Specify the statistical techniques to be used; explain the assumptions and the rationale of the techniques if they are new or extremely advanced. The proposal should demonstrate sufficient familiarity with the proper uses of techniques and their limitations; more complex formulae or statistical issues can be covered in the appendix.

A clear rationale should exist to justify the particular choice of methodology.

Significance of study

The *significance of objectives* of the study includes discussion of the importance and contributions to the field that are expected as a result of the

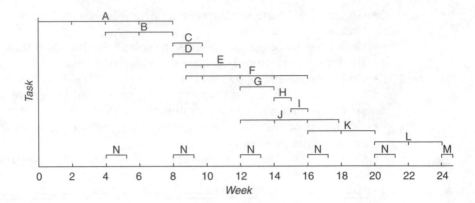

Tasks

A. Develop instruments and pilot test (completed by Week 8).
B. Select sample (completed by Week 8).
C. Train interviewers (during Weeks 9–10).
D. Interim report to NET staff (during Weeks 9–10).
E. Collect data from Summarized Dispatcher Logs (during Weeks 10–12).
F. Household interviews with users and nonusers (during Weeks 10–16).
G. Telephone survey of agencies (during Weeks 12–14).
H. Nonreactive, participant observation on buses (during Week 15).
I. Selected interviews with agency representatives (during Week 16).
J. Coding and keypunching all data (during Weeks 13–18).
K. Theoretical and data analyses (during Weeks 17–20).
L. Prepare final report (during Weeks 21–24).
M. Submit final report (completed by Week 25).
N. Submit monthly reports on work accomplished, task progress, and financial expenditures (Weeks 4, 8, 12, 16, 20).

Figure 13.3 Example of a Time Frame Describing Proposed Periods of Performance. (_Source:_ Rowland, Douglas, and Frank E. Hagan. "Research Proposal to Evaluate Neighborhood Elderly Transportation Project, City of Cleveland." Cleveland: Case Western Reserve University, School of Applied Social Sciences, June 16, 1975, p. 10.)

Facilities   proposed work. The _facilities_ in which the project will be housed should be described. Sufficient detail regarding the organizational management of the project should be given to permit the proposal reviewers to judge the capabilities of the supporting services of the project director(s) to properly perform the proposed work. Included should be a description of the parent physical plant, office, equipment, computer facilities, consulting services and any other arrangements that are anticipated. For small research projects a description might read "Arrangements have been made to utilize the computer facilities of _X_ university or corporation which consists of _____."

Personnel   Under _personnel,_ the proposal should list the qualifications of the applicant(s) for the particular project, as well as the specific role to be played by each investigator. The principal investigator (chief person responsible for directing the project), any co-principal investigators, associates, assistants, part-time technicians, and supportive staff are described here. Biographical sketches, with curricula vitae or resumes attached, should be included for the principal researchers. These brief biographies summarize key relevant items from the resume, placing particular emphasis on previous as well as current or pending research that may be relevant to the proposed work.

In project planning it is particularly important for the researcher to make a realistic appraisal of his or her ability to undertake the project.

> [E]valuate your qualifications in relation to the requirements of the project. Be realistic in assessing whether you have the necessary experience, interest, and ability not only to carry out the project but also to compete for funding. It is equally important to assess how the project fits with your institution's mission, size, and resources. Grants are generally made to institutions, not individuals; in many cases, sponsors require evidence of institutional commitment before they will consider supporting a project, however impressive an individual's proposal may be (Sponsored Programs, 1990, p. 4).

References   The reference section is a list of major books, articles, and monographs cited in the proposal or mentioned as important documents to be utilized during the course of the project. Additionally, a *bibliography* subsection can be included for materials that are not directly consulted in the proposal, but are likely to be used during the project.

As suggested previously, *appendixes* are used to present detailed information that is too long or complex to justify its inclusion in the main body of the proposal.

Ethical protections   Appropriate forms or assurances should also be included in the proposal with respect to the *steps the researcher has taken to protect the privacy, confidentiality, and personal security of human subjects.* This subject was discussed in greater detail in Chapter 2. In considering potential ethical hazards, researchers should describe potential risks to subjects and alternate methods that have been considered to avoid such risks. If applicable, informed consent procedures for protecting subject confidentiality should be detailed, along with a relative risk–benefit ratio, which weighs the relative benefits to the world of knowledge against the potential harm to subjects. Such considerations are usually assured through university review committees.

Budget   The *budget* section of a proposal is the part where the beginning researcher may require the greatest assistance. This help can be obtained from university offices of research administration (or grants person), others who have had research funded, or, to some extent, from contact people at the funding agency. A particularly useful practice is for the proposal writer to consult copies of the budget sections of other previously funded proposals. At any rate, for larger proposals, if the researcher is housed within a larger organization, the office in charge of research should be contacted with respect to certain specifics

The components of the budget section are usually specified by the funding organization which often includes the required forms within the proposal package. Some specifics of the budget are personnel costs (such as salaries and fringe benefits), consulting fees, equipment, supplies, materials, computer costs, telephone and correspondence costs, travel, indirect costs, university overhead, and other categories dependent on the administrative location of the project.

A very useful suggestion is for proposal writers to obtain copies of previously funded proposals. One should seek advice from successful grant recipients. The final proposal should not exceed the number of pages specified in the applications procedures in the program announcement. MacKenzie and McCarthy (1990, p. 10) suggest that rather than viewing this requirement as a limitation and playing fruitless games with single spacing and narrow margins, you should

> instead, work the page limit to your advantage; use it to force a determination of what is needed in the body and what can be placed in an appendix. Avoid wasting space in arguing the need for research on the merits of "the crime crisis," "violent crime," or "prison overcrowding." These arguments will fail to convince the reviewers and will cost valuable page space. Also be careful about citing dollar losses for particular problems unless these statements can be supported with facts and truly help to build the argument.

Some very practical advice includes (ibid., p. 11):

- Number the pages of the proposal, since pages may rip off. Numbering the pages also makes it easier for reviewers to discuss items.
- Present a nice package by using both good word processing software and a good printer.
- Do not use any fancy means of binding the proposal; instead use a simple staple. Uniformly stapled copies are more manageable for reviewers.
- One may give serious consideration to employing a copyeditor to improve readability.
- Use the required signature page (which requires signatures of institutional officials approving the program) as the cover page, thus eliminating the need for a title page.

NIJ Proposal Format and Content

NIJ proposals   As we have indicated, each organization has specific requirements—specifications regarding forms, format, content, and the like that vary somewhat from the basic elements of a proposal just discussed. The research priorities of NIJ were indicated earlier in this chapter. These areas outline the particular research areas the Institute is most interested in funding. To illustrate proposal requirements we now discuss the application procedures and requirements of NIJ (1991, pp. 7–9):

1. Various *federal forms* (for example, federal standard forms for assistance) are specified and must be included in the proposal.

2. A *budget narrative* should detail salaries, materials, and cost assumptions used to estimate project costs. Narratives (explanations of costs) and cost estimates should be presented under the following standard budget categories: personnel, fringe benefits, travel, equipment, supplies, contracts, other, and indirect costs.

3. *One-page abstract* of the full proposal should highlight purposes, goals, research methods, and location of experiments. Ordinarily, the abstract should not exceed one page.

4. A *program narrative* is the technical portion of the proposal and should consist of the following:

   a. A clear, concise statement of the issues surrounding the problem area and of the research hypotheses or questions to be explored. A discussion of the relationship of the proposed work to the existing literature also is expected.

   b. A statement of the project's anticipated contribution to criminal justice policy, practice, theory, and/or research.

   c. A detailed statement of the proposed research design and analytical methodologies. Delineate carefully and completely the proposed data sources, data collection strategies, variables to be examined, and analytical procedures to be employed. If access to particular data sources or the cooperation of operational agencies is proposed, written assurances of cooperation and availability must be attached.

   d. A wide range of research designs and methodologies, including simple descriptive studies and secondary data analysis. When appropriate, the Institute encourages experimental designs because of their potential relevance to policymaking and because of the strength of the evidence they can produce.

   e. A thorough description of the expected research products (reports, journal articles, data sets, etc.).

   f. A description of the organizational capability of the potential grantee.

   g. The organization and management plan to conduct the study. Include a list of major milestones of events, activities, and products; and a timetable for completion, including the time commitments to individual project tasks. All grant activities, including writing the final report, should be completed within the duration of the fellowship.

   h. The name of the author of the proposal.

5. *Copies of the applicant's curriculum vitae* (resumés) should summarize education, research experience, and bibliographic information related to the proposed work.

Other proposal requirements specify such matters as deadlines for submission and proposal length. Finally, of interest is the requirement that all generated data sets must be submitted to NIJ at the end of the project period, along with codebooks and documentation. All applicants are also expected to abide by U.S. Department of Health and Human Services guidelines for protection of human subjects, which require approval of proposals by the applicant's Institutional Review Board.

Evaluation of Research Proposals

NIJ is fairly typical in its proposal evaluation operations. Most funding agencies utilize a peer review process by which they obtain written evaluations from both "in-house" reviewers (those who work for the agency) and outside experts (professionals in the field). The following considerations act as evaluative **guidelines for peer review in assessing the adequacy of research proposals** that have been submitted:

Peer review

Impact of the proposed project
Feasibility of the approach to the issue including technical merit and
    practical considerations
Originality of the approach, including creativity of the proposal and
    capability of the research staff
Economy of the approach (NIJ Research Plan, 1994, p. 27).

In elaborating on these criteria, the National Institute of Justice (ibid.) indicates:

> Applicants bear the responsibility of demonstrating to the panel that the proposed study addresses the critical issues of the topic area and that the study findings could ultimately contribute to a practical application in law enforcement or criminal justice. Reviewers will assess applicants' awareness of related research or studies and their ability to direct the research or study toward answering questions of policy or improving the state of criminal justice operations.
>
> Technical merit is judged by the likelihood that the study design will produce convincing findings. Reviewers take into account the logic and timing of the research or study plan, the validity and reliability of measures proposed, the appropriateness of statistical methods to be used, and each applicant's awareness of factors that might dilute the credibility of the findings. Impact is judged by the scope of the proposed approach and by the utility of the proposed products. Reviewers consider each applicant's understanding of the process of innovation in the targeted criminal justice agency or setting and knowledge of prior uses of criminal justice research by the proposed criminal justice constituency. Appropriateness of products in terms of proposed content and format is also considered.
>
> Applicants' qualifications are evaluated both in terms of the depth of experience and the relevance of that experience to the proposed research or study. Costs are evaluated in terms of the reasonableness of each item and the utility of the project to the Institute's program.[1]

[1]Petersilia, Joan, and Susan Turner. "Evaluating Intensive Supervision Probation/Parole: Results of a Nationwide Experiment." *National Institute of Justice Research in Brief,* May 1993.

Although specific evaluation criteria may change, NIJ employed the following for 1995–1996 proposals. A review panel of researchers and practitioners constituted the peer review panel. They reviewed all proposals and made recommendations to the director, who made all final decisions. Applicants received written comments (critiques) on their proposal, including suggestions on how subsequent proposals may be improved.

NIJ Evaluation of Proposals

Proposal
evaluation
process

Five criteria are used in the NIJ *evaluation process:* the applicant's understanding of the problem, the importance of the research or study, its technical merit, the qualifications of the applicant, and the project's costs. Applicants must demonstrate that the proposed research contributes to current knowledge and has practical policy applications in criminal justice.

Technical merit considerations include (NIJ, 1991a, p. 9):

> [I]s the research design adequate and reasonable? Reviewers take into account the logic and timing of the research or study plan, the validity and reliability of measures proposed, the appropriateness of statistical methods to be used, and the applicant's awareness of factors that might dilute the credibility of the findings.

Is the applicant's experience relevant to the proposed research? Both the depth and relevance of his or her experience are considered, while costs are examined for both reasonableness and usefulness to NIJ's program.

Our presentation of points related to policy analysis, evaluation research, and proposal writing is simplified and limited in scope because more thorough coverage is beyond the limits or intent of this volume. It is hoped that this brief encounter will serve as an interest-inciting device and will encourage the reader to consult some of the more specialized works that have been cited in this text. Appendix A provides more specialized guidelines on "How to Write a Research Report."

Summary

Policy analysis is the study of government behavior. It includes proposals, programs, decisions, and effects. The policy process involves identification, formulation, legitimation, implementation, and evaluation. *Policy experiments* are applied field experiments with immediate practical policy implications. *Evaluation research* is an applied branch of social science that evaluates policies and programs to determine whether and how well they work. The NIJ's research program emphasizes policy-oriented programs and attempts to link researchers with practitioners. A *systems model* of evaluation research consists of inputs, activities, results, outcomes, and feedback.

Before an evaluation is undertaken, three crucial questions must be answered: Will the findings be used? Is the project evaluable? Who can do this work? Formative research, or an evaluability assessment, addresses these questions before an evaluation is agreed to be undertaken.

The *steps in evaluation research* are problem formulation, design of instruments, research design (evaluation model), data collection, data analysis, findings and conclusions, and utilization. *Some obstacles or pitfalls in evaluation research are* poor evaluation design and methodology, poor data analysis, unethical evaluations, naive or unprepared evaluation staff, poor relationships between evaluation and program staff, co-optation of evaluation staff and/or design, poor-quality data, poor literature reviews, and focus on method rather than process. Much evaluation research exemplifies some of these problems, particularly the politics of evaluation.

Of particular importance in effective evaluation is the need for effective relationships between the researcher and the host agency (site to be evaluated). The National Advisory Committee on Criminal Justice Standards and Goals (1976) suggests clear agreements beforehand, assistance from funding agencies in bringing the two parties to suitable agreements, and training programs to acquaint researchers with agency problems and needs. Additional problems in evaluation research were illustrated by Garwood's (1978) application of "Murphy's Law" to evaluation research, while a nationwide experiment on intensive supervision served as an example of evaluation research.

A very general introduction to *proposal writing* was presented with the suggestion that researchers obtain and follow the specific guidelines of the organizations to which the proposal is to be submitted. The basic elements of a proposal are title page, abstract, table of contents, introduction, and description of the proposed study. The description includes statements of past and proposed work, methodology, the significance of objectives, facilities, personnel, references, bibliography, appendices, guarantees of confidentiality, and budget.

The evaluation of research proposals varies according to funding agency. Guidelines employed by NIJ include compatibility with NIJ's mandate and priorities, originality, adequacy and economy of design and methods, experience and competence of proposers, and probability of obtaining new knowledge applicable to solving the crime problem.

Key Concepts

Policy Analysis	Assessment	Obstacles to Evaluation
Evaluation Research	Monitoring	Research
Policy Experiments	Evaluability Assessment	Basic Elements of
Systems Model	Steps in Evaluation	Proposal Writing
Process Evaluation	Planning	Guidelines for
Impact Evaluation		Evaluation of Research
		Proposals

Review Questions

1. How does evaluation research fit into the general scheme of policy analysis? Using the NIJ program, what role can research have in public policy debates in criminal justice?
2. Describe the "systems model" of evaluation research. In what way can such a model inform public policy in criminal justice?
3. Evaluation research seldom takes place as planned. Using the discussions in the chapter, elaborate on obstacles to evaluation research in criminal justice.
4. What are some essentials in proposal writing as well as criteria employed in the evaluation of research proposals?

How to Write the Research Report

The nature, style, and substance of the research report will vary with audience and purpose. A number of the features of a research report have been discussed previously, first in our analysis of the steps in research, then in our analysis of the steps in evaluation research and proposal writing. Does the audience consist of other professionals or laypersons? Is it a paper for a course, for professional meetings, or for a popular publication, a professional journal, or a funding agency? Although differences will exist depending upon the answer to these questions, enough similarities exist that similar guidelines with minor modification will suit each situation.

General Advice

The best way to start to learn how to do anything is to *"just do it"*—practice. Getting started by putting pencil to pad or fingers to keyboard is often the worst part. Howard Becker (1986, p. 167) advises: "Try it! As a friend once said to me, the worst that can happen is that people will think you're a jerk. It could be worse." Before examining specifics of the research report some general advice includes:

- Read some journal articles in the field for a sense of style, language, and format.
- Do not be afraid to start putting your thoughts on paper (or screen). Just assume that you will have to rewrite and polish later.
- Avoid plagiarism by giving proper acknowledgment—provide a citation for the words, ideas, or paraphrases of others. To avoid plagiarism, be careful to record sources in your notetaking while preparing to write the paper.
- Avoid sexist language. Avoid nouns ending in "man," such as policeman or chairman. Use police officer or chair, for example. When using

a pronoun for an antecedent that applies to neither sex specifically, use he or she or him or her (Macmillan, 1988, pp. 9–10).

- Avoid prejudicial language. Be careful to guard against stereotypes or attributions that are offensive to any race, creed, or nation.
- Avoid libel, that is, writing something that is not truthful and could be interpreted as damaging to another party. A publisher once talked this author out of including a section on a celebrated child sexual abuse case in a book he had written because the case had not been adjudicated. Fortunately, it was eliminated; but it turned out to be the longest such trial in American history and the defendants were eventually found not guilty.
- Generally avoid using the first person pronoun "I" in formal papers.
- Proofread the paper. This can be done efficiently with spell checking software, which is available for most wordprocessing programs.

The function of scientific writing is not so much to entertain as it is to objectively inform, and although the style need not be boring, it is generally more technical and geared to a professional audience.

Steps in the Research Report

There are a number of variations in steps in a research report, depending upon whether the report is qualitative or quantitative and depending upon its intended audience. The steps in a research report include:

- The Research Problem and Literature Review
- The Methodology: Research Design and Data Collection
- The Analysis and Presentation of Findings
- Discussion and Conclusions
- References

Preceding the actual body of the paper are the title and abstract. A good title and abstract are succinct and to the point. Abstracts should be less than 200 words. The following is an example (McElrath, 1990, p. 135):

Standing in the Shadows: Academic Mentoring in Criminology
by Karen McElrath
Abstract

Survey data were used to explore the effect of mentoring on publications by faculty members in criminology and criminal justice. The initial analysis showed that mentored faculty were significantly more successful at publishing than nonmentored faculty. Further examination revealed gender differences with respect to being mentored: among new faculty members, publication success was associated with being mentored by males. Explanations for these findings focused on the well-established male network in criminal justice and criminology and on structural disadvantages encountered by female faculty members.

Because many reviewers scanning bibliographic abstracts in search of information will decide on the basis of the abstract's content what the report deals with, it is essential that the abstract be a succinct rendering of the paper's content. Abstracts are written after the entire report has been completed.

Research Problem and Literature Review

Included in this initial section of the research paper is a clear identification of the purpose of the research project. The writer should address why this research and its findings may be useful to criminal justice and/or criminology. A beginning topic is narrowed down into a formalized and specific research problem. The introduction should also include a brief overview of what is to come.

Howard Becker (1986, p. 135) uses the phrase, "terrorized by the literature," to refer to the tendency of some researchers to become so overwhelmed by and deferential to the past literature that they become almost immobilized when trying to get on with their own work. As discussed in Chapter 1, a good literature review can be considerably enhanced by the use of a computerized search service such as DIALOG or the National Criminal Justice Reference Service. Because research papers, unlike books, must be succinct, the literature review must of necessity be abbreviated to permit space for the other sections of the report. In most instances research report writers should avoid relying upon the mass media and popular literature—for example *Time* or *Newsweek*—and they should, as much as possible, use sources from professional journals such as *Criminology* or *Justice Quarterly.*

If there is a specific hypothesis to be examined in the paper, the writer should state this as clearly as possible. In the methodology section one can describe how the measurements are intended to address and test the hypothesis. Kerlinger (1973, p. 694) indicates: "The report should be so written that the reader himself can reach his own conclusions as to the adequacy of the research and the validity of the reported results and conclusions."

Methodology

The methodology section, which includes descriptions of research design and data gathering, should be as specific as possible in order to permit replication. Actual instruments used, such as questionnaires, may be added at the end of the report if they are brief enough. Student reports for class may require that instruments as well as calculations and raw data be appended.

The methodology part should also detail the sampling procedures, the subjects and setting, ethical protections, operationalization of key variables, and the measuring instruments that were employed. The writer basically explains how the study was done. If the report is also to be submitted to the media, it is advisable to cut some of the professional jargon and methodological detail that might not be understood by a general audience. These items should be retained in the original report for submission to a professional audience. Finally, an important question to be discussed is whether the research intends to replicate in any way previous research.

Analysis and Findings

Presentation of tables and results are the subject of this portion of the research report. Berg (1989, p. 150) explains that this section might vary with qualitative data. In some cases the data might be presented throughout the report because qualitative studies are often organized around conceptual themes, ethnographic narratives, and observations.

For quantitative analysis, researchers should explain in detail any scoring and analysis procedures that were used. For qualitative analysis, researchers select quotes and indirectly connote the field experience to the reader (Lofland, 1976).

Discussion and Conclusions

The discussion section usually reiterates the initial research problem and how the analysis and findings addressed it. The writer now goes beyond reporting findings and speaks to how these findings bear upon broader theoretical and substantive concerns. Some typical questions include:

What are the limitations of the study?
Of what significance are these results to issues in the field or to practical criminal justice concerns?
What should future research of this type address?
What conclusions can be drawn?

Writers should avoid getting carried away and generalizing beyond the level of the data that they have gathered. Such sweeping generalizations should be avoided.

References

Most social science journals and writers prefer using what is called the APA style or some variation for referencing materials. This style is spelled out in the *Publication Manual* of the American Psychological Association

(1994). This approach eliminates the traditional style of footnotes at the bottom of the page in addition to a separate bibliography. Instead references are cited directly in the body of the text as has been the case throughout this textbook. For example:

> The number of doctoral programs remain small (Flanagan, 1990, p. 195).

For the reference section, the item would be included in an alphabetized list that has some variation:

> Flanagan, T. (1990). "Criminal Justice Doctoral Programs in the United States and Canada: Findings From a National Survey." *Journal of Criminal Justice Education* 1(2): 195–213.

Another variation is:

> Flanagan, Timothy J. "Criminal Justice Doctoral Programs in the United States and Canada: Findings From a National Survey," *Journal of Criminal Justice Education* 1 (Fall, 1990),195–213.

Such formats are usually detailed near the front or back of journals. The research report should provide a reference for each source that is actually cited in the report.

Appendix

The Appendix contains any tables or figures that are considered too detailed or distracting to include in the main body of the text. While most published journal articles are slim on appendixes because of page space limitations, student research reports that fulfill class requirements should include as much supporting material as possible. For more detail on preparing a research report, the reader is referred to: Brown and Curtis, 1987; Strunk and White, 1979; and Turabian, 1967.

A final piece of advice for academic writers is offered by Howard Becker (1986, p. 121)—"get it out the door." There is something to be said for completing a project within a reasonable period of time. If one is afraid of criticism or seeks absolute perfection, do not write. Research is a dynamic process and critiques and reviews can be very helpful in improving a research report.

References

American Psychological Association. *Publication Manual of the American Psychological Association.* 4th ed. Washington, D.C.: American Psychological Association, 1994

Becker, Howard S. *Writing for Social Scientists: How to Start and Finish Your Thesis, Book, or Article.* Chicago: University of Chicago Press, 1986.

Berg, Bruce L. *Qualitative Research Methods for the Social Sciences.* Boston: Allyn and Bacon, 1989.

Brown, Stephen E., and John H. Curtis. *Fundamentals of Criminal Justice Research.* Cincinnati, Ohio: Pilgrimage, Anderson, 1987.

Flanagan, Timothy J. "Criminal Justice Doctoral Programs in the United States and Canada." *Journal of Criminal Justice Education.* 1 (Fall 1990): 195–213.

Kerlinger, Fred N. *Foundations of Behavioral Research.* 2d ed. New York: Holt, Rinehart and Winston, 1973.

Lofland, John. *Doing Social Life: The Qualitative Study of Human Interaction in Natural Settings.* New York: John Wiley, 1976.

Macmillan. *Author's Guide.* New York: Macmillan, 1988.

McElrath, Karen. "Standing in the Shadows: Academic Mentoring in Criminology." *Journal of Criminal Justice Education* 1 (Fall 1990): 135–151.

Strunk, William, Jr., and E. B. White. *The Elements of Style.* New York: Macmillan, 1979.

Turabian, Kate. *A Manual for Writers.* 3d rev. ed. Chicago: University of Chicago Press, 1967.

Table of Random Numbers

Line/Col.	(1)	(2)	(3)	(4)	(5)	(6)
1	53182	25016	29379	06362	56264	18456
2	62977	55825	65752	53800	15876	47671
3	52707	14924	71846	60633	71877	86471
4	49506	59597	33253	68337	26011	05905
5	62522	87697	89468	11991	31143	74085
6	47967	36735	14328	66359	92592	83369
7	90337	55260	32461	37011	33394	70258
8	68175	81456	51852	07004	60112	14596
9	81204	89541	09655	07004	14002	67115
10	44561	84002	72056	27040	83811	08813
11	34037	09713	28077	15634	36525	26164
12	05040	51825	93494	44669	79764	79207
13	22221	31460	18804	00675	57565	97923
14	70782	14238	04333	04135	53143	06821
15	70260	80002	23998	05749	45538	91204
16	48443	50561	93294	60636	69116	64409
17	04020	00112	24737	05512	47451	66254
18	45974	75158	94918	40441	75549	37582
19	58683	04096	89594	63308	18424	32161
20	68672	97126	23514	99419	32523	71387
21	75642	47774	24915	61419	49356	36692
22	07259	35997	76395	76784	69328	95021
23	79876	78345	22645	13444	09119	29524
24	44379	12780	86861	84838	17030	81101
25	80137	73898	53986	92733	25262	39595
26	22500	26528	27421	73356	53397	26196
27	10725	07664	92595	78723	10328	29456
28	72929	37954	33393	30109	42005	77947
29	11322	66495	60304	56587	92842	10001
30	28254	72057	14900	71602	74683	10939
31	52015	97123	70904	12031	29842	56502
32	69836	43296	32645	47977	42325	30123
33	26453	65591	66983	29645	19238	78223
34	00794	55154	55201	26016	53608	73311
35	77044	46849	90939	74638	71607	41492

Line/Col.	(1)	(2)	(3)	(4)	(5)	(6)
1	18772	49913	60102	50000	83333	51160
2	60983	83941	33300	56591	03004	55620
3	15333	03414	92008	43888	60416	22990
4	91169	60410	27994	72123	79500	37386
5	26854	78500	46492	44913	00892	03799
6	68229	38616	24502	80488	15242	74551
7	24862	15794	72795	80020	49996	20975
8	45930	98571	71452	57415	07972	27613
9	95188	71102	70365	31484	18201	90511
10	52833	89737	63555	81594	88935	85610
11	09310	11580	95081	58554	67233	91188
12	72454	06427	86128	20007	72430	33322
13	89862	79735	73144	48849	73729	30952
14	15046	44025	70616	76288	98658	29868
15	64257	21425	55848	90109	87180	28007
16	63258	38848	16341	31720	95215	75729
17	19380	47663	68298	13935	82606	05517
18	70351	49140	25396	47383	40949	35951
19	45679	16595	74271	56882	68585	25104
20	49424	07655	22348	41576	89990	99812
21	85064	83551	64341	74618	65661	96591
22	80895	93454	30174	59903	70008	18851
23	36953	25851	00242	39367	59905	36510
24	94500	60012	80378	65870	65773	50953
25	39440	01007	15730	08616	29372	34449

An Overview of SPSS/PC+

Laure Weber Brooks

The purpose of this appendix is to familiarize the novice with some fundamental commands and procedures in SPSS/PC+. This appendix is not intended to be an exhaustive discussion of SPSS/PC+; rather, it is designed to discuss only some rudimentary issues in utilizing this canned software. More detailed and additional information can be found in the *SPSS/PC+ Base System User's Guide Version 5.0* (1992). This appendix will cover two basic areas: (1) File Management, which will include information on general procedures for creating files, saving files, and the running of SPSS/PC+ program files; and (2) Programming Commands, which will cover the actual and utilization of SPSS/PC+ programming commands.

File Management

In this section certain aspects of managing files in SPSS/PC+ will be addressed. These aspects include the issues of file, types, naming files, creating files, saving files, executing files, examining files, dealing with errors, and exiting SPSS/PC+.

Types of Files

There are several different types of files that are utilized in SPSS/PC+. Some commonly used files include: data files, which contain raw data; include files, which contain a group of SPSS/PC+ programming commands; and listing files, which contain the output from an executed include file.

Naming Files

File names contain three parts: the pathname, the filename, and an extension. The pathname indicates the drive that the computer is to use, typically the "A" drive. The filename indicates the primary name of the file, and can be no longer than eight characters with no blanks permitted. The filename is followed by a period. The extension directly follows the period and contains three characters that generally refer to the type of file being named (i.e., DAT for a data file, INC for an include file, and LIS for a listing file). For example, A:POLICE.DAT would refer to a data file of police officers stored on a diskette in drive "A."

General Information

SPSS/PC+ uses a split-screen approach in that the top half of the screen contains read-only information (a menu and a Help window) and the bottom half contains a "scratchpad" (an area to write in).

When the SPSS/PC+ user first logs on to the system and occasionally thereafter, the user is placed in the "Menu mode". In this mode, the cursor appears as a box that does not flash. The user must switch from this mode into the "Edit mode" by the key combination of ALT and E. The cursor will then flash and become smaller.

SPSS/PC+ allows for the use of the Insert key, the Delete key, all four arrows, as well as the majority of traditional word processing keys. It is very simple to correct mistakes as well as to move around in files. In addition, SPSS/PC+ utilizes several "Key Combinations" that involve striking two keys simultaneously.

Creating or Retrieving Files

To create or retrieve files in SPSS/PC+, one must be in the Edit mode. Next, follow these instructions: (1) press F3, (2) choose "Edit a Different File" by pressing Enter, and (3) type in the name of the file you want to create or edit (retrieve) and enter this request. You must use the complete filename as discussed above. If the name you have typed in is a new file name, the words "New File" will appear at the bottom of the screen. At this point, a new file has been created and you will begin to enter your programming commands (to be discussed later) in the scratchpad. If you have simply retrieved an old file, your file will appear in the scratchpad.

Saving Files

To save a file, the cursor must be at the very beginning of the first line in your file. The file will only be saved from the point at which the cursor is placed until the end of the file. Next, press F9. Select "Write the Whole File" option by striking the Enter key. The computer will request the name by which you want to call this saved file, and the name you originally called it will be displayed at the bottom of your screen. If you want to keep this name, hit Enter. If not, type a new, complete file name and hit Enter.

Executing Programs

In order to run a program (execute a set of commands), the cursor needs to also be at the very beginning of the first line in a file. Next, press F10. Select "Run from Cursor" by striking the Enter key. Information will flash on the screen and you may be placed in the Menu mode which will require the ALT E key combination to return to the Edit mode. At this point, the program has been executed and your output has been placed in a special Listing file designated in the Include file (discussed in a later section).

Examining the Listing (Output) File

To examine the results of the executed program before printing, press F2. Select "Switch" by pressing Enter. The cursor will now move to the upper half of the screen and the output of the submitted run will be displayed. Move through the output with the arrows, key combinations of CTRL HOME or CTRL END, or use PAGE UP and PAGE DOWN. Examine the Listing file for errors or warnings. Move back down to the scratchpad by pressing F2 again. Select "Switch" to switch back to your original position in the bottom half of the screen.

Errors and Warnings

When errors and warnings occur in processing, they will be indicated either at the bottom of the scratchpad or inside the top half of the screen and will be detected in the examination of your listing file. Errors and warnings need to be corrected in the actual Include file and cannot be changed in the Listing file. The user needs to exit SPSS/PC+ (instructions will follow) and enter the system again to avoid the retention of a Listing file with old errors and warnings. Once the system is entered again, the user needs to edit the Include file (F3), correct the mistake, save the corrected version (F9), and rerun the program (F10).

Exiting SPSS/PC+

To exit the system, press F10. Select "Exit to Prompt" by using the right arrow to highlight this choice and enter this command. When the response, "SPSS/PC," is displayed, type "FINISH" and hit Enter.

Printing Files

The actual technique of printing a file will depend on the operating system available to the user. Typically, Listing files are retrieved in a word processing environment, reduced in size, and otherwise edited. They are then generally printed in that word processing system.

SPSS/PC+ Programming Commands

Before we begin with a discussion of specific commands, it is necessary to highlight one procedural rule. SPSS/PC+ commands are made up of two parts: a command part and a specification part. The command part refers to the unique word or sets of words that indicate the task being requested by the user. SPSS/PC+ requires that commands begin in the first column on a line in a program. The *specification* part of an SPSS/PC+ command refers to additional information necessary to provide details of the command and may not begin in the first column in a program. At least one space must be left before the specification or subcommand part may begin. Additionally, if the user needs to continue on to another line in a program at least one space must be inserted before beginning on the new line. During the course of this appendix, the parts of the SPSS/PC+ commands, that constitute both command and specification parts will be indicated.

Secondly, SPSS/PC+ requires a "command terminator," in the form of a period (.) , to be placed at the end of a command or any further specification of it.

Data Definition

In this section we will discuss five basic data definition commands: DATA LIST, VARIABLE LABELS, VALUE LABELS, SET, and MISSING VALUE. All of these commands center around giving the computer instructions on how to read and interpret data by providing information on the names and locations of data and of variables in the data, as well as indicating missing data. These five commands will be discussed in the typical order they might appear in an SPSS/PC+ program.

Data List

The purpose of the DATA LIST command is to identify the name of the data file to be used, as well as the names and locations of the variables that the user wishes to utilize in the present analysis. A typical format is as follows:

DATA LIST FILE= 'A:CA1.DAT'
/ GENDER 3 RACE 4 SES 10
/ CRIMES 8–11 ARRESTS 14–16.

The phrase DATA LIST is a command, while the remainder of the three lines constitute the specification part of the command. After the command, DATA LIST, the user needs to leave a space and then include the word FILE with an equal sign directly after it and, in quotes, the complete name of the data set to be utilized is listed. The second line of this statement begins with a /. This tells SPSS/ PC+ that the user is ready to refer to variables located on card one, or the first line of data. The user must leave a space and then may list the first variable that is to be utilized with a space and the appropriate column listed next. Additional variables that are found on the first record may be listed with their columns indicated using the same format. The next line begins with another / which indicates that the second card will be discussed and any variables located on that card will then follow. In this example, the variable GENDER is located on the first line of data in column 3, RACE is found in column 4, and SES is in column 10. Additionally, the variables of CRIMES and ARRESTS are found on the second line of data in columns 8–11 and 14–16 respectively. Only the variables that the user wishes to examine should be mentioned and the cards need to be discussed in numerical order. If a card/record is to be skipped, simply put a / and do not list any variables after it (e.g., // GENDER 6. would skip the first card and read Gender on the second card in column 6; / GENDER 6 /. would read GENDER on the first card in column 6 and would skip the second card). Remember to end with a command terminator after the last variable on the last card is listed. There are some rules concerning the naming of variables in SPSS/PC+, such as: (1) variable names must be unique, (2) they cannot be longer than eight characters, and (3) the first character must be a letter of the alphabet or a #, @, or $ (Norusis, 1992).

Variable Labels

The purpose of the VARIABLE LABELS command is to attach a longer name to a variable to allow for ease in interpretation of that variable. Since the maximum length of a variable name is eight characters, this is often not long enough to adequately identify the nature of the variable; thus, it is helpful to attach variable names. A typical format is as follows:

VARIABLE LABELS GENDER 'SEX OF PERSON'
RACE 'RACIAL STATUS'
SES 'SOCIOECONOMIC STATUS'
CRIMES '# CRIMES COMMITTED'
ARRESTS '# TIMES ARRESTED'.

VARIABLE LABELS is the command, while the remainder constitute the specifications. A space is left after the command, the variable name comes next with a space to follow, and finally the label for the variable is enclosed in quotes. At least one space must separate the second quote from the next variable to be labeled. The maximum length including the quotes and any blanks inside the label is forty characters per variable. Remember to use the command terminator at the very end.

Value Labels

The purpose of the VALUE LABELS command is to attach a label to the values or codes of variables measured at the nominal or ordinal level of analysis. These labels allow the researcher to know how the variable was coded and what the codes stand for. A typical format is as follows:

VALUE LABELS GENDER 1 'FEMALE' 2 'MALE'/
RACE 1 'WHITE' 2 'BLACK' 3 'OTHER'/
SES 1 'LOW' 2 'MIDDLE' 3 'UPPER'.

The phrase VALUE LABELS is a command and the remainder of the statements contain the specifications. A space must follow the command and then the programmer may list the first variable that requires a label for its values. This is followed by a space and then the values and the appropriate labels are listed according to the above format. If there is more than one variable to be labeled, a / must be inserted between the end of the value list and the next variable. Additionally, a space must be left in the first column of any line that is a continuation. The allowed length of the VALUE LABEL is a maximum of twenty characters per label including the quotes and spaces.

Set

The SET command has multiple purposes and three will be discussed in this appendix. One purpose is to send output continuously to the screen without pausing to give the "More" prompt when the screen lists files. This would be accomplished with the following command:

SET MORE=OFF.

A second purpose is to direct the output to a file by specifying a complete file name, including the pathname, filename, and extension. For example:

SET LISTING='A:STUDENT.LIS'.

This command would create a listing or output file to contain the results from this run. This would be the file to eventually be examined (as discussed earlier) or to be printed.

A third purpose concerns the treatment of blanks in data sets. Generally, when SPSS/PC+ encounters a blank field in a numeric variable, it treats the blank as equivalent to a zero or as a system missing value. If the programmer wishes the blanks to be treated as something else, the SET command may be used to accomplish this. A typical format dealing with blanks is as follows:

SET BLANKS = -1.

In this example, the SET command requests that all blanks be treated as a value of −1. The user may request any numeric character after the equal sign. This command is generally used in conjunction with the MISSING VALUE command to be discussed next. For other purposes of the SET command, the reader should consult the *SPSS/PC+ Base System User's Guide* (Norusis, 1992).

Missing Value

The purpose of the MISSING VALUE command is to inform SPSS/PC+ of missing codes for the variables in a program and to ultimately exclude the missing data from the performance of various statistical procedures. The MISSING VALUE command should follow the SET command if one is used in the treatment of blanks. The MISSING VALUE command allows for a variety of approaches in the listing of variables and their missing codes. Consider the following format:

MISSING VALUE GENDER (−1) RACE (9,8) SES (−8).

In this example, the variables of GENDER, RACE, and SES all have different codes that indicate missing data. If this is the case, each variable must be listed separately with the missing codes listed in parentheses with commas between missing codes, and with spaces between the variable and the parentheses. If all the variables in the program have the same missing code (such as when SET is used to treat blanks as −1), then an alternate form of MISSING VALUE may be used:

MISSING VALUES GENDER TO ARRESTS (−1).

In this case, all of the variables on the DATA LIST card have the same missing code, −1. If this is the case, instead of listing all of the variables, the programmer can use the keyword TO and list the first variable on the DATA LIST card (GENDER in this example), the keyword TO, and the last variable on the DATA LIST card (ARRESTS in this example) with spaces between. Additionally, the missing value code needs to be enclosed by parentheses with a space before the open parenthesis. Other forms of the MISSING VALUE command and further specifications are provided in the *SPSS/PC+ Base System User's Guide* (Norusis, 1992).

Transformations

This section will explore some of the major ways that SPSS/ PC+ users can transform and manipulate variables and data. In this section we will discuss five commands that deal in some capacity with the transformation of data and/or variables: RECODE, COMPUTE, IF, SELECT IF, and PROCESS IF.

Recode

The purpose of the RECODE command is to collapse response codes of variables into more useful categories. Many times the way a variable is originally coded is in a form that is not conducive to certain types of analysis. RECODE allows the user to change the structure of a variable without actually editing the data. A typical format is as follows:

RECODE ARRESTS (0=1) (1,2=2) (3 THRU HI=3).

In this example the variable, ARRESTS, is recoded into three groups: those who were never arrested are recoded with a score of 1, those arrested one or two times are recoded with a score of 2, and those arrested three or more times are recoded with a score of 3. RECODE is a command and must be typed in the first column followed by a space and the variable to be recoded. After a space, the programmer inserts the original code followed by an equal sign and the new code, all of which are enclosed in parentheses. If more than one code of a variable recoded, spaces must separate the code lists as shown above. There are several keywords that can be used in the RECODE command, such as: LO, HI, ELSE, and THRU. In the example above the keyword HI was used to indicate the upper limit of the third set of values, but a number could have been used instead to indicate the maximum value. A separate RECODE command may be used, or the use of a slash to separate one variable from another is also permitted. If a string of variables is used, they need to be separated by commas and listed before the first open parentheses.

Compute

The COMPUTE command allows the user to create a new variable using a variety of arithmetic operations. This command is helpful when researchers create scales or need to refine an existing variable. The new variable can be easily created using simple addition (as in the case of Likert scales) or it can be as complicated as using a combination of numerical operations. A typical format is as follows:

COMPUTE NEWVAR=VAR1+VAR2+VAR3.

In this example a new variable named NEWVAR would be created by summing the codes of VAR1, VAR2, and VAR3. Some of the standard numeric operations that could be utilized include: + (addition), − (subtraction), * (multiplication), / (division), and ** (exponentiation). Other more complicated arithmetic functions that can be utilized with the COMPUTE command are discussed in the *SPSS/PC+ Base System User's Guide* (Norusis, 1992).

If

The IF statement is often used in conjunction with COMPUTE and is used to transform a newly created variable. Programmers may create a new variable with COMPUTE and specify with the IF command certain situations in which the newly created variable takes on different values. For example:

COMPUTE CRIMINAL=0.
IF (CRIMES NE 0 OR ARRESTS NE 0)CRIMINAL=1.

In this example, a new variable, CRIMINAL, is created with the COMPUTE statement and is set to equal 0. At this point, all cases would have a score of zero on this new variable. The IF statement then selects certain cases and changes their values to equal 1. For example, cases which have a score on CRIMES other than 0 or cases with a score on ARRESTS other than 0 will get a score of 1 on the variable CRIMINAL. Spaces must be placed after the IF statement and between the words/symbols inside the parentheses. Some possible "operators" that may be utilized in the IF statement include: EQ (equal to), NE (not equal to), LT (less than), GT (greater than), LE (less than or equal to), and GE (greater than or equal to). Additional operators are discussed in the *SPSS/PC+ Base System User's Guide* (Norusis, 1992). In the above example, the word OR was used to identify cases for which the IF statement applied. The word AND is also permitted or one condition (CRIMES NE 0) can be used.

Select If

SELECT IF is used to select out certain cases for analyses. If the expression identified in the SELECT IF command is true, the case is selected. If the expression is not true, the case is excluded. For example:

SELECT IF (GENDER EQ 1).

This command would select individuals who have a score of 1 on the variable GENDER; in this case, females. Only those individuals would be included in this analysis. The same operators discussed above in the IF statement may be used in the SELECT IF, as well as the words AND and OR.

Process If

The command, PROCESS IF, may be inserted in a program before a transformation and/or a procedure to indicate a temporary transformation that is only in effect for the next procedure. This command is helpful if users want to analyze different sets of cases within one SPSS/PC+ program. For example:

PROCESS IF (GENDER EQ 1).
FREQUENCIES VARIABLES=CRIMES.
PROCESS IF (GENDER EQ 2).
FREQUENCIES VARIABLES=CRIMES.

This set of commands would result in two separate analyses. The first would include only females and would provide frequencies on the variable CRIMES, while the second would include males and would also provide frequencies on the variable CRIMES. The FREQUENCIES command will be discussed later.

Statistical Procedures

In this section we will examine five basic statistical procedures in SPSS/PC+. Only selected options and/or statistics associated with each will be discussed here. The user should consult the *SPSS/PC+ Base System User's Guide* for additional information regarding these procedures and for other available statistical procedures in SPSS/PC+ (Norusis, 1992). The procedures to be discussed in this section are: FREQUENCIES, CROSSTABS, T TEST, CORRELATIONS, and REGRESSION.

Frequencies

The FREQUENCIES command produces a table of values with the number of cases associated with each value for identified variables. It will also, upon request, provide certain statistics for each variable. A typical format is as follows:

FREQUENCIES VARIABLES=CRIMES ARRESTS/
STATISTICS=MEAN MEDIAN MODE.

This hypothetical FREQUENCIES command will produce a frequency listing of all values for the variables CRIMES and ARRESTS, and will provide the mean, median, and mode for each distribution. If statistics are requested (as above), the user must place a / after the variable list. If the user wishes to have a frequency table of all of the variables on the DATA LIST card, then the keyword ALL can be inserted in lieu of a variable list (VARIABLES=ALL). Additionally, the keyword TO may be used to list strings of variables. Available statistics include: MEAN, MEDIAN, MODE, STDDEV (standard deviation), VARIANCE, SKEWNESS, KURTOSIS,

SEKURT (standard error of the kurtosis statistic), SESKEW (standard error of the skewness statistic), SEMEAN (standard error of the mean), RANGE, MINIMUM, MAXIMUM, SUM, DEFAULT (mean standard deviation, minimum, maximum), ALL (all available statistics), and NONE (no statistics) (Norusist 1992). Barcharts and histograms are also available by specifying BARCHART or HISTOGRAM after the slash following the variable list. Other options and output are also available (Norusis, 1992).

Crosstabs

The procedure CROSSTABS produces cross-tabulations for variables. In addition to printing the raw numbers of cases that fall into the cells, CROSSTABS can also produce cell percentages, row percentages, column percentages, etc. A typical format is as follows:

CROSSTABS GENDER BY ARRESTS/CELLS.

This example would result in a cross-tabulation of two gender types by the number of times they have been arrested. The cells specification would result in row, column, and total percents, as well as the count for each category. Other options are also available. The user may also specify more than one separate cross-tabulation within the CROSSTABS command by placing a / between lists. Additionally, more than a two-way table may be requested (i.e., GENDER BY ARRESTS BY CRIMES). In addition, with a STATISTICS command the user can request statistics such as: chisquare (CHISQ), Phi and Kramer's V (PHI), contingency coefficient (C), Lambda (LAMBDA), Kendall's Tau-b (BTAU), Kendall's Tau-c (CTAU), Somer's d (D), Eta (ETA), Pearson's r and Spearman's correlation coefficient (CORR), Kappa's coefficient (KAPPA), and all available statistics (ALL) (Norusis, 1992). For example:

CROSSTABS GENDER BY ARRESTS
/STATISTICS=CHISQ.

T-Test

The procedure, *T*-TEST, compares two means by group. *T*-TEST calculates the student's t to determine if means are significantly different from each other. It can be used with both independent samples and paired samples. A typical format for an independent samples test is:

T-TEST GROUPS=GENDER/VARIABLES=ARRESTS.

The grouping variable must be divided into two groups and if more than two groups exist, the user must specify the two values to be examined (e.g., GROUPS=GENDER(1,2)) In the above example, there are only two groups of GENDER and the mean of arrests for females would be compared to the mean of arrests for males. Additional *T*-TESTS may be requested for the same groups by listing other variables on the VARIABLES= specification (VARIABLES=ARRESTS CRIMES). If paired samples are used, the programmer would use PAIRS= instead of the GROUPS and VARIABLES specification.

Correlations

The command, CORRELATIONS, computes Pearson correlations and significance levels for requested variables in the form of a correlation matrix. A typical format is as follows:

CORRELATIONS SES CRIMES ARRESTS.

This example would produce a correlation matrix that examines the correlations between SES and CRIMES, SES and ARRESTS, and CRIMES and ARRESTS. The keyword WITH can also be used to request a series of correlation matrices. More than one matrix can be requested by inserting a / between the first list and any additional list of variables (i.e., SES CRIMES/CRIMES ARRESTS). Additionally, the keyword TO can be used to examine a string of variables. See the *Base System User's Guide* for additional possibilities (Norusis, 1992).

Regression

The command, REGRESSION, requests the performance of multiple regression on selected variables and offers several methods of variable selection. Numerous options and statistics are also available in this procedure. Only some of the variations will be discussed in this appendix. A typical format is as follows:

REGRESSION VARIABLES=ARRESTS CRIMES INCOME AGE
/DEPENDENT=ARRESTS
/ENTER.

This hypothetical REGRESSION request will examine four variables (ARRESTS, CRIMES, INCOME, and AGE). Variables may be listed separately with spaces between them or may be listed as a string with the keyword TO. Additionally, if the user wishes to include all of the variables defined on the DATA LIST command, the word ALL may be used in place of a list of variables. The second line in this example specifies which variable is to be considered the dependent variable in this analysis. If more than one regression model is requested, then the user may leave a space after the first dependent variable and include another. A / must also appear at the beginning of this line. The third line in this example is the line which requests the method to be used in the regression and it must begin with a /. In this example, the programmer is requesting forced entry to be used. If no variables are listed on the ENTER line, then all variables that pass the tolerance level will be included. Otherwise, the entry of only certain variables can be requested by listing the selected variables with commas between them. Additionally, multiple ENTER commands with slashes between them may be used if the user wishes to specify the order of the variable inclusion regardless of tolerance. Other options concerning the METHOD are available such as: FORWARD (forward entry), BACKWARD (backward elimination), STEPWISE (stepwise selection), REMOVE (forced removal), and TEST (test of subsets of independent variables). Multiple methods can be requested for a set of variables by listing the methods with slashes between them (i.e., /STEPWISE/ENTER). Additionally, the user may request certain statistical criteria to be used in lieu of the default (PIN (0.05), POUT (0,1), and TOLERANCE (0.01)). The /CRITERIA=specification is used to accomplish this and must be placed before the /DEPENDENT command.

A variety of STATISTICS are available with REGRESSION and several are included in the default mode (multiple R, analysis of variance, regression coefficients, and coefficients and statistics for variables not yet in the equation). See the *Base System User's Guide* for additional statistics (Norusis, 1992). If additional statistics are requested, the statistics subcommand must appear before the DEPENDENT subcommand.

Analysis of residuals can be achieved by the following subcommands: RESIDUALS, CASEWISE, SCATTERPLOT, PARTIALPLOT, and SAVE. These can be specified in any order. Each of these has a variety of specifications that are too lengthy to be discussed here. The complete description of these subcommands are discussed in the *Base System User's Guide* (Norusis, 1992).

The above discussion of REGRESSION is not meant to be exhaustive but rather to simply highlight some of the options available to the SPSS/PC+ user in the REGRESSION command.

Miscellaneous Issues

In this section we will discuss three main issues regarding the use of SPSS/PC+ which merit some attention. These include: using in-line data, systems files, and interpreting errors and warnings.

In-line Data

Instead of utilizing a data set contained in a separate file, it is also possible to put one's data directly into the Include file that contains the SPSS/PC+ commands. This approach is referred to as using "in-line data." To use in-line data, two commands in addition to the data must be included in the program. Before the first line of data is typed, the command, BEGIN DATA must be inserted. Next, the data will be entered in their appropriate columns, followed by the command, END DATA, and the command terminator. For example:

BEGIN DATA
2345 376 34
6583 098 21
2487 976 17
END DATA.

It is possible to use the BEGIN DATA and END DATA commands without including a procedure card in the program. In this case, SPSS/PC+ will simply read the data. However, if procedure commands are used in the program, the BEGIN DATA command must directly follow the first procedure command and any options or statistics commands that are associated with it.

System Files

The command, SAVE, allows the programmer to create a system file for future use. All information on data definition and transformation is kept in this file. Therefore, the programmer does not need to include commands such as DATA LIST, VARIABLE LABELS, VALUE LABELS, SELECT IF, IF, COMPUTE, RECODE, and the like, as long as they were included in the original program that generated the system file. Using a system file results in a great savings of time for the SPSS/PC+ user as well as an increase in convenience. The user may create a system file even when no procedure is requested in a program, as long as the command SAVE is used. A typical SAVE command is as follows:

SAVE OUTFILE='A:OFFICER.SYS'.

This SAVE command will save the file in a system file called OFFICER.SYS on the "A" drive. It is also possible to save more than one system file within one program by using multiple SAVE commands, each listing a different OUTFILE handle.

Once a system file has been created, the user by the command:

GET FILE='A:OFFICER.SYS'.

In this case, the system file called "OFFICER.SYS" would be accessed.

A helpful command that often accompanies a GET command is the DISPLAY command. This command displays all the documentation for the system file. For example:

GET FILE='A:OFFICER.SYS'.
DISPLAY ALL.

Errors and Warnings

When SPSS/PC+ finds a problem or an error in a program, it responds by usually giving the user an error message or a warning message. These messages are accompanied by numeric digits that correspond to a particular problem. Warnings typically occur when nonfatal problems are involved. In this case, the user may have failed to identify missing data or perhaps misspelled a variable name on an optional command. Generally, warnings do not affect the processing of a procedure but rather may affect the labeling or treatment of a variable. Errors are more serious problems and may affect the output substantially or may cause the processing to cease. These may also occur because of a spelling error, failure to correctly set up procedure cards, failing to identify variables, and many other possibilities. In either case of an error or a warning, SPSS/PC+ provides information on the cause of the problem. After an error or warning has been identified, the user must exit SPSS/PC+, reenter the system, go back to the Include file, make the correction, save the corrected Include file, and resubmit the program to SPSS/PC+.

Summary

The preceding has been a fairly brief overview of rudimentary SPSS/PC+ commands to assist the novice in writing and running SPSS/PC+ programs. It is clearly not meant to cover every possible command, nor every variation of even the covered SPSS/PC+ commands. It is strongly recommended that the SPSS/PC+ user consult the *Base System User's Guide* for additional and more comprehensive discussions of SPSS/PC+.

Reference

Norusis, Marija J. *SPSS-PC+ Base System User's Guide Version 5.0.* Chicago: SPSS Inc., 1992.

Statistics: An Addendum to Chapter 12

This appendix is intended to go into more detail than Chapter 12, "Data Analysis: A User's Guide to Statistics," on various matters requiring more explanation.

Measures of Central Tendency for Grouped Data

For the following data, calculation of the median and mean is made more complicated because we are dealing with group data.

The *mode for grouped data* is simply the midpoint of the class interval that has the most cases. In our example, the interval 26–50 has the most cases (16). The midpoint of this interval can be easily obtained by adding the highest and lowest score of the interval and dividing by 2. Thus, 26 + 50 = 76 ÷ 2 = 38. *The mode for this distribution = 38* (see Table D.1). Note that this is not different from our previous procedure except that the data are grouped; for example, to obtain the mode of categories 1–5, calculate 1 + 5 = 6 ÷ 2 = 3 or 3rd category, assuming values 1, 2, 3, 4, 5.

TABLE D.1

Crime Rate	t^a
76–100	4
51–75	8
26–50	16
0–25	10
	$N = 38$

[a]Frequency.

The *mean for a grouped distribution* can be calculated in the following manner (see Table D.2):

1. Calculate the midpoint for each interval. In our example, 76 + 100 ÷ 2 = 88.
2. Obtain ΣfX by multiplying each X or midpoint by each frequency.
3. Calculate the mean using the formula for frequency distribution.

$$\overline{X} = \frac{\Sigma fX}{N} = \frac{1,594}{38} = 41.9$$

The *median for a grouped distribution* can be obtained in the following manner:

1. Construct a cumulative frequency distribution for the data (see Table D.3, column 3).
2. Calculate the simple median position using the standard formula: median = $(N + 1)/2$. In our example, 39/2 = 19.5th case.
3. Find the interval that contains the median position. In our example, counting up we find that the interval 26–50 contains the 11th through 26th cases; thus, our median, 19.5th case, lies within this interval.
4. Now calculate the exact median for a grouped frequency distribution using the formula

$$\text{median} = LL + \left(\frac{(N/2) - CF_{below}}{f \text{ in median interval}} \right) i$$

TABLE D.2

Crime Rate	X^a	f	fX
76–100	88	4	352
51–75	63	8	504
26–50	38	16	608
1–25	13	10	130
		$N = 38$	$\Sigma fX = 1,594$

[a]Midpoint.

TABLE D.3

Crime Rate	f	cf^a
76–100	4	38
51–75	8	34
26–50	16	26
1–25	10	10

[a]Cumulative frequency.

where

LL = lower limit of the class interval that contains the median (this is the true limit, for example, the true limits of interval 1–5 are 0.5 and 5.5)

CF_{below} = cumulative frequency below the class interval that contains the median

f in median interval = frequency in the interval that contains the median

i = size of interval (again, use true limits; thus, the size of interval 1–5 is 5, because 0.5–5.5 contains 5 units)

Calculating for Table D.3

$$\text{median} = 25.5 + \left(\frac{19-10}{16}\right)25$$

$$= 25.5 + 14.1 = 39.6$$

Thus, for the grouped data in Table D.1, the mode = 38, the mean = 41.9, and the median = 39.6. Only when the data resemble a perfect normal curve such as in Figure D.1 will the mean, median, and mode be equal.

The distribution for our data is slightly positively skewed; that is, there is a positive tail, or extreme scores that cause the mean to be higher than the median and mode, and thus a less useful measure of central tendency (Figure D.2).

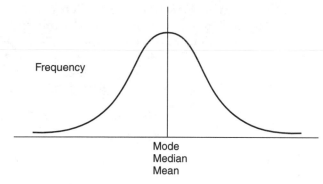

Frequency

Mode
Median
Mean

Figure D.1 A Perfect Normal Curve.

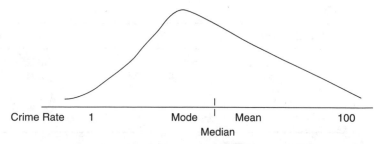

Crime Rate   1   Mode   Mean   100

Median

Figure D.2 Frequency Curve for Data in Table D.1.

Standard Deviations for Grouped Data

Calculation of the standard deviation for grouped frequency data is at times both difficult and time consuming. Fortunately, the advent of computer software programs, which do much of the work, has improved the situation. The reader should be aware that the formulas for simple distributions are not applicable to grouped data. For the same example employed for measures of central tendency, the standard deviation for grouped frequency data can be calculated by means of either a raw score or a deviation score formula.

Raw Score Approach

The raw score formula for grouped data

$$\sigma = \sqrt{(\Sigma fX^2 / N) - \overline{X}^2}$$

is obtained in the following manner (see Table D.4):

1. Calculate the midpoint (X) for each interval. In our example, 76 + 100 ÷ 2 = 88, and so on.
2. Calculate fX ($f \times X$): 4 × 88 = 352 and so on.
3. Calculate with *CAUTION fX²*, which is obtained by multiplying each midpoint X by fX, 88 × 352 = 30,976, and *not fX × fX*, $(352)^2$.
4. Plug these values into the formula:

$$\sigma = \sqrt{(87,522/38) - (41.95)^2}$$
$$= \sqrt{2,303.21 - 1,759.80}$$
$$= \sqrt{543.4105}$$
$$= 23.31$$

TABLE D.4

Crime Rate	f	X	fX	fX^2
76–100	4	88	352	30,976
51–75	8	63	504	31,752
26–50	16	38	608	23,104
1–25	10	13	130	1,690
	$N = 38$		$\Sigma fX = 1,594$	$\Sigma fX^2 = 87,522$

Deviation Score Approach

The deviation score formula for grouped data

$$\sigma = \sqrt{\frac{(\Sigma(fx')^2 - [(\Sigma fx')^2 / N])i^2}{N}}$$

is sometimes called the "guessed mean" approach to calculating the standard deviation (Table D.5) and comprises the following steps:

1. Guess which interval contains the mean, in our example, 26–50.
2. Each interval is expressed as deviation units, x' (or "x prime"), above or below the guessed mean. In our example, 51–75 is 1 deviation unit above 26–50; 76–100 is 2 deviation units above; and so on.
3. Multiply each deviation unit (x') by each frequency (f), $f \times x - fx'$. In our example $4 \times 2 = 8$, and so on. Then sum these, $\Sigma fx'$, in our example, $\Sigma fx' = 6$.
4. Calculate with *CAUTION* $(fx')^2$, which is obtained by multiplying each x' by each appropriate fx', $2 \times 8 = 16$, and *not $fx' \times fx'$*.
5. i = interval size; in this case data were grouped into intervals of 25, obtained as (highest score – lowest score) + 1, or in our example, $100 - 76 = 24 + 1 = 25$.

$$\sigma = \sqrt{\frac{(\Sigma(fx')^2 - [(\Sigma fx')^2 / N])i^2}{N}}$$

$$- \sqrt{\frac{(34 - [6^2 / 38])(25)^2}{38}}$$

$$= \sqrt{\frac{(34 - .9474)625}{38}}$$

$$= \sqrt{\frac{20,657.875}{38}}$$

$$= \sqrt{543.6283}$$

$$= 23.32 \text{ (differs from raw score result because of rounding error)}$$

TABLE D.5

Crime Rate	f	x′	fx′	fx′²
76–100	4	2	8	16
51–75	8	1	8	8
26–50	16	0	0	0
1–25	10	−1	−10	10
			$\Sigma fx' = 6$	$\Sigma(fx')^2 = 34$

Calculation of ANOVA

The following calculations are for the ANOVA example discussed in Chapter 12. (See Tables D.6. and D.7.)

1. Calculate the sum of squares (SS_{total}).

$$SS_{total} = \Sigma X_{total}^2 - \frac{(\Sigma X_{total})^2}{N_{total}}$$

In our example,

$$SS_{total} = 548 - \frac{(80)^2}{15}$$
$$= 121.33$$

TABLE D.6   Professionalism in Three Police Departments[a]

	High	Medium	Low
	10	9	5
	9	7	3
	8	5	3
	7	3	3
	6	1	1
$\overline{X}$	8	5	3

[a]1 = low professionalism, 10 = high professionalism.

TABLE D.7

High		Medium		Low		
X_1	X_1^2	X_2	X_2^2	X_3	X_3^2	
10	100	9	81	5	25	
9	81	7	49	3	9	
8	64	5	25	3	9	
7	49	3	9	3	9	
6	36	1	1	1	1	
$\Sigma X_1 = 40$	$\Sigma X_1^2 = 330$	$\Sigma X_2 = 25$	$\Sigma X_2^2 = 165$	$\Sigma X_3 = 15$	$\Sigma X_3^2 = 53$	$\Sigma X_{total}^2 = 548$
$\overline{X} = 8$		5		3		$\Sigma X_{total} = 80$

2. Calculate the sum of squares for between groups (SS_{between}).

$$SS_{\text{between}} = \left(\frac{(\Sigma X)^2}{N}\right) - \frac{(\Sigma X_{\text{total}})^2}{N_{\text{total}}}$$

$$= \left(\frac{(40)^2}{5} + \frac{(25)^2}{5} + \frac{(15)^2}{5}\right) - \frac{(80)^2}{15}$$

$$= 490 - 426.67 = 63.33$$

Regression Calculations

A regression equation enables us to predict, on the basis of one variable, a person's score on another variable. The following calculations refer to our example on regression in Chapter 12 for the scores of five correctional officer recruits on mathematical (X) and verbal (Y) ability.

$$b = \frac{N(\Sigma XY) - (\Sigma X)(\Sigma Y)}{N(\Sigma X^2) - (\Sigma X)^2}$$

$$a = \overline{Y} = bX$$

For our example,

$$b = \frac{5(104) - (15)(30)}{5(65) - (15)^2}$$

$$= \frac{520 - 450}{325 - 225}$$

$$= \frac{70}{100} = .7$$

$$a = 6 - .7(3)$$
$$= 6 - 2.1$$
$$= 3.9$$
$$Y' = a + bX$$
$$= 3.9 + .7X$$

Thus, if a new recruit scores 8 on verbal ability, using our prediction equation we could predict that this same recruit would score $Y = 3.9 + .7(8)$, or 9.5, on the math portion.

The regression line is calculated with the deviation score formula:

$$b = \frac{\Sigma xy}{\Sigma x^2}$$
$$a = 0$$

The Y intercept (a) is set at zero because we are expressing the data as deviation scores; thus, $Y' = bX$. For the data in our example,

$$b = \frac{14}{20} = .7$$
$$Y' = bX$$

In the same example that we used for raw data, a person with a verbal score of $8[Y' = .7(8)]$ would have a mathematical score of 5.6, which (added to the intercept of 3.9) equals 9.5.

A Test of Significance for Gamma

In this case, gamma is converted into a Z score and its probability assessed:

$$Z = G\sqrt{\frac{A - D}{N(1 - G^2)}}$$
$$= .76\sqrt{\frac{4,268 - 579}{225(1 - .58)}}$$
$$= .76\sqrt{\frac{3,689}{94.5}}$$
$$= .76\sqrt{39.037}$$
$$= .76(6.25) = 4.75$$

Using a table of Z values from any statistics text we would find a Z of 4.75 highly significant at least exceeding the .001 level, or in less than one time out of a thousand could such a relationship be due to chance.

Answers to Pop Quizzes in Chapter 12

12.1

X		
	1.	Mode = 2
2	2.	Median = 5
2		
5	3.	$\overline{X} = 5$
6		

$$\text{Median} = \frac{N+1}{2} = \frac{5+1}{2} = 3\text{rd case} = 5$$

$$\overline{X} = \frac{\Sigma X}{N} = \frac{25}{5} = 5$$

$$\Sigma X = \frac{10}{25}$$

12.2

1. 70 and 80
2. 66 and 78

X	x	x^2	X	X^2
1	−2	4	1	1
1	−2	4	1	1
3	0	0	3	9
5	+2	4	5	25
5	+2	4	5	25
$\Sigma X = 15$		$\Sigma x^2 = 16$		$\Sigma X^2 = 61$

3a. $\overline{X} = 3$ $\qquad \overline{X} = \dfrac{\Sigma X}{N} = \dfrac{15}{5} = 3$

3b. Median = 3 $\qquad \text{Median} = \dfrac{N+1}{2} = \dfrac{6}{1} = 3\text{rd}$

3c. Mode = <u>1 and 5</u>

3d. $\sigma = 1.79$

$$= \sqrt{\frac{\Sigma x^2}{N}} = \sqrt{\frac{16}{5}} = \sqrt{3.2}$$

$$\sigma = 1.79$$

or

$$\sigma = \sqrt{\frac{\Sigma X^2}{N} - \overline{X}^2}$$

$$= \sqrt{\frac{61}{5} - (3)^2}$$

$$= \sqrt{12.2 - 9}$$

$$= \sqrt{3.2}$$

$$= 1.79$$

12.3

	X	Z	Table Value	Percentile
1.	13	$\dfrac{13 - 10}{3} = \underline{+1}$	$.3413 + .50 = (.8413) \times 100 = 84.13\%$
2.	7	$\dfrac{7 - 10}{3} = \underline{-1}$	$.3413 - .50 = (.1587) \times 100 = 15.87\%$
3.	8	$\dfrac{8 - 10}{3} = \underline{-.67}$	$.2486 - .50 = (.2514) \times 100 = 25.14\%$
4.	12	$\dfrac{12 - 10}{3} = \underline{+.67}$	$.2486 + .50 = (.7486) \times 100 = 74.86\%$

12.4

1. a. Chi-square equal 1.6, with one degree of freedom, and is not significant (calculated value did not exceed expected or table value 3.84) at .05 level.

   b. Chi-square equals 6.4, with two degrees of freedom, and is statistically significant; that is, the probability exceeds the expected or table value (5.99) at the .05 level.

2. a. $(2 - 1)(2 - 1) = 1$

   b. $(4 - 1)(3 - 1) = 6$

   c. $(5 - 1)(4 - 1) = 12$

3. a. Yes, $4.8 > 3.84$

   b. No, $4.2 < 5.99$

   c. No, $2.6 < 3.84$

12.5

1. $\phi^2 = \dfrac{\chi^2}{N} = \dfrac{5}{10} = .50$

2. 50 percent of the variance is explained.

12.6

$$t = \frac{10-5}{\sqrt{(2^2/30)+(2^2/40)}}$$

$$= \frac{5}{\sqrt{(4/30)+(4/40)}}$$

$$= \frac{5}{\sqrt{.1333+.1}}$$

$$= \frac{5}{\sqrt{.2333}}$$

$$= \frac{5}{.48}$$

$$t = 10.4 \qquad p < .05$$

12.7

A calculated *F* value in analysis of variance equaled 7.61 at 12 and 4 degrees of freedom, and the differences between groups were statistically significant at the .05 level of probability.

12.8

1. Pearson's correlation equals .70 (a fairly high relationship), and it is statistically significant at the .05 level of probability. r^2 equals variance explained; thus $(.70)(.70) = .49$, or 49 percent of the variance is explained.

2.

	Deviation Score Approach								Raw Score Approach			
X	**Y**	**x**	**x²**	**y**	**y²**	**xy**		**X**	**Y**	**X²**	**Y²**	**XY**
1	3	−2	4	−1	1	2		1	3	1	9	3
3	3	0	0	−1	1	0		3	3	9	9	9
5	6	+2	4	2	4	4		5	6	25	36	30
			8		6	6		9	12	35	54	42

$$\overline{X} = 9/3 = 3 \qquad\qquad \overline{Y} = 12/3 = 4$$

$$r = \frac{\Sigma xy}{\sqrt{\Sigma x^2 \Sigma y^2}} \qquad r = \frac{N\Sigma XY - \Sigma X \Sigma Y}{\sqrt{[N\Sigma X^2 - (\Sigma X)^2][N\Sigma Y^2 - [\Sigma Y)^2]}}$$

$$= \frac{6}{\sqrt{(8)(6)}} \qquad = \frac{(3)(42) - (9)(12)}{\sqrt{[3(35) - (9)^2][3(54) - (12)^2]}}$$

$$= \frac{6}{\sqrt{48}} \qquad = \frac{126 - 108}{\sqrt{(105 - 81)(162 - 144)}}$$

$$= \frac{6}{6.9282} \qquad = \frac{18}{\sqrt{(24)(18)}}$$

$$= .87 \qquad = \frac{18}{\sqrt{432}} = \frac{18}{20.7846} = .87$$

12.9

1. This is regression equation for predicting score for *Y* based on *a* (the *Y* intercept), and *b* (the slope), and *X*.

2. **a.** 10.9

$$Y' = 3.9 + .7X$$
$$= 3.9 + .7(10)$$
$$= 3.9 + 7$$
$$= 10.9$$

   b. 7

$$Y' = 3.9 + .7(5)$$
$$= 3.9 + 3.5$$
$$= 7.4$$

12.10

1. $G = \dfrac{A - D}{A + D}$

$$= \frac{200 - 125}{200 + 125} \qquad A = 10(5 + 10) + 5(10)$$
$$= 200$$
$$= \frac{75}{325} \qquad D = 10(5 + 5) + 5(5)$$
$$= 125$$
$$= .23$$

2.

X*	Y	D	D²
1	3	−2	4
2	2	0	
4	1	3	9
3	2	1	1
		$\Sigma D^2 =$	14

*Note that *X* and *Y* are already ranked.

$$r_s = 1 - \left(\frac{6(\Sigma D^2)}{N(N^2 - 1)} \right)$$

$$= 1 - \left(\frac{6(14)}{4(16 - 1)} \right)$$

$$= 1 - \left(\frac{84}{60} \right)$$

$$= 1 - 1.4$$

$$= -.40$$

Final Quiz

1. Chi-square equals 4.67, with one degree of freedom, and is statistically significant at the .05 level.
2. Correlation equals .71 and is statistically significant at the .01 level of probability. A correlation of .71 is fairly high [$r^2 = (.71)(.71) = .50$, or 50 percent of the variance is explained].
3. Gamma (an ordinal measure of relationship) equals .32 and is not statistically significant. Gamma is a PRE measure (a proportional reduction in error measure); thus, 32 percent of the variance is explained.
4. The mean (average) equals 3.6 and the standard deviation is 1.2, which means that about 68 percent of the scores were between 2.4 and 4.8.
5. Z (standard) score or standard deviation unit score) equals 3.01, which is statistically significant at the .01 level of probability.

Normal Curve Areas

(A) z	(B) Area between Mean and z	(C) Area beyond z	(A) z	(B) Area between Mean and z	(C) Area beyond z
0.00	.0000	.5000	0.25	.0987-	.4013
0.01	.0040	.4960	0.26	.1026	.3974
0.02	.0080	.4920	0.27	.1064	.3936
0.03	.0120	.4880	0.28	.1103	.3897
0.04	.0160	.4840	0.29	.1141	.3859
0.05	.0199	.4801	0.30	.1179	.3821
0.06	.0239	.4761	0.31	.1217	.3783
0.07	.0279	.4721	0.32	.1255	.3745
0.08	.0319	.4681	0.33	.1293	.3707
0.09	.0359	.4641	0.34	.1331	.3669
0.10	.0398	.4602	0.35	.1368	.3632
0.11	.0438	.4562	0.36	.1406	.3594
0.12	.0478	.4522	0.37	.1443	.3557
0.13	.0517	.4483	0 38	.1480	.3520
0.14	.0557	.4443	0.39	.1517	.3483
0.15	.0596	.4404	0.40	.1554	.3446
0.16	.0636	.4364	0.4t	.1591	.3409
0.17	.0675	.4325	0.42	.1628	.3372
0.18	.0714	.4286	0.43	.1664	.3336
0.19	.0753	.4247	0.44	.1700	.3300
0.20	.0793	.4207	0.45	.1736	.3264
0.21	.0832	.4168	0.46	.1772	.3228
0.22	.0871	.4129	0.47	.1808	.3192
0.23	.0910	.4090	0.48	.1844	.3156
0.24	.0948	.4052	0.49	.1879	.3121

(A) z	(B) Area between Mean and z	(C) Area beyond z	(A) z	(B) Area between Mean and z	(C) Area beyond z
0.50	.1915	.3085	0.90	.3159	.1841
0.51	.1950	.3050	0.91	.3186	.1814
0.52	.1985	.3015	0.92	.3212	.1788
0.53	.2019	.2981	0.93	.3238	.1762
0.54	.2054	.2946	0.94	.3264	.1736
0.55	.2088	.2912	0.95	.3289	.1711
0.56	.2123	.2877	0.96	.3315	.1685
0.57	.2157	.2843	0.97	.3340	.1660
0.58	.2190	.2810	0.98	.3365	.1635
0.59	.2224	.2776	0.99	.3389	.1611
0.60	.2257	.2743	1.00	.3413	.1587
0.61	.2291	.2709	1.01	.3438	.1562
0.62	.2324	.2676	1.02	.3461	.1539
0.63	.2357	.2643	1.03	.3485	.1515
0.64	.2389	.2611	1.04	.3508	.1492
0.65	.2422	.2578	1.05	.3531	.1469
0.66	.2454	.2546	1.06	.3554	.1446
0.67	.2486	.2514	1.07	.3577	.1423
0.68	.2517	.2483	1.08	.3599	.1401
0.69	.2549	.2451	1.09	.3621	.1379
0.70	.2580	.2420	1.10	.3643	.1357
0.71	.2611	.2389	1.11	.3665	.1335
0.72	.2642	.2358	1.12	.3686	.1314
0.73	.2673	.2327	1.13	.3708	.1292
0.74	.2704	.2296	1.14	.3729	.1271
0.75	.2734	.2266	1.15	.3749	.1251
0.76	.2764	.2236	1.16	.3770	.1230
0.77	.2794	.2206	1.17	.3790	.1210
0.78	.2823	.2177	1.18	.3810	.1190
0.79	.2852	.2148	1.19	.3830	.1170
0.80	.2881	.2119	1.20	.3849	.1151
0.81	.2910	.2090	1.21	.3869	.1131
0.82	.2939	.2061	1.22	.3888	.1112
0.83	.2967	.2033	1.23	.3907	.1093
0.84	.2995	.2005	1.24	.3925	.1075
0.85	.3023	.1977	1.25	.3944	.1056
0.86	.3051	.1949	1.26	.3962	.1038
0.87	.3078	.1922	1.27	.3980	.1020
0.88	.3106	.1894	1.28	.3997	.1003
0.89	.3133	.1867	1.29	.4015	.0985

(A) z	(B) Area between Mean and z	(C) Area beyond z	(A) z	(B) Area between Mean and z	(C) Area beyond z
1.30	.4032	.0968	1.70	.4554	.0446
1.31	.4049	.0951	1.71	.4564	.0436
1.32	.4066	.0934	1.72	.4573	.0427
1.33	.4082	.0918	1.73	.4582	.0418
1.34	.4099	.0901	1.74	.4591	.0409
1.35	.4115	.0885	1.75	.4599	.0401
1.36	.4131	.0869	1.76	.4608	.0392
1.37	.4147	.0853	1.77	.4616	.0384
1.38	.4162	.0838	1.78	.4625	.0475
1.39	.4177	.0823	1.79	.4633	.0467
1.40	.4192	.0808	1.80	.4641	.0359
1.41	.4207	.0793	1.81	.4649	.0351
1.42	.4222	.0778	1.82	.4656	.0344
1.43	.4236	.0764	1.83	.4664	.0336
1.44	.4251	.0749	1.84	.4671	.0329
1.45	.4265	.0735	1.85	.4678	.0322
1.46	.4279	.0721	1.86	.4686	.0314
1.47	.4292	.0708	1.87	.4693	.0307
1.48	.4306	.0694	1.88	.4699	.0301
1.49	.4319	.0681	1.89	.4706	.0294
1.50	.4332	.0668	1.90	.4713	.0287
1.51	.4345	.0655	1.91	.4719	.0281
1.52	.4357	.0643	1.92	.4726	.0274
1.53	.4370	.0630	1.93	.4732	.0268
1.54	.4382	.0618	1.94	.4738	.0262
1.55	.4394	.0606	1.95	.4744	.0256
1.56	.4406	.0594	1.96	.4750	.0250
1.57	.4418	.0582	1.97	.4756	.0244
1.58	.4429	.0571	1.98	.4761	.0239
1.59	.4441	.0559	1.99	.4767	.0233
1.60	.4452	.0548	2.00	.4772	.0228
1.61	.4463	.0537	2.01	.4778	.0222
1.62	.4474	.0526	2.02	.4783	.0217
1.63	.4484	.0516	2.03	.4788	.0212
1.64	.4495	.0505	2.04	.4793	.0207
1.65	.4505	.0495	2.05	.4798	.0202
1.66	.4515	.0485	2.06	.4803	.0197
1.67	.4525	.0475	2.07	.4808	.0192
1.68	.4535	.0465	2.08	.4812	.0188
1.69	.4545	.0455	2.09	.4817	.0183

(A) z	(B) Area between Mean and z	(C) Area beyond z	(A) z	(B) Area between Mean and z	(C) Area beyond z
2.10	.4821	.0179	2.50	.4938	.0062
2.11	.4826	.0174	2.51	.4940	.0060
2.12	.4830	.0170	2.52	.4941	.0059
2.13	.4834	.0166	2.53	.4943	.0057
2.14	.4838	.0162	2.54	.4945	.0055
2.15	.4842	.0158	2.55	.4946	.0054
2.16	.4846	.0154	2.56	.4948	.0052
2.17	.4850	.0150	2.57	.4949	.0051
2.18	.4854	.0146	2.58	.4951	.0049
2.19	.4857	.0143	2.59	.4952	.0048
2.20	.4861	.0139	2.60	.4953	.0047
2.21	.4864	.0136	2.61	.4955	.0045
2.22	.4868	.0132	2.62	.4956	.0044
2.23	.4871	.0129	2.63	.4957	.0043
2.24	.4875	.0125	2.64	.4959	.0041
2.25	.4878	.0122	2.65	.4960	.0040
2.26	.4881	.0119	2.66	.4961	.0039
2.27	.4884	.0116	2.67	.4962	.0038
2.28	.4887	.0113	2.68	.4963	.0037
2.29	.4890	.0110	2.69	.4964	.0036
2.30	.4893	.0107	2.70	.4965	.0035
2.31	.4896	.0104	2.71	.4966	.0034
2.32	.4898	.0102	2.72	.4967	.0033
2.33	.4901	.0099	2.73	.4968	.0032
2.34	.4904	.0096	2.74	.4969	.0031
2.35	.4906	.0064	2.75	.4970	.0030
2.36	.4909	.0091	2.76	.4971	.0029
2.37	.4911	.0089	2.77	.4972	.0028
2.38	.4913	.0087	2.78	.4973	.0027
2.39	.4916	.0084	2.79	.4974	.0026
2.40	.4918	.0082	2.80	.4974	.0026
2.41	.4920	.0080	2.81	.4975	.0025
2.42	.4922	.0078	2.82	.4976	.0024
2.43	.4925	.0075	2.83	.4977	.0023
2.44	.4927	.0073	2.84	.4977	.0023
2.45	.4929	.0071	2.85	.4978	.0022
2.46	.4931	.0069	2.86	.4979	.0021
2.47	.4932	.0068	2.87	.4979	.0021
2.48	.4934	.0066	2.88	.4980	.0020
2.49	.4936	.0064	2.89	.4981	.0019

(A) z	(B) Area between Mean and z	(C) Area beyond z	(A) z	(B) Area between Mean and z	(C) Area beyond z
2.90	.4981	.0019			
2.91	.4982	.0018	3.15	.4992	.0008
2.92	.4982	.0018	3.16	.4992	.0008
2.93	.4983	.0017	3.17	.4992	.0008
2.94	.4984	.0016	3.18	.4993	.0007
			3.19	.4993	.0007
2.95	.4984	.0016			
2.96	.4985	.0015	3.20	.4993	.0007
2.97	.4985	.0015	3.21	.4993	.0007
2.98	.4986	.0014	3.22	.4994	.0006
2.99	.4986	.0014	3.23	.4994	.0006
			3.24	.4994	.0006
3.00	.4987	.0013			
3.01	.4987	.0013	3.25	.4994	.0006
3.02	.4987	.0013	3.30	.4995	.0005
3.03	.4988	.0012	3.35	.4996	.0004
3.04	.4988	.0012	3.40	.4997	.0003
			3.45	.4997	.0003
3.05	.4989	.0011			
3.06	.4989	.0011	3.50	.4998	.0002
3.07	.4989	.0011	3.60	.4998	.0002
3.08	.4990	.0010	3.70	.4999	.0001
3.09	.4990	.0010	3.80	.4999	.0001
3.10	.4990	.0010	3.90	.49995	.00005
3.11	.4991	.0009	4.00	.49997	.00003
3.12	.4991	.0009			
3.13	.4991	.0009			
3.14	.4992	.0008			

From Runyan, Richard P. and Audrey Haber. *Fundamentals of Behavioral Statistics.* Homewood, Ill.: Richard D. Irwin,1982. Reprinted by permission of the publisher.

G Distribution of Chi-Square (χ^2)

Degrees of Freedom	.05 Level	.01 Level
1	3.84	6.64
2	5.99	9.21
3	7.82	11.34
4	9.49	13.28
5	11.07	15.09
6	12.59	16.81
7	14.07	18.48
8	15.51	20.09
9	16.92	21.67
10	18.31	23.21
11	19.68	24.73
12	21.03	26.22
13	22.36	27.69
14	23.69	29.14
15	24.99	30.58
16	26.29	32.00
17	27.59	33.41
18	28.87	34.81
19	30.14	36.19
20	31.41	37.57
21	32.67	38.93
22	33.92	40.29
23	35.17	41.64
24	36.42	42.98
25	37.65	44.31
26	38.89	45.64
27	40.11	46.96
28	41.34	48.28
29	42.56	49.59
30	43.77	50.89

(Calculated values must exceed those in the table at the appropriate degrees of freedom in order to be significant.)

Factor Analysis

Factor analysis is a statistical procedure by which underlying patterns, factors, or dimensions are identified among a series of scale items. It observes the interrelationships of data to locate commonalities (factors held in common) that may explain the basis of response. Despite the apparent complexity of the technique, the advent of "canned" computer programs has made statistical procedures such as factor analysis quite popular (Nie et al., 1975). Hirschi and Selvin (1973, p. 210) correctly observe that often the use of such techniques as factor analysis is a "confession of ignorance," because one constructs a scale and, through factor analysis, the underlying dimensions or clusters are identified. The purpose of this presentation is to give the reader a general understanding of the technique. For a more detailed presentation the reader is advised to consult Nie et al. (1975, pp. 468–514) and Harmon (1967).

Generally, factor analysis generates dimensions (factors) or hypothetical clusters that different items seem to have in common. To simplify the presentation, let us examine an attitudinal scale that has been administered to respondents. Rather than assuming that all items tap the same dimension, let us say police cynicism, we might assume that a number of dimensions are being measured. Regoli (1976) was concerned with the fact that despite much theoretical discussion regarding police cynicism, only one attempt had ever been made to measure this entity: Niederhoffer's index (1967). Niederhoffer administered a twenty-item scale to police officers in New York City. Each item had three response patterns: (1) a professional view, (2) a middle-of-the-road view, and (3) a cynical view.

The average arrest is made because of the following:

1. As a result of hard work and intelligent dedication to duty.
2. As a result of good information from an informer.
3. The officer could not avoid it without getting into trouble.

Regoli (1976) modified the Niederhoffer scale by adding Likert responses and appropriate reversals and administered it to police officers in Washington and Idaho.

To perform a factor analysis, an intercorrelation matrix of each item with all other items is generated. These correlation coefficients (*r*) are discussed in Chapter 12. Each factor to be identified can be viewed as a yet-undefined underlying variable that has some relationship to the actual variables in the study (Bailey, 1978, p. 354). When a number of variables have something in common, vary together, or are highly related to the same underlying dimension, then a factor or subscale has been identified. Table H.1 reproduces the results of Regoli's replication and analysis of Niederhoffer's police cynicism scale.

According to this analysis, five yet-unidentified factors exist among the twenty items. The correlation between each question and each factor is a *factor loading.* It is up to the researchers, based on their knowledge of the theoretical intent of the questions, to name these factors. A correlation of .00 would be considered a low loading or relationship, whereas a correlation of

TABLE H.1   Regoli's Factor Analysis of Niederhoffer's Cynicism Scale[a,b]

Question Content	Item	Factor				
		1	2	3	4	5
Superior interested in subordinates	1	.13	.36	.33[a]	.06	−.07
Complaint result of pressure	2	.08	.29	−.07	.23	.12
Arrest due to dedication	3	.05	−.02	.52[a]	.07	.06
Arrest due to hard work	4	−.12	.07	.30[a]	.18	.03
College makes better department	5	.07	.04	.01	.05	.54[a]
Department inept	6	.05	.46[a]	.14	.02	.11
Police academy training	7	.07	.19	.08	.45[a]	.25
Professionalization here	8	−.05	.04	.10	.27[a]	−.07
Department trial stacked	9	.06	.46	.03	.39[a]	.11
Work overtime—dedication	10	.03	.18	.47[a]	.18	.22
Police work regulations fair	11	.07	.42[a]	.18	.21	.02
Social service training	12	.12	.02	.03	−.10	.42[a]
Who you know	13	.08	.71[a]	.25	−.08	−.02
Detectives superior	14	.03	.03	.29	−.20	.14
Summonses sensible	15	.05	−.04	.00	.22	−.08
Public respect	16	.66[a]	.17	.09	−.01	−.04
Public obstructs	17	.65[a]	.04	−.07	.27	.17
Police peculiar view	18	−.01	.39[a]	−.06	−.01	.09
Newspapers help	19	.39[a]	.06	.04	−.07	.18
Police treated badly in court	20	.26	.41[a]	.12	.08	.23

[a]Indicates best item–factor correspondence.

[b]Orthogonal Varimax Rotations from Principal Axes Solutions for Five Factors: Niederhoffer's Police Cynicism Scale.

Source: Modified from Robert M. Regoli, "An Empirical Assessment of Niederhoffer's Police Cynicism Scale." *Journal of Criminal Justice* 4 (Fall 1976): 236. Reproduced by permission of the author and Pergamon Journals Limited.

+ 1.0 or − 1.0 would represent the highest loading and explain the largest proportion of variance. It is also desirable that the item display *simple structure;* that is, that it load highly on only one factor and low on all of the rest. If this is not the case, then the question may be measuring a multidimensional entity and may not fit neatly into any of the scales. In examining Table H.1, we find that items 16, 17, and 19 loaded highest on factor 1. These items dealt with public respect, cooperation, and newspaper coverage of police work. Regoli gave this factor the name CYNPUB, or cynicism toward relations with public. Factor 2 had five items, 6, 11, 13,18, and 20, and was tagged CYNORG or cynicism toward organizational functions. Items 1, 3, 4, and 10 (factor 3) were labeled CYNED, cynicism about police dedication to duty. Factor 4 (items 7, 8, and 9) was called CYNSOL, an acronym for cynicism about police solidarity. CYNEDU (cynicism about training and duty) was used to describe factor 5 (items 5 and 12). Questions 2, 14, and 15 did not load sufficiently on any of the factors to justify their inclusion and thus were dropped from the subscales. Regoli concludes his analysis by questioning the reliability and validity of Niederhoffer's scale and suggesting the multidimensional nature of the concept cynicism (Regoli, 1976, p. 237).

Factor loadings can now be utilized to calculate weighted scale scores for respondents. That is, the relative importance of each item can be taken into account in the calculation of subscale scores. Suppose that for factor 5, CYNEDU, the subject scored 3 ("don't know") to item 5 and 2 ("somewhat disagree") to item 12. Their weighted score would be .54(3) + .42(2) = 2.46.

Factor analysis can, to use Hirschi and Selvin's term, become a fetish, an automatic ritual researchers go through as a substitute for theoretical and logical thinking, a "data dredging" or "ransacking" device in which large numbers of items are bound to turn up something. It is nearly impossible to perform without a computer.

With the availability of computer programs, factor analysis represents a powerful tool for developing and analyzing scales. It enables the identification of independent subscales, relative variable weights that provide far greater sophistication and discrimination than more simplistic scaling procedures. Sophisticated technology and statistics are no substitute, however, for logic, sound theoretical thinking, and substantive knowledge. Gottfredson (1980) indicates that the use of highly sophisticated methods with poor data, such as official case files, may merely compound error. It may be analogous to using a battering ram when a mere knock on the door would do.

References

Bailey, Kenneth. *Methods of Social Research,* 3d ed. New York: Free Press, 1978.

Gottfredson, Don M. Roundtable Discussion on "Classification." National Workshop on Research Methodology and Criminal Justice Program Evaluation. Baltimore, Md., March, 1980.

Harmon, Harry H. *Modern Factor Analysis.* Chicago: University of Chicago Press, 1967.

Hirschi, Travis, and Hanaan C. Selvin. *Principles of Survey Analysis.* New York: Free Press, 1973.

Nie, Norman H., et al. *Statistical Packages for the Social Sciences.* 2nd ed. New York: McGraw-Hill, 1975.

Niederhoffer, Arthur. *Behind the Shield: The Police in Urban Society.* Garden City, N.Y.: Doubleday, 1967.

Regoli, Robert M. "An Empirical Assessment of Niederhoffer's Police Cynicism Scale." *Journal of Criminal Justice* 4 (Fall 1976): 231–241.

References

Chapter 1   Introduction to Criminal Justice Research Methods: Theory and Method

Ad Hoc Committee on the Future of Justice Research: Report and Recommendations. Washington, D.C.: National Institute of Justice, March 1982.

Adler, Freda. *Nations Not Obsessed by Crime.* Littleton, Colo.: Fred B. Rothman, 1983.

Bayley, David H. "Comment: Perspectives on Criminal Justice Research." *Journal of Criminal Justice* 6 (1978): 287–298.

Bernard, Thomas J., and R. Richard Ritti. "The Role of Theory in Scientific Research." In *Measurement Issues in Criminology,* edited by Kimberly L. Kempf, 1–20. New York: Springer–Verlag, 1990.

Black, Thomas. *Evaluating Social Science Research.* Thousand Oaks, Calif.: Sage, 1993.

Blankenship, Michael B., and Stephen E. Brown. "Paradigm or Perspective?: A Note to the Discourse Community." *Journal of Crime and Justice* 16 (1993): 167–175.

Blumer, Herbert. *Symbolic Interactionism: Perspective and Method.* Englewood Cliffs, N.J.: Prentice-Hall, 1969.

Blumstein, Alfred, and Joan Petersilia. "NIJ and Its Research Program." In *25 Years of Criminal Justice Research,* 1–42. Washington, D.C.: National Institute of Justice, December 1994.

Bohm, Robert M. "Myths about Criminology and Criminal Justice: A Review Essay." *Justice Quarterly* 4 (December, 1987): 631–642.

Brown, Stephen E., and John H. Curtis. *Fundamentals of Criminal Justice Research,* Cincinnati: Anderson, 1987.

Chesney-Lind, Meda. "Girls' Crime and Woman's Place: Toward a Feminist Model of Female Delinquency." *Crime and Delinquency* 35 (1989): 5–30.

Clinard, Marshall B. *Cities with Little Crime: The Case of Switzerland.* Cambridge, Eng.: Cambridge University Press, 1978.

Clinard, Marshall B., and Peter C. Yeager. *Illegal Corporate Behavior.* Washington, D.C.: Law Enforcement Assistance Administration, 1979.

Comte, Auguste. *System of Positive Policy.* London: Longmans, Green, 1877.

Crano, William D., and Marilynn B. Brewer. *Principles of Research in Social Psychology.* New York: McGraw-Hill, 1973.

Denzin, Norman. "An Interpretation of Recent Feminist Theory: Review-Essay." *Sociology and Social Research* 68 (1984): 712–718.

_____. *The Research Act: A Theoretical Introduction to Sociological Methods.* Englewood Cliffs, N.J.: Prentice-Hall, 1989.

Dorworth, Vicky, and Marie Henry. "Optical Illusions: The Visual Representation of Blacks and Women in Introductory Criminal Justice Textbooks." *Journal of Criminal Justice Education* 3 (Fall 1992): 251–260.

Durkheim, Emile. *Suicide: A Study in Sociology.* Translated by John A. Spaulding and George Simpson. New York: Free Press, 1951.

Eichler, Magrit. *Nonsexist Research Methods: A Practical Guide.* Boston: Allen and Unwin, 1988.

Evans, Bergen. *The Natural History of Nonsense.* New York: Anchor Paperbacks, 1958.

Friedman, Herman P. Roundtable Discussion: "Classification," National Workshop on Research Methodology and Criminal Justice Program Evaluation. Baltimore, Md., March 1980.

Garfinkel, Harold. *Studies in Ethnomethodology.* Englewood Cliffs, N.J.: Prentice-Hall, 1967.

Haar, Robin N. "Examining Police Drug Corruption: Where to Go From Here." Paper presented at the Academy of Criminal Justice Sciences Meetings, Pittsburgh, Pa., March 1992.

Hagan, Frank E. "Comparative Professionalization in an Occupational Arena: The Case of Rehabilitation." Ph.D. dissertation, Case Western Reserve University, 1975.

Hagan, Frank E. *Introduction to Criminology: Theories, Methods and Criminal Behavior.* 2d ed. Chicago: Nelson-Hall, 1990.

Hagan, Frank E. "The Global Fallacy and Theoretical Range in Criminological Theory." *Journal of Justice Issues* 2 (Winter 1987): 19–31.

Hills, Stuart L. *Corporate Violence: Injury and Death tor Profit.* Totowa, N.J.: Rowman and Littlefield, 1987.

Hirschi, Travis, and Hanan Selvin. *Principles of Survey Analysis.* New York: Free Press, 1973.

_____, and Rodney Stark. "Hellfire and Delinquency." *Social Problems* 17 (Fall 1969): 202–213.

Kappeler, Victor E., Mark Blumberg, and Gary W. Potter. *The Mythology of Crime and Justice.* Prospect Heights, Ill.: Waveland Press, 1993.

Kuhn, Thomas. *The Structure of Scientific Revolutions.* 2d ed. Chicago: University of Chicago Press, 1970.

Light, Stephen C., and Theresa K. Newman. "Awareness and Use of Social Science Research Among Executive and Administrative Staff Members of State Correctional Agencies." *Justice Quarterly* 9 (June 1992): 299–324.

Mann, Coramae Richey. *Unequal Justice: A Question of Color.* Bloomington: Indiana University Press, 1993.

Martinson, Robert. "What Works?—Questions and Answers about Prison Reform." *The Public Interest* 35 (Spring 1974): 22–54.

_____. "Martinson Attacks His Own Earlier Work." *Criminal Justice Newsletter* 9 (December 1978): 4.

McCaghy, Charles. *Deviant Behavior.* New York: Macmillan, 1976.

McDermott, M. Joan. "The Personal is Empirical: Feminism, Research Methods, and Criminal Justice Education." *Journal of Criminal Justice Education* 3 (Fall 1992): 237–249.

Merton, Robert K. "The Matthew Effect." *Science* 159 (January 1968): 56–63.

Morris, Norval. "Insanity Defense." *Crime File.* Washington, D.C.: National Institute of Justice, 1987.

National Institute of Justice. *Research Program Plan: Fiscal Year 1995–1996.* Washington, D.C.: National Institute of Justice, 1994.

O'Block, Robert. *Criminal Justice Research Sources.* Cincinnati: Anderson, 1992.

"PAVNET Online User's Guide." National Institute of Justice Research in Action, March 1995.

Pepinsky, Harold E., and Paul Jesilow. *Myths That Cause Crime.* Cabin John, Md.: Seven Locks Press, 1984.

Prewitt, Kenneth, and David L. Sills. "Federal Funding for the Social Sciences: Threats and Responses." *Footnotes* (American Sociological Association) (December 1981): 4–8.

Rabow, Jerome. "Research and Rehabilitation: The Conflict of Scientific and Treatment Roles in Corrections." *The Journal of Research in Crime and Delinquency* 1 (January 1964): 67–79.

Reiff, Robert. "The Danger of the Techni-pro: Democratizing the Human Service Professions." *Social Policy* (May/June 1971): 62–64.

Reinharz, Shulamit. *Feminist Methods in Social Research.* New York: Oxford University Press, 1992.

Renzetti, Claire M. "On the Margins of the Malestream (Or, They Still Don't Get It, Do They?): Feminist Analyses in Criminal Justice Education." *Journal of Criminal Justice Education* 4 (Fall 1993): 219–234.

Russell, Katheryn K. "Development of a Black Criminology and the Role of the Black Criminologist." *Justice Quarterly* 9 (December 1992): 667–683.

Simon, Julian L., and Paul Burstein. *Basic Research Methods in Social Sciences: The Art of Empirical Investigation.* 3rd ed. New York: Random House, 1985.

Sobel, David. "The Matthew Effect." *Omni* (August 1989): 27.

Sontheimer, Henry, and Lynne Goodstein. "An Evaluation of Juvenile Intensive Aftercare Probation: Aftercare Versus System Response Effects." *Justice Quarterly* 10 (June 1993): 197–227.

Stanko, Elizabeth. *Everyday Violence: How Women and Men Experience Sexual and Physical Dangers.* London: Pandora, 1990.

Stewart, James K. *Justice Research: The Practitioner's Perspective.* Washington, D.C.: National Institute of Justice, June 1983.

Survey of Inmates of State Correctional Facilities—Advance Report. Special Report No. SD-NPS-SR-Z, Washington, D.C.: U.S. Government Printing Office, March 1976.

Sutherland, Edwin H. "White Collar Criminality." *American Sociological Review* 5 (February 1940): 1–12.

Taylor, Ralph B. *Research Methods in Criminal Justice.* New York: McGraw-Hill, 1994.

Turner, Jonathan H. *The Structure of Sociological Theory.* Homewood, Ill.: Dorsey, 1974.

U.S. Department of Justice. *Myths and Realities About Crime.* Washington, D.C.: Law Enforcement Assistance Administration, National Criminal Justice Information and Statistics Service, 1978.

Velikovsky, Immanuel. *Worlds in Collision.* New York: Doubleday, 1950.

Walker, Samuel. *Sense and Nonsense about Crime: A Policy Guide.* 2d ed. Monterey, Calif.: Brooks/Cole, 1989.

Weber, Max. *The Methodology of Social Sciences.* Translated by Edward A. Shils and Henry A. Finch. New York: Free Press, 1949.

Wilkins, Leslie T. "The Unique Individual." In *Crime in Society.* edited by Leonard D. Savitz and Norman Johnston, 233–238. New York: Wiley, 1978.

_____. "The Concept of Cause in Criminology." In *Classes, Conflict and Control: Studies in Criminal Justice Management,* edited by J. Munro. Cincinnati: Anderson, 1976.

Williams, Frank III. "The Demise of Criminological Imagination: A Critique of Recent Criminology." *Justice Quarterly* (March 1984): 91–106.

Willis, Cecil. "Criminal Justice Theory: A Case of Trained Incapacity." *Journal of Criminal Justice* 11, no. 5 (1983): 447–458.

Wilson, James Q. *Varieties of Police Behavior.* Cambridge: Harvard University Press, 1968.

Wolfgang, Marvin E., R. M. Figlio, and M. E. Thornberry. *Evaluating Criminology.* New York: Elsevier North-Holland, 1978.

Wright, Kevin N. *The Great American Crime Myth.* Westport, Conn.: Greenwood Press, 1985.

Additional Useful Sources

Albright, Ellen, et al. *Criminal Justice Research: Evaluation in Criminal Justice Programs, Guidelines and Examples.* Washington, D.C.: National Institute of Law Enforcement and Criminal Justice, 1973.

Bohm, Robert M. "Crime, Criminal and Crime Control Policy Myths." *Justice Quarterly* 3 (June 1986): 193–214.

Brantingham, Paul, and Patricia Brantingham. *Patterns in Crime.* New York: Macmillan, 1984.

Champion, Dean J. *Research Methods for Criminal Justice and Criminology.* Englewood Cliffs, N.J.: Regents/Prentice Hall, 1993.

Cordner, Gary W. "Police Patrol Work Load Studies: A Review and Critique." *Police Studies* 2 (Summer 1979): 50–60.

Fitzgerald, Jack D., and Steven M. Cox. *Research Methods in Criminal Justice.* 2d ed. Chicago: Nelson-Hall, 1994.

Geis, Gilbert, and Arnold Binder. *Methods of Research in Criminology and Criminal Justice.* New York: McGraw-Hill, 1986.

Glaser, Daniel. "Achieving Better Questions: A Half Century's Progress in Correctional Research." *Federal Probation* 39 (September 1975): 3–9.

Isaac, Stephen, and William B. Michael. *Handbook in Research and Evaluation for Education and the Behavioral Sciences.* 2d ed. San Diego, Calif.: Robert R. Knapp, 1981.

Maxfield, Michael G., and Earl Babbie. *Research Methods for Criminal Justice and Criminology.* Belmont, Calif.: Wadsworth, 1995.

Menheim, Gerald, and Richard C. Rich. *Empirical Political Analysis: Research Methods in Political Science.* 2d ed. New York: Longham Press, 1986.

Miller, Delbert C. *Handbook of Research Design and Social Measurement.* 5th ed. New York: McKay, 1991.

Nachmias, David, and Chava Nachmias. *Research Methods in the Social Sciences.* 6th ed. New York: St. Martin's Press, 1992.

National Advisory Committee on Criminal Justice Standards and Goals. *Criminal Justice Research and Development.* Report of the Task Force on Criminal Research and Development, December 1976.

Reid, Susan Titus. "Research Methodologies in Criminology." In *Crime and Criminology,* 4th ed. New York: Holt, 1985, pp. 95–120.

Reppucci, N. D. "Methodological Issues in Research with Correctional Populations." *Journal of Consulting and Clinical Psychology* 46 (August 1978): 727–746.

Rhodes, Robert P. *The Insoluble Problems of Crime.* New York: Wiley, 1977.

Selltiz, Claire, Lawrence J. Wrightsman, and Stuart W. Cook. *Research Methods in Social Relations.* 3d ed. New York: Holt, 1976.

Wellford, Charles, ed. *Quantitative Studies in Criminology.* Beverly Hills, Calif.: Sage, 1978.

Chapter 2   Ethics in Criminal Justice Research

Adamitis, James A., and Bahram Haghighi. "Ethical Issues Confronting Criminal Justice Researchers in the United States." *The Criminologist* 13 (July 1989): 235–242.

Altman, Laurence K. "Revisionist History Sees Pasteur as Liar Who Stole Rival's Ideas." *New York Times,* 16 May 1995, B5, B8.

American Correctional Association. "The Use of Prisoners and Detainees as Subjects of Human Experimentation: Position Statement Officially Adopted." *American Journal of Corrections* 38, no. 3 (1976): 14.

American Sociological Association. "Toward a Code of Ethics for Sociologists." *The American Sociologist* 3 (November 1968): 318.

Babbie, Earl R. *The Practice of Social Research.* Belmont, Calif.: Wadsworth, 1983.

Bailey, Kenneth. *Methods of Social Research.* 3rd ed. New York: Free Press, 1987.

Barnes, J.A. "Some Ethical Problems in Modern Fieldwork." In *Qualitative Methodology,* edited by William J. Filstead, 235–251. Chicago: Markham, 1970.

Bloomberg, Seth A., and Leslie T. Wilkins. "Ethics of Research Involving Human Subjects in Criminal Justice." *Crime and Delinquency* 23 (October 1977): 435–444.

Boruch, Robert F., and Joe S. Cecil, eds. *Solutions to Ethical and Legal Problems in Social Research.* New York: Academic Press, 1983.

Brandt, A. M. "Racism, Research and the Tuskegee Syphilis Study." *Hastings Center Report* 7 (1978): 15–21.

Branson, R. "Prison Research: National Commission Says 'No,' Unless . . . ." *Hastings Center Report* 7 (February 1977), 17–21.

Broad, William, and Nicholas Wade. *Betrayers of the Truth: Fraud and Deceit in the Halls of Science.* New York: Simon and Schuster, 1983.

Cassell, Joan, and Murray L. Wax. "Editorial Introduction: Toward a Moral Science of Human Beings." *Social Problems* 27 (February 1980): 259–264.

Chambers, Eve. "Fieldwork and the Law: New Contexts for Ethical Decision Making." *Social Problems* 27 (February 1980): 330–341.

Code of Federal Regulations, Title 45, A. Department of Health, Education, and Welfare, General Administration, Part 46, Protection of Human Subjects, in *Federal Register* 40 (March 13, 1975): 11854–11858.

Code of Professional Ethics and Practices of the American Association for Public Opinion Research, 1977.

Code of Professional Ethics and Practices of the American Association for Public Opinion Research, in Kenneth D. Bailey, *Methods of Social Research.* New York: Free Press, 1978, 449–452.

Comprehensive Drug Abuse Prevention and Control Act. Public Law 91–514, 84 Statute 1271 as amended by the Comprehensive Alcohol Abuse and Alcoholism Prevention, Treatment, and Rehabilitation Act of 1974, Public Law 93–282, 88 Statute 125, 1970.

Cook, Fred J. *Maverick Ethics: Fifty Years of Investigative Reporting.* New York: G. P. Putnam's Sons, 1984.

Cousins, Norman. "How the U.S. Used Its Citizens as Guinea Pigs." *Saturday Review,* 10 November 1979, 10.

Dahmann, Judith, and Joseph Sasfy. *Criminal Justice Information Policy: Research Access to Criminal Justice Data.* Washington, D.C.: Bureau of Justice Statistics, 1982.

Dalton, Melville. "Preconceptions and Methods in *Men Who Manage.*" In *Sociologists at Work,* edited by Philip E. Hammond, 50–95. New York: Basic Books, 1964.

Denzin, Norman K. *The Research Act: A Theoretical Introduction to Sociological Methods.* 3rd ed. New York: McGraw-Hill, 1989.

Department of Health, Education, and Welfare. *Institutional Guide to DHEW Policy on Protection of Human Subjects.* Washington, D.C.: U.S. Government Printing Office, 1971.

_____. *Report and Recommendations on Institutional Review Boards.* Washington, D.C.: U.S. Government Printing Office, 1978.

_____. "Protection of Human Subjects: Institutional Review Boards." *Federal Register* 43 (November 30, 1978): FR 56174.

Diener, Edward, and Rick Crandall. *Ethics in Social and Behavioral Research.* Chicago: University of Chicago Press, 1978.

Douglas, Jack D. "Major Tactics of Investigative Research." In *Focus: Unexplored Deviance,* edited by Charles H. Swanson, 206–221. Guilford, Conn.: Dushkin, 1978.

_____. "Living Morality versus Bureaucratic Fiat." In *Deviance and Decency,* edited by Carl B. Klockars and Finbarr O'Connor, 13–33. Beverly Hills, Calif.: Sage, 1979.

Duster, Troy, David Matza, and David Wellman. "Field Work and the Protection of Human Subjects." *The American Sociologists* 14 (August 1979): 136–142.

Erez, Edna. "Randomized Experiments in Correctional Context: Legal, Ethical and Practical Concerns." *Journal of Criminal Justice* 14, no. 5 (1986): 389–409.

Erikson, Kai T. "A Comment on Disguised Observation in Sociology." In *Focus: Unexplored Deviance,* edited by Charles H. Swanson, 240–244. Guilford, Conn.: Dushkin, 1978.

_____. "Letter to the General Membership of the American Sociological Association on Behalf of Mario Brajuha's Legal Defense," 1984.

"Ethical Aspects of Experimentation with Human Subjects." *Daedalus* (Spring 1969).

Federal Register. "Department of Health and Human Services Guidelines" (January 26, 1981), 389–392.

Fichter, Joseph H., and William L. Kolb. "Ethical Limitations on Sociological Reporting." *American Sociological Review* 18 (1953): 455–550.

"Final Research Regulations Approved: Most Social Science Research Exempt." *Footnotes* (American Sociological Association) 9 (March 1981): 1, 9.

Fletcher, Ronald. *Science, Ideology and the Media: The Cyril Burt Affair.* New Brunswick, N.J.: Transaction Publishers, 1991.

"Fraud in Research." *Society* 31 (March/April 1994), series of articles, 5–63.

Freund, Paul, ed. *Experimentation with Human Beings.* New York: Braziller, 1970.

Fund to Protect Scholars from Defamation. "*Solicitation Letter,*" Box 263, Augusta, Mich., April 22, 1980.

Galliher, John F. "The Protection of Human Subjects: A Reexamination of the Professional Code of Ethics." *American Sociologist* 9 (August 1973): 93–100.

_____. "Social Scientists' Ethical Responsibilities to Superordinates: Looking Upward Meekly." *Social Problems* 27 (February 1980): 298–308.

Gans, Herbert. *The Urban Villagers.* New York: Free Press, 1962.

Geis, Gilbert. *Correctional Rehabilitation.* Washington, D.C.: Joint Commission on Correctional Manpower and Training, 1967.

Hagan, Frank E. *Goals in New Town Planning: The Case of Columbia, Maryland.* Master's thesis, University of Maryland, 1968.

_____. *Comparative Professionalization in an Occupational Arena: The Case of Rehabilitation.* Ph.D. dissertation, Case Western Reserve University, 1975.

_____. *Introduction to Criminology: Theories, Methods and Criminal Behavior.* 3rd ed. Chicago: Nelson-Hall, 1994.

Hearnshaw, Leslie S. *Cyril Burt, Psychologist.* Ithaca, N.Y.: Cornell University Press, 1979.

Henslin, James M. "Studying Deviance in Four Settings: Research Experiences with Cabbies, Suicides, Drug Users and Abortionees." In *Research on Deviance,* edited by Jack D. Douglas, 35–70. New York: Random House, 1972.

Holmes, K. A. "Problems and Pitfalls of Rape Victim Research: An Analysis of Selected Methodological, Ethical, and Pragmatic Concerns." Rockville, Md.: National Institute of Mental Health, 1978.

Homan, Roger. *The Ethics of Social Research.* London: Longman, 1991.

Horowitz, Irving L. "The Life and Death of Project Camelot." *Transaction* 3 (1965): 3–7, 44–47.

Humphreys, Laud. *Tearoom Trade.* Chicago: Aldine, 1970.

Inciardi, James A. "In Search of the Class Cannon: A Field Study of Professional Pickpockets." In *Street Ethnography,* edited by Robert S. Weppner, 55–77. Vol. 1, Beverly Hills, Calif.: Sage, 1977.

Irwin, John. "Participant-Observation of Criminals." In *Research on Deviance,* edited by Jack D. Douglas, 17–138. New York: Random House, 1972.

James, Jennifer. "On the Block: Urban Research Perspectives." *Urban Anthropology* 1 (1972): 125–140.

Jones, J. H. *Bad Blood: The Tuskegee Syphilis Experiment.* New York: Free Press, 1982.

Joynson, Robert B. *The Burt Affair.* London: Routledge, 1989.

Katz, Jay. *Experimentation with Human Subjects.* New York: Russell Sage Foundation, 1972.

Klockars, Carl B. "Field Ethics for the Life History." In *Street Ethnography,* edited by Robert S. Weppner, 201–226. Vol. 1, Beverly Hills, Calif.: Sage, 1977.

_____, and Finbarr W. O'Connor, eds. *Deviance and Decency: The Ethics of Research with Human Subjects.* Beverly Hills, Calif.: Sage, 1979.

LaFollette, Marcel C. *Stealing into Print: Fraud, Plagiarism, and Misconduct in Scientific Publishing.* Berkeley: University of California Press, 1992.

Law Enforcement Assistance Administration. *Confidentiality of Research and Statistical Data.* Washington, D.C.: National Criminal Justice Information and Statistics Service, 1979.

Lawrence, Jill. "Feds Used Human Subjects in Radiation Exposure Experiments." Erie Times–News, 25 October 1988, 1A, 12A.

Lee, Raymond. "Doing Research on Sensitive Topics." Newberry Park, Calif.: Sage, 1993.

Longmire, Dennis R. "Ethical Dilemmas in the Research Setting." *Criminology* 21 (August 1983): 333–348.

Maldonado, Lionel, "Ofshe Wins Case against Synanon." *Footnotes* (American Sociological Association), 15 (April 1987), 3.

Marks, John. *The Search for the Manchurian Candidate: The CIA and Mind Control.* New York: Times Books, 1979.

Marshall, E. "Anthropologists Debate Tasaday Hoax Evidence." *Science* 246 (1989): 1113–1114.

Menges, Robert J. "Openness and Honesty Versus Coercion and Deception in Psychological Research." *American Psychologist* 28 (1978): 1030–1034.

Milgram, Stanley. *Obedience to Authority: An Experimental View.* New York: Harper, 1974.

Mitford, Jessica. *Kind and Unusual Punishment.* New York: Random House, 1973.

_____. "Experiments Behind Bars: Doctors, Drug Companies and Prisoners." In *Focus: Unexplored Deviance,* edited by Charles H. Swanson, 167–175. Guilford, Conn.: Dushkin, 1978.

National Advisory Committee on Criminal Justice Standards and Goals. *Criminal Justice Research and Development,* Report of the Task Force on Criminal Justice Research and Development, Washington, D.C.: Law Enforcement Assistance Administration, December 1976.

National Commission for the Protection of Human Subjects of Biomedical and Behavioral Research (NCPHSBBR). *Transcript of Proceedings,* 16th meeting, Bethesda, Md., 1976.

_____. *The Belmont Report: Ethical Principles and Guidelines for the Protection of Human Subjects of Research,* DHEW OS 78-0012, Washington, D.C.: U.S. Government Printing Office, 1978a.

_____. Appendix Vols. I and II, DHEW OS 78-0013, 78-0014, Washington, D.C.: U.S. Government Printing Office, 1978b.

_____. *Report and Recommendations on Institutional Review Boards,* DHEW OS 78-0008, Washington, D.C.: U.S. Government Printing Office, 1978c.

National Institute of Justice. "Data Confidentiality and Human Subjects Protection," Research Program Plan: Fiscal Years 1995–96, Washington, D.C.: National Institute of Justice, 1994.

Nejelski, Paul, ed. *Social Research in Conflict with Law and Ethics.* Cambridge, Mass.: Ballinger, 1976.

_____, and Lindsey M. Lerman. "What to Do before the Subpoena Arrives." *Wisconsin Law Review* (1971): 1085–1148.

Neuman, W. Lawrence. *Social Research Methods: Qualitative and Quantitative Methods.* Boston: Allyn and Bacon, 1991.

O'Connor, Finbarr W. "The Ethical Demands of the Belmont Report." In *Deviance and Decency,* edited by Carl B. Klockers and Finbarr W. O'Connor, 225–250. Beverly Hills, Calif.: Sage, 1979.

Polsky, Ned. *Hustlers, Beats and Others.* Chicago: Aldine, 1967.

Punch, Maurice. *The Politics and Ethics of Fieldwork.* Beverly Hills, Calif.: Sage, 1986.

Rabow, Jerome. "Research and Rehabilitation: The Conflict of Scientific and Treatment Roles in Corrections." In *Criminal Justice Research: Approaches, Problems, and Policy,* edited by Susette M. Talarico, 237–254. Cincinnati: Anderson, 1980.

"Regulations on the Protection of Human Subjects." *Federal Register,* Book 2, Section 8366 (January 26, 1981).

Reiman, Jeffrey H. "Research Subjects, Political Subjects, and Human Subjects." In *Deviance and Decency,* edited by Carl B. Klockars and Finbarr O'Connor, 35–61. Beverly Hills, Calif.: Sage, 1979.

Reiss, Albert J., Jr. "Governmental Regulation of Scientific Inquiry: Some Paradoxical Consequences." In *Deviance and Decency,* edited by Carl B. Klockars and Finbarr O'Connor, 61–95. Beverly Hills, Calif.: Sage, 1979.

Reynolds, Paul D. *Ethical Dilemmas and Social Science Research.* San Francisco: Jossey-Bass, 1979.

_____. *Ethics and Social Science Research.* Englewood Cliffs, N.J.: Prentice-Hall, 1982.

Rivlin, Alice, and Michael Timpane. *Ethical and Legal Issues of Social Experimentation.* Washington, D.C.: Brookings Institution, 1975.

Roth, Julius A. "Comments on 'Secret Observation'." *Social Problems* 9 (1962): 283–284.

Sagarin, Edward, and James Moneymaker. "The Dilemma of Researcher Immunity." In *Deviance and Decency,* edited by Carl B. Klockars and Finbarr O'Connor, 61–95. Beverly Hills, Calif.: Sage, 1979.

Sanders, William B., ed. *The Sociologist as Detective: An Introduction to Research Methods.* 2d ed. New York: Praeger, 1976.

Scheflin, Alan W., and Edward M. Opton, Jr. *The Mind Manipulators.* New York: Paddington Press, 1978.

Simon, David R., and Stanley D. Eitzen. *Elite Deviance.* 6th ed. Boston: Allyn and Bacon, 1996.

Soloway, Irving, and James Walters. "Workin' the Corner: The Ethics and Legality of Ethnographic Fieldwork among Active Heroin Addicts." In *Street Ethnography,* edited by Robert S. Weppner, 159–178. Vol 1, Beverly Hills, Calif.: Sage, 1977.

Spencer, F. *Piltdown: A Scientific Forgery.* New York: Oxford University Press, 1990.

Talarico, Susette M., ed. *Criminal Justice Research: Approaches, Problems and Policy.* Cincinnati: Anderson, 1980.

Thaler, Ruth E. "Fieldnotes Case Resolved; Scholars' Rights Supported." *Footnotes* (American Sociological Association) 13 (May 1985): 1.

Thorne, Barrie. "You Still Takin' Notes? Fieldwork and Problems of Informed Consent." *Social Problems* 27 (February 1980): 284–297.

Trend, M. G. "Applied Social Research and the Government: Notes on the Limits of Confidentiality." *Social Problems* 27 (February 1980): 342–349.

Wade, Nicholas. "I.Q. and Heredity: Suspicion of Fraud Beclouds Classic Experiment." *Science* 194 (1976): 916–919.

Wax, Murray L. "Paradoxes of 'Consent' to the Practice of Fieldwork." *Social Problems* 27 (February 1980): 272–283.

Weiner, J. S. *The Piltdown Forgery.* London: Oxford Press, 1955.

Weppner, Roberts S. "Street Ethnography: Problems and Prospects." In *Street Ethnography,* edited by Robert S. Weppner, 21–51. Beverly Hills, Calif.: Sage, 1977.

Wexler, Sandra. "Ethical Obligations and Social Research." In *Measurement Issues in Criminology,* edited by Kimberly L. Kempf, 78–107. New York: Springer–Verlag. 1990.

Whyte, William Foote. *Streetcorner Society.* Chicago: University of Chicago Press, 1955.

Witt, Howard. "CIA Sued for Attempts at Brainwashing." *Erie Daily Times,* 3 October 1988, 2A.

Wolfgang, Marvin B. "Ethical Issues of Research in Criminology." In *Social Research in Conflict with Law and Ethics,* edited by Paul Nejelski, 25–34. Cambridge, Mass.: Ballinger, 1976.

_____. "Confidentiality in Criminological Research and Other Ethical Issues." *Journal of Criminal Law and Criminology* 72 (1981): 75–86.

_____. "Ethics in Research." In *Ethics, Public Policy and Criminal Justice,* edited by Frederick Elliston and Norman Bowie, 391–418, Cambridge, Mass.: Oelgeschlager, Gunn and Hain, 1982.

Wolfgang, Marvin E., et al. *Delinquency in a Birth Cohort.* Chicago: University of Chicago Press, 1972.

Yablonsky, Lewis. *The Hippie Trip.* New York: Pegasus, 1968a.

_____. "On Crime, Violence, LSD and Legal Immunity for Social Scientists." *Criminologica* 3 (May 1968b): 148–149.

Zimbardo, Philip G. "Pathology of Imprisonment." *Society* 9 (1972): 4–6.

Zimbardo, Phillip. "On the Ethics of Intervention in Human Psychological Research: With Special Reference to the Stanford Prison Study." *Cognition* 22 (March 1973): 243–246.

Zimbardo, Philip G., et al. "The Psychology of Imprisonment: Privation, Power and Pathology." In *Doing Unto Others,* edited by Zick Rubin. Englewood Cliffs, N.J.: Prentice-Hall, 1974.

Chapter 3 Research Design: The Experimental Model and Its Variations

Adams, Stuart. *Evaluative Research in Corrections: A Practical Guide.* Washington, D.C.: National Institute of Law Enforcement and Criminal Justice, 1975.

"Albuquerque Study Confirms KC Findings." *Criminal Justice Newsletter* 10 (September 10, 1979): 4–5.

Binder, Arnold, and James Meeker. "Experiments as Reforms." *Journal of Criminal Justice* 16 (1988): 347–358.

_____. "Arrest as a Method to Control Spousal Abuse." In *Domestic Violence: The Changing Criminal Justice Response,* edited by Eve S. Buzawa and Carl G. Buzawa, Dover, Maine: Auburn House, 1991.

Brown, Barry S., et al. "Released Offenders' Perceptions of Community and Institution." *Corrective Psychiatry and Journal of Social Therapy* 16, nos. 1–4 (1970).

Buzawa, Eve S., and Carl G. Buzawa, eds. *Domestic Violence: The Changing Criminal Justice Response.* Dover, Maine: Auburn House, 1991.

Campbell, Donald T. "Reforms as Experiments." In *Readings in Evaluation Research,* 2d ed., edited by Francis G. Caro, New York: Russell Sage, 1977.

_____, and H. Laurence Ross. "The Connecticut Crackdown on Speeding: Time-Series Data in Quasi-Experimental Analysis." In *Criminal Justice Research,* edited by Susette M. Talarico, 70–88. Cincinnati: Anderson, 1980.

_____, and Julian C. Stanley. *Experimental and Quasi-Experimental Designs for Research.* Chicago: Rand McNally, 1963.

Carey, Alex. "The Hawthorne Studies: A Radical Criticism." *American Sociological Review* 32 (June 1967): 403–417.

Chalken, Jan M. "What's Known about Deterrent Effects of Police Activities." Santa Monica, Calif.: Rand Corp., paper presented at the Joint National Meeting of the Operations Research Society of America and the Institute of Management Sciences, Miami, November 3, 1976.

Charalampous, K. D., and Thelma J. Skinner. "Alcoholism and the Courts: Experience with a Traffic Safety Project." *Hospital and Community Psychiatry* 28 (January 1977): 33–35.

"Community Policing in the 1990s." *National Institute of Justice Journal,* August (1992): 2–8.

Cook, Thomas D., and Donald T. Campbell. *Quasi-Experimentation: Design and Analysis Issues for Field Settings.* Chicago: Rand McNally, 1979.

Cooper, William H. "Ubiquitous Halo." *Psychological Bulletin* 90 (September 1981): 218–244.

Cressey, Donald R. *Other People's Money: A Study in the Social Psychology of Embezzlement.* Belmont, Calif.: Wadsworth, 1957.

Cresswell, John W. *Research Design: Qualitative and Quantitative Approaches.* Thousand Oaks, Calif.: Sage, 1994.

Davis, Edward M., and Lyle Knowles. "A Critique of the Report: An Evaluation of the Kansas City Preventive Patrol Experiment." *The Police Chief* 42 (June 1975): 31–32.

Denzin, Norman K. *The Research Act.* 3rd ed., New York: McGraw-Hill, 1989.

Deschenes, Elizabeth P. "Longitudinal Research Designs." In *Measurement Issues in Criminology,* edited by Kimberly Kempf, 152–166. New York: Springer–Verlag, 1990.

Dunford, Franklyn W., David Hiuzinga, and Delbert S. Elliott. *The Omaha Domestic Violence Police Experiment.* Final Report, Washington, D.C.: National Institute of Justice, 1989.

_____. "The Role of Arrest in Domestic Assault: The Omaha Police Experiment." *Criminology* 28 (1990): 183–206.

Empey, Lamar T., and Maynard L. Erickson. *The Provo Experiment: Evaluating Community Control of Delinquency.* Lexington, Mass.: Heath, 1972.

_____, and Steven G. Lubeck. *The Silverlake Experiment: Testing Delinquency Theory and Community Intervention.* Chicago: Aldine, 1971.

Erez, Edna. "Randomized Experiments in Correctional Context: Legal, Ethical and Practical Concerns." *Journal of Criminal Justice* 14 (1986): 389–400.

Esbensen, Finn, and Scott Menard. "Is Longitudinal Research Worth the Price?" *The Criminologist* 15, no. 2 (March–April 1990): 1, 3–5.

Fagan, Jeffrey A. "Natural Experiments in Criminal Justice." In *Measurement Issues in Criminology,* edited by Kimberly Kempf, 108–137. New York: Springer–Verlag, 1990.

Farrington, D. P. "Effectiveness of Sentencing." *Justice of the Peace* 142 (February 1978): 68–71.

_____. "Longitudinal Research on Crime and Delinquency." In *Crime and Justice: An Annual Review of Research,* edited by Norval Morris and Michael Tonry, 289–348. Vol. 1, Chicago: University of Chicago Press, 1979.

_____. "Randomized Experiments in Crime and Justice." In *Crime and Justice: An Annual Review of Research,* edited by Michael Tonry and Norval Morris, 257–308. Vol. 4, Chicago: University of Chicago Press, 1983.

Feinberg, S. B., B. Singer, and J. M. Tanur. "Large Scale Social Experimentation in the United States." In *A Celebration of Statistics,* edited by A. C. Atkinson and S. B. Feinberg. New York: Springer-Verlag, 1985.

Field, H. S. "Simulated Jury Trials: Students Versus 'Real' People as Jurors." *Journal of Social Psychology* 104 (April 1978): 287–293.

Finckenauer, James O. *Scared Straight! and the Panacea Phenomenon.* Englewood Cliffs, N.J.: Prentice-Hall, 1982.

Garwood, David W. "Edsel Murphy's Law: Anything That Can Go Wrong Will Go Wrong." *The Loop: A Newsletter for Evaluators* 8 (December 1978): 17–22.

Gelles, R. J. "Etiology of Violence: Overcoming Fallacious Reasoning in Understanding Family Violence and Child Abuse," manuscript available through National Criminal Justice Reference Service, 1977.

Glaser, Daniel. "Correctional Research: An Elusive Paradise." In *Probation, Parole and Community Corrections,* 2d ed. edited by Robert M. Carter and Leslie T. Wilkins, 765–777. New York: Wiley, 1976.

Glueck, Sheldon, and Eleanor Glueck. *Later Criminal Careers.* New York- The Commonwealth Fund, 1937.

_____. *Juvenile Delinquents Grown Up.* New York: The Commonwealth Fund, 1940.

Gordon, Andrew C., et al. "Critique by Four Illinois Researchers Questions Validity of UDIS Evaluation." *Criminal Justice Newsletter* 9 (July 31, 1978): 1–6.

Gramckow, Heike. "Community Prosecution in the United States and Its Relevance for Europe." *European Journal on Criminal Policy and Research* 3 (2 1995): 112–121.

Hackler, James C. "Dangers of Political Naivete and Excessive Complexity in Evaluating Delinquency Prevention Programs." *Evaluation and Program Planning* 1 (1978): 278–283.

Heussenstamm, F. K. "Bumper Stickers and the Cops." *Trans-action* 8 (1971): 32–33.

"Hidden Cameras Project, Seattle, Washington." *Exemplary Projects: A Program of the National Institute of Law Enforcement and Criminal Justice.* Washington, D.C., August 1978.

Hirschi, Travis, and Hanan C. Selvin. "False Criteria of Causality in Delinquency." *Social Problems* 13 (Winter 1966): 254–268.

Holmes, M., and W. A. Taggart. "A Comparative Analysis of Research Methods in Criminology and Criminal Justice." *Justice Quarterly* 7(1990): 421–437.

Hood, Roger, and Richard Sparks. *Key Issues in Criminology.* New York: McGraw-Hill, 1971.

Hyman, Herbert H. *Survey Design and Analysis.* New York: Free Press, 1955, Chs. 5–7.

Isaac, Stephen, and William B. Michael. *Handbook in Research and Evaluation.* 2d ed. San Diego, Calif.: EdITS Publishers, 1981.

Josephson, E., and M. A. Rosen. "Panel Loss in a High School Drug Study." In *Longitudinal Research on Drug Use: Empirical Findings and Methodological Issues,* edited by Denise B. Kandel. Washington, D.C.: Hemisphere, 1978.

Kelling, George L. "Foot Patrol." In *Crime File,* Washington, D.C.: National Institute of Justice, 1985.

Kelling, George L., et al. *The Kansas City Preventive Patrol Experiment: A Summary Report and a Technical Report.* Washington, D.C.: The Police Foundation, 1974.

_____, and Tony Pate. "Response to the Davis-Knowles Critique of the Kansas City Preventive Patrol Experiment." *The Police Chief* 42 (June 1975): 33–34.

Langan, Patrick A., and Christopher A. Innes. *Preventing Domestic Violence against Women.* Washington, D.C.: Bureau of Justice Statistics Special Report, August 1986.

Larson, Richard C. "What Happened to Patrol Operations in Kansas City? A Review of the Kansas City Preventive Patrol Experiment." *Journal of Criminal Justice* 3 (Winter 1975): 267–297.

Loranger, A. W., C. T. Prout, and M. A. White. "The Placebo Effect in Psychiatric Drug Research." *Journal of the American Medical Association* 176 (June 17, 1961): 920–926.

Luskin, M. L. "Building a Theory of Case Processing Time," *Judicature* 62 (September 1978): 115–127.

Mackenzie, Doris L., and James W. Shaw. "The Impact of Shock Incarceration on Technical Violations and New Criminal Activities." *Justice Quarterly* 10 (September 1993): 462–488.

Mackenzie, Doris L., and Claire Souryal. Multisite Evaluation of Shock Incarceration, Rockville, MD: National Criminal Justice Reference Service, NCJ #150062, 1994.

Mastrofski, Stephen D. "What Does Community Policing Mean for Daily Police Work?" *National Institute of Justice Journal* (August 1992): 23–27.

McCord, William, and Joan McCord. *Origins of Crime: A New Evaluation of the Cambridge Somerville Youth Study.* New York: Columbia University Press, 1959.

Menard, Scott. *Longitudinal Research.* Newbury Park, Calif.: Sage, 1991.

Monahan, John, and Laurens Walker. *Social Science in Law: Cases and Materials.* 2d ed. Westbury, N.Y.: The Foundation Press, 1990.

Morris, Norval, and Michael Tonry. *Between Prison and Probation: Intermediate Punishments in a Rational Sentencing System.* New York Oxford University Press, 1990.

Murray, Charles. "Reply from Principal Author of UDIS Study." *Criminal Justice Newsletter* 9 (July 31, 1978): 4–5.

Orne, Martin T. "Demand Characteristics and the Concept of Quasi-controls." In *Artifacts in Behavior Research,* edited by Robert Rosenthal and Ralph L. Rosnow, 147–177. New York: Academic Press, 1969.

Ostrom, Elinor, Roger B. Parks, and Gordon Whitaker. "Do We Really Want to Consolidate Urban Police Forces? A Reappraisal of Some Old Assertions." *Public Administration Review* (September/October 1973): 423–432.

Pate, Tony, et al. "A Response to 'What Happened to Patrol Operations in Kansas City.'" *Journal of Criminal Justice* 3 (Winter 1975): 299–320.

Petersilia, Joan, and Sue Turner. *Intensive Supervision for High-Risk Probationers.* Santa Monica: Rand Corporation, 1990.

Pierce, Glenn, and William Bowers. *The Impact of the Bartley—Fox Gun Law on Crime in Massachusetts.* Boston: Northeastern University Center for Applied Social Research, 1979.

Police Foundation. *Domestic Violence and the Police: Studies in Detroit and Kansas City.* Washington, D.C.: The Police Foundation, 1977.

Police Foundation. *Newark Foot Patrol Experiment.* Washington, D.C.: The Police Foundation, 1981.

Ray, Maria. "Four Thousand Partners in Violence: A Trend Analysis." In *The Abusive Partner: An Analysis of Domestic Battering,* edited by Maria Ray. New York: Van Nostrand Reinhold, 1982.

Reid, Susan, T. *Crime and Criminology.* 3d ed. New York: Holt, Rinehart and Winston, 1982.

Roethlisberger, F. J., and William J. Dixon. *Management and the Worker.* Cambridge, Mass.: Harvard University Press, 1939.

Rosenberg, Milton J. "The Conditions and Consequences of Evaluation Apprehension." In *Artifacts in Behavioral Research,* edited by Robert Rosenthal and Ralph L. Rosnow, 280–348. New York: Academic Press, 1969.

Rosenthal, Robert. *Experimenter Effects in Behavioral Research.* New York: Century, 1966.

"Scared Straight Found Ineffective Again." *Criminal Justice Newsletter* 10 (September 10, 1979): 7.

Schneider, Anne L., and L. A. Wilson, "Introduction to Interrupted Time Series Designs." in *Handbook of Resources for Criminal Justice Evaluators,* edited by Anne L. Schneider, et al., 2–66. Washington, D.C.: National Institute of Law Enforcement and Criminal Justice, 1978.

Schneider, Anne L., et al., eds. *Handbook of Resources for Criminal Justice Evaluators.* Washington, D.C.: National Institute of Law Enforcement and Criminal Justice, 1978.

Schneider, Victoria, and John Smykla. "War and Capital Punishment." *Journal of Criminal Justice* 18 (1990): 253–260.

Sherman, Larry. "Neighborhood Safety." in *Crime File,* Rockville, Md.: National Institute of Justice, 1985.

Sherman, Larry, and Richard A. Berk. *The Minneapolis Domestic Violence Experiment.* Washington, D.C.: The Police Foundation, 1984a.

Sherman, Larry, and Richard A. Berk. "The Specific Deterrent Effects of Arrest for Domestic Assault." *American Sociological Review* 49 (1984b): 261–272.

Sherman, Larry, James W. Shaw, and Dennis P. Rogan. "The Kansas City Gun Experiment." National Institute of Justice Research in Brief, January 1995.

Smykla, John, et al. "Effects of Prison Facility on the Regional Economy." *Journal of Criminal Justice* 12 (1984): 521–539.

Solomon, R. L. "Extension of Control Group Design." *Psychological Bulletin* 46 (1949): 137–150.

Steffensmeier, Darrell J., and Robert M. Terry. "The Experimental Study of Human Behavior." In *Examining Deviance Experimentally,* Port Washington, N.Y.: Alfred 1975, pp. 38–49.

Sykes, Gary W. "Saturated Enforcement: The Efficacy of Deterrence and Drunk Driving." *Journal of Criminal Justice* 12 (1984): 185–197.

Thomas, W. I., and Dorothy Swaine. *The Child in America.* New York: Knopf, 1928.

Thorndike, R. L. "A Constant Error in Psychological Ratings." *Journal of Applied Psychology* 4 (1920): 25–29.

Tontodonato, Pamela. "Explaining Rate Changes in Delinquent Arrest Transitions Using Event History Analysis." *Criminology* 26 (August 1988): 439–459.

Tracy, Paul E., Marvin E. Wolfgang, and Robert M. Figlio. *Delinquency in Two Birth Cohorts: Executive Summary.* Philadelphia, Pa.: Center for Studies in Criminology and Criminal Law, The Wharton School, University of Pennsylvania, 1985.

Travis, Jeremy. "Researchers Evaluate Eight Shock Incarceration Programs." National Institute of Justice Update, October 1994.

Trojanowicz, Robert C., and Dennis W. Banas. *Perceptions of Safety: A Comparison of Foot Patrol versus Motor Patrol Officers.* East Lansing: National Neighborhood Foot Patrol Center, School of Criminal Justice, Michigan State University, 1985.

Visher, Christy A. "Understanding the Roots of Crime: The Project on Human Development in Chicago Neighborhoods." *National Institute of Justice Journal,* November (1994): 9–15.

Weubben, Paul L., Bruce C. Straits, and Gary F. Shulman, eds. *The Experiment as a Social Occasion.* Berkeley, Calif.: Glendessary Press, 1974.

Widom, Cathy Spatz. "The Cycle of Violence." National Institute of Justice Research in Brief, October 1992.

_____. "Victims of Childhood Sexual Abuse—Later Criminal Consequences." National Institute of Justice Research in Brief, March 1995.

Wilkins, Leslie T. "The Concept of Cause in Criminology." In *Classes, Conflict and Control: Studies in Criminal Justice Management,* edited by J. Munro. Cincinnati: Anderson, 1976.

Wilson, James Q., and George L. Kelling. "Broken Windows: The Police and Neighborhood Safety." *The Atlantic* (March 1982): 27–38.

Witkin, Herman A., et al. "XYY and Criminality." In *Crime in Society,* edited by Leonard D. Savitz and Norman Johnston, 275–291. New York: Wiley, 1978.

Wolfgang, Marvin, et al. *Delinquency in a Birth Cohort.* Chicago: University of Chicago Press, 1972.

Wycoff, Mary Ann, and Wesley K. Skogan. "Community Policing in Madison: Quality from the Inside Out—An Evaluation of Implementation and Impact." In "Update on NIJ-Sponsored Research: Six New Reports," National Institute of Justice Research in Brief, April, 1994, 4–5.

Wycoff, Mary Ann, Wesley Skogan, Anthony Pate, and Lawrence W. Sherman. *Personal Contact Patrol: The Houston Field Test.* Washington, D.C.: The Police Foundation, 1985a.

_____. *Police Community Stations: The Houston Field Test.* Washington, D.C.: The Police Foundation, 1985b.

Zimring, Franklin E. "Firearms and Federal Law." *Journal of Legal Studies* 4 (January 1975): 133–198.

Chapter 4 An Introduction to Alternative Data-Gathering Strategies and the Special Case of Uniform Crime Reports

Albini, Joseph. "The Guardian Angels: Vigilantes or Protectors of the Community?" Paper presented at the Academy of Criminal Justice Sciences Meeting, Orlando, Fla., March 1986.

Black, Donald J. "Production of Crime Rates," *American Sociological Review* 35 (August 1970): 733–748.

Bouchard, T. J., Jr. "Field Research Methods: Interviewing, Questionnaires, Participant Observation, Systematic Observation, Unobtrusive Measures." In *Handbook of Industrial and Organizational Psychology,* edited by Marvin D. Dunnette. Chicago: Rand McNally, 1976.

"Burying Crime in Chicago." *Newsweek,* 16 May 1983, 63.

Cameron, Mary Owen. *The Booster and the Snitch: Department Store Shoplifting.* Glencoe, Ill.: Free Press, 1964.

Carter, Robert M., and Leslie T. Wilkins, eds. *Probation, Parole and Community Corrections.* 2d ed. New York: Wiley, 1976.

Clinard, Marshall B. *The Black Market: A Study of White Collar Crime.* New York: Holt, 1952.

Dodenhoff, Peter C. "LEN Salutes Its 1989 People of the Year, the UCR Redesign Team." *Law Enforcement News* 15, no. 307 (January 31, 1990): 1, 10–11.

Filstead, William J., ed. *Qualitative Methodology.* Chicago: Markham, 1971.

Glaser, Barney, and Anselm Strauss. *The Discovery of Grounded Theory: Strategies for Qualitative Research.* Chicago: Aldine, 1967.

Glaser, Daniel. *Crime in Our Changing Society.* New York: Holt, 1978.

Hackler, James C. "Dangers of Political Naivete and Excessive Complexity in Evaluating Delinquency Prevention Programs." *Evaluation and Program Planning* 1 (1978): 278–283.

Ianni, Francis A. *A Family Business: Kinship and Social Control in Organized Crime.* New York: Russell Sage, 1972.

Jackson, Patrick D. "Assessing the Validity of Official Data on Arson." *Criminology* 26 (February 1988): 181–195.

King, Harry, and William J. Chambliss. *Harry King: A Professional Thief's Journal.* New York: Wiley, 1984.

Kitsuse, J. I., and A. V. Cicourel. "A Note on the Use of Official Statistics." *Social Problems* 11 (Fall 1963): 131–138.

Klockars, Carl B. *The Professional Fence.* New York: Free Press, 1974.

Lejins, Peter. "Uniform Crime Reports." *Michigan Law Review* 64 (April 1966): 1011–1030.

Maas, Peter. *The Valachi Papers.* New York: Bantam Books, 1968.

Poggio, Eugene C., et al. *Blueprint for the Future of the Uniform Crime Reporting Program: Final Report of the UCR Study.* Washington, D.C.: U.S. Department of Justice, May 1985.

Polsky, Ned. *Hustlers, Beats and Others.* Chicago: Aldine, 1967.

President's Commission on Law Enforcement and the Administration of Justice. *The Challenge of Crime in a Free Society.* Washington D.C.: U.S. Government Printing Office, 1967.

Reaves, Brian A. "Using NIBRS Data to Analyze Violent Crime." Bureau of Justice Statistics Technical Report, October 1993.

Reiss, Albert J., Jr. *The Police and the Public.* New Haven, Conn.: Yale University Press, 1971.

Rhodes, Robert P. *The Insoluble Problem of Crime.* New York: Wiley, 1977.

Rosenthal, Robert. *Experimenter Effects in Research.* New York: Appleton, 1966.

Rovetch, Emily L., Eugene C. Poggio, and Henry H. Rossman. *A Listing and Classification of Identified Issues Regarding the Uniform Crime Reporting Program of the FBI.* Cambridge, Mass.: Abt Associates, Inc., 1984.

Savitz, Leonard D. "Official Police Statistics and Their Limitations." In *Crime in Society,* edited by Leonard D. Savitz and Norman Johnston, 69–81. New York: Wiley, 1978.

Seidman, David, and Michael Couzens. "Getting the Crime Rate Down: Political Pressure and Crime Reporting." *Law and Society Review* 8 (Spring 1974): 457–493.

Sellin, Thorsten. "Crime in the United States." *Life Magazine* 9 September 1957, 48.

Shaw, Clifford. *The Jack-Roller.* Chicago: University of Chicago Press, 1930.

_____. *The Natural History of a Delinquent Career.* Chicago: University of Chicago Press, 1931.

Sherman, Larry, and Barry Glick. "The Quality of Arrest Statistics." *Police Foundation Reports* 2 (1984): 1–8.

Skogan, Wesley. "The Validity of Official Crime Statistics: An Empirical Investigation." *Social Science Quarterly* 55 (June 1974): 25–38.

_____. "Dimensions of the Dark Figure of Unreported Crime." *Crime and Delinquency* 23 (January 1977): 41–50.

Skolnick, Jerome H. *Justice without Trial: Law Enforcement in Democratic Society.* New York: Free Press, 1966.

Snodgrass, Jon. *The Jack-Roller at Seventy: A Fifty-Year Follow-up.* Lexington, Mass.: D.C. Heath, 1982.

Stamp, J. *Some Economic Factors in Modern Life.* London: P. S. King and Sons, Ltd., 1929.

Sutherland, Edwin H. *The Professional Thief.* Chicago: University of Chicago Press, 1937.

Teresa, Vincent, with Thomas C. Renner. *My Life in the Mafia.* Greenwich, Conn.: Fawcett, 1973.

U.S. Department of Justice. *FBI Uniform Crime Reports: Crime in the United States, 1990.* Washington, D.C.: U.S. Government Printing Office, 1991.

U.S. Department of Justice. *FBI Uniform Crime Reports: Crime in the United States, 1993.* Washington, D.C.: U.S. Government Printing Office, December 1994.

U.S. Department of Justice. *FBI Uniform Crime Reports: Crime in the United States, 1986,* Washington, D.C.: U.S. Government Printing Office, July 25, 1987, p. 42.

Webb, Eugene, et al. *Unobtrusive Measures: Nonreactive Research in the Social Sciences.* Chicago: Rand McNally, 1966.

Webb, Eugene, et al. *Nonreactive Measures in the Social Sciences.* 2d ed. Boston, Mass.: Houghton Mifflin, 1981.

Weber, Max. *The Methodology of Social Sciences.* Translated by Edward A. Shils and Henry A. Finch. New York: Free Press, 1949.

Whyte, William Foote. *Street Corner Society.* Chicago: University of Chicago Press, 1943.

Wilbanks, William. "Professor Disputes Crime Rate Rankings." *The Miami News* 30 January 1986, 1H.

Wolfgang, Marvin E. "Uniform Crime Reports: A Critical Appraisal." *University of Pennsylvania Law Review* 11 (1963): 708–738.

Yablonsky, Lewis. *The Tunnel Back: Synanon.* New York: Macmillan, 1965.

Chapter 5 Sampling and Survey Research: Questionnaires

Alex, Nicholas. *Black in Blue: A Study of the Negro Policeman.* New York: Appleton, Century Crofts, 1969.

American Statistical Association. "Report on the ASA Conference on Surveys of Human Populations." *The American Statistician* 28 (February 1974): 30–34.

Archer, Dane, and Rosemary Gartner. *Violence and Crime in Cross-national Perspective.* New Haven, Conn.: Yale University Press, 1984.

Babbie, Earl R. *The Practice of Social Research.* 6th ed. Belmont, Calif.: Wadsworth, 1992.

Bachman, G. G. *Monitoring the Future.* Ann Arbor, Mich.: University of Michigan, Institute for Social Research, 1987.

Bachman, G. G., P. M. O'Malley, and J. Johnston. *Youth in Transition,* 4. Ann Arbor, Mich.: University of Michigan, Institute for Social Research, 1978.

Barton, A. J. "Asking the Embarrassing Question." *Public Opinion Quarterly* 22 (1958): 67–68.

Biernacki, P., and Dan Waldorf. "Snowball Sampling: Problems and Techniques of Chain Referral Sampling." *Sociological Methods and Research* 10 (1981): 141–163.

Bogue, Grant. *Basic Sociological Research Design.* Glenview, Ill.: Scott, Foresman, 1981.

Brantingham, Paul, and Patricia Brantingham. *Patterns in Crime.* New York: Macmillan, 1984.

Brehm, John. *The Phantom Respondent: Opinion Surveys and Political Representation.* Ann Arbor: University of Michigan Press, 1993.

Camilli, Gregory, and Lorrie A. Shepard. *Methods for Identifying Biased Test Items.* Thousand Oaks, Calif.: Sage, 1994.

Chilton, Roland. "Twenty-Five Years After the Crime Commission Report: Is the Field Still Data Starved?" *The Criminologist* 18 (September/October 1993): 1, 6–8.

Clark, John P., and Larry L. Tifft. "Polygraph and Interview Validation of Selfreported Deviant Behavior." *American Sociological Review* 31 (August 1966): 516–523.

Coleman, James S. *The Adolescent Society.* Glencoe, Ill.: The Free Press, 1961.

Criminal Victimization Surveys in Milwaukee. National Crime Survey Report No. SD-NCS-C-12, Washington, D.C.: National Criminal Justice Information and Statistics Service, July 1977.

Cullen, Francis T. "Public Support for Punishing White-Collar Crime: Blaming the Victim Revisited?" *Journal of Criminal Justice* 11 (1983): 481–494.

Dentler, Robert A., and Lawrence J. Monroe. "Social Correlates of Early Adolescent Theft." *American Sociological Review* 26 (October 1961): 733–743.

Deutscher, Irwin. "Words and Deeds: Social Science and Social Policy." *Social Problems* 13 (Winter 1966): 235–265.

Dillman, Don A. "Increasing Mail Questionnaire Response in Large Samples of the General Public." *Public Opinion Quarterly* 36 (Summer 1972): 254–257.

_____. *Mail and Telephone Data Collection Methods.* New York: Wiley-Interscience, 1976.

_____, and James H. Frey. "The Contributions of Personalization to Mail Questionnaire Response as an Element of a Previously Tested Method." *Journal of Applied Psychology* 59 (1974): 297–301.

Edwards, Alba L. *The Social Desirability Variable in Personality Assessment and Research.* New York: Appleton-Century-Crofts, 1957.

Elliott, Delbert S., and Suzanne S. Ageton. "Reconciling Race and Class Differences in Self-reported and Official Estimates of Delinquency." *American Sociological Review* 45 (February 1980): 95–110.

Elliott, Delbert S. and David Huizinga. "Social Class and Delinquent Behavior in a National Youth Panel: 1976–1980." *Criminology* 21 (May 1983): 149–177.

Empey, Lamar T., and Maynard L. Erickson. "Hidden Delinquency and Social Status." *Social Forces* 44 (1966): 546–554.

Erez, Edna, and Pamela Tontodonato. "Victim Participation in Sentencing and Satisfaction with Justice." *Justice Quarterly* 9 (September 1992), 393–415.

Erickson, Maynard L., and LaMar T. Empey. "Court Records, Undetected Delinquency and Decision-Making." *Journal of Criminal Law, Criminology and Police Science* 54 (1963): 456–469.

Fagan, Jeffrey. "The Social Organization of Drug Use and Drug Dealing Among Urban Gangs." *Criminology* 27 (November 1989): 633–669.

Farrington, David P. "Self-Reports of Deviant Behavior: Predictive and Stable?" *Journal of Criminal Law and Criminology* 64 (1973): 99–110.

Fitzpatrick, Kevin M., Mark E. LaGory, and Ferris J. Ritchey. "Criminal Victimization Among the Homeless." *Justice Quarterly* 10 (September 1993): 353–368.

Garofalo, James. *Public Opinion about Crime: The Attitudes of Victims and Nonvictims in Selected Cities.* Washington, D.C.: U.S. Department of Justice, 1977.

Gertz, Marc G., and Susette M. Talarico, "Problems of Reliability and Validity in Criminal Justice Research." In *Criminal Justice Research: Approaches, Problems and Policy,* edited by Susette M. Talarico, 166–176. Cincinnati: Anderson, 1980.

Glaser, Daniel. *Crime in Our Changing Society.* New York: Holt, 1978.

Gold, Martin. "Undetected Delinquent Behavior." *Journal of Research in Crime and Delinquency* 3 (January 1966): 27–46.

Gold, Martin, and D. J. Reimer. *Changing Patterns of Delinquent Behavior Among Americans 13 to 17 Years Old—1972.* Report Number 1 of the National Survey of Youth, 1971, Ann Arbor: University of Michigan, Institute for Social Research, 1974.

Goldkamp, John S., and Michael R. Gottfredson. *Final Report of the Judicial Guidelines for Bail: The Philadelphia Experiment Project.* Washington, D.C.: National Institute of Justice, 1984.

Goodman, Leo A. "Snowball Sampling." *Annals of Mathematical Statistics* 32 (March 1969): 148–170.

Goodstein, Lynne I., et al. "Defining Determinancy: Components of the Sentencing Process Ensuring Equity and Release Certainty." *Justice Quarterly* 1 (1984): 47–74.

Greenberg, David, and N. J. Larkin. "Age-Cohort Analysis of Arrest Rates." *Journal of Quantitative Criminology* 1 (1985): 227–240.

Greenberg, Stephanie J., J. R. Williams, and W. M. Rohe. *Safe and Secure Neighborhoods: Physical Characteristics and Informal Territorial Control in High and Low Crime Neighborhoods.* Washington, D.C.: National Institute of Justice, 1982.

Greenwood, Peter W., and Allan Abrahamse. *Selective Incapacitation.* Santa Monica, Calif.: Rand Corp., August, 1982.

Gross, Martin. *The Brain Watchers.* New York: New American Library, 1962.

Hagan, Frank E. *Comparative Professionalization in an Occupational Arena: The Case of Rehabilitation.* Ph.D. dissertation, Case Western Reserve University, 1975.

_____, Marie R. Haug, and Marvin B. Sussman. *Comparative Profiles of the Rehabilitation Counseling Graduate: 1965 and 1972.* 2d series. Working Paper No. 5. Cleveland: Case Western Reserve University, Institute on the Family and the Bureaucratic Society, 1975.

Hamilton, Henry, and John Ortiz Smykla. "Guidelines for Police Undercover Work: New Questions About Accreditation and the Emphasis of Procedure Over Authorization." *Justice Quarterly* 11 (March 1994): 135–151.

Hamm, Mark S. "Legislator Ideology and Capital Punishment: The Special Case for Indiana Juveniles." *Justice Quarterly* 6 (June, 1989): 219–232.

Hardt, Robert H., and Sandra Peterson Hardt. "On Determining the Quality of the Delinquency Self-report Method." *Journal of Research in Crime and Delinquency* 14 (July 1977): 247–261.

Hazelwood, Robert R., and Janet Warren. "The Serial Rapist: His Characteristics and Victim." *FBI Law Enforcement Bulletin* 60 (1989): 10–17.

Heberlein, Thomas A., and Robert Baumgartner. "Factors Affecting Response Rates to Mailed Questionnaires: A Quantitative Analysis of the Published Literature." *American Sociological Review* 43 (August 1978): 447–462.

Hindelang, Michael J., Travis Hirschi, and Joseph G. Weis. "Correlates of Delinquency: The Illusion of Discrepancy between Self-report and Official Measures." *American Sociological Review* 44 (December 1979): 995–1013.

Hirschi, Travis. *Causes of Delinquency.* Berkeley: University of California, 1969.

Holmes, Ronald M. *Profiling Violent Crimes: An Investigative Tool.* Newbury Park, Calif.: Sage, 1989.

Hood, Roger, and Richard Sparks. *Key Issues in Criminology.* New York: McGraw-Hill, 1971.

Huizinga, David, and Delbert S. Elliott. *Self-Reported Measures of Delinquency and Crime: Methodological Issues and Comparative Findings.* Boulder, Colo: Behavioral Research Institute, 1984.

Inciardi, James A. "Heroin Use and Street Crimes." *Crime and Delinquency* 25 (July 1979): 335–346.

Isaac, Stephen, and William B. Michael. *Handbook in Research and Evaluation.* 2d ed. San Diego, Calif.: EdITS Publishers, 1981.

Jackson, Patrick G. "Sources of Data." In *Measurement Issues in Criminology,* edited by Kimberly L. Kempf, 21–50. New York: Springer-Verlag, 1990.

Jacob, Herbert. *The Frustration of Policy: Response to Crime in American Cities.* Boston, Mass.: Little, Brown, 1984.

Japha, Tony. *The Nation's Toughest Drug Law: Evaluating the New York Experience.* Washington, D.C.: National Institute of Justice, 1978.

Kish, Leslie. *Survey Sampling.* New York: Wiley, 1965.

Koenig, Daniel J., et al. "Routine Activities, Impending Social Change and Policing." *Canadian Police College Journal* 7 (1983): 96–136.

Krueger, Richard A. *Focus Groups: A Practical Guide for Applied Research.* 2d ed. Newbury Park, Calif.: Sage, 1994.

Kulik, James A., et al. "Disclosure of Delinquent Behavior Under Conditions of Anonymity and Nonanonymity." *Journal of Counseling and Clinical Psychology* 32, no. 5 (1968): 506–509.

Lab, Steven B., and Roy B. Allen. "Self Report and Official Measures: A Further Examination of the Validity Issue." *Journal of Criminal Justice* 12 (1984): 445–455.

LaPiere, Richard T. "Attitudes vs. Actions." *Social Forces* 13 (March 1934): 230–237.

Lazarsfeld, Paul F. "The Art of Asking Why: Three Principles Underlying the Formulation of Questionnaires." In *Public Opinion and Propaganda,* edited by Daniel Katz et al., 675–686. New York: Holt, 1954.

Levine, James P. "The Potential for Overreporting in Criminal Victimization Surveys." *Criminology* 14 (November 1976): 307–330.

Loether, Herman J., and Donald G. McTavish. *Descriptive and Inferential Statistics for Sociologists: An Introduction.* 2d ed. Boston: Allyn and Bacon, 1980.

Loftin, Colin. *Data Resources of the National Institute of Justice.* Washington, D.C.: U.S. Department of Justice, May 1987.

McCandless, Boyd R., et al. "Perceived Opportunity, Delinquency, Race and Body Build Among Delinquent Youth." *Journal of Consulting and Clinical Psychology* 38, no. 2 (1972): 281–287.

Miller, Delbert C. *Handbook of Research Design and Social Measurement.* 5th ed. New York: McKay, 1991.

Morgan, David L. *Successful Focus Groups.* Thousand Oaks, Calif.: Sage, 1993.

Morin, Richard. "A Pollster's Worst Nightmare: Declining Response Rates." *The Washington Post National Weekly Edition,* 5–11 July 1993, 37.

Nettler, Gwynn. *Explaining Crime.* 2d ed. New York: McGraw-Hill, 1978.

Norusis, Marija J., and SPSS-Inc. SPSS/PC+V.20 Base Manual. Chicago: SPSS Inc., 1988.

Nurco, David N., et al. "Crime as a Source of Income for Narcotic Addicts." *Journal of Substance Abuse Treatment* 2 (1985): 113–115.

Nye, F. Ivan, and James F. Short, Jr. "Scaling Delinquent Behavior." *American Sociological Review* 22 (1956): 326–331.

O'Donnell, John A., et al. *Young Men and Drugs: A Nationwide Survey.* Rockville, Md.: National Institute on Drug Abuse, 1976.

O'Keefe, Garret J., et al. *Taking a Bite Out of Crime: The Impact of a Mass Media Crime Prevention Campaign.* Unpublished report, University of Denver, Center for Mass Communications Research and Policy, 1984.

Osgood, D. Wayne, et al. "Time Trends and Age Trends in Arrests and Self-Reported Illegal Behavior." *Criminology* 27 (August 1989): 389–417.

Panel for the Evaluation of Crime Surveys. *Surveying Crime.* Washington, D.C.: National Academy of Sciences, 1976.

Pate, Anthony, et al. *Final Report of the Effects of Police Fear Reduction Strategies: A Summary of Findings from Houston and Newark.* Washington, D.C.: The Police Foundation, 1986.

Petersilia, Joan, Peter W. Greenwood, and Marvin Lavin. *Criminal Careers of Habitual Felons.* Santa Monica, Calif.: Rand Corp., 1977.

Polsky, Ned. *Hustlers, Beats and Others.* Chicago: Aldine, 1967.

Porterfield, A. L. *Youth in Trouble.* Austin, Tex.: Leo Polishman Foundation, 1946.

Schuerman, Leo A., and Solomon Kobrin. "Community Careers in Crime." In *Communities and Crime,* edited by Albert Reiss and Michael Tonry. Crime and Justice series Vol. 8, Chicago: University of Chicago Press, 1986.

Schuman, Howard, and Stanley Presser. *Questions and Answers in Attitude Surveys: Experiments on Question Form, Wording and Context.* Orlando: Academic Press, 1981.

Sheley, Joseph F., and James D. Wright. "Gun Acquisition and Possession in Selected Juvenile Samples." Research in Brief, National Institute of Justice, Office of Juvenile Justice and Delinquency Prevention, December 1993.

Short, James F., and F. Ivan Nye. "The Extent of Unrecorded Juvenile Delinquency." *Journal of Criminal Law, Criminology and Police Science* 49 (1958): 296–302.

Short, James F., and Fred L. Strodtbeck. *Group Process and Gang Delinquency.* Chicago: University of Chicago Press, 1965.

Sigler, Robert T., and Donna Haygood. "The Criminalization of Forced Marital Intercourse." In *Deviance and the Family,* edited by Frank E. Hagan and Marvin B. Sussman. New York: Haworth Press, 1988.

Sigler, Robert T., and Ida M. Johnson. "Public Perceptions of the Need for Criminalization of Sexual Harassment." *Journal of Criminal Justice* 14 (1986): 229–237.

Slocum, W. L., and C. L. Stone. "Family Culture Patterns and Delinquent-Type Behavior." *Marriage and Family Living* 25 (1963): 202–208.

Solomey, Joseph. *The Glory Boys: Notes on the Police Underground.* Senior Thesis, Mercyhurst College, 1979.

Sparks, Richard F. *Massachusetts Statewide Criminal Justice Guidelines Evaluation, 1979: Sentencing Data.* Washington, D.C.: National Institute of Justice, 1982.

Stewart, D. W., and P. N. Shamdasani. *Focus Groups: Theory and Practice.* Newbury Park, Calif.: Sage, 1990.

Sudman, Seymour, and Norman M. Bradburn. *Asking Questions: A Practical Guide to Questionnaire Design.* San Francisco, Calif.: Jossey-Bass, 1982.

Tittle, Charles W., and Wayne J. Villemez. "Social Class and Criminality." *Social Forces* 56 (December 1977): 474–502.

Toborg, Mary. *Pretrial Release: A National Evaluation of Practices and Outcomes.* Washington, D.C.: National Institute of Justice, 1981.

Toy, Calvin. "A Short History of Asian Gangs in San Francisco." *Justice Quarterly* 9 (December 1992): 647–665.

Voss, H. L. "Ethnic Differentials in Delinquency in Honolulu." *Journal of Criminal Law, Criminology and Police Science* 54 (September 1963): 322–327.

Wallerstein, James S., and Clement J. Wyle. "Our Law-Abiding Law-Breakers." *Probation* 35 (April 1947): 107–118.

West, D. J., and D. P. Farrington. *The Delinquent Way of Life.* London: Heinemann 1977.

Chapter 6   Survey Research: Interviews and Telephone Surveys

Albini, Joseph L. *The American Mafia: Genesis of a Legend.* New York: Appleton, 1971.

Bachman, Ronet, and Bruce M. Taylor. "The Measurement of Family Violence and Rape by the Redesigned National Crime Victimization Survey." *Justice Quarterly* 11 (September 1994): 499–512.

Berg, Bruce L. *Qualitative Research Methods for the Social Sciences.* 3d ed. Boston: Allyn and Bacon, 1995.

Biderman, Albert. *Time Distortions of Victimization Data and Mnemonic Effects.* Washington, D.C.: Bureau of Social Research, 1970.

Biderman, Albert D., et al. *Report on a Pilot Study in the District of Columbia on Victimization and Attitudes toward Law Enforcement.* Field Surveys I, Commission on Law Enforcement and Administration of Justice, Washington, D.C.: U.S. Government Printing Office, 1967.

Black, Donald J. "The Production of Crime Rates." *American Sociological Review* 35 (August 1970): 733–748.

Bucher, Rue, Charles E. Fritz, and E. L. Quarantelli. "Tape Recorded Interviews in Social Research." *American Sociological Review* 21 (June 1956): 359–364.

Bureau of Justice Statistics. *Report to the Nation on Crime and Justice: The Data.* Washington, D.C.: U.S. Department of Justice, 1983.

Bureau of Justice Statistics. "Households Touched by Crime." *Bureau of Justice Statistics Bulletin.* Washington, D.C.: U.S. Department of Justice, 1987.

Bureau of Justice Statistics. *Redesign of the National Crime Survey.* Washington, D.C.: Bureau of Justice Statistics, February, 1989.

Bureau of Justice Statistics. "Domestic Violence: Violence Between Intimates." *Bureau of Justice Statistics Selected Findings.* November 1994a, p. 10.

Bureau of Justice Statistics. "Technical Background on the Redesigned National Crime Victimization Survey." U.S. Bureau of Census, October 30, 1994b.

Burnham, David. "New York Is Found Safest of 13 Cities in Crime Study." *New York Times* 15 April 1974, 1, 51.

Clinard, Marshall B. "Comparative Crime Victimization Surveys: Some Problems and Results." *International Journal of Criminology and Penology* 6 (1978).

Converse, Jean M., and Howard Schuman. *Conversations at Random: Survey Research as Interviewers See It.* New York: Wiley, 1974.

Cressey, Donald. *Other People's Money.* New York: The Free Press, 1953.

Crittenden, Kathleen S., and Richard J. Hill. "Coding Reliability and Validity of Interview Data." *American Sociological Review* 36 (December 1971): 1073–1080.

Dodge, Richard W. "Response to Screening Questions in the National Crime Survey." *Bureau of Justice Statistics Technical Report.* Washington, D.C.: U.S. Department of Justice, June 1985.

Douglas, Jack. *Investigative Social Research.* Beverly Hills, Calif.: Sage, 1976.

Eigenberg, Helen M. "The National Crime Survey and Rape: The Case of the Missing Question." *Justice Quarterly* 7 (December 1990): 655–671.

Ennis, P. H. *Criminal Victimization in the United States: A Report of a National Survey.* Field Surveys II, the President's Commission on Law Enforcement and Administration of Justice, Washington, D.C.: U.S. Government Printing Office, 1967.

Fox, James A., and Paul E. Tracy. *Randomized Response: A Method for Sensitive Surveys.* Newbury Park, Calif.: Sage, 1986.

Frey, James H. *Survey Research by Telephone.* 2d ed. Newbury Park, Calif.: Sage, 1989.

Garofalo, James, and Michael J. Hindelang. *An Introduction to the National Crime Survey.* Analytic Report SD-VAD-4, Washington, D.C.: National Criminal Justice Information and Statistics Service, 1977.

Glaser, Daniel. *Crime in Our Changing Society.* New York: Holt, 1978.

Glasser, Gerald J., and Dale D. Metzger. "Random-Digit Dialing as a Method of Telephone Sampling." *Journal of Marketing Research* 9 (February 1972): 59–64.

Gordon, Raymond L. *Interviewing: Strategy, Techniques and Tactics.* Homewood, Ill.: Dorsey, 1969.

Gottfredson, Michael R., and Michael J. Hindelang. "A Consideration of Telescoping and Memory Decay Biases in Victimization Surveys." *Journal of Criminal Justice* 5 (Fall 1977): 205–216.

Groves, Robert M., and Robert L. Kahn. *Surveys by Telephone: A National Comparison with Personal Interviews.* New York: Academic Press, 1979.

Groves, Robert M., et al. *Telephone Survey Methodology.* New York: John Wiley and Sons, 1988.

Guerts, M. D., R. R. Andrus, and J. Reinmuth. "Researching Shoplifting and Other Deviant Customer Behavior Using the Randomized Response Research Design." *Journal of Retailing* 51 (Winter 1976): 43–47.

Hagan, Frank E. *The Rural Elderly in Erie County, Pennsylvania,* a report prepared for the Appalachian Regional Commission and Greater Erie Community Action Committee, Erie, Pa., September 1972, p. 8.

Hoinville, Gerald, Roger Jowell, et al. *Survey Research Practice.* London: Heinemann, 1978.

Institute on the Family and the Bureaucratic Society. *Interviewer's Handbook.* Cleveland: Case Western Reserve University, 1974.

Jensen, Gary F., and Maryaltani Karpos. "Managing Rape: Exploratory Research on the Behavior of Rape Statistics." *Criminology* 31 (August 1993): 363–385.

Klockars, Carl B. "A Theory of Contemporary Criminological Ethics." In *Ethics, Public Policy and Criminal Justice,* edited by Frederick Elliston and Norman Bowie, 419–458. Cambridge, Mass.: Oelgeschlager, Gunn and Hain, 1982.

Laub, John H. *Criminology in the Making: An Oral History.* Boston: Northeastern University Press, 1983.

Lavrakis, Paul J. "Citizen Self-help and Neighborhood Crime Prevention." *American Violence and Public Policy.* New Haven, Conn.: Yale University Press, 1984.

_____. *Telephone Survey Methods: Sampling, Selection and Supervision.* 2d ed. Beverly Hills, Calif.: Sage, 1993.

Lehnen, Robert G., and Albert J. Reiss. "Response Effects in the National Crime Survey." *Victimology* 3 (1978): 110–124.

Lehnen, Robert G., and Wesley G. Skogan. *The National Crime Surveys: Working Papers,* Vol. 1: *Current and Historical Perspectives.* Washington, D.C.: U.S. Department of Justice, December 1981.

Levine, James P. "The Potentials for Crime Over-reporting in Criminal Victimization Surveys." *Criminology* 4 (November 1976): 307–330.

Liu, P. T., and L. P. Chow. "A New Discrete Quantitative Randomized Response Model." *Journal of the American Statistical Association* 71 (1976): 72–73.

Loftin, Colin. *Data Resources of the National Institute of Justice.* Washington, D.C.: U.S. Department of Justice, May 1987.

Mackay, H. and John Hagan. "Studying the Victims of Crime: Some Methodological Notes." *Victimology* 3 (1978): 135–140.

McDermott, M. Joan. "The Personal is Empirical: Feminism, Research Methods and Criminal Justice Education." *Journal of Criminal Justice Education* 3 (Fall 1992), 237–249.

Menard, Scott. "Short-Term Trends in Crime and Delinquency: A Comparison of UCR, NCS and Self-Report Data." *Justice Quarterly* 4 (September 1987): 455–474.

Merton, Robert K., M. Fiske, and P. L. Kendall. *The Focused Interview.* New York: Free Press, 1956.

Monette, Duane R., Thomas J. Sullivan, and Cornell R. DeJong. *Applied Social Research: Tools for the Human Services.* Fort Worth: Harcourt, Brace, 1994.

Morin, Richard. "From Confusing Questions, Confusing Answers." *Washington Post National Weekly Edition,* 18–24 July 1994a, p. 37.

_____. "Ask and You Might Deceive." *Washington Post National Weekly Edition,* 6–12 December 1994b, p. 37.

_____. "When the Method Becomes the Message." *Washington Post National Weekly Edition,* 19–25 December 1994c, p. 33.

Mutchnick, Robert J. "Criminology: The Use of Oral History as an Educational Tool." Paper presented at the Academy of Criminal Justice Sciences Meetings, Orlando Fla., March 1986.

National Advisory Committee on Criminal Justice Standards and Goals. *Criminal Justice Research and Development.* Report of the Task Force, Washington, D.C.: Law Enforcement Assistance Administration, 1976.

"National Crime Victimization Survey Redesign." *Bureau of Justice Statistics Fact Sheet,* October 30, 1994.

Nettler, Gwynn. *Explaining Crime.* 2d ed. New York: McGraw-Hill, 1978.

Neuman, W. Lawrence. *Social Research Methods: Qualitative and Quantitative Approaches.* Boston: Allyn and Bacon, 1991.

Panel for the Evaluation of Crime Surveys. *Surveying Crime.* Washington, D.C.: National Academy of Sciences, 1976.

Payne, Stanley J. *The Art of Asking Questions.* Princeton, N.J.: Princeton University Press, 1951.

Reiss, Albert J., Jr. *Studies in Crime and Law Enforcement in Major Metropolitan Areas.* Field Surveys III, President's Commission on Law Enforcement and Administration of Justice, Washington, D.C.: U.S. Government Printing Office, 1967.

"Renshaw Memo Advocated NCS Suspension." *Criminal Justice Newsletter* (October 24, 1977): 4.

Sanders, William B. "Pumps and Pauses: Strategic Use of Conversational Structure in Interrogations." In *The Sociologist as Detective,* edited by William B. Sanders, 273–281. New York: Praeger, 1976.

Selltiz, Claire, et al. *Research Methods in Social Relations.* New York: Holt, 1976.

Singer, Simon I. "Comment on Alleged Overreporting." *Criminology* 16 (May 1978): 99–103.

Skogan, Wesley G. "Measurement Problems in Official and Survey Crime Rates." *Journal of Criminal Justice* 3 (Spring 1975): 17–31.

_____. *Victimization Surveys and Criminal Justice Planning.* monograph. Washington, D.C.: National Institute of Law Enforcement and Criminal Justice, July 1978.

_____, and M. G. Maxfield. *Coping with Crime: Individual and Neighborhood Reactions.* Beverly Hills, Calif.: Sage, 1981.

Smykla, John O. "The Human Impact of Capital Punishment: Interviews with Families of Persons on Death Row." *Journal of Criminal Justice* 15 (1987): 53–68.

Sparks, Richard F., Haxel G. Genn, and David J. Dodd. *Surveying Victims: A Study of the Measurement of Criminal Victimization, Perceptions of Crime and Attitudes to Criminal Justice.* New York: Wiley, 1977.

Stanko, Elizabeth. *Everyday Violence: How Men and Women Experience Sexual and Physical Danger.* London: Pandora, 1990.

Sudman, Seymour. *Applied Sampling.* New York: Academic Press, 1976.

_____. "Eliciting Sensitive Information by Telephone Survey." Paper presented at the National Workshop on Research Methods and Criminal Justice Evaluation, Baltimore, Md., March 17–19, 1980.

Survey Research Center. *Interviewer's Manual.* Ann Arbor: University of Michigan, May 1969.

"Suspension of LEAA Victim Surveys Opposed." *Criminal Justice Newsletter* (October 24, 1977): 3–4.

Sussman, Marvin B., and Marie R. Haug. "Human and Mechanical Error: An Unknown Quantity in Research." *American Behavioral Scientist* 2 (November 1967): 55–56.

Sutherland, Edwin H. *The Professional Thief.* Chicago: University of Chicago Press, 1937 (reissued 1956).

Taylor, Bruce M. "New Directions for the National Crime Survey." *Bureau of Justice Statistics Technical Report,* Washington, D.C.: Bureau of Justice Statistics, March, 1989.

Thomas, William I., and Dorothy Swaine. *The Child in America.* New York: Knopf, 1928.

Tracy, Paul E., and James Alan Fox. "The Validity of Randomized Response for Sensitive Measurement." *American Sociological Review.* 46 (April 1981): 187–200.

Tuchfarber, Alfred J., and William R. Klecka. *Random Digit Dialing—Lowering the Cost of Victimization Surveys.* Washington, D.C.: Police Foundation, 1976.

_____, et al. "Reducing the Cost of Victim Surveys." In *Sample Surveys of the Victims of Crime.* edited by Wesley G. Skogan. Cambridge, Mass.: Ballinger, 1976.

U.S. Bureau of Census. "Victim Recall Pretest (Washington, D.C.: Household Surveys of Victims of Crime)." Washington, D.C.: Bureau of Census, Demographic Surveys Division, mimeograph, 1970.

U.S. Department of Justice. *Crime in Eight American Cities.* Washington, D.C.: Law Enforcement Assistance Administration, National Criminal Justice Information and Statistics Service, July 1974a.

_____. *Crimes and Victims: A Report on the Dayton—San Jose Pilot Survey of Victimization.* Washington, D.C.: Law Enforcement Assistance Administration, 1974b.

_____. *Criminal Victimization Surveys in the Nation's Five Largest Cities.* Washington, D.C.: Law Enforcement Assistance Administration, National Criminal Justice Information and Statistics Service, April 1975a.

_____. *Criminal Victimization Surveys in 13 American Cities.* Washington, D.C.: Law Enforcement Assistance Administration, National Criminal Justice Information and Statistics Service, June 1975b.

_____. *Criminal Victimization in the United States.* Washington, D.C.: Law Enforcement Assistance Administration, National Criminal Justice Information and Statistics Service, 1976.

_____. *Criminal Victimization in the United States, 1977.* Washington, D.C.: Law Enforcement Assistance Administration, National Criminal Justice Information and Statistics Service, December 1979.

Vasu, M., and G. D. Garson. "Computer-Assisted Survey Research and Continuous Audience Response Technology for the Political and Social Sciences." *Social Science Computer Review* 8 (1990): 535–557.

Warner, S. L. "Randomized Responses: A Survey Technique for Eliminating Evasive Answer Bias." *Journal of the American Statistical Association* 60 (1965): 63–69.

Whitaker, Catherine J. "The Redesigned National Crime Survey: Selected New Data." *Bureau of Justice Statistics Special Report,* Washington, D.C.: Bureau of Justice Statistics, January, 1989.

Chapter 7   Participant Observation and Case Studies

Abadinsky, Howard. *The Mafia in America: An Oral History.* 3d ed. New York: Praeger, 1993.

_____. *The Criminal Elite: Professional and Organized Crime.* Westport, Conn.: Greenwood Press, 1983.

Adler, Patricia A., and Peter Adler. *Wheeling and Dealing: An Ethnography of Upper Level Drug Dealing and Smuggling Community.* New York: Columbia University Press, 1985.

Agar, Michael H. *Ripping and Running: A Formal Ethnography of Urban Heroin Addicts.* New York: Seminar Press, 1973.

_____. "Ethnography in the Streets and in the Joint: A Comparison." In *Street Ethnography,* Vol 1, edited by Robert S. Weppner 143–156. Beverly Hills, Calif.: Sage, 1977.

Albini, Joseph. "The Guardian Angels: Vigilantes or Protectors of the Community?" Paper presented at the Academy of Criminal Justice Sciences Meetings, Orlando, Fla., March 1986.

Allen, John. *Assault with a Deadly Weapon: The Autobiography of a Street Criminal,* Diane Hall Kelly and Philip Heymann, eds. New York: Pantheon, 1977.

Anderson, Annelise G. *The Business of Organized Crime.* Stanford: Hoover Institution Press, 1979.

Becker, Howard S. *Outsiders: Studies in the Sociology of Deviance.* New York: Free Press, 1963.

_____. "Practitioners of Vice and Crime." In *Sociological Methods: A Sourcebook,* edited by Norman K. Denzin, 85–101. New York: McGraw-Hill, 1978a.

_____. "The Relevance of Life Histories." In *Sociological Methods: A Sourcebook,* edited by Norman K. Denzin, 289–295. New York: McGraw-Hill, 1978b.

Bennett, James. *Oral History and Delinquency: The Rhetoric of Criminology.* Chicago: University of Chicago Press, 1981.

Berg, Bruce L. *Qualitative Research Methods for the Social Sciences.* Boston: Allyn and Bacon, 1995.

Bernard, H. Russell. *Research Methods in Anthropology.* Thousand Oaks, Calif.: Sage, 1994.

Bertaux, Daniel, ed. *Biography and Society: The Life History Approach in the Social Sciences.* Beverly Hills, Calif.: Sage, 1981.

Bigus, Odis E. "The Milkman and His Customer: A Cultivated Relationship." In *Interaction in Everyday Life,* edited by John Lofland, 85–119. Beverly Hills, Calif.: Sage, 1978.

Blok, Anton. *The Mafia of a Sicilian Village: 1860–1960.* New York: Harper and Row, 1975.

Bryan, James H. "Apprenticeships in Prostitution." *Social Problems* 12 (Winter 1965): 287–297.

Campbell, Donald T., and Julian C. Stanley. *Experimental and Quasi-experimental Designs for Research.* Chicago: Rand McNally, 1963.

Carey, James T. "Problems of Access and Risk in Observing Drug Scenes." In *Research on Deviance,* edited by Jack D. Douglas, 71–92. New York: Random, 1972.

Caudill, William A. *The Psychiatric Hospital as a Small Society.* Cambridge, Mass.: Harvard University Press, 1958.

Cavan, Sheri. *Liquor License.* Chicago: Aldine, 1966.

Chambliss, William J. *The Box Man: A Professional Thief's Journal, by Harry King.* New York: Harper and Row, 1975.

Cressey, Donald R. *Other People's Money.* New York: Free Press, 1953.

Davis, Fred. "The Cabdriver and His Fare: Facets of a Fleeting Relationship." *American Journal of Sociology* 65 (September 1959), 158–165.

Deming, W. Edwards. "On Errors in Surveys." *American Sociological Review* 9 (August 1944): 359–369.

Denfield, Duane, ed. *Streetwise Criminology.* Cambridge, Mass.: Schenkman, 1974.

Dennis, D. L. "Word Crunching: An Annotated Bibliography on Computers and Qualitative Data Analysis," *Qualitative Sociology* 7 (1984), 148–156.

Denzin, Norman K., and Yvonna S. Lincoln, eds. *Handbook of Qualitative Research.* Thousand Oaks, Calif.: Sage, 1993.

Deutscher, Irwin. "Words and Deeds: Social Science and Social Policy." *Social Problems* 13 (1966), 233–254.

Douglas, Jack D. *Research on Deviance.* New York: Random, 1972.

_____. *Investigative Social Research.* Beverly Hills, Calif.: Sage, 1976.

Festinger, Leon, Henry Riecken, and Stanley Schachter. *When Prophecy Fails.* New York: Harper, 1956.

Fielding, Nigel G., and Raymond M. Lee. *Using Computers in Qualitative Research.* Newbury Park, Calif.: Sage, 1991.

Fox, Renee C. "Bill Whyte: In Essence a Participant Observer." *Footnotes* (American Sociological Association) (August 1980): 2.

Fujisaka, S., and J. Grayzel. "Partnership Research: A Case of Divergent Ethnographic Styles in Prison Fieldwork." *Human Organization* 37 (1978): 172–179.

Gans, Herbert J. "The Participant Observer as a Human Being: Observations on the Personal Aspects of Field Work." In *Institutions and the Person: Essays Presented to Everett C. Hughes,* edited by Howard S. Becker, Blanche Greer, David Riesman, and Robert S. Weiss, 300–317. Chicago: Aldine, 1968.

Gardiner, John, and David J. Olson. *Wincanton: The Politics of Corruption.* President's Commission on Law Enforcement and Administration of Justice Task Force Reports: Organized Crime, Appendix B, Washington, D.C.: U.S. Government Printing Office, 1968.

Garfinkel, Harold, ed. *Studies in Ethnomethodology.* Englewood Cliffs, N.J.: Prentice-Hall, 1967.

Gittings, James A. *Life Without Living: People of the Inner City.* Philadelphia: Westminster Press, 1966.

Glaser, Barney G., and Anselm Strauss. *The Discovery of Grounded Theory.* Chicago: Aldine, 1967.

Goffman, Erving. *Asylums.* Garden City, N.Y.: Doubleday, 1961.

Gold, Raymond L. "Roles in Sociological Field Observations." *Social Forces* 36 (March 1958): 217–223.

Hagan, Frank E. "The Rural Elderly in Erie County, Pennsylvania," a survey report prepared on behalf of the Appalachian Regional Commission and the Greater Erie Community Action Commission, Erie, Pennsylvania, 1972.

_____. "Single Subject Designs: A Strategy for Quantitative Case Studies." Paper presented at the Academy of Criminal Justice Sciences Meetings, Washington, D.C., March, 1989.

Haley, Alex. *Roots.* Garden City, N.Y.: Doubleday, 1976.

Hamm, Mark S. *American Skinheads: The Criminology and Control of Hate Crime.* Westport, Conn: Praeger, 1993.

Holzman, Harold R., and Sharon Pines. "Buying Sex: The Phenomenology of Being a John." Paper presented at the American Society of Criminology Meetings, Philadelphia, Pa., November 1979.

Hopper, Columbus B. "The Changing Role of Women in Motorcycle Gangs: From Partner to Sexual Property." Paper presented at the American Society of Criminology Meetings, San Francisco, Calif., November 1991.

Humphreys, Laud. *Tearoom Trade: Impersonal Sex in Public Places.* Chicago: Aldine, 1970.

Hurwitz, Jacob I. "The Idiographic Evaluation Model in Crime Control." *Journal of Offender Counseling Services and Rehabilitation* 8 (Summer 1984): 41–48.

Ianni, Francis A., and Elizabeth Ianni. *A Family Business: Kinship and Social Control in Organized Crime.* New York: Russell Sage, 1972.

Inciardi, James A. "In Search of the Class Cannon: A Field Study of Professional Pickpockets." In *Street Ethnography,* edited by Robert S. Weppner, 55–78. Beverly Hills, Calif.: Sage, 1977.

Irwin, John. "Participant Observation of Criminals." In *Research on Deviance,* edited by Jack D. Douglas, 117–138. New York: Random, 1972.

Jackson, Bruce, ed. *In the Life: Versions of the Criminal Experience.* New York: Mentor Book, 1972.

Jankowski, Martin Sanchez. *Islands in the Streets: Gangs and American Urban Society.* Berkeley: University of California Press, 1991.

Johnson, Jeffrey C. *Selecting Ethnographic Informants.* Newbury Park, Calif.: Sage, 1990.

Kazdin, A. E. *Single-Case Research Designs.* New York: Oxford University Press, 1982.

Keiser, R. Lincoln. *The Vice Lords: Warriors of the Streets.* New York: Holt, 1969.

King, Harry, and William J. Chambliss. *Harry King: A Professional Thief's Journal.* New York: Wiley, 1984.

Kirkham, George. *Signal Zero.* New York: J. B. Lippincott, 1976.

Klein, J. F., and A. Montague. *Check Forgers.* Lexington, Mass.: Lexington Books, 1977.

Klockars, Carl P. *The Professional Fence.* New York: Free Press, 1974.

_____. "Field Ethics for the Life History." In *Street Ethnography,* Vol. 1, edited by Robert S. Weppner, 201–226. Beverly Hills, Calif.: Sage, 1977.

Kobrin, Solomon. "The Use of Life History Documents for the Development of Delinquency Theory." In *The Jack-Roller at Seventy: A Fifty-Year Follow-up,* edited by Jon D. Snodgrass, 153–165. Lexington, Mass.: D.C. Health, 1982.

LaPiere, Richard, "Attitudes vs. Actions." *Social Forces* 13 (March 1934): 230–237.

Laub, John H. *Criminology in the Making: An Oral History.* Boston: Northeastern University Press, 1983.

_____. "Talking About Crime: Oral History in Criminology and Criminal Justice." *Oral History Review* 12 (1984), 29–42.

Lee, Nancy Howell. *The Search for an Abortionist.* Chicago: University of Chicago Press, 1969.

Letkemann, Peter. *Crime as Work.* Englewood Cliffs, N.J.: Prentice-Hall, 1973.

Levine, James P. "The Potential for Overreporting in Criminal Victimization Surveys." *Criminology* 14 (November 1976), 307–330.

Liebow, Elliot. *Tally's Corner.* Boston: Little, Brown, 1967.

Lofland, John. *Analyzing Social Settings.* Belmont, Calif.: Wadsworth, 1974.

Maas, Peter. *The Valachi Papers.* New York: Bantam Books, 1968.

Malinowski, Bronislaw. *Argonauts of the Western Pacific.* New York: Dutton, 1922.

_____. *Crime and Custom in Savage Society.* London: Routledge and Kegan Paul, 1926.

———. *A Diary in the Strict Sense of the Word.* New York: Harcourt, 1967.

Manning, Peter K. "Observing the Police: Deviants, Respectables, and the Law." In *Research on Deviance,* edited by Jack D. Douglas, 213–268. New York: Random, 1972.

_____, and John Van Maanen, eds. *Policing: A View from the Streets.* Santa Monica, Calif.: Goodyear, 1979.

Marquart, James W. "Doing Research in Prison: the Strengths and Weaknesses of Full Participation as a Guard." *Justice Quarterly* 3 (March 1986): 15–32.

McCall, George J. *Observing the Law: Field Methods in the Study of Crime and the Criminal Justice System.* New York: Free Press, 1978.

_____, and J. L. Simmons, eds. *Issues in Participant Observation.* Reading, Mass.: Addison-Wesley, 1969.

McKinney, John C. *Constructive Typology and Social Theory.* New York: Appleton, 1966.

McLuhan, Marshall. *The Medium is the Massage.* New York: Touchstone Press, 1989.

Miller, Eleanor. *Street Woman.* Philadelphia: Temple University Press, 1986.

Mills, James. *The Underground Empire: Where Crime and Government Embrace.* Garden City, N.Y.: Doubleday, 1986.

Monette, Duane R., Thomas J. Sullivan, and Cornell R. DeJong. *Applied Social Research: Tool for the Human Services.* 3d ed. New York: Holt, Rinehart and Winston, 1994.

Mutchnick, Robert J. *"Criminology: The Use of Oral History as an Educational Tool." Paper presented at the Academy of Criminal Justice Science Meetings, Orlando, Fla., March 1986.*

National Advisory Committee on Criminal Justice Standards and Goals. Criminal Justice Research and Development. Report of the Task Force on Criminal Justice Research and Development, Washington, D.C.: Law Enforcement Assistance Administration, December 1976.

Orenstein, Alan, and William R. F. Phillips. *Understanding Social Research: An Introduction.* Boston: Allyn, 1978.

Orne, Martin T. "On the Social Psychology of the Psychological Experiment: With Particular Reference to Demand Characteristics." In *The Experiment as a Social Occasion,* edited by Paul L. Wubben, Bruce C. Straits, and Gary I. Schulman, 139–152. Berkeley, Calif.: Glendessary Press, 1974.

Phillips, Derek L. *Knowledge from What? Theories and Methods in Social Research.* Chicago: Rand McNally, 1971.

Plate, Tom. *Crime Pays: An Inside Look at Burglars, Car Thieves, Loan Sharks, Hit Men, Fences and Other Professionals in Crime.* New York: Ballantine, 1975.

Plimpton, George. *Paper Lion* (1981 Edition). New York: Holtzman Press, 1965.

_____. *The Open Net.* New York: Norton, 1985.

Polsky, Ned. *Hustlers, Beats and Others.* Chicago: Aldine, 1967, especially pp. 117–149.

Reichel, Philip L. "Regulating the Criminal Justice Snooper." *Journal of Criminal Justice* 13 (1985): 75–84.

Reiss, Albert J., Jr. *The Police and the Public.* New Haven, Conn.: Yale University Press, 1971.

Rettig, Richard P., Manuel J. Torres, and Gerald R. Garrett. *Manny: A Criminal-Addict's Story.* Boston: Houghton Mifflin, 1977.

Robinson, Elizabeth, Denise E. Bronson, and Betty J. Blythe. "An Analysis of the Implementation of Single-Case Evaluation by Practitioners." *Social Service Review* 62 (June 1988), 285–301.

Sanders, William B. *Detective Work.* New York: Free Press, 1977, especially pp. 190–207.

Schwartz, Morris S., and Charlotte G. Schwartz. "Problems in Participant Observation." *American Journal of Sociology* 60 (January 1955): 343–353.

Shaffir, William B., and Robert A. Stebbins. *Experiencing Fieldwork: An Inside View of Qualitative Research.* Newbury Park, Calif.: Sage, 1991.

Shaw, Clifford R. *The Jack-Roller.* Chicago: University of Chicago Press, 1930.

_____. *The Natural History of a Delinquent Career.* Chicago: University of Chicago Press, 1931.

_____, Henry D. McKay, and James F. McDonald. *Brothers in Crime.* Chicago: University of Chicago Press, 1938.

Sherizen, Sanford. "Videotaping as a Method of Dialogue: A New Teaching and Research Method in Criminal Justice." *Journal of Criminal Justice* 4 (Spring 1976): 63–68.

Shils, Edward A. "The Calling of Sociology." In *Theories of Society,* edited by Talcott Parsons et al., 1405–1448. New York: Free Press, 1961.

Silverman, David. *Interpreting Qualitative Data.* Newbury Park, Calif.: Sage, 1993.

Skipper, James K. "Stripteasers: A Six Year History of Public Reaction to a Study." In *Sociological Footprints,* edited by L. Cargan and J. Ballantine. Boston: Houghton Mifflin, 1979.

Skolnick, Jerome H. *Justice without Trial: Law Enforcement in Democratic Society.* New York: Wiley, 1966.

Smykla, John Ortiz. "Placing Uruguayan Corrections in Context, 1973–1984: A Note on the Visiting Criminologist's Role." *Journal of Criminal Justice* 17 (1989): 25–37.

Snodgrass, Jon. *The Jack-Roller at Seventy: A Fifty Year Follow-up.* Lexington, Mass.: D.C. Heath, 1982.

Soloway, Irvine, and James Walters. "Workin' the Corner: The Ethics and Legality of Ethnographic Fieldwork among Active Heroin Addicts." In *Street Ethnography,* edited by Robert S. Weppner, 159–178. Beverly Hills, Calif.: Sage, 1977.

Spradley, James P. *You Owe Yourself a Drunk: An Ethnography of Urban Nomads.* Boston: Little, Brown, 1970.

Steffens, Lincoln. *The Shame of the Cities.* New York: McClure, Phillips, 1904.

Steffensmeier, Darrell J. *The Fence: In the Shadow of Two Worlds.* Totowa, N.J.: Rowman and Littlefield, 1986.

Stein, Martha L. *Lovers, Friends, Slaves . . . : The Nine Male Sexual Types.* Berkeley, Calif.: Berkeley Publishing Corp., 1974.

Sullivan, Mercer. *Getting Paid: Youth Crime and Work in the Inner City.* Ithaca, N.Y.: Cornell University Press, 1989.

Sullivan, Mercer. "Mapping the Streets of Crime." *Newsweek* 19 (December 1983), 68.

Sussman, Marvin B., and Marie R. Haug. "Human and Mechanical Error: An Unknown Quantity in Research." *American Behavioral Scientist* 11 (November 1967): 55–56.

Sutherland, Edwin H. *The Professional Thief.* Chicago: University of Chicago Press, 1937.

_____, and Donald Cressey. *Principles of Criminology.* 10th ed. Chicago: Lippincott, 1978.

Talese, Gay. *Honor Thy Father.* Greenwich, Conn.: Fawcett, 1971.

_____. *Thy Neighbor's Wife.* Greenwich, Conn.: Fawcett, 1979.

Tawney, J. W., and D. L. Gast. *Single Subject Research in Special Education.* Columbus, Ohio: Charles C. Merrill, 1984.

Taylor, Laurie. *In the Underworld.* Oxford, England: Blackwell, 1984.

Teresa, Vincent, with Thomas C. Renner. *My Life in the Mafia.* New York: Doubleday, 1973.

Terkel, Louis (Studs). *Hard Times: An Oral History of the Great Depression.* New York: Avon, 1970.

_____. *Working.* New York: Pantheon, 1974.

_____. *American Dreams: Lost and Found.* New York: Pantheon, 1980.

_____. *The Good War: An Oral History of World War II.* New York: Pantheon, 1984.

Tesch, Renata. *Qualitative Research: Analysis Types and Software Tools.* New York: The Falmer Press, 1990.

_____. "Introduction." *Qualitative Sociology* 14 (3 1991): 225–243.

Thompson, Hunter. *Hell's Angels.* New York: Ballantine Books, 1967.

Thrasher, Frederick M. *The Gang: The Study of 1313 Gangs in Chicago.* Chicago: University of Chicago Press, 1927.

Toby, Jackson. "Going Native in Criminology" (Letter to the Editor). *The Criminologist* 11 (May–June 1986): 2.

Travis, Lawrence F. III. "The Case Study in Criminal Justice Research: Applications to Policy Analysis." *Criminal Justice Review* 8 (Fall 1983): 46–51.

Trice, H. M. "The 'Outsider' Role in Field Study." In *Qualitative Methodology,* edited by William J. Filstead, 77–82. Chicago: Markham, 1970.

Walker, Andrew L., and Charles W. Lidz. "Methodological Notes on the Employment of Indigenous Observers." In *Street Ethnography,* edited by Robert S. Weppner, 103–124. Beverly Hills, Calif.: Sage, 1977.

Wambaugh, Joseph. *The Onion Field.* New York: Delacorte, 1973.

Webb, Eugene, D. T. Campbell, R. D. Schwartz, and L. Sechrest. *Unobtrusive Measures: Nonreactive Research in the Social Sciences.* Chicago: Rand McNally, 1966.

Weber, Max. *The Methodology of Social Sciences.* Translated by Edward A. Shils and Henry A. Finch. New York: Free Press, 1949.

Weinberg, Martin. "Sexual Modesty: Social Meanings and the Nudist Camp." In *Sociology and Everyday Life,* edited by Marcello Truzzi. Englewood Cliffs, N.J.: Prentice-Hall, 1968.

Weinberg, Martin S., and Colin J. Williams. "Fieldwork Among Deviants: Social Relations with Subjects and Others." In *Research on Deviance,* edited by Jack D. Douglas, 165–186. New York: Random, 1972.

Weppner, Robert S., ed. *Street Ethnography,* Vol. 1, Beverly Hills, Calif.: Sage, 1977.

Wheeler, Stanton, ed. *On File: Records and Dossiers in American Life.* New York: Russell Sage, 1970.

_____. "Trends and Problems in the Sociological Study of Crime." In *Readings in Criminology,* edited by Peter Wickman and Philip Whitten, 3–10. Lexington, Mass.: D.C. Heath, 1978.

Whyte, William Foote. *Street Corner Society.* Chicago: University of Chicago Press, 1943.

_____. "Report of the President: Whyte Reviews Term; Emphasizes Field Work." *Footnotes* (American Sociological Association) (October 1981), 6.

Wolff, Kurt H. "The Collection and Organization of Field Materials: A Research Report." In *Human Organization Research: Field Relations and Techniques,* edited by R. N. Adams and J. J. Preiss, 240–254. Homewood, Ill.: Dorsey, 1960.

Wright, Richard, and Trevor Bennett. "Exploring the Offender's Perspective: Observing and Interviewing Criminals." In *Measurement Issues in Criminology,* edited by Kimberly Kempf, 138–151. New York: Springer–Verlag, 1990.

Yablonsky, Lewis. *The Violent Gang.* Baltimore: Penguin, 1962.

_____. *Synanon: The Tunnel Back.* Baltimore: Penguin, 1965a.

_____. "Experiences with the Criminal Community." In *Applied Sociology,* edited by Alvin W. Gouldner and S. M. Miller. New York: Free Press, 1965b.

Yin, Robert K. *Case Study Research: Design and Methods.* 2d ed. Beverly Hills, Calif.: Sage, 1994.

Chapter 8 Unobtrusive Measures, Secondary Analysis, and the Uses of Official Statistics

---

Abadinsky, Howard. *Organized Crime.* 4th ed. Chicago: Nelson-Hall, 1993.

Albini, Joseph. *The American Mafia: Genesis of a Legend.* New York: Appleton, 1971.

Anderson, Annelise G. *The Business of Organized Crime: A Cosa Nostra Family.* Stanford, Calif.: Stanford University Press, 1979.

Anspach, Donald F. "Installment Plan Mutual Funds—The Legal Taking of Other People's Money: Some Problems with the Concept of Crime." Paper presented at the American Society of Criminology Meetings, Baltimore, Maryland, November 1990.

Archer, Dane, and Rosemary Gartner. *Violence and Crime in Cross-national Perspective.* New Haven, Conn.: Yale University Press, 1984.

Asch, Solomon E. "Effects of Group Pressure upon the Modification and Distortion of Judgment." In *Groups, Leadership and Men,* edited by Harold Guetzkow. Pittsburgh: Carnegie Press, 1951.

Bailey, William C. "Murder, Capital Punishment, and Television: Execution Publicity and Homicide Rates." *American Sociological Review* 55 (October 1990): 628–633.

Banton, Michael. *The Policeman in the Community.* New York: Basic, 1964.

Becker, Howard S. "Practitioners of Vice and Crime." In *Sociological Methods: A Sourcebook,* edited by Norman K. Denzin, 143–156. Beverly Hills, Calif.: Sage, 1970.

Bennett, Richard R., and James P. Lynch. "Does a Difference Make a Difference? Comparing Cross-National Crime Indicators." *Criminology* 28 (February 1990): 153–181.

Berelson, Bernard. *Content Analysis in Communication Research.* New York: Free Press, 1952.

Bielby, William T., and Richard A. Berk. "Source of Error in Survey Data Used in Criminal Justice Evaluations: An Analysis of Survey Respondents' Reports of 'Fear of Crime'." Paper presented at the National Workshop on Research Methodology and Criminal Justice Program Evaluation, Baltimore, Md., March 17–19, 1980.

Black, Donald J. "Police Encounters and Social Organization: An Observational Study." Ph.D. dissertation, University of Michigan, 1968.

_____. "Production of Crime Rates." *American Sociological Review* 35 (1970): 733–748.

Block, Alan A. *East Side-West Side: Organizing Crime in New York.* Swansea, United Kingdom: Christopher Davis, 1979.

Bonanno, Joseph, with Sergio Lalli. *A Man of Honor: The Autobiography of Joseph Bonanno.* New York: Simon and Schuster, 1983.

Bouchard, Thomas, Jr. "Unobtrusive Methods: An Inventory of Uses." *Sociological Methods and Research* 4 (February 1976): 267–300.

Brantingham, Paul, and Patricia Brantingham. *Patterns in Crime.* New York: Macmillan, 1984.

Buckner, H. Taylor. "The Police: The Culture of a Social Control Agency." Ph.D. dissertation, University of California, 1967.

Bureau of Justice Statistics. "Criminal Cases in Five States, 1983–1986." *Bureau of Justice Statistics Special Report.* Washington, D.C.: Bureau of Justice Statistics, September, 1989.

Burnham, Kenneth P. "Mark-Recapture Techniques for Estimating Animal Populations: What Has Been Done in Ecology." Paper presented at the National Workshop on Research Methodology and Criminal Justice Program Evaluation, Baltimore, Md., March 1980.

Cameron, Mary Owen. *The Booster and the Snitch: Department Store Shoplifting.* Glencoe, Ill.: Free Press, 1964.

Caudill, William C., et al. "Social Structure and Interaction Processes on a Psychiatric Ward." *American Journal of Orthopsychiatry* 22 (1952): 314–334.

Cavoir, Norman, and L. Ramona Howard. "Facial Attractiveness and Juvenile Delinquency among Black and White Offenders." *Journal of Abnormal Child Psychology* 1 (1973): 202–213.

Chappell, Duncan, and Marilyn Walsh. "No Questions Asked: A Consideration of the Crime of Criminal Receiving." *Crime and Delinquency* (April 1974): 157–168.

Chermak, Steven M. "Body Count News: How Crime is Presented in the News Media." *Justice Quarterly* 11 (December 1994): 561–582.

Clarke, James W. *American Assassins: The Darker Side of Politics.* Princeton, N.J.: Princeton University Press, 1982.

Clinard, Marshall B. *The Black Market: A Study of White Collar Crime.* New York: Holt, 1952.

_____, and Richard Quinney. *Criminal Behavior Systems.* 2d ed. New York: Holt, 1973.

_____, and Peter C. Yeager. *Illegal Corporate Behavior.* Washington, D.C.: U.S. Government Printing Office, 1979.

_____. *Corporate Crime.* New York: Macmillan, 1980.

Colasanto, D., and J. Sanders. "Methodological Issues in Simulated Jury Research." Paper presented at the Annual Meeting of the Law and Society Association, May 1978.

Conley, John A. "Historical Research in Anglo-American Criminal Justice," In *Criminal Justice Research: Approaches, Problems and Policies,* edited by Suzette Talarico, 129–146. Cincinnati: Anderson, 1980.

Courtright, Kevin E. "An Overview of the Use and Potential Advantages of the Diary Method." Paper presented at the Academy of Criminal Justice Sciences Meetings, Boston, Mass. March 1995.

Cox, Edward R., Robert C. Fellmeth, and John E. Schulz. *Nader's Raiders: Report on the Federal Trade Commission.* New York: Grove Press, 1969.

Davies, Margaret Gay. *The Enforcement of English Apprenticeship: A Study in Applied Mercantilism, 1563–1642.* Cambridge, Mass.: Harvard University Press, 1956.

Davis, F. James. "Crime News in Colorado Newspapers." *American Journal of Sociology* 57 (January 1952): 325–330.

DeFranco, Edward J. *Anatomy of a Scam: A Case Study of a Planned Bankruptcy by Organized Crime.* Washington, D.C.: National Institute of Law Enforcement and Criminal Justice, 1973.

Demaree, Robert G. "Estimating the Size of Drug User Populations." Paper presented at the National Workshop on Research Methodology and Criminal Justice Program Evaluation, Baltimore, Md., March 17–19, 1980.

Denzin, Norman K. *The Research Act.* 3rd ed. Englewood Cliffs, N.J.: Prentice-Hall, 1989.

Douglas, Jack D. "Observing Deviance." In *Research on Deviance,* edited by Jack D. Douglas, 3–34. New York: Random, 1972.

Durkheim, Emile. *Suicide: A Study in Sociology.* Translated by John A. Spaulding and George Simpson. New York: Free Press, 1951.

Erickson, Kai T. *The Wayward Puritans.* New York: Wiley, 1966.

Erickson, M. L., and J. P. Gibbs. "Further Findings on the Deterrence Question and Strategies for Future Research." *Journal of Criminal Justice* 4 (Fall 1976): 175–189.

Esposito, John C., and Larry J. Silverman. *Vanishing Air: Ralph Nader's Study Group Report on Air Pollution.* New York: Grossman, 1970.

Farrington, David P., and Barry J. Knight. "Two Nonreactive Field Experiments on Stealing from a 'Lost' Letter." *British Journal of Social and Clinical Psychology* 18 (1979): 277–284.

Feldman, Roy E. "Response to Compatriot and Foreigner Who Seeks Assistance." *Journal of Personality and Social Psychology* 10 (1968): 202–214.

Formby, William A., and John O. Smykla. "Citizen Awareness in Crime Prevention: Do They Really Get Involved?" *Journal of Police Science and Administration* 9 (1981), 398–403.

_____, and John O. Smykla. "Attitudes and Perceptions towards Drinking and Driving: A Simulation of Citizen Awareness." *Journal of Police Science and Administration* 12 (1984): 379–384.

Glaser, Daniel, and Max S. Zeigler. "The Use of the Death Penalty v. the Outrage at Murder." *Crime and Delinquency* October 1974: 333–338.

Glass, Gene V. "Primary, Secondary, and Meta-Analysis of Research." *Educational Researcher* 5 (1976): 3–8.

Glass, Gene, B. McCraw, and Mary Lee Smith. *Meta-analysis in Social Research.* Beverly Hills, Calif.: Sage, 1981.

Glueck, Sheldon, and Eleanor Glueck. *Delinquents and Nondelinquents in Perspective.* Cambridge, Mass.: Harvard University Press, 1968.

Gosch, Martin A., and Richard Hammer. *The Last Legacy of Lucky Luciano.* New York: Dell, 1974.

Gottschalk, Louis, Clyde Kluckhohn, and Robert Angell. *The Use of Personal Documents in History, Anthropology and Sociology.* New York: Social Science Research Council, 1945.

Graff, M. J. "Crime and Punishment in the Nineteenth Century: A New Look at the Criminal." *Journal of Interdisciplinary History* 7 (1977): 477–491.

————. "Systematic Criminal Justice History: Some Suggestions: A Reply." *Journal of Interdisciplinary History* 9 (Winter 1979): 465–472.

Green, Bert F., and Judith A. Hall. "Quantitative Methods for Literature Reviews." *Annual Review of Psychology* 35 (1984): 37–53.

Green, Mark J., et al., ed. *The Monopoly Makers: Ralph Nader's Study Group Report on Regulation and Competition.* New York: Grossman, 1973.

Guetzkow, Harold, ed. *Simulation in Social Science.* Englewood Cliffs, N.J.: Prentice-Hall, 1962.

Hagan, Frank E. "Comparative Professionalization in an Occupational Arena: The Case of Rehabilitation." Ph.D. dissertation, Case Western Reserve University, 1975.

_____. "Comparative Attitudinal Professionalism in Nine Occupations: Some Empirical Findings." Paper presented at the Pennsylvania Sociological Society Meetings, Bloomsburg, Pa., October 1976.

_____. "The Organized Crime Continuum: A Further Specification of a New Conceptual Model." *Criminal Justice Review* 8 (Fall 1983): 52–57.

_____. *Introduction to Criminology: Theories, Methods and Criminal Behavior.* 2d ed. Chicago: Nelson-Hall, 1990.

Haney, C. "Play's the Thing: Methodological Notes on Social Simulations." In *The Research Experience,* edited by Patricia Golden. Itasca, Ill.: F. E. Peacock, 1976.

_____, Curtis Banks, and Philip Zimbardo. "Interpersonal Dynamics in a Simulated Prison." *International Journal of Criminology and Penology* 1 (1973): 69–97.

Heussenstamm, F. K. "Bumper Stickers and the Cops." *Trans-action* 8 (1971): 32–33.

Holsti, Ole. *Content Analysis for the Social Sciences and Humanities.* Reading, Mass.: Addison-Wesley, 1969.

Howson, Gerald. *Thief-Taker General: The Rise and Fall of Jonathan Wild.* London: Hutchinson, 1970.

Huang, W. S. Wilson, and Charles F. Wellford. "Assessing Indicators of Crime Among International Crime Data Series." *Criminal Justice Policy Review* 3 (March 1989): 28–48.

Humphreys, Laud. *Tearoom Trade: Impersonal Sex in Public Places.* Chicago: Aldine, 1970.

Hyman, Herbert. *Secondary Analysis of Sample Surveys: Principles, Procedures and Potentialities.* New York: Wiley, 1972.

Ianni, Francis A., and Elizabeth Ianni. *A Family Business: Kinship and Social Control in Organized Crime.* New York: Russell Sage, 1972.

Inciardi, James A., Alan A. Block, and Lyle A. Hallowell. *Historical Approaches to Crime: Research Strategies and Issues.* Beverly Hills, Calif.: Sage, 1977.

Jacob, Herbert, et al. "The Study of Governmental Responses to Crime." Paper presented at the National Workshop on Research Methodology and Criminal Justice Evaluation. Baltimore, Md., March 17–19, 1980.

Kalish, Carol B. "The Beginning of Wisdom." Paper presented at the International Society of Criminology Meetings, Hamburg, Germany, September 1989.

Kenadjian, Berdj. "Estimating the Amount of Unreported Income." Paper presented at the National Workshop on Research Methodology and Criminal Justice Program Evaluation, Baltimore, Md., March 1980.

Klofas, John, and C. Cutshall. "Unobtrusive Research Methods in Criminal Justice: Using Graffiti in the Reconstruction of Institutional Cultures." *Journal of Research in Crime and Delinquency* 22 (1985): 355–373.

Knox, Robert E., and Timothy J. McTiernan. "Lost Letters and Social Responsibility in Dublin." *Social Studies* 2 (1973): 511–518.

Landy, David, and Elliot Aronson. "The Influence of the Character of the Criminal and His Victim on the Decisions of Simulated Jurors." *Journal of Experimental Social Psychology* 5 (1969): 141–152.

Laub, John H., Robert J. Sampson, and Kenna Kiger. "Assessing the Potential of Secondary Data Analysis: A New Look at the Gluecks' *Unraveling Juvenile Delinquency Data.*" In *Measurement Issues in Criminology,* edited by Kimberly Kempf, 241–257. New York: Springer–Verlag, 1990.

Lieber, Arnold L., and Carolyn R. Sherin. "Homicides and the Lunar Cycles: Toward a Theory of Lunar Influence on Human Emotional Disturbance." *American Journal of Psychiatry* 129 (July 1972): 101–106.

Loeber, Rolf, and Magda Stouthamer-Loeber. "Family Factors as Correlates and Predictors of Juvenile Conduct Problems and Delinquency," In *Crime and Justice: An Annual Review of Research* 7, edited by Michael Tonry and Norval Morris, 334–355. Chicago: University of Chicago Press, 1986.

Lupscha, Peter A. "Networks vs. Networking: An Analysis of Organized Criminal Groups." Paper presented at the American Society of Criminology Meetings, Toronto, Ontario, Canada, November 1982.

Lutzker, M., and E. Ferrall. *Criminal Justice Research in Libraries: Strategies and Resources.* New York: Greenwood Press, 1986.

Maas, Peter. *The Valachi Papers.* New York: Bantam Books, 1968.

Mandel, Jerry. "Hashish, Assassins and the Love of God." *Issues in Criminology* 2 (1966): 149–156.

Mann, Coramae Richey. "Getting Even? Women Who Kill in Domestic Encounters." *Justice Quarterly* 5 (March 1988): 33–51.

Manning, Peter. "Observing the Police." In *The Ambivalent Force,* edited by Arthur Niederhoffer and Abraham Blumberg. Hinsdale, Ill.: Dryden Press, 1976.

McDonald, William F., and James A. Cramer. *Plea Bargaining.* Lexington, Mass.: D. C. Heath, 1980.

Messner, Steven F. "Economic Discrimination and Societal Homicide Rates: Further Evidence on the Cost of Inequality." *American Sociological Review* 54 (August 1989): 597–611.

Miles, Matthew B., and A. Michael Huberman. *Qualitative Data Analysis.* 2d ed. Thousand Oaks, Calif.: Sage, 1994.

Milgram, Stanley. "The Lost-Letter Technique." *Psychology Today* 3 (1969): 30–33, 60–68.

_____. *Obedience to Authority: An Experimental View.* New York: Harper, 1974.

Miller, Herbert S., William F. McDonald, and James A. Cramer. *Plea Bargaining in the United States.* Washington, D.C.: National Institute of Justice, 1980.

Miller, Walter. *Violence by Youth Gangs and Youth Groups as a Crime Problem in Major American Cities.* Washington, D.C.: Law Enforcement Assistance Administration, 1975.

Mockridge, N. *The Scrawl of the Wild: What People Write on Walls—And Why.* Cleveland: World Publishing Co., 1968.

Monkkonen, E. "Systematic Criminal Justice History: Some Suggestions," *Journal of Interdisciplinary History* 9 (Winter 1979): 451–464.

_____. *Crime and Justice in American History* (A 16-volume series). Westport, Conn.: Mockler, 1000.

National Advisory Committee on Criminal Justice Standards and Goals. *Criminal Justice Research and Development.* Report of the Task Force on Criminal Justice Research and Development, Washington, D.C.: Law Enforcement Assistance Administration, December 1976.

"Not So Quietly Flows the Don: The Mafia Memoirs of Joe Bonanno are Seized by the Law." *Time,* 11 June 1979, 24.

Olson, Sheldon. *Ideas and Data: The Process and Practice of Social Research.* Homewood, Ill.: Dorsey Press, 1976.

Page, Joseph, and Mary Win O'Brien. *Bitter Wages: Ralph Nader's Study Group Report on Disease and Injury on the Job.* New York: Grossman, 1973.

Pearson, Edmund, ed. *The Autobiography of a Criminal: Henry Tufts.* New York: Duffield, 1930 (originally published 1807).

Phillips, David P. "Motor Vehicle Fatalities Increase Just after Publicized Suicide Stories." *Science* 196 (1977): 1464–1465.

_____. "Airplane Accident Fatalities Increase Just after Newspaper Stories about Murder and Suicide." *Science.* 201 (1978): 748–750.

Pileggi, Nicholas. *Wiseguy: Life in a Mafia Family.* New York: Simon and Schuster, 1985. Pool, Ithiel de Sola, ed. *Trends in Content Analysis.* Urbana: University of Illinois Press, 1959.

Reinharz, Shulamit. *Feminist Methods in Social Research.* New York: Oxford University Press, 1992.

Reiss, Albert, J. Jr., "Stuff and Nonsense About Social Surveys and Observation." In *Institutions and the Person,* edited by Howard S. Becker, 351–367. Chicago: Aldine, 1968.

Riis, R. W. "The Repair Man Will Gyp You If You Don't Watch Out." *The Reader's Digest* 39 (1941a): 1–6.

_____. "The Radio Repair Man Will Gyp You If You Don't Watch Out." *The Reader's Digest* 39 (1941b): 6–10.

_____. "The Watch Repair Man Will Gyp You If You Don't Watch Out." *The Reader's Digest* 39 (1941c): 10–12.

Rosenhan, D. L. "On Being Sane in Insane Places." *Science* 179, no. 19 (1973): 250–258.

Rosenthal, Robert. *Experimenter Effects in Behavioral Research,* enlarged ed., New York: Wiley, 1976.

_____. "How Often Are Our Numbers Wrong?" *American Psychologist* 33 (November 1978): 1005–1007.

Roth, Julius A. "Comments on 'Secret Observation.' " *Social Problems* 9 (1962): 283–284.

Sampson, Robert J., and John H. Laub. *Crime in the Making: Pathways and Turning Points Through Life.* Cambridge, Mass: Harvard University Press, 1992.

Sanders, William B., ed. *The Sociologist as Detective.* 2d ed. New York: Praeger 1976.

Sawyer, H. G. "The Meaning of Numbers." Speech before the American Association of Advertising Agencies, cited in Eugene Webb et al., *Unobtrusive Measures.* Chicago: Rand McNally, 1961.

Scheff, Thomas J. *Being Mentally Ill.* Chicago: Aldine, 1966.

Schwartz, Richard D., and Jerome H. Skolnick. "Two Studies of Legal Stigma." *Social Problems* 10 (1962): 133–142.

Sechrest, Lee, ed. *Unobtrusive Measurement Today.* San Francisco: Jossey-Bass, 1980.

_____, and A. K. Olson, "Graffiti in Four Types of Institutions of Higher Education." *Journal of Social Research* 7 (1971): 62–71.

Shakur, Sanyika. *Monster: The Autobiography of an L.A. Gang Member.* New York: The Atlantic Monthly Press, 1993.

"Sharp Blows at the High Bench." *Time,* 10 March 1980, 48–49.

Sherick, L. G. *How to Use the Freedom of Information Act (FOIA).* New York: Arco, 1980.

Sherif, Muzafer, and Carolyn Sherif. *Groups in Harmony and Tension.* New York: Octagon, 1966.

Simon, Julian L. *Basic Research Methods in Social Science,* 3d ed. New York: Random, 1989.

Singer, Max. "The Vitality of Mythical Numbers." *The Public Interest* 23 (Spring 1971): 3–9.

Smith, Mary Lee, and Gene Glass. "Meta-analysis of Psychotherapy Outcome Studies." *American Psychologist* 32 (September 1977): 752–777.

Steffensmeier, Darrell, and Renee H. Steffensmeier. "Who Reports Shoplifters? Research Continuities and Further Developments." *International Journal of Criminology and Penology* 5 (1976): 79–95.

Steffensmeier, Darrell, J., and Robert M. Terry. "Deviance and Respectability: An Observational Study of Reactions to Shoplifting." *Social Forces* 5 (1973): 417–426.

Stein, Martha L. *Lovers, Friends, Slaves . . . The Nine Male Sexual Types.* Berkeley, Calif.: Berkeley Publishing Corp., 1974.

Stewart, David W. *Secondary Research: Information Sources and Methods,* Beverly Hills, Calif.: Sage, 1984.

Stewart, James. "Foreword." In *Data Resources of the National Institute of Justice,* edited by Colin Loftin et al., iii–iv. Washington, D.C.: U.S. Department of Justice, May 1987.

Stewart, John E., and Daniel A. Cannon. "Effects of Perpetrator Status and Bystander Commitment on Response to a Simulated Crime." *Journal of Police Science and Administration* 5 (1977): 318–323.

_____. "Defendant's Attractiveness as a Factor in the Outcome of Criminal Trials: An Observational Study." Paper presented at the Southeastern Psychological Association Meetings, New Orleans, La., 1979.

Stricker, L. J. "The True Deceiver." *Psychological Bulletin* 68 (1967): 13–20.

Sutherland, Edwin, H. *White Collar Crime.* New York: Dryden, 1949.

Taylor, C. B., L. Fried, and J. Kenardy. "The Use of a Real-Time Computer Diary for Data Acquisition and Processing." *Behavior Research and Therapy* 28, no. 1 (1990): 93–97.

Teplin, Linda A. "Managing Disorders: Police Handling of the Mentally Ill." In *Mental Health and Criminal Justice,* edited by Linda A. Teplin, 157–175. Beverly Hills, Calif.: Sage, 1984.

Teresa, Vincent, with Thomas C. Renner. *My Life in the Mafia.* Greenwich, Conn.: Fawcett, 1973.

Thomas, W. I., and Florian Znaniecki. *The Polish Peasant in Europe and America.* Boston: Badger, 1918.

Tittle, Charles R., Wayne Villemez, and Douglas A. Smith. "The Myth of Social Class and Criminality: An Empirical Assessment of the Empirical Evidence." *American Sociological Review* 43 (1978): 643–656.

Tracy, Paul E., and James Alan Fox. "A Field Experiment on Insurance Fraud in Auto Body Repair." *Criminology* 27 (August 1989): 598–603.

Tracy, Paul E., Marvin E. Wolfgang, and Robert M. Figlio. *Delinquency in Two Birth Cohorts: Executive Summary.* Philadelphia: Center for Studies in Criminology and Criminal Law, The Wharton School, University of Pennsylvania, 1985.

Truzzi, Marcello. "Sherlock Holmes: Applied Social Psychologist." In *The Sociologist as Detective,* edited by William B. Sanders, 50–86. 2d ed. New York: Praeger, 1976.

Tucker, Lyle, et al. "The Effects of Temptation and Information about a Stranger on Helping." *Personality and Social Psychology Bulletin* 3 (1977): 416–420.

Turner, James S. *The Chemical Feast: Ralph Nader's Study Group Report on the Food and Drug Administration.* New York: Grossman, 1970.

Uchida, Craig D., Laure Brooks, and Christopher S. Kopers. "Danger to Police During Domestic Encounters: Assaults on Baltimore County Police, 1984–86." *Criminal Justice Policy Review* 2 (December 1987), 357–371.

Vaughn, Ted R. "Governmental Intervention in Social Research: Political and Ethical Dimensions in the Wichita Jury Recordings." In *Ethics, Politics and Social Research,* edited by Gideon Sjoberg. Cambridge, Mass.: Schenkman, 1967.

Volz, Joseph, and Peter J. Bridge, eds. *The Mafia Talks.* Greenwich, Conn.: Fawcett, 1969.

Von Hoffman, Nicholas. "Sociological Snoopers." *Washington Post* 30 January 1970.

Wallis, W. Allen, and Harry V. Roberts. *The Nature of Statistics.* Rev. ed. New York: Free Press, 1966.

Wanat, John, and Karen Burke. "Estimating Juvenile Recidivism by Cross-level Inference." Paper presented at the National Workshop on Research Methodology and Criminal Justice Program Evaluation, Baltimore, Md., March 1980.

Webb, Eugene, D. T. Campbell, R. D. Schwartz, and L. Sechrest. *Unobtrusive Measures: Nonreactive Research in the Social Sciences.* Chicago: Rand McNally, 1966.

Webb, Eugene J., et al. *Nonreactive Measures in the Social Sciences.* 2d ed. Boston: Houghton Mifflin, 1981.

Weber, Robert P. *Basic Content Analysis.* Newbury Park, Calif.: Sage, 1990.

Wells, L. Edward. "The Utility of Meta-Analysis in Criminal Justice Research." Paper presented at the Academy of Criminal Justice Sciences Meetings, Nashville, Tennessee, March 1991.

_____, and Joseph H. Rankin. "Families and Delinquency: A Meta-Analysis of the Impact of Broken Homes." *Social Problems* 38 (February 1991): 71–93.

Wessel, David. "Racial Bias Against Black Job Seekers Remains Pervasive, Broad Study Finds." *Wall Street Journal* 15, May 1991, A9.

Wheeler, Stanton, ed. *On File: Records and Dossiers in American Life.* New York: Russell Sage, 1970.

Whitehead, John T., and Steven P. Lab. "A Meta-Analysis of Juvenile Correctional Treatment." *Journal of Research in Crime and Delinquency* 26 (1989): 276–295.

Wolf, George, and Joseph DiMona. *Frank Costello: Prime Minister of the Underworld.* New York: Bantam Books, 1975.

Wolfgang, Marvin E., R. M. Figlio, and T. P. Thornberry. *Evaluating Criminology.* New York: Elsevier/North-Holland, 1978.

_____, Robert Figlio, and Thorsten Sellin. *Delinquency in a Birth Cohort.* Chicago: University of Chicago Press, 1972.

Woodward, Bob, and Scott Armstrong. *The Brethren: Inside the Supreme Court.* New York: Simon and Schuster, 1979.

Zimmerman, Don H., and D. Lawrence Wieder. "The Diary: Diary Interview Method." In *Social Science Methods: A New Introduction,* edited by Robert Smith. New York: Free Press, 1974.

Chapter 9   Validity, Reliability, and Triangulated Strategies

Albini, Joseph L. *The American Mafia: Genesis of a Legend.* New York: Appleton, 1971.

Bailey, Kenneth. *Methods of Social Research.* 2d ed. New York: Free Press, 1987.

Bailey, William C. "Correctional Outcome: An Evaluation of 100 Reports." In *Crime and Justice,* Vol. III, edited by Leon Radzinowicz and Marvin E. Wolfgang. New York: Basic, 1971.

Ball, John C., et al. "Lifetime Criminality of Heroin Addicts in the United States." *Journal of Drug Issues* 1 (1982): 1–12.

Block, Alan A. "The History and Study of Organized Crime." *Urban Life* 6 (January 1978), 455–474.

Bownas, D. A., and Marvin D. Dunnette. *The Development of the Police Career Index.* Minneapolis, Minn.: Personal Decisions, Inc., 1975.

Brantingham, Paul, and Patricia Brantingham. *Patterns in Crime.* New York: Macmillan, 1984.

Brewer, John, and Albert Hunter. *Introducing Multimethod Research.* Belmont, Calif.: Wadsworth, 1983.

Campbell, Donald T., and Donald W. Fiske. "Convergent and Discriminant Validation by the Multitrait-Multimethod Matrix." *Psychological Bulletin* 56 (1959): 81–105.

Carmines, Edward G., and Richard A. Zeller. *Reliability and Validity Assessment.* Newbury Park, Calif.: Sage, 1979.

Chaiken, Jan, and Marcia R. Chaiken. *Varieties of Criminal Behavior.* Report prepared for the National Institute of Justice, Santa Monica, Calif.: Rand Corp. 1982.

Chilton, Roland J., and Adele Spielberger. "Increases in Crime: The Utility of Alternative Measures." *Journal of Criminal Law, Criminology and Police Science* 63 (March 1972): 68–74.

Clarke, James W. *American Assassins: The Darker Side of Politics.* Princeton, N.J.: Princeton University Press, 1982.

Collins, James J., and Marianne Zawitz. "Federal Drug Data for National Policy." *Drugs and Crime Data.* A Report from the Drugs and Crime Data Center and Clearinghouse, Washington, D.C.: Bureau of Justice Statistics, April, 1990.

Crano, William D., and Marilynn B. Brewer. *Principles of Research in Social Psychology.* New York: McGraw-Hill, 1973.

Cronbach, Lee J. "Coefficient Alpha and the Internal Structure of Tests." *Psychometrika* 16 (1951): 297–334.

Cronbach, L. *Essentials of Psychological Testing.* 3d ed. New York: Harper and Row, 1970.

_____. and Paul E. Meehl. "Construct Validity in Psychological Tests." *Psychological Bulletin* 52 (1955): 281–302.

Drug Use Forecasting, 1993, Annual Report on Adult Arrestees. Washington, D.C.: National Institute of Justice, November 1994.

Epstein, Edward J. *Agency of Fear.* New York: G. P. Putnam, 1977.

Erickson, Maynard L., and Lamar T. Empey. "Court Records, Undetected Delinquency and Decision-Making." *Journal of Criminal Law, Criminology and Police Science* 54 (December 1963): 456–469.

Farrington, David P. "Self Reports of Deviant Behavior: Predictive and Stable?" *Journal of Criminal Law and Criminology* 64 (March 1973): 99–110.

Fishman, J. E. *Measuring Police Corruption.* Monograph No. 10, New York: John Jay College of Criminal Justice, 1978.

Gross, Martin L. *The Brain Watchers.* New York: New American Library, 1962.

Guilford, J. R, and B. Fruchter. *Fundamental Statistics in Education and Psychology.* New York: McGraw-Hill, 1978.

Hardt, Robert H., and Sandra Peterson Hardt. "On Determining the Quality of the Delinquency Self-report Method." *Journal of Research in Crime and Delinquency* 14 (July 1977): 247–261.

Hebert, Eugene E. III, and Joyce A. O'Neill. "Drug Use Forecasting: An Insight into Arrestee Drug Use." *National Institute of Justice Reports.* (June 1991), 11–13.

Hood, Roger, and Richard Sparks. *Key Issues in Criminology.* New York: McGraw-Hill, 1971.

House, Ernest R. *Evaluating with Validity.* Beverly Hills, Calif.: Sage, 1980.

Kerstetter, Wayne A., and A. M. Heinz. "Pretrial Settlement Conference: Evaluation of a Reform in Plea Bargaining." *Law and Society Review* 13 (1979): 349–366.

Kirk, Jerome, and Marc L. Miller. *Reliability and Validity in Qualitative Research.* Beverly Hills, Calif.: Sage, 1986.

Kuder, G. Frederic, and Marion W. Richardson. "The Theory of the Estimation of Test Reliability." In *Principles of Educational and Psychological Measurement: A Book of Selected Readings,* edited by William A. Mehrens and Robert L. Ebel. New York: Rand McNally, 1967.

Lupscha, Peter A. "Networks vs. Networking: An Analysis of Organized Criminal Groups." Paper presented at the American Society of Criminology Meetings, Toronto, Ontario, Canada, November 1982.

Maas, Peter. *The Valachi Papers.* New York: Putnam, 1968.

Maltz, M. D., and R. McCleary. "The Mathematics of Behavioral Change: Recidivism and Construct Validity." *Evaluation Quarterly* 1 (August 1977): 421–438.

Martinson, Robert. "What Works? Questions and Answers about Prison Reform." *The Public Interest.* 35 (Spring 1974): 22–54.

Mash, Eric J., and David A. Wolfe. "Methodological Issues in Research on Physical Child Abuse." *Criminal Justice and Behavior* 18 (March 1991): 8–29.

Miller, Herbert S., William F. McDonald, and James A. Cramer. *Plea Bargaining in the United States.* Washington, D.C.: National Institute of Justice, 1980.

National Advisory Committee on Criminal Justice Standards and Goals. *Criminal Justice Research and Development.* Report of the Task Force on Criminal Justice Research and Development, Washington, D.C.: Law Enforcement Assistance Administration, December 1976.

Orenstein, Alan, and William R. F. Phillips. *Understanding Social Research.* Boston: Allyn and Bacon, 1978.

Reed, R. S. "Three Approaches to the Study of Jury Trials: Observation, Interview and Experimentation." Ph.D. dissertation, Florida State University, 1976.

Reppucci, N. Dickson, and W. Glenn Clingempeel. "Methodological Issues in Research with Correctional Populations." *Journal of Consulting and Clinical Psychology* 46 (August 1978): 727–746.

Reuter, Peter. "The (Continued) Vitality of Mythical Numbers." *The Public Interest* 75 (Spring 1984): 135–147.

Schlesinger, Stephen E. "Prediction of Dangerousness in Juveniles: A Replication." *Crime and Delinquency* 24 (January 1978): 40–48.

Schneider, Anne L., et al. *Handbook of Resources for Criminal Justice Evaluation.* Washington, D.C.: National Institute of Law Enforcement and Criminal Justice, 1978.

Selltiz, Clair, et al. *Research Methods in Social Relations.* New York: Holt, 1959.

Shaw, Clifford D., and Henry D. McKay. *Social Factors in Juvenile Delinquency.* National Commission on Law Observance and Enforcement, Report on the Causes of Crime, Vol. 2, Washington, D.C.: U.S. Government Printing Office, 1931.

Shusman, Elizabeth J., and Robin E. Inwald. "A Longitudinal Validation Study of Correctional Officer Job Performance as Predicted by the IPI and MMPI." *Journal of Criminal Justice,* 19, no. 2 (1991): 12–180.

Singer, Max. "The Vitality of Mythical Numbers." *The Public Interest* 23 (Spring 1971): 3–9.

Slavin, Robert E. *Research Methods in Education: A Practical Guide.* Englewood Cliffs, N.J.: Prentice-Hall, 1984.

Thorndike, R. L., and E. P. Hagen. *Measurement and Evaluation in Psychology and Education.* New York: Wiley, 1977.

Traub, Ross E. *Reliability for the Social Sciences: Theory and Applications.* Thousand Oaks, Calif.: Sage, 1994.

Turkus, Burton B., and Sid Feder. *Murder, Inc.: The Story of the Syndicate.* New York: Farrar, Straus and Young, 1951.

Walters, Glenn D., and Thomas W. White. "Heredity and Crime: Bad Genes or Bad Research." *Criminology* 27 (August 1989): 455–485.

Webb, Eugene J., et al. *Unobtrusive Measures: Nonreactive Research in the Social Sciences.* Chicago: Rand McNally, 1966.

Wish, Eric W., and Joyce A. O'Neill. *Drug Use Forecasting (DUF) Research Update, January to March, 1989.* Washington, D.C.: National Institute of Justice, September 1989.

Chapter 10   Scaling and Index Construction

Akman, D. D., et al. "The Measurement of Delinquency in Canada." *Journal of Criminal Law, Criminology and Police Science* 58 (1967): 241–243.

Arnold, William R. "Continuities in Research: Scaling Delinquent Behavior." *Social Problems* 13 (Summer 1965): 59–66.

Baumer, Terry, and Dennis Rosenbaum. "Measuring Fear of Crime." Paper presented at the National Workshop on Research Methodology and Criminal Justice Program Evaluation, Baltimore, Md., March 1980.

Blumstein, Alfred. "Seriousness Weights in an Index of Crime." *American Sociological Review* 39 (December 1974): 854–864.

Blumstein, Alfred, et al., eds. Criminal Careers and "Career Criminals." Vol. 2. Washington, D.C.: National Academy of Sciences, 1986.

Bogardus, Emory, S. "A Social Distance Scale." *Sociology and Social Research* 17 (January 1933): 265–271.

Brodsky, Stanley, and O'Neal Smitherman, eds. *Handbook of Scales for Research in Crime and Delinquency.* New York: Plenum Press, 1983.

Cavior, Norman, and L. Ramona Howard. "Facial Attractiveness and Juvenile Delinquency among Black and White Offenders." *Journal of Abnormal Child Psychology* 1 (1973): 202–213.

Christie, Richard and F. L. Geis, eds. *Studies in Machiavellianism.* New York: Academic Press, 1970.

Cloward, Richard, A., and Lloyd E. Ohlin. *Delinquency and Opportunity: A Theory of Delinquent Gangs.* London: Routledge and Kegan Paul, 1961.

Cohen, Albert K. *Delinquent Boys: The Culture of the Gang.* Glencoe, Ill.: Free Press, 1955.

Cohen, Jacqueline. "Incapacitation as a Strategy for Crime Control: Possibilities and Pitfalls." In *Crime and Justice: An Annual Review,* Vol. 5, edited by Michael Tonry and Norval Morris. Chicago: University of Chicago Press, 1983a.

_____. "Incapacitating Criminals: Recent Research Findings." *NIJ Research in Brief.* Washington, D.C.: National Institute of Justice, December 1983b.

Cole, Stephen. *The Sociological Method.* Chicago: Markham, 1972.

Cullen, Francis T., Bruce G. Link, and Craig W. Polanzi. "The Seriousness of Crime Revisited." *Criminology* 20 (May 1982): 83–102.

Dentler, Robert A., and Lawrence J. Monroe. "Social Correlates of Early Adolescent Theft." *American Sociological Review* 26 (October 1961): 733–743.

Dunnette, Marvin D., and Stephan Motowidlo. *Police Selection and Career Assessment.* Washington, D.C.: National Institute of Law Enforcement and Criminal Justice, November 1976.

Edwards, Allen. *Techniques of Attitude Scale Construction.* New York: Appleton, 1957.

Farrington, David P. "Self-Reports of Deviant Behavior: Predictive and Stable?" *Journal of Criminal Law and Criminology* 64 (1973): 99–110.

Farrington, David, and Roger Tarling. *Criminological Prediction.* London: Home Office Research and Planning Unit, 1983.

Fritz, Sara. "Is Consumer Price Index 'Loaded'?" *U.S. News and World Report,* 4 February 1980, 86.

Glueck, Sheldon and Eleanor Glueck. *Unraveling Juvenile Delinquency.* New York: The Commonwealth Fund, 1950.

_____. *Predicting Delinquency & Crime.* Cambridge, Mass.: Harvard University Press, 1960.

Gottfredson, Don M., and Kelley M. Ballard. "Differences in Parole Decisions Associated with Decision Makers." *Journal of Research in Crime and Delinquency* 3 (1966): 112–119.

Greenwood, Peter W., and Allan Abrahamse. *Selective Incapacitation.* Santa Monica Calif.: Rand Corp., August 1982.

Guttman, Louis L. "A Basis for Scaling Qualitative Data." *American Sociological Review* 9 (April 1944): 139–150.

_____. "The Basis for Scalogram Analysis." In *Studies in Social Psychology in World War 11, Vol. 4, Measuring and Prediction,* edited by Samuel A. Stouffer et al. Princeton, N.J.: Princeton University Press, 1950.

Harmon, Harry H. *Modern Factor Analysis.* Chicago: University of Chicago Press, 1967.

Hirschi, Travis, and Hanaan C. Selvin. *Principles of Survey Analysis.* New York: Free Press, 1973.

Hoffman, Peter. "Screening for Risk: A Revised Salient Factor Score." *Journal of Criminal Justice* 11 (1984): 539–547.

_____. "Predicting Criminality." *Crime File Series.* Washington, D.C.: National Institute of Justice, 1985.

Hood, Roger, and Richard Sparks. *Key Issues in Criminology.* New York: McGraw-Hill, 1971.

Hsu, Marlene. "Cultural and Sexual Differences on the Judgment of Criminal Offenses: A Replication Study of the Measurement of Delinquency." *Journal of Criminal Law and Criminology* 64 (September 1973): 348–353.

Jacoby, Joan E. "Case Evaluation: Quantifying Prosecutorial Policy." *Judicature* 58 (1975): 486–493.

Klaus, Patsy, and Carol B. Kalish. "The Severity of Crime." *Bureau of Justice Statistics Bulletin.* Washington, D.C.: U.S. Department of Justice, January 1984.

Kratcoski, Peter C. "The Functions of Classification Models in Probation and Parole Control or Treatment-Rehabilitation?" *Federal Probation* 49, no. 4 (1985): 49–56.

Likert, Rensis. "A Technique for the Measurement of Attitudes." *Archives of Psychology* 140 (1932).

Machiavelli, Niccoló. *The Prince.* New York: New American Library, 1952.

Mannheim, H., and Leslie T. Wilkins. *Prediction Methods in Relation to Borstal Training.* London: Her Majesty's Stationery Office, 1955.

Maranell, Gary M., ed. *Scaling: A Sourcebook for Behavioral Scientists.* Chicago: Aldine, 1974.

Martin, Susan, and Larry Sherman. *The Washington Repeat Offender Project.* Washington, D C.: The Police Foundation, 1985.

Miller, Delbert C., ed. *Handbook of Research Design and Social Measurement.* 5th ed. New York: Longman, 1991.

Monahan, John. *Predicting Violent Behavior: An Assessment of Clinical Techniques.* Beverly Hills, Calif.: Sage, 1981.

Norusis, Marija J., and SPSS Inc. *SPSS/PC+V2.0 Base Manual.* Chicago: SPSS Inc., 1988.

Nye, F. Ivan, and James F. Short, Jr. "Scaling Delinquent Behavior." *American Sociological Review* 22 (June 1957): 326–331.

Ohlin, Lloyd E. *Selection for Parole.* New York: Russell Sage, 1951.

Oppenheim, A. N. *Questionnaire Design and Attitude Measurement.* New York: Basic, 1966.

Orenstein, Alan, and William R. F. Phillips. *Understanding Social Research.* Boston: Allyn, 1978.

Osgood, Charles, et al. *The Measurement of Meaning.* Urbana: University of Illinois Press, 1957.

Robinson, J. P., P. R. Shaver, and L. S. Wrightsman, eds. *Measures of Personality and Social Psychological Attitudes.* San Diego: Academic Press, 1991.

Rossi, Peter H., and J. P. Henry. "Seriousness as a Measure for All Purposes?" In *Handbook of Criminal Justice Evaluation,* edited by M. Klein and K. Teilmann, 489–505. Beverly Hills, Calif.: Sage, 1980.

Rossi, Peter H., et al. "The Seriousness of Crimes: Normative Structure and Individual Differences." *American Sociological Review* 39 (April 1974): 224–237.

Samuelson, R. "Riding the Monthly Escalator: The Consumer Price Index." *New York Times Magazine* (December 8, 1974): 34–35.

Scheussler, Karl B., and Donald B. Cressey. "Personality Characteristics of Criminals." *American Journal of Sociology* (1950): 476–484.

Scott, John Finley. "Two Dimensions of Delinquent Behavior." *American Sociological Review* 24 (April 1959): 240–243.

Sellin, Thorsten, and Marvin E. Wolfgang. *The Measurement of Delinquency.* New York: Wiley, 1966.

Shaw, Marvin E., and Jack M. Wright. *Scales for the Measurement of Attitudes.* New York: McGraw-Hill, 1967.

Sherman, Larry. "Repeat Offenders." *Crime File.* Rockville, Md.: National Institute of Justice, 1985.

Short, James F., Jr., and F. L. Strodtbeck. *Group Process and Gang Delinquency.* Chicago: University of Chicago Press, 1965.

Simon, Frances H. *Prediction Methods in Criminology.* Home Office Research Studies, No. 7, London: Her Majesty's Stationery Office, 1971.

Snider, J. G., and C. E. Osgood, eds. *Semantic Differential Technique.* Chicago: Aldine, 1969.

Stephenson, W. *The Study of Behavior: Q-Technique and Its Methodology.* Chicago: University of Chicago Press, 1953.

Summers, Gene F., ed. *Attitude Measurement.* Chicago: Rand McNally, 1970.

Tennenbaum, David J. "Research Studies of Personality and Criminality: A Summary and Implications of the Literature." *Journal of Criminal Justice* 5 (Spring 1977): 1–19.

Thielbar, Gerald W., and Saul D. Feldman. "Images of Deviants and Their Behavior: Stereotypes and Social Context." In *Deciphering Deviance,* edited by Saul D. Feldman, 265–281. Boston: Little, Brown, 1978.

Thurstone, Louis L., and E. J. Chave. *The Measurement of Attitudes.* Chicago: University of Chicago Press, 1929.

Torgerson, W. *Theory and Methods of Scaling.* New York: Wiley, 1958.

Vito, Gennaro F. "Felony Probation and Recidivism: Replication and Response." *Federal Probation* 50, no. 4 (1986): 17–25.

Waldo, Gordon P., and Simon Dinitz. "Personality Attributes of Criminals: An Analysis of Research Studies, 1950–1965." *Journal of Research in Crime and Delinquency* 4 (1967): 185–202.

Wilkins, Leslie T. *The Evaluation of Penal Measures.* New York: Random, 1969.

Wolfgang, Marvin E., et al. *The National Survey of Crime Severity.* Washington, D.C.: U.S. Department of Justice, 1985.

Wright, Benjamin D. "The Objective Construction of Scales." Paper presented at the National Workshop on Research Methodology and Criminal Justice Program Evaluation, Baltimore, Md., March 1980.

Chapter 11   Data Analysis: Coding, Tabulation, and Simple Data Presentation

Babbie, Earl R. *The Practice of Social Research.* 6th ed. Belmont, Calif.: Wadsworth, 1992.

Broom, Leonard, and Philip Selznick. *Essentials of Sociology.* 2d ed. New York: Harper, 1979.

Bureau of Justice Statistics. *Criminal Victimization in the United States.* 1991, Washington, D.C.: U.S. Department of Justice, 1993.

Cole, Stephen. *The Sociological Method.* Chicago: Markham, 1972.

Dixon, W., et al. *BMDP Statistical Software.* Berkeley, Calif.: University of California, 1981.

Hagan, Frank E., Marie R. Haug, and Marvin B. Sussman. *Comparative Profiles of the Rehabilitation Counseling Graduate: 1965 and 1972.* Working Paper No. 5, 2d series, Cleveland: Case Western Reserve University, Institute on the Family and the Bureaucratic Society, 1975.

Hirschi, Travis, and Hanan C. Selvin. *Principles of Survey Analysis.* New York: Free Press, 1973.

Huff, Darrell. *How to Lie with Statistics.* New York: Norton, 1954.

Lazarsfeld, Paul, Ann Pasanella, and Morris Rosenberg, eds. *Continuities in the Language of Social Research.* New York: Free Press, 1972.

Monette, Duane R., Thomas J. Sullivan, and Cornell R. DeJong. *Applied Social Research: Tool for the Human Services.* 3rd ed. New York: Holt, Rinehart and Winston, 1994.

Norusis, Marija J., and SPSS Inc. *SPSS/PC+4.0 Base Manual.* Chicago: SPSS Inc., 1990.

Rosenberg, Morris. *The Logic of Survey Analysis.* New York: Basic, 1968.

Roth, Julius. "Hired Hand Research." *American Sociologist* 1 (August 1966): 190–196.

SAS User's Guide. Cary, N.C.: SAS Institute, Inc., 1982.

SPSS, Inc. *SPSS-X User's Guide.* New York: McGraw-Hill, 1983.

Stewart, John. "Defendant's Attractiveness as a Factor in the Outcome of Criminal Trials: An Observational Study." Paper presented at the Southeastern Psychological Association Convention, New Orleans, La., 1979.

Sussman, Marvin B., and Marie R. Haug. "Human and Mechanical Error: An Unknown Quantity in Research." *American Behavioral Scientist* 11 (November 1967): 55–56.

Tracy, Paul E., Jr. "Prevalence, Incidence, Rates, and Other Descriptive Measures." In *Measurement Issues in Criminology,* edited by Kimberly L. Kempf, 51–77. New York: Springer–Verlag, 1990.

Wallis, W. Allen, and Harry V. Roberts. *Statistics: A New Approach.* New York: Free Press, 1956.

Wilbanks, William. "Is Violent Crime Intraracial?" *Crime and Delinquency* 31 (January 1985), 117–128.

_____. *The Myth of a Racist Criminal Justice System.* Monterey, Calif.: Brooks/Cole, 1986.

Zeisel, Hans. *Say It with Figures.* 4th ed. New York: Harper, 1957.

Chapter 12   Data Analysis: A User's Guide to Statistics

Binder, Arnold. "Restrictions on Statistics Imposed by Method of Measurement: Some Reality, Much Mythology." *Journal of Criminal Justice* 12 (1984): 467–481.

Brent, Edward E., Jr., and Ronald E. Anderson. *Computer Applications in the Social Sciences.* New York: McGraw Hill, 1990.

Dometrius, Nelson C. *Social Statistics Using SPSS.* New York: Harper Collins, 1992.

Elzey, Freeman F. *Introductory Statistics: A Microcomputer Approach.* Monterey, Calif.: Brooks Cole, 1987.

Fox, James Alan, and Jack Levin. *Elementary Statistics in Social Research.* 6th ed. New York: Harper Collins, 1994.

Fox, William. *Social Statistics Using Microcase.* Chicago: Nelson-Hall, 1992.

Franzblau, Abraham N. *A Primer of Statistics for Non-statisticians.* New York: Harcourt, 1958.

Hirschi, Travis, and Hanan C. Selvin. *Principles of Survey Analysis.* New York: Free Press, 1973.

Huff, Darrell. *How To Lie with Statistics.* New York: Wiley, 1966.

Kanji, Gopal K. *100 Statistical Tests.* Thousand Oaks, Calif.: Sage, 1993.

Kinsey, Alfred, et al. *Sexual Behavior in the Human Female.* Philadelphia: Saunders, 1953.

Loether, Herman J., and Donald G. McTavish. *Descriptive and Inferential Statistics for Sociologists: An Introduction.* Boston: Allyn and Bacon, 1980.

Malcolm, D. "Statistical Navigator Professional." *Social Science Computer Review* 10 (1992): 121–123.

Mueller, John H., Karl F. Schuessler, and Hebert L. Costner. *Statistical Reasoning in Sociology.* Boston: Houghton Mifflin, 1970.

Niederhoffer, Arthur. *Behind the Shield: The Police in Urban Society.* New York: Doubleday, 1967.

Reckless, Walter C. *The Crime Problem.* 4th ed. New York: Appleton-Century-Crofts, 1967.

Robertson, O. Zeller, Jr., and Charles B. Fields. "Criminal Justice Statistics Use Survey." Preliminary results of survey mailed to participants, University Center, Mich.: Saginaw Valley State College, June 23, 1986.

Robinson, W. S. "Ecological Correlations and the Behavior of Individuals." *American Sociological Review* 15 (June 1950): 351–357.

Siegel, Sidney. *Nonparametric Statistics for the Behavioral Sciences.* New York: McGraw-Hill, 1956.

Sussman, Marvin B., Marie R. Haug, Frank E. Hagan, and Gay C. Kitson. *Staying Power in Rehabilitation: The Impact of Rehabilitation Services Administration*

Support in Nine Occupations. Cleveland: Institute on the Family and the Bureaucratic Society, Case Western Reserve University, 1975.

Thorndike, Edward L. "On the Fallacy of Imputing the Correlations Found for Groups to the Individuals or Smaller Groups Composing Them." *American Journal of Psychology* 52 (1929): 122–124.

Vito, Gennaro F., and Edward J. Latessa. *Statistical Applications in Criminal Justice.* Newbury Park, Calif.: Sage, 1989.

Vogt, W. Paul. *Dictionary of Statistics and Methodology: A Nontechnical Guide for the Social Sciences.* Thousand Oaks, Calif.: Sage, 1993.

Yule, Udny G., and Maurice G. Kendall. *An Introduction to the Theory of Statistics.* 14th ed. New York: Hafner, 1950.

Chapter 13   Policy Analysis, Evaluation Research, and Proposal Writing

Abt, Clark C. *Supply, Demand, Motives and Constraints of the Evaluation Producing Community.* Monograph, Cambridge, Mass.: Abt Associates, Inc., 1976.

Adams, Stuart. *Evaluative Research in Corrections: A Practical Guide.* Washington, D.C.: National Institute of Law Enforcement and Criminal Justice, 1975.

Albright, Ellen, et al. *Criminal Justice Research: Evaluation in Criminal Justice Programs: Guidelines and Examples.* Washington, D.C.: National Institute of Law Enforcement and Criminal Justice, June 1973.

Boruch, Robert F. "On Common Contentions about Randomized Field Experiments." In *Evaluation Studies Review Annual.* Vol. 1, edited by Gene V. Glass, 158–194. Beverly Hills, Calif.: Sage, 1976,

Cain, Glen G. "Regression and Selection Models to Improve Non-experimental Comparisons." In *Evaluation and Experiment,* edited by Carl A. Bennet and Arthur A. Lumsdaine, 297–317. New York: Academic Press, 1975.

Cochran, N. "Cognitive Processes, Social Mores, and the Accumulation of Data." *Evaluation Quarterly* 2 (May 1978): 343–358.

Cook, T. D., F. L. Cook, and M. M. Mark. "Randomized and Quasi-Experimental Designs in Evaluation Research: An Introduction." In *Evaluation Research Methods: A Basic Guide,* edited by Leonard Rutman. Beverly Hills, Calif.: Sage, 1977.

Dye, Thomas R. *Understanding Public Policy.* 8th ed. Englewood Cliffs, N.J.: Prentice-Hall, 1995.

Fagan, Jeffrey A. "Natural Experiments in Criminal Justice." In *Measurement Issues in Criminology,* edited by Kimberly Kempf, 108–137. New York: Springer–Verlag, 1990.

Franklin, Jack L., and Jean H. Thrasher. *Introduction to Program Evaluation.* New York: Wiley, 1976.

Finckenauer, James. *Scared Straight! and the Panacea Phenomenon.* Englewood Cliffs, N.J.: Prentice-Hall, 1982.

Fry, Lincoln J. "Participant Observation and Program Evaluation." *Journal of Health and Social Behavior* 14 (September 1973): 274–278.

Garner, Joel, and Christy A. Visher. "Policy Experiments Come of Age." *National Institute of Justice Reports.* September/October, 1988, 2–8.

Garwood, David D. "Edsel Murphy's Law: Anything That Can Go Wrong Will Go Wrong: Murphy's General Law as Applied to Program Evaluation." *The Loop: A Newsletter for Evaluators.* 8 (December 1978): 17–22.

Glaser, Daniel. *Routinizing Evaluation: Getting Feedback on Effectiveness of Crime and Delinquency Programs.* Rockville, Md.: Center for Studies of Crime and Delinquency, 1973.

_____. "Remedies for the Key Deficiency in Criminal Justice Evaluation Research." *Journal of Research in Crime and Delinquency* 11 (July 1974): 144–154.

_____. "Correctional Research: An Elusive Paradise." In *Probation, Parole and Community Corrections,* 2d ed. edited by Robert M. Carter and Leslie T. Wilkins, 765–777. New York: Wiley, 1976.

Hudzik, John K., and Gary W. Cordner. *Planning in Criminal Justice Organizations and Systems.* New York: Macmillan, 1983.

Jones, Charles O. *An Introduction to the Study of Public Policy.* Boston: Duxbury, 1977.

Levine, James P., Michael C. Musheno, and Dennis J. Palumbo. *Criminal Justice: A Public Policy Approach.* New York: Harcourt, 1980.

Locke, Lawrence F., Waneen W. Spirduso, and Stephen J. Silverman. *Proposals that Work: A Guide for Planning Dissertations and Grant Proposals.* Thousand Oaks, Calif.: Sage, 1993.

Logan, Charles H. "Evaluation Research in Crime and Delinquency: A Reappraisal." In *Criminal Justice Research: Approaches, Problems and Policy,* edited by Susette M. Talarico, 29–44. Cincinnati: Anderson, 1980.

MacKenzie, Doris L., and Belinda McCarthy. *How to Prepare a Competitive Grant Proposal: A Guide for University Faculty Members Pursuing Criminal Justice Research Grants.* Highland Heights, Ky.: Academy of Criminal Justice Sciences, 1990.

Maida, Peter R., and Jeanne E. Faucett, eds. *Crime and Delinquency Prevention Reader.* 2d ed. College Park: University of Maryland, 1978.

Morris, Norval, and Michael Tonry, eds. *Crime and Justice: An Annual Review of Research,* Vol. 1. Chicago: University of Chicago Press, 1979.

National Advisory Committee on Criminal Justice Standards and Goals. *Criminal Justice Research and Development: Report of the Task Force on Criminal Justice Research and Development.* Washington, D.C.: Law Enforcement Assistance Administration, 1976.

National Criminal Justice Reference Service. *How Well Does It Work? Review of Criminal Justice Evaluation, 1978.* Washington, D.C.: National Institute of Law Enforcement and Criminal Justice, June 1979.

National Institute of Justice. *Research Plan: 1991.* Washington, D.C.: National Institute of Justice, May, 1991.

NIJ Research Plan: 1995–96. Washington, D.C.: National Institute of Justice, 1994.

Office of Juvenile Justice and Delinquency Prevention. *Evaluation Issues.* Washington, D.C.: U.S. Department of Justice, June 1978.

Office of Research Administration. *Proposal Preparation Guide.* Cleveland: Case Western Reserve University, July 1971.

Petersilia, Joan, and Susan Turner. "Evaluating Intensive Supervision Probation/Parole: Results of a Nationwide Experiment." *National Institute of Justice Research in Brief.* May 1993.

Posavec, Emil J., and Raymond Carey. *Program Evaluation: Methods and Case Studies.* 4th ed. Englewood Cliffs, N.J.: Prentice-Hall, 1992.

Rabow, Jerome. "Research and Rehabilitation: The Conflict of Scientific and Treatment Roles in Corrections." *The Journal of Research in Crime and Delinquency* 1 (January 1964): 67–79.

Rowland, Douglas, and Frank E. Hagan. "Research Proposal to Evaluate Neighborhood Elderly Transportation Project, City of Cleveland." Cleveland: Case Western Reserve University, School of Applied Social Sciences, June 16, 1975.

Rossi, Peter H., and Howard E. Freeman. *Evaluation: A Systematic Approach.* 5th ed. Newbury Park, Calif.: Sage, 1993.

Rudestam, Kjell E., and Rae R. Newton. *Surviving Your Dissertation: A Comprehensive Guide to Content and Process.* Thousand Oaks, Calif.: Sage, 1992.

Rutman, Leonard. "Formative Research and Program Evaluability." In *Evaluation Research Methods: A Basic Guide,* edited by Leonard Rutman. Beverly Hills, Calif.: Sage, 1977.

Schneider, Anne L., et al. *Handbook of Resources for Criminal Justice Evaluators.* Washington, D.C.: U.S. Department of Justice, 1978.

Schulberg, Herbert C., and Frank Baker. "Program Evaluation Models and the Implementation of Research Findings." *American Journal of Public Health* 58 (July 1977): 1248–1255.

Schwarz, Paul A. "Program Devaluation: Can the Experiment Reform?" Paper presented at the National Workshop on Research Methodology and Criminal Justice Program Evaluation, Baltimore, Md., March 1980.

Shanahan, Donald T. *Patrol Administration: Management by Objectives.* 3d ed. New York: Longwood, 1985.

Sponsored Programs and Contracts Office. *Faculty Guide to Sponsored Programs.* University Park, Pa.: Pennsylvania State University, 1990.

Strasser, S., and O. L. Deniston. "Pre- and Post-Planned Evaluation: Which is Preferable?" *Evaluation and Program Planning* 1, no. 3 (1978): 195–202.

Suchman, Edward A. *Evaluative Research: Principles and Practice in Public Service and Social Action Programs.* New York: Russell Sage, 1067.

Turabian, Kate L. *A Manual for Writers of Term Papers, Theses and Dissertations.* 4th ed. Chicago: University of Chicago Press, 1973.

Vito, Gennaro F. "Does It Work?: Problems in the Evaluation of a Correctional Treatment Program." *Journal of Offender Counseling, Services and Rehabilitation* 7 (1983): 5–21.

Waller, John D., et al. *Monitoring for Criminal Justice Planning Agencies.* Washington, D.C.: National Institute of Law Enforcement and Criminal Justice, March 1975.

Weiss, Carol H. "The Politicization of Evaluation Research." *Journal of Social Issues* 26, no. 4 (1970): 57–68.

———. *Evaluation Research: Methods for Assessing Program Effectiveness.* Englewood Cliffs, N.J.: Prentice-Hall, 1972.

Wholey, Joseph S. "Evaluability Assessment." In *Evaluation Research Methods: A Basic Guide,* edited by Leonard Rutman. Beverly Hills, Calif.: Sage, 1977.

———. *Evaluation and Effective Public Management.* Boston: Little, Brown, 1983.

Wilson, James Q. "On Pettigrew and Armor." *The Public Interest* 31 (Spring 1973), 132–134.

Glossary

Arbitrary scales. Scales developed by the researcher based primarily on face validity and personal judgment.

Bounding (in victim surveys). The initial interview in a panel serves as a boundary or means of establishing exactly when events have taken place.

Branching procedure. Interview technique used to narrow down sensitive responses such as income into less threatening categories or ranges.

CAPI. Computer-assisted programmed interviewing in which portable laptop computers are used in field interviews.

CART. Continuous audience response technology in which respondents register their reaction to various stimuli on a continuous basis using a hand-held keypad.

Case study (life history). In-depth investigation of a single case (individual, group, or community).

CATI. Computer-assisted telephone interviewing.

Codebook. Guidebook for numerically classifying each question to be coded.

Coding. Assignment of numbers to responses.

Compensatory equalization of treatment. Desirable services (treatment) in the experimental group cause complaints and demands that the control group be supplied with this same treatment.

Concepts. Abstract or symbolic tags placed on reality.

Confederates. Research assistants who pose as subjects in a study.

Confidentiality. Requirement that any information obtained in research be treated as confidential and not be revealed in any manner that would identify or harm subjects.

Construct validity. Accuracy of the scale or measurement in tapping the correct concept or construct.

Contamination of data. Unanticipated events or experiences that differentially impact on the experimental or control group, but not in the same way with both.

Content analysis. Systematic classification and analysis of data such as the content of mass media.

Content validity. Accuracy of individual items in a scale in measuring the concept being measured.

Convergent-discriminant validity. Different measures of the same concept should yield similar results (convergence), whereas the same measure of different concepts should yield different results (discrimination).

Crime dip. The decline in recorded crime in the 1980s believed to be caused primarily by demographic change.

Crime index. Part I Uniform Crime Report offenses divided by population, then multiplied by 100,000.

Crime rate. Number of crimes divided by population, per 100,000 population.

Crime seriousness scales. Procedures that assign weight or severity rating to various crimes .

Criminal profiling. An attempt to construct typical characteristics of certain types of criminals.

Criterion problems. Problems related to the measurement of outcome in which different measures show different outcomes.

Cross-sectional design. Study of one group at one time.

"Dark figure" of crime. Crime that is unmeasured by official statistics or that has not come to the notice of police.

Data archives. Data libraries or organizations that store data resources (raw data) from previous studies.

Debriefing. After completion of a study (particularly one involving deception), reassurance of subjects and explanation of the purposes of the research.

Demand characteristics. Overagreeableness on the part of those surveyed; respondents give the researcher the response they believe is demanded (expected).

Diffusion of treatment. The control group learns about and imitates the experimental group.

Disguised observation. Informed consent of subjects is not sought and researchers pretend to be part of the study group.

Double-blind experiment. Neither the subjects nor administrators in an experiment know which group is receiving the treatment.

Drug Use Forecasting (DUF). NIJ research program that asks volunteer arrestees to provide urine specimens to test for drug usage.

Dummy tables. Blank tables that are constructed prior to gathering data to suggest the type of data needed in the analysis.

Ecological fallacy. Error of assuming that relationships proven true of groups are true of individuals.

Elaboration. Examination of a relationship on introduction of a third variable.

EPSEM. An acronym to describe probability sampling that uses an *e*qual *p*robability of *s*election *m*ethod.

Erosion of treatment effects. Deterioration of the effects of treatment over time.

Evaluation research. Measurement of the effects of a program in terms of its specific goals, outcomes, or program criteria.

Experimental mortality. Loss of subjects over the course of time.

Explanation. In elaboration, the relationship observed in the original bivariate table weakens or disappears in the partial tables.

Ex post facto study. Study that looks at existing outcomes and, after-the-fact, traces back and determines what may have predicted these outcomes.

External validity. Accuracy in the ability to generalize or infer findings from a study to a larger population.

Face validity. Accuracy of the instrument in measuring (on face value) that which is intended.

Factor analysis. Statistical procedure that identifies underlying patterns, factors, or dimensions among a series of scale items.

Field experiment. Experiment conducted in a natural (field) setting.

Focus groups. Purposively selected groups brought together in order to measure their reaction to some stimuli (for example, a commercial).

Gatekeepers. In field research, those who will vouch for the researcher's presence and serve as an entree to the field setting.

Guttman scales. Scaling procedure that insists on unidimensionality (measures only one dimension) and that on the basis of the total score one should be able to predict the pattern of response on each item.

Halo effect. Observer bias; observers follow an initial tendency to rate certain objects or subjects in a biased manner.

Hawthorne effect (named for an experiment at the Hawthorne plant of Western Electric Company). Subjects behave atypically if aware of being studied.

HHS guidelines. Ethical guidelines of the Department of Health and Human Services which provide a model for most other federal agencies with respect to informed consent and protection of human subjects in social and biomedical research.

Historicism. View of all social events as a distinct chronicle of unique happenings.

History. Specific events other than the treatment that during the course of a study may be responsible for producing the results.

Hypotheses. Specific statements or predictions regarding the relationship between two variables.

Impact evaluation. Examination of relationship between outcome and input, activities and results of a program.

Informed consent. Agreement of subjects to participate in research after they have been briefed.

Institutional review boards. College/university research committees that oversee and ensure ethical research standards.

Instrumentation. Changes in the measuring instrument during the course of a study that invalidate comparisons.

Internal validity. Accuracy within the study itself.

Interpretation. In elaboration, the partial table relationships weaken or disappear and the control variable is an intervening one (occurs between X and Y).

Interrupted time series. Multiple measurements at time points before and after the treatment (interruption).

Interval level measurement. Measurement in which equal distance (or intervals) between objects on a scale is assumed.

Interviewer effect. Biases introduced by the interviewer.

Item analysis. Procedure employed in Likert scaling in which questions (items) that do not discriminate (distinguish) high and low scores are eliminated from the scale.

Known-group validation (reverse record checks). Involves validation of reported behavior by studying groups whose behavior is already known.

Levels I and II. New categories for police departments reporting under the revised Uniform Crime Report program in which Level II sample departments report crime incidents more extensively.

Lie scales (truth scales). Series of questions that measure truthfulness of respondents in answering a survey.

Likert scales. Simple summated attitude scale consisting of a 5-point bipolar response scheme for each item ranging from strongly agree to strongly disagree.

Local history. Special case of "history" in which an event happens to the experimental or the control group, but not both.

Longitudinal study. Study involving the collection of data over a period of time.

Mark-recapture technique. Marked (tagged) samples are used to estimate the size of an unknown population.

Masking effects. Experimental treatments may have opposite effects on different kinds of subjects.

Maturation. Biological or psychological changes in the respondents during the course of a study that are not due to the treatment variable .

Meta-analysis (the analysis of analysis). Statistical analysis of data from many different studies dealing with the same research question in order to determine general findings.

Methodological narcissism. Fanatical adherence to a preferred method at the expense of substance; view that there is one and only one way of doing research, that is, by employing the one, best method.

Methodology (methods). Collection of accurate facts or data; attempt to address the issue of "what is."

Mnemonics. Simple memorizing devices that are particularly useful in field studies.

Monitoring. Similar to auditing; assessment of whether a program is doing what it is supposed to be doing in terms of process or program activities.

Multiple-form reliability. Administration of alternate forms of an instrument to the same group should produce similar results, thus demonstrating consistency (reliability) of measurement.

Multiple-treatment interference. Outcome produced by combinations of treatments; it may be difficult to isolate the specific combination(s) responsible.

National crime survey (NCS). Victim surveys conducted by the Census Bureau on behalf of the Bureau of Justice Statistics. The survey consists of a rotating crime panel of 60,000 households.

National Incident-Based Reporting System. The unit-record reporting system used in the redesigned UCR in which each local law enforcement agency reports on each individual arrest.

Needs assessment. Enumeration of some activity or resource, for example, measuring the need for a particular service in some target area.

Nominal level measurement. Measurement that places responses in mutually exclusive categories and has no mathematical meaning.

Nonparametric statistics. Statistics that are appropriate for ordinal and nominal data and are "distribution free," that is, few assumptions need to be made regarding the normality of the distribution.

Nonprobability sample. Sample that is not chosen by an equal probability of selection method.

Nonreactivity. Research conducted in such a manner that subject reactivity, or awareness of being studied, is eliminated.

Normal distribution (curve). Bell-shaped curve that describes a variety of phenomena, for example, a large sample of a population will be normally distributed and resemble a normal curve.

Null hypothesis (symbolized by H_0) Statement of no difference between groups being compared or a statement of no relationship in the general population. In other words, any differences observed are due to random error.

Objectivity. Basic canon of research; approach to subject matter from an unbiased, ethically neutral or value-free perspective.

Offender-Based Transaction Statistics. A program that collects felony arrest records with details of cases from booking to final disposition.

Operationalization. Definition of concepts on the basis of how they are measured; "I measured it by _____ ."

Ordinal level measurement. Placement of objects into ranks, for example, 1st, 2nd, and 3rd.

Panel study. A type of longitudinal study involving examination of the same select group over time.

Paradigm. A model or schema that provides a perspective from which to view reality.

Participant observation. Temporary participation in group activity by researchers for the purpose of observing the group.

Physical trace analysis. Type of unobtrusive measurement that involves the analysis of deposits, accretion of matter, and other indirect substances produced by previous human interaction.

Placebo effect ("sugar pill effect"). Tendency of control groups to react to believed treatment in a positive manner.

Policy analysis. Study of the causes and consequences of government behavior (what governments do or do not do).

Positivism. A natural science, empirical, or quantitative approach to research methodology.

Post hoc error. Incorrect assumption that because one variable precedes another in time, it is the cause of the outcome.

Pragmatic validity. Accuracy of the measuring instrument in predicting current status (concurrent validity) or future status (predictive validity).

PRE measure. *Proportional reduction in error* measure. Reduction in error of predicting or explaining a given proportion of one variable because of knowledge of the other variable.

Prediction scales. Attempts to forecast crime commission or success or failure on probation/ parole.

Pretest (pilot study). Exploratory test of an instrument on subjects who are similar to the group to be studied.

Primary sources. Raw data, unaccompanied by analysis or interpretation.

Probability sample. Sample chosen by an equal probability of selection method.

Probing. Follow-up question(s) that focuses, expands, or clarifies the response given.

Problem formulation. Selection, identification, and specification of the research topic to be investigated.

Process evaluation. Establishment of relationships between results and project inputs and activities.

Pseudonyms. Aliases used in research reports to protect the identity of respondents.

Q sort (question sort). An attitudinal scale procedure in which the respondents sort questions (on cards) into predetermined categories.

Random digit dialing. Sampling procedure employed in telephone surveys in which random numbers are used to obtain unlisted numbers.

Randomized response technique. Means of coping with resistance to sensitive questions by using indeterminate questions, ones in which the actual question answered is known only to the respondent.

Reactivity. Atypical or artificial behavior produced by respondent's awareness of being studied.

Reciprocity. A system of mutual obligation between subjects and researchers; because the subject's cooperation assisted the researcher, the researcher owes the subject professional regard.

Reliability. Consistency and/or stability of a measuring instrument.

Replication. Repetition of experiments or studies utilizing the same methodology.

Research, applied. Research concerned with solving or addressing immediate policy problems.

Research, pure. Acquisition of knowledge for science's sake; acquisition of knowledge that contributes to the scientific development of a discipline.

Research, qualitative. Research for the purpose of developing "sensitizing concepts" and verstehen (understanding) rather than quantitative measurement.

Research, quantitative. Operationalization and numerical measurement of variables.

Researchese. Language of research.

Reverse record check. Validation of reported behavior on the basis of studying a group whose behavior is already known.

Rival causal factors. Variables other than X, the independent variable that may be responsible for the outcome, for example, history, maturation, selection bias.

Rotation. In NCS panels, replacement of subsamples in order to control for maturation.

Salient factor score. Sentencing/parole prediction scheme used by the U.S. Parole Commission to predict recidivism.

Sampling frame. Complete list of the universe or population under investigation.

Scales. Attempts to increase the complexity of the level of measurement of variables from nominal to at least ordinal and hopefully interval/ratio level.

Scientism. View that, if one cannot quantitatively measure a phenomenon, it is not worth studying.

Screening questions. Preliminary questions employed to determine appropriate respondents for the main portion of a survey. For example, in victim surveys they are used to locate victims, who are then asked the incident questions.

Secondary analysis. Reanalysis of data that were gathered for other purposes.

Secondary sources. Sources that analyze, synthesize, and evaluate information.

Selection bias. Involves choosing nonequivalent groups for comparison.

Selection-maturation interaction. Combination of errors introduced by selection bias plus the differential maturation of groups.

Self-report surveys. Surveys in which subjects are asked to admit to the commission of various delinquent and/or criminal acts.

Semantic differential. Attitude scaling procedure that consists of usually a 7- or 9-point bipolar rating scale; respondents are asked to indicate their perception of the tag or description provided.

Sellin-Wolfgang Index. Procedure for assigning crime seriousness weights.

Serendipity. Surprising and unanticipated discoveries.

Shield laws. Laws that protect researchers from being forced to reveal sources in a court of law.

Simulation. Situation or game that attempts to mimic key features of reality.

Single-subject designs. Quantitative case studies that involve longitudinal measurement of a dependent variable on a single subject or case.

SPSS. *S*tatistical *P*ackage for the *S*ocial *S*ciences; canned or prewritten computer programs for statistical analysis in the social sciences .

Spuriousness. A false relationship that can be explained away by other variables.

Statistical regression. Tendency of groups that have been selected for study on the basis of extreme high or low scores to regress (fall back) toward the mean (average) on second testing.

Suppression. In elaboration, when despite no relationship in the original bivariate table, a relationship occurs in the partial tables.

Systems model. Model in which all parts of an organism, organization, or program are interrelated and consist of a series of inputs and outputs.

Telescoping. Tendency of respondents to move forward and report as having occurred events that actually occurred before the reference period.

Testing effects. Pretest effects or bias that is introduced as a result of having been pretested. Testing effects may also invalidate the ability to generalize to larger populations.

Test-retest reliability. Ability of the same instrument, when administered twice to the same population, to produce the same results, thus demonstrating the stability (reliability) of the measure.

Test of significance. Determination of whether the findings are due to chance (sampling error) or are statistically significant at a given probability level.

Theory. Plausible explanation of reality (why and how do things occur).

Thurstone scales. Attitude scales that rely on ratings by judges of scale items.

Time-series design. Measurement of a single variable at successive points in time.

Triangulation. Use of multiple measures of the same concept.

True experimental design. Design in which randomization, pretests and posttests, and experimental and control groups are employed.

Unidimensionality. Requirement of the Guttman scales that the items measure only one dimension (or concept); this is assumed if 90 percent reproducibility is achieved.

Uniform Crime Report (UCR). Annual FBI publication of official statistics of crimes recorded by police.

Unobtrusive measures (nonreactive methods). Ways of studying groups so that they remain unaware of being studied, thus eliminating reactivity.

Validity. Accuracy of measurement; does the instrument in fact measure that which it purports to measure.

Variable, dependent. Outcome variable (Y); or the subject of study.

Variable, independent. Predictor variable (X); precedes in time and causes change in the dependent variable.

Variables. Concepts that can vary or take on different numerical values; operationalized concepts.

Variables list. A list of variables being measured keyed to the question number in the questionnaire which are designed to measure each variable.

Verification. Confirmation of the accuracy of findings; attainment of greater certitude in conclusions through additional observations.

Verstehen. Weber's notion that the purpose of research is to gain a qualitative "understanding" of phenomena from the perspective of the subjects.

Name Index

Subject Index

15560